THE PENNY-A-LINE MAN

THE PENNY-A-LINE MAN

Reg Shay

ATHENA PRESS
LONDON

THE PENNY-A-LINE MAN
Copyright © Reg Shay 2007

ISBN (10-digit): 1 84401 713 3
ISBN (13-digit): 978 1 84401 713 3

First Published 2007 by
ATHENA PRESS
Queen's House, 2 Holly Road
Twickenham TW1 4EG
United Kingdom

Printed for Athena Press

Dedicated to my courageous late wife, Margery, and to our children, Robert, Annette, Peter and progeny

Many thanks for the helpful advice from Peter Munro and Peter Shay

Thanks also to Mike Collins

Special thanks to the staff of Bromley Library

Go for it now so that you'll never look back with regret

Of my Scotch on the Rocks: '*How can you measure a goal, an attainment in life, in terms of lumps of ice?*'

'How can I help you, sir?' asked the unsuspecting police sergeant. '*Well sergeant, I have here an unexploded bomb!*'

Of Robert Kennedy: '*Then I shook the former American Attorney General by the leg and called, "Wakey, Wakey!" I doubt if anyone had ever awakened him like that before perhaps Marilyn Monroe but not a man and instinctively I knew it was not appreciated.*'

On a Zambezi river crocodile attack: '*Steel-like hide tore into the thin (rubber) flesh of the Klepper boat and we spun like a leaf in the cone of a tornado as death incarnate stopped and lashed its tail angrily.*'

A panicking Portuguese soldier: '*I tried to shoot you. I tried to kill you but my safety catch was on!*'

Of a Rhodesian concentration camp I discovered and forced the authorities to close: '*Children were dying on average five a day!*'

The US Consul-General in Luanda: '*I feel you would like to know that Henry Kissinger (then US Secretary of State) has sent a message to say he is relying solely on your AP reports!*'

AP photographer Horst Fass: '*He says the MPLA are looking for you and that you are to be tried as a spy, and executed!*'

The leading French author of James Bond-type books, Gerard de Villiers, once described Reg Shay in a novel as 'A journalist who sits behind a big desk in Salisbury (Rhodesia) whose feet don't quite touch the ground!' Shay had been a shy undemanding little boy, not scholarly, who had left school aged thirteen years and was orphaned. He worked as a messenger in Fleet Street in WW2 with no prospects and yet he beat the odds. 'I wrote this book partly to inspire others who despair the future,' he said.

De Villiers is a known critic of the book *Papillion* and its authenticity but he had no doubt about Shay following a visit to Rhodesia at the time of the Ian Smith rebellion. Shay was taking him down a new unmapped security road leading into the forbidding Zambezi Valley when his car was stopped by armed men wearing camouflage uniforms who had been hiding in the grass. 'We didn't know if they were Rhodesian soldiers or guerrillas,' Shay said later. In fact, they were Rhodesian paramilitary police and the pair found themselves under arrest and taken to a police station before being released.

The chief of Rhodesia's secret police said later that if he had known at the time that Shay was involved he would have had him shot. In de Villiers' subsequent novel, the journalist, named Reg, is the second hero who is shot dead in the streets of Salisbury (now Harare) by the Special Branch.

In Angola, Shay was accused of being a spy by the communists who were taking over the country by force and escaped by the skin of his teeth. 'I can't think why people want me dead,' he says. 'I have only ever done an honest reporting job that any journalist should have done.'

It wasn't only people who were after his blood. In this exciting book of many hair-raising escapes which include the jaws of a crocodile and a lone fight with three gunmen in his office, Shay found himself making several forceful stands for freedom of speech which included resigning his job twice against censorship. At great personal risk in which he put his life in permanent danger, he forced the Rhodesian government to close a concentration camp where children were dying on average five a day; and gave evidence against the Special Branch in camera in the High Court after he had taken photographs inside a secret police torture chamber.

Foreword

If you can survive the opening of this book, then you can survive anything. Like most of the story of Reg Shay's life, it has you hanging on to your seat, wishing you'd prepared yourself for the roughest of rollercoaster rides. And that's the way it goes on, until you reach the last chapter and heave a sigh of relief that Reg has at last reached what looks – very unexpectedly – like a safe retirement in Birmingham.

This book is about one of the most infectiously disarming characters in British journalism. He tells his own story without any pretensions to grandeur – full of the self-mockery and casual humour that endears him to so many of his friends and colleagues. He tells the stories of his many escapes – this man is endowed not with nine lives but at least fifty – with the verve and skill of a writer who has seen it all. And he has. Central Africa has been one of the biggest stories in recent history, and no British correspondent has covered it without valuing Reg's knowledge and advice about the flow of events. Nothing was too dangerous for him, as you'll soon learn the moment you begin to read; nothing was beneath him, as I remember all too well when the President of Rhodesia's press corps was reduced to lugging around the great tangle of valves and cables that allowed my ITN camera crew to operate during the guerrilla war on the Mozambique border.

Most of all this is an honest view – told largely anecdotally but with a keen and unbiased knack of getting at the truth – of the way black and white leaders have mishandled the job of creating modern countries in Africa.

Peter Snow

My crazy world – a dangerous and irritable African buffalo and a thirsty giraffe! Picture: Marion Kaplan.

Contents

Introduction

It's not often that you have a chance to look at your own death rising before you, a serpent writhing in hatred at what you might represent – I have had that experience more than once. Much of my life has had an almost Hollywood-aura of disbelief pervading it – a feeling that what has happened to me is, in a way, extraordinary and that an ordinary life would be almost mundane. Take Angola as just one example...

When I looked into the face that I'd come to know so well over the last few months, the transformation was terrifying; but I knew that remaining cool, however difficult it might be, could save me. Then the face had been calm and collected, friendly even during our many chats. Now it was contorted into a hatred and fury-filled expression of betrayal as he screamed, 'You're a spy! My God, you're a spy...'

There was almost a question of disbelief hovering like a wasp. But the death sentence was pronounced and it was devastating.

'That's absurd,' I replied. My voice was disembodied as I stood accused and condemned by those few words. I was in deep, deep trouble, like a fish trapped in a trawler's net with no way of escape.

Everything would have been all right but for the telex; that damned machine and my alcoholic PA at the other end of it. Luis had been angry enough when he came into the office but nothing like he was now. Until that moment I could have expected arrest and a month or so incarcerated in jail treating vampire mosquitoes to liquid lunches before certain deportation. That had all changed and suddenly it was Luis who wanted my blood. I was facing someone who couldn't be reasoned with and all the evidence was there in black and white. He seemed to have lost his mind as he continued, 'You're a spy! I would never have believed it!'

Fervently I wished he wouldn't believe it. The yelling was unsettling and those brown eyes of his were blazing pure hatred. The urbane and likeable party spokesman, Dr Luis d'Almeida, had changed with schizophrenic intensity into a raving fanatic.

We'd always got on well. Only a month ago he'd discussed Angola's MPLA party and its flirtation with Marxism. 'We're not Marxist,' he'd insisted disarmingly, 'how can I be a Marxist? I'm a Roman Catholic.' My mind had flashed to the thousands of Cuban troops, bristling with weapons, who were disembarking down the coast; perhaps they too would have Roman Catholics amongst them. The MPLA, created from an ideology when there was an emphatic east-west divide, had found its aid from the Eastern bloc. With the connivance of well-placed moles in the Portuguese army and navy, it had used treachery, even murder, to gain control. I'd watched it happen; stood in the street as mortars showered bombs at dawn on the homes of genuine African nationalists with whom they were supposed to be sharing power until the time of a free and fair election they could not hope to win.

I'd seen the FNLA offices in Luanda, the capital, after the MPLA had smashed rockets into it, killing and wounding the occupants. This is what they did to people who were their allies in the war of independence against the Portuguese; I had no illusions about what they would do to an enemy, which is what I was accused of being – a CIA spy! Caught in the act, too!

I asked myself: What the hell am I doing here anyway? I'd been approached to come by the Associated Press of America but I couldn't blame them for the trouble I was in. I was the last British journalist left in the capital city unless the woman reporter from the *Financial Times* was still around. She'd been welcomed with open arms by the MPLA and I was warned that though I'd never even talked to her, she hated my guts. Perhaps it was she who had fingered me; I didn't know. Could it be the *Daily Telegraph* and *New York Times* correspondents? They'd certainly believed that I was responsible for their exposure which caused them to hurriedly leave the country with their tails between their legs. I suppose that in an indirect way I was, but it was the CIA man who had accompanied me to the battlefront who'd exposed them to the Consul General which would subsequently result in the American Secretary of State, Henry Kissinger, sending a message that he relied solely on my reports of the fighting. I could hardly tell d'Almeida that!

With Luis was a tall African who had been introduced as an intelligence officer. He was such a dedicated member of the silent service that throughout the whole proceedings he didn't open his mouth. Instead, he took part in rummaging through my files and waste paper baskets searching for incriminating evidence but I decided he really hadn't a clue what he was looking for. His sinister presence was frightening all the same.

Why was I so scared, more than I'd ever been in my life? Only two weeks ago I wasn't bothered when in this very room, three African bandits held me up at gunpoint. I'd attacked them and laughed when they ran away; it was *their* nerves that cracked. Perhaps it was because the accusations against me were as unjust as they were deadly. Some spy I'd make; I even feel guilty of intrusion when someone asks me to read a personal letter they've received. Come to think of it, by that yardstick it's surprising I'd even become a journalist.

Slowly I realized there was another reason for my concern; not only had nearly all my colleagues gone but there was also no western government representative to turn to. The British had closed their consular offices four months hence and even the brave American Consul-General had gone, personally ordered out by Kissinger two weeks ago – just seven days before Independence. I was very vulnerable, I knew that, and spelt out the uncomfortable truth to myself as Luis continued to scream. My accusers would be only too happy to put a western journalist on a mock trial before a kangaroo 'People's Court', especially as they knew about the country where I lived. First the torture, then the 'trial', followed by a public execution by a trigger-happy firing squad. They had already shot some of their own 'freedom fighters' on the local soccer pitch for taking part in what is still considered a victors' natural bounty in so much of Africa – rape and pillage. These charges were only minor compared to those levelled against me. To the MPLA, shooting an adopted Rhodesian would be a pleasure; shooting a reactionary, a duty; shooting a spy, mandatory. To d'Almeida, I was all three!

The vision of my fate moved in front of me like a hologram – hands tied behind the back, eyes blindfolded, an order shouted in Portuguese and the Cheshire Cheese would turn to Emmental as I crumbled into the dirt. It wouldn't be a nice way to go, I'd always thought I would succumb peacefully in bed or, like my dad, die from a sudden heart attack.

As I stood there, I reflected on my life: the little chap who took risks when he needn't have done, the honest crusader who would always win through in the end. Now, because of thoughtlessness or even malicious treachery by respected members of my profession, I wasn't so sure…

Zambezi river crocodile: 'Steel-like hide tore at the thin flesh of the Klepper...' Picture: Tony Down.

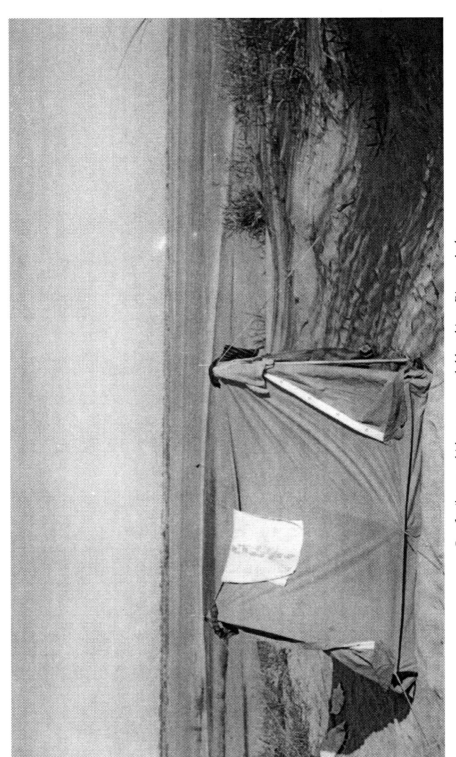

Our fragile tent, which was surrounded by a hippo Picture: Author.

A hippo jumped out of the water! Picture: Tony Down.

A cyclone approaches Dona Ana. Picture: Author.

The Zambezi adventure begins. Picture: Alan Allen, Rhodesia Herald.

Large goods, tiny boat! Picture: Rhodesia Herald.

The Zambezi, the Rubber Boat and an Angry Crocodile

During February/March 2001, the Zambezi River flooded causing death and destruction throughout central Mozambique. On the first day of March, Sophia Pedro, perched high in a tree in cyclonic conditions above the flooded lands of southern Mozambique, gave birth to a daughter, Rositha, before they were rescued by helicopter to enter the world of celebrities. Until this unusual feat of parturition, with which no man can ever compete, I'd firmly believed that my friend Tony Down and I, who had also overcome hurricane-type conditions on the Zambezi River, were possibly Mozambique's ultimate water survivors.

When I first met Tony Down he was an ambitious police sergeant in Southern Rhodesia. We couldn't have been more opposite in stature or thought and therefore an attraction of the opposites. He was born in England as was I and that's where the similarities ended: I was dark haired, diminutive and idealistic, he was blond, 6ft 2in tall and seemingly contemptuous of nearly everyone he met. His toughness manifested itself with a chiselled face and the glinting flinty eyes of a hunter but he was an honest and fearless man of the macho breed often condemned by lesser mortals but with whom it's good to be in an emergency. Tony once mentioned that he'd been the helmsman on a sailing ship which had got into serious difficulties in a storm. Fearing for the lives of the passengers and crew, he dived overboard and swam seven miles through rough seas to the shore to get help. In another terrifying incident he was crouching on the edge of the Zambezi River during a very personal moment when he saw a crocodile lumbering from the water and coming straight towards him. Even though he was literally caught with his pants down, his reaction was quicksilver: 'I grabbed my revolver and shot it between the eyes before I realized it was a leguan,' he told me. The unfortunate creature would have done him no harm and probably did my friend a service by accelerating his bowel evacuation.

Shortly after my return from circumnavigating Botswana's Okavango Swamps for *Life* magazine, Tony broached a proposition with seemingly feigned indifference: 'How about sailing down the Zambezi from Tete to the coast? It'll only take four days.' While the Zambezi may not be the longest river in the world, it is one of the most exciting but as I didn't want to be away from the family for a long period, I gave the suggestion slightly greater thought than usual. It was the 'four days' that persuaded me. 'Okay,' I replied in similar nonchalant vein. 'When do we go?' His face creased into a broad grin: 'January.'

January? Was he raving mad? Even winter in the Zambezi Valley is hot and as humid as newly manufactured elephant dung, yet he was advocating that we should undertake the 300-mile sail in mid-summer. Even worse, it would be at the height of the wet season! This meant that while on the water we would be sweating in temperatures of around 150 degrees Fahrenheit in the sun. I argued that the intense humidity would be so debilitating that we could be likened to chickens crammed into a steaming casserole, but my plea to change the date fell on unsympathetic ears. 'We can't go at any other time,' he said adamantly, 'as it's the only period when I can get leave.' By now he'd left the police and was representing the Swiss drugs company, Sandoz, for the whole of Africa and therefore had little time for holidays. 'Do you have a craft?' I ventured. 'Not yet but I have one coming from Germany, a twelve-foot Klepper sail boat.' That was small and when he saw the dubious look on my face he decided to reveal all, which wasn't reassuring. 'It's portable, it comes in three sections and is made of rubber.' I did a rapid mental check on the chances of surviving one of the world's most highly dangerous waterways in an outsized latex banana and concluded they were not very good. If I'd known in advance what would happen I'd never have agreed to go – or would I? Life is a very precious commodity and perhaps adventurous people like Tony and me take awful risks in order to appreciate and enjoy it all the more.

It's common knowledge in Africa that an angry hippo can mangle even a metal boat and its occupants without even scraping the plaque off its incisors, or it can just overturn a small vessel when it rises from the depths. Facing us, too, would also be a poisonous water snake and equally less known about by the general public was the Zambezi shark which I knew could go into a frenzy in temperatures of about eighty degrees Fahrenheit upwards and could tear our rubber boat and us to pieces. I'd learned quite a bit about the shark during a spell in Durban, South Africa, with Professor David Davies, the late Director of Oceanic Research Institute there, and its exploits would seem to put the much-publicised and feared Great White into the shade. He told me how they breed in river estuaries and had been found over 300 miles upstream from the coast on the very stretch of water we were to travel. Davies was convinced they were responsible for the carnage off the South African coast during WW2 when a ship carrying 765 Italian prisoners and 134 South African troops plus crew was torpedoed and sunk off Natal. There were only 192 survivors and they all spoke fearfully of horrendous attacks in the water and even on lifeboats by sharks crazed by blood. This particular shark is a world traveller and is known variously as the Shovelnose Grey, Slipway Grey and van Rooyen's Shark in South Africa, the Bull Shark, Cub Shark and Ground Shark in the USA, Lake Nicaragua Shark in Central America and the Whaler Shark in Australia. Other problems to face us would be the branches of submerged trees which could tear through the boat's thin skin like a butcher's blade, leaving us to helplessly splash about amongst the predators without a snowball's chance of surviving. Then there was the pre-dinosaur reptile, the crocodile, a 200-

million-year-old (give or take a few million years) survivor of the holocaust that changed life on earth. This monster could bite our rubber boat in half or, like the Zambezi shark, could leap out of the water and snatch one of us from it. Men armed with guns could be a problem, too, as the forbidding area through which we would travel gave cover to gangs of Frelimo guerrillas who were causing untold murder and mayhem downstream in their fight for Mozambique's independence.

Because of all these formidable odds, it was a challenge that I knew I'd have to face, like it or not; somehow there was always a challenge with Tony Down and I was never sure what he was trying to prove. He was a solitary man who didn't seem to have nor want any friends outside of myself and even that was an anomaly because he was particularly contemptuous of journalists. Sometimes he'd seemingly try to unnerve me, possibly because of my profession, and there were occasions his attempts would rebound and so I wondered if he found in me a challenge. Take the time that nearly got us both written off when driving at 60 mph on a corrugated dirt road towards Lake McIlwaine, just outside Salisbury (Harare) while reading a newspaper. This was a party piece but as he was a superb driver I was quietly confident that even when reading he kept one eye on the road ahead. Big, big mistake! As we neared a level crossing I saw a train approaching but waited before speaking and it was only when there was no sign of deceleration that I said, casually, 'There's a train coming.' He grunted, and carried on reading. What incredible bravado, I thought, and paused before repeating, a little anxiously, 'You really should slow down, otherwise we'll smack into it.' He glanced up from the newspaper just twenty-five yards from the track, with the car and train heading straight for each other; twisted metal and two mangled bodies only a second or two away. He slammed on the brakes and we pirouetted in a circle. For once he looked shame-faced and surprisingly vulnerable while I, smiling indulgently and without raising my voice, commented, 'Close!' He didn't utter a word but I knew Tony well enough that inwardly he was reproaching himself. While he didn't seem to care much for his own life, he'd never deliberately endanger someone for whom he was responsible. As for me, my overall attitude is that if you don't have confidence in the driver what the hell are you doing in the car?

While I've sailed single-handed I don't claim to be a good yachtsman even though some of my sailing experience was gained aboard Tony's Dunkirk veteran sailboat, *Snowgoose*. An example of why I admired him is the time he saved my life in a surreal situation when I was too laid-back to help myself. We were coming in at speed towards the jetty at McIlwaine in a high wind and he suggested I jump ashore with a rope and tie up. I jumped, slipped on the wet deck and hurtled beneath the water before entering into the feathery comfort of a dream world where reality slipped away and my brain comatosed into slow motion. As I gazed up, death loomed towards me at bone-crushing speed but I felt only complete detachment and a serenity; surreal enough for me to believe that I could slip out of danger as fast as an eel should I want to. As the craft came on sideways and I was about to be pulverised, I saw Tony's arm reach out and grab an upright wooden post on the jetty and hold it tight. How he did it I shall never know for it was with Herculean strength that he stopped the half-ton *Snowgoose* dead with its sails still billowing.

Since the building of Kariba Dam, the majestic Zambezi had become un-navigable to downstream shipping in Mozambique except for a few miles from the Indian Ocean coast. Tony's invitation had given me an opportunity to traverse its course before the Portuguese completed a dam of their own at Kebrabassa, to be named Caborra Bassa, which I believed would turn the river into something of a canal. I had wanted to go down before such an anticipated ecological disaster occurred. The start of the new damming had already given me a chance to look around Kebrabassa, the very same gorge that had defeated the missionary explorer, Dr David Livingstone, when he failed to navigate through it on his smoke belching, asthmatic-wheezing boat, the *Ma Robert*. His river launch, with its funnel protruding as an upright chimney stack, had put the fear of God into the watching tribesmen until he assured them that God was actually with him and that He was on their side. It was on that brief Kebrabassa visit that I came across huge hollowed-out boulders protruding from the river and Livingstone, I was told later, had also come across the same boulders and entered them and so it's possible that we were the only two white people to have done so or ever will. Kariba Dam had destroyed the Kebrabassa rapids, which had been rated as the most dangerous in the world, and as I now climbed into one boulder I felt privileged to look down in wonder and to marvel at how a tumble-drier spinning effect had reduced large stones inside into tiny pebbles. They are all sunken treasures now, hidden beneath the lake waters held back by the great Caborra Bassa dam.

It was on this brief visit, too, that I also appreciated with incredulity the awesome determination and ability of flora to survive in extreme conditions even greater than cacti and baobab have to contend with. Having clambered some distance down into the steep gorge, I happened across the single living root of a dwarfed tree straddled over fifteen feet of bare rock. The stumped tree even bore dust-covered green leaves, which was an outstanding achieve-ment when considering that the excessively high temperature of the rock in summer would severely cauterize a human hand within seconds of touching it. As I paused to gaze in wonder and admiration at this wonderful heat-mangled survivor, I reflected that despite all its efforts to live, Man would eventually drown it in the same manner as the trees at upstream Kariba lake had also been drowned. Only their skeletal mummified fingers are left to point accusingly and eternally at those who had drowned them in their prime.

My own survival was brought into jeopardy even on that innocent Caborra Bassa visit thanks to an act of gross stupidity by the pilot of a private plane. As my charter Piper Cub aircraft was preparing to land on a narrow airstrip hewn from a rock jutting 3,000 ft high above the river chasm, a dismembered voice on the radio gave us the go-ahead to touch down. Without warning, another small plane shot ahead, crossing our flight path in what would be officially termed a 'near miss' and caused us to swerve sharply. The queue jumper landed and we touched down immediately afterwards before the voice crackled over the radio, 'There seems to have been a mistake but you can land now.' My pilot hissed with undisguised contempt and frustration, 'We're already on the bloody ground!'

Now, a year after the plane incident, Tony and I stood on the banks of the Zambezi River at Tete and began to assemble the boat, drawing the rubber sheath over the wooden framework. We'd practised doing this many times before in Salisbury until we were proficient in getting it together in twenty minutes but we hadn't anticipated the heat and humidity so early in the morning and the effect it would have on the wood and rubber. The 7 a.m. temperature at Tete was 120 degrees Fahrenheit and it took four and a half hours of sweat and toil before the boat was ready! A major setback to the trip was the absence of sail even though Tony had made several frustrating attempts to get a mast for the Klepper but without success owing to world sanctions imposed upon Rhodesia. We had a mast built locally but when this proved to be too heavy for the craft we reluctantly decided to rely upon the boat's five-hp outboard engine which meant we would carry a heavy load of extra fuel to cramp still more our limited space. For supplies we took only salt, biltong (dried meat), tinned food, rice, tea, coffee and medicated coconut oil to protect us from sunburn, fishing rods and a small supply of fresh water, Halazone tablets for water purifying, a small patrol tent and two sleeping bags. The basic plan was to live off the water.

I gazed across the Zambezi and it was a daunting sight. 'They've opened the Kariba floodgates,' I observed dejectedly as water rushed past but as Tony stared across the mile-wide stretch of river he seemed quite happy at the fast flow, declaring, 'It will save fuel.' As we eased ourselves into the heavily laden three-foot-wide flimsy craft, a *Rhodesia Herald* photographer recorded the start of what was rated an historic adventure that no one had dared to do before (nor since). 'We'll make Dona Ana tonight,' declared Tony confidently and I looked at him quizzically until he explained that Dona Ana was not a Portuguese lady of easy virtue but a settlement downstream. The first day went smoothly enough and as evening approached the ever-widening river became placid, shimmering with enough deceit to lure us into believing there were no dangers lurking below the surface. Gently we floated along the beautiful African waterway in a near hypnotic trance until we realised it would soon be dark and we were a long way from either bank. As Tony started the engine the boat suddenly rocked and shook haphazardly as if a subterranean volcano had burst beneath us and we gazed up in astonishment at the most amazing sight I have ever seen in my life, or ever will see again: poised only yards ahead and ten to fifteen feet in the air was a gigantic 5,000 lb bull hippopotamus! Instinctively, Tony swerved the boat to avoid us being crushed on its return to the water while I grabbed my camera and hastily whipped off the lens cap but I was far too late for a world-class photo as the hippo came down with the splash of a depth charge before submerging to hidden depths. Even though we rode across the spot where the *grand jeté en avant* took place and Tony turned the boat around to travel back over it again and again, there were no encores for me to photograph and share our incredibly privileged experience with others.

Slowly we made our way to the south bank as Dona Ana was clearly further away than Tony had anticipated, and my fantasy of being embraced by the clean sheets of well-sprung beds of an hotel became a wistful daydream. Instead we came to a grinding halt and found ourselves firmly wedged on a submerged sandbank. Gingerly we disembarked and pulled the boat for several yards before the sand ran out and we now found ourselves struggling in deep, fast-moving water as we hit the mainstream, desperately clinging for our lives to the rubber craft. The situation was critical as we hung on to the heavily laden Klepper while at the same time tried to struggle aboard, knowing that with the slightest false move the boat would overturn. As I was the lightest and a poor swimmer, Tony helped me aboard and then I helped pull him up. Imagined lurking crocodiles were an incentive to get aboard quickly and we made the south bank without further trouble, just as the giant red globe over which many have eulogised, turned the Zambezi into a tropical paradise before disappearing behind the raised curtain of a distant escarpment.

My friend began to cook as I put up the tent and while they don't usually give me trouble, this one was an aggravation. In Africa the wind tends to drop at sunset yet now it was rising and the condescending smile from Tony quickly turned to anger as sand on the canvas landed in his cooking pot. Eventually we both worked on the small green tent but it took forty minutes to erect. After we dined, Tony magically produced a bottle of cognac for himself and for me, a Glenlivet (it appropriately means, 'The Valley of the Flooding River') accompanied by a box of cigars. He was, and is, a very tough character and would never suffer a fool but he has a caring streak and clearly took pleasure in my look of appreciation. 'You're a genius,' I murmured.

Our first night beside the river was a mere foretaste of things to come. Because of sand fleas – there is always something to bite you in Africa – we found it more comfortable to sweat in our warm quilted sleeping bags than stay outside them in a sublime ninety degrees Fahrenheit. During the night I heard a noise above the sound of cicadas and snorting hippo and I put my hand out to turn on a tape recorder. If I hadn't, I knew my companion would never just take my word for what I would tell him. Come the dawn, we were up at 6.30 a.m. 'You snored,' I said. Tony looked vexed and self-righteous. 'I don't snore,' he snapped. I wonder what it is about snoring that people refuse to admit to it as if they've been accused of a heinous crime and yet cannot possibly know whether they are doing so when they're in the land of nod. I wasn't going to argue and switched on the tape recorder; it may not have been the most tactful way to start the day but it had been an insufferable night, especially for a flea and mosquito-bitten person like myself who doesn't snore.

As I tucked into a boiled egg for breakfast, Tony casually pointed to a nearby sandbank which we would have to pass and what I saw was indigestible. Seven crocodiles were resting there and all seven pairs of green evil eyes were staring directly at us. I'm not clairvoyant but I could read their minds: they were hungrily awaiting a breakfast of their own and we were on the menu! I was surprised they hadn't tried to take us during the night – possibly our tightly closed tent had deterred them. After we had eaten we repacked our supplies neatly into the boat and manoeuvred it away without touching the nearby sandbank but I was concerned that we might run onto another which was submerged: then we'd be sitting ducks for the crocs which we watched slide quietly into the water.

Severe heat rapidly became oppressive and tortuous and we were soon hanging over the side pouring saucepanfuls of warm Zambezi water over our sweat-soaked heads. Our precious clean water supply had quickly vanished and we were forced to begin drinking from the river which we cleansed with purifying tablets. Purifying? What a misnomer! The water was full of sand, mixed with crocodile and hippo uppings for flavour and I soon had awful visions of my intestines being clogged with animal waste. At 9 a.m. we glided into the narrow Lupata Gorge where a major fortune in silver is reputed to be stashed away. Only two senior Manica tribesmen reputedly know at any one time where it is and they hand down the information through successive generations. The water was now moving at the speed of rapids through the narrow gorge and after half an hour of being pressure cooked we pulled over to some rocks where Tony diagnosed a swim to ease our sunburn. So intense was the sun that it had tanned the skin through our shirts. 'What about crocs?' I asked with incredulity, believing that swimming was the most absurd suggestion I'd ever heard. 'You don't have to worry about them,' Tony said, airily. 'They don't operate in fast-moving water but will wait at the end of the gorge for whatever titbit comes along.' I wasn't totally convinced but he tied a mooring rope around his waist and asked me to hold the other end as he plunged into the water with supreme confidence. After ten minutes, I hauled him towards me and when he came out I was consoled to see that he still had all his limbs attached. 'Beautiful,' he declared, 'that was just beautiful.' Then it was my turn and I too spent about ten minutes in the water before he pulled me to the rock. All the water from the upstream Victoria Falls and Kariba was moving so fast through the narrow gap that no one could have swum against the current; the taut rope had also kept me afloat.

Later, two weeks after our return to Salisbury, I was enjoying a quiet drink and related the incident to a hunter friend who looked at me in a strange kind of way, sideways and disbelieving but with a respectful air of admiration. 'You swam in Lupata Gorge?' he said. 'That gorge contains some of the largest crocs in Africa!' I then thought of something else: the Zambezi shark had been seen further upstream than Lupata and the water's temperature while we were swimming was above that needed to send the shark berserk!

As evening approached and the river had broadened and slowed to an almost static pool we saw our first signs of civilisation, a fortress perched on top of a hill. 'Dona Ana?' I asked. 'Well, er…' mumbled Tony. 'Can you see a suspension bridge?' 'Come on, it's much too wide here for a suspension bridge,' I replied. Tony had made his point. We'd arrived at Tambara, a settlement we thought we must have passed many miles back. A group of Africans waved, and forgetting crocodiles and my inability to swim well, I dived overboard and made for the bank thirty yards away. Ruling Tambara was the Portuguese Provincial Administrator, Senhor Jasconuno Carmelo da Cunha, who, despite such an ostentatious name, was a very nice chap. 'I heard on the radio that you were coming down,' he smiled, holding up his arms at the water's edge. 'I thought you might need these.' In his hands were the very reason for my rashness in swimming ashore and he handed each of us a freezing cold bottle of Manica beer. Never before nor since have I felt such gratitude to one person as I tasted the finest lager ever to befriend Man!

We spent a well-protected night as guests at da Cunha's nineteenth-century fortress which, he told us with pride, was one of only two triangular forts in the world. It seemed to be an absurd place to put such an historical treasure but then, I thought, only the Portuguese would want to cling to such a God-forsaken area. The fortress had been built 150 years before during the 'War of Pacification' and I was sorry for the young da Cunha living out there alone with his wife, child and a Portuguese estate manager. An intelligent couple, they had little chance of outside conversation and their only entertainment was an old crackling radio and a few gramophone records. He told me that he looked after 11,000 rural, uneducated Africans and I noticed that a loaded rifle was propped against the wall in every room I visited. 'I'm dead,' he confided with an oblique smile over dinner where we had been joined at the table by his African domestic staff. 'The other day I was listening to Radio Tanzania and heard a report that terrorists had crossed the river from Malawi and killed both me and my family.' I looked over to his young attractive Portuguese wife and wondered how she coped, knowing they were prize targets and if they had made a death pact should they be reduced to a handful of bullets.

From the buttress next morning we stared across the Zambezi River which was now five miles wide and pockmarked with sandbanks, some no larger than our boat while others covered more than 100 yards. It didn't look inviting and I appreciated Tony's wisdom in bringing a compass; something I had thought irrelevant until now, seeing that we were going downstream all the way. Soon after we bade our farewells we were lost – totally, completely and utterly lost despite the compass. We'd been admiring the courage of an African who braved the crocs by standing up to his neck in water setting fish traps and an hour later, as we approached one of the interminable vegetated islands, I pointed, 'There's another man doing the same thing!' Something was uncannily familiar about him and also the surrounding area which gave me a despondent sense of *déjà vu*: it was the very same man! Because of the width of the water, there'd been no noticeable downstream and as we manoeuvred around the scores of islands and visible sandbanks, thus wasting our valuable fuel, the compass had shown us to be going in all directions. Another hour passed and we were back at the same spot but the African had disappeared. Two more hot and sticky hours were to pass, while I contemplated his fate, before we found our way out of the giant millpond maze.

'Look at that!' cried Tony with the enthusiasm of a schoolboy finding a stickleback in a stagnant pond. I glanced to where he was pointing only to see the forbidding 'V' shape of a large crocodile swimming just below the surface. By the laws of survival, any sane and intelligent person would immediately alter course to the opposite direction but when our boat turned I realised that Tony, with gung-ho enthusiasm, was actually 'buzzing' it. Backwards and forwards we criss-crossed, our rubber boat just skimming its snout in an attempt to force the reptile to divert its course but with admirable dignity and contempt it completely ignored us. My companion became so engrossed with the creature that he wasn't looking where he was going and there was a grinding crunch as we landed onto a sandbank. 'That was clever,' I commented dryly and turned to see if the croc would attack but happily the reptile just didn't want to know and snootily carried on its way. Tony grinned sheepishly and it took a full half an hour of wading and pulling through six inches of water under the ever-blazing sun before we were on our way again. That night, my companion reproduced the goodies of the night before and we quietly sat and drank. It was our last truly convivial night together and the next day an incident took place which would make us members of a very exclusive band of survivors.

We had just spent another exhausting period of pulling the heavily laden craft off a submerged sandbank when it happened. Unknown to us a crocodile was watching our every movement, waiting for its moment to strike. Hot, sweating and tired, we dragged the boat into three feet of water and as I began to struggle aboard we hit the mainstream and started to move away fast. I was almost aboard with only my legs waving just above the water when Tony yelled and literally hurled himself out of the water and into the boat without overturning us. As his 230 lbs crashed into the frail craft I saw, fascinated, the familiar and sickening 'V' shape slicing through the water at less than ten feet away. Its speed defied belief and it all happened so quickly that within a fraction of a second it had sped under the boat missing Tony's legs by inches. Steel-like hide tore at the thin flesh of the Klepper and we spun like a leaf in the cone of a tornado as death incarnate stopped and lashed its tail angrily. 'Missed,' I commented somewhat amused for I was genuinely unperturbed: Tony, on the other hand, glared and I could see that he was livid. He grabbed a paddle and began lashing out at the croc, cursing it for having the audacity to attack us. We humans all react differently to danger and Tony was far more upset than me; perhaps it was something personal between him and the crocodiles for he treated them with disdain. The thought of being outwitted by this reptile, no matter how many millions of years of ancestral experience in killing and survival it might have, would be too much for my friend. A later examination of the boat showed ridges on the rubber where the crocodile's rough hide had scored it. Had we been in any shallower water the hull would have been torn to shreds and so would we, very shortly afterwards. The incident said much for the hardiness of the Klepper which was not built to withstand the full impact of a crocodile attack and our craft was probably the only one ever to have done so. The attack also displayed the awesome strength of the crocodile that it could turn around a heavily laden sailboat (as opposed to a flat-bottomed dinghy) with two men aboard. I felt the incident and my spontaneous remark had perhaps soured our relationship as we hardly said a word all the way down the river but in reality Tony's disposition had nothing to do with me. The sun, intense heat and humidity and perhaps even the filthy drinking water, were physically and psychologically affecting my companion very badly indeed. He was feeling very ill and I was worried for him.

That night we slept on a small island because of a strong wind and choppy waters which came up in late afternoon and fight it as we may, it prevented us from reaching either bank. Our diminishing petrol supply, which had never been intended to last this long, was also causing grave concern and did nothing to ease our tensions. An indication of Tony's sickness was evidenced when we left the island next morning two hours later than usual but he insisted on manning the tiller. By now it was our fifth day on the water and just forty minutes after departure our spirits rose as we spotted the suspension bridge of Dona Ana! She was an incredible structure with over thirty spans looped like a mythical sea monster across the glimmering expanse of river. As the fiery sun hung above it to create a vast heat haze, the bridge became the mirage of a snarling medieval dragon with nostrils that exhaled a flame of such intensity that even our boat quivered and with a loud belch the engine stopped. It was at this very moment of sighting the bridge our precious fuel supply ran out! There were wooden paddles aboard but our boat, which was built for graceful sail, protested at the indignity we inflicted upon her and she reacted like a cow in labour when we used them. Fortunately, we quickly found the mainstream but shortly afterwards we pulled off it with difficulty to what was believed to be the town only to discover a small Portuguese settlement with no petrol.

Back in the boat we struggled to the mainstream again and fought hard to stay in it with a bucking craft that refused to be paddled. Two desperate miles further on, we reached Dona Ana where a small group of Portuguese were standing on the bank to greet us with big smiles and a hand clap, telling us that they, like the keeper of the fort at Tambara, had heard of our trip on the national radio. To them we were heroes and they regarded us with awe, something I enjoyed to the full, but it did cross my mind that if everyone we met had listened to the radio, so too would the local guerrilla bands who might want to attack us for the publicity they would gain. Ever an hospitable people, the Portuguese bystanders took us to the nearest café for a beer and sandwiches and we were then driven two and a half miles inland to a petrol pump.

I wanted Tony to spend the night at Dona Ana in order to recuperate but he declined, saying he preferred to cross to the far side of the Zambezi before setting up camp. As we prepared to leave, a man came across to me and he looked grave. 'You must stay here tonight, it is very dangerous to go on,' he warned. 'Don't worry about us,' I answered, 'we know all the about crocodiles, we met one.' He put a concerned hand on my shoulder, 'No, no, you must understand that you cannot leave. There is a big cyclone coming towards us and it is too dangerous to go on to the river!' Cyclone Daphne, he told me, had been moving back and forth for several hours and was now raging just ahead of us in the Indian Ocean! That was a hazard I hadn't reckoned on when I first weighed up our chances of success but it explained the unexpected evening winds. I recalled reading a book which stated that cyclones frequently travelled up the Zambezi and once, seventeen years previously during the night of 18 February 1950, the wind swept along the waterway and deposited fifteen inches of rain. At Kariba Gorge, four surveyors camping on the banks had been swept away and drowned while at Chirundu, just upstream from Tete where we had started out, the river rose an incredible twenty-four feet! The deaths amongst tribespeople was not known but carnage amongst the animals was appalling and the rotting carcasses in varied stages of decomposition ranged from elephant, buffalo and lion on the ground to cheetahs and leopards in the trees. 'Are you sure you want to go?' I asked Tony but he was adamant and I suspected he was concerned that his health might give up totally if we rested up. Tony was a man who had to drive himself into the ground if need be in order to achieve his objective and I couldn't argue too much as he was, after all, the skipper.

When we left Dona Ana the water was placid and the warm breath of a breeze brushed gently across my sun-blistered cheeks like a woman's lips with a blissful promise of the passion to come. For a while I sat for'ard in the boat soaking in its gentle caress; oblivious of anything but the serenity of the moment until a voice jolted me out of my reverie of self-indulgence, 'We're in trouble!' I looked about me and saw the glistening waters were becoming restless while soft velvety clouds were starting to scud and harden into ominous crazy shapes. A monk dressed in black stared at me and to his right was the figurehead of the *Flying Dutchman* itself, defiantly fighting God and the treacherous seas to the south of us off the Cape of Good Hope. Even as I watched the cloud formations the waters of the Zambezi whipped up into a frenzy and torrential rain struck us with the penetrating force of steel-tipped arrows while waves furiously slapped the sides of our pathetically frail craft. I grabbed a small saucepan, the only utensil to hand, and baled furiously to combat the attack from all sides by waves, wind and rain.

During the unequal struggle for our lives, the boat ran aground on a small, palm-fringed island and despite our exhaustion we battled to make camp before enduring an insufferable night of hell with the wind so strong that it savagely and repeatedly pulled our the tent stanchions from the loose sand. I wished we had the experience of Bedouins for most of the hours of darkness were used up trying to keep the shelter over our heads. The trouble with keeping a 'Ship's Log' is that you are aware of the date and next morning's had a fearful reputation: Friday thirteenth!

The storm had abated before dawn but the day started badly as Tony was still very unwell and his mood didn't improve when the engine began to play up; I wondered if the change of petrol at Dona Ana was responsible. We'd only been on the water for an hour before it spluttered and with a final snort broke down completely. Reluctantly we produced the paddles again and struggled towards yet another island, wondering if this was where it would all end, ignominiously and in a place known only to God. The wind had dropped but the sun reflecting off the water showed no compassion and as there was no place on the island to pull the boat ashore, I stood on board holding a paddle ready to repel all crocodiles while Tony stood bravely in the water trying to carry out repairs. I felt a little foolish standing upright with a thin wooden paddle, knowing full well that should a fifteen or twenty-foot monster attack at speed, I might as well be waving a wafer biscuit. Tony detected the fault in the fuel pipe which was leaking at a joint and this he glued before we set off once more without much confidence, expecting the engine to peter out again. It was a time to keep our fingers crossed as neither of us had any idea how the glue would stand up to such high temperatures and we expected the worst.

Throughout the day we edged our way slowly downstream but the weather changed and the recurring storm blew up. Cyclone Daphne was getting closer yet again as she restlessly danced a chassé around the Indian Ocean with her tentacles ominously reaching out, probing, searching for the mouth of the Zambezi River. Four-foot waves pounded and lapped aboard our fragile craft as tropical rain lashed our faces and helped to swell the water above our ankles. We seemed to be fighting a losing battle and I looked back at Tony, his bull-like shoulders hunched forward and his face set in stone. 'Keep baling,' he ordered gruffly in a voice that could be hardly heard yet its tone was more of an order than a request. My mind went to the family and wondered what possessed me to get into such desperate situations. Perhaps it was the children for they, I knew, would be proud of their dad. It couldn't be for Margery as she would much prefer that I was at home like any normal husband. No, there was more to it than that and I realised as I battled against the odds the true reason: I needed the excitement and the flow of adrenalin; the taking of risks. Here, I was living an open life and to the full and I knew that despite the odds we would make the shore provided I kept baling frantically with the pathetically small saucepan. An hour after the storm began we reached another small island which appeared through the rain as if from nowhere. As we went ashore, Sod's Law prevailed; the rain stopped and the wind died down as Daphne's long arms withdrew out to sea until tomorrow when she would call upon us again!

Tony slept well but I was cruelly attacked by mosquitoes despite using re-pellent. My blood is their nectar as I long ago discovered to my cost, whereas my companion was left alone. Mosquito tension always begins from the moment I hear a whine as a mossie flies along the flight path and this is followed by an aphonic silence after it settles on to an untraceable landing area; I know it is poised to strike and the tautness within me builds up to screaming pitch as I hold my hand at the ready until it noiselessly glides and settles on me like a feather. There is a sudden sharp smack on my face as I try to kill it and miss, and the mental torture of hit-and-miss chess between human and killer insect continues throughout the night.

I'd dozed off into a fitful sleep but was awakened when the ground began to tremble with an earthquake intensity of point five on the Richter scale accompanied by the chomping sound of a giant masticating. What was it? Gingerly and silently I untied the thin ropes and poked my head outside the tent and what I saw was daunting; we were surrounded by hippo – I counted eight – and they were so close I could have reached out and touched one of them. They had risen from the murky depths of the Zambezi River and come ashore without making a sound until their cavernous mouths chomped on nearby reeds. Being fully aware that hippopotamus accounted for more human deaths than any other animal in Africa, I shook Tony to consciousness and whispered, 'We're surrounded by hippo!' He looked out of the tent, nodded drowsily, and turned back to sleep. 'What do you suggest we do?' I asked, hesitantly. Tony was equal to my belief in his fearlessness and I suspected he had a malicious grin when he turned back and answered, 'They have a nasty habit of playfully running through tents but if they don't want to play they'll go back into the water!' Very comforting, I thought and I repeated the question, 'So what do we do?' 'Go back to sleep,' he whispered drowsily. 'We're trapped and there is nothing else we can do.' With that, he turned over again in his sleeping bag. I had to give him credit: what panache! Furthermore, I was sure he was absolutely right and I did the same; shut out the immediate worries and dangers of the outside world. The hippos slipped away during the night as quietly as they had arrived but I had an object lesson, well learned, that would come in useful years later when I was covering a very nasty and bloody civil war in Angola.

Next morning, even before easing myself from the sleeping bag, I annihilated thirteen mosquitoes in the tent in less than two minutes, none of them on Tony's side. My face was mutilated by their bites between the sores which were appearing because of the heat and undernourishment. I knew we were suffering some of the agonies pioneers, explorers and missionaries experienced as they opened up the hinterland for the Europeans. Four hundred years earlier the Portuguese had called the Zambezi 'The River of Promise' and sent an army of 1,000 conquistadores upstream wearing shining breastplates and high domed morion helmets. To me, the thought of wearing breastplates in that sun was mind-boggling. Battling against malaria, sleeping sickness and the great African king, Monomatapa, all took their toll on the Portuguese soldiers and history records that very few survived. As if to emphasize their experiences, Tony's stomach and now his back were getting worse and his moods became very dark indeed. My sometimes humorous friend was becoming a regular Captain Bligh; perhaps this was not surprising when taking into consideration his suffering and acute sense of responsibility, and the only relief to the tension between us came when we reached Vila Fontes, a pleasant small town where we collected fresh water, mangoes and pawpaw. Further downstream we realised that we were at last edging towards civilisation and the logbook noted: 'We passed Laconia at 2.15 p.m. which appeared attractive with its little railway station on a hill.' I made a further observation, 'It's strange, but the African women we have seen here nearly all wear blue skirts. Some trader must have sold them on the idea.' I was wrong: it was the Roman Catholic missionaries who were responsible and they seemed not to know about the needs of those they converted as dark blue skirts are far from conducive to the African climate. Amusingly, the white missionaries discouraged the ladies from walking around bare-breasted and with rings through their noses and other parts of the body. One now has to visit Britain to witness the culture swap!

The cyclone returned like a magnet and throughout the afternoon we again desperately battled for our lives against heavy waves until it was dark when we reached the safety of the south bank. Our attempts at fishing throughout the trip had been poor; to be precise, we hadn't caught a damned thing. At the tiny settlement of Chupanga, a fantastic sight awaited us: a ferry made of oil drums, yet powered by Perkins diesel engines. As we pressed on the cyclone returned like a magnate. That afternoon we battled for our lives yet again through heavy waves to reach the safety of the shore where tribespeople, led by their chief or headman, Harry, stood on the bank to greet us. Harry didn't sound like much of a Portuguese or African name, but it was dark and we were too exhausted to ask questions. Quite suddenly, there was no wind and the waves receded once more.

Surprisingly, Harry spoke excellent English and insisted that he provide food and despite African superstitions about going out on the water at night, he sent off a group of boatmen to catch some. Ah! The awesome power of being a chief! Soon they returned and triumphantly produced catches of bream but being too tired to cook on a spit, we fried them in the only fat we had – medicated coconut oil. The wonderful fresh fish tasted foul but we had to consume them with broad smiles; we could not disappoint our genial host and his followers who watched us eat the lot. Then it became a night of enchantment beside the camp fire as the throbbing of drums beat out their message that Harry was entertaining European guests for dinner. This, I thought, is the Africa that I know and love and I slept contentedly and soundly to the pulsating rhythm. Because we had mentioned to Harry that we would be leaving early, he awakened us at dawn and we found the whole village surrounding our tent carrying mangoes to see us on our way. Very reluctantly, we made our farewells and a couple of hours later we stopped on an island to make tea. I walked over the sand and saw spoor coming from the water: it was easy to identify – crocodile! Without giving my next action a thought, I followed it unarmed to a freshly dug hole and coming out of eggshells scattered around it were baby crocs. Mother, I quickly realised, had disappeared by another route otherwise she might well have provided them with their first-ever meal and I called Tony across. He picked up one shell to help a baby out and was rewarded with a bite on the finger. Making a hostile squeaking sound, five of them lined up and tried to attack us, their sharp little teeth snapping angrily and then another came from some scrub. Clearly, even at birth, crocodiles are nothing but anti-social. It was a unique find and fortunate for us to be in the right place at the right time.

In the crocodile world, the mother buries her eggs and then returns to scoop them out when her time clock says they are due to hatch. Usually only about twenty per cent survive, the rest being taken by large fish which have to make the most of the situation before the crocs are big enough to take the initiative. Similar breeding practices were carried out by dinosaurs such as the ninety-foot long, thirty-ton Diplodocus, over 130 million years ago. The crocodile was around at that time, and during the Zambezi's 150-million-year history it was home to many dinosaurs whose skeletal remains have been found there. They include the Syntarsus, a small feathered creature that hopped about and shared common physiological characteristics with present-day birds. A suspected warm-blooded creature, the feathers were needed to insulate it against extremes of climate and later, its descendants used the feathers for flight. The valley, which is older than its famous neighbour, the Great Rift Valley, had also been the home of another prehistoric creature, the seventy-five-foot-long brachiosaurus which stood as tall as a two-storey building and weighed fifty tons, thus comparing the hippo outside our tent to Lilliputian children's toys.

Our epic journey was approaching its end and next day we arrived at the Marromea sugar estates. Even then there was a surprise as we saw a Mississippi-type paddle steamer which was used to carry sugar to the estuary but it also carried passengers. If Paul Robeson had appeared singing 'Ol' Man River' it wouldn't have surprised me. 'Tie-up,' growled Tony, still oppressively Bligh-like, as we pulled alongside the jetty. 'That's it!' I muttered to myself, jumping ashore and stalking off, leaving the boat to swing back with Tony sitting on its edge. I glanced back and smiled malevolently as his head emerged from oily water. Inside the offices of the sugar estate, fans whirling from the ceiling brought the temperature down to a blissfully cool 112 degrees Fahrenheit. But the heat outside was not the reason we didn't return to the river even though we were only a mile from the coast. Cyclone Daphne was still around and we agreed that to go further would be suicide. I'd been ready to chance it until Tony pointed out that as the boat could hardly contain the Zambezi's waves, we would not have made a quarter of a mile in the Indian Ocean. Instead we took the sugar estate train back to Vila Fontes and then went on to Beira where I telephoned home to give an assurance that we were safe. This was met with unexpected relief as I learned that the *Rhodesia Herald* had been publishing alarmist stories that we were missing. We had, after all, been on the water for ten days instead of the expected four.

Tony Down's present boat. Picture: Tony Down.

At Beira, Tony tested the boat in the sea to see if the Marromea decision had merit. A wave overturned the craft within minutes and threw him into the water with the engine still running and I winced as the propeller blade just missed chopping off his head. As he pulled the boat ashore I walked to the water's edge and held out a Manica Lager, 'Come on, let's have a beer,' I said. He grinned, the first time I had seen him do so since Tambara. Later, I would become best man at his wedding to Laura.

At the end of our trip, Tony mentioned his childhood and how he had stood on a quay at Plymouth and tied up the yachts of the wealthy who moored in the harbour. He had a dream that one day he would have a yacht of his own and it was an ambition that would be realized. The last time I saw him was at Plymouth where he owned a large waterborne 'gin palace' and an impressively big penthouse overlooking the harbour. We went offshore and winched down the boat's rubber dinghy to wallow on the Solent for half an hour; our thoughts thousands of miles and a few decades away and I reflected upon how I came to be in Africa in the first place. Unlike Tony, my only dreams had been nightmares so fearful that as a small child I was terrified to go to sleep. The nightmares were always recurring – I was either being chased by lions and other wild animals or by tribesmen wielding spears. As I grew older the nightmares faded and there seemed little chance that these fears would ever be realised until the crocodile attack. Take away the spears and replace them with Russian-made AK-47s and the nightmares would become reality.

Much later, the BBC series of derring-do entitled *Epic Journeys* was led with a canoe trip down the whole length of the Zambezi by a lady then unknown in Britain, Sandi Toksvig. I estimated that she was actually on the Zambezi by herself for about four minutes, and that was where the river rose as a stream. When I pooh-poohed the programme, saying it belittled the other epic features which were genuine, I was accused by acquaintances of sour grapes and belittling the woman. After writing a letter of complaint, I received the following response from the BBC:

> Dear Mr Shay, You are quite right to say that Sandi Toksvig did not canoe down the Zambezi. In fact, she admitted as much several times during the programme. She certainly set out to canoe the river, but part of the humour of the film was in her inability to do so. I hope this clarifies the situation.
>
> Yours sincerely, Alan Bookbinder, Series Editor.

I and others who saw the show must have missed the admissions and the humour of a programme which was to launch this overbearing 'celebrity' on her successful British career.

Early Influences

When it happened, our small terraced home in Tooting, South London, shook to the foundations with volcanic ferocity and sound. 'What was that?' cried Mum in alarm as Warren dashed into the hallway quickly returning with his face and clothes as white as a Persil ghost.

'It's in the front room,' he panted excitedly, 'the ceiling's collapsed!'

'The front room?' Mum whispered, her face transformed with a mixture of shock and horror. The parlour was her temple, the holiest of shrines, so sacred that only rare visitors were entertained within its confines except at Christmas when it became a treasure house of presents and the stage for the annual incineration of the pine tree. This was a ritual that began when flames from tiny coloured candles ignited the tree's thin green needles and the branches, too, from which small presents and decorations hung. As the flames blazed and crackled our mum would courageously race with the eyebrow-singeing inferno out through the back door and into the garden where I would watch the wind-swept flames consume all the mouth-watering colourfully wrapped chocolates that were meant for my brother and me. The room, with its polished floor, blue patterned rug, *chaise longue*, lonely aspidistra and an upright piano that none of us could play (Tooting in the twenties wasn't noted for its *soirées*) also included a French-polished table which had held the coffin encasing Dad's body before, to Mum's extreme anguish and humiliation, it was spirited away to Streatham cemetery for interment beside his first wife.

Now, in that very shrine of such poignant memories, something bizarre had happened.

'Come on,' urged my big brother as he led us forward to the room which had been transformed into an Alpine winter scene, with decades of whitewash glistening like stardust through beams of light filtered from the sash windows. 'Look,' cried Warren. He dramatically pointed aloft to where the heavy Victorian plaster ceiling had been. We stared in bewilderment but all we could see was a hole.

'What are we supposed to be looking at?' snapped Mum. Her voice didn't mask her irritation for she knew it would take days to clear the mess and cost her the precious money she had worked so hard for, to pay for the repairs. 'Can't you see?' said my brother, dramatically wiping the white dust from his metal-rimmed spectacles. 'The hole! Look at the hole – it's shaped like a map of Africa!'

Africa? Warren was a pupil at the nearby Smallwood Road School and knew about such places whereas I'd heard of the dark forbidding continent only a week or so earlier after a man with a black skin sauntered down the road and neighbours had come out of their houses to stare at him. Even though I'd seen a photograph on a wall at the doctor's of black children sitting in the bush around a portable gramophone with its outsized ear trumpet-type horn, he was the first such man I'd ever seen in the flesh.

'Africa,' repeated Mum, 'that is strange!' She had deeply held superstitions that had made her easy prey for any itinerant hawker (especially if he wore a turban), who chanced to knock at the door with a bag of Talismans. Was the fallen ceiling an omen? Was there a message about Africa being sent to us? She would have thought it possible but for whom was it intended? Mum would never live long enough to travel overseas even if she had wanted to, which she didn't, and any message would not have been for Warren either as the only time he was to stay abroad was during WW2 when he served with the army in India. There was only one of the trio left – the diminutive shy and uncomprehending little boy whose eyes were filling with dust by the minute. With no clear vision to the meaning of the riddle, the fallen ceiling episode lapsed into the recesses of distant memory.

The memory recall has helped to reinforce my belief that infancy (for me and possibly most of us) is a mere dress rehearsal for future performances to be acted out in the adult world; that experience is merely the catalyst to developing our personalities. There are assuredly some aspects of my life that haven't changed one iota since I was an infant; my thoughts and ideals have merely developed and dovetailed with the realities of adulthood. 'Give me a child until he is seven and I will show you the man,' the Jesuit priests boast. They talk, of course, of developing and moulding the character of the child into a recognisable and hopefully civilised being. My character was determined long before the age of seven, possibly through genes while I was still in the womb. I was only three years old or less when this first openly manifested itself. 'What are you doing?' cried Mum in dismay as she saw me pour a glass of water over my costly roast beef Sunday lunch, transmuting it from a perfectly edible meal into slush and dumplings. To me, the action was quite practical and I couldn't understand the fuss our mum was making as I'd reckoned that physical effort could be saved by combining food and drink on the same plate. Mum saw things quite differently – to her I was a self-indulgent idiot child who ruined the good food she had selflessly bought from the pittance she earned as a dressmaker. 'How dare you waste food like that! Do you think money grows on trees?' The mandatory verbal scolding was one thing but what followed was far less digestible as I was then obliged with lack-lustre enthusiasm to demolish the rest of the meal at teatime, supper and breakfast next day. On reflection she was probably right as I've never been squeamish about eating any type of food and I too have an intolerance toward waste of any kind. But at the time, this was an injustice: a trial and sentence without the chance of presenting my defence. Injustice! I really hate that. It has always stuck in my craw and I can pinpoint the origins of this lifelong aversion to that soggy childhood meal.

At the time of the food incident, I decided that chastisement was a poor reward for displaying such initiative and that other imperative, retaliation, was mentally clocked. Only weeks later, I struck the retaliatory blow by playing on Mum's superstitious nature. Knowing that she firmly believed it was unlucky to have a wild bird in the house (a childhood incident concerning a wild grouse in the fens probably started this particular heterodoxy), I caught her off-guard as she was putting washing out on the line and my news was disturbing: 'Quick, Mum, you must come at once! There's a bird in the kitchen!' Her complexion turned ashen and long wooden gipsy-pegs fell from her mouth as she clutched the washing line to compose herself. Then, with her fingers wrapped around a pronged tree-branch clothes prop, she gingerly made her way through the backdoor poised like a lancer warrior ready to ward off an impending attack. 'Where is it?' she cried. 'There, Mum!' I answered, pointing to a yellow-and-blue toy bird perched on a stick which protruded from an empty milk bottle in the centre of a small table. I laughed nervously after studying her expression and realised that I'd gone right over the top, that she did not think it was funny at all. Was this to be the camel's straw that would send me into the home for naughty children that she'd always threatened me with? Had I, with cavalier abandonment, pushed my luck too far in spite of the fearful consequences? After a long pause my mother looked hard at me, turned and then walked thoughtfully into the backyard.

My birth had been a disappointment to Mum for within seconds of viewing my winkle she sighed – she had desperately wanted a girl! My post-natal cries of bewilderment at the change of environment were drowned by the noise of traffic, motorised and horse-drawn, which bustled along London's Strand beneath the grime-covered walls of Charing Cross Hospital. Across the road, a morose newsvendor was perched uneasily on a rickety wooden stool at the entrance to the railway station. His crutches and the fading campaign ribbons pinned to his crumpled blue jacket declared how lucky he was to be alive as a wounded survivor of the Great War. With a thin cry of '*Standard*', the Old Contemptible could have been heralding my lowly birth as a great non-event rather than hinting that at some time in the future there'd be work waiting for me on that very newspaper.

The world I'd entered had been one of optimism but the excitement of the Armistice ten years earlier was being diluted by the beginnings of the Great Depression and its pessimistic reality that peace does not necessarily lead to prosperity.

For women, the war had been a disaster with the wasting of the lives of so many young men on the murderous battlefields of Belgium and France who knew they were dying for King and country but someone had forgotten to tell them the reason why. Their deaths brought about a disastrous shortage of men to marry and procreate with, but Mum must have had something special going for her as she had married a WW1 survivor, a physically unmarked Company Sergeant Major in the King's Shropshire Light Infantry who carried the rank throughout the war and had retired with a small pension and a bristling waxed moustache with which he would face the civvy world with outward confidence. While senior officers retired to company directors' positions (Mum told me that young subalterns drawn from the ranks in the trenches had an average life expectancy of six weeks so not too many of them were around), he became a commissionaire for the organisation which produced their executive cars, Rolls Royce. Despite being a widower eleven years older than Mum and the proud father of five surviving children, his instincts to reproduce never failed him. One year after their marriage, Warren arrived; two years later, Tommy, and two years after that came me. I never met Tommy; he and Warren were both seriously ill with pneumonia and only one lived. It wasn't long after my arrival that she fell pregnant again and knew with complete conviction that this time it would be a little girl. Such was her maternal and intuitive instinct that even while in the womb my sister was named June. This time, surely, nothing could go wrong?

I was only seventeen months old when the next disaster happened and it began downstairs in our Tooting home which was in joyous mood with hand-made paper chains decorating the ceilings and hallway. On a top shelf in the kitchen was a special treat which Mum had planned to take down tomorrow and scrape the mildew off to provide the best Christmas pudding anywhere in the whole of Merry England. There was nothing to suggest that anything out of the ordinary would happen on that crisp winter's morning until Dad declared, 'I feel very strange, Nellie!'

'What is it?'

'I don't know… I just feel very strange. I can't explain.'

He was disorientated and Mum suspected a bout of 'flu. 'Go and lie down, darling,' she said soothingly, 'and I'll make you a nice cup of tea. You'll soon feel better.' 'No, come with me,' he said. Gone was any sign of the parade ground demagogue and as he put his hand to his chest there was an uneasy urgency in his voice, 'There's something wrong!' With his back now bent, his face ashen and the dagger edges of his waxed moustache seeming to droop, the sharp-eyed grey-haired soldier slowly made his way up the narrow creaking wooden staircase followed by Mum who put him to bed. As the pain increased she cradled his head soothingly. It was the last time that my mother would hold her husband in her arms. They had been ardent lovers from which I was one of the offspring, and in her arms he died. Just fifteen minutes after that fateful trip up the narrow winding stairs she came down stunned and bewildered, a widow who would now have only her memories to cling to and the two young children who were looking forward with excitement to the presents Father Christmas would bring them down the chimney during the night. Dad left my mother just the one present, for six months later my sister was born but that happy event, too, turned to tragedy as she expired within minutes of coming into the world. As Mum's own mother had died while she was carrying me, her happy wedding bells had tolled four immediate family deaths in just seven and a half years.

Dad had been a distinguished-looking man and as I grew up I'd gaze at relics and wonder about him. He comprised a large photograph in uniform as a sergeant beside the Great Pyramid of Cheops, two Ghurkha kukris with ivory encrusted handles, a short military swordstick, an ebony walking stick with silver top, a row of medals, a KSLI bugle, a Benson's watch with heavy chain presented on his leaving the regiment and a clock with the legend, 'Presented to Mr Robert Shay by the Metropolitan Police with grateful thanks'. The thanks, Mum told me, had extended to an additional award of £5. A gang of thugs, it seems, was beating hell out of a young policeman on Blackfriars Bridge when my father waded into the rescue and punched the consciousness out of a couple of them before the other three ran away. Dad was a brave man and while in France in WW1 he evaded the Germans by being hidden in a haystack by a French girl named Yvonne. A niece of mine bore that name. I did know, inwardly, that I wasn't at all brave; not a bit like him and that really worried me. I was a very nervous and frightened little boy when it came to facing up to bullies and this worried me as I wanted to be as courageous as my dad. But there was another side to him which I didn't like. As a strict disciplinarian, my father wouldn't allow Warren to wear spectacles despite an urgent need for them and so I've little doubt that had Dad lived, Warren's sight would have worsened and my relationship with my father would have been, quite literally, one of not seeing eye to eye.

Mum would never marry again and I doubt the thought of it ever crossed her mind. Fashion photographers would not have fallen over themselves to catch her wistful smile and even I, as a child, disliked her harshly swept-back raven-and-grey peppered hair which was knotted at the back in a severe Victorian bun. Perhaps someone with the acumen of Karsh might have created a black and white study of her contoured face for it was etched with the lines of suffering relentless physical torture from chronic asthma, bronchitis and six attacks of rheumatic fever. But she had something more important than the transient cosmetic of physical glamour claimed by present-day so-called 'celebrities'; there existed in her the unsung beauty of a very kind, loving, gentle and compassionate mother who would stay alive for just two precious reasons: 'I promise that I won't die until both you children have started work,' she said to Warren and me. It was a pledge that she repeated and a pledge that she kept, only just, even though it cost her so much. Our poor, very dear, mum. For my part, while I was as mischievous as any other boy, I soon learned that because she was living on a knife's edge, some levity and pranks had to be kept constrained or I would send her into a frenzied asthmatic attack. I was still an infant when I became aware that my mum wasn't like other children's; that I had to be careful when I pulled pranks because they might kill her. 'You've got a cough coming,' she said one day when a frog got stuck in my throat, 'I'll get some sulphur.'

'No, Mum, not that! It's 'orrible!'

'Don't be so childish,' she admonished, before carefully making a cone from a scrap of newspaper. I watched anxiously as the sulphur was poured into it.

'Open your mouth!' came the command. With the bloated cheeks of Cab Calloway, she blew! I choked and gasped for water as the yellow powder clung to my vital air passage. Wonder cure it may have been but I didn't like sulphur one bit and knew that if the practice was to be terminated, I'd have to take the initiative. 'Open your mouth,' came the order the next time I cleared my throat in her presence. 'No, Mum, I'm orl right, really.'

'Open your mouth or I'll put you away into a Home!' she ordered, using her ultimate and only weapon. That threat of terror again; a prison for naughty boys from which there was no escape. A place which I dreaded more than anything else in the whole world well, almost more than having sulphur blown down my throat. Reluctantly I opened my mouth and as Mum inserted the cone I watched her cheeks begin to bulge. At the critical moment, I blew. It was a very stupid thing to do for immediately after I'd done it I thought she was going to die and she might well have done, too. Her face transformed as she desperately struggled for breath like a jumping jack on the end of a Tyburn rope, choking and reeling around the kitchen with arms flailing as she pointed to a small green rectangular tin. I hastily grabbed the object, knowing it contained the elixir that would keep her alive but my inadequate tiny fingers couldn't prise open the tightly closed lid. I ran to a drawer and grabbed a kitchen knife and slipped it between the lid and the tin itself but still it wouldn't budge. Mum, coughing and wheezing, looked on helplessly and I felt her eyes desperately boring into me as I frantically turned the tin upside down and struck the lid each side with the knife until it began to move. Again and again I inserted the blade and at last it opened and I poured out some of the herbal contents. Grabbing a box of matches with trembling hands, I struck one and ignited the herbal powder and within a second Mum bent over the lid and was enveloped in a halo of smoke which she sucked into her lungs until the crisis passed. She never ventured anywhere without her tin of Potter's Asthma Cure and even though I reckon it saved her life during the cruel attacks, it wasn't a cure and the wording was subsequently amended to an 'Asthma Remedy'. Nevertheless, it was the only palliative that could relieve her intense physical and mental suffering.

My repressed, deep-rooted sense of fun became a fountain of trouble for me on a cold winter's evening when Mum's youngest sister, Lillie, came to stay. While knitting woollen socks in front of a blazing coal fire beneath a hissing gaslight, my maiden aunt rested her weary slippered feet on to a rubber hot-water bottle. She dropped a steel needle which pierced the bottle but as she leaned forward to retrieve it, her added pressure on the bottle forced boiling water to gush upwards and scold her legs. Uttering a loud shriek she stood bolt upright in pained surprise and horror while her feet, still planted firmly on the bottle, increased the pressure causing the water to jet its way right up her skirt. It was very funny but my laughter was as instantaneous as the lighting of a candle which I held in disgrace while dejectedly making a lonely trek upstairs to bed, its flickering flame being my only protection to ward off the fearsomely terrifying creatures in the hollows of surrounding darkness that waited malevolently to come out and grab me. I slept in the same room in which Dad had died and as I lay in bed petrified at being there alone while listening to the chatter of conversation downstairs, I could hear the relentless ticking of his clock which told me that time was passing: I couldn't wait for the dawn of tomorrow.

When the new day dawned it would sometimes bring excitement to the cheerless Khartoum Road with the arrival of a horse and cart carrying a kaleidoscope of colour and music resembling a fairground carousel. It cost either a ha'penny or a jam jar for a ride but the Virgil adage that there is no such thing as a free meal was epitomised by what happened later. After this mini version of a Lord Mayor's Show I was dispatched along the road armed with a bucket and shovel to collect the horse droppings to be used as fertilizer for plants in the near wasteland we called the backyard. While the plants were hidden from public view, they may just have caught the eyes of some unexpected visitors a year or so earlier who appeared overhead. I was in the backyard with Warren when they arrived, suspended in the gondola of a blimp. 'That's an airship,' said Mum, 'the R101.' Common sense tells me that I could not have remembered the airship and yet I have a vivid recollection of it arriving from the north east. I was only fifteen months old when she made her maiden voyage over London in October 1929 and little more than two years old in October 1930 when she made her ill-fated passage to India only to crash at Achy, near Beauvais, in France. During a discussion many years later I mentioned the incident to Warren who was astonished at my recall and confirmed that it appeared from the direction I gave him. It's because of this incident that I believe that something quite out of the ordinary will focus any toddler's attention enough to memorise it.

My state education began when the trees on Tooting Bec Common had seen the passing of summertime and were bracing themselves for the elements, starting with the autumn winds which would strip off their ochre-and-red foliage and leave them to stand and face the snow and blizzards of winter with statuesque and naked defiance. Mum, a creative dress designer, had been treading overtime on her Singer sewing machine to produce the outfit I'd wear to school. The tools of her trade included a tape measure, scissors and pins which she lodged between her lips until she could contain herself no longer: 'Oh, do stay still, Reggie, otherwise I'll stick a pin in you.' After standing motionless for an eternity, she declared, 'All right, you can take them off now.' Then came a quick snip of her scissors, a neat tuck in the material, a burst on the machine and perfection was brought a little closer. 'There,' she cried at last as she held up my new attire, 'put it on.'

I duly dressed and turned around to show off the completed work with grave misgiving. 'I don't like it, Mum. None of the other boys dress like this.'

'Don't be silly,' she remonstrated. 'You look very nice.'

My brother, Warren, and me as children – Mum had wanted a daughter. Studio photo.

My first chat-up line

On the day my state education began both Mum and Warren led me on my first steps to embrace the elements of learning. We turned right out of our home and right again until we came to a formidable establishment which was protected by a high wall. After breaching the battlements though an entrance marked 'Boys' we approached the Colditz-like building and walked up stone steps where my brother left us. Two women teachers waited to greet the newcomer and they beamed friendliness as one introduced herself as Mrs Lloyd and the other was Miss Birkett who, Mum told me much later, was the sister of the famous defence lawyer. 'Reggie can tell the time,' said Mum proudly when they asked why I was wearing a five shilling Ingersoll pocket watch and chain. 'But he's only three years old!' exclaimed Mrs Lloyd excitedly. 'I shall see that he tells the time to the whole class.' Reassured by pleasantries from the two ladies, I was led to a play room and invited to ride on the toy scooters and tricycles, being given a free rein on the choice of conveyance. Soon I realised life was good and if this was education I liked it. A bell rang and all infants were shown the playground where we were told more fun was to be had. I was on a roll.

"'Ere, look at that sissy!' called a voice and immediately a group of older boys gathered and began to jeer menacingly. "'E finks 'e's a girl, let's bash 'im!' The gang got closer and I knew I was in trouble as a misfit in society which must either be exorcised or eliminated. It was a tense moment and the playground erupted with excitement as a wall of bloodthirsty children prepared to watch their first ever execution. They knew it wouldn't be a fair fight but neither cared nor tried to intervene until Warren heard the noise and investigated. 'What do you think you're doing?' came his familiar voice and the gang moved back in the face of someone bigger than themselves. 'You leave my brother alone,' he said, menacingly. With the tables turned the bullying gang shamefacedly melted away from the formidable seven-year-old who then gave up his own break with friends to stay with me throughout playtime. It was the moment when I fully appreciated my brother and from then on there has always been an unbreakable bond between us.

School over for the day, I remonstrated with Mum about my clothes, 'They all laughed and wanted to bash me up. I want proper trousers with fly buttons.' I never again wore the offending garment that had caused me so much trouble – a pink tunic! I didn't go to school next day but was taken to a shop in Tooting where I was bought a shirt and shorts with fly buttons. It was a sad realisation for Mum as she would no longer live with the illusion that I was really the dimpled girl that she had craved for and lost. I learned something too from the playground incident which wasn't in the school curriculum: it was that a tough and nasty world awaited anyone whose sexuality was in question. Rightfully dressed, I began to receive female attention both overt and furtive and it started when a group of infant girls called enticingly, 'Come over here!' I looked suspiciously at them and began to walk away. A voice from behind cried, 'Grab 'im!' and suddenly I found myself being forced towards their loo with the undisguised intention of finding out what was hidden behind the buttons. Clearly, they were anxious to learn what the future held for them but being less unworldly than the inquisitive girls I broke away, leaving them to stamp their feet crossly in frustration. Another girl tried a different tack, far more subtle. As we stood for assembly and morning prayers she offered to show me her wares in time-honoured fashion on a reciprocal basis. I looked down her openly held knickers and could see nothing. Assuming that I was being cheated, I indignantly refused to uphold my end of the bargain.

On an enticingly beautiful Spring morning I'd expected to jump out of bed to face another new day of school surprises when a dank humid mist as thick as pea soup enveloped me and I became a hot, sweating floppy doll. The doctor called and put a thermometer under my arm before he gave a diagnosis which was worse than Mum had already dreaded – I didn't have just one deadly disease but three! 'He has gastric flu, pneumonia and measles and is running a dangerously high temperature,' said the doctor, gravely. Asked about my chances of survival, the doctor nodded his head sideways and told Mum the worst could happen at any time and that I was now in God's hands. After I had been laid low for several days the familiar figure of my schoolteacher, Mrs Lloyd, appeared through the haze and in her hands was a token gift of young fresh Spring flowers which Mum placed in a tall glass vase beside my bed as solemnly as if I were already dead. I'd never looked closely at flowers before but now, peering at them with heavy aching eyes through the semi-darkened room, I was captivated by their colours and inhaled their lightly scented breath until the magic of their purity insinuated itself into my senses with such fragrant power that I felt a compelling urge to recover. The sweating stopped and reality returned almost at once as the fever broke and I could hear again the steady imperative ticking of my father's clock as it urged me to regain my strength as quickly as possible. With a croaking voice I called out for the first time in several days, 'Mum, I'm thirsty.' Her footsteps came hurriedly up the stairs and to my surprise she burst into tears.

My half brother, Willie, who years later would be killed in WW2 parachuting into a Japanese ambush in Burma, called with a toy railway engine which ran on methylated spirits (I was never allowed to use it and it quietly disappeared) and I overheard Mum talking to him downstairs. 'I'd given him up for lost but then the flowers arrived and he just stared at them,' she said. 'Even when I moved him to change the damp sheets and make him comfortable he wouldn't take his eyes away. It's as though they were communicating with each other and they kept him alive. I've never seen anything like it in all my born days.' There has always been an almost Pagan-deep affinity with flora since that illness and when I am bruised by people or situations, I like to find a quiet spot where there are trees and flowers so that I can recharge myself through the tranquillity and beauty that only Nature can give me. The *Reader's Digest*, I suspect, would have called my recovery 'The Miracle of the Flowers'. Yaach!

Classical music, too, played an early role in my life with Warren agonising over his violin and the instrument's catgut strings screaming in retaliation as he struggled with Rubenstein's 'Melody in F' and Handel's 'See the Conquering Hero'. 'Can't you get him to stop?' I complained to Mum on a regular basis but without success and it was only when I went to the Royal Albert Hall where Warren played with the Combined Schools Orchestra that I showed even the slightest appreciation of the classics. He also played at another venue inside a gigantic building made of glass where dinosaur sentinels stood guard outside, while within the construction were trees, shrubs, escalators and fountains with pools containing giant goldfish. Not long after we had left Tooting I saw a red glow in the sky several miles away and our walnut-brown Ultra wireless set told us that the Crystal Palace was being razed in a terrifying inferno. To many the destruction ended an era, for the glass palace had been the centrepiece of the first ever World Trade Fair, symbolizing Britain's greatness under Queen Victoria. 'What's happening to the goldfish?' I asked Mum, but she did not know the answer and I was deeply distressed some time later to learn that they had been slowly and agonisingly boiled alive.

A Change of Home, a Change of Life

Mum was being mysterious. She had never left us alone before but one morning she put on her pale eggshell-blue suit with white blouse and contrasting deep red cut-glass necklace and departed, saying, 'I'll be home at four o'clock.' With incredible concentration, Warren sat for hours watching the hands of Dad's clock go round until, sure enough, she arrived home to the minute. Her face was wreathed with undisguised triumph for on that day she had committed herself to a deed that would change our lives, our culture and even our future perspectives on life. But she never let on her secret until the furniture van arrived.

Our departure from London had come to me as a surprise but it was something Mum had been working towards from the day she became a widow. She loathed Tooting and its environment of noise and urban decay and had no time for inquisitive neighbours whose prying eyes scrutinized their inhibited world and its inhabitants through furtively raised lace curtains. Sometimes she would stop on the pavement by our front door and defiantly point towards a house where the veils would shimmer and hastily fall into place. Yet Tooting, a name with a bicycle bell ring to it, had once been beautiful and rural and according to the nineteenth-century *London Encyclopaedia*, it was 'A very pretty district of hills and woods and tiny streams.' Regretfully, urban development had seen little value in retaining such extravagances so close to central London and there existed no longer a single tree in our road, the next road and many more beyond. There was a fountain a short distance away in Garrett Lane but it was The Fountain pub where the only resemblance to a stream was the flow of beer being pumped from the cellar into pint glasses. Further along the road towards the Broadway was a pet shop which stank of straw and animal faeces as mangy lice-ridden kittens, puppies, rabbits, hamsters and white mice huddled piteously in cages of tea-chest wood and chicken wire waiting for someone to pay a few coppers to take them home as toys for the children until the bob-tailed bunnies would eventually make a useful meal. Only the newly built Granada cinema which I watched being opened was to offer respite from the dullness with its Versailles-like mirrors and Wurlitzer organ deftly played by Harold Ramsey. Until the advent of the Granada we occasionally went into the cellar of a house which had been converted into a cinema with such attractions as a film which showed hundreds of flies crawling up a window pane accompanied with the jolly tune, *'The flies few up the window, that's all they had to do; they went up in their thousands and came back two by two.'*

'We are going to live in Surrey,' said Mum as we closed the front door for the last time. 'It's a place called Fetcham and Mrs Lloyd lives there.' I asked in surprise, 'My teacher?' 'Yes.' I hadn't known they were close friends and it explained how we were moving to a place whose name doesn't spring immediately to people's minds. Because of rural development between the two world wars which included the building of our bungalow, Fetcham is not so much country now. A village with Saxon links, it is surprisingly shown on some old maps where large towns are not mentioned. Unlike neighbouring Leatherhead, it has little recorded history. At Leatherhead, John Wesley preached his last sermon in 1791 at Kingston House. Handel reputedly played on the church organ, while in the churchyard is buried Sir Anthony Hope Hopkins, author of *The Prisoner of Zenda*. Churchyards always fascinated me as a child and there was nothing morbid about it; my interest was in the age of the graves and tombs, the inscriptions, and a curiosity about those interred such as what they were like (probably desperately dull, but who knows?) and the clothes they wore.

Until we went to Fetcham, I had never even seen the inside of a new house and our bungalow at 111 Nutcroft Grove had an agreeable smell of newly sawn wood, cement and a mixture of paint and garden-fence creosote. For Mum it was a personal triumph as her children would grow up in a clean, healthy environment away from London. We had hot and cold running water which I didn't even know existed, a proper bath, electricity, and something else unheard of – an inside loo. I'd always hated the outside privy and especially at night in the winter. Until now we had always had our Friday night scrub in the front room where hot water from the kettle and saucepans was poured into a long tin bath. When it was Mum's turn to bath, Warren and I would be ordered to face the wall and ordered not to look round. I did once risk a peep and having spotted a breast that had suckled three children I wondered what all the fuss was about.

From the outset Mum confessed that she knew nothing about electricity except for one golden rule: 'Always remember, Reggie,' she confided knowingly, 'if you are touching electric wires or changing a light bulb, you must have a damp cloth in your hand.' Despite this misinformation, electricity opened up a whole new world of excitement and a favourite pastime occurred when the bulb expired. With damp cloth in hand I'd remove the bulb and smash the glass, join the two filament wires together and push the bayonet back into the socket before switching on. The flash and bang were most rewarding and well worth mending the fuse afterwards – or was it? That water-on-the-dinner inventive brain clicked again and asked the question: why should the fuse blow each time? The answer was quite clear – the wire was too thin. Without pondering that thin fuse might have something to do with safety, I applied extra wire really thick and it worked. A flick of the switch, the expected flash and bang, and the fuse remained intact. By a remarkable coincidence it was at that very instant that all the street lights went out.

After electricity, gunpowder became a force to be reckoned with and the knowledge on how to make it was imparted amongst schoolboys with enthusiasm. The keenest partakers were my neighbours, Peter and Ray Lambeth, who decided upon one big bang which would let the whole estate know of their presence. On the other side of the Lambeths lived the Shirley Temple of Nutcroft Grove, pretty Betty Tett, and she was on her garden swing when the Lambeth boys chose to ignite their bomb in a two-foot-high tin packed tight with explosives. The loud bang that followed was a foretaste of the bombs that were to come and I watched aghast and mesmerised as Betty, wearing a pink and white dress, swung back and forth as the splintered drum made its way towards her. Would the secret love of my life be blasted away to eternity? As she was coming down the lethal jagged-edged metal container shot between the swing ropes, missing Betty's head by inches and she carried on as if nothing had happened, possibly not realising the danger she had been in. And it was with the Lambeth kids that I was the passenger in a feat which might have found a place in the *Guinness Book of Records*, had it existed at the time. While living in Tooting my remarkable mother had bought me a toy racing car complete with pumped-up tyres, handbrake, headlights and a hooter. The car was similar to a Bugatti and we called it the Silver Bullet. While it was of little use in Khartoum Road the potential for excitement in Fetcham had few limitations. 'Let's take it up Marden Hill,' said Warren and together we pushed the large toy car up the hill and I sat on the back as he drove down the incline. Shortly afterwards I took the Lambeths up the hill and let Peter drive down. He had just started the run when a bus overtook us but as we began to roll fast and because the handbrake was not powerful enough to stop the car with three children on board, one up front, one driver and one on the back, we quickly caught up with the bus and overtook it to the bemused gaze of the driver and passengers. Neither before nor since have I heard of a toy car overtaking a bus at speed.

Paradise: we humans have our subjective interpretations of what it is, whether it is here on earth or a post-mortal target for which to aim. I actually discovered it was Fetcham, a place which had everything a child could wish for and 'The Splash' on the River Mole was a favourite venue in summer where my friends and I would play and fish. In winter, another idyllic spot was the millpond with swans and coots and sparkling springs, and the water froze over especially for children so that we could either skate, slide or ride bicycles on it. Then, for countryside tranquillity, there were broad-chested shire horses which patrolled the fields beside the pond in unified pairs, their bodies steaming sweat but their heads held high with dignified defiance as they drew ploughs through unyielding sun-baked earth or rain-sodden mud. Finally, there were Surrey woods at Bookham Common, while only a short cycle ride away was Box Hill, as tall as a mountain and only scalable by fearlessly crossing a moat that was bridged by ancient paving stones.

Aunt Lillie, of the hot-water-bottle incident, had married and came to visit us with her two children, Jack and Barbara. Jack was about six years old and I took him to the Splash which had a man-made waterfall containing a slime-coated concrete shelf below at the water's edge. In flood, a torrent would cascade over the fall, hit the concrete and then continue downstream taking its flotsam of tree branches, dead swans, moles, dogs and any other plant or creature captured in its lethal embrace. Now, as the water level was low without even a trickle flowing over the top, I eased Jack down the drop to the shelf and followed him. Until the moment I put my feet on its surface I hadn't realised the shelf was as slippery as a winter ice slide and danger signals flashed in my brain: we could cross the river provided we kept close to the fall itself. 'Keep away from the edge and stay with me,' I warned Jack sternly, sound advice which was contemptuously unheeded. He approached the brink of slippery slope and fell in. Desperately I looked around for help but there was no one in sight and then, as I went to the edge, hoping to pull him out, there was a second splash. The situation was critical for Jack had never been near deep water before and I had only a faint chance of saving him. During school swimming lessons, I'd attempted the breaststroke and been picked up by my trunks from the bottom, still performing frog-like motions. Now I kept submerging under Jack to try to keep him on the surface while nudging him towards the waterfall without any certainty that he would be able to scramble up on to the treacherous concrete. Incredibly, while I was frantically sub-merging and surfacing like a demented porpoise in order to suck in precious air, he just lay flat on his back and floated like a corpse despite the water sometimes passing over his face. I knew that if he panicked we'd both drown.

Then, as if by a miracle, a tall gangling youth appeared from nowhere carrying a fishing rod and I called him over to splutter that we were in serious trouble. Without uttering a word he pushed the rod towards us and Jack, making the first movement to confirm that he was alive, caught it and was eased over the concrete and given a helping hand to the top of the fall. In order to stay afloat, I conversely dived again into the murky waters and then grabbed the fishing rod on my return. The youth had a good catch that day by saving the lives of two children and yet throughout the ordeal he never uttered a word and quietly walked away as I went to thank him. Apart from illness, this was my first brush with death.

If the Splash could be lethal – I'd made a reed raft downstream which dis-integrated as I entered deep water on the Mole leaving me to apply my unusual swimming technique to reach the safety of a bank – it was also the place where water was not the only danger. Shortly after the start of WW2 French-Canadian soldiers were stationed at Leatherhead and two of them stood on a brick bridge and by their behaviour I sensed they were trouble. They looked tough and mean and approached two children who were walking past with their pet dog. Without warning they grabbed the mutt and threw it from the bridge high into the air before it crashed into the fast-moving swirling waters racing through a lock below. The soldiers ignored the tearful cries of the youngsters who ran down to try to retrieve and revive the hapless animal. Then an elderly lady leaning heavily on a walking stick went past and despite protestations her pet Jack Russell was thrown in too. 'If you don't shut up you'll go in as well,' one of them snarled as she demanded they rescue the animal. I was stunned and went home wondering why anyone should want to do such a thing.

Some time later, as a fourteen-year-old, I was travelling to London by train when a soldier got into the compartment where I was the only passenger. On the shoulder of his khaki uniform was one word, 'Canada'. I'd always felt at ease on the restful trains which were painted green to blend in with the countryside and even the name, Southern Railway, had a homely ring to it which I'd subconsciously associated with safety and friendliness. Now, as the train serenely snaked its way past the still-intact homes of middle-class suburbia towards the bomb devastated rail-track houses of south London, the pleasing ambience became supercharged with tension.

The soldier sat opposite and I watched uncomfortably as his giant fists opened and closed. He glared at me with hostility, his eyes blazing hatred so intense that I was inwardly afraid I'd be plucked from the seat and thrown out of the open window and onto the rails. Then he spoke. His accent was heavy and I recognised him as a French-Canadian: 'You fucking English, you're a bunch of fucking cowardly shits!' he snarled. It was 1942, and by now I'd witnessed quite a bit of the war. I'd watched the Battle of Britain, seen the destruction by bombs of all types – incendiary, oil, HE and aerial 'land mines', and with patriotic fervour I knew first-hand that as a race there was *nothing* cowardly about the British. There was, however, something decidedly cowardly about me. I was alone with a big man under terrible mental stress, perhaps shell-shocked, whose ever twisting hands had been trained to strangle German sentries. He turned away quickly to look out of the window, his face twitching until slowly his head moved round to face me again, the eyes smouldering volcanoes of hatred. 'You bastards sent us into a trap.'

'Where was that?' I ventured.

'Dieppe. I've just come back from fucking Dieppe and the Germans were waiting for us!' There had been reports of a landing at Dieppe but censorship of the day, which tended to highlight victories, not losses, merely admitted that casualties were likely to have been heavy because of fierce fighting. In my brainwashed nationalistic innocence, it never occurred to me that we could ever lose a battle. Even the remarkable and gallant escape from Dunkirk following France's capitulation, had been turned from a hasty retreat into a victory of the little boats. I didn't reply to the soldier because I didn't know what to say. As the train meandered on he looked out of the window again but I knew now that he wasn't looking at the devastation of the outskirts of London we had now reached; all he could see were the mined beaches of Dieppe, the wire, the machine guns, exploding shells and Stuka dive-bombers.

He turned back and those eyes bore into me before he said, accusingly, 'All my buddies are dead!' This would be the first person I'd met who'd just come out of a battle, and he was not the macho returning hero either he or I had expected him to be. He was a man who had been to hell and back and he was frightened, bitter and alone and he knew without a doubt that he and his dead buddies had been betrayed.

Post-war revelations disclosed there were 5,100 Canadians who took the brunt of the assault plus 1,000 British Commandos, and 50 US Rangers. The Canadians were largely cut down before they reached the sea wall and the overall toll was 4,384 dead, wounded or missing (some reports say 3,670) compared to 591 German dead. The Dieppe raid, codenamed 'Operation Jubilee', was a rehearsal for the North African landings which were to take place three months later; and for D-Day.

Perhaps the worst aspect of 'Operation Jubilee' was that the Germans did know of the operation and, according to a 1945 monograph by the National Security Agency in Washington, the British knew that they knew yet didn't call it off! 'Were you stationed at Leatherhead?' I asked. The soldier looked surprised, and nodded, 'Yeah, how did you know?' – 'I lived there,' I said, simply. For a moment I thought I had briefly taken him away from Dieppe until he said, 'We were all stationed around Leatherhead.' My mind went back to the Splash and the two soldiers who delighted in throwing pet dogs off a bridge. They would have gone to Dieppe; perhaps they were his buddies.

At home, it was incumbent upon me to peel the potatoes and sometimes cook the dinner, depending upon Mum's state of health. Most of my immature thinking was done over a kitchen sink with potato peeler in hand. I was Sir Reginald, a knight in shining armour galloping out to right all wrongs; a crusader against those who would do evil. There was a drawback to these thoughts: because of my lack of courage whereby I'd rather walk away from a bully or talk my way out of conflict, I couldn't possibly have guessed that when I was older this outlook would stand me and my colleagues in much better stead than by adopting an aggressive posture. I'd only fight my way out of a corner when there was no other option. As for standing up for other people; that ideal would lapse into the subconscious and become dormant until unexpected life-threatening challenges arose.

Warren, who grew the potatoes that I cooked, had a preschool job to supplement the family income and I could only admire his good fortune. He was actually paid for doing a milk round on the back of the horse-drawn cart of Curtis Dairies where he'd stand imperiously in the light of dawn like a novice Roman charioteer. It was a different brother in winter though when he and the milkman would crouch like lepers, their bodies hunched and drawn with vapour rising through snow blizzards as every breath from man, boy and beast erupted into the air with the velocity of steam escaping the spout of a kettle. Their small brown horse would then trudge dejectedly forward at a jerk of the reins, reluctant to trust its steel-shod hooves on the treacherous snow and ice-packed thoroughfares. 'There'll be a nice cup of tea waiting for you when you get home,' Mum would say comfortingly when my brother set off wearing a knitted balaclava helmet and sure enough, on his return with blue fingers protruding from his hand-knitted ice-sodden mittens, a piping hot cup would be waiting.

For my part, in addition to peeling potatoes, one of my tasks was to feed up to a dozen chickens at the bottom of the garden and to clean the hutches of the most incontinent of all God's creatures. I got to know the chickens well and had names for them but accepted that sometimes one would be chosen for the table. For those wretched creatures the axe would literally fall and as no one at home was capable of dispatching them we would call upon the robust lady next door, Mrs Snook, to perform the *coup de grâce* while we cowered indoors away from the place of execution. Our neighbour was not at all squeamish and to prove that she could 'Snook a Cock' she sometimes put my feathered friends' necks into a doorway and slammed the door while I offered a silent prayer for them. At other times she preferred the axe and one day after Mum had handed Madame Guillotine a victim, there was a cacophony of commotion and noise and we raced outside to be met by a scene from a Wagnerian opera. The buxom Mrs Snook, her flaxen hair swept back in Valkyrian flow, was chasing a chicken around the garden with bloodstained axe held high yelling, 'Come back!' The poor creature could not possibly have heard her even if it had any masochistic desire to return – its head was lying some distance away! Many people have seen headless chickens running but what I found truly curious was that it never once bumped into the surrounding garden fence but veered away when it got close.

While I was never squeamish about eating the birds, nor even plucking them when they were still warm when the feathers were easy to pull (if my life had taken another course I might have become a Grade 'A' chicken plucker!) there was one incident with chickens which did cause me deep shock and distress and introduced me to a world I'd never suspected existed – sadism! With its discovery went a childish innocence that I cherished. The 'Gentle Jesus meek and mild, look upon the little child' I'd been taught at Sunday school bore no relationship to the stark reality that faced me. We had bought half a dozen day-old-chicks and they were put into a small compound of wire mesh at the end of the garden which bordered an open field. I went up to them with a bowl of bran one sunny spring afternoon and the sight that met me numbed by brain with horror; I stood transfixed with bowl of food in one hand and water in the other. They were all dead with their heads severed, seemingly hacked off with a blunt penknife. The sight was totally alien to my nature which was always to help and not hurt. Killing in anger I could understand and Mrs Snook's axing for the pot was acceptable, but vicious wanton slaying was beyond my comprehension. We had a good idea who the culprit was, a boy who lived in a road beyond the end of the field, but there was no proof. The child suspect was aged eleven years and I have sometimes wondered what the little bastard did later in life; he could have been robust in business and perhaps he now has a knighthood. More chilling, however, is the knowledge that because he took pleasure in killing he had the attributes of a serial murderer.

And it was a serial bird killer in the form of a fox that broke into the chicken run one night and in a moment of frenzied bloodlust tore to pieces every one of our hens. Not one of them was eaten or taken away by the fox. We never kept chickens after that and I feel no sympathy for foxes; the only non-human animal I know of, other than the domestic cat that kills for killing's sake.

So far as I'm aware I've not killed anybody but as a little boy I did cause some acute discomfort to a lady and she may have choked to death; I just don't know. Throwing accurately, and later shooting, were two of my attributes and the throwing was demonstrated one winter's evening when the Surrey countryside took on a harsh Edvard Munch scene of light, brittle snowfall. Standing beside a small footpath in nearby woods, I watched as two women approached and one was talking animatedly about the weather. 'Yes, it is cold. I'm glad I put on my woollens,' she said. She wore a woollen hat, woollen coat, woollen scarf, woollen stockings and no doubt a woollen cardigan, woollen jersey and woollen vest underneath. Her knickers, I suspected, would be woollen, too, although schoolboys knew red flannel was the vogue of the elderly. Neither had noticed the diminutive boy standing close to some trees, who had stooped to gather snow. As the fall was thin, it became the smallest snowball I'd ever made, no larger than a bantam's egg and it was the one item the woollen clad lady had not counted on to protect herself against. When they came into range, I threw and then stood transfixed and mesmerised as the missile headed towards the voluble one's open mouth. It was a marksman's shot and as it entered the orifice and passed beyond her dentures, her eyes bulged while she spluttered and choked. From this I could only assume that the snowball had gone straight down a tonsil-less throat. Clearly it was a superb shot but a lucky one and so I didn't wait for plaudits but I did wonder with something of a conscience whether she had died before the snow melted in her throat. With no evidence of a missile to be seen at an autopsy, it would have been a mystery death to baffle even the great investigative brain of Sherlock Holmes!

Trouble was again my companion when Mum chose to visit her other sister, Maggie, at Felbridge, also in Surrey, near East Grinstead. On reflection, they were marvellous if unimaginative names for three sisters: Nellie, Maggie and Lillie, quite worthy of a dirty ditty. Cousin Albert was a Boy Scout and his troop visited a pasture some miles away to play cricket. Dressed in my best Sunday suit, I was sternly ordered to observe play from the sidelines. As I watched with little enthusiasm, a fair-haired lad squared up to the bowler with a large cricket bat that almost grazed his chin. Suddenly he struck the ball hard and it skied into the air and hurtled towards me like a Halley's comet. Instructions and boredom were forgotten and I raced forward with eyes heavenwards and arms outstretched. Directly in line with my own trajectory and totally unobserved, were two large mounds of newly manufactured cow dung. As my foot touched the first pat I skidded forward in a headlong position and catapulted into the second, which was pie crust hard at the top and as soft as custard inside. I parted this pat with my nose and flattened it with the rest of my body before being bundled ignominiously into the blue Wolesey car of my usually jovial Uncle Ted and driven back to Felbridge with windows wide open. An unkind colleague to whom I once related this story suggested that some of the bull droppings had never washed off. It was certainly the day I learned a salutary lesson: if you land in the crap only a loving mother wants to know you!

A few years later, during the early part of WW2 when Mum had another of her innumerable painful stays in Epsom Hospital, I was again in Felbridge and stood in a field next to uncle's home and looked up to see a Lysander spotter aircraft diving towards me. I waved, thrilled that the pilot should bother to make a friendly dive at a mere schoolboy and the thought that he may be in peril never crossed my mind. After the incident I ran indoors to tell Aunt Maggie and she smiled indulgently but later that day Ted returned home and said a Lysander had crashed nearby. Maggie looked across and while she didn't say a word, we were on the same wavelength; the pilot was killed and so I shall never know the answer to the haunting unasked question.

Happiness was at Leatherhead Poplar Road School where I even enjoyed studying and was well rated. I was also a good sprinter but running is only mentioned because it led to a furtherance of my sex education. Sex was taboo at school and yet it was a schoolmistress who gave me a demonstration of the sex act. She was blonde, pretty and in her early twenties; and she was not the type to waste her lunchtimes on small talk in the staff room. Gambolling innocently through knee-high grass I accidentally stumbled across her with her boyfriend. My 'Sorry Miss' did not alleviate the confusion at the horrified recognition of her pupil and feeling as welcome as a voyeur in a harem, I raced off. The teacher resigned immediately and went to South Africa, possibly wishing to avoid the embarrassment of facing the little creep in class who knew of her private passion. Even at that age I wasn't interested in gossip and never talked of the incident and as it has taken me many years to write about it, I doubt I shall ever make the grade as a gossip columnist.

The weekly attendance at church was a bore until the day I was invited to pump the organ. A wide-eyed inspection of the instrument and the instruction on my duties created a whole new world of opportunity. The organist took me aside for a short lecture on the privilege bestowed upon me and he then pointed to a long wooden handle which, he explained, I must push up and down when he played. The organist was a sincere fellow; slim, balding and studious with a lifelong dedication to playing the organ. Despite this enlightened calling, I found him to be a petty dictator, someone who felt that little boys should be kept firmly in their place and out of sight. My instruction on organ pumping began with him pointing to a dangling lead weight and two crudely scratched notches on the side of the instrument. Imperiously, he declared, 'If you pump too hard the weight will rise above the top notch and the organ will squeak, and if you don't pump hard enough the weight will remain below the lower notch and I won't be able to play. Therefore,' he commanded, 'the lead weight must be kept even between the two notches – do you understand, boy?' I understood the implications substantially more than he realised, for the potential was enormous and was even worth a silent prayer of thanks as it was a gift from God which was actually presented to me by Him in church!

We didn't have a rehearsal and I was plunged in at the deep end and because of my enthusiasm during the first hymn, the lead weight and the organ scaled new heights. The hymn was Charles Wesley's 'Jesu Lover of my Soul' but the organist's bespectacled eyes contained neither compassion, love nor even affection as his dismembered head appeared round the side of the organ. 'Not so fast, child,' he cried in a voice that gave resonance to the old Norman church. The choir had stopped in discord but once the offending weight had taken up its correct position, they restarted. The next hymns went well and the organist had reason to relax, convinced that he had contained the mini-monster around the corner. Only while playing the last hymn, No. 483, to the words of Tennyson's 'Strong Son of God, Immortal Love' was there a notice-able loss of composure. It was in verse three that I slowed down. 'Our wills are ours, we know not how,' sang the choristers in concert with the deflating organ. The organist proved not to be word perfect for I distinctly heard him transpose the words of the hymn title to 'For the love of God'!

At the end of the service the vicar made a small apology, with the assurance that the blessed organ would be all right next week. And so it was for from then on the organist beamed and the vicar beamed with good reason as I never mis-pumped again, having decided it was better to be cooped up around the side than face the music in front. Sometimes in my little cubbyhole my eyes would even rise heavenwards but the reason wasn't that I'd found God – I was interested in the bells beyond the ropes which hung tantalisingly from the belfry. As the Sundays passed, the interest strengthened into fascination until, during one sermon, curiosity overcame obedience and I began to climb a steel ladder that led to the belfry. I used the hanging ropes for support knowing that I was not heavy enough to ring the bells, that was until I slipped off the ladder. People in the village said later that far from ringing out wild bells, they were really quite muted. But being directly overhead, they were heard by the vicar, the choir, the congregation and the organist. My possible career as a campa-nologist ended abruptly as the bespectacled face, this time accompanied by the whole body, loomed before me and lifted me away for ever, leaving the vicar to take my place. It was the first time I was given the sack but far from the last.

Not long after my possible bell-ringing career came to its abrupt halt, campanologists throughout Britain were banned from the belfries unless the country was invaded, or a victory had been secured as happened at El Alamein. Then they could ring their hearts out like the clappers hanging above them. The edict came after the gamp-toting, cadaverous-looking prime minister, Neville Chamberlain, with the melancholy air of a Birmingham undertaker, solemnly told us on the wireless that we were at war with Germany. Chamberlain's voice presaged doom with every word; not the voice of a potential victor set to destroy one of history's great tyrants in mortal combat but one of a dejected and tired man who had tried desperately for peace and whose precious piece of paper signed by Hitler heralding 'Peace in our time', was now being metaphorically shredded under jackboots marching into Poland. At home we felt desperately sorry for Chamberlain. I sat on the doorstep in the sunshine listening to his speech and gazed at the rear garden we had developed over the past three years. I looked at the fruit trees Warren and I had planted, Cox's apples mixed with Victoria and Greengage plums and wondered if any of us would be alive after the day was over. Warren had reported for duty at the council offices where he would be on stand-by to start the air-raid siren in the event of enemy bombers being spotted.

My Entry into the Real World

She had always known there would be a war and had told us so with the same apocalyptic conviction that she said the world would be destroyed by fire during hostilities in the Middle East. Even though this Armageddon would seem impossible, we both believed Mum. In the event, she was to die before the advent of the atom bomb and the proliferation of nuclear weapons. For two years my mother had surreptitiously gathered food in preparation for the day there would be rationing and she kept it in a wafer-thin wooden tea chest thus ensuring that our small family would not starve during the war ahead. She had been in London during WW1, and had watched Kaiser Wilhelm's Zeppelins drop their deadly cargoes on unsuspecting civilians in the capital city. A reminder of the first London Zeppelin raid can still be seen on the Thames Embankment beside Cleopatra's Needle where shrapnel embedded itself into the river wall. Her home had been just a short distance away on the other side of the river and the scars of those raids were still with her, as I was soon to learn.

Ten minutes after Chamberlain's speech Warren pressed the red alert button and as the air-raid siren wailed, Mum called me to her. We stood huddled in the hallway of our cherished bungalow waiting to be blown to smithereens as explosions shattered the peace of Fetcham to propel me into the violence of my first war. The earth shook, the bungalow trembled and I could see Mum's eyes were closed as if she was praying. 'Can I go outside and have a look?' I asked adventurously. While Mum gave an adamant 'No', I wasn't so sure that staying indoors when bombs were dropping was a good idea. As quickly as the bombardment had started, it stopped and all was quiet. Tensely we waited for the next wave of destruction until Warren pressed the green button and the siren sounded again, this time heralding the 'All Clear'. By so doing, he told all of Leatherhead and the surrounding villages that hostilities were temporarily at an end and I raced outside anticipating total destruction and was truly disappointed to see all the houses were standing undamaged. There were no piles of rubble, no mangled bodies lying in the street, no ambulances – nothing! Neighbours came out, and each of them looked surprised and relieved. 'Where did the bombs fall?' inquired the talkative Mrs Reed from three doors away, for even the chickens she kept for company and loudly chatted to each day hadn't even shed a feather. News soon filtered back that the sirens were a false alarm and there were no bombs. The explosions, Warren explained when he came home, had been caused by an anti-aircraft gun on the railway line whose jittery crew had mistaken woodpigeons for enemy planes. My introduction to war was thrilling, but an anti-climax.

Accompanying the advent of hostilities was the ARP Warden, Home Guard and Civil Defence and at the top of the road living in a house, as opposed to a bungalow, was Mr Major who immediately took charge of any civil defence operations that were needed in the vicinity. Possibly his commanding name helped to get him the appointment as it suggested unquestioned leadership, a man who made critical decisions and stuck to them. Mr Major quickly confirmed this status by deciding that in preparation for air-raid casualties his own home should be used for rescue practice. He sensibly reasoned that there was no advantage in dragging wounded victims through the window of any of the surrounding single-storey buildings when they could be quite easily taken through a front or back door. What Mr Major needed was a volunteer to be 'rescued' from an upstairs window and he would prefer, he said, someone who wasn't too heavy. He surveyed the gathering crowd until his eyes alighted on the raised hand of a little boy and his face lit up. Everyone's head turned in my direction and I nodded. 'Splendid, my boy,' beamed Mr Major to polite applause from the onlookers. 'What a brave little chap!'

Brave? My initial reaction was to swell with pride but I had misgivings and my apprehension grew when Mr Major added, 'Just run upstairs and lie on the stretcher; it's in the front bedroom.' I'd been expecting an exciting fireman's lift which was the true reason for volunteering but upstairs was a stretcher and two men I didn't know strapped me tightly onto it with comforting reassurances and knowing winks, just to let me know that each possessed a safe pair of hands. My arms were strapped down so tight that I could have been in a straitjacket and I knew that I would be unable to move them in an emergency. 'Have you done this before?' I asked one of the men, hoping for reassurance. 'No, son,' came the reply, 'but you've nothing to worry about.' I had the distinct impression that the man himself was actually more worried than me. A grating sound told me that my means of escape was being placed against the window outside and soon I was hauled upwards from the floor. Amid heaves, grunts and cries of 'Watch it!' the stretcher was eased to the opening and over the sill, a difficult manoeuvre which I felt they should have tried with an empty stretcher first. This hypothesis was quickly confirmed when I heard an alarmed cry from below, 'The bloody ladder's slipped!'

'We'll hold on to him,' said a confident voice from behind me as I wavered precariously and helplessly in the air until the moment I was hauled back inside to the accompanying sound of the ladder crashing to the ground. This was followed by a collective gasp of 'Ooh' and 'Aah' from the crowd below and a woman even cried out, helpfully, 'Be careful! Make sure you don't hurt the child.' The offending ladder was returned and I was raised again and put feet first out of the window so that one second I was looking at light feathery clouds above, followed by the roofs of bungalows of the estate and then at the ground seemingly hundreds of feet below as I was swung over into the semi-vertical position of a helter-skelter. Perhaps I was too heavy or possibly the men's hands were sweating with nervousness for amid the turmoil, the next utterance that came from the male 'voice of confidence' seemed worryingly to have lost its reassurance: 'Christ, we've dropped him!' A man at the bottom, who was supposed to climb up and ease me down, had only reached a quarter of the way as I rocketed towards him. There were two split-second decisions he could have made: the obvious one was to stop me but this he declined and chose the second option by jumping out of the way. Another man instinctively leapt forward and caught the base of the stretcher as it was about to make its power dive into the earth with a spine-jarring crash. 'Are you all right, son?' cried out Mr Major anxiously. 'Yes thanks,' I replied, and this time it was I who was reassuring. 'It was fun.'

With that, his face creased into a grin. 'Yes, wasn't it?' Everyone laughed and all the rescue team exchanged glances. As a couple of men unstrapped me I thought it was good that Mum hadn't been watching. 'Lucky the stretcher didn't come off the ladder,' I ventured. No one replied, for had it done so, I would have been Fetcham's first war victim, something of an own goal. Instead, I felt I'd done my bit for the war effort and didn't volunteer to go up again and nor did anyone else. The practice of hauling 'casualties' on stretchers from upstairs windows was quietly dropped from Mr Major's Civil Defence curriculum but the incident made a profound impression upon me for I became aware of the fallibility of adults whom, until then, I had always innocently trusted. It was at that moment I vowed that I would never again allow my arms to be tied so that I would not be helpless when I most needed them.

'I reckon we should dig an air-raid shelter,' said Warren enthusiastically and I jumped at the idea. No sooner had this brilliant suggestion been transmitted to me than two eager beavers got out our spade and fork and began digging a wide hole in the garden, the idea being that we would then make concrete walls and a roof, topped by sandbags. 'It's heavy going,' I complained as the soil got heavier and damper. 'Just get on with it,' ordered my big brother, 'and stop moaning.' The more we dug the damper the soil became until we reached three punishing feet down and came to the water table. All we had to show for our hours of sweat and toil was a pool of water and I came up with the suggestion of turning it into a swimming pool. This idea was rejected next day when we examined the site and decided that a drowned mole floating face down was not a good omen and the project was abandoned.

The air-raid shelter was a good idea for Leatherhead and Fetcham had more than their fair share of incendiary bombs with an estimated 5,000 dropping one night with most of them landing in fields. Several times my friends and I tried to relight them as bright magnesium flames would be fair compensation for the lack of fireworks on Guy Fawkes Night, but our efforts were disappointing. Not all the clusters that showered down upon us were incendiaries for mixed with them were high explosives (HEs) and oil bombs and there was no way of telling one from another as they murderously screamed towards us bearing their message of hate. Yet the most unnerving bomb to date was the

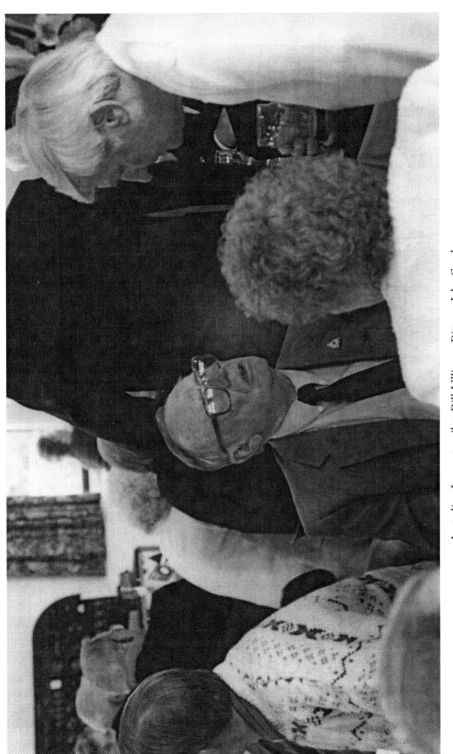

Australian Lancaster pilot, Bill Ullinger. Picture: John Sanderson.

parachute 'landmine' which declined to announce its presence. There were many people in Britain going about their chores at home during the dark evenings unaware that death was suspended above them like a Satanic claw, their lives depending on a sudden wisp of wind, an unseen air current or an updraught which would determine the final destination of these lethal packages that held enough explosive to demolish several houses. One such mine landed in Leatherhead and according to people who knew, had caught a lady blissfully soaking herself in the officially permitted five inches of bath water. The blast, which destroyed many houses and killed people, blew both her and the bath into the air and they landed in a tree. The lady was found sitting upright, unabashed, unclad, unwashed and unharmed!

While news of the lady's miraculous escape was uplifting, it was a German, however, who became a big morale booster to the villagers of Fetcham. According to local gossip he was a pilot with an Iron Cross who had managed to bomb the local sewage plant with a high explosive. His story had a moral if local gossip could be believed: having bombed the plant, he was brought down by AA guns and baled out, landing in the middle of the excrement he had just stirred. The moral is obvious but he didn't survive to learn the lesson! Many years later I got to know an Australian bomber pilot, Bill Ullinger, who baled out over England and definitely did land in a sewage plant and returned to his base covered in muck. Bill, with his British crew that included my war decorated chum, Don Brown, had been on a bombing trip over Germany when at 15,000 feet an American bomb dropped from above and wedged itself in the wing of their Lancaster. His bomb aimer, nicknamed 'The Duke', recognised the missile as one with a barometric fuse which was set to explode below a certain altitude and Ullinger, having dropped his own bombs over the target, flew back to England to let his crew bale out. Bill estimated that the Lancaster still had enough fuel on board to fly back to Germany, and so he turned the aircraft round and thus ensured that the American bomb would not be wasted. With that he dropped into the sewage. (Footnote: After the war Bill Ullinger went home to Western Australia and created the Redgate vineyard whose high-class Margaret River wines are exported worldwide).

I'd familiarised myself with the engines of various aircraft, friend and foe alike, and was surprised one afternoon to hear the familiar sound of a Heinkel flying towards me as there had been no air-raid warning. With a satchel on my back and gasmask nestling in a brown cardboard box hanging from my neck, I was returning home from school and had taken a route which went under a railway bridge and led me towards the millpond. The bridge was a few paces behind me when, directly ahead and emerging just feet above the treetops, came the Heinkel with its bomb doors open. I could see the crew quite clearly and as I stood and watched a cluster of high explosive bombs fell from the plane and exploded in a field less than seventy yards away, just missing the railway line. I did wonder if the machine gunner might take a shot at me although I didn't think he would, me being a child. But as I wandered home I did wonder, also, if the plane would still have dropped its bombs had it been a few yards off course with the bridge and me in sight. The decision on whether the life of a child was more important than the bridge would have been split second and in the light of the terrible risk the crew had taken to be there I was sure I knew the answer.

It was while delivering newspapers early one morning that I heard the drone of another oncoming aircraft whose engine sound was identifiable as an Airspeed Oxford. On looking up I easily recognised the familiar outline of the RAF's yellow-painted training plane but what I didn't know, and the pilot didn't know, was that the insistent throbbing rhythm of the engine was for him a pulsating cadence of death. We were both listening to the countdown, me on the ground with a shoulder bag of newspapers and he in the air enjoying an early morning flip at sunrise. Tragically, the finger of Fate pointed skyward that rapturous spring morning as the vibrating rear framework of the fragile plane began to fall apart. As I stood watching it fly overhead the tail blew off with a small puff of dust, followed by a muffled bang. In awful fascination I gazed transfixed as the wings and fuselage started to spin in unhurried windmill rotation. The frustration and confusion of the young pilot can only be guessed as he struggled helplessly to gain control of his stricken aircraft without even knowing what had happened. I could see the outline of his helmeted head but not the expression on his face which could only have registered total disorientation and sheer terror. He knew he was about to die but couldn't do anything about it and soon the plane crashed into a back garden, narrowly missing a row of suburban homes as people were awakening from an air-raid free night. Only ten minutes before I'd delivered newspapers to the house where he died and the bedroom curtains were still drawn together; in homage, they would remain drawn for another week. The following morning, on my next delivery, I saw the crumbled shell of the plane lying amongst flowers in the rear garden where it had fallen. As the body of the hapless young RAF trainee pilot had been removed, I never did see the face or know the name of the man whose agonies and fears I had shared. At that young age I had no thoughts of becoming a reporter and yet one basic ingredient was already showing itself – the knack of being in the right place at the right time.

I was also in the right place at the right time when I went truanting from school. 'Some of us are taking the afternoon off,' said Bertie Bennett, a friend whose grandmother made the best bread pudding I'd ever tasted. A small group of us schoolmates were walking across a field when we came to a deep unprotected hole in the ground. Bertie found a stone and dropped it down and we all listened as it took a long time before hitting the bottom. 'That's deep,' said Bertie knowingly and we all nodded in agreement. It was then that the small brother of one of my friends chose to look in the hole and as he began to topple forward I somehow, through sheer instinctive reaction, leapt forward and pulled him away. It was the only time I played hooky from school and my being there was quite a coincidence. Other lives would also be saved through similar extraordinary coincidences.

The war brought a fervour of patriotic zeal and when I was legitimately away from school during the summer holidays I volunteered to help the war effort by working in the fields of Lord Beaverbrook's nearby Cherkley Court. Day after day was spent picking up potatoes and sorting out the chats from the wares which, to non-yokels, means separating small potatoes from their larger siblings after they've been churned out of the earth by tractor. Beaverbrook, who was Minister for Aircraft Production, had advanced his farming methods beyond the need for shire horses. On a dim miserable day the heavens opened as monsoon-like rain turned the fields into quagmires causing school kids and farm labourers alike to rush for shelter in a barn and wait for the weather to ease up. Unexpectedly the barn door burst open and in strode a man resplendent in his be-medalled RAF uniform. I guessed who he was and expected him to crack a joke about the weather, which is mandatory in England. We kids had been led to believe that the Spitfire and Hurricane pilots were a jolly lot who just dropped what they were doing when a red alert sounded and flew up to do battle with a few Jerries before coming back to laugh about how many each had shot down. But this man didn't in any way fit the image of my schoolboy comic hero such as fighter pilot-cum-boxer, Rockfist Rogan. This man's face was as clouded as the skies above and he thundered, 'What the hell are all of you doing here? Get out and work or I'll deduct the time wasted off your wages!' The 'wage' I was earning for giving up my holiday to do voluntary farm work was a paltry sixpence an hour. The officer: Beaverbrook's son, Max Aitken. I doubt he would have won first prize for industrial relations at that time and I was to remember the incident when I became a minor trade union official on Beaverbrook's London *Evening Standard*.

Lord Beaverbrook was a Canadian and Mum had to make a terrible decision at the outbreak of war regarding me and his country of origin. She came to me and asked, 'How would you like to live in Canada? There's a plan to evacuate children and I've booked you on a ship to Toronto. You'll be safe there and well looked after but,' she added, 'the choice is yours.' Canada? My heart leapt as I thought of the American continent, the Rockies, the Great Lakes. The prospect of going to Toronto was wonderful... the excitement of it... the adventure! Then I looked at her troubled eyes; we were a very close-knit family and I asked if I would be travelling alone. 'Yes,' she said with a forced a smile, 'but don't worry about that. We'll meet up after the war which shouldn't last long.' With that assurance, I agreed to go on the adventure of a lifetime. Only Mum knew that she would never see me again, and that for her, like the trainee pilot, time was fast running out. And having lived through WW1 with the assurance that it would all be over by the first Christmas, she would have had reservations about how long WW2 would really last.

I didn't go to Canada. It hadn't occurred to her at the time what an appalling risk she was taking by giving her consent. Perhaps it hadn't occurred to the government, either. Yet they, at least, should have known. They knew that U-boats were lurking in the Atlantic to destroy convoys between Britain and America and yet were prepared to evacuate shiploads of schoolchildren to safety, even if they were killed on the way. On 17 September 1940, the unescorted *City of Benares* the 11,081 ton flagship of the Ellerman Line, was sailing towards Canada in rough seas with children aboard under the official Children's Overseas Reception Board scheme. Lying in wait 600 miles from shore beneath the Atlantic waves was the U-48 commanded by Kapitän Heinrich Bleindrodt and into the sights of his periscope came the *City of Benares*. He gave the order to fire torpedoes, an order which was to haunt both himself and members of his crew for the rest of their lives for as the ship went down waves swamped and sank many of the lifeboats. Some reports said the children had been more disciplined than some of the Indian crew and walked in file towards lifeboats while many crewmen made off without them. Only thirteen evacuees survived, plus six other children who were travelling privately. Of the ship's company, 248 were drowned, including eighty-five evacuee children.

When the U-48 returned to its base in France the crew learned of the horror of the attack. Said one of them, Wilhelm Kruse, many years later, 'It was a dark day for all of us, thinking of the women and children swimming for twenty hours in a rough sea, on a black night.' Future evacuation to Canada and other Commonwealth countries was abandoned shortly after the attack even though the Minister responsible for the evacuation wanted to send another boatload. I can't think what was on his mind as it's inconceivable that any loving parent would risk putting their child in such dangerous circumstances. It had been a shock to Mum as I was booked to go on the next ship.

While Leatherhead was a high-risk area enough to send children overseas for safety, the powers-that-be chose Leatherhead as a safety zone for evacuees sent down from two London high schools, the Strand for boys and St Martin's for girls. Despite her illness Mum had insisted on taking some in from both schools, possibly to supplement her meagre income. There was a special approach made to her about one child to see if she would accept him. 'He's a Jew,' she was told. 'So what?' she asked, somewhat surprised at the question. 'He's a German Jew!' 'He is also a child,' she countered, and I thought she looked angry. It was all a little over my head for I had no idea that children of my own age were being butchered in Germany just because someone didn't like them. And so it was that Walter Valk came to stay with us. His father ran a carpet business in the City of London and I once stumbled across his seedy looking shop near St Paul's Cathedral. Walter's claim to fame was that his Uncle Fritz was a film star under the name of Frederick Valk who played a prominent role in the British wartime film, *Night Train to Munich*. In another wartime film, *Gasbags*, with the Crazy Gang, he played the unlikely role of a

Wartime as a Leatherhead schoolboy, aged eleven years and five months, with gas mask. School photograph.

Nazi *Sturmführer*, a role he must have taken with some misgivings. Later he was in *The Colditz Story*. Walter didn't look any different from any other child and we got on well but he never once spoke to me of Germany or of relatives he left behind. I knew nothing of concentration camps or of Hitler's attitude towards Jews, not even from Walter; nor could I even suspect that our evacuee would be murdered if England was successfully invaded. Even in Leatherhead life wasn't always easy for him and on one occasion Warren intervened to stop him being beaten up by local children.

Mum's life-ebbing asthmatic and bronchial attacks were becoming ever more frequent, brutal and unabated for days on end and I'd cycle home from school in trepidation of the constant wheezing, coughing, gasping for breath and choking that she suffered. The dreadful agonies of the twin diseases were wretched for everyone and particularly for her but I would often wonder if the next gasp would be her last and whether, on opening the front door, I would find her dead. Sometimes I'd find a note from our neighbour, Mrs Lambeth, saying she had been rushed by ambulance to hospital and this was something of a relief for it meant I wouldn't have to nurse her when she was bedridden; I loathed dealing with her toilet facilities when she was physically incapable of leaving her bed. She was very Victorian and must have hated asking me for the chamber pot but only later would I realise that the indignity was much worse for her than for me.

I'd been home for a few days looking after her and when I returned to school I was told the headmaster wanted to see me. Apprehensively I knocked on his door but as I entered the formidable Mr Moore, who had a fearsome reputation for giving six of the best, rose from his desk and smiled. His secretary brought me a chair and I was invited to sit down. My immediate appraisal was that corporal punishment was off his menu. 'How is your mother today?' he asked. 'She's a bit better, sir,' I replied, cautiously. Always at the back of my mind was the thought that if things got bad, I would be packed off to a children's home. 'Did you do your paper round this morning?' he asked. 'Yes, sir,' I answered, wondering how he knew that I did a newspaper round. 'And what did you cook for dinner yesterday?' This was becoming truly ominous and the question really caught me off guard as I'd never even told my friends that I cooked. It could only be the education authorities checking up on me to see if I should be sent away. 'Lamb, potatoes, carrots and cabbage,' I replied. 'Do you like cooking?' I didn't, but I wasn't going to tell him. I smiled broadly as I've always done when in a tight corner: 'It's all right except for the cabbage, I don't like the smell of it being cooked.' He laughed back, 'You remind me of a Cheshire Cheese. Do you know what that is?' 'No, sir. I've heard of a Cheshire Cat.' With that, he picked up a pencil and drew a large round circle and put a laughing face on it. 'That's just like you,' he said. 'You're always laughing, never stop doing that.' It was an extraordinary interview. I was now thirteen years of age and in many ways far more worldly than my classmates yet I was being talked to rather like a six-year-old. I knew with a stomach churning inner trepidation that something was very wrong and I felt sure now that my suspicions were correct and that I was definitely destined for a home.

A month after my chat with the headmaster Mum said, casually, 'I've managed to get you a job with Dyers starting next week. You are to become an apprentice compositor.' By law I should have remained at school with all my classmates if only to improve my game of cards in the shelters during air raids, but Destiny and the Law are not always compatible. Dyers was a pedestrian newsagents and printers and on reporting for work I was told, stiffly, that my wages would be 17/6d a week which was fractionally more than double the amount I received from my morning and Sunday newspaper rounds. I was led from the shop and into a dingy cobbled alley at the side where there was a small door. 'You won't be allowed into the shop any more at any time, this will be your entrance in future,' said Ted Dyer loftily, a tall, bespectacled man who was as dour as the machine room I'd just entered. His words and demeanour impressed upon me that I was now lower than third class and I recalled that even as a paper boy working for a rival newsagents (which had appreciated me) there was never any question of not being allowed into the shop. I looked around at the darkened walls of the machine room that had once been covered with lime green but that was a distant memory and I felt a suffocating depression as I sniffed the air. There was a smell I hadn't come across before, of oil, rubber, ink and paper and it was accompanied by the noise of an Arab printer turning out visiting cards and a Heidelberg used for printing official documents and posters. The machine rooms of newspapers, I was to discover later, had a more urgent sound but the aroma was exactly the same and, like pre-war school desks which housed generations of stale bread crumbs, tomato, cheese, oranges and apples, once the smell permeates the senses it never completely leaves them.

Upstairs, resting on bare wooden floorboards in the typesetting room was a large organ which I was forbidden to go even near, its keys were those of a typewriter and the type itself was set in hot molten lead. When Ted Dyer took to the keyboard he was Bach playing a Toccata for the Deaf on a silent fire-fed organ, but whatever my aspirations to emulate him had been I was never destined to become such a maestro. Instead, I was escorted to a plain, unvarnished table where I stood on a creaking wooden platform. In front of me on the table was a series of open boxes which contained lead type, one box for each letter of the alphabet and figures, while others had punctuations and thin sheets of lead used for spacing between words. I have subsequently seen identical boxes in a print of a European typesetting firm of about the year 1600. A metal holder was placed in my hand and I was shown how to set type for visiting cards by putting the type upside down into the holder. Nearly every facet of my work was pre-Dickensian as day after dreary day I stood there, setting up type.

I went home one evening to find the bungalow was empty and when

Warren came in he asked our neighbour to telephone Epsom Hospital. We were told that Mum was 'comfortable', an irritating meaningless term used to fend off worried callers. Next day, a Sunday evening, the neighbour received a telephone call from the hospital asking for Warren to go over. He cycled the long, hilly five miles to Epsom with dire misgivings but fully expecting to see Mum while in the meantime the neighbour, Mr Lambeth, took me for a short walk. It couldn't have been easy for him and we chatted generally until we approached some arches at the entrance to the housing estate when he turned and said, 'Your mother is dead!'

I froze in disbelief at the awful truth that I would never see Mum again. The finality of his words was devastating and I tried desperately to visualise and retain images of her as she had always been: her face, her voice, and the way she stood and walked. Her Victorian morals with their strong sense of honesty, integrity and loyalty which she'd imparted to us, one way or another. Mum, who was quite well-educated and had lived in a large house in Chippenham, Cambridgeshire, before it and the whole village burned down, had been strict but kind and fair and the centre of our small family for which she had struggled so hard to keep together. As I stood speechless beside the arches I remembered our trip to the Ideal Home Exhibition in London where she bought the demonstration washing machine so that she could launder other people's washing; I recalled the way she worked to clean Mrs Lloyd's house and came home wheezing and exhausted only to tidy ours before designing dresses for people and running them up on her sewing machine. Then there was the time we stood in the garden as she gazed up thoughtfully at the sky before saying with utter conviction, 'I know I've lived on earth before.' Mum's life had been the triumph of incredible willpower over adversity for she had just managed to keep her solemn promise from my infancy; that despite all her suffering, she would not die until we were both working. She made it with just two months to spare!

Shortly after the funeral in Fetcham churchyard, Ted Dyer, whose son had been my best school friend told me, 'Roy will be leaving school at the end of the year and I'm bringing him into the business. As there won't be room for the two of you – and I don't think you are suited here – I feel you should leave right now!' With those few words of dismissal I was taken to the back door and handed a small brown envelope containing thirty-five shillings, or two weeks' pay. 'I would also like you to have this little gift,' he said. The Dyers were devout Jehovah's Witnesses and my going-away present was a red-covered cheap copy of the New Testament. At least Ted Dyer had assured himself, that his action would be looked upon with approval by The Lord but it didn't seem very Christian to me that the Dyer brothers, who had wanted Mum to become a member of the sect, could promise to give me an apprenticeship when she was alive and then sack me as soon as she died. I walked out through the back door and down the cobbled grimy alley for the last time and wondered dejectedly about the future, for I'd been given the firm impression by the

Dyers that I was really quite useless. My initial reaction was that I had let down my very special, wonderful mum.

When the axe falls it has never left a chip on my shoulders but the oozing blood has manifested into a thick deep-red cloak of despondency and a total lack of confidence. Already I had good reason to feel these twin emotions and worse was to follow. 'Do you realise, Reg, that I'll be called up any day now,' said my brother. Warren had been the last pillar of stability in a crazy world, who I'd thought had been rejected from the army as medically unfit through poor eyesight. If he went, our home would go too, for the do-good authorities certainly wouldn't allow me to live there alone, no matter how capable I might be at looking after myself. I was quite resilient but the past three months had been catastrophic for I had lost my mother, my schooling, my friends, my job, my home, my village and my brother to the army, too. But there were kind people around and my protective eighteen-year-old brother, who was employed in the Finance Department of Leatherhead Council, approached the Deputy Treasurer, Bill Jarvis, and his wife who generously offered to let me live with them at Craddocks Avenue, Ashtead, for a while. A prominent councillor, Blaxland Stubbs, who was deputy editor on Sir Walter Hamilton's historical books about WW1, was told of the problem and found me work. I was to report to the Amalgamated Press at the Fleetway House, Farringdon Street, London. As I took my first train to Waterloo I finally left any semblance of my childhood behind me. It was a journey into a different world, a world of total war where even the electric train seemed to be imbued with nationalist passions. As its wheels ran over joins in the track they emitted the sound of three dots and a dash, the Morse 'V' for Victory sign. The closer to London we travelled, the greater the signs of intense bombing where walls stood like ancient ruins; empty shells of homes with their insides scooped out by archaeologists' shovels. These had been homes where families had lived, some house-proud with shining brass knobs on the corners of their beds, a polished table downstairs and dusted chairs; others more slovenly with dirty shoes and boots dropped where they'd been removed, towels left on the bathroom floor and beds unmade. It made little difference now to the house-proud or the dilatory, for they had suffered the same fate.

My thoughts were interrupted as the train entered Waterloo Station and the importance of the British Isles as a strategic base for winning the war became instantly apparent. A mass of humanity bustled about the concourse, mostly in uniform and many wearing shoulder identity strips of different nationalities. I made my way through the crowd to the bewildering Underground where the tube train notices warned that 'Careless Talk Costs Lives', and 'Coughs and sneezes spread diseases, trap the germs in your handkerchiefs'. There was one commercial break to the gloom but still with a war theme which showed a happy girl with a young Brylcreemed RAF pilot and the poignant words, 'Cheers, Cheers, I've got my wings, now we can look for some Bravington rings.' I thought of the pilot who had died in front of me getting his wings and of the others I'd seen shot down in dogfights and wondered with melancholy how many of them had read the advert and bought Bravington rings.

From Blackfriars Station I began to walk towards Ludgate Circus and gazed in wonder and horror at the devastation. Charred walls stood precariously in crazy patterns, held up by invisible puppet strings and ready to collapse into the piles of rubble. Up Ludgate Hill on the right was St Paul's Cathedral which rose majestically above the ruins; until now I'd only seen newspaper photographs of it surrounded by flames and smoke. In its crypt were the remains of two men who knew a lot about war, Nelson and Wellington, and the bomb which exploded above their heads and near the body of General Gordon of Khartoum, would possibly have revived post-mortal nostalgia. I reached the Amalgamated Press and pondered what my duties would be. Because a deputy editor had found me the job, I knew they would require some sort of intelligence and I looked forward to the challenge. Perhaps I'd be given some important work on a famous magazine or even a comic to start with. As I climbed the marble steps and passed through the swing doors, I could see that the foyer of the Fleetway House was tastefully decorated with a highly polished wooden counter, velvet curtains and flowers. A smartly uniformed member of the Corps of Commissionaires (on seeing him I ruefully thought of my dad) invited me to take the lift to the first floor where I was to make my presence known. This was definitely more my style – the back-alley entrance of Dyers was already a distant and disagreeable memory.

A trim-suited lady stood waiting to greet me with a smile as I left the elevator and she quickly confided my duties and income while we walked briskly to a long drab-brown varnished bench where some youths were sitting. My heart sank with shame for whatever my hopes had been, they were dashed from under me: I was to become a messenger at twenty-one shillings a week. There couldn't be any job more demeaning than a messenger…

"Ere, wot's yer name?' asked a tall, gangly ginger-haired boy whose very attitude told me that he was streetwise. I told him. 'Well, I'm the chief messenger, see, and I've got a job for yer.' There was a smirk on his face which I didn't like but because I didn't know the ropes I could only do as he said. 'I want yer to go along to Boots, the chemist just up the road, and get me wot's written on this 'ere bit of paper.' I looked hard at the word but did not understand it. 'What is it?' I inquired. The boy sniggered and looked at the others. They sniggered too and looked away. "Ere's 'alf a crown,' he said without answering the question, and handed me a coin. So there was something lower than being a messenger boy – I was a messenger's messenger! At the chemist shop I handed over the piece of paper to an attractive young girl who smiled sweetly. Then she looked at me curiously, and blushed. 'You won't get those in any Boots,' she said. Then I blushed, instinctively knowing what I had been sent to buy. My vocabulary had improved on my very first day of work and now I was familiar with the word 'contraceptives'.

Once my pride had sunk, being a messenger had compensations. There was plenty of time to read and I could go out frequently to fulfil a fascination for historical places – and there were still plenty left, despite the bombing. Walking up Fleet Street, I gazed up in awe at the *Daily Express* and *Daily Telegraph* buildings which imposed a magic of their own. Even as an adult, I would take a nostalgic look at those edifices, reminiscent of Tom Brown returning to Rugby, but the comforting feeling of its permanence has disappeared for ever. Arthur Mee, whose books were published by the Amalgamated Press, once said the *Daily Telegraph* building was 'As sound and solid as the paper it produces.' The building is still there but the solid newspaper went to the dogs, the Isle of Dogs, that is. Gone elsewhere too, is the *Daily Express* and others which made the street the exciting and dynamic newspaper nerve centre of Britain. As a lowly messenger it never occurred to me that I would outlive the mighty Fleet Street, per se. Beyond the *Telegraph* was a pub, a very old building which immediately caught my eye. It is possibly the most famous pub in Fleet Street and even though I didn't know it existed, when I saw the name I somehow knew my destiny would be tied up with that strip of road and at once I felt at home. The pub bore the strange name my headmaster had bestowed upon me: The Cheshire Cheese!

The Fleetway House gave an instant insight into old London; it was built on the site of the Fleet Prison, the famous debtors' jail. A favourite book of mine as an impressionable youngster was *Northwest Passage*, in which Major Robert Rogers, 'Late Commander of His Majesty's Rangers in North America, late Captain Commandant of the garrison of Michiulimackinac,' had found himself incarcerated. A few lines that opened Chapter Seventy-Nine aroused my interest:

> I had thought of the Fleet Prison as I had thought of all jails – as a stone building filled with straw-strewn cubicles from whose iron-barred doors peered wan prisoners in chains, and before which paced morose guards in uniform, jingling huge keys on iron rings, but it wasn't like that. When I reached Ludgate Hill and walked down Farringdon Street I found a grated window in a blank wall. Above the window were cut the words, 'Pray Remember Poor Debtors Having No Allowance' and behind the grating stood a man hopefully rattling pennies in a tin cup. The cup came out of the bars appealingly toward me as I passed and dropped a few shillings in. A few paces beyond the window was an arched doorway – as busy a doorway as I ever saw. Messengers raced in and out; waiters with trays and hampers hurried anxiously through. Ladies whose profession was dubious made small talk with cadaverous-looking doorkeepers who stared fixedly at those who came and went.

And what was I now doing? I was a messenger: only time, the building and the use of the site had changed. Life was looking more interesting than I could have imagined or ever hoped for!

Opposite the Fleetway House was another piece of London's history which was to interest me so much that I found myself becoming something of an authority on the immediate area. I inquired why the building across the street was so narrow in appearance and learned that during the plague of 1665, the overflow of bodies from the churchyard of the original St Bride's Church in Fleet Street (where Samuel Pepys was baptized) was so large, that a communal grave pit was dug nearby. It was forbidden to build on the pits nearly 300 years later, more for health than sacrilegious reasons. The hidden pit meant that Farringdon Street had seen bodies thrown on to carts and heard hand bells and the mournful cry of 'Bring out your dead!'. I'd seen sketches of the pitiful scene and now I was fascinated at the visual evidence of a pit's existence.

Near our building was the Memorial Hall where the Labour Party was founded while behind us was the site of the formidable Newgate Prison, a drab louse-ridden hole where human dignity was denied; where the grim tolling of the great bell from the nearby Old Bailey church of St Sepulchre's would let Londoners know that they were awakening to execution morning at Newgate. The ashes of Sir Henry Wood now rest at St Sepulchre's and are a shrine to many of the millions who attend the Royal Albert Hall promenade concerts that he initiated; even the bold Captain John Smith of Pocahontas fame is interred there. Years later, as a journalist, I covered the anniversary of Pocahontas's sailing from Woolwich on her fatal last voyage when Edwina Mountbatten disclosed for the first time in public that she was a descendant of the princess. The *Daily Mail* used my story with the eye-catching headline, 'I am a Red Indian – Countess Mountbatten.'

Then there was the Old Bailey on the site of Newgate, whose scales of justice above the green dome have sometimes proved to be fearfully unbalanced by the fallibility of the lawmakers, the police and the judiciary itself. Sometimes I'd take an early lunch and stroll up Fleet Street to the Law Courts and listen to criminal appeals. Lord Chief Justice Goddard conjured up visions of a latter-day Judge Jeffreys: I don't know if he enjoyed playing God as his name might suggest, for his cold-chiselled granite face showed only dispassionate indifference which I found disturbing. Richard Crossman, years later, was to describe him succinctly as 'This astonishing old monster.' What a disappointment these wretched murderers were who would end a life with a broken bottle, a knife or even just kick their victims to death; nothing like the sophisticated villains in Whodunit? books. While I liked detective books, my fellow messengers would look askance at some of my other literature: Thackeray, Austen, Schute, Dickens, Tolstoy, and in particular A J Cronin who greatly influenced me through his insight into the frailty of human nature and his portrayals of life's injustices; of the condemnation by manipulative people of influence against others who were idealistic.

I was promoted from the messengers' bench to the Sales Department where my triple duties were to remain as a messenger but also use an addressograph machine for addressing envelopes, and a comptometer for writing out cheques.

Hardly exciting stuff, but there was an increase in wages – and in my confidence.

An incident took place during this brief period that produced a social habit later in my life. I was asked to deliver some papers to the home of the Sales Director, named Hufton, and found him and his wife sipping G & Ts on the lawn on a brilliant cloudless day. It was the first time I'd seen or heard of ice in a drink or come across anyone who owned a refrigerator and when I was offered an orangeade with ice I realised that this was another dimension to the world I had grown up in. People today sometimes comment on the large amount of ice in my gins or Scotch-on-the-rocks (not good malts) and when they put it down to my many years in Africa I nod in agreement. How can you measure a goal, an attainment in life, in terms of lumps of ice? While cubed ice was my yardstick of success, the impetus also came from disillusioned people with unrealised ambitions. Many times in my youth I would listen incredulously to men in their thirties who would say, dejectedly, 'If only I was your age, the things that I would do!' It was hard to believe that men with a reasonable education could look upon me with envy, especially as my view of the future was clear as a misty crystal ball. I resolved there and then that *I would try to live life to the full, and never ever look back with regret.*

I met Sid Creek in the Army Cadets after I'd moved from Surrey to live with Aunt Lillie in New Barnet, Hertfordshire. Sid's arms fascinated me as they were much longer than anyone else's I had seen until I met his father whose arms hung like a gorilla's, below his knees! Sid explained that his dad was a signalman on the railway and his arms had been stretched by pulling long levers in junction boxes and Sid, it transpired, used to help him. My friend's long arms came in particularly useful when we went to a local cinema to see the film *Lost Horizon*. He was agitated when a lady wearing an eggshell blue hat with a long feather chose to sit directly in front of him. Tapping the lady lightly on the shoulder he asked politely, 'Would you mind removing your hat, Madam, as I can't see the film?' The lady was not amused and turned in her seat to glare at the impudent youth: 'Certainly not,' she answered tersely and turned back to view the film which she had denied to Sid. My friend was taken aback but he was a resourceful fellow and clearly determined not to move from his own seat to accommodate the bad manners of the lady in front. From a pocket he produced a pair of scissors which surprised me as it was one of the last things I'd have expected him to carry. Ronald Colman's plane had just crashed in the Tibetan mountains but my attention was distracted away from the Himalayan snowstorm and Shangri-La and was riveted instead to the drama taking place beside me. Fascinated, I watched those long arms stretch out and with a quick surgical snip, which the lady did not hear, he cut three-quarters off the offending feather, leaving the rest to stand erect like the middle finger in an obscene gesture. After the performance, the lady strutted from the cinema with the great confidence of a latter-day Madame du Barry but actually resembling Countess Mountbatten's forebear.

'I wonder if it's ticking,' I said to Sid as we were strolling through nearby Hadley Wood. We'd come across a large unexploded bomb lying flat on the mud-soaked ground. It was about five feet long without a fin and as rounded as a fat pig, not like anything I'd seen before. 'Perhaps it's a landmine,' I added.

'I dunno,' my companion replied, 'let's have a look!'

We sauntered across to investigate and were disappointed to find that the answer to my question about ticking was in the negative. 'Perhaps if we kick it we might start the clock going?' I ventured but no amount of kicking or any futile attempts to roll it made the slightest difference. In the end we gave up in disgust and wandered off. The bomb was of a type still being dropped when I first started work in London but it was followed by the V-1, doodlebug, buzz bomb, or whatever names people preferred to call the impersonal fiery-winged killer. Even though Londoners could see these outsized mosquitoes dropping from the skies *ad nauseum* and they slaughtered hundreds of innocent people, I found them more a curiosity than a threat, with one exception…

Unlike bombs raining down in clusters, the doodlebugs were loners which crashed one at a time with plenty of warning. The practice of potential victims was to watch the direction of the flight of the flying bomb and wait for the engine to cut out. Then the robot would either glide or nosedive into the ground, tip its stubby wings to fly either to the left or right or sometimes double back on itself. To add to the cat-and-mouse game, there were occasions when the engine did not cut out at all and the monster flew straight into a building.

I was rinsing my hands in the men's cloakroom at the Fleetway House, when I heard the familiar staccato of the bomb's engine and as it came nearer the jet cut out. My throat lost its moisture as I waited expectantly for an explosion; and I waited. Then came the sinister swishing sound of the Grim Reaper's scythe, the slipstream of the bomb's wings as it flew towards me. Almost inaudible at first, the whispering grew louder and excruciatingly close until it was immediately overhead and only a few feet above the building. I had only seconds to live and I realised the same knowledge must be flashing through the minds of other people in the office who were also waiting to die. With the tingle of fear came a sensuality and intensity of orgasmic proportions as adrenalin pumped throughout my body while I stood helplessly with my hands resting on the washbasin. After an eternity the loud swishing passed until it once more became a brief whisper and I waited for the monster to double back. It came to earth with a shattering explosion less than a hundred yards from me, killing other people who were working in their offices near the Appeal Courts.

Tragedy to most people is the death of someone near or even a pet. To others can be added the loss of a beautiful piece of architecture or furniture. Many Londoners mourned the loss of famous works of art, albeit temporarily. While not a connoisseur, I enjoy paintings and it was during the early 1940s that I strolled up Fleet Street and the Strand at lunchtime and entered the National Gallery which borders Trafalgar Square. I walked into a curator's nightmare; a depressing, melancholy sight. Hideously barren were faded walls with bright patches to show where they had been graced by masterpieces of the world's greatest artists. Slowly I wandered through the cavernous building and heard, faintly at first, haunting music echoing through the empty chambers. It was unmistakably Bach and in the distance was a gallery with a grand piano and people, a few of them in uniform, either sitting on collapsible chairs or standing around listening to the playing of a grey-haired lady who had become a national figure through her lunchtime concerts, Dame Myra Hess. I contemplated the mixed-up, crazy state the world was in. Hess! That was the name of Hitler's deputy, a Nazi leader more used to Wagner and concentration camps. Yet here was this lady, his namesake, comforting people with her gentle music, playing to the people of London and the soldiers, sailors and airmen of many lands who called in to hear her. With all the destruction that had taken place in London, I wondered if her famous party piece, 'Jesu Joy of Man's Desiring' was really appropriate. After the recital and as I walked out of the building into bright sunlight, there standing opposite and singing beside a fountain in Trafalgar Square was Beatrice Lillie with another anomaly. Her choice of song was, 'Three Little Fishes' which she had popularized at the time but her venue was bizarre: the fountain she stood beside was both waterless and fishless. Other popular musical anomalies I counted were: 'Praise the Lord, and pass the Ammunition' (presumably in order to blow the opposition into oblivion in the name of God); and the opening bars of Beethoven's Fifth Symphony which propaganda suggested could have been written to boost Churchill's 'V' sign. Beethoven? Wasn't he German? Ah, well, that's war for you.

'I've got some rather bad news, Reg,' said Warren who came home on leave. Warren had been drafted into the Recce Corps (Reconnaissance Corps) and the bad news he was about to impart wasn't good for him, either. 'Our colonel gave a pep talk the other day and said that seventy-five per cent of us would become casualties!' As he passed this titbit to me I didn't need much education to know this was very bad news; and if this was a 'pep talk' I wondered how the colonel behaved when he had really bad news to impart and I still have a fearful memory of those Recce Corps teenagers who trained with my brother. In February 1943, they arrived in cheerful mood at Waterloo Station on transfer to Kent. I stood under the big clock whistling our chosen tune, 'Story of a Starry Night', so that we could find each other in the crowd and it was possibly the wrong tune to whistle, coming from Tchaikovsky's Sixth Symphony (Pathetique), the composer's own swan song.

The following year, as D-Day approached, I doubted I would ever see my brother again but Fate stepped in once more in its own peculiar way. Because of his poor eyesight, Warren was transferred to the Royal Army Pay Corps which created the unusual position between us that throughout most of the war my soldier brother was safe (or comparatively so) in some remote area while he was deeply concerned that his civilian brother was in London in a nasty war. This was brought home to me when he was on leave and visited me in Barnet. We walked down a street at night in the middle of an air raid and the Ack-Ack boys were having a ball; vicious jagged pieces of shrapnel kept sparkling around us as they crashed into the street and ricocheted. 'I say, Reg,' Warren declared apprehensively, 'I don't think much of this!' Many years later he was attending a flower show in Surrey and met one of his old Recce comrades. The man was in a wheelchair and said that he was badly wounded and crippled for life during the D-Day landing but many others were killed.

While the German V-1s only once disturbed my metabolism, I had a fearful respect for the V-2s and with two good reasons: they came without warning and their explosive force was terrifying. The first one I heard explode was in Barnet where Aunt Lillie had a Morrison shelter in her lounge-cum-dining room. It was not Chippendale but nevertheless could claim some distinction in the furniture world as being the ugliest yet safest table ever made. Comprising a solid steel roof with steel supports in which people encased themselves in steel mesh sides, the roof acted as a dining-room table during the day but not even a tablecloth could disguise its hideousness. While Lillie and my two cousins slept in the shelter, I opted for the comfort of bed. For some like me who adopted this cavalier attitude there were tragic consequences but I felt that if I was to die, God let it be in a soft bed. Creature comforts can be of paramount importance for morale but one night I questioned my wisdom, or lack of it. My bedroom windows were criss-crossed with strips of brown paper, in a pattern copied from the attractive small lead variety, which were expected to reduce the murderous effects of splintered flying glass. During the still of night the windows shattered and this was followed by a deafening explosion. My face, blankets and pillow were covered with broken glass and the brown strips of paper and yet, miraculously, I was not beheaded and came out unscathed. The missile had landed some distance away but its 1,654 lbs of high explosive had caused the freak blast which disturbed my slumbers. Wernher von Braun had left his visiting card; his next would be delivered to my office in indelible print.

Smithfield, London's largest meat market, is a bustling place and so it was during the war, despite the meat shortage. Queues of people lined up expectantly, like Antarctic penguins with ration cards in hand, waiting for morsels of food while Bummarees trundled their barrows of carcasses through the rows of newly hung beef, pork, lamb and poultry; their snow-white overalls daubed with crimson blood.

Outwardly Smithfield, whose original market dates back to 1183, has always been a cheerful place and once boasted its own fair, St Bartholomew's. Even today, the Cockney humour of the butchers and porters is never far away but underlying this bustling light-heartedness is a toughness which, one senses, verges on the brutal. Perhaps this feeling is encouraged by the sight of the slaughtered animals, their skins peeled to reveal bare flesh, which hang row upon row, waiting to be collected. In medieval times, during the reign of Queen 'Bloody Mary' Tudor, the carcasses of human Protestant martyrs would hang from gibbets where the Brugel-type fair was held. The former St Bartholomew's fairground site is now a pleasing small park for lovers who meet for a lunchtime kiss and an ear-nibble, and for lonely secretaries whose only nibble is on their sandwiches. They are unlikely to know much of its history, of the Peasants' Revolt, of Wat Tyler's confrontation with King Richard II at Smithfield on 15 June 1331 when, during an altercation with one of the king's attendants, Tyler was attacked and badly wounded by the mayor of London, William Walworth. Tyler was carried into St Bartholomew's hospital for treatment but Walworth had him dragged out and beheaded. The Scottish hero, Sir William Wallace, also died there after being declared a traitor to King Edward I to whom he had never sworn allegiance. The poor chap was hanged, disembowelled, beheaded and quartered before his head was displayed on London Bridge and his limbs exposed at Newcastle, Berwick, Stirling and Perth.

This brutality of Smithfield past was matched towards the end of the war when I was preparing to visit the market for some sandwiches of my own. Each morning I would make a decision: should I turn left out of the office and buy sandwiches at Manzies in Ludgate Circus or should I turn right and go to Smithfield? On this day I was wearing a new suit for the first time, which had cost my meagre savings and all my clothing coupons as well. I decided upon Smithfield, where I would sometimes have a pleasant chat with an elderly colleague's wife as we took our place in the queue. I was about to stand up to leave the dimly lit general office when the room was dazzled by the effulgence of sunlight as one of its walls crumbled in a cloud of sparkling dust. As bricks and mortar were flung across the desks there came the sound of an explosion, as deafening as a nearby clap of thunder and so intense that it shook the whole of the building. Incredibly, no one in the office was hurt and I hurried downstairs, and turned right. Eighty yards away, just beyond Holborn Viaduct, was a large pall of dust and I knew the explosion had been caused by a V-2 rocket. Oh God, I thought, it's Smithfield Market!

Walking at the double – one should never get excited in an emergency and running suggests panic – I wondered what horrors were in store and yet on arrival the sight was nothing like I had expected. My first impression was of stillness and emptiness. Buildings had disappeared, others were half collapsed, and even though there was plenty of rubble it was less than I had anticipated. What particularly struck me was that no one else was around, no bodies, no wounded, nothing. It was as silent as a grave. As I stood in the dustbowl, the appalling truth began to manifest itself – it was a grave! I realised that much of the market had collapsed through the surface to become enveloped in the network of roads underneath. I began to pull at a pile of wooden beams and bricks, trying not to tear my priceless and irreplaceable blue pin-striped suit, but I knew that alone I was less than useless. Where was everybody? Possibly those inside the precariously standing buildings were either trapped, or too shocked to move. But what about the ordinary pedestrians and more important of all, the services?

Gradually, or so it seemed to me, people began to arrive, the ARP, Civil Defence, police, firemen, off-duty soldiers and others in civilian clothes. I'd been doing my inadequate best for over half an hour when a man came up and helped with the clearing, saying, 'I feel sick at just thinking about what we will find under here.' Until that moment I hadn't given the matter a thought but suddenly I felt disorientated and ill and staggered away. In my school days I had always been excused First Aid lessons as I would become dizzy at the mere mention of blood and arteries. I feel today that I would not have turned a hair at what I might find at Smithfield. I've subsequently seen many massacres and mutilated, tortured bodies usually without any problem but paradoxically, I still cannot listen to a First Aid lecture or watch a surgical operation on television. The rocket on Smithfield which killed 120 people was the second worst single disaster in the whole of London during the war and amongst the victims was my colleague's wife.

I made my way back towards the Amalgamated Press where my life had been happy but where my employment was coming to an end without either myself or the company realising it. Shortly after the V-2 incident I was called upstairs for a cordial meeting with the Sales Director who declared that he was sending me on promotion into the provinces as a trainee sales representative. Would I prefer Manchester or Cardiff? Promotion? I'd been unaware that my work was under review. Having seldom been north of London, it didn't matter where I went and a mental pin on the map chose Manchester. It was a fateful decision. Had I gone to Cardiff I might indeed have become a sales representative and remained at the job to retire with a pension. Shortly before my promotion I'd been going through an office cupboard and came across a book on sex and it being a subject of which I was conscious but not well informed, despite the schoolmistress incident, I glanced through the pages when a voice said over my shoulder, 'What are you reading?' The owner of the voice, a senior clerk who was dodging his national service, then shouted for all to hear, 'You don't read that filth,' and grabbed the offending publication and threw it into a waste-paper basket like shaking off a venomous snake. Everyone stared at me, a pervert in their midst even though they must have known the book was there and had read it themselves. One of them must even have put it in the cupboard as it wasn't an Amalgamated Press publication. When news got around that I was being sent to Manchester, the same man glared at me, 'Keep your nose clean,' he said in a loud voice. 'He doesn't mean your nose,' sniggered another of the clerks and I went away wondering what he did mean.

Manchester is a city which makes many exalted claims and is not shy to self-promote. It even prides itself on its friendliness and neighbourliness but this was not my experience. My new job there was to sort out magazines and tie them together for delivery by the sales representatives to various news agents: sort out magazines? Deliver them? This was familiar. I'd been sorting out newspapers each morning as a child before starting my paper round; now I was to do it on promotion! Miss Paxton, an ice maiden, ran the show and while I have always enjoyed women's company, Paxton loathed me from the start. Slim, bespectacled with short iron-grey hair, I soon learned she was paranoid over southerners. Manchester, she once declared, should be the capital of England, and my immediate unspoken reaction was that perhaps it should have borne the Battle of Britain blitz instead of London. It wasn't in my nature to curry favour and mention that my father actually came from the Manchester suburb of Salford and had once served as a sergeant in the Manchester Regiment.

Before arriving at work one morning, I watched a black and white cat run over by a car and in agony, the wretched creature jumped up and down in the middle of the busy road until another car mercifully killed it. I must have looked pale and shaken as my condition elicited a rare question from Paxton. After I had explained about the cat, she retorted before stalking off, 'Oh, so you have some feelings then!' On another morning I bought my first-ever gramophone record on the way to the office and put it on a table. I felt a pair of eyes boring into me and saw that I was being watched through Paxton's observation window. Quickly she left her office, brushed past me and went straight to the record which she picked up. She was momentarily speechless for whatever she had been expecting it certainly wasn't Tchaikovsky's First Piano Concerto. 'I wouldn't have thought you would know anything about good music,' she sneered and delicately placed the recording down. 'At least there is something in your favour.'

I'd been booked into a boarding house and quite unknown to me, the seemingly friendly owners kept a record of my comings and goings, especially the time I arrived home at night. I was now just seventeen years of age and had been totally independent for three of them. It came as some surprise, there-fore, when I was called before the iron lady to be told, 'I have a report here on the disgraceful hours you have been keeping. I am sending you back to London where you will be instantly dismissed.' So much for promotion; it had lasted exactly ten weeks. I mentioned to Hufton that my so-called late hours had been spent helping to decorate the home of a family which had befriended me but the knife had sunk too deep and my dismissal was a formality. He refused to hand over to me the sheaf of papers he held containing the other alleged misdemeanours. I went down to the sales office to pick up some belongings. Everyone watched me but no one said a word. Even though I'd done no wrong, I knew that one man there would certainly believe Paxton. He was sure I hadn't kept my nose clean.

Sacked again! In addition to the very deep sense of injustice, in the back of my mind, too, was the feeling of incompetence, of having no skill, no trade, no prospects but my knowledge of life and people, the good, the bad, the jealous, the negative and the positive, was growing daily.

I called into the office of the Natsopa trade union, as membership was mandatory. They weren't bothered with the reasons why people were sacked; they found members jobs and the work they found me was with the London *Evening Standard*, in the Greyhound Department. The greyhound tips of the *Evening Standard* were renowned for their excellence and it was all because their reporters went to race meetings and jotted down on cards whether a dog was bumped, baulked or just bewildered. All this information, together with its placing in each race, was meticulously logged into large ledgers by male clerks from the morning when the office opened to the evening when it closed. I was now one of the Greyhound Department's Bob Cratchits whose futures seemed even more bleak than my own. Not having the slightest interest in greyhounds and never having been to a meeting to this day, I found the work tedious. But I was now on a Fleet Street newspaper!

Within the year I was called to arms at a most enviable time as the second world war was now over but what would happen for the next two years of my life would be decided at an interview by a one-man selection committee with the rank of colonel who reminded me of the *Evening Standard* cartoonist David Low's caricature, Colonel Blimp. He carried a fruit salad of medal ribbons above his left breast; he was chubby with flushed cheeks and I was fascinated by the soft strawberry centrepiece of his countenance which was displaying unmistakable signs of fermentation. The application of handkerchief to it might, I suspected, have had catastrophic results and throughout our discussion I waited expectantly for the moment when he needed to blow his nose. His speech was a little slurred and my suspicions of his inebriation were reinforced by brandy fumes which pervaded the small, utilitarian interview room. At 10 a.m. it was difficult for an unsophisticated lad of eighteen years to conceive that anyone might imbibe so soon after breakfast, but he was amiable enough and who was I to be critical of a serving officer who may have been through all kinds of hell during the war? 'And what regiment would you like to go into, my boy?' he beamed benevolently.

'The Pay Corps.' My innocuous answer brought about an immediate convulsion. Bushy eyebrows shot heavenwards, while his dilated fading blue eyes almost departed their sockets as if he had been poleaxed. Then, as if suffering an auditory malfunction he asked, 'What did you say?' – 'The Royal Army Pay Corps.'

'Good God.' He recovered slowly with a smile of pained condescension: 'Surely a young man like you doesn't want to go into the Pay Corps?' The very words caused him suffering and I knew, instinctively, that he would not have got on with Warren. 'The British army is full of fine regiments, any one of which you could join,' he said but as he looked reflectively at the diminutive figure facing him, he abruptly amended his statement as he had obviously ruled out the Coldstream and Grenadier Guards for starters. 'Well,' he said, slowly, 'most of them.' I was adamant and he was puzzled. 'But why the bl... (pause), why the Pay Corps?' Had he known of my father's military record and my own time in the Army Cadets, he would have asked the question with even more perplexity.

But he didn't know, and I merely replied, 'My brother is a serving officer in the corps, he recommended it.' I didn't add that Warren had also said it would get me away from all the bullshit of the infantry regiments. As a sop I added profoundly, 'There's not much point in joining the infantry now that the war is over.' That caused him to ponder and he wrote on a sheet of paper. I didn't go into the Royal Army Pay Corps, nor the infantry. He had found a sober compromise – the Royal Army Service Corps.

The first six weeks' initial military training were at Devizes, Wiltshire, and my first night of sleeping in a hut with other youths was one of utter bewilderment. Several were crying for their mothers blubbering that they were homesick and didn't want to be in the army. Not having had a mother for the past four years it was inconceivable to me that eighteen-year-old strapping youths should be crying for theirs. As for being homesick, I hadn't exactly had a home for quite some time either. The weeping carried on for three nights until I could stand it no more and shouted, 'For Christ's sake, shut up!' Perhaps because they were becoming used to taking orders or possibly fearing they would be beaten up by the rest of us, the wimps did as they were told. Having got the recruits quiet, I was next to become the centre of hostile reaction when there came another interruption, this time from under my bed. Because I was physically exhausted from the day's training I pretended not to notice but the sounds became agonising, which wasn't helped by the uproar from my comrades, 'Who've you got in your fucking bed, mate?' I got out from the blanket with great reluctance and turned on the lights amid more hostility. Beneath the bed was a creature in some sort of agony and I replied in the lingua franca of the army which had been almost foreign to me before call up, 'There's a fucking pussy cat under my bed and it's having kittens!' Despite our extreme exhaustion from the day's labours no one had the heart to throw out the young mother who was having labours of her own. At 3.30 a.m. we all watched, awestruck at the wonder of nature before retiring again to try to sleep. All too soon there was a banging on the door and the morning cry, 'Stand by your beds!' The early morning inspection began and the inevitable question was asked by a curious sergeant: 'What the 'ell is that under your fucking bed, Private?' 'Hmm Humph,' demurred the captain beside him. 'Sorry, Sah!' And then to me, 'Wot's under yer bleeding bed?' 'It's a pussycat with kittens, Sarge,' I confided. 'It had them during the night but I haven't got a box for them. Is it possible to get one?' The sergeant had a flinty look in his eyes which indicated that he didn't have a fucking box either and that I was being presumptuous for even suggesting that he might have. I was also given to understand that animals were not allowed to be kept as pets on military establishments unless they were regimental mascots. He advised me that this was all written down in King's Regulations, something of which I had not been aware. That morning we rookies were taken on a route march tour of the Wiltshire countryside and on our return the cat and kittens had disappeared. I feared the worst had happened to them, suspecting that the only wonder of nature to interest the sergeant would be a quite different type of pussy.

My next port of call in the army was an RASC clerical training depot at Cirencester in Gloucestershire and my presence there was due to a mechanical aptitude test which proved me to be so inapt or inept with machinery that there was only one course left open – to train as a clerk. I might just have well have been in the Pay Corps! The clerical course had one advantage which has stood me in good stead all my life; we were taught to touch type but on machines that would have taken pride of place in many museums. Having fingered around typewriters before, I knew what to look for and as there were no Remingtons I settled for an old Victorian upright Underwood. One oafish soldier had an Olivetti which was possibly a priceless original. His untrained podgy fingers forcibly sought out the correct keys with the delicacy of a bare-knuckle pugilist until the Italian-crafted typewriter, which had courageously survived scores of other recruits with great stoicism, finally gave up in the most dramatic way. The carriage had carried on moving along the framework until, in a magnificent gesture of defeat, it waved the typing paper as a white flag and leapt from the machine to make its suicidal plunge to the classroom's concrete floor.

I too was suffering but it had nothing to do with typewriters. Three warts had appeared and they were definitely in the wrong place at the wrong time. The *Concise Oxford Dictionary* describes them as 'Small, hardish roundish excrescence on skin caused by virus-induced abnormal growth of papillae and thickening of epidermis.' My own description of them at the time was more prosaic even if flavoured by military adjectives. Some warts go down in history: Oliver Cromwell's, for instance, were renowned and his death mask at Warwick Castle confirms they were not a pretty sight. Mine went down to the base of my right foot, two up front and one on the heel. On route marches they were total agony although some soldiers believed I was malingering for when it came to running I would always outstrip everyone without any sign of a limp, the simple reason being that my feet hardly touched the ground.

An army doctor provided corn pads after hacking away at the warts with a sharp blade and after several weeks of suffering, I asked if there was nothing else he could do. He thought for some time before replying, 'I could burn them out with acid.' Because of our rank disparity I couldn't demand to know why he hadn't thought of this in the first place but he produced a small bottle and applied the acid and within hours the weeks of pain, and the warts, disappeared.

It was because of my difficulty in marching that I'd sometimes be ordered to take a parade between lessons on the barrack square. It soon became clear that my father's leather lungs had been inherited and my drill orders could be heard reverberating around the classrooms seventy-five yards away. It was a wonderful discovery for this same voice projection was in later years to be used in a most diabolical act of retaliation that resembled my childhood prank of putting the bird in a jam jar, for in perpetrating the act I would mischievously if unintentionally turn the award of the Freedom of a capital city into a Gilbertian fiasco.

With the completion of my clerk's course, Aldershot beckoned, that hallowed shrine of many a dedicated military policeman whose Bible was King's Regulations and whose temple of worship was called 'The Glasshouse'. Having arrived at night as stiff as a penguin in freezing cold and deep snow, I was directed by an orderly sergeant to my quarters and on arrival at the barrack room. I was dismayed to discover the bed was missing certain items that help to create a tranquil comatose such as paillasse, blankets and pillow. Back at the Orderly Room I demanded blankets from the sergeant. 'Wait until the morning,' came the terse reply and when I protested the sergeant glared at me as if I was a maggot that had just crawled out of an apple. 'The quartermaster has gone to bed and I'm not going to wake him up just for you,' he said. There was no point in arguing with an Aldershot sergeant nor in asking for a higher authority and so I tried to sleep on bed springs wearing greatcoat and boots. The winter of 1946/7 was one of the coldest ever recorded in Britain and next morning on parade, another sergeant announced there was a posting to the Isle of Wight; he needed a volunteer and I made a fateful decision that would improve my army lot. Despite tiredness, caution was thrown to the winds and I was right out in front without giving the matter a second thought. Aldershot I did not need although others didn't seem to mind it as I was the only soldier to volunteer. That same day a ferry took me across a choppy Solent to Ryde where an army truck was waiting to chauffeur me to the barracks. This is the life, I thought, I'm going places at last. And so I was – all the way to the camp switchboard!

Being such an important personage as a switchboard operator without which the camp would come to a halt, I was excused all other duties except one: once a week it was incumbent upon me to light the cookhouse fire in time for breakfast. The first morning I tried for over half an hour without success until the thought of the whole camp being deprived of their morning porridge in mid-winter's thick snow was too much for me to stomach. In near frenzy, I called one of my new comrades who succeeded in getting it going. The next week I was determined to succeed. In still freezing cold I kept striking matches, partly to keep my hands warm but mainly to light the fire. The paper would ignite but the damp wood refused to succumb to the flames. I had run out of matches when the cook arrived and he showed no compassion for the frozen hapless figure huddled despondently over the unlit stove. So far, I have faithfully recorded the general barrack-room language of the British army. Cooks, it seems, have their own varied diet of words and at 5.30 a.m. I was treated to an unparalleled education into some of the lesser-known vulgarities of English vocabulary. Camp breakfast was subsequently an hour and a half late.

The switchboard had early advantages in contacting girlfriends on the island. I'd been out with a few girls, but one, whose soldier boyfriend had been posted the day before, telephoned me to take her out. This came as a surprise as I hadn't really noticed her. I went to her address and she called, 'Come in.' She was lying stark naked on the carpeted floor – it was the first time I had seen a girl naked. The effect on me was quite contrary to what she had expected as I walked out. Subsequently I was to realise that far from enjoying sex handed to me on a plate, I prefer the frills and thrills of seduction.

Manning the switchboard had been an amenable task until the man who shared the duty was posted away and not replaced. My bed was transferred into the switchboard room and for three weeks the only day I had off was Sunday, never a Saturday afternoon, which was to bring about my transfer. Warren had flown in from India and was due in Ryde to see me and I asked the Staff Sergeant ('Staff') for the Saturday afternoon off and when this was refused I walked out of the camp and met him anyway. As it was an early spring day we went to the far end of the island to Alum Bay, near the Needles. The beach was nearly deserted and while my brother stayed on a bench gazing out to sea, I climbed a multi-coloured sandy cliff to take a look around. With my romantic penchant for history, I envisaged the incredible sight of the Spanish Armada back in August 1588 as it sailed in its crescent formation to be met by the English navy. I then walked across the top of the cliff and jumped over a small muddy pool. Everyone in camp knew the island had quicksands but didn't know where they were. Suddenly I was in deep trouble as mud gurgled around my shins and soon it was up to my knees. Despite childhood fears following a warning from Mum about quicksands which were to be found in the fens, faced with the reality I was totally unperturbed although I doubt I would have been so calm had the blue sludge been creeping up my nose. Perhaps it's only a bog, I consoled myself, but my feet had not touched the bottom and I was sinking. I could see about ten yards of the beach and by chance two youths and a girl came into view and I waved, 'Can you give me a hand? I think I'm in quicksand!' The girl waved back and they moved on. Perhaps it was the casual way I had asked, or possibly the friendly grin suggested I was kidding. I shouted again as they, like me, were disappearing from view and the girl stopped and called back, 'What did you say?' 'I'm in quicksand!' They looked at each other and scrambled up the cliff. 'Mind that puddle,' I warned as I held out my arms. The men grabbed one wrist apiece and pulled hard. Very little happened as the mud clung to its victim and the girl held one of my rescuers around the waist and began pulling too. I felt sure the suction would pull off my army boots and arched my feet to try to keep them on. I would be in enough trouble when I got back to camp without being charged with losing government property. In truth, I was more concerned about those damned boots than my life! Gradually my rescuers were winning and after many heaves and grunts I was out. After clambering down to the beach I approached Warren and the look on his face was not encouraging; it verged on contempt. 'What the hell have you been up to this time?' This time? Yes, of course. He had known me since I was a baby. 'Nothing much, I jumped into a bog.' 'Well, you had better dry out and then brush off that mud. I can't be seen with you looking like that!' And that was it. One minute I'm being sucked down into treacherous sand and the next the next I'm being dressed down by my own brother for being untidy.

There were two sequels to the incident. Some years later when I was taking down telephoned news copy on the *Evening Standard*, our Isle of Wight correspondent reported that a man had been rescued from quicksands. He had been fortunate to be near a tree and hauled himself out before they caught hold. I read a report much later in which another man wasn't so lucky as he disappeared. Neither incident was near Alum Bay where I got into trouble and I am assured by the Needles Pleasure Park, which took over some of the area above the Alum Bay, that it has no quicksands and is perfectly safe. Jean Newnham of the Isle of Wight County Press, quoting the IoW Museum of Geology told me it was probably not quicksand but Reading clay which moves about and can be found above cliffs both to the north and south of Alum Bay. 'This can behave just like quicksand,' she said. I can endorse that and you cannot tell the difference when you are alone and stuck in it.

'And where the bloody hell have you been?' The staff sergeant didn't look even remotely pleased to see me alive and well. 'Do you realise that in your absence the whole camp has been without a telephone?' He advised me I would be facing several charges and I was not allowed out of camp. The following Monday morning I appeared at the CO's office: 'Left, right, left, right, left, right, 'alt!' My khaki beret was snatched off my head and I stood before the Commanding Officer. He was a youngish chap who very soon quite understood why I had wanted to leave camp. My brother had flown in from India to see me, had he? Flown? Was he an officer? The CO had become chatty and had not known I was all alone on the switchboard for so long and something must be done about that immediately. But rules have to be obeyed, etc. For breaking out of camp, breaking into camp, absent from duty and absent for parade, I was confined to barracks for a mere seven days. And I didn't have to go near the switchboard any more, either. In fact, the CO directed that I was forbidden to do so. Did I detect an inaudible groan beside me as the order was given? I'm not sure, but there was only one other person in camp who knew how to use the switchboard: the very man who had taught me. To his chagrin, the staff sergeant had to personally man it until someone else was brought in by ferry and trained. I, in turn, was kept busy cleaning out Staff's quarters, sweeping, polishing and washing up. When he told me with some delight that he had arranged for me to be posted overseas, I was equally pleased and thanked him cordially, explaining I had volunteered to go abroad before being posted to the island.

I left the beautiful chocolate-box isle to go to a transit camp at Thetford, Norfolk, naively believing that a transit camp was where soldiers waited around, smoking and drinking and reading books until their ship or plane arrived. It wasn't like that at all. Having been shown my quarters and bed, complete with blanket – at least that was one up on Aldershot – the bed came to be something to dream about and not to dream in as my weary head would never be enticed to its pillow and my fatigued limbs and body would also be cheated from succumbing to the seductive luxury of the paillasse. I was immediately ordered to the cookhouse.

The cookhouse proved to be a tearjerker as for three days and nights I peeled onions without sleep. My tear ducts had dried out after the first hour or two and it was only after I was physically drained that I was discharged from the onion peeling and immediately put on twenty-four-hour guard duty. This was followed by my marching orders to the War Office in Northumberland Avenue, London, where a stocky, sandy-haired Major Rankin introduced himself. The department was ST-6 and, the major explained, it held many secrets because it contained the displacement of all British troops throughout the world. To prove this importance, he showed me books which detailed supply ships and their cargoes. I looked down casually, 'Isn't that rather a lot of herrings for Malta?' It was meant to be a conversation piece as I knew nothing of ships, the tons of food required in any specified area, or even for how long herrings could be kept aboard ship. But I struck a cord for the major's face blanched and he stood motionless, his army career disappearing before him as his eyes became transfixed on the ledger. 'My God, you're right!' he exclaimed, as he hastily retreated to an inner office carrying the offending ledger with him. Someone, possibly himself, had written in an extra nought on the cargo tonnage to be sent and if his assessment was correct, the ship was now laden with enough herrings to feed half the British army abroad. Urgent (panic) messages were sent to the cargo ship to drop only the required amount of herrings to Malta and then alter course for Cyprus, Alexandria, Gibraltar, anywhere! My casual but timely question must have impressed Rankin as I became a corporal within weeks and a sergeant shortly afterwards and as a perk of being at the War Office I was permitted to wear civilian clothing so few people knew of my elevated rank. Wearing civvies could cause problems, I knew, for on my second week at the WO, Private Shay dropped some documents into the Brigadier's office. Bending over his desk was an unkempt-looking man whom I took to be a messenger. He was scanning some papers marked 'Secret' through pince-nez spectacles which, I knew, was outside the jurisdiction of such lowly vassals. 'What are you doing?' I demanded suspiciously. The messenger looked up, his eyes studying me over the top of the specs. 'I'm Brigadier Whittie.' Oh, shit, I thought. Then he held out his hand, which I took. What a charming fellow; he was the first brigadier I'd had the pleasure of shaking hands with.

I went back to the Isle of Wight one weekend to look up some old friends and at the army camp I ran into 'Staff' who was taken aback at seeing both me and three stripes on my arm, only one rank below his own. 'Christ, how did you get those?' he asked. 'They were going spare,' I replied. 'Where are you stationed?' 'The War Office.' He paled, 'The War Office?' I had known the WO held the same reverence for him as the Vatican has for a priest. He paused, as though summing up courage to ask the next question. 'What department?' There was something else I knew about 'Staff' when I was stationed on the IoW; he was worried about a certain department in the War Office which bore the initials 'ST' to which he had to submit all his supply returns. He was probably working a fiddle as quartermasters through the centuries have been known to do such things. 'ST-6,' I replied. There was a look of awe, mingled with apprehension. Not only was I at his Vatican, I was clearly a cardinal with the ear of his Pope. He had no conception of how cumbersome the War Office could be as he had never been near it. But he felt his whole military career, as a regular soldier, could hinge on what I might say about him. It was too good an opportunity to miss. I said, ambiguously, 'I've just come down to see how things are working out.' There was no doubt in my mind that he had automatically assumed that I was personally receiving all of his returns from Ryde. In reality, I was associated only with the overseas contingents. 'You know, Reg, you must have lunch with me!' *Reg*? He knew my Christian name. I could only assume he had remembered that the man who had the effrontery to walk out on the switchboard was Private 19059037 Reginald Robert Shay. 'Yes,' I said, 'I'd like to.' He cooked a surprisingly good meal and it was a congenial lunch.

Me as a National Service Sergeant in the War Office, aged nineteen

My brother, Warren, in India

Elizabeth Becomes Queen and Later Complains to Me

My return to the *Evening Standard* was an inauspicious frustrating disappointment, for having become accustomed to some measure of authority, I learned that I would now be employed in the Correspondence Department. 'The what?' I inquired with disdain and good reason for it turned out that this was a department that didn't matter and anyone who worked there didn't matter; a newspaper department of such insignificance that even I can't even recall its function. My superior and the only other person there was Miss Doe, a middle-aged lady small in height but gargantuan in stature, with elephantine posterior cheeks that hung like balloon ballast each side of her protesting secretarial chair. Being head of a department that didn't matter, it's unlikely that any of the journalists and sub-editors who occupied the floor had even spoken to her. But there was one day when Miss Doe did matter and she became the most important person on the *Evening Standard*; when typewriters were silenced and even the chief sub, 'Parky' Parkinson stopped shouting 'Boy!' at which a youngster would dash forward and clutch upheld copy before dropping it down a hole into the compositors' room below. Sometimes Parky would call 'Boy, Fudge' and the messenger ran even faster to catch the 'Stop Press'.

The spotlight was on Miss Doe because of her ring. I'd sometimes ponder over her love life: was there ever a lover? With a name of such rabbit-like overtones she could have expected to attract a predatory young buck's animal instincts at some time in her life and the ring may have been a love token. On that fateful day, she had been sitting with only her nostalgic thoughts to occupy her when she removed the ruby-and-diamond encrusted ring from a podgy finger for whatever reason and accidentally dropped it on the floor. In the subsequent search for it, she pushed her desk aside. Walking past at the time was a militant trade unionist from the machine room who was easily identifiable by his ink-stained shirt tucked carelessly beneath a thick leather belt and down into grimy blue trousers which hung over, surprisingly, well-polished boots. His nails harboured cakes of oil and paper dust which disappeared into a clenched fist and his belligerent face showed only anger with no sign of compassion or gallantry towards the unsuspecting Miss Doe. Instead of offering to help her, his narrow-set eyes expanded and bulged until he hissed with the venom of a striking cobra, 'What the 'ell do yer think you're doing?' Replied Miss Doe, with the innocence and uncertainty of a newly deflowered virgin, 'I've lost my ring!' Aghast at the breach of trade union rules which no one on the editorial floor had heard about, the petty dictator snarled before raising his voice with the clarity of a soap-box orator for all to hear: 'And who gave yer permission to move yer desk?' Before she had a chance to answer, he looked around the general office and having ensured he had gained absolute attention he pointed to Miss Doe, 'If this woman even touches her desk I'll call a strike right now!'

Editorial staff sat uncomfortably and silently with their heads cowed reminiscent of miscreant children facing their headmaster. There wasn't the slightest doubt in anyone's mind that the machine-room shop steward would have kept his word had she argued reason, or moved the desk again. With the spotlight upon her for the first time in her life, the hapless Miss Doe faltered without uttering another word and the tyrant marched off triumphantly, leaving her to wait for over half an hour before two men in overalls arrived and allowed her to pick up the offending ring before they pushed her desk nine inches back to where it belonged. Years later, on a visit to England, I thought of the arrogant 'Gentleman of the presses' when I chanced along members of Sogat '84 marching down Fleet Street with bleeding-heart placards pleading for sympathy for themselves and their children after they had been sacked by the upstart Rupert Murdoch.

Being a glorified office boy had an upside when I was asked to accompany well-known writers who were covering particular events. Rebecca West was amongst the first – famous authoress, mistress of intrigue and ex-mistress of H G Wells, she was also a close friend of Beaverbrook. I was interested to meet the great lady and read through her newly spun pearls of wisdom and possibly have an informative chat with her. The venue was the Lynskey Tribunal at the Memorial Hall, Westminster, which related to the major scandal of the day when the Parliamentary Secretary to the Board of Trade, John Belcher, was being questioned about his dealings with a slimeball of mid-European origin, Sidney Stanley. The inquiry was into whether Belcher had received 'presents' from Stanley and done favours in return, thus compromising his position. The sleaze inquiry was also interesting to me because I wanted to see in action the most famous barrister of the day, Sir Hartley Shawcross, who was leading the inquiry for the Crown. Shawcross had built his reputation as a British prosecutor at the Nuremburg trials and his displays of pomposity and showmanship at the tribunal suggested that he felt he now had no peers. My reaction to the beleaguered Belcher, however, was one of sorrow for he came across as a gullible man who had been catapulted out of his league as railway ticket clerk and into a world of intrigue he didn't fully comprehend. He had been given his post by the President of the Board of Trade, Harold Wilson (who knew all about intrigues and was one of the witnesses to give evidence), when the Labour Party came to power after the war. The crunch came for Belcher when he accepted presents from Stanley of a new suit, a gold cigarette case and a bucket-and-spade holiday trip to sandy Margate. In turn, he was introduced to the Sherman brothers of Shermans' Pools, who were facing certain prosecution charges. In appreciation of Stanley's 'kindness' Belcher had the charges dropped.

Commissioned to write a daily column of colourful deathless prose on the progress of the tribunal, Rebecca West breezed into the hall with the air of an imperious hospital matron and the only piece of colour I can recall came on the first day when her pen revealed how easy it was to recognise the attendant Labour supporters by their red ties which hung down as if their throats had been cut. The article was as in-depth as the mythical wounds Rebecca had fantasised, mainly because she was clearly bored with the proceedings. More than once she spoke to me with enthusiasm about a new gadget she had bought for her spectacles. 'It's wonderful,' she enthused as she demonstrated how her new toy worked. Commonplace today is the thin chain or piece of cord around the neck to which spectacles are attached; to Rebecca West it was far more important than the repercussions of the Lynskey Tribunal on the Attlee government. I daresay Dame Rebecca, as she later became, never lost her spectacles again whereas the hapless Belcher lost his reputation and his job for ever.

While Rebecca West was toying with her spectacle chain my thoughts had been more subjective, focusing on a brown stigma in my right eye which had been there since birth. It had never bothered me until I began taking a healthy interest in girls and convinced myself that the blemish was moving closer to the pupil. My doctor's interest was aroused and he promptly sent me to a specialist, who in turn directed me to another specialist at the Royal Cancer Hospital. The thought that I might go blind if the stigma reached the pupil had occurred to me; the thought that I might have the Big 'C' didn't cross my mind as I was merely told that the cancer hospital had the most up-to-date equipment for studying brown spots. The day of the operation arrived and two young nurses with long steel needles approached me and my look of apprehension gave way to alarm as one invited me to sit in a chair and relax. 'I'm only going to clear your tear duct,' smiled the prettiest of the pair and as I quaked at the notion she pushed the needle into the corner of my eye socket. Then she pulled the needle out, looked at in frustration and pushed it back in again. After four attempts she gave up and turned to the other nurse: 'I can't get any tears out,' she said. 'I'll gave a go,' came the response and she too pushed the needle down until it scraped against my nose bone. 'I hope I'm not hurting you,' she said, 'but you can't have an operation until the tears are removed from your eye.' I decided to react against another foray and pleaded that I had spent three days and nights peeling onions in the army and that this had permanently dried my tear ducts. To my relief they aborted their unrewarding task.

The operation was for a melanoma, which was a meaningless medical term to me. With only a local anaesthetic for protection against pain, I watched with fascination as the surgeon's scalpel scraped away the offending blemish. Later, while sitting up in the hospital bed with the bandaged eye, I chatted up the nurses and one of them said cheerfully, 'The tissue has been sent away to the pathologist to see if it is malignant.' Even that didn't mean a great deal until I left the hospital and looked up 'malignant' in the dictionary. In effect, my lack of schooling had left me in a position where a nurse had told me that I might soon die of cancer and I hadn't the first idea what she was talking about! I was now faced with two choices: to approach the surgeon and ask him outright if I had cancer or I could wait until he told me himself. The latter of the agonising options was chosen largely because I was far too cowardly to hear the awful truth but also because I wasn't sure he would give an honest answer. The medical profession at the time was not forthcoming and cancer itself amongst the hoi polloi was as unmentionable as gonorrhoea or syphilis, the very existence of which were uttered in hushed, disapproving tones. My first visits to the hospital were daily, then weekly, and then monthly and the doctor who took over the case never once mentioned the word cancer. In the meantime I went into the country whenever possible, listening to the birds and enjoying the landscapes. If I wasn't going to be around much longer I was going to appreciate Nature to the very end. A quick death from a bomb or a sudden heart attack, as my father had suffered, was infinitely better than death by deterioration as had happened to my mother. There was one practice I did give up, however, and that was walking through graveyards. After a year of mental agony and on the very day I had decided to question the doctor about my condition, he elicited the answer to my unspoken inquiry: 'We thought you had cancer but I'm happy to say that you haven't.' The doctor would never know the anguish he had caused by not telling me earlier. And the nurse would never know the distress she had caused by innocently passing on a titbit of information…

A vacancy arose in the Telephone Reporters' department which was a euphemism for typists who take down news and feature copy over the telephone. I applied for the job and to my utter surprise was accepted despite not having typed since leaving the Cirencester army school. The TRs were housed in a long glass cubicle and in order that we could be seen but not heard, only Remington Noiseless typewriters were used and once mastered, they were the fastest manual typewriters I've ever encountered. My colleagues were an all-male mixed bunch of different personalities and backgrounds and each disliked being holed up but some were more aware of the confinement than others and would pace up and down like frustrated predatory tigers in a zoo. One such man was Laurie Edmonds, a quiet, well-educated self-effacing man who, I felt, should not be there because of his high intellect. He had started work for a publishing house that produced comics which was employment but not exactly his scene and with the outbreak of war he became a conscientious objector and was sent to jail for standing up for his anti-war principles and couldn't understand why all the prison inmates hated him so much while they accepted murderers as friends.

'The fact that by being in jail they weren't in the Forces either was conveniently ignored,' he confided to me. 'I was hated as much as any child murderer or sex pervert.' Laurie also found himself despised after the war and work was hard to obtain. He was the first conscientious objector I'd met and I found myself admiring him for standing up for his principles in the sure knowledge that they would cost him very dearly. Until we met I'd only been concerned with getting on in life through hard work without giving much thought of anything beyond that: everything had been clear-cut in black and white without any grey areas. But then, my background had been to take orders without asking questions; taking life's hardships for granted rather than looking for reasons. Conversely, another caged colleague who unknowingly helped with reassessing my early beliefs was 'Smudger' Smith who had been called into the army and was therefore totally acceptable both socially and to his employers. It was Smith who shocked my naivety that not all our troops were glory boys when he told me how he was in the western desert moving forward with a British tank squadron when they saw a single German Tiger tank coming towards them. 'It was much bigger than us with better and longer range fire power,' he said. When I asked him what happened next, expecting him to say that the British tanks raced forward with the same fortitude of the famous Polish cavalry charge, he replied, 'Knowing that we would be shot to pieces and that our guns would be like peanuts against the Tiger, we got out of our tanks and ran!' I was stunned: the man of the type I'd always assumed to be a coward had shown incredible courage while the Desert Rat I had expected to be courageous had fallen short of my expectations. I should mention here, just in case my comments are misinterpreted, that I had and still have the greatest respect for the British fighting forces.

There were seven of us shut up together and each had quite a different personality ranging from idealists like Edmonds and myself to Ron Coulbert who frequently fretted over the loss of his cylindrical recordings by Caruso which meant more to him than his house that had also vanished when hit by a German bomb. Another man had gall-bladder problems and treasured a gall-stone he brought in for us to admire. One bright young man of about my age, Jack Surridge, looked as though he might break out of the glass menagerie and he actually emigrated to the American Midwest to become a reporter. Many years later, I was telexing from Africa a story for the *Daily Express* when he identified himself as the telex operator at the receiving end. This meant that he had eventually only advanced from a typist to a telex operator with little hope of going further and that I, the least qualified of the bunch, was the only one to beat the system. I know of only three people, including myself, who have ever worked their way up from lowly positions in Fleet Street to become reporters, one of them being the remarkable Derek Jameson who became editor of three national newspapers, and the other was Philip Grune who became a war correspondent and subsequently picture editor of the *Evening Standard*.

Taking down copy, by definition, is uninspiring but to me it was also a tortuous nightmare after I realised that reporters reading their stories over the telephone could speak at over twenty-one words a minute. Adamantly refusing to look at the keyboard, I slowly began to pick up speed until it averaged 100 wpm and was no longer a problem, but my spelling disability was a monumental disaster. Being semi-literate, I spent painful hours trying to brush up my orthography but was dubbed the 'fancy speller' by Evelyn Irons, the first woman western journalist into Berlin after its fall to the Russians, and the tag stuck. I'm convinced that I am partly dyslectic for while my spelling has greatly improved, I can still inexplicably transpose letters and numbers and I usually turn water and gas taps the wrong way when there is the slightest lapse of concentration. The sub-editors nodded their heads at my poor spelling until the axe fell and the Editor, Herbert Gunn, demanded, 'He goes!' This was now my third sacking but at least I considered it to be fair and the decision, I believe, had been made reluctantly and upset some people. While working my month's notice it almost appeared as if 'someone up there' objected to my dismissal for a miracle happened: Herbert Gunn was given his instant marching orders by Beaverbrook! On advice from the news editor's PA, Arthur Whitehall, I carried on as if nothing had happened. I didn't know at the time that the suggestion had come from the news editor himself.

One of many major stories I was to take down was from Evelyn Irons, phoning from the Tree Tops Hotel in Kenya when the young Princess Elizabeth, who was on a Royal tour with her new husband, was told of her father's death and that she was now the Queen. Later, our wandering Irons lady was in New York when she came through to say she had been held up at gunpoint by a bandit in her hotel room. When I asked her what she did, she replied, 'I gave him the money, of course.' I wondered what I would do under similar circumstances…

Our news editor was the legendary Ronnie Hyde who was tall, languid and impressive and frightened most of the reporters to such a degree that he was the only news editor in Fleet Street I have known who was not called by his Christian name. But while the 'Street' knew him as the formidable 'Mr Hyde' who once fired over a dozen reporters in a week, (one of his three wives committed suicide by jumping out of a window of their Eaton Place, home), to me he was a Jekyll. He was top class at his job as rival newspapers would grudgingly concede, and while our backgrounds were totally different, (he was a Cambridge MA and his father Sir Harry Hyde had given up his parliamentary seat to Beaverbrook) we got on well and there was a genuine mutual respect. For the first time in my life, when I was to resign the job as his Personal Assistant on my steady march upward, he asked me sincerely not to leave and years later with many *Evening Standard* and other newspaper front-page leads to my credit, and several television appearances, he would leave his busy desk for an hour or so for a chat.

It came as a surprise when I was invited to become deputy to Hyde's PA in the knowledge that through Whitehall's retirement, I'd take over the job which entailed a fair amount of responsibility and verged on reporting. One task was to totally control the newspaper's coverage of local government

Reader's Digest

August 1966

Book of the Month

THE WORLD'S LARGEST CIRCULATION
Over 26 Million Copies in 14 Languages Bought Each Month

BAHRAIN Rs. 2 • CYPRUS Mils. 150 • DUBAI Rs. 2 • EIRE 3/3 incl. Tax
ETHIOPIA E$ 1.10 • GAMBIA 3/- • GHANA 36p • IRAN Rls. 35 • IRAQ Fls. 150
JORDAN Fls. 150 • KENYA Shs. 3 • KUWAIT Fls. 150 • LEBANON LL. 1.25
LIBERIA 40c • LIBYA LL. 150 • MALAWI 3/- • NIGERIA 3/- • QATAR Rs. 2
SAUDI ARABIA S.R. 2.00 • SIERRA LEONE 30c • SUDAN PT. 15 • SYRIA SL. 2.00
UGANDA Shs. 3 • UNITED REPUBLIC OF TANZANIA Shs. 3 • ZAMBIA 3/-
ALL OTHER COUNTRIES: 3/- sterling

My first-ever feature

elections by employing the use of our 850 correspondents countrywide (for whom I was responsible with hire-and-fire status) whose results had to be telephoned in before 8 a.m. It was a major task but the *Evening Standard* results were satisfyingly way ahead of the rival newspapers, the *Evening News* and the *Star*. Such was the turnaround in my fortunes that Herbert Gunn's replacement, Percy Elland, actually sent me a personal letter of congratulations!

I'd also regularly call at Caxton Hall to break stories on marriages of interest – one big scoop was the wedding of Ingrid Bergman. The Chief Registrar at the time was on a real money spinner, for in addition to receiving a regular backhander from me for tips, he also supplemented his official income by putting his hand out for a gratuity from every happy wedding couple without even the hint of a blush. And there was more! His biggest scam was having several arrangements of flowers placed in all the wedding rooms and in addition to claiming for them on expenses he would charge each bride and groom the full price for them too. There were dozens of weddings over the Easter period and he found the lucrative tax-free income from flowers alone to be most rewarding.

Despite my change of status I was still occasionally asked to look after leading journalists on assignment and one was Sir Beverley Baxter who was invited to write on the Labour Party conference at Scarborough. 'Would you care to join me for dinner tonight?' asked 'Bev' on the second day of the conference. It was an invitation I couldn't refuse and I don't know what brought it about but Baxter was in expansive mood and we dined well. During the meal, and afterwards with cigars and brandies, he gave me a long discourse on feature writing and my ears strained to catch every word. It is unfortunate that he spoke *sotto voce* because I have always been deaf to a certain pitch, and I wasn't in a position to say, 'Speak up, man!' I didn't hear a word he muttered, but I certainly thought of him when my first-ever feature led the *Reader's Digest*.

Sir Beverley, former editor of the *Daily Express*, was later to have his own problems, which showed me how even men with considerable influence can get the sack. He became the theatre critic of the *Evening Standard* and while he was reviewing one play, he criticised an actor for a stumbling performance. The actor wrote a stinging letter in reply and it was given prominence in the newspaper. The letter was so good that Bev was given his marching orders and the actor replaced him as the theatre critic: he was Kenneth Tynan.

I'd also become very friendly with one of the *Evening Standard*'s parliamentary reporters, Don 'Robbie' Robertson. Edinburgh University educated, he was nevertheless a good down-to-earth reporter of the kind that Scotland so often breeds. Robbie had his share of scoops and once told me of the day he had jumped on to Stanley Baldwin's train, with a nod from the security guard whom he knew, and faced the prime minister: 'Are you going to resign?' he demanded. Baldwin looked horrified as if he was about to be assassinated and he was asked the question again. 'Yes,' replied the quivering prime minister who'd been at the centre of the Edward VIII abdication crisis. My reporter friend also covered a fire for the *Daily Express* and naturally went into a pub, where he found customers talking about an army officer being locked up in the Tower of London. He ignored the fire and broke the famous pre-war story of a lieutenant in the Seaforth Highlanders, Norman Baillie-Stewart, who had been locked up in the Tower while awaiting trial for passing military secrets to Nazi Germany. He was cashiered by court martial and jailed for five years. On his release in 1939 he fled to Germany to broadcast Nazi propaganda to Britain thus becoming the first Lord Haw-Haw, a sobriquet given to him because of his upper-class accent. Captured in 1945 in Austria he was brought back to England to face the music but the Attorney General, Hartley Shawcross, felt the charge of high treason would not stick and he was jailed for five years on a lesser charge, much to the fury of MI5 who wanted him hanged. Illogically, his US-born Irish successor as Lord Haw-Haw, William Joyce, *was* topped.

Robbie had led an exciting life and I subconsciously, or even consciously, modelled a part of mine on his exploits. For the hell of it, he had once joined the French Foreign Legion and had even gone on an expedition up the River Amazon and found a lost city. 'Read this,' he said and showed me a newspaper cutting with a Rio de Janeiro dateline which told of an unusual Amazonian tribe with blue eyes. The cutting was shown furtively as Robbie's wife, Marie, was in the next room of their Chiswick flat. The story only merited a few paragraphs but it told of an Irishman who had made his way up the river and befriended the local native girls. The Scottish blue eyes of Robbie twinkled as I read but from what I have seen of some of the maidens of the Amazon on television, I feel he must have been away from home for a very long time to have shown his munificence to them. A man of many parts, he told me he had also played violin with the London Symphony Orchestra and sometimes talked of an open invitation he had to meet Jean Sibelius. It was an appointment he never kept. Robbie died from too much Scotch, followed by Marie a week later without her knowing she had cancer. Sibelius died shortly afterwards.

The news desk telephone rang. We on the desk had been feeling very smug and amused that morning as the *Evening Standard* first edition carried a front-page splash with pictures of the young Prince Charles playing football at Cheam School. It was a scoop by photographer, Vic Drees, who had climbed a tree and used a telephoto lens. Sneak pictures of royalty were unheard of and telephoto lenses were a novelty, even to news photographers. Vic was the originator and unheralded founder of the royal paparazzi although I have never heard his name mentioned in that context nor, indeed, in any other. It was a lady's voice on the phone: 'This is the Queen and I wish to protest most strongly about the photographs you have taken of Prince Charles at school. You had absolutely no right…' etc. etc.

Was this a joke? It sounded like the Queen herself, for I'd listened each Christmas to her 'My husband and I' homilies and had visions of her standing at the other end wearing crown and gown with a sceptre in one hand and telephone in the other. It was unfortunate that she should be so upset for under normal circumstances I'd have enjoyed a chat, perhaps with a discussion on our different lifestyles and the problems of bringing up young children. This was not the time for small talk, however, for in my hand was a steaming telephone and every instinct told me there was no point in hanging on to it for I'd no intention that the buck from Buck House would stop with me. There was an audible gasp followed by stunned silence at the other end when I interrupted the verbal flow to say that the editor might be able to help and that I would put her through to him. It took some time to contact the switchboard and I could sense a growing foot-tapping impatience. At last the operator came through: 'Put the Queen through to Percy, would you?'

'What did you say, Reg?'

'The Queen, she's holding on. Would you put her through to the editor?'

I replaced the telephone and turned to the reporters sitting in front of me at an uninspiring long dark varnished table: 'The Queen doesn't like Vic's pix!'

'How do you know?' I was asked.

'She's just phoned and told me!' There were guffaws because it would be normal for the Queen's press secretary to make the call but I knew it wasn't a hoax. 'Okay, just watch Percy's door in a couple of minutes.' The reporters carried on typing out their respective stories but they were not concentrating and shortly afterwards a door burst open and all heads turned as Percy Elland rushed out of his office. His thinning hair was scattered, his face was salmon pink, his eyes were glazed and I formed the impression he was in an absolute panic. He rushed to his desk in the general office and looked around, suffering the torments of pressure and indecision that most Fleet Street editors go through many times during their stewardship. Nervously he picked up the telephone and I was surprised that the Queen had not thought of making that same call as she would have known the proprietor, Lord Beaverbrook. To his credit, Beaverbrook stood by his enterprising editor.

Over thirty years later there was a sequel to the incident when the *People* newspaper photographed Charles's son, Prince William, at school. Once again there was a royal objection and the editor, Wendy Henry, was fired by her proprietor, Robert Maxwell. Perhaps the ambitious late Cap'n Bob did not know that above all else, the Queen believes in loyalty, something the swindled *Mirror* pensioners would say Maxwell knew nothing about.

An incident occurred on a telephone which was bizarre and quite inexplicable. I was living in Bexley, Kent, and heavy snow was so thick that I rang the office to say it would be impossible for me to be there on time. I had stopped at a public call box and as I picked up the receiver a familiar voice said, '*Evening Standard*.' Despite my surprise I was able to ask to be put through to the news desk which was quite remarkable because I had not put any coins in the box – and I had not dialled the number!

Another strange coincidence originated when I was relying on public transport to commute to and from work. Because of the pace under which we operated, producing eight editions a day – nine on Saturdays – there was seldom time to read the feature section of the newspaper until travelling home by Underground and train; a crushed vertical sardine in its tin coffin. While these travelling conditions were not conducive to newspaper readers, I would nevertheless enjoy a weekly short story by an author otherwise unknown to me, John Appleby. The stories were well written as Whodunits? and I thought of them as being scorpion yarns because of their sting in the tail. Incredibly, Appleby and I were to meet years later in a far off land and become good friends, but our close association was to end with a tragic scorpion finality involving myself that even he could never have dreamed of...

At the time of the Hungarian uprising a newcomer appeared on the *Evening Standard* and I was told he had been on the communist *Daily Worker* but had resigned in protest against Soviet intervention, and that Beaverbrook was always interested in recruiting bright young people such as him even if they opposed his views. Having subsequently read the man's own autobiography in which there is no mention of the *Daily Worker*, the information gleaned by the *Evening Standard* journalists was quite untrue. But he did turn up at an inopportune time. We met in the cloakroom and he walked across and shook hands. 'My name's John Junor,' he said. 'I've been appointed editor of the Readers' Letters column.' We chatted for a while and during the conversation he told me how mundane the letters were and that he preferred to write his own. He then asked if I would sign one for him and possibly get my colleagues to do the same. Clearly this was a very ambitious young man who was far more interested in putting across his own views than reading anyone else's. Years later he didn't have to scavenge around as he became editor of the *Sunday Express* where he could write his own leader articles if he wished. He got a knighthood too; you just never know what will happen to people you meet by chance in a loo.

Streatham's nationally famous ballroom, the Locarno, was the place to meet the opposite sex and I was there when an acting competition was being held. A girl approached me declaring with Shakespearian passion that she wished to take part but needed a partner. How could I refuse? We won the heat. The following week, film star Valerie Hobson, arrived to judge the final and, surprise, surprise, we had to read from the script of her current film, *The Silent Voice*, a movie which introduced Howard Keel to the screen. The winners would be given a prize and a screen test. To the dismay of the other participants, all amateur London thespians who came in from miles around, we won despite neither of us having any previous theatre experience. As a magnanimous gesture, Valerie invited everyone to Elstree film studios but none of us had a screen test. And the great prize was just £5, to be shared between the joint winners. Mecca, owners of the Locarno, clearly felt that budding stars should suffer a little first. Valerie asked me if I intended to take up acting as a career. It was something I'd always been interested in and I had taken the lead in school productions going right back to my infant days but I couldn't see it as a way of paying the rent. 'No,' I replied, 'I'm planning to become a journalist.' Possibly she didn't really believe or care that it would happen and considered it to be a young man's dream with about as much chance as the local thespians had of making the West End. But I've sometimes wondered what she subsequently thought about journalists after those front-page leads about her husband, Defence Minister John Profumo, and call girls Christine Keeler and Mandy Rice-Davies – well, I would, wouldn't I? As for my career, I'm glad that I became a journalist who acted out the realities of life to the full rather than an actor who fantasized life through the playwright's thoughts and words. While some of them may glory in so-called 'celebrity' status, the more thoughtful must question if their lives have been less than a meaningful façade.

On another foray to the same dance hall I saw a really beautiful girl with gorgeous legs, sylphlike figure and long natural golden hair and I wondered why she was by herself. She was a goddess. Whenever she moved, people turned their heads and it was clear that the young men were either too shy to ask her to dance or were put off by the sparkling diamond ring on the third finger of her left hand. I swallowed twice and took the plunge. She was a good dancer, very good, and we stayed together for the rest of the evening with an agreement to meet again. Her name was Margery and she was engaged to an amateur boxer who had foolishly left her alone that night in order to don a pinafore at the local Masonic Lodge. We started meeting once a week, and then twice until life became cruel if there was not a night when we were together. Boxer or not, this was one fight her fiancé would not win and she broke off the engagement. I was in love.

Margery, I soon learned, was a girl of tremendous courage. She had been attacked in the street by a man whom she left lying on the road having known where to kick him. This wasn't bad for a slip of a girl weighing a mere seven stone.

I also learned that while she might use her toes as a weapon, she harboured a terrible secret which was her Achilles heel and I discovered it at a cinema one evening where an inevitable British war film was being screened. The usual scene-setter was to precede bombing sequences with a wailing of sirens and when this happened I turned to Margery and was stunned to find her seat was empty! She hadn't gone out and as she couldn't have been spirited away I looked anxiously along our row of seats and then behind at the rows of faces that flashed like black-and-white neon signs as the film sequences changed. The sirens continued to wail their warnings of danger and as a last resort I checked beneath her seat and was bewildered to find Margery huddled on the floor like a little girl hiding with her hands over her head, her delicate body convulsing with fear. Gently I took her hands and as I drew them towards me I shuddered at seeing her delicate face contorted with sheer terror in the flickering light from the film projector. Clearly something appalling must have happened to scar her young life and I loved her all the more for it as I protectively led her from the cinema. I didn't press her to say anything and she didn't enlighten me but some day, I knew, she would pluck up the courage to relive the experience to me.

War films were taboo after that, but inevitably we would occasionally see an unadvertised 'B' movie in which an air-raid siren sounded and Margery would always be stopped from sliding under the seat but she would still be shaking and petrified as her nails sank into my arm. It was some months before she revealed her nightmare ordeal and strangely it had nothing to do with sirens.

At the start of the war she'd been evacuated to relatives at Newhaven on the south coast of England and when the bombing of London had eased, she returned to the family home in London's East Dulwich where she lived with her maternal grandparents and youngest brother. It was towards the end of the conflict when Margery's father was out on ARP duty that a rocket dropped without warning and destroyed their home. Margery and her mother slept in the same bed upstairs with her younger eight-year-old brother in another bed beside them. Their own bed was lifted into the air and came down on top of the rubble without either Margery or her mother being injured but ironically, her grandparents who had slept under the stairs for safety were killed outright. From beneath the rubble of wood, brick, cement and tiles mother and daughter could hear the little boy's cries, 'Mummy, Mummy, please help me!'

As Margery related her story she was in tears, her fingernails tearing into the flesh of my hand while she gripped a small embroidered tear-dampened handkerchief in her other hand. I listened with awful fascination as she continued her ordeal. 'Dad and the other ARP workers were quickly on the scene and tore away at the rubble,' she said, and I could visualise the scene of them working frantically clawing with ever more desperation as the tiny frightened voice grew thinner. Their hopes were raised when the boy was reached and it seemed their prayers had been answered as he was still alive. It was a cruel deceit for all those present as the little boy died while they were pulling him out. The terror suffered by the youngster can only be imagined, and even years later the torment of both mother and father was etched upon their kindly faces, their smiling eyes giving only a hint of deep tragedy that had befallen them. Margery never forgot, either.

Despite our love or perhaps because of it, our engagement had been far from happy. According to the unwritten rules as I had understood them, once the engagement ring was slipped on the finger the girl could contentedly plan for the wedding. By nature I am not very jealous and therefore couldn't believe the transformation in Margery who had become obsessively possessive which was extraordinary considering that she was the prize catch, not me. Endless quarrels were caused if I happened to even glance in the direction of a girl walking down the street. Was this the reason for the break-up of her previous engagement with her fiancé being so smothered by possessiveness that he was finding excuses not to be with her? Had I turned up as a knight in shining armour for him rather than her? I hoped not, but I did begin to wonder and because I'd been a free agent long before becoming an adult I had an aversion to being stifled. Would married life be as intolerable as this?

Matters nearly reached a climax outside the Royal Festival Hall following a gala concert attended by the Queen Mother. There were many attractive girls around whom I hadn't even noticed until I was subjected to another tirade. 'That's it, we're finished,' I said, and stormed off in anger. Even though I had some chauvinistic satisfaction in Margery chasing after me to apologise, it wasn't what I wanted and I was totally disillusioned with our relationship. Towards the end of November while walking along a quiet rain-washed road during another upset for the very same reason, I made an instant decision and turned to Margery, facing her squarely, 'That's it,' I said, 'let's get married now!'

'Now?' she asked and her hand went to her mouth. 'Now?' she repeated.

'Yes, before Christmas.'

Three weeks later, on 15 December, we were wed – the first to be married in the East Dulwich Congregational Church after the war where a special effort was made to clear away bomb rubble. Warren was my best man and as we sat in the pew up front the wedding march struck up and my beautiful bride entered wearing a white wedding dress of her own design. Suddenly her lack of confidence in our relationship came to the fore for the last time and I smiled as a distraught voice could be heard throughout the church, 'Where is he? I can't see him. Dad, he's not here!'

My brother and I were sitting and chatting while keeping an eye on the entrance. As my jealous Margery made her way down the aisle, even then not confident that I hadn't run off with some other girl to leave her alone at the altar, we grinned knowingly at each other: 'I think we'd better stand up, old chap,' said Warren. With the security of marriage, the jealousy fell away and we lived together idyllically. The *Evening Standard* management, which was not noted for its largesse, allowed me the Saturday and Monday off for the wedding which limited the distance we could travel for the honeymoon and we settled for Canterbury. During a sightseeing tour of the cathedral I spoke to a dog-collared churchman who appeared to be agitated. 'We were burgled last night,' he said. 'Good heavens,' I replied thoughtfully, having uttered the appropriate words to be used in England's premier cathedral. 'Was anything stolen?'

'We don't know yet but the burglar has left his footprints everywhere,' came the reply. He pointed to a raised tomb and sure enough there were footprints on it. As we left the cathedral I headed towards a telephone box. 'Where are you going?' asked my bride. 'To phone the *Standard* with the story.'

'On our honeymoon?' she cried. 'Can't you forget your work just for once?' Every journalistic instinct told me to use the telephone. This could be the first crime to have taken place in Canterbury Cathedral since the murder

Attending an Evening Standard *dinner with Margery – minus fingernail!*

of Thomas à Becket 781 years earlier. Judging by the way our first married night of bliss had gone, I knew that on average there was no chance that I would live long enough to report the next crime to take place there. Prudence and every instinct of a honeymooner told me that I must leave the phone alone and so the attempted plundering of that great historical cathedral was never reported. It was one of only two stories that I never wrote.

Being in love and married to Margery were amongst the happiest and saddest years of my life and she proved her mettle time and again. In some ways, I suppose, our lives together were of the stuff from which novels and operas are written and it was an opera experience that showed me how she could put vanity aside when the occasion demanded. 'Here's a couple of tickets to Covent Garden, dear boy,' said Ronnie Hyde as he handed me a pair of complimentary tickets for the first night of *Aida*. Next night, with Margery on the pillion of my 125 cc BSA Bantam motorcycle, I headed towards London. It was a night when the capital city would revert to its sinister past of Victorian melodrama; when ghouls rose from cemeteries to appear through the blending of mist and soot which shrouded the capital city in one of its infamous pea-soup fogs – the cover of the notorious Jack the Ripper; and the mythical demoniacal Sweeney Todd who would murderously slice the throats of customers attending his Fleet Street barber's shop before sending their blood-soaked mortal remains through a trapdoor until they were transformed into delicious meat pies. As we rode towards the West End, our faces became blacker by the second from the clinging damp grime and when we reached Covent Garden I shed my riding gear in the foyer, leaving it with a disdainful but polite commissionaire as we retreated to the washrooms for a hasty clean-up.

The gold velvet curtain hung expectantly and was about to rise on the production's first night as we left the washrooms looking much the same as we had entered. Margery's long rich honey-coloured hair particularly suffered and I know of no other woman who would walk into a Covent Garden premier with head held high the way she did that night. Being the last to arrive, we felt all eyes upon us as we made our way to the stalls the second row from the front. Sitting on our left was a red-tabbed army general and on the right, next to Margery, was a lady whose head sparkled with a bejewelled tiara. Each of our neighbours would cast a sly disdainful eye to the side and shudder. In turn, we Bisto Kids would have been happy to be right up on stage incarcerated in the pyramid that was on display.

On yet another obscene night we went to a function but this time in torrential rain. Margery, radiant in glamorous evening dress chose to wear the latest women's fashion: false fingernails. After parking the car I'd recently bought, we ran towards the venue, with the protection of only one umbrella when my wife stopped in her tracks and cried, 'I've lost a fingernail!' As rain tumbled, the pair of us peered into the gutter beneath a London street lamp where the water rushed past with the speed of a Colorado River rapid. There was no sign of the offending nail substitute but we kept looking as no beautiful woman can go to a party with aplomb wearing only nine fingernails. From out of the wet came a helpful man with an umbrella who joined us in the search. With heads tucked under our portable shelters which exposed only our bottoms to the rain he asked, casually, 'What are we looking for?'

'My wife's fingernail.'

His benevolent smile disappeared, and he didn't even bid us goodnight.

Shortly after our marriage when we lived in Bexley, Margery expressed the wish to learn to drive the motorcycle. The road led down to a T-junction and on the other side was a kerb, a large grass area which had formerly been a meadow, and then a stream. She went down the hill, accelerated over the road, up the kerb, across the grass and into the water. She never tried again.

Margery had always said she would like to have four children and, despite private fearful reservations of bringing children into the nuclear world (an East-West future confrontation was on the cards and the proliferation of nuclear weapons seemed inevitable), I entered our union with such enthusiasm that she became pregnant one month after marriage. Robert was born at over nine pounds, boisterous and beautiful with such a full crop of hair on his head that it resembled a black mop. He was very intelligent and soon showed a determination to crawl up and down stairs even if it killed him. We were sitting in the lounge when he crawled out of the room and unknown to us climbed up the stairs on a voyage of discovery. With horror we heard an explosion and raced upstairs fearing the worst but were astonished to see him sitting upright staring at an electric wall fitting. Protruding from it was a hairpin as discoloured as the fitting itself, caused by a surge of electricity. Rob was quite unharmed and it appeared he would share some of the charmed life I'd enjoyed for I too had a narrow escape days earlier when putting in new lights in the lounge. Using a cold chisel, I'd hammered through a wall and pierced just one of the two wires which were twisted together!

Two years after Robert's arrival our second son, Alan, was born and weighed in at seven pounds. Like Rob, he was a beautiful child but unlike his brother he was serene with a contented smile, almost angelic. While I was a proud father who accepted children as a natural part of family life and was far from dispassionate towards them, being a male I was content to have provided the means for the birth and left their mother to take over without interference. I didn't have the close bond that a mother has after she physically experiences the creation of another human being inside her body but my attitude towards my children underwent a fundamental change when Alan was three months old and developed an eye infection. 'I'd like him to spend some time in hospital,' said our doctor. 'Is his eye that bad?' asked Margery.

'It does need hospital treatment,' the doctor replied. 'He may have to stay a couple of weeks and as you are breastfeeding him I've made arrangements for you to stay too.' We hadn't realised that it was not just Alan's eye that was at risk for during his stay in hospital it never dawned upon us that his very life was in danger. I visited the Crayford Hospital every evening after work and knew there would always be a ready smile of recognition despite his pain. Eventually the eye cleared up and as the danger had gone he was allowed home and as time passed, he was put into Robert's bedroom next to ours where we would hear him gurgling contentedly during the night. Because of his brush with death he'd become something special and he was nearly six months old on the night that is forever etched on my memory; when Margery put him to bed after he waved me goodnight.

A few hours later we went to our room and I felt a surge of warmth and contentment as I moved on to the bed beside my beautiful wife. The moon shone through a crack in the curtains and illuminated the face of an angel. She looked up at me steadily and whispered the same words she had uttered when we enjoyed our first day of rapture in Epping Forest. 'I love you so much,' she said as she took me in her arms and drew me towards her tightly and with a passion that no one else in the world possessed. It was 6.30 a.m. when Margery gently pulled herself away from my arms and said, 'Alan's very quiet.' Knowing that he would always be the first to awaken with happy gurgles, she left the bed and walked unsuspectingly into his room while I froze with a sudden premonition: I knew without a shadow of a doubt what she would find. She opened the children's door and called, 'Wake up, darling.' There was a pause, silence, and I cringed as the hairs on my arms stood upright and I heard a chilling scream. I rushed through to the bedroom and found myself holding a classically crafted ice-cold porcelain doll.

The autopsy revealed bronchitis as the cause of death although today it would be described by many as a cot death with maliferous theories and recriminations as to how it came about without even a thought for the distressed parents. One person even pronounced his theory in the newspapers that such deaths were caused by murderous parents. Bronchitis had helped to kill my mother and the twin disease, asthma, was already affecting Robert. I considered them the curse of the family and if Margery hadn't been pregnant again we would never have had more children. That would have been a mistake, for Alan was followed by my adorable daughter, Annette, and then came another Cheshire Cheese, Peter.

My tortuous climb up the rungs of the flailing rope ladder to success was given an unexpected boost on my short walk home from Bexley Station. Standing at the gate of a large Victorian house on the crest of a small hill was a most unlikely heaven-sent soul who was waiting to point me in my next direction. The man was thickset with a thick mop of curly black hair, thick spectacles and sported a thick Italian-style mustachio reminiscent of a street-corner organ grinder. Lino 'Dan' Ferrari was a high-powered freelance journalist and one of the men on my list of *Evening Standard* correspondents. While we had met a couple of times before that fateful evening I hadn't realised that he was such a big-time operator with the best news agency in the south London and Kent area, writing for all the national newspapers and major agencies. 'I've been offered a job as deputy night news editor on the *Daily Mirror*,' he told me, 'and as there is no one to run my agency, I wondered if you would care to come in with me on a partnership basis?'

While I had newspaper experience aplenty and frequently manned the *Standard* news desk alone, my reporting knowledge was almost nil and I didn't even know if I could write! I also recognised that twenty-eight years of age is not the wisest time to take up professional reporting from scratch and especially freelancing when I had a dependent young family to support. A true freelance, I knew, survived or fell solely on his ability to recognise and write a story. There were very deep qualms but I claim no wisdom and facing me was a once-in-a-lifetime opportunity which, had I rejected the offer, I would have become one of the 'If I was only your age' brigade. Margery baulked that I was taking such a high risk and I didn't get her vote of confidence but I knew I must move forward and her reward would be an improvement in our standard of living – provided I succeeded. It was the proudest moment of my working life because I was making a quantum leap into a different employment status and I was determined to prove to myself and everyone else that I was at least as good as my peers and would be better than many. To anyone who has been handed journalism on a plate it is just another job; to a person who as a child had delivered newspapers over many miles, sometimes in deep snow (I once started delivering one Sunday at 6 a.m. and arrived home at 10.30 p.m.) that I would one day be writing for these very newspapers was beyond my wildest fantasies. Now I would become a fully committed journalist, naive perhaps, but totally dedicated and honest and ready to take on any task regardless of the dangers and sacrifices. I had to prove myself more than others, partly because of my lack of education, but also to show that I was no less a man than the next. Even though I didn't know if I had any reporting ability I was fully aware that the unexpected still tended to happen when I was around. This had been demonstrated only a few weeks ago when I made an unusual discovery.

The water pipes at home had become frozen and I made my way into the loft to find out what could be done. As I gazed down into the water tank I was startled to see a fish reflecting back from the bottom, grey and as still as the pike I remembered that never seemed to move from a clear spring in the millpond at Fetcham. Questions raced through my mind: how long had it been there? How had it survived and had it contaminated the drinking water? I took a closer look and realised it was not a pike at all, nor was it like any other fish I'd ever come across before; something of an aquatic oddity with a long tailfin. Plunging my arm into the depths I grabbed the object, cold, thin and metallic and immediately identifiable – an unexploded incendiary bomb. I could only assume that during the war that it had crashed through the roof and into the tank and the wartime house owners had probably believed their tiles had been shattered by glancing shrapnel from an anti-aircraft shell. To keep the missile at home was a criminal offence and the only sensible way to dispose of it was to put it into a carrier bag and take it to the local police station. 'How can I help you, sir?' asked the unsuspecting sergeant at the desk. I delved my hand into the bag and began to slowly produce the contents with words that should have haunted the policeman for the rest of his life, 'Well you see, sergeant,' I said, 'I have here an unexploded bomb!'

A Leap into Journalism – the Hard Way

Until recent years, freelance contributors to newspapers were known as 'Penny-a-liners', always depicted as grubby men in dirty crumpled raincoats who were paid a penny for every line of their copy that appeared in a national newspaper. Most of them padded their stories to elicit a few more coppers in order to survive and sustain their families and they were deemed offensive to the late Lord Hartwell, former editor-in-chief of the *Daily* and *Sunday Telegraph*, who contemptuously declared of them as '…the generation that prided itself on having started as office boys on fifteen shillings a week who had all retired twenty years ago.' When he wrote the article in the *Sunday Telegraph*, he hadn't even checked elementary facts with his own newspaper for I was certainly writing news features under my own byline in his *Sunday Telegraph* less than eight years before the article appeared. I was, of course, paid considerably more than a penny a line.

The antithesis of Hartwell was Ferrari, an incredible ideas man who re-mained something of a legend amongst journalists long after his early death. He was tough and a natural for the tabloids and once told me he would not climb on to the roof of a house with anyone else because he was overwhelmed with an urge to push the other person off. It was the classic attitude for success in Fleet Street! Some good advice from Ferrari to any aspiring reporters made it clear that everything said in an interview should be on the record and he pointed out that he was not interviewing for his own sake but for public interest. I have used the same tactic and found that people were soon telling me exactly what they would have said off the record. A further piece of journalistic advice given by Ferrari with which I didn't wholly agree was that I should go out on every story with an angle in mind; in other words, mentally write the story and put words into the mouth of the interviewee as confirma-tion. On his own admission I made more money for the agency than even he had done and I always came back with a story, but he was a great tutor with a fantastic imagination.

While I didn't feel the need to participate in his stunt stories, their insight into human greed or even self-seeking publicity was most revealing. The manager of the local Granada cinema was looking for publicity and approached Ferrari and the pair of them put their heads together before going to a pet shop and buying a baby crocodile which was placed on a cinema seat after the audience had left. A primed usherette walked down the aisle checking the seats when she saw two beady eyes looking at her. The subsequent story and photos made good publicity for Granada in the national dailies and posed the follow-up question, 'Where is the owner of the crocodile?' No one in his right mind would believe the story, of course, yet there were seventeen claimants from people as far north as Huddersfield, Yorkshire, who just happened to be in Woolwich and at the Granada cinema with their pet croc!

The area covered by the Ferrari agency encapsulated and mirrored the lives of people anywhere in the world: their frailties, beliefs, actions – everyone was there from the rich, semi-rich and poor; the upper class, middle class and would-be class, to the lunatic, prostitute, murderer, con-merchant and ordinary, mundane, but usually nice person. The Greenwich and Woolwich magistrates' courts saw all of these people and more of every aspect of human life once a week than most people see in a lifetime. First in court came the detritus of society from a nearby dosshouse at Greenwich who swilled methylated spirits because it was cheaper than beer while those who could afford a little more blew what was left of their brains on strong cider. Each morning the ritual was the same: 'I'm sorry, your worship, I was on Merrydown.' And the magistrates would hand down fines with robot-like uniformity; 'Ten and six' (pence). 'Thank you, your worship.'

On the other side of the drunk spectrum came a man of a different ilk whose brain was not blown by alcohol – the author, Arthur Koestler. A subject that interested Koestler was 'coincidence' and I've already indicated that the coincidences in my life are above average. It was something of a coincidence that I should have been in court as I always ignored attending the drunk cases. Only after reading Koestler's *Roots of Coincidence* did I learn that coincidences had been a subject for study.

While the break-in at Canterbury Cathedral was the first story I never wrote, the second was at the Greenwich court after a man approached me and asked if I would ignore his case. I replied with extreme self-righteous pomposity that everyone is treated equal and that if it was a story of interest I would expose it to the world. 'What are you up for?' I asked and when he said it was for speeding, I replied almost offhandedly, 'You don't have to worry. I never bother with speeding cases.' He was filled with joy and gratitude and clutched my hand in his sweaty palm, 'Thank you,' he gushed with relief. 'If that had been in the newspaper I'd have lost my job.' I felt an inner disquiet; a sudden feeling that I'd been too hasty when I had virtually given my word not to write. 'How can you lose your job for speeding?' I asked.

'Well, you see, Guv, I was driving a hearse at seventy miles per hour down Greenwich High Street.' I knew the worst before bothering to ask the obvious question. 'And you had a corpse on board?' 'Yes!'

With my constant observation of the human psyche I realised that in addition to the types I've already mentioned, there were some extremely strange people and often very lonely people walking the streets, usually motivated by greed and sex. While I've never been interested in brothels, per se, my work at the agency soon converted me into believing that they should exist for the safety of the general public. This was particularly illustrated by a man with a hunchback who walked with a pronounced limp and whose general appearance suggested that chances of finding romance were beyond his reach and he therefore approached a prostitute to relieve his burning desire. What happened next resulted in a charge of attempted murder and when the case came to Greenwich magistrates' court, it brought into the picture another and unexpected part of the psyche.

After the sex-hungry Quasimodo had agreed a price they went back to her home but to his surprise the whore's boyfriend was waiting behind a door and the unfortunate man was beaten and kicked so badly that he was taken for dead. After relieving the 'body' of its wallet, the couple bundled the hunchback into a broom cupboard and while they were counting their new wealth the woman had a pang of conscience. 'We can't just let 'im go like that,' she said. 'We've got to give 'im a decent send off, it's only right an' proper.' When her boyfriend protested she countered, 'How would you like to be murdered and then just bundled into a bleeding cupboard without anyone giving a toss?' It was a tricky problem because they couldn't go off and report their evil deed to the authorities just so that the victim could have a suitable burial. Being an enterprising couple, as their initiative had shown, they came up with the unlikely solution that the victim should be sent off with full honours. From a cupboard drawer they produced a Union Jack which was carefully placed over the supposed corpse and then they solemnly sang the national anthem before going off to a pub to spend their ill-gotten gains. The recipient of their attention who had feigned death was aggrieved that he had lost his money without any sexual gratification and did not feel that the funeral rites were anything approaching compensation for the unfulfilled passion, loss of money and physical pain he was suffering. Unappreciative so far as the would-be killers were concerned, he escaped and reported the incident to the police.

I wrote of a man in the Dartford, Kent, area who was so sex deprived and depraved that he dug up the corpse of an eighty-year-old unmarried lady and ravaged it. He was never caught so far as I know. There were other instances of a frustrated sex drive where men, unattractive to women, would push their penises into milk bottles where they remained trapped until, to the delight of giggling young nurses, they were compelled to put on concealing raincoats and call red-faced into hospital casualty departments. Without being attractive to the opposite sex or even possibly their own, and having been humiliated by the failed projection into an early sperm bottle bank, I wonder what they turned to next.

A weirdo I did interview had decided to remarry after his wife died but he left his bride in no doubt where his heart and also where his late wife was. When I visited their home the second wife, a simple soul, objected to the veneration accorded to the deceased and as I sat on a settee in the front room the current wife brought in tea and cakes which she placed on a long table that I could have sworn was a coffin. 'Not there,' he ordered, 'don't you have any respect for the dead?' I lifted the teacup and saucer off the polished woodwork as the distraught spouse cried out, 'I hate her! Isn't it about time you started thinking of me and put her under the ground?' The cakes were almost indigestible but it had nothing to do with the baking…

Among other south London unfortunates were members of Woolwich's cat population who fell into the clutches of a mysterious catnabber and were whisked away for vivisection. Their constant disappearance for over a year was nationally reported and the police were under pressure to find the monster moggie snatcher. To the local newspapers it was a scandal equal to Burke and Hare; to the cat owners there was obvious distress, and to the police there was a major challenge. 'Something must be done!' trumpeted the indignant local press, and so it was.

The police set several traps until one night the culprit was caught in the act of whisking a cat off the streets and forcing it into a wicker basket. On the day of the trial the courtroom was filled with meowing cats in boxes which had been found at the snatcher's home and as the bedraggled down-at-heel wretch stood in the dock, wringing his sweaty hands with remorse, he was questioned about his motivation. 'It was the money, your worship,' he whined to the magistrate.

'You must have known that these thefts were causing great distress to the owners?' said the magistrate as he looked imperiously over his glasses and glared at the accused. The small courtroom was hushed and all those present leaned forward to hear the reply. Most of the observers were women whose cats had disappeared for ever while others were members of an anti-vivisection group for whom it was a *cause célèbre*. They were all after the blood of this demon in their midst and a hundred eyes bored into him like searing arrows with everyone knowing that the only true and just sentence would be to boil him in oil or even send him alive for the same treatment their pets had suffered. 'It's like this, your worship,' he whimpered. 'I was on me uppers, yer see, and so I took one cat to the hospital where they paid me. Then I realised I could make quite a bit of cash out of it.'

The magistrate, dressed in black morning coat and pin-striped trousers, topped with a starched shirt, butterfly collar and bow tie, was remorselessly frigid as he played to the gallery and the press, assured with the knowledge that his measured words would be reported throughout Great Britain. 'And so you continued to steal these unfortunate creatures knowing that they would be used for vivisection and knowing also the distress it would cause their owners!' The reply from the dock was as unexpected as it was immortal, a reply that every court reporter dreams of: 'I didn't think about that, your worship. All I could see was ten-and-sixpence walking around on four legs!'

Court reporters often have a rapport with magistrates without ever talking to them. Greenwich and Woolwich had two stipendiaries, one named Pereira and the other Hutchinson. Pereira was warm and compassionate and would often look across the press box with twinkling eyes after passing sentence to see if we agreed. In my view he had a perfect assessment of the person in the dock and his humane judgments could not be faulted, except in law. After I'd left Ferrari he was harshly criticised by the Appeal Court which was a great pity. Hutchinson would qualify as 'Mr Frigidaire' with judgments given without feeling, tolerance or understanding of the real world, but correct in law. In yesteryear, I felt, he would recommend deportation to a starving child for stealing a loaf of bread. His harsh sentences were never criticised by officialdom but they were by everyone in the courtroom watching the dispensation of justice.

Another unbending magistrate, in Dartford, was Mrs Minnie Ling, a Justice of the Peace and chair of the bench. I was unimpressed by Justices of the Peace because so many were amateurs – 'county' stock – while others were just ambitious and wished to make their mark, whose contributions to human understanding were not usually notable. Minnie Ling was a tyrant who sentenced a widowed sixty-five-year-old pensioner to six months' jail for stealing a pair of shoelaces. My deputy, Malcolm Stewart, was present and wrote the story of poor 'Poor Little Miss Dolly' and the tabloid newspapers went berserk over the judgment. They were even more up in arms when the *Daily Sketch* baled her out, gave her some money and hid her in an hotel from other reporters before her appeal, which she won. Chequebook journalism was in its infancy and perhaps the petty thief had unwittingly contributed to its expansion. It meant that the Ferrari agency which had broken the story and thought up the catchy phrase would not benefit any further from the story which had been hijacked. As for the *Daily Sketch*… The *Daily* what? When was that last published?

One newspaper in the whole of Fleet Street defiantly refused to condemn Minnie Ling – the *Sunday Express*. This wasn't because the journal believed she had been right to pass the stiff sentence; moral issues didn't come into it. Minnie Ling happened to be the news editor's mother-in-law!

Years later, I came to know an elderly lady in Ascot and sometimes stayed at her home. She had formerly been chair of the Ascot bench and I told her about Minnie Ling. 'You know,' she said sweetly, 'they used to call me a tyrant, too!'

My naive belief that it was my job to take dangerous risks for exclusive stories first manifested itself after a report came in that a man had gone berserk and battered his mother to death with a flat iron and that he was holed up in woods near Woolwich. I wanted to interview him before he was caught by the police and the thought that he might become difficult had crossed my mind but I reckoned on being fleet-footed enough to outpace him in a difficult situation. Stealthily I entered the woods, hoping not to be spotted by the police, and over an hour was spent looking for the murderer without success. Disappointed, I came from the trees and returned to the office only to learn some hours later the man was arrested in adjacent woods! He appeared in court next day and he was a brute, big and nasty: I was relieved that our paths hadn't crossed.

I was perusing the charge sheet at Greenwich when the grey-haired sergeant on the desk, 'Sarge' to one and all, called me across. 'There was one helluva fight in Deptford last night,' he said.

Seedy pub brawls in Deptford were not uncommon and seldom reported and I was a little surprised he even bothered to mention it. 'It was a race riot,' he said. 'About sixty whites were at one end of the road and sixty blacks at the other.' Post-war race riots were as yet unheard of in Britain and I was soon filing copy. Great stuff, I thought, far less concerned with the political implications than the fact that it was a good story. I bought all the newspapers anticipating a splash lead on the front pages but to my astonishment there was nothing, not in the *Evening News, Star* nor *Evening Standard*. I had also filed to the morning newspapers for their first editions with the same negative result. Why? No one ever said and I wondered if there was a Government 'D' notice on the story. It was a time of smugness in Britain; racism existed in America and South Africa, but not at home! Some time later another race riot broke out and this time it couldn't be brushed under the carpet. And so, officially, the first post-war race riots were at Notting Hill a few months later, not Deptford.

The *Daily Express* telephoned to say that a man had left his London office four days ago to travel home by bus to Welling, Kent, and hadn't been seen since. Would I call on the family? I was surprised, as missing adults are seldom news stories but this proved to be the most tactless interview I have ever undertaken. A boy of about fourteen years opened the door of a 1930s semi-detached house and I asked him the number of the bus his father usually travelled home on. He told me and without a moment's thought I said, 'But a man died on that bus four days ago and he's in the Dartford mortuary!' Tears welled into the boy's eyes before I came to the shocked realisation of what I had done so brutally. My thoughts had been of the total lack of liaison between the Metropolitan and Kent police and that I had just solved the mystery of the dead man on the bus and yet here I was casually telling the youngster that his father was an unidentified corpse on a cold slab in the morgue. Sadly, my deduction was all too accurate.

Another story. The police were searching for a fifteen-year-old youth after a stabbing incident at his home. The alarm had gone out together with a description and warning over the radio that he was known to be still carrying a knife. Pruning the roses in my front garden, I watched a youngster walking up the hill who fitted the description in every way and a few questions confirmed that he was the wanted lad. 'You'd better give me the knife,' I said and it was an awkward and tense moment as I'd no idea how he would react, especially when he pulled out the blade. I held out my hand and to my relief he handed it over. I drove him to the police station and my story merely mentioned that he had been found and detained but it was surely a coincidence that he should walk up my road?

Being a freelance reporter meant I had to be prepared to do unpalatable jobs such as interviewing, say, the parents of a child who had just been killed. A law came about to put a stop to this practice which was roundly condemned – and yet I'd always found that the newly bereaved generally wanted to talk and would welcome me into their homes. At that stage I was still a shy person who had to pluck up courage to knock on doors but my approach was always direct and genuinely sympathetic because I had been through a similar ordeal. It is something, I suspect, that trained welfare officers lacking personal experience will never understand. It has to be pure chance, but of the many welfare officers I've met, none have been married or have children. News editors are not stupid and they would telephone, tongue in cheek: 'A girl has just been murdered and it's a sex job. Would you pop round and talk to the neighbours to see if they have any pix?' I'd talk to the neighbours to find out about the girl; whether she was happy, attractive (I've never read a newspaper report of an ugly one), and had boyfriends, etc. But I have not yet met a neighbour who kept photographs of the children next door and the only way to get the all-important photos is by talking to the parents. Should there be a complaint to the newspaper, it would be met by a pained response and the reply that the irresponsible freelancer must have gone too far. It is ironic that I was in great demand for the job I hated: knocking on the doors of the bereaved. While I wrote for nearly all the Fleet Street newspapers, it was the popular press that kept the money flowing. On one occasion, three youths were killed in an horrific car crash and I interviewed all three bereaved mothers for the *Mirror* and each of them gave me a photograph of their beloved sons. One had even been taken off the body that day. It was a compliment that the *Mirror* used my story as a middle-page spread; galling that they ignored the photos they had asked for and used one of the crash instead.

In truth, I never received a single complaint – quite the reverse, and what angers me today is the number of distressed people who are dragged by the authorities in front of television cameras to plead for witnesses to come forward when their child or loved one has been found murdered. It is a type of exposure I find quite tasteless, tactless, embarrassing, cruel and unnecessary. I've noted with interest the police creating within the public a suspicion of their competence by putting forward on TV so-called distressed people who have embarrassingly turned out to be the actual murderers.

By contrast to the alleged press intrusion, in one incident I covered, a youth had stabbed his elder sister to death. She was a very beautiful girl and her father, an amateur photographer, adored her. I wondered if jealousy had been involved, but the police treated the case as an accident and no charge was brought. I spoke to the distressed father and he showed me a very large selection of photographs of the girl before taking me into another room. It was filled with Leica cameras, tripods, an enlarger, and a mass of other photo-graphic equipment. 'You take them away,' he said. 'I shall never take another photograph.' The temptation was great but that's not why I was there. 'You keep them,' I replied. 'One day you will take photographs again.' I settled for a picture of the girl and hoped that the next reporter or photographer to see him would react the same way.

The telephone rang and it was the *Daily Express*. 'Reg, just slip along to Bellingham (South-East London) and interview Henry Cooper. We hear he's having an affair with Diana Dors.' I didn't know much of 'Our 'enry' and what a great character he was, but I did know that he was the British heavyweight boxing champion and that I was to ask him about his sex life with the buxom married film star. I also knew that one punch from him would have put me through his front door and across the street even if the door was closed at the time. That fist was to knock down Mohammed Ali in a world title fight some time later. ''enry's in bed,' said his mother who answered the door. 'Will you get him up?' This was worse than I had expected. I'd half hoped he wouldn't be there and now I was getting him out of bed! Henry bounded downstairs in his dressing gown and began jabbing away with his hambone fists while bobbing and weaving, shadow boxing with nasty little jabs. These were big paws he was throwing around and rather than try to interview him dancing around on uneven terms, I cautiously eased myself into a chair. Thus, out of immediate fist range, I came straight to the point with an uppercut that might have floored him, 'We hear you are having an affair with Diana Dors.' For a second his guard almost dropped and I thought I had landed the sucker-punch until his fists began flailing the air, jab, jab, jab. 'Nah,' he said, simply.

'Are you saying you are not having an affair?' 'That's right. I ain't 'aving no affair wiv Diana Dors.'

By now his fists were pummelling an unseen punch bag as he danced around the tiny lounge. 'Do you know Diana Dors?' There was a pause before he began jabbing again. 'Yeah.' I cast a glance at his mother who sat in another chair watching the dual between the pugilist and the journalist. 'Do you know her well?' 'Yeah.' Then I pushed my luck. 'How well?' Henry Cooper continued to dance up and down without a flinch. He'd got the measure of his challenger and his lethal fists never stopped jabbing out. 'We're just good friends,' he answered. 'Just good friends.' His mother smiled indulgently; she had known all along that her 'enry was a good boy.

Interviewing people after a divorce was an anathema to me because of the acrimony and animosity which so often occurs. It is a time when people relive the worst moments of their marriage, totally disregarding the happier events which had brought them together. Bitterness is very sad but it makes good copy. The *Daily Express* asked me to see a very distraught fading star in Dulwich whose husband had just left her for a younger model. She was very upset and very drunk. 'After all I have done for him,' the woman drawled as she staggered to a garden seat. I can't say that I took to her, but in fairness she was being interviewed under the worst possible conditions and some years later she had the guts to put her own money into a successful comeback at the London Palladium to a full house. There is no doubt she had done a lot for her handsome husband but looking at this blousy lady swaying in front of me brought out sympathy for the man.

He was already idolised by millions of women cinemagoers throughout the world who readily took him to their hearts but he was unknown before his marriage to the lady in front of me. She was Dorothy Squires, the songstress whose tune 'The Gipsy' foretold her lover would come back again – he didn't, although he did help her later in life. He was Roger Moore.

There had been a serious outbreak of polio and the *Telegraph* asked me to visit a house where two people had contracted the disease and died, while another member of the family was in hospital with it. The outbreak had happened so fast that the authorities had not time to distribute the new American Salk vaccine – it turned up a week after the ordered story. The request had presented me with a personal crisis. If I went to the house and contracted the disease I could transmit it to my family, yet if I found this an excuse not to go, the chances were that in future I would find excuses for not covering other unpleasant stories. I went into the house where a youth told me he had just lost his mother and brother. A terrible tragedy, but I didn't stay long or make close contact for fear of another occurring at my home.

'Let's go home before the fog really closes in,' said Margery. We were shopping in Lewisham, south London, when the fog came down and as we left a furniture store, police cars, ambulances and fire engines raced past. I knew she was antici-pating that I might want to go after a possible story. 'Okay,' I replied with some reluctance; my journalistic hunch told me that I was in the right place at the right time but I was walking away from a big story. As we reached home I checked the office and was surprised that Ferrari answered the phone. He seldom looked into the newsroom. 'There's been a rail pile up at St John's station near Lewisham,' he said. 'I've sent Malcolm to cover it and you'd better come in.' 'Sure, I'll come over,' I replied, feeling Margery's eyes boring into me. We didn't see as much of each other as we had wanted because of what she termed 'Your damned job!' 'I'll be back soon,' I told her, but neither of us believed it.

As I arrived at the office, Malcolm Stewart came on the phone with copy. 'It's awful,' he said and his voice was shaking, 'there are so many bodies.' The self-confident bespectacled young man had gone to the tragedy expecting to cover it dispassionately but he hadn't anticipated the enormity of the crash in which ninety-two people were killed in one of England's worst rail disasters. The following day I hired a car to take me to the site and the fog by now had turned into a pea-souper. On the way the driver told me he had been with the British army in post-war Germany where he had spent most of his time as a smuggler. With that knowledge, I felt quite happy; I knew he would be intrepid enough to get me to the crash scene if anyone could.

We started off in his heavy black Humber Super Snipe and travelled fast, considering that he had to keep his eyes on the kerbs all the way. There was a disturbing factor to which I felt obliged to draw his attention: 'Tell me, why are we driving on the wrong side of the road?' I asked in a feigned casual and almost uninterested way, imagining that it was perhaps an oversight, given that he had driven for so long on the Continent. 'What do you expect me to do?' he replied. 'It's the only way I can see the kerb.' This was reasonable; there was only about a yard of visibility. 'Aren't you bothered that we might hit something coming the other way?' I ventured. His reply was instant: 'There's not much hope of that. You don't think that any other bloody fool would be out in a fog like this!' We didn't encounter any parked or abandoned cars, not even in south London.

The crash involved three trains and a collapsed bridge but the human interest story centred on a very courageous and badly injured young woman who was trapped hanging upside down. Her spirits were high and eventually oxyacetylene equipment managed to cut her away from the twisted wreckage, but she died. For myself, it was back to knocking on doors, some of the rich and some of the poor who were briefly united by the tragedy. I interviewed about a quarter of the victims' next-of-kin, all of whom invited me into their homes. I'm not going into the details of the crash but there was a sequel a year later when I carried out my only discreditable act of journalism. Well, I thought so.

Ferrari had suggested that I go back to the scene to see if anyone was on the platform saying a one-year anniversary prayer for the deceased. This was absolutely typical of him and he knew that I would never come back without a story so it was up to me to find one. As St John's station was deserted I took a train to London and went to Fleet Street. At Ludgate Circus I bought a posy from a florists and took it back to St John's waiting room where the bodies had been piled up in a make-shift mortuary. I wrote a brief note, 'To Daddy, I love you very much, Wendy' and telephoned the newspapers. Lino Ferrari, who would dare most things, was very concerned that the Sunday papers might carry out some investigating on the authenticity of the story and expose the agency. The *Daily Mail* photographed the flowers and played up the story with the question, 'Who is Wendy?' A few days later came a message allegedly from a rich man in California who had read the report and said that Wendy, if she could be found, would be invited to a free holiday with him in the United States. At least, I thought, that can't happen. There is truth in the cliché that nothing should be taken for granted. I had felt myself a conscience-stricken ragbag right up to the time when a young Miss came forward and claimed that she was Wendy. It wasn't her real name, 'But that's what Daddy called me.' So far as I know, she didn't even have a relative in the crash as the *Mail* story was extremely vague. Almost certainly the *Mail* reporter had guessed the original report was phoney and he decided to let someone, perhaps a niece, take the trip. Certainly, either the fraudulent Wendy went on holiday to California or the whole of the *Mail* story was fictitious too! Ironically, I may have started a trend. While poppies became the symbol of grief and remembrance after the first world war, I can't recall flowers being placed on the sites of rail and road crashes by groups of people before the Lewisham crash. At Potters Bar, where seven people were killed in a rail crash many years later, a memorial garden has even been built.

If I had stayed with Ferrari I would have gone back to Fleet Street at some stage and may have done well, but Robert was suffering heavy asthma attacks which would last for two weeks, then a week off, followed by another two weeks of agony. To watch him going downhill was devastating – then Annette started to wheeze. Nightmare memories of my mother's suffering flooded back. My doctor, who had the appropriately phonetic name of Goulstone, was in the RAF in Southern Rhodesia during the war and it was a place, he said, with a perfect climate which was especially good for asthma sufferers. I knew little about the country other than that the prime minister of the Federation of Rhodesia and Nyasaland was Sir Roy Welensky, a huge genial man who had been feted recently at a filmed banquet in London. His policy was known to be one of multi-racialism as opposed to apartheid and as the British government was encouraging people to emigrate there, I wrote to the London editor of the *Rhodesia Herald* and fixed an appointment to see him in Fleet Street. It was a fateful move.

By coincidence, the day before the interview I was chatting to Leslie Meehan, a police constable, who was waiting for a colleague opposite Woolwich Magistrates' Court. Because of my court reporting, I was on a nodding acquaintance with most of the policemen in the 'manor' and while the chat lasted only a few minutes before we went our separate ways, it was memorable – as his murder a couple of hours later would ensure that I would be offered a job in Rhodesia.

A truck driven by a local twenty-six-year-old scrap dealer, Leslie 'Gipsy' Smith, was travelling along a road in Woolwich with scaffolding on the back. Suspecting that it was stolen, Meehan questioned Smith and as the driver tried to get away he jumped on to the truck and clung there until he was hit by an oncoming car and killed instantly. There is no doubt about the immediacy of his death as his brains were left in the road for several hours, surrounded by a wood-and-rope cordon. It was my first experience of personally knowing a murdered man and I felt queasy looking down with fascination at his grey jellyfish-like brains. There seemed to be no reason to leave them there for passers-by to stare at. Smith was charged with murder and found guilty but he won his appeal and was jailed for ten years for manslaughter.

Dissatisfied with the appeal, the police took the case to the House of Lords and because Smith had won his appeal, he became 'The man they cannot hang.' It was a celebrated case and the Law Lords decided Smith had actually murdered the policeman and therefore should have been topped.

The morning after Meehan's death, I went to the *Rhodesia Herald* offices in Fleet Street having telephoned that I would be late. The editor, named Noble, was courteous and asked me for my qualifications. No journalist could ever have gone for a job interview better equipped. First I threw the daily newspapers on to his desk with my story of Meehan's death on the front pages. 'And this is why I was late,' I said. I put down the three evening newspapers I had just bought from a seller outside his office, with the splash front page lead in all three of Smith's being charged with murder. 'Do you need any other qualifications?' I asked. 'Can you fly out tomorrow?' he replied. My modest request was to travel out by sea as the cruise would give the whole family a good treat. This was readily agreed to but now there was the question of telling Margery. I telephoned. 'Hello, darling. I thought you should know straight away that I've got the job and we are travelling to Salisbury in two weeks.' 'That's nice,' she said, 'I like the west country.'

Hadn't she been listening to what I had told her about my job application? This could be difficult. 'No, sweetheart, not Salisbury in Wiltshire, *Salisbury*, Southern Rhodesia!' There was silence followed by a faint, 'Oh... Oh!'

She was tremendous. First she had to suffer the fact that the man she married had worked regular hours whereas I was now out half the day and night. Now she would have to uproot everything, leave her parents and our first-ever home and go to the foreign continent of Africa. In fairness to myself, I did not think I'd get the job on the turn and had planned to tell her that evening about the interview but the breaking of the major story, of actually knowing Meehan, and now the enormity of changing my job and emigrating, had stimulated the adrenalin. It was the second time I had thrown up a job on a gamble but the health of the children was paramount and so too was their education. Both Margery and I had been disturbed at junior schools encouraging children to go wild for about twenty minutes a day in what was called, 'self-expression'. We felt that lessons in self-discipline would have been better taught if our youngsters were to face the future with dignity and we were also concerned that the school discouraged parents from teaching their children to read and write in favour of an experimental untried system. Our emigration, therefore, was for more than one reason.

A touching moment came when I was approached by Gwen Parrish, a reporter on the *Kentish Mercury* who handed me a silver beer tankard. 'Your leaving us has come so quickly that we didn't have time to get it inscribed but it's from all three papers, the *Mercury*, *Kentish Times* and *Kentish Independent*,' she said. It was a surprise gesture as reporters on local newspapers generally dislike the presence of freelancers who cut their supplementary incomes from tipping off the dailies with stories. Even the chairman of Dartford Council rose to make a speech of farewell although, being a Labour councillor, he questioned my wisdom in going to Rhodesia. Thus began the start of an incredible adventure for which I had been inexplicably and thoroughly groomed; a journey that would give meaning to my life.

Emigration, Apartheid and I Become Rebellious

It was a good day to leave England for ever. Cold, damp, miserable, the weather complemented the glum looks of those standing on the Southampton quayside who watched with concern as my little family struggled up the gangplank of the RMS *Edinburgh Castle*. As I looked back and waved at the upturned faces, knowing that forced smiles belied their thoughts, a deep pang of guilt gnawed inside my stomach at the enormity of what I had done and the gauche way I'd gone about it. I hadn't given Margery much time to dwell about being torn from her parents who had meant so much to her as I'd feared she might feel the ties too strong to leave.

Would Margery ever see them again? It would be the last time she would kiss her father goodbye; the slightly built, quiet but humorous gentle man whom I'd frivolously nicknamed 'Jumbo' would drop dead while tending the garden and be given a quiet funeral. Her brother, Harry, would also drop dead in the street within weeks of returning from climbing in the Himalayas. His funeral, by contrast, would be attended by all the very top brass of the Parachute Regiment who eulogized over Corporal 'Smokey' Holter's work in arranging reunion tours to Europe where comrades had fought and died, and the annual Paras' march past at the Whitehall Cenotaph. Standing there was my mother-in-law, grey haired, bespectacled and plumpish, who had suffered so much tragedy and yet watched over us like a kindly matriarch whom we all loved and respected. There was Warren with his wife, Rosa. Warren had always protected me as a big brother and without his finding me work under the most difficult of circumstances, I would almost certainly have been put into a children's home when I was sacked after the death of Mum. I'd been best man at his wedding which fell on Derby Day at nearby Epsom and had prepared a good speech to coincide with the event but had been too shy and unsure of myself to deliver it and made a hash of the impromptu alternative. As I now looked down, the laughter and the tragedies in our lives were all there standing on the docks and I was glad it was drizzling with rain.

The ship's farewell horn blasted me out of the reverie for a final wave and as we edged away into a sullen sea the coast of England reluctantly released its magnetic pull and the liner began to knife through the waters as if answering the seductive call of a Siren whose outstretched arms were luring us inexorably towards another continent and unknown destinies. Two days later as I leaned over the ship's rail pensively watching a shoal of porpoises playing, there was a brief moment of apprehension, but then I looked up at the cloudless sky and quickly dismissed it for the rest of the cruise.

Shortly before the dawn following our last night aboard, all passengers mustered on deck to gaze ahead with awe as the stars of the southern hemisphere gave ethereal light to a giant flat-topped monument seemingly placed by Hercules himself while tinselled maidens pirouetted with ecstasy beneath it. As the sun emerged from the sea, the twinkling lights of Cape Town faded and the mighty pillar transmogrified to reveal itself as the most famous sailors' landmark anywhere in the world – the imperious Table Mountain which majestically gazes down upon two mighty oceans as they confront each other in titanic clashes. This was the morning where the curtain would be raised on an historical tragicomedy in which even I was found a small part to play and the first act of the drama began within minutes of our stepping on to South African soil. Our spirits were high as we came ashore and I picked up our suitcases to make my way across a railway bridge, a little surprised that there were no porters. I was halfway up and struggling when a voice growled from behind, 'You come down from there, Man!' I turned to see a burly thug in a blue uniform glaring at me. His accent was heavy and his face was thunder. 'What did you say?' I asked, not believing what I had heard.

'You go over there,' he snarled, nodding in the direction of another bridge some distance away. 'That's all right,' I answered innocently, 'this will do.' There was a finality in his voice and the manner in which he rubbed the palm of his hand on the heavy gun holstered at his side warned me not to argue, 'I said you go to that bridge over there.' This was very different from England and a type of man whose outlook was totally foreign to me – I knew of apartheid but hadn't realised the intensity and absurdity could be so total. As I looked across to Margery, standing frozen to the platform with Peter in her arms, I knew what she was thinking but it was too late to turn back now. I had burned our bridges financially and the South African Rubicon had to be crossed! 'Come on, Sweetheart,' I called as I struggled with the heavy cases towards the 'Whites Only' bridge, and, in a loud voice called, 'Don't get worried about him, he's not worth it.' Once across we were met by African porters and I wondered why our luggage should be so sacred that it could not have been taken across the bridge reserved for Africans. A journalist from the *Cape Argus* arrived to take care of our luggage and disappeared before putting in a phoney expense account for providing a meal and drinks for the five of us which I was later obliged to pay. As there was time to spare before our 2,000-mile-journey, we strolled to the public gardens beside the parliament buildings and white fantailed doves attracted our attention to some park benches. We sat in the sunshine beneath shade trees and I noticed brown squirrels running up the branches. The squirrels were a pleasant surprise as I'd always mourned their near-demise in England. As chance would have it, that brief visit to the gardens would bring me into controversy many years later with the South African authorities.

Slowly we ambled back to the station where a train was waiting. 'It's filthy,' snapped Margery as we entered our compartment but before she could remonstrate further about the powdered soot which covered our seats, the carriage shuddered, chains protested loudly and with the belch of a hippo, thick black smoke rose into the air to eclipse the sun as the massive engine powered its way forward. Slowly it trudged into the vast barren Karoo, a depressing and untenable stretch of desolate void where even vultures found no easy pickings. As black smut flew in through the open windows and settled like hot black lava dust on the whole family I decided that if hell was an actual place it was confined to railway compartments of a steam train that ran through the Karoo; if it was a state of mind this was to suffer the journey with a mortified wife and three small children. 'Close the windows, for God's sake,' snapped Margery as she hastily brushed a hot cinder off Peter whom she was cradling. With her recently pristine frock now blackened and smudged, she added with caustic satisfaction as though I was responsible for everything that had gone wrong, 'Your hair's on fire!' As the top of my head began to smoke I hastily brushed off a burning cinder before rushing to close the windows, despite the searing heat outside. Accusingly, Margery looked at me and uttered, 'Did you say we have three days of this?'

Four hours out of Cape Town, a morose white waiter appeared and his attitude was no different from the policeman on the docks. Instead of a dinner menu, he produced a greasy mixture of mashed potatoes, ageing greens, meat of an unidentifiable origin and boiled pumpkin which I suspected had been a leftover several months from Halloween. When he reappeared to take away the plates, I asked, 'Where do we sleep?'

'You sleep here!' he said in a strong Afrikaans accent which suggested that he liked the English even less than the Africans.

'So where are the bed bunks?'

'You sleep on the seats, this isn't the Blue Train, Man!' With that he left us only to return with unlaundered sheets which were tossed across to me before he disappeared again. The Blue Train? I'd never heard of it but concluded, rightly, that it had to be better than this and wondered why we were not on it? Margery's misery was complete: 'We're going back home as soon as we reach Bulawayo,' she snapped. It was an ultimatum and I couldn't blame her. 'Rhodesia must be better than this,' I parried, fervently hoping that I was right.

I thanked God and Margery for our well-behaved children for despite being cooped up in a railway carriage for three days and two nights, they never complained. I also concluded when we stopped eventually en route that the Relief of Mafeking had less to do with the Anglo-Boer War but was an expression of gratitude by passengers of South African Railways as they alighted from the train halfway through the journey. After the sun-baked sand of the Karoo we crawled through the Kalahari Desert of Bechuanaland (Botswana) suffering the torments of that tedious barren land for hour upon hour in oppressive heat before seeing our first mud-huts. A change in the atmosphere was instantaneous, for instead of the oppressive sullenness of South Africa, laughing black children waved as they ran beside the train. We crossed the border into

Southern Rhodesia and on to Bulawayo where another train was waiting. I looked anxiously at Margery, 'As we've come this far, we may as well carry on and see what Rhodesia's like,' I ventured. Reluctantly she stepped aboard the Salisbury train and the transformation in her came straight out of Cinderella. The carriages were spotless and they even provided overnight sleepers with clean sheets and towels. A smiling black waiter welcomed us aboard and later brought a meal of highly edible steaks with fresh vegetables and a sweet of freshly picked tropical fruits. We were still on a high next day when we arrived at Salisbury station to a warm welcome by a Congregational Church minister, Geoffrey Thrussell (later to become chaplain to Leeds University), a *Rhodesia Herald* representative, and a friend-of-a-friend. As we were driven to our hotel I noticed a relaxed-looking white policeman and I was impressed that he did not carry a gun. 'None of the police carry guns,' said Thrussell, 'and no one has been shot in anger by the police for over fifty years!' I was relieved that the assurances I had received in London were true, that unlike South Africa, Rhodesia was not a police state.

My first confrontation in our new country was at our hotel, The New Manor, which had been new at the turn of the century, but like an ageing film star, it demanded a facelift. And unlike its transient guests who would stay for a week or two, it also had permanent residents who took advantage under cover of darkness to move across uncarpeted wooden floors. I heard them on the first night and next morning asked the owner for rat traps as we were concerned for the safety of Peter in his cot. 'There are no rats in this hotel,' snorted its proprietress, a formidable woman who enhanced her disagreeable personality with a bottle of whisky which she secreted in a cupboard above the reception desk. 'Here, have this,' she said truculently as she threw a mousetrap on to the counter. The next morning I went downstairs with a dead mouse and was in no mood for an argument having heard the padded feet of a heavier animal after the trap had been sprung. 'Now for a rat trap,' I demanded. This time one was provided and the following day I presented myself at the reception counter and placed a large dead rat on it. 'Thank you,' I said with satisfaction. A small group of would-be guests at the reception looked at my offering and then at each other before hurriedly disappearing out through the swing doors. With that, I was invited to leave as soon as I could find other accommodation with the words, 'You are nothing but trouble!' Shortly afterwards I rented a house with an acre of garden for the children to play in.

We knew it was the 'thing' to have servants but the whole concept was initially embarrassing to us until a stream of Africans knocked on the door for work. We employed one as a domestic for the house and another for the garden. My newly appointed gardener told me his name was 'Gate' and I hoped the next houseboy to call would be named Cowan but it was too much to ask for.

Shortly after taking over the property I bought a highly pedigreed German Shepherd puppy but at six months, to everyone's distress, Sheba disappeared.

It was unlike her to leave the garden where she was a perfect companion to the three children and we had almost given up hope of ever seeing her again, when Annette looked out of the window several weeks later and shouted that Sheba was coming down the road. Excitement ran high as we raced out but we could see that she was limping badly and as we ran out to meet her I saw a chain was tight around her neck and one eye was closed. Examination showed she had been held by a chain lead which she had somehow managed to break but I had to remove the strangling-tight chain with a hacksaw. Clearly she had been badly beaten and the vet just managed to save her eye. 'If you had come here tomorrow it would have been too late,' he said. 'She would have been blind.' Many people claim that high pedigree causes instability but this was not the case with Sheba. She was always gentle with the children with whom she played and protected. She escaped the house one firework night and ran around with a jumping cracker in her mouth, thoroughly enjoying the minor explosions without any fear of the consequences, contradicting the belief that all dogs are terrified of Guy Fawkes Night. But the day she returned home she was a racist, except with the servants. I had often thought of Sheba's kidnapper being a white because there were twelve world champions in her strain which made her pedigree obvious, but her reaction to the blacks now caused me to suspect otherwise.

What disturbed me was that had a white man stolen Sheba, I would have condemned just him but if it had been an African would I, like so many other whites, condemn the whole black race? It was clear to me that in the years to come, if I was to carry out my work in a fair manner, the road ahead would be laced with potholes and I'd discovered some on my first day at the *Rhodesia Herald*. An interview with the news editor, Charles Still, a South African, was most revealing. 'It is the policy of the newspaper to side with the government of the day,' he confided. 'It is also our policy never to carry a report involving an African on the front page!' There were four million blacks in the country at the time and a quarter of a million whites with just one daily newspaper. I said with incredulity, 'You're not serious?'

'I certainly am, it's management policy.'

'Management? What have they to do with the editorial?'

'The Anglo American Corporation own the newspaper's shares and they control the policy.'

'My God,' I answered bitterly, realising what I had let myself in for. After some discussion I asked, 'What if there is an African murder and it's a big one? Will that go on the front page?' The news editor blanched visibly but instantly recovered and said in a patronising tone that having come from England I did not understand politics of the country with its unwritten laws (which I was concluding were promulgated and promoted by the *Herald*). 'Least of all a murder – they happen all the time and are quite sordid.'

'And what about quoting African political leaders?' I asked. The current nationalist leader, Joshua Nkomo, was frequently quoted in the British press.

He was away in voluntary exile at the time. Charles Still looked hard at me as though I had come from another world – which was true. 'They have very little support amongst their own people,' he said. 'We occasionally quote them if someone like Nkomo says something overseas but no one takes any notice. He might have a paragraph or two on an inside page.'

'But surely the leaders are interviewed by the political correspondent?' 'Never. They live in the townships and no one goes there.'

'What about at the airport?'

'They are never interviewed by the *Herald*.'

It was the proverbial red rag to a bull and I had already started snorting. Until that time I was seldom rebellious but I was inwardly angry with myself for leaving the twentieth century and moving into the nineteenth. I was not intending to carry any torch for African nationalism and never have to this day (some people have suggested otherwise), but there was a question of journalistic integrity which deeply bothered me. This was a form of self-censorship to please one small section of the population whereas a strong percentage of the *Herald* readership was black. My new-found rebellious nature struck the news editor forcibly when he told me on reading my copy how to open a story starting with the name and address of the person being interviewed. 'Do you realise that for the past three and a half years I have survived the biggest rat race in the world by writing good opening paragraphs which sell stories?' I snapped.

'Maybe, but that's how I want it,' he replied. 'Then you do it!' I threw my copy in his face and stormed off. On any other newspaper I would have been sacked on the turn. Instead, I had a victory on my hands and my opening paragraph remained; it was the *Herald* that began to change its style. Charles and I became quite friendly for the storm was over a professional matter, not personal, but at this time his journalism was as anachronistic as the newspaper itself.

I'd been told that I would be a court reporter and Charles hoped that I might be able to produce a story every couple of days. 'Of course, there will be times when you won't be able to get one a week,' he said. Court reporting again? I was hoping for something better. The chief court reporter was a tall, portly, grey-haired man, Douggie Campbell-Watt, and his entrance to the office each morning was unusual for a journalist, for on his arm was a wicker basket filled with farm produce of eggs, cabbage and potatoes which he sold first to the reporters and secretaries, and later to the magistrates' court staff. Douggie was a delightful man but despite his grandiose title he was less of a reporter than a farmer! Inoffensive, with a wry sense of humour, he came into the office one Monday morning laden with his usual agricultural wares and told me of an incident at his farm the previous day. 'I went to the outside loo and just before sitting down I noticed a cobra in the pan,' he said. My mind boggled at the thought of what could have happened. Douggie's broad beam would have been a sitting target for the reclining asp; and the subsequent sight of him trying to cross his lands with trousers down, clutching a dangerously swelling posterior, would have destroyed his credibility with his farm labourers for ever. 'What did you do?'

'I shot it,' he replied.

'But I thought you said it was curled up in the pan?'

'Yes, it was. That's why I used my 12-bore shotgun. I had to be sure of killing it.'

And did you?'

'Yes, I blew it to bits.' His eyes twinkled as he answered the unasked question. 'And the pan, too!'

Court reporting in Southern Rhodesia, as in South London, had its special moments, and one of them was when a grey-haired man with thick lens spectacles stood in the witness box and I was surprised by his presence. An African burglar had entered his bedroom, he said. 'I was asleep in bed but was awakened by a noise in my room and saw the accused.' That too was surprising on two counts: in addition to being half blind, he was also as deaf as a post and had to wear a hearing aid which he would turn off if he didn't wish to listen to a parliamentary debate. Seeing and hearing the black man in the dark of his bedroom must have been extremely difficult for him. When questioned, he said he always slept naked and was nude when he chased the burglar out of the house and across the lawn. It was a good story, for not every day does one have a bachelor of such eminence as the Prime Minister, Sir Edgar Whitehead, giving evidence of running naked over the lawns of his official residence.

In addition to the court work, I also became the newspaper's crime reporter and it was exactly one year since my arrival in the country that I achieved the impossible – an African murder appeared on the front page. A killer was running amok having axed to death and cut the throats of a black woman and her three children. With tongue in cheek, I suggested that as the maniac was near to Salisbury, white women might be attacked too and they should be warned. The ruse worked but was aided by a bonus to the story which cried out for front page treatment. The murders had been committed on a farm where the British premier, Harold Macmillan, had stayed the previous year on his historical 'Winds of Change' tour of Africa.

Even though the *Rhodesia Herald* found the rise of African nationalism to be irrelevant, I persuaded the news editor to send me into the black townships on Sundays to attend political gatherings. I wasn't a political animal per se, merely a journalist looking for a good story and it seemed obvious that there was a nascent force soon to be reckoned with which was being totally ignored. Up to 5,000 blacks attended the meetings and I always sat alone near the leaders whose rhetoric would be against the white government but never the whites as such and even though there would be verbal attacks on the *Rhodesia Herald*, their leaders would point to me and declare, 'At least one man from the *Herald* comes to hear us.' That acknowledgment was to stand me in good stead and even save my life.

Two other white men also attended and sat some distance away. They were members of the Special Branch, Detective Chief Superintendent 'Robbie' Robinson, who resembled the forgotten breed of genial London bobby, and his assistant, Detective Inspector Piet Moores, a giant and pleasant Afrikaner. Because I was both the court and crime reporter I knew them quite well and was grateful that they never acknowledged me at the nationalist meetings. I particularly liked Robbie: he never once asked me for information and I was sorry that in later years some of his staff were to indulge in sadistic torture to such an extent that I would eventually give evidence against them in a secret court hearing. Robbie was known to Royalty, to Harold Macmillan and to other politicians who visited Rhodesia and it is difficult to believe that he approved some of the antics of his junior officers. Perhaps he didn't; he was just one of many pawns who would be overtaken by events. Piet Moores died at an early age of a heart attack while sitting at his desk before the liberation war began and was not involved in torture. The three of us were the first white men in the country, sitting like losing white pawns on a chess board, to hear the haunting anthem, 'Nkosi Sikelele Africa' 'God Bless Africa'. I've never since heard it sung so well and emotionally than when thousands of African male voices blended to pour out their evocative prayer for freedom. Many of those attending would die from bullets and firebombs, some would probably be hanged as terrorists, while most of the others would be disappointed with their lot after the armed struggle was over when they realised that they, too, were only black pawns in the political power game, that 'freedom' and improved standard of living under Robert Mugabe was just a cynical ploy.

The bubbling, irrepressible, nationalist volcano inevitably erupted on several occasions when serious rioting took place and whenever there was an uprising, I drove into the townships to watch events. Because of an insane habit of leaving my car, it was inevitable that I would become caught up in them and on one foray I found myself in the centre of a surging mass of blacks, the one white man present, who were throwing rocks and destroying everything and anything in sight as they made their way through a township and up a hill leading towards Salisbury city centre. At the top of the hill armed police blocked the road and as thousands of blacks surged forward they opened fire. I wondered if they might pinpoint me as a 'kaffir boetie' and take a shot as they had sharpshooters who picked off the ringleaders hiding in the crowds, urging the masses forward. When I returned to the office and heard the government statement on the radio stating that one black had been killed by police rifle fire, I knew it to be a blatant lie. 'That's very strange,' a police contact told me later that evening. 'I shot two myself!'

During another riot which lasted over several days, a lorry filled with Africans bussed in from another part of the country couldn't believe their luck at seeing a 'European' casually watching the action. The lorry screeched to a halt and as they jumped off they hurled insults and rocks at me. It was a desperate moment and I wished I hadn't been so stupid as to leave my car too far away to run to. Here was a truckload of blacks against one white but martyrdom was far removed from my thoughts and I began throwing their own rocks back. None of their stones hit me but that was sheer chance and I knew it was only a matter of time before they did. St Stephen, the first of the Christian martyrs to be stoned to death, didn't appear to have a guardian angel – I did! He came in the form of a diminutive, bespectacled African who had arrived in a small, dilapidated blue banger which was so old that it could have been propelled by his tiny feet through the flooring. 'Here, Baas, jump in.' His voice was music and I knew he was taking an enormous risk. I ran for my life and climbed into the car as stones whistled around me. Thank God, I thought, that my assailants were terrible shots. As we drove away to safety my rescuer held out his hand and grinned broadly. 'You were lucky, Baas,' he said. 'I've seen you at our meetings!' I'd no idea how much my life was worth but to me it was more than the gratuity he gratefully received.

Jim Biddulph (later shot and wounded in Congo), myself and John Parker.
Picture: Rhodesia Herald.

While driving into African riots I've been conscious of an eerie atmosphere which emanates from entering a human whirlpool as a seething mass of men and women appear to slowly circle around and around. Once in the vortex escape is difficult and yet while inside the people seem to be hardly moving. While I have come out unscathed, others were hurt and even killed and on one occasion, rocks were thrown through the windscreen of a car only minutes after I'd passed and a white man and his wife were critically injured. They hadn't used my natural form of defence – to laugh and wave as though I'm one of them. Who can bring themselves to kill someone as dumb as that?

Having broken down one of the *Herald*'s cardinal rules by getting a black murder on the front page, the other, of leading the newspaper with a story on an African political leader, was soon to follow. Michael Mawema, who was standing in for Joshua Nkomo, was put on trial for making seditious utterances during a political meeting. The trial was political dynamite and instead of holding it in the supercharged atmosphere of Salisbury, the authorities moved it to Inkomo Barracks, seventeen miles away. The authorities decreed that only one reporter would be allowed to cover the proceedings and he or she must be from the *Rhodesia Herald*. They could not know that the *Herald* had acquired a Fleet Street-standard court reporter who could write verbatim shorthand. The courtroom was a tiny classroom with a concrete floor that was so dusty that Mawema clowned to me by cynically sweeping it with a broom, like a domestic, raising clouds of dust just before the court session started. Considering that a hangman's noose could be his future, he showed incredible composure and humour.

A leading South African counsel, Aaron Maisels, SC, defended and made a far more profound impression upon me than Hartley Shawcross had done at the Lynskey Tribunal. Two African lawyers who helped in the defence and whom I knew well, Herbert Chitepo and Dr Edson Sithole, would later both be murdered. Chitepo, who has a street named after him in Harare, had slipped across the border into Zambia after Ian Smith seized independence but he was blown to pieces by a mine in Lusaka. As he drove out one morning the car detonated the bomb outside his garage which was so large that much of the vehicle landed on the roof of a house across the road.

Maisels decimated the police evidence against Mawema and it was clear that the principal witness for the Crown, a black policeman, had not personally written the report on which the charges were based. He had attended a Mawema meeting and then verbally told a white policeman what went on. It soon transpired that the report was written up with the white officer inserting words and phrases which his black colleague didn't even understand. Then the African constable obediently signed it. The Mawema trial could not be ignored and led the front page of the *Herald* each day. Behind the scenes the prosecutor complained bitterly to me first, and then to the *Herald*, about my verbatim accounts of the trial. He knew they were accurate; what bothered him was they were *too* accurate. 'You are making the police appear to be a bunch of idiots,' he complained. 'No,' I replied, 'Maisels and the police themselves are doing that.' What had frustrated the prosecutor was that if Maisels and I had not been there, Mawema would almost certainly have lost his case and been hanged. But my reports were being milked by a local freelance agency and used in the overseas newspapers, too, so the outcome was being watched with international interest. Such was the sycophancy of the *Rhodesia Herald* to authority that they took me off the case and I was replaced by a woman reporter with little journalistic experience and no shorthand. The story was immediately dispatched to the middle pages but to my personal satisfaction the prosecutor lost and Mawema was acquitted, thus averting any miscarriage of justice.

Charlie Still had the unenviable task of telling me that I was being pulled out and he did it well. As he tactfully put it, 'You have done such a great job on the trial that we now need you to clean up the city council. We know it's corrupt and we want you to prove it.' I was most suspicious. 'Has the prosecution asked for me to be taken off?' I demanded. Charlie blushed and lied, but the truth was in his eyes.

The council was indeed corrupt and my experience of council reporting with Ferrari was invaluable. A new suburb was to be built for Africans outside Salisbury at Crowborough near the city's crematorium and vast sums of money were involved. The lowest building tender had been put in by the international contractors, Richard Costain, but the tender went to a local firm, Posselt and Coull. The deal meant that African tenants would have to pay an extra ten shillings a month rent, causing financial hell for people already living below the poverty line. I didn't have to be clever to smell and find a rat as Henry Posselt was the previous mayor of Salisbury and even now he was deputy mayor. My campaign exposing the dealings of the council and the lobbying which had taken place by Posselt lasted a month. The exposés were front page leads as the *Herald* had little option but to back me to the hilt. And while it might support the government of the day, this did not extend to the city council. After a month, the council called an emergency meeting, rescinded its decision, and gave the contract to Costain. Posselt resigned and the name Crowborough was changed to Mufakose, partly because it was an African name but also to ensure that no one would be reminded of the corruption.

Another former mayor had built a dam which collapsed while I was covering the council, causing extensive flooding of houses. He was upset that I didn't report his farewell party whereas he should have been grateful.

Being taken off the Mawema trial didn't stop me watching the African political scene. Joshua Nkomo returned from his voluntary exile and thousands of Africans throughout the country lined the streets to greet him. A meeting was held at Stoddardt Hall in one of the townships and he was already on the platform when I arrived. A teenager, Sketchley Samkange, whispered to Nkomo who was addressing the meeting and Nkomo stopped his speech. Every face in the hall turned in my direction and I felt like an intruder, the one white face amongst a seething mass of blacks. I hadn't even seen Nkomo before and wondered what had been said about me to stop the oration. Sketchley came down from the stage and walked the length of the hall to where I was standing. He took me by the hand and led me up on to the stage to meet the big man. Amid a deafening applause, Nkomo warmly shook hands and said a few complimentary words to the audience about my reporting. For me, the incident was deeply embarrassing as I was strictly neutral and intended to remain that way but a chair and table were quickly found and I sat down to cover the proceedings from the stage, like an honoured guest. It was the last place I wanted to be. Looking around, I could see there were no white secret police present but their black colleagues would be there and from now on the reports they took would be accurate. As a direct result of the Mawema trial it became mandatory for every public political meeting to be tape recorded. The likeable Sketchley Samkange was drowned a few months later during a fishing trip on Lake Malawi.

Occasionally I'd go into the Highfield township to meet a man who telephoned to see me. Our drab rendezvous was at a small, dusty Dickensian store which sold bacon, eggs, cabbage, cooking pots, shirts, trousers, dresses, shoes, cold Cokes and rusting tins of food. Paraffin was a popular commodity and children frequently arrived clutching dented petrol cans or bottles which would be filled from an old drum with a leaking tap. Beneath the tap was a bowl to catch the drips, thus ensuring that the store was a potential incinerator. The man I met was a bespectacled nationalist party spokesman and we'd have a soft drink while we talked and even eat a dubious cheese roll. At that time I believe that I was the only white journalist living in the country who knew him to talk to, and probably who'd ever heard of him. He never looked me in the eye, always turning his gaze from one side to the other and because of this I didn't trust him but some people explained it was an African custom not to look into the eyes of someone they considered superior. I didn't believe a word of it but I did recognise that behind his spectacles was a well-educated (far better than I'd had the chance to be) intellectual but a very ruthless and arrogant man. Years later we met at his brother's grubby home and as we sat in the kitchen with squawking chickens running around our feet, it was clear that after eleven years in detention he hadn't remembered me and he now gazed straight into my eyes with extreme confidence. I thought of that little store and its ever-pervading smell of paraffin; of the dingy house and the hens when I was listening to the BBC news and an announcement that President Robert Mugabe would be dining with the Queen.

On a visit to Zimbabwe I'd see this now corrupt despot who succeeded in turning a lush, well organised country into a land of chaos, fear and destitution when a cavalcade of outriders passed followed by three cars, (one containing Mugabe) a truck load of troops and an ambulance. We had to stop the car or risk being shot or severely beaten up, something that had nearly happened to my little grandson when my daughter stopped near Mugabe's residence to pick up her husband. A guard walked down the road and menacingly ordered her to move on while, at the same time he smashed the butt of his rifle against the car, and aimed at the quickly withdrawn fingers of four-year-old Tim. Confided little Tim to me as the cavalcade passed us when I was in Zimbabwe on a visit, 'That's the president.'

'Yes,' I replied.

In January 2002, Tim visited Zimbabwe from England and was driving with friends from Lake Kariba when their car was stopped by Mugabe's so-called 'war veteran' thugs. Fortunately, they got away lightly.

A Gun-Crazed Wife and the Rescue of Some Very Brave Children

I was always the first journalist to arrive at the *Rhodesia Herald* offices but as I pushed open the heavy brown swing doors one morning I was surprised to see someone there before me. She was rummaging through the desk drawers of a colleague, Ian Mills, and as I entered she quickly snatched something lying on top of the desk and turned to face me: it was then I recognised his wife. She was smartly dressed in a pale eggshell-blue suit but it wasn't her outfit that caught my attention. My eyes fell on her beautiful right hand with its long classical fingers and I was hypnotized by the index finger: it was curled around a sliver of grey metal – the trigger of a Berretta. Jill was pointing the gun at my temple. 'Hey, what's this all about?' I asked, my brain racing to assess the surrealistic situation which instantly reminded me of my confrontation with the knife-carrying youth in Bexley, 'Where's Ian?' she demanded. 'Ian? How should I know?'

She looked at me coldly and there was murder in her hazel eyes. 'He phoned to say he was going out last night for a drink with you!'

'I don't know what you're talking about,' I answered truthfully but she shook her head and I could tell she suspected a conspiracy to cover up for her husband's philandering. 'He didn't come home and when I drew back the sheets they were stained,' she said. 'He took her to our bed yesterday while I was at work.' Jill had discovered something appalling to any faithful wife – that her husband was being unfaithful. And to add to the insult, her treasured matrimonial bed had been invaded and abused by another woman. The shock had changed her overnight from being a devoted wife into a potential killer. Tears welled into her eyes and the gun wavered slightly but while I felt surprisingly calm and detached, I watched the emotion tightening Jill's wretched face. A greater increase in her own tension would, I knew, transfer itself down to the trigger finger and as I made a step forward to put an avuncular arm around her she stopped me in my tracks. 'Don't move or I'll shoot you!' she snapped. Her eyes told me she meant it. As I'd only been in Africa a couple of months with little time to know my colleagues socially, I had no idea that Ian was paying attention to the sensuous, breathtaking young brunette sitting a few desks away from him on the women's features desk. The first I was aware of it was this very moment, just seconds after I'd entered the cavernous newsroom. Jill had come across as a wife to whom marriage and fidelity meant everything. With mousey hair and a prominent nose which dominated an otherwise featureless face, she was a very nice person but no beauty. Her husband was a likeable young journalist who had briefly introduced me to Jill and I'd wondered even then at the matrimonial match. Slim, tallish with fair wavy hair, he had a confident air with a whisper of the intellectual; I was sure he would be attractive to women especially as he was also a part-time band leader and a good clarinettist. 'Do you really want to shoot him?' I asked.

'Yes!'

It was the wrong question and the wrong answer and as I awaited my fate I watched the knuckle of her long finger grow whiter. My own emotions were mixed: I didn't want to be killed and leave Margery to bring up the children and I would not have liked Jill to be strung up on the gallows for my murder. 'Is he really worth hanging for?'

'I love him!' Love, I thought, the emotion that produces the irrational in all of us; Jill was certainly that and my life hung in the balance because of it.

I guessed that when I entered the room she had been looking for incriminating evidence but love letters were unlikely to have passed between the illicit pair, seeing as they were working almost side by side. 'Can I help you to find what you're looking for?' I asked, clasping at straws in the hope that I might grab the gun. She declined the offer but my mind raced as I kept her talking. If Ian walked through those doors, and he was due to at any second, he would have a bullet smack between the eyes. He had to be stopped yet there was nothing I could do about it as she made me keep my distance. I thought of the war years and the seemingly inane question asked to anyone suffering stress during or after a bombing raid: 'Would you like me to make you a nice cup of tea?' I asked it, and she paused for a moment and her face softened: 'Yes, please,' she said, simply. I held out my hand and said, softly. 'And let me take the gun, too, just in case you accidentally shoot me when I come back. We don't want to spill tea all over the floor!' My humour missed its mark and her face froze again.

'No!'

'Okay, I'll get the tea,' I said and slowly turned to make my way to the swing doors, conscious of the gun pointing at my back. I had to warn Ian...

The doors closed behind me and with relief I stood in the corridor stopping another reporter from entering and told him to call the editor. The editor, a retired police colonel, did not personally enter the field of conflict but his deputy, who had just arrived for work, went pale-faced through the swing doors and talked her into handing him the gun. I waited outside until Ian arrived for work late with his girlfriend, quite oblivious of the drama that was taking place or of the courage of the deputy editor, Malcolm Smith, who had saved his life.

There was some reconciliation but it didn't stop Ian's steamy affair with his mistress and eventually there was a divorce without blood letting. But for the innocent victim of the tryst, Jill, there was worse to follow. Believing that her looks and particularly the nose were responsible for losing her feckless husband to the young Women's Page editor, she decided to have a nose job. This was such a complete failure that the long proboscis, which had given her face and herself character, was reduced to a budgerigar's beak and she flew to Johannesburg to escape the double humiliation of losing both her husband and her nose!

My truly uncanny knack of being on the spot at the right time happened yet again when one quiet evening when I was walking with Margery close to the main Salisbury police station. I was taking her out for a Chinese meal to her favourite restaurant. 'The cowboys are at it again,' I said with a grin as we heard the wail of a police siren approaching at speed along nearby Railway Avenue. 'They're like children with new toys,' Margery smiled back. 'It's just as well they're not armed, they'd be shooting up the town!' The words died on her lips as a shot rang out. In less than a second a patrol car turned the corner, sped across the road, mounted the pavement, leapt a false moat and crashed into the wall of the police station. Behind came another police car, the one with the siren. I turned to Margery and shrugged before hurrying across the road, 'Go on to the restaurant and I'll see you there in a while,' I called back. It would be another late meal; she knew all about them. Margery may have stopped me on our honeymoon from reporting the break-in at Canterbury Cathedral but that had been only an initial warning to her of the sort of person she had married. As I stood by, a man was eased out of the crashed car and carried into the station on a stretcher where he died twenty minutes later. I entered the police station to discover the dead man was actually a policeman and that this was another domestic scene only this time the results were a double tragedy. The policeman had quarrelled with his wife who then left the house declaring, 'I'm going home to mother!' He then followed her to his mother-in-law's, stood on the lawn and cold bloodedly shot his wife through the French windows; she dropped dead on the lounge carpet at her mother's feet.

What happened next was, I suspect, unique in police history worldwide. After the devastated mother telephoned for help there was the astonishing scene of one police car chasing another but the following car driver was reluctant to close in as caution had overtaken any thoughts of valour, as the murderer was known to be a marksman! Perhaps the gunman had intended to give himself up and might have done so if he hadn't been chased, for he was heading straight for the police station. As the chase continued at high speed along Railway Avenue the errant policeman used his gun for the second time, shooting himself in the head – the shot we heard.

I telephoned the *Herald* to dictate the story in true Fleet Street fashion only to be met with the frustration of being in a backwater. 'Sorry, Reg, we don't have any room for it in the paper this evening,' came the night news editor's voice. 'We might find some space for it tomorrow.' In disgust I telephoned SAPA, the local news agency subscribed to by Reuters and the Associated Press, and the story was published in Britain and America before it was seen in

Rhodesia. I was wryly amused at being paid ten shillings by SAPA for my trouble and immediately returned the cheque, suggesting it be sent to charity. Had the incident taken place in London it would have been worth a few hundred pounds, even in those days.

The present-day attempt in Africa to seduce men into using condoms as part of the great highly unsuccessful anti-AIDS drive must inevitably come up against major difficulties in rural areas of Africa where the disease, like Man, is said to have been cradled. I'm basing this assessment on the true story told to me in an interview with a woman who did much work to further family planning amongst the indigenous population, the comely Mrs Paddy Spillhouse. We were discussing the problems of educating Africans into the advantages of having small families, instead of something like ten to twelve children per wife. Politics were against Paddy as African nationalists proclaimed it was a plot by the whites to reduce the multiplying African population. She found, however, that black women were generally enthusiastic towards family planning for having spent most of their married lives in pregnancy, they felt it was time to enjoy some respite. But nationalism was not Paddy's only problem; ignorance too played its part. One couple went to see her and the wife made it abundantly clear that she was not interested in any more offspring. This having been established, Paddy gave a talk on the various preventative measures that could be taken and the lady, suspicious of the pill and the loop, settled for the condom which had been produced. Paddy placed the condom on the husband's thumb to demonstrate how it worked. Sombrely the couple took away several packs-of-three and they were not seen again for six months. When they returned it was a very belligerent wife, obviously heavy with child, who complained that the white man's magic had not worked. The proof was in the pudding! Paddy was puzzled, 'Did you do as I instructed and put on the condom?' she asked the man. 'Yes,' he replied with a frown, 'I haven't taken it off.' With that, he produced his thumb.

Soon after my arrival in Africa I discovered a group of people who were a particular embarrassment to the whites and were shunned from society. Many Africans didn't want to know them either yet they were the result of a blending of the two races who had come together without condoms – the Coloureds. As in South Africa, they proudly considered themselves to be a separate race of Coloureds but only in the time of the civil war that was to come was the loyalty of the Coloureds ever wanted – by both sides. Some were called up to fight for the continuance of white dominance while others joined the African nationalist movements. Such was the tragedy of the forthcoming civil war that the brothers of some soldiers were hanged as terrorists.

The leader of their community was a softly spoken and courteous man, Gerry Raftopolos, and I occasionally called at his home where I was made very welcome. Unlike Gerry, his wife, who became a member of Zimbabwe parliament after independence, was fired with a militancy born of deep resentment. I liked her too and understood the reason for the chip on her shoulder for she had been a little girl who had known her dad and, like most little girls, had wanted to identify herself with him. Years ago, it was the practice that Coloured and African people must get off the pavement and on to the road if a white man or woman was walking towards them. 'Whenever my father came along my mother and I would have to leave the pavement and he wouldn't condescend to even spare us a glance even though he knew who we were,' she confided to me. Sometimes she would go to her father's house and look longingly across his large beautifully landscaped garden but she was never allowed past the gate. The experience of rejection by her dad built up the deep resentment that would eventually take her into politics.

This hypocrisy towards the Coloureds struck me when I was given a homily by Charlie Still after I visited a school in their Arcadia township; a name given by a cynical wag as there was nothing pastoral about it. I interviewed a lady teacher, Miss Selous, and her name rang bells: Frederick Courteney Selous was a world-famous hunter and there had been the corpses of thousands of butchered elephants to prove his dexterity with a gun. He had led the 1890 Pioneer Column of the first white settlers up from South Africa into what eventually became Rhodesia. 'Were you related to him?' I asked. 'Yes,' said Miss Selous, 'he was my grandfather.'

She invited me into her home to look at some of the relics she had of him and they were so interesting that I went back to the office to write the story. I strolled over to the news editor and told him of my discovery of an actual descendant of Selous. Charles Still looked at me benignly; it was clear the newcomer from England still had not grasped the realities of Africa, one of which was not to admit to visiting the home of a single Coloured woman, not even as a journalist. 'Reg, that's a good story and it would be marvellous to find the granddaughter of Selous, but it just isn't true,' he said. There was something about his patronising voice and manner which warned me that I was about to be delivered another piece of bigotry and I bristled: 'What do you mean, "it isn't true"?'

'Selous was a very highly respected man in this country, a friend of the American president, Theodore Roosevelt, and he didn't go around having it off with African women,' said Charles. 'He wasn't that sort of person.' It wasn't for me to question how the news editor knew anything about Selous's sex life, but I posed the question, 'Then how did she get her name?' Charles smiled indulgently and I felt my heckles rising. 'When you've been here for a while, Reg, you will find that many African servants have a tremendous respect for their white employers and even name their children after them.' I accepted that this might happen as some African children *did* bear English names but pointed out that as she was Coloured, either her father or grandfather had to be white or Asian. The observation irritated Charles, possibly because of its simple logic; it caused the mask to slip a little to bring out the true South African attitude in him towards recognition of any sexual integration of the races having taken place by whites, especially those they revered. 'Just take it from me that she is not the granddaughter of Courteney Selous!'

'Okay, Charles, if you say so,' I said, 'but tell me, how do you explain her having some of his possessions?' The news editor asked me to explain: 'Well, for starters, she owns his guns. She showed them to me.' Charles looked startled for there had to be exceptional reasons for anyone other than a white to get a licence to possess a gun and the fact that she had shown them to a journalist proved that Miss Selous had nothing to hide. I was about to walk away and write the story but Charles was not finished. 'That still doesn't prove that the guns belonged to Selous,' he said. 'Really?' I was equally irritated that my word had been questioned like a cub reporter. I wrote the story but, as expected, it was never used despite the conclusive proof that the guns had belonged to Selous – his name was engraved on them! Much later I was to learn, although it was never publicised in Rhodesia, that Selous was recorded as fathering a child by an African lady of the court of Lobengula, the Matabele king whom Cecil Rhodes had cheated out of his country in the name of Queen Victoria. As for the guns, I don't know what happened to them but in the materialistic world of today they would be worth a great deal of money.

I'd gone to Arcadia at Charles's suggestion to look for any possible stories as this was another area not visited by *Herald* journalists. The first story stared me in the face as I drove into the small township; a disused quarry pit on an area known as Nicodemus Plot which was deep, full of water and very dangerous. I learned from the locals that several people, including children, had fallen in and drowned and I was taken by one resident to see a man who was something of a local hero. He was small and thin and his clothes could have been handed down by a charity; a shy nobody who lived alone like a hermit because life had seemingly passed him by. Yet this same man frequently risked his life by diving into the murky depths of the pit to save people's lives despite two handicaps: he could only dog paddle; and he suffered serious spasms of epilepsy. Charles Still backed me into campaigning to the council to clean up the quarry area and thanks to the *Herald* initiative the pit was quickly filled in. My personal satisfaction was that the life saver was presented with an award by the Royal Humane Society and that as a journalist, I'd been directly responsible. No one had bothered to mention this to me until long after the event otherwise I would have attended the ceremony but by the time I got to hear about it the man had died during an epileptic fit.

While I was finding good and even worthwhile stories, deep down inside me was the gnawing despondency that I had thrown away my whole career, that everything I had worked for was to finish up with me as a hack on a second-rate newspaper. I hadn't realised how much I would miss the vitality of Fleet Street journalism. Conversely, there was the wonderful consolation that Robert's asthma attacks were on the wane and both Annette and Peter had none at all.

In order to collect my thoughts and perhaps see if there were stories outside the capital city, I decided to take Robert on a tour of Southern Rhodesia. I soon learned that much of the countryside was covered by strip roads – two strips of tarmac for the tyres to grip on to – which called for intense concentration when driving for hundreds of miles. The main roads were fine and I was on one of these nearing the last leg of our journey when we came at night to a sign marked 'Deviation'. The main road, it appeared, was being widened and I turned off on to a strip road but despite the brilliant half-moon under the clear southern sky, I missed the turn-off back on to the main highway and just carried on for mile after mile. I was quite lost and anxious to get home, knowing that Margery would become worried by our non-appearance. My tired thoughts were simply that if I drove long enough I must come to some sort of town sooner or later but the gnawing question was, when? Perhaps the hand of Fate had taken over and pointed me along that strange path, a road that I didn't even know existed. Whatever the reason, I was heading towards an unscheduled rendezvous with both life and death and by another extraordinary coincidence I even had the music for the occasion.

To help keep me awake and to concentrate we began singing and while I kept trying to think of different songs, one theme kept returning, 'The Ghost Riders in the Sky'. I'd been concerned at the number of low, narrow bridges we kept coming across with the ominous warning signs such as 'Deadly Hazard' but there was no reason to believe that the one we were now approaching would be any different from the rest. The bridges had no barriers on the sides, just evenly placed marker bricks indicating the edges and as with their larger counterparts on Alpine passes in Europe, they were painted white. Halfway across, with eyes concentrated on the narrow edges, I glimpsed to the left when my headlights picked up the outline of a vehicle in the river below. Its wheels were in the air and I wondered if the person in the wreck had been badly hurt. That it might be a recent accident did not occur to me, not even when I noticed that white marking stones towards the far end of the bridge were missing. As I looked at the overturned van again, two faces appeared at the water's edge and my dulled brain told me it was a strange time of night to be examining an old wreck. Then one waved and my brain clicked into gear; something was wrong, very wrong. I waved back before carrying on over the perilous bridge.

As I reached the other side I swung the car round and drove down towards the river so that the headlights dipped down to the bank but because of the steepness of the slope, the trees and the scrub blocking the view, they did not pick up the wreck or those standing below. Grabbing a torch, with Rob behind me, I edged my way down the bank. Whatever I may have half expected to find could not compare with the scene that came into the focus of the torchlight on that memorable night. Before me were the pallid white faces of two little children who were standing together holding hands. The boy, who had a nasty gash on his face was wearing blue striped pyjamas while the girl was in a pink nightdress. Both were soaking wet and it was clear they had been in the river. 'Where are your parents?' I asked, shocked that they should be left alone while their mother and father had presumably gone for help. Seven-year-old Alan Somers, his wet pyjamas covered in blood, looked back at me and said in a quiet, matter-of-fact voice, 'Daddy is dead!' He pointed to the water. 'Rob, help me get some blankets from the car,' I ordered, and we raced up the bank while the two children remained without moving.

Shock, I half thought to myself, was why they stood there so close to the water and not beside the road but when I went back with the blankets I took a closer look at them and saw why they hadn't moved. In addition to Alan's facial injury, I saw his hip bone protruding through the flesh above his pyjama trousers. I marvelled that while he must be suffering excruciating agony, brave little Alan was showing no sign of it. Ingrid, his sister, who was only six years old, had a badly gashed finger but was otherwise all right and she, too, showed no sign of distress. I carried Alan up to the car while Robert brought Ingrid and then I went back down to the upturned van to confirm that there was no one else trapped inside. Close to where the children had been standing was the outstretched body of a man lying on his back and as I shone the torch I could see that his head was resting on a rock in the water while his lifeless eyes stared back at me. The hour was 1 a.m. and the post-mortem would show he had died at 10.30 p.m. As we drove off for help, Alan told me that he and his sister had been asleep in the back of the van when it went over the bridge. 'We landed upside down in the water and I pulled Ingrid out to the bank,' he said. It seems he had been able to use his legs initially and the broken one had seized up after he had made sure his sister was safe.

The trauma of waking up in a river to find their father dead beside them, and then to stand beside the waterway for two and a half hours at night with only the body for company was greater than any fearful nightmare I'd experienced as a child. In reality, they had *lived* my nightmares. There were crocodiles in the river and the children knew there was a very real threat of an attack by leopards, lions and other nocturnal predators. Later, I was told by a doctor that if I had not found them, the children would almost certainly have died from exposure by the morning. I hadn't the first idea where I was and neither had the children but my immediate reaction was that they needed medical treatment urgently for both injuries and shock. They also needed dry clothes, even though they were wrapped in warm blankets. After six miles we came to a group of houses. 'Umvuma,' said Alan as he recognised a small mining town which I'd never heard of. I found a house which served as the local police station and hammered on the front door but there was no reply. 'Wake up,' I shouted but it became clear that when people go to sleep in Umvuma they don't believe in waking up until dawn. I hammered and shouted for ten minutes before the policeman roused from his slumbers and another ten minutes for a doctor to arrive.

'We'll put them into my car and take them to Enkeldoorn Hospital,' said the doctor. 'With his leg like that?' I said, taken aback. 'It's better they should stay together with me.' The doctor was driving a Chevy, and so was I and I'd expected a gentle run to the hospital so as not to cause more pain to the children. The quick spin of the doctor's rear wheels was early warning of what was to follow and we did not travel under 70 mph at any stage on the strip road. It's fine for him, I thought, he knows the bloody road and has his headlights on full. I didn't know the road and my lights were on dip so as not to blind him in his rear-view mirror. I knew, too, that one of my tyres had become frayed which I could handle travelling at a reasonable speed but that if it blew at this pace we could all become ghost riders in the sky. After thirty miles we reached our destination where the children were taken into casualty. Not once did they cry or complain of the pain they were suffering even though neither had been given sedatives or pain-killing injections.

With Rob beside me, I slowly drove the final hundred miles home but we didn't indulge in any more singing.

Armed with bags of sweets, we travelled down to Enkeldoorn Hospital the following weekend and went to the children who were sitting up in their beds. Beside them was a woman dressed from head to foot in widow's weeds. To see her there came as a shock. I had realised they had lost their father but hadn't given much thought to the lady beside the bed and the black attire came as a sharp realisation of her loss. Both children were very quiet, as calm as they had been when we first met and even though I'd introduced myself, it wasn't until we were leaving that realisation dawned upon the mother who the two unknown visitors were. 'It was you who found them?' she asked. 'Yes. They were very brave.'

'Thank you,' she said, simply. Not wishing to intrude any more than five minutes, we said our goodbyes and walked to the ward door. We left as we had met, complete strangers who were not likely to see each other again. We would never have met in the first place if a wooden sign with a pointed finger had not caused me to turn off from the main road and traverse that very long, lonely road.

In the bar of the old Meikle's Hotel in Salisbury where lean prospectors of another era parted with gold dust over the counter in return for a few days of blissful drunkenness, I was taken by a colleague to meet someone who had been telling a yarn that had engrossed all who listened. 'If you really want to know something about what goes on in the bundu you'd better come with me,' said the colleague. 'There's an old prospector who has one hell of a story to tell.' It was a tale cloaked in one of the many mysterious legends of the African interior; an awesome story that ended in tragedy. As I was introduced to the storyteller (I'll call him Fred) I could see he was a true man of the bush, a prospector who survived years in the sun through sheer willpower and a determination to be rich. His flint-hardened darting eyes were set into a face of untanned hide and as he nodded his head to acknowledge my outstretched hand those eyes flashed like tiny inset diamonds. The breast pocket of his creased sun-bleached shirt was stained by samples of fool's gold, pyrite and other minerals he'd stumbled across in his relentless quest for the big bonanza which would buy a palace, a place where he could rest and probably die as a bored social outcast.

He told me he had farmed at Inyanga and while there he had tried to climb a sacred mountain named Muozi. Inyanga is a beautiful mountainous region in the country's Eastern Highlands and he described the mountain as having a flat top from which the local chief would have subjects hurled to their deaths should they cross his path. 'One day I set out with the local Native Commissioner to climb the mountain,' the prospector told me. 'We camped on the foothills and during the night the Chief's Council came to us with a warning to stay away. They said Muozi was sacred and that if we attempted to climb, the spirit of the mountain would beat us back with heavy rain. If we continued, we would die.' The pair ignored the warning but as they prepared to climb next morning they were barred by the chief himself. He repeated the ominous threat of the spirit but while the chief had power over all his subjects he was subservient to the Native Commissioner who ordered him to move aside. A quarter of the way up, the pair were disturbed by the rumbling of thunder and looked up to see heavy black clouds centred on the mountain top, the only clouds in sight. Soon they were in trouble as lightning struck the rocks around them, attracted by their iron content. Then the heavens opened and within seconds the two men were saturated. Believing it to be an out-of-season tropical storm which would soon pass, they agreed to move on upwards but had inched forward only a few paces when they found themselves staring into the eyes of a huge leopard which glared down at them baring its naked fangs. It was a rare confrontation, for the leopard is an animal of the night.

The old prospector quickly downed his beer at the very recollection of it and I ordered another pint. 'The Native Commissioner had a rifle which he aimed at the leopard and pulled the trigger. The gun didn't fire and so he pulled the trigger again, again and again but nothing happened,' he recalled. It was a touch-and-go stand-off as the hapless pair with a defective weapon faced one of the most malevolent carnivores in Africa. With the menacing predator poised on a rock above them, a tropical storm all around and no protection from either, they edged their way back down the mountain.

Said the prospector, 'When we got to the bottom the chief was waiting for us, grinning from ear to ear. He looked at our soaked clothing and then pointed to the ground which was bone dry. The sun, too, was shining brilliantly. The Native Commissioner then pointed his rifle to the sky and pulled the trigger – it fired immediately!' The prospector had reason to be convinced about the voracity of the legend. 'Two days later my companion died of pneumonia caused by the drenching,' he said. 'I am very lucky to be alive.' This was too good to ignore; a Tarpeian forbidden rain mountain with a forbidding legend. 'Could you find Muozi again?' I asked. It had been forty years since he had farmed in that area. 'I reckon so.'

'Then let's climb it. How about next weekend?' His whole demeanour changed as one shaking hand clutched a scrawny neck while the other helped to down his beer. He then said hoarsely, 'Go *back*?' He looked at me before his eyes fell on to the empty glass and I nodded to the barman before answering, 'I'm free next weekend and it sounds an interesting story. If you don't want to go up I'll climb it myself but you can show me where it is.' It was a trap and he knew it. For years he had lived off the story but now, in addition to putting a beer where his mouth was, he'd been challenged to prove the efficacy of it in front of the bar, many of whose regulars had heard the story several times before. Fear crossed his face, the fear of a man who was not afraid of dying and was not afraid of wandering through thousands of miles of dangerous country by himself but who knew the dark forces that inhabited Inyanga (it means 'The Place of the Witchdoctors'); the same area that inspired Rider Haggard to write *King Solomon's Mines*.

Although he was in his sixties, the prospector was as wiry and tough as a steel hawser. As a deep believer in African superstitions, some of them taught to him by his black wife, I reckoned there could be more problems for him in defying sorcery than the physical problem of climbing. We set out early on a Saturday morning and drove 200 miles to Inyanga and then, after travelling a further forty miles on a dirt road beneath a mountain range, we stopped beside a dried-up hot spring. Sulphur had turned some nearby stones green and believing he had struck pay dirt, Fred furtively slipped some of them into his pocket, hoping that I wouldn't notice.

'What are they?' I asked. He looked hard at me and then whispered with reverence, 'Emeralds.' I'd seen emeralds in their raw state surrounded by matrix and they looked nothing like these. They had been produced as evidence in a fraud case at Salisbury Magistrates' Court where the accused was found guilty of trying to salt a worked-out mine. The attempt to defraud had taken place in autumn and the mindless fraudster had thrown the raw emeralds on top of fallen leaves which defied the credulity of the intended buyer. Fred listened suspiciously to my description of emeralds but didn't believe a word. It surprised me that he hadn't seen them uncut before; perhaps his search had always been for gold. If he believes they are emeralds, I thought, no wonder he's still looking for his El Dorado. My interest was in something else by the dried spring. Several boulders had been placed symmetrically only yards from each other and as they appeared to be facing east I pondered whether it had been a Muslim burial ground. If so, it would give some small credence to those who claim that the world-renowned Zimbabwe Ruins, which inspired Rider Haggard to write his second famous novel, *She*, were built by Arabs and not Africans. It is a suggestion which is taboo today in the country they now call Zimbabwe and something on which I have no strong views. One personal observation I have, however, is that when Muslims face the east to pray, they flagrantly raise their posteriors to the west!

We drove on until the prospector pointed and I saw a flat-topped mountain which was not as tall as I had expected. Once it would have been of formidable height but millions of years of erosion had given it the appearance of having been pressed down into the earth by an unseen hand until it resembled a squat domestic ironing board. As darkness fell I looked around and wondered at the enormity and beauty of the heavens that could be seen so clearly. A shooting star had dropped earthwards just as the cicadas ceased their noisy tumbril vibrations to create an eerie silence as if commanded by a conductor's raised baton. Then the prospector spoke, 'Here they come!' His keen eyes had not been on the stars; instead they had picked out flaming torches in the distance which slowly, menacingly, moved across the veld towards us. I hadn't been expecting guests and asked, 'Who are they?'

'The Chief's Council,' came the reply. 'They know what we're up to and are coming to warn us not to climb the mountain.' It was half an hour before the grim-faced men arrived, their ebony faces and the whites of their eyes and teeth gleaming by the light of their flaming torches. These were Manica tribesmen and I could see their faces were more distinctive than those of the Mashonas and their long noses and thin lips hinted at an Arab influence. They greeted us cordially but the only warmth I felt came from our dull fire which they crouched around. Fred was fluent in the Manica dialect and they all spoke at length. Then came a long argument and an hour passed before they rose slowly shaking their heads and I looked at their eyes as they stood to stare back at us like doomed men. As quietly as they arrived, they melted into the shadows with only the flames from their torches to give indication of their whereabouts and soon they were mere specks against Muozi that now loomed large and forbidding in the stillness of the night. 'They warned me that the mountain is sacred and that we will be beaten back by heavy rain, or die at the top,' said the prospector. Nothing had changed in forty years!

From the distance came a sound, deep and throbbing, which echoed around the mountain and through the vast chamber of the African interior. It came from a large unseen drum and gave warning by bush telegraph to the surrounding area of our proposed intrusion into the sanctity of something they held more sacred than all else: the mountain. Is this really happening to me? I wondered, as I felt a tingle of excitement. More drums all around us began to pass on the message in unison with a pulsating beat and I pondered if impis might creep up in the night and spear us to death rather than let us attempt to break the timeless spell of this hallowed place. Here in Inyanga anything could happen, a frightening place where the witchdoctor held an unhealthy sway over all the tribespeople with such awesome power that even though patrolling policemen had discovered the entrails of ritually slaughtered babies hung out on trees, they had never received a complaint from bereaved parents. I asked, 'Did the council say the chief would stop us in the morning?'

'Yes,' said the prospector, uneasily. He had committed himself and had to go on, but he remembered the past; that his companion had died because they had ignored the chief's warning. Perhaps Fred had a charmed life. That was cold comfort to me now that I was his companion. I said, 'We'd better try to get some sleep.'

'With all that fucking noise?' he snapped back. His voice was gruff, mingled with a trace of fear: I knew that deep down he was a very disturbed man. As the fire gave out little heat and we were out in the open without tents, I felt cold and vulnerable. Perhaps it was better if the flames were allowed to die than to act as a beacon pin-pointing our exact location. The drums continued their vigil all night, keeping us awake and as I watched the moonlit bush for any sign of movement, I wondered if I would live to see the dawn. When it eventually arrived the sun catapulted skywards to quickly disperse our misgivings but as we ate our meagre breakfast of fresh fruit we knew that hundreds of eyes were upon us, brown eyes, impassively waiting and watching. The air was charged with electricity, like the lull before a tropical storm. But where would the storm break? On the mountain itself? 'Let's go,' I said, anxious to get moving. Waiting, for me, has always been worse than the action and I wanted to start climbing. It hadn't occurred to me until then that Allan Quatermain could have been a pint-sized reporter.

When we approached the mountain a solitary figure barred our way. I had expected him to be in a leopard skin holding an assegai with a shield, possibly made from lion or zebra skin. Instead, he was fully dressed in the traditional scarlet uniform of a chief loyal to Her Imperial Majesty, Queen Victoria, which was topped incongruously with a white pith helmet. A brass chain hung around his neck holding a large medallion which symbolised his office and as we walked towards him he held up his hand for us to halt. 'You must go no further, otherwise you will die,' he told us. 'If you attempt to climb the mountain you will walk to your deaths.' He repeated the rest of the message of the past. The prospector was still nervous but was angry, too. He had lived with this legend for most of his adult life and he had known it to be true but didn't want to be reminded. There had been too many times when it had haunted him and now he must break the spell once and for all, or die in the attempt. 'We're going,' he said and we walked past the chief in silence: now we were fully committed!

Our ascent began in brilliant sunshine, a perfect day for climbing and right at the beginning we came across stone terracing from a long-lost age. There was no time for close examination for we had to beat the clock and whatever else we might come across, and be down again before dark. The terracing was a nuisance as it had to be scrambled over which caused scratching and bruising. For me, some of the terracing was high enough to be a climb in itself. 'Look at that!' I called when we were a third of the way up and had come to a long plateau. Spread out before me was a huge carpet of colourful wild protea, the national flower of South Africa. This was the first and only time I have seen it growing wild in any other country and there was something else, too. 'What's that over there?' asked the keen-eyed prospector. We walked across the carpet and were soon staring down at a slave pit which was in mint condition, as if it had just been built. The only other such pits in the area, which I've subsequently visited many times, have always been very old. 'Slave pit' is the name given by Europeans to unusual circular pit dwellings, their structure originally thought to have been used for housing slaves by the Moors of North-West Africa. Perhaps the possible graves I found earlier might hold the key. It is likely that the structures were actually used for keeping goats or other small animals. Access is gained through a lintel entrance which leads to a tunnel before opening into a circular pit which is cunningly drained so that it never holds water. The other pits I have been to always had the stone top entrances worn, as if guards with curvaceous buttocks had sat on them over the centuries. This one was different as there was no sign of wear.

We had climbed further up the mountain than my companion and his late friend achieved and so far there wasn't a cloud in sight but I noticed, as we continued our ascent, that he kept looking upwards nervously. 'That's interesting,' I commented, staring down at my feet. We were nearing the summit and I stooped and began scraping at the ground: ashes! Why would anyone build a fire up here, and how long ago? This had not been a one-off bonfire, the ashes ran deep and as I scraped something glistened in the sun – a red glass bead. Then there was another. Soon I had a handful of coloured beads and began to wonder how they came to be there. They were not local and the find suggested to me a trade at some time with the east coast of Africa, suggesting they had come down the East African coast to Mombassa or further south by Arab dhow, originally from India. I could see that my companion wasn't the slightest bit interested as he kept looking towards the summit, only a hundred yards away, and at the sky. We moved forward and upward until we reached the top without incident; I had half hoped to be fighting through an electric storm but that great ball of fire was still visible in the sky and there wasn't even the wisp of a cloud. I looked over the edge and drew back quickly at the realisation that the drop was sheer. Spread out before us was land as far as the eye could see and it was as I had always imagined a moonscape to be. The climb took place before the American Apollo astronauts landed on the moon to send back happy snaps of the lunar surface first hand; even so their pictures were not unlike the Inyanga I saw that day. Fred turned to me and there was moisture in his eyes and excitement in his voice as he held out his hand with the cry, 'We've done it!' As we shook hands he suddenly threw his arms around me and I could feel that he was trembling with an emotion which would have been rare for he was not an obviously emotional man.

Before we left I scouted around a wooded area at the summit and found large clay pots, or urns, with holes in them, one in each. There was also a rusted wide-faced spearhead and I called the prospector across for his opinion and he froze in his tracks. 'Those are burial urns,' he said. 'So that's it,' I answered. 'This must be the chiefs' burial ground.' Everything was falling into place. Traditionally, when a chief is buried a large black oxen is killed and so at Muozi it would have been taken up the mountain alive and then ceremonially slaughtered. There would be hungry people to feed and that would explain the ashes: it was a barbecue site that had been used for centuries. 'It's time we went,' suggested the prospector as he looked anxiously at his watch. We had chanced our arm quite enough; we didn't want to be trapped overnight on this high-rise cemetery as the legend would not be broken until we got down safely. Slowly we made our descent of the sacred Mount Muozi and at the bottom, just on the foothills, we came to a hut with the sign, 'Marist Brothers Mission'. We entered, and sitting at a table was a man in an off-white cassock who introduced himself in a strong French-Canadian accent as Brother Ernest.

Overcome with pent-up excitement, Fred spilled out the story of the terrifying legend he'd related in the bar: the death of his friend forty years before; how the scene of the chief's council and the arrival of the chief himself had been re-enacted. The Roman Catholic brother listened with deep interest and then smiled as the prospector told of the superb panoramic view at the top. 'Yes,' said Brother Ernest. 'The view is very beautiful.' There was a stillness in the air as I watched the prospector's face pale with the slow realisation that the thunderbolt he'd been expecting at the top had just arrived in the confines of this small wooden hut at the bottom. He spluttered, 'What do you mean?'

'The view at the top, it really is quite beautiful.'

Fred's face had undertaken a metamorphosis and he turned into a gargoyle as he hissed the words between gritted teeth in a manner that suggested gases escaping from Vesuvius prior to an eruption. 'How do you know that?' Without realising the agony and the torment that was fomenting inside my companion's head, Brother Ernest replied, 'I like to climb it at weekends!'

The final words were too much for Fred who stood up and smashed his fist on the rickety wooden table that stood precariously between himself and the man of God. He then uttered three words I had never expected to hear in such circumstances for he denied both the priest's celibacy and integrity.

I've climbed the mountain twice subsequently, once with my chum, Richard Lindley, formerly of ITN and BBC's *Panorama* programme, together with a chubby little pink-faced girl named Polly Toynbee. Polly struggled hard to get to the top and needed encouragement but she was gutsy and she made it. I'd quickly organised the trip for her as a brief outing to relieve some of the pressure she was under after Richard, who was currently working for *Panorama*, approached me to help get her out of Salisbury for a break as she feared she was about to be arrested by Ian Smith's government for her work with Amnesty International. She was expelled immediately on returning to Salisbury after I'd taken her to the summit but I believe her mountain climb combined with her Amnesty work and its subsequent consequences helped to prepare her for the tough journalistic future that was to lie ahead.

When I returned to the mountain again it was with my son, Rob, and while the mission station had grown beyond recognition, Brother Ernest was still there. I quickly gained the disquieting impression that he was as untamed as some of those wartime French-Canadians who were stationed at Leatherhead, for Brother Ernest had a secret: he was a firebug! There had been no rain for some months and the whole of the Inyanga area was tinder dry. As we walked together through the scrub he kept striking matches and throwing them into the dried grass which was disturbing to me as I've seen many bush fires and know how quickly they can take off. Nearby was a small area of smooth granite and I hurried towards it with my son as the flames began to rise. Soon the fire caught hold and Brother Ernest, now walking by himself and still dropping lighted matches, suddenly realised the danger he was in as flames surrounded him before they raced up the mountain from which Rob and I had just descended. I still have a vivid vision of Brother Ernest in his cassock as he climbed a tree with the flames of damnation raging above and below: a most impressive and symbolic sight.

Other people have climbed Mount Muozi subsequently and, I'm told, have run away in terror when they searched around the chief's burial ground claiming they had heard heavy footsteps coming towards them through the trees, so loud that they could not have been made by human feet on the soft grass and granite.

A member of one such group, businessman Mr Chamiso Mapfunde, told Rob that he had attended the Marist Brothers school and all the children there feared the spirits. With some friends, he nevertheless ventured forth and near the summit they too heard the footsteps and ran away terrified, never daring to return.

I Resign Over Censorship and Become a Congo War Correspondent

The *Rhodesia Herald* was an unparalleled career stepping-stone as I'd been served on a golden plate a rare insight into a country of deep-rooted passions which would eventually result in two rebellions: one of them blacks against whites and the other of whites against their mother country. I had also become rebellious and surprised myself at the depth of my feeling over the compelling need for integrity and fair play, brought about in part by the Mawema trial and the Crowborough affair. These were not petty issues as an innocent man's life had been put on the line in a country which professed to be teaching civilisation, and the capital city's council had sleazily approved a financial rip-off of such magnitude that it would have financially disadvantaged hundreds, even thousands of poor people in order to facilitate the greed of a corrupt company.

The *Herald* itself was not untarnished for although it had given me my lead for a while, its leanings were still towards a dangerous policy of deception which had cocooned the whites into raising hands to shield their eyes like innocent children, truly believing the unpleasant realities would either go away or could be handled without interruption to their paradisiacal lifestyles. Five important stories in a row that I'd written were killed by the deputy editor, Malcolm Smith, and the last was penned after I'd driven along a major highway in Salisbury where I noticed piles of boulders behind trees bordering a cemetery. There was no doubt in my mind why the rocks were there; that a riot was in the offing and they would be thrown through the windscreens of passing cars whose drivers and passengers would be either maimed or killed. I telephoned the police and called for a photographer who took good pictures of policemen throwing the stones over the cemetery fence. The story and pix were an obvious clear warning to motorists to keep their eyes open but when the deputy editor telephoned from home to ask about the stories to be used, he immediately ordered that mine should be killed. This was intolerable for by killing this particular story he was putting people's lives in terrible jeopardy and I strolled over to the chief sub to say the editor himself (whom I never met) had phoned to countermand Smith's order. While I was sure the chief sub didn't believe me, when we made eye contact it was clear that he too, wanted the story to appear and knew that he would be in the clear when the flak hit the fan. With that, the story and pix were displayed prominently and next morning I waited with some trepidation to be called into the editor's office for either a severe dressing down or instant dismissal but to my astonishment nothing happened. Even so, I'd had enough and my letter of resignation did not endear me to the deputy when I complained of 'That frightened little voice which rings up every evening to kill my stories.' I had come to realise just how strongly I was opposed to news censorship and especially self-censorship by the media.

Even while working with Ferrari in England I'd resolved that I would rather go to jail than reveal the names of sources of information so the protection of journalistic freedom was passionately entrenched in my thoughts and beliefs.

Now that I was out of work and out of money and with a wife and three children to support I pondered over my future. The resignation had meant a serious financial loss as the *Herald* demanded that as I had not fulfilled my two-year contract (all the reported events took place in just eighteen months), I must now pay my own fare from England having already paid the family's before I left for Africa. 'I don't understand you,' admonished Margery in desperation. 'Surely you could have just protested and kept your job. What's going to happen to us?' It's difficult to explain principles to a young mother who is totally reliant on her husband working to bring in the rent, food and clothing money. The problem of resigning in Rhodesia at that time was that there was no other newspaper in the country of any consequence outside the Argus group. I have believed, naively perhaps, that if you make an honest stand on your principles and lose your job, something else will turn up. I was wondering what the hell to do next when I met someone who was a well-known voice on the national radio, John Appleby, the Head of News for the Federal Broadcasting Corporation. A smallish, amiable man, John had at one time been seconded by the BBC to Cyprus during the troubles there. The very nature of his work had made him a terrorist target and he was the first journalist I ever knew who admitted to carrying a gun in a war situation. At the time of our meeting I didn't know he knew me and was surprised when he stopped to talk. 'I've heard that you have left the *Herald* and the reasons for it and I wondered if you would care to join the FBC newsroom?' he asked. My best job offers, it seems, occur when people stop me in the street as in the case of Ferrari. 'Are there any restrictions on reporting?' I asked. 'No,' replied John, firmly. 'We don't have censorship.' It was the beginning of a good relationship and I learned with pleasure and astonishment that he was the same John Appleby whose short stories with the scorpion sting-in-the-tail I had read avidly each week on my way home from the *Evening Standard*.

A war in the former Belgian Congo was raging, the prototype of many to follow amongst emergent post-colonial African countries and one of my colleagues, Jim Biddulph, was sent there. In an outstanding report he broadcast on an air raid on the provincial capital of Katanga, Elisabethville, where planes shot up the city. Jim had calmly sat on the veranda of the Leopold II Hotel, speaking into his tape recorder with bullets whistling around him. We were all worried for his safety but were still stunned when we received the shock news: the cherubic face of John Appleby was grave as he spelled out what had happened. A Swiss financier was driving down to Northern Rhodesia in his Land Rover and Jim, anxious to get some tapes to our studios there, hitched a lift. Unarmed, they were driving south when Swedish United Nations troops turned an anti-aircraft gun on to the moving vehicle and shot it to pieces. The financier was killed outright and Jim's condition was critical with a piece of shrapnel lodged in his skull. It was an unforgivable, outrageous, callous and cowardly attack and Sandy Gall mentions in his memoirs that he and fellow journalists, Peter Younghusband and John Monks were also shot at by the Swedes only a couple of hours earlier. Conor Cruise O'Brien, who was in charge of the gung-ho UN force, made no bones that he despised the colonialist Rhodesian Federation but he knew there was only one option open to him – Jim needed urgent medical attention and Salisbury was only one place he could have it. Either to his credit or because the incident had given the UN a bad international press, O'Brien rose to the occasion and ordered his personal aircraft to fly Jim home. I went to the airport to see him brought off the plane and on to an ambulance and then drove at speed to his home to break the news to his wife, Marie.

As I raced along the open road a motorcycle came alongside and I was waved down by a man in a familiar uniform – a speed cop. 'You're the last person I need,' I said. After explaining the situation the policeman declared, 'Thank God Mr Biddulph is safe, sir. I shall personally escort you to the home of Mrs Biddulph. Where does she live?' This was an attitude I felt that all policemen should have towards the media and I was impressed. It was the first (and last) time I had been offered a police outrider escort and the presumption of self-importance almost outweighed the reason for it. Could this really be happening to me and could it last?

We sped along the road and then slowed to make a right turn with the speed-cop's hand smartly outstretched in regulation manner to indicate that he was turning. Another car driver chose this critical moment to overtake and as the policeman started his turn there was the grating sound of metal fusing with tarmac as the motorcycle and cop were sent sprawling. My foot welded to the brake pedal and I was about to get out of my car to offer assistance when the policeman staggered to his feet. 'Are you all right?' I called, anxiously. 'Don't you worry about me, sir, you just go to Mrs Biddulph.' He forced a smile to show that he was taking it bravely and then his face changed and his eyes hardened as he approached the hapless driver of the car that had hit him. Through the rear-view mirror I saw the caring policeman taking out his notepad and pencil; he had only been going to nab me for a mere speeding offence but now, in return for his good deed, he had a bonus!

Jim survived but it was touch and go and when he eventually left hospital it was with a permanent tin plate in his head. I took his place and my flight from Southern to Northern Rhodesia was my first-ever trip in a big white bird and was totally uneventful and any qualms I may have harboured about flying were quickly dispelled. A car was waiting at the airport and I was whisked to the plush Edinburgh Hotel in Kitwe where a room had been booked. This was red carpet treatment and I began to feel like the next sacrificial lamb after Biddulph who would be a hard act to follow. Next morning, a charter plane flown by a legendary African bush pilot, Alan Kearns, was standing by to whisk me across the Congo border to a small air strip in Katanga used by the giant Union Minere copper mine company. A Belgian approached me and said he was the driver of my next transport and suggested I should get in the back. I looked in disbelief. 'You're joking!'

'I'm afraid not. You don't have United Nations accreditation and so I have to smuggle you in.' Our conversation was limited because of the nature of the vehicle but it did seem like a page from Evelyn Waugh's book *Scoop* that the intrepid Cheshire Cheese should start his first assignment as a war correspondent in Africa in the back of a municipal trash cart!

'Sometimes I drive ambulances and sometimes they contain automatic rifles and not people,' said my driver who explained that the guns were for Tshombe's mercenaries. The civil war was being fought following the decision by Moise Tshombe to take the mineral-rich Katanga province away from the rest of the Congo, led by the communist president, Patrice Lumumba.

Not smelling of roses, I entered the Leo Deux Hotel (Leopold II) and was escorted to the hotel bar to be briefed by a group of journalists on the latest situation. 'It's a bit scary here,' said one, darkly. 'Armed African troops often march into the hotel and take people away and they're never seen again.' I went to bed early, hoping to get off to a good start in the morning and as I slept I dreamed of heavy gunfire similar to that I'd experienced during the blitz and it was so loud that I awoke with a start. Someone was banging urgently on my bedroom door. Who would be calling on me at this time of night? Were there troops outside wanting to take me off as a Rhodesian spy? I didn't know and I didn't like the idea of opening the door. 'Who's that?' I shouted. An African voice yelled back in French and my brain clicked into gear. If it had been the United Nations they would have answered in English; if it had been another journalist he wouldn't have banged so hard in the first place. It had to be the Congolese troops! Reluctantly, I opened the door and outside stood a huge African who glared down angrily at me. He began to shout aggressively and pushed at the door, trying to force himself into my bedroom and my bare foot took the shock before I shouldered it shut. The hammering began again and I stood at the door naked and with clenched fists until he went away.

Within an hour I was awakened again and felt oppressively damp and uncomfortable with the sure knowledge that I was not alone in bed. My unclothed body was being shared with others in a humid orgy of blood letting and the bedside lamp revealed bugs, thousands of them that had crawled from hidden crevices and converged on my bedroom for a vampires' nocturnal orgy. The pale blue walls had become a living montage of crawling black lice while others moved en masse over the floor, the bed and me, one lodging itself in my ear. Blood covered the sheets and pillow and every drop of it was mine! As

I leapt from the bed they crackled like breakfast cereal beneath my bare feet and when I frantically brushed them off my skin and returned to the blooded sheets, I decided to leave the light on to discourage further assaults. I felt dirty, really dirty and waited for hours before dawn which came as a blessed sight. I sauntered along the corridor to the bathroom to shower off the blood but as I turned on the tap the shower elicited a choking sound – the death rattle of the town's water supply which had been sabotaged during the hours of darkness. Despondently I wandered back to my bedroom, deciding that the lot of a war correspondent was an unhappy one and was sure this was true when I went to the bedroom basin and the same throttling noise came from the tap. As a discipline I shave every morning and I had no intention of being defeated now. Initiative was called for and after I dressed I went downstairs before returning to my room with several bottles of the only liquid I could find. My first full day as a war correspondent began with shaving and cleaning my teeth in Congolese brewed lager.

The management proved sympathetic and nostalgic about times gone by and the pinafored Belgian housemaid who came to fumigate my bedroom with a tin of insect repellent confided to me with disdain, 'This room was previously occupied by Miss Katanga, our local beauty queen. She was very dirty, we never had bugs before she came here.' Miss Katanga? It explained why one big African had defied death by breaking the curfew to be with the young lady who had previously occupied my room. Because of his anger, I could only guess that in his agitated state of concupiscence, he thought I had beaten him to her sexual charms. What was crystal clear to me was that the only bang he had that night was on my bedroom door.

Later in the day I learned that mercenary troops were on the move from Elisabethville travelling north towards Jadotville and that a couple of journalists had already set off. John Spicer, the grey-haired young-faced editor of the Argus News Service volunteered to take me to the action. 'We'll go in my car,' he said. We set off when the afternoon sun was well past the zenith which did not cause any immediate concern and we did not even think about it when we reached a swollen river, but as we approached a bridge the car screeched to a halt and we left the vehicle to stare in dismay. 'They've blown the bloody bridge,' muttered John as we gazed down at railway trucks filled with ballast which were resting upright in water. The fast-flowing river lapped impatiently, only inches from the top of the trucks and John and I looked at each other before he said, 'Hold on a minute.' Curiously, I watched him stroll back to the car from which he produced a brown bottle and I admired his advanced planning. We jumped down on to the first truck and then the next with my companion tenaciously clutching the bottle of Castle lager which he had carried lovingly all the way from Kitwe. As we leapt from truck to truck we knew that a false move or a slip on the wet sand-and-stone ballast would have seen us washed us away and disappear beneath the raging torrent as food for submerged crocodiles.

Soaking with sweat and spray, we reached the other side and looked long-ingly at the beer bottle before realising with desperation that neither of us had brought an opener. As I'd recently chipped a tooth removing the cap off a bottle some months ago I'd vowed to give up the practice. Salvation came to us in the form of an old mortar case which stood at the river's edge. 'Give me the bottle,' I said and tried vainly to ease off the bottle cap on the metal casing. 'Here, give it to me,' said John but his attempts were no better. The situation was serious: two journalists hot in the Congo sun with a drink but no bottle opener, comparable to a camel caravan train reaching a dried-up desert oasis. In frustration he kicked the mortar case and it rolled over to reveal that it still contained its lethal cargo of mortar bombs! With respect we removed a couple of bombs before John wedged the offending bottle between the metal squares of the case where the mortar bombs had been, and yanked hard. 'Bugger,' he cried in despair as the neck of the bottle broke and warm beer gushed out. Despite the jagged edges we eagerly finished off the contents of the bottle before moving forward on foot. Ahead of us in the far distance we saw two men approaching and one was carrying a heavy camera. 'George and Ernie,' said John and as they came closer, he added, 'They're looking pleased with themselves.' Journalist George Clay, and his cameraman, Ernie Christie, were two South Africans employed by NBC. Both were known womanisers with redoubtable reputations and there was many a time, on mentioning that I was a journalist, women asked me excitedly, 'Do you know George Clay?' George and Ernie were almost inseparable and did superb work for their American television company.

As we stopped to talk on that lonely Congo road, it became clear that John and I had just missed all the action – and that these two veterans were very much a part of it. 'Ernie has some great shots,' said George. His words epito-mised the way competitive journalists think in war situations; not so much the slaughter they have witnessed but the very fact they have the story first hand and, in television terms, got the 'film in the can' no matter what the risk to themselves. They told us of a new United Nations atrocity, similar to that in which Jim Biddulph's car was shot up, and it was Ernie who had heroically brought the carnage to an end. A Volkswagen had been travelling down the Jadotville Road and the occupants were the Belgian driver, his wife, and a woman friend. Without warning or reason, UN-Indian troops opened fire on the car, killing both women instantly. Ernie, holding his camera to his eyes, ran in front of the automatic guns which forced the troops to stop shooting. The driver left the car on his knees with his hands held in supplication as he pleaded with the United Nations troops not to murder him too. The film was flown to America for processing and later the newsreel was shown at a Kitwe cinema where dramatic music in the background highlighted the tension. Said a dazed Ernie, as he left the cinema, 'Fucking hell, I didn't know it was like that!' For his great piece of filming he received the *Encyclopaedia Britannica* Award; for saving a life so selflessly he received nothing. Ernie had started work as a dentist and knowing his temperament, I'm glad I was never a patient of his for he had a very wild streak. Once, when he was with South Africa's top freelance reporter, Peter Hawthorne, he took off from an airstrip, turned the plane and dived straight at me and waved as I ducked before shooting back up into the air. I mention the incident because of the bizarre way he was to kill himself, and others.

John Spicer and I walked on for a couple of miles and it was dark before we turned back without reaching the scene of the tragedy. Fireflies darted about and it was the first time I'd seen them and they reminded me that despite the silence, there was life all around us. The walk reminded me of my childhood when Warren took me by bus to a cinema in Cobham, five miles from home. He was probably twelve years of age and I was eight and as we left the cinema we raced to the last bus which disappeared into the distance. In the dark we made our way along the long lonely road with only the sound from telephone wires and hooting owls to keep us company until we reached a distraught mother who was standing in the road at about midnight. Now my companion was named John and I was much older and on another continent but I felt the same sense of menace as we made our return trip which was even more hazardous and dangerous than the outward one. We had to cross the swollen river by the light of the stars before returning to the Leo Deux where I hurriedly did a voice piece into my tape recorder for the FBC.

Pre-recorded tapes, news film and most of journalists' copy were sent daily, either by road to Kitwe or to the Union Minere airstrip, where they were flown out by Alan Kearns. The FBC had an office in Kitwe run by a local broadcaster, Alistair McKenzie, and the day I managed to get through to Salisbury by telephone, John Appleby came on the line and was furious. 'Where have you been?' he demanded. 'I thought you were dead!' Clearly the Biddulph incident was still weighing heavily upon him. 'What are you talking about?' I replied, dumbfounded and equally testily. 'I've been filing voice pieces every day.' I'd been sending the tapes to McKenzie and it meant that all the work I had done and all the risks I'd taken had been in vain. An inquiry was carried out and it was found that McKenzie had been getting so much money stringing for all the other companies such as CBS, NBC, ABC, CBC, BBC, and any other broadcasting company in the world anxious for news, that he totally ignored his own employers and their staff correspondent. In truth, he didn't ignore the copy; he merely milked it and broadcast to everyone else under his own name. No one's story, which had often been obtained by risking life and limb, was sacred or exclusive as everything was broadcast by him to their opposition companies.

In a smouldering rage I flew down to Northern Rhodesia to confront McKenzie who was waiting at Ndola Airport and as I began to remonstrate he merely smiled, urbanely, 'You're coming home to dinner tonight, my wife's cooking trout especially for you.' Nice touch! As I got into his heavy Wolesey car we drove off into the warm balmy afternoon but the atmosphere in the car was freezing. As we sped along a main road I watched a small sports car race towards us from a side street to our left and expected McKenzie to slow in anticipation of trouble: he didn't. The smaller car crashed into us lifting the Wolesey into the air before it came down facing in the opposite direction. The centre of the impact was inches from my left hip and the sports car finished up sixty yards away in a ditch, the driver being seriously injured. My mood had not improved and I didn't even bother to go over to see if the maniac who had so nearly killed me was still alive. I'd also decided that McKenzie's driving was as poor as his integrity for only a blind man would not have foreseen that the sports car wasn't going to stop. A policeman drove up and spoke to McKenzie, whom he seemed to know well. Then he came over to talk to me, 'I understand that you have just come out of the Congo?' I nodded. With almost reverence, he then asked 'Tell me, sir, what's it really like up there?' Still furious, my reply was spontaneous and said with feeling but it sent McKenzie into spasms, 'It's a bloody sight safer there than it is down here!'

Some time later the driver of the sports car was charged with dangerous driving and the defence lawyer cheekily called me as a witness. A rail ticket was sent down to Salisbury and I was booked into a cheap hotel and refused to go unless I was flown up and able to stay at the Edinburgh Hotel with all expenses paid. Having sorted that out, I flew to Zambia and arrived at the hotel in the evening in time for dinner and then decided to call it a day. When I appeared in court the defence lawyer only asked me two questions: 'How fast would you say my client was travelling at the time of impact?'

'About sixty miles an hour.'

'Don't you feel you are overestimating the speed?'

'I was being conservative!'

'Thank you, Mr Shay. That will be all.' I wondered how he explained my bill to his client.

Among many of the fine journalists who visited the Edinburgh Hotel during the Congo War was the gentlemanly John Osman of the BBC. On one of my overnight stays in Kitwe, John turned up and asked for a room and as these were at a premium, he was surprised and delighted that there was indeed one to spare. His round, bespectacled face lit up with pleasure and he signed the hotel register before he inquired, 'What number?' He was told room 214. As he walked across to the lift I watched him stop dead in his tracks and he came over to me to ask the name of the journalist who had been the previous occupant. 'I thought so,' he said, and handed back the key preferring to spend the night on the settee in the foyer. Somehow, before he had even reached the hotel he had found out what we all knew – that the previous occupant of 214 had pediculosis pubis (crabs).

Another visitor to the hotel was the legendary French mercenary Colonel Bob L'Afreux 'The Terror' Denard of the French 4th Commando who was in a room close to mine. As the former legionnaire was a close rival of the British mercenary, Mike Hoare, I knew he was worth an interview. I knocked on his door and although there was no reply, I sensed that someone was on the other side and stooping, I peered through the keyhole and was startled at what I saw. Fixed to the other end of the keyhole was another eye and as we gazed at each other, eyeball-to-eyeball only inches apart, I said I would like to talk to him. There was silence. I asked, 'Why are you here?' The eye moved away and later, under cover of darkness, he left the hotel. That was all I ever saw of the man who would later topple governments and replace heads of state – just one eye!

Back in Elisabethville, shortages of most goods were getting worse and there was a petrol crisis. Because there had been an incident at the Katangese border post on the Kasumbaleza Road between Kitwe and Elisabethville the road was closed and some journalists asked if I would fly down to Kitwe and try to open it up again, bringing petrol back at the same time. My chances of getting through were better than most, they explained, and I kidded myself that this was true. Because I worked for the FBC, I felt that I should be acceptable to the Katangese as their president, Moise Tshombe, was friendly with Sir Roy Welensky. When I arrived in Kitwe I learned that an American journalist had been nearly shot while driving towards Elisabethville which was why no one was now allowed on the road. The American had been saved by the intervention of John Monks, a fiery red-haired, pink-faced Australian, unkindly known as the Pink Pig, who worked for the *Daily Express*, and Peter Younghusband, a giant South African who was writing for *Newsweek* and the *Daily Mail*, the two who were shot at with Sandy Gall. We knew each other well and I called on them in John's room where they were about to start writing a joint story. 'We were driving along the Kasumbaleza Road when we were stopped at a Katangese checkpoint before we were allowed to drive on,' John told me, 'and just after leaving the control post we saw a hut and noticed a white arm waving from it.' They left their car and walked across, curious to find the owner of the arm and ask him what he was up to. It was then that they found Evelyn Waugh's nature correspondent who'd been mistakenly sent to cover a war in Africa, William Boot of the Beast. But this was an American. 'Who are you and what are you doing in there?' boomed Big Pete.

The reply left even these two seasoned veterans speechless: 'I'm the music critic of the *Baltimore Sun*!'

'You're *what*?' thundered Pete in disbelief.

The man was trembling with fear as he repeated, 'I'm from the *Baltimore Sun*. I am their music critic.' After digesting this snippet they asked incredulously what he was doing in the Congo, and more particularly, in the hut? 'I was in Rome covering a music festival,' quavered the man. 'My newspaper came through on the phone and said that as Rome was nearer to the Congo than Baltimore, I had been assigned to cover the war!' Having flown to Northern Rhodesia and knowing nothing of the politics of the war, he had driven up the road and was arrested on handing over his passport. There were two passports which were particularly out of favour with Tshombe's troops –

the Irish and the American. The Irish, who had suffered terrible casualties, were as popular as a suckling pig at a bar mitzvah because their troops were part of the UN peace-keeping force; and the Americans because they supported the United Nations. 'What are they planning to do with you?' was the next question. 'They said they would shoot us all.' The two journalists could see that the American was not alone for in the hut were some Africans who had also been promised a firing squad. Peter Younghusband chose to stay with the frightened man while John Monks dashed off for help. While he was away, Katangese troops arrived and marched off the occupants of the hut, together with Younghusband. A firing squad was being formed and the prisoners were removing their clothes when Monks returned with a Katangese army officer who ordered the squad to hold their fire while the music critic and Peter were ushered away to safety. On returning to Kitwe, the music critic went straight to bed suffering from shock and stayed there for days before he tried to write his story. It began, 'Three days ago I was rebuffed at the border.' Said Peter on scrutinizing the output, 'That's terrible.'

'Let's write it for you,' offered John, magnanimously. That is when I came on to the scene. 'I'll type if you would like to dictate,' I suggested.

And so an Australian, a South African, and an Englishman domiciled in Southern Rhodesia sat down to write a news story for an American. John Monks began, 'Today my American passport nearly cost me my life.' Peter did much of the rest while my contribution, other than typing, was merely to throw in the odd word when they were stuck, which wasn't often with those two pros. As we came to the end I read the story back aloud and we liked it. 'I reckon we should get the Pulitzer Prize for this,' joked John. Some time later we heard that the music critic had indeed been nominated for the Pulitzer. We kept our mouths shut so as not to embarrass him but he was an honest fellow and gave credit to the two men who richly deserved it. I was surprised that Peter Younghusband had not come up with the opening sentence for as a freelance, he was an expert. He had once opened a story for the *Daily Mail* with the words: 'I like it here,' a line which was possibly picked up by Kingsley Amis as the title of a book. Where was the place that Peter liked so much? In Swaziland, at a natural cleavage between two moulded hills datelined: Sheba's breasts!

The following day a group of 'war correspondents' who clearly felt it imprudent for them to accompany me into the Congo themselves, hired a Land Rover complete with an African driver, and put a large drum of petrol aboard. I bought cartons of cigarettes, just for protection. Eric Robins, a freelance in Salisbury and a chief correspondent for *Time* magazine, was there to shake hands gravely as he saw me off. The entrance to the Kasumbaleza Road sliced through a giant anthill where man had invaded and destroyed the home of billions of insects which had taken untold years to create. The two sides that were left stood like sentinels and beyond was a long narrow swathe sliced out seemingly by a giant scythe along which I would travel through a forbidding gauntlet of tall trees, bushes and scrub, seemingly with each side waiting to close in on claustrophobic travellers and soldiers alike. I was on an adrenalin super highway.

A little way up the road, Katangese troops waved us down and pointed their guns at me. They were not a firing squad and merely wanted a lift but I had already heard, disturbingly, that they frequently squeezed the trigger acciden-tally and shot each other. Giving a lift was no problem until some more stopped us and I soon had one sitting on my lap, so cramped was the vehicle. My lack of formal education meant that my French was appalling but I knew how to say, goon-like, 'Vive Tshombe, Vive Welensky.' I handed out cigarettes but my mind was more concentrated on producing the right pass when reached the border control post which could not be far away. The United Nations pass was stuck firmly down my right sock, and my FBC identity card down the left and my passport in a pocket. It was vitally important to make sure I had it correct when the checkpoint came up; my life depended upon it. As we came to the control post where the music critic had nearly come to grief, I felt it had been a good move to have the hitch-hiking troops waiting in the truck. Slowly I advanced to the hut containing the border officials, turning to wave at the soldiers before entering the checkpoint hut.

'Bonjour,' I said with a big stupid grin. 'Vive Tshombe, Vive Welensky!' I refrained from adding the sentence my schoolmistress jocularly declared to the class: 'Monsieur Shay a un nez grand!'

The men manning the post didn't respond to the smile but looked back grimly and one held out his hand for my passport. It was British and they thumbed through it slowly, checking on which countries I had visited. As the British Government had supported the United Nations I wasn't too sure of my ground and so I bent down as if to scratch my leg and retrieved the FBC pass which, like the passport, contained my photograph.

'Roy Welensky's Radio Rhodésie,' I explained, and casually proffered some cigarettes which they took but without response. Then I pointed to myself, 'Je représente Radio Rhodésie,' and held out my hand. 'Ah, ah!' they exclaimed as the penny dropped, 'Radio Rhodésie!' Their faces lit up as quickly as their cigarettes and it was smiles all round. 'Bon voyage, Monsieur,' they said as I made my way back to the Land Rover where the soldiers were waiting, happy that they did not have to kill me.

Some got off further up the road while others, looking more hardened, climbed aboard and I told myself they certainly deserved some cigarettes, like cartons of them. I'd given my driver explicit instructions not to tell the troops that we were carrying petrol as they may believe we were taking it up to the United Nations soldiers but as we drove northwards the heavily smoking dishevelled soldiers pointed to the drum with curiosity.

'Paraffin,' I said, wondering if we would all go up with a great big bang from the lighted cigarettes and petrol fume mixture. My driver took his eyes off the road and turned round nervously. 'It's petrol,' he corrected.

'Stop!' ordered one of the soldiers and as we screeched to a halt. I knew that if they shot me now and took the petrol, no one would be any the wiser as my body would never be found. While they were alighting from the truck I quickly gave them some more cigarettes to take their minds off any nasty thoughts they may be harbouring. They nodded grimly like men about to receive the last cigarette before they die and I knew the crisis had passed. 'Merci,' they said, and waved us on. The reason for the sudden departure and their grimness was soon apparent. We were now uncomfortably close to the United Nations lines which were manned by Ethiopian troops, some of the meanest soldiers in Africa. According to some journalists I'd spoken to, they had gone into one unarmed village and completely wiped it out, just for the joy of killing and now, only a couple of miles further along we were waved down by the surly Ethiopians at a checkpoint. I dug into my right sock as they looked over the truck and appeared surprised to see the petrol and talked amongst themselves. One of them spoke English and asked about the petrol drum. There was no point in lying, especially as I was the holder of a United Nations pass. 'It's petrol I'm taking to Elisabethville for journalists with the United Nations,' I said. These were words that could have put me in front of a firing squad only a short while ago. The Ethiopian soldier handed back my UN pass and soon the long, frightening journey was over.

Outside the Leo Deux was the same group of journalists who had given me money for the petrol. 'The road's all right now,' I said, feeling physically and mentally drained, 'and here's your petrol.' They looked at me with embarrassment. 'Thanks for taking the trouble, Reg, but you needn't have bothered after all. We've managed to get a fresh supply through the United Nations!'

'Really,' I replied, annoyed that the journey had been wasted. 'Well you paid for it so you can have it.' I was at least cynically amused that they were stuck with a large amount of petrol they did not want and didn't know how to dispose of it. As I stood at the hotel reception, they were trying to explain to the truculent Swiss manager, M. Blatter, why they had rolled a drum of highly inflammable fuel into the carpeted foyer of the best hotel in Elisabethville.

While the United Nations had tarnished its reputation with the killing of innocent people, its attempt to save lives had not always fared much better. In Elisabethville the UN produced cans of meat to distribute free to the hungry Katangese and were astonished when the starving masses refused to take them. To the Katangese, most of whom were illiterate, the only way to tell the contents of a tin of meat was to look at the bull, chicken or pig depicted on the outside and the photograph on these tins of a laughing black man with sparkling teeth was clear proof that the United Nations' troops were killing innocent happy Africans and then canning their bodies for distribution as food. Had the officials used their intelligence they would have torn off the wrappers and then handed out the tins. Instead, they gave the lot to an enterprising Indian entrepreneur from Kitwe who stripped off the wrapping paper and had fresh ones printed. Being a shrewd businessman and not a philanthropist, he sold the lot in Northern Rhodesia at a huge profit.

While cannibalism still existed in some parts of the Congo, it seemed to be the exception rather than the rule and much of it in Katanga was confined to the Baluba tribe. There was a sick joke amongst journalists who knew their fate if the Balubas escaped from a nearby encampment. Should the name Baluba be mentioned, war correspondents would puff out their cheeks knowing that the Balubas had a reputation of cutting of a victim's testicles, ramming them into his mouth, and then sewing the lips together. When hordes of them, armed only with bows and arrows, wiped out an Irish contingent, they actually left all the bodies except a machine gunner whom they ate as an accolade of honour, believing his bravery would pass on to them. The Katangese were not cannibals and were rated the most sophisticated of the Congolese, and yet they had devised a diabolical torture which involved the worst kind of cannibalism by compelling prisoners to eat themselves to death. First, they tied their victim to a tree where he stood all day in the blazing sun while his tormentors would always generously ladle out water but no food. After a couple of days the terrified hapless captive would cry out from starvation and obligingly a captor would cut a slice off the man's rump and give it to him until the starving man gradually devoured himself.

The Congo crisis and the United Nations' bad press brought a Very Important Person to Africa in a bid to meet Tshombe and reach an agreement which would stop the fighting. There was tension and irritation amongst journalists as we stood anxiously at Ndola Airport, just south of Kitwe, keeping a close eye on both the sky and our watches. His plane was overdue and soon it would be too late to send off dispatches in time for some newspaper deadlines. I wasn't too concerned as the FBC produced regular news bulletins and an important news flash would occasionally interrupt a broadcast which was a sure way of capturing the interest of listeners. 'What has delayed him?' were the words on everyone's lips. 'Where is Hammarskjöld?'

Reluctantly, some reporters drifted away to file their stories of his late arrival. They feared that he might suddenly appear from out of the sky, leaving those who stayed behind with a scoop interview. Editors don't take kindly to journalists who miss world-shattering events, no matter the reason and as history records, Dag Hammarskjöld, the UN Secretary General, never did arrive at Ndola as his plane crashed and he was killed. The crash was somewhat humiliating for one leading British journalist, Clive Sanger, who had to leave early and subsequently earned the sobriquet, 'Clive Clanger' as he not only filed his report of Hammarskjöld's arrival but also an interview with him! His story was based on an earlier interview using the touchdown as his peg for using it but Sanger was not the only one to suffer. In Oslo there was a newspaper telex operator who was bored with hanging on to an open line when he wanted to go home to enjoy the comforts of his wife and family. The nervous Norwegian staff reporter at the airport pleaded with the operator to keep the line open, saying, 'I'm sure that something has happened to Hammarskjöld.' 'Nothing has happened to Hammarskjöld,' came the belligerent retort from Oslo as the telex was cut off for the night.

When I returned from the Congo, John Appleby took me aside before I got down to work. 'You have a new colleague, he's an Italian nobleman, a prince no less,' he said, adding, 'I thought it was time we brought a little class into the newsroom!' I'm seldom surprised but John managed to hit the mark. 'Does he speak English?' I inquired. 'Perfectly, but he doesn't have much news sense.' I was curious that an Italian prince should have come to Rhodesia to live and take a fairly lowly job when there was plenty of sunshine with a lot more culture in Italy. 'I think he has woman problems back home and just wanted to get away,' explained John with amused empathy for his own spouse had left him. 'He's had something like five wives.'

'He must be either a masochist or they weren't all his own,' I retorted before the thought struck me. 'If he's an Italian nobleman he must be a Roman Catholic. How does he get away with the divorces?' John was still grinning, 'It's worse than you think, he's a prince of the Vatican and he's totally out of favour with Rome.' I was taken to be introduced to Prince William Rospiliosi who was tall, grey and totally charming. ''ello Reg,' he said using the hard 'g' and extending his hand. 'Call me Bill.' I liked Bill but felt John had been rash to take on the prince for he proved to be too vague to be working in the Federal capital's newsroom but he was such a nice chap that no one wanted to lose him. Fortunately for Bill our staff man in Nyasaland (Malawi), Alan Hart, had shot himself in the foot by sending us a story about the youth wing of Dr Hastings Banda's Congress Party building a sports pavilion. Three weeks later came another story stating that the pavilion had been blown down by a gust of wind. To us it was petty stuff but amusing while to Banda, who would become Malawi's first president (and criminal dictator) it was a fabricated slur upon himself, his party and its magnificent youth wing. Not only had the pavilion not blown down – it had never been built!

Prince William was duly sent to Blantyre as a replacement in our one-man Nyasaland news operation but the only story we received was that Bill himself had come to grief – he had been thrown from a horse! The accepted view of the newsroom was a little different in that he over-indulged in wine consumption one night and tottered downstairs, breaking a leg. Whatever the cause of his injuries, he was flown to Salisbury, leaving behind three cats and a small Fiat car. Unwisely, I offered to bring them back and flew to Blantyre but my patronage to the papal hierarchy nearly ended on viewing the cats. The first was a Siamese whose demeanour was one of utter disdain and inbred arrogance, she was contemptuous of humans below princely status as socially inferior beings whose presence was only permitted to serve her food and act as chauffeurs. That she disapproved of her journey to come was clear, for while being devoid of social intercourse her protests were contained in perpetual meowing. 'She's about all I need when we reach the border posts,' I commented to Bill's housekeeper. The next cat was digitally disadvantaged through an earlier confrontation with a car – she had only three legs! I was told that she was a stray who had made her own way in life until she had appeared at the prince's palace where she was treated like Cinderella by the other cats but welcomed by the prince. The third feline was Persian, well fed, relaxed and demure, not demanding but appreciative of life's pleasures, rather like Prince William himself. Unlike her Siamese cousin, she did not need to demand recognition but accepted her role in life without question and with dignity.

The 300-odd mile drive even without cats would be troublesome enough for it would involve travelling down through Nyasaland (Malawi) to Mozambique, then carrying on along a rut-pitted dirt road through that country until I would cross the Zambezi by car ferry. It meant that borders were to be negotiated and borders meant veterinary certificates for the cats. They could not be found! Under normal circumstances I would not even consider crossing a border with animals without a vet's certificate but I salved my conscience in the sure knowledge that these cats had been vaccinated and they would not leave the car while travelling from one part of the Federation to another. I was also aware that wild animals such as elephant and buck were not stopped to produce certificates when they passed through frontiers which made the whole issue a bureaucratic farce.

The only worthwhile containers for the journey that I could lay my hands on at the home of Prince William were two empty Mateus Rosé bottles and I filled one with milk and the other with water for the Siamese. The bottles would only be used if the cats appeared to be really thirsty and the thought of letting them out of the car for natural functions and then trying to get them back on the day-long trip was daunting. Two of them, I knew, I would never catch if they ran into the bush and it would be awkward returning with just the one triple-legged moggie.

The cats were ensconced on the back seat and as I drove towards Mozambique the Siamese objected every mile of the way, whining with untold despair. Perhaps, I wondered with malevolent inspiration, would it matter so much if I granted it one last wish and gave the misery guts the freedom it craved for? Out in the wild it might find another animal it would respect, a superior king of beasts perhaps, for they are plentiful in Mozambique. It would be difficult to explain this to Bill, of course, and put me in a position rather like the poor bastard on the BBC who picked up Doug Willis's ashes. As I drove on I thought of Doug who was a regular caller to the FBC newsroom around lunchtime to ask who would join him at a nearby pub for gins and tonic or lager. I seldom went, knowing that drinking during the day lulls me into contented somnambulism whereas at night it rejuvenates me into a desire for ecstasy. Sadly, Doug died while he was in Southern Rhodesia and was cremated before the BBC despatched a colleague with the unenviable responsibility of taking home what was left of him. Disaster struck during the flight back when the plane stopped at Khartoum for refuelling and the passengers disembarked into the searing heat of the Sudanese capital. Either as a nostalgic gesture to Willis or fearing that a cleaner might appropriate the silver urn, the courier made his way to the airport bar and placed the container on the counter before ordering a drink to relieve the stress. The flight was called and the guardian of the precious casket duly downed a couple of scotches before reboarding the plane for London Airport.

The BBC man had been twitching nervously on the plane for some time, long before being asked to fasten his seat belt for landing; it started from the moment of enlightenment when he realised with horror that the very object of his expensive mission was not aboard. He had to report with impending doom to his BBC overlords and the grieving widow waiting at the airport that he had mislaid Doug Willis in a bar in Khartoum! After frantic international telephone calls and telexes, a search for the ashes was mounted and they were recovered from beneath the bar a few days later amongst unopened bottles of wines and spirits. Knowing Doug Willis as well as I did, I'm sure he would have been quite happy to have been left there as his final resting place.

With my contingent of cats, I came to the Nyasaland border post which presented no problems but as I was travelling through the stretch of no-man's land I saw possible trouble ahead. 'Damn,' I muttered as the Mozambique border post came into view some distance away for only twenty yards ahead was a hitchhiker and he wore the uniform of a man I couldn't refuse to help. 'Shut up or you'll be dead meat!' I hissed to the Siamese. As I wound down the window the uniformed man, an Immigration officer, asked me to drop him off for work. Never before or since have I been requested a lift by an Immigration official; it's called Sod's Law! The cat had got the message through a sixth sense or by the tone of my voice as it was silent all the way to the frontier post. While I was filling in the Customs declaration forms the same Immigration official must have slipped back to the car and made off with a Mateus Rosé bottle, the one containing the water. Having seen the cats he knew I could not complain but there was some mean feeling of satisfaction when I visualised the thieving official's face after his first swig.

I cleared the border post without difficulty and began the seventy-mile trek towards the Zambezi River but because the dark blue car attracted the sun's rays, they turned the small vehicle into a mobile glasshouse. For me the searing heat was unpleasant but for my companions with their coats of fur it was intense and yet I could only slightly open the windows as a mere apology for their lack of ventilation. I had to drive fast to give them air and when I did open the driver's window wider, the result was nearly catastrophic. Unknown to me, the three-legged hybrid had been biding its time and now decided this was the moment to make its bid for freedom and I felt claws pierce into my skin like eagle's talons as it pounced from the rear seat. With one hind leg missing, it then lost its balance and as it struggled to stay on my now-bloodied shoulder, the car swerved and nearly overturned as I attempted to shake it off. 'Not again,' I muttered to myself as a recent stomach churning memory recalled one of the worst moments of my life.

I'd been sitting quietly at home with Annette and Peter when Merle Fadness, an attractive girl I had worked with on the *Rhodesia Herald*, rang the doorbell to say her car had broken down and could I help? The heavens had opened as a tropical storm broke around us and after I'd sorted out Merle's problems, I began to drive back home. I was in Margery's small car as she had borrowed the Chevy and I didn't know the brakes had been recently adjusted and were very sharp. There were just three of us in the car – Annette was beside me and little Peter was in the rear seat when I noticed through the sheets of rain that a car was speeding towards us on our side of the road. My foot touched the pedal brake and the car immediately spun round and reversed out of control on a slippery camber. Automatically I took my foot off the brake to arrest the skid but it was too late and I instinctively cradled Annette with my left arm as the car rolled over before righting itself again. I glanced behind me to ensure that Peter was all right and to my horror realised that he wasn't even in the car. The full significance of his disappearance quickly registered with me and I was devastated: if he wasn't in the car he had to be outside. And if he was outside, either our vehicle or some other car must have rolled over him. What I might find outside filled me with dread. For a couple of seconds I sat numbed, hardly daring to get out. All too clearly I recalled the same mental paralysis I had felt years ago before I heard Margery's scream on finding Alan dead in his cot. Had I killed Peter? I forced open the door and once outside I looked around to where I expected to find his crushed body. He wasn't there! My blood ran cold and then I went into a sweat and my mouth felt hollow for there was only one alternative – he was lying pulverized under the car. I looked beneath, dreading what I would find but there was still no sign of him. Then I heard a cry from the far side of the vehicle and I dashed around to be met by the most wonderful sight in my life: Peter was alive!

He was sitting in the middle of the road with cars trucks and buses racing past but he was on the opposite side to where we had rolled. Nothing made sense. Firstly, he'd been ejected from the vehicle with all its doors and windows closed and secured. Secondly, as the car rolled one way he was thrown out in the opposite direction to the roll. His survival could only be described as miraculous for he didn't even receive a scratch. Annette suffered a gash in her leg while my only injury was to my wrist where my watch had torn into it. Once I'd ensured that my children were safe, my arm seized up and I stood for thirty minutes in the torrential rain waiting for an ambulance.

As the memory of the near-tragedy flashed through my mind, I was now struggling once again to stop a car overturning whilst trying to shake off a stupid cat! I clutched it beneath the forelegs and tossed it onto the back seat before gaining control and continuing to head south. Half an hour later I saw sparkling strips of tinfoil which slowly materialised into the glistening waters of the Zambezi River. The shimmering mirage of a first-world-war tank was sitting on the water but as I approached the mirage slowly transformed into a raft of oil drums and wooden planks. An African wearing a seaman's ill-fitting blue-striped T-shirt waved to me as I gingerly approached the water's edge. 'Aqui,' he said and indicated to where I must drive aboard. I looked at the ferry with trepidation and half closed my eyes as the car wheels grudgingly found their way on to the strips of wood on which my life would depend for the next half an hour. The ferry lurched forward with the weight of the car and I braked sharply to avoid running over the open edge. I got out of the Fiat and looked to where the ferry would tie up and wondered at the principles of getting an engineless outsized raft across as there was no obvious means of propulsion. I was still waiting for a tug to arrive when I realised that we had cast off and were speeding downstream. A thick rope for'ard rose from the water and we swung like an archer's bow until strong men with sweating bodies heaved at the rope to take up the slack, fighting the fast-moving waters until we arrived at the opposite bank.

An anti-climax of the trip came during mid-afternoon when I arrived at the last two border posts, for passing through them didn't even invite a lazy cursory glance at the vehicle but there was still a surprise in store before the journey was over. As I meandered along the road towards Salisbury, congratulating myself that I would soon be home and that the worst of the journey was past, an explosion rocked the car. I looked round to see three cats with their hair standing on end staring at me in fright but by the colour of their fur I knew what had happened. Like my companions, I too was wet and a glance in the car mirror showed premature white hair while a survey of the floor revealed shards of the remaining Mateus Rosé bottle, possibly the very same bottle which had caused the prince's downfall following an intimate candle-lit dinner. The bottle, I concluded, had been so outraged and humiliated that its noble contents should be replaced by milk that it rebelled in kamikaze-style by blowing itself to pieces.

'Please, Daddy, will you take us to the circus?' pleaded Annette soon after I'd arrived home from Nyasaland. I've never been much of a circus fan but circuses are for children and one was in town. The advertised climax of the show was the human cannonball and during a trapeze performance I looked back to see a young man in a silver suit adjusting nuts on the cannon. 'He's not happy,' I said to Margery, feeling that something was very wrong; my intuition being so strong that he would be killed I felt almost compelled to walk over and suggest he call off the act. Finally he got into the cannon and after the Master of Ceremonies made a short speech there was a loud bang. Adults as well as children, put their hands to their mouths as the helmeted young man soared above them and landed into a net some distance away. There was unbridled applause and he rose unharmed with open arms to accept the plaudits. He had, of course, done the act many times before and I realised then that there was really nothing to worry about, that my intuitive suspicions were not justified. My intuition wasn't entirely at fault, however, for it was the following night that he missed the net and was killed instantly with a broken neck.

It was while I was still with Federal Broadcasting that I travelled to Lusaka, the Northern Rhodesia capital, to relieve our staff correspondent, Langley Brown, who was married on the fateful day President Kennedy was assassinated. The honeymoon venue was a secret but those at the reception party learned that the nuptial pleasures would take place upstairs at the Ridgeway Hotel, where we all just happened to be celebrating. 'That's their room,' said one of my companions. We looked up with fixed voyeur inquisitiveness and saw that the bedroom light was still on, which seemed odd. With enthusiasm, we guests drank to the success of the happy couple in the belief that soon the light would be extinguished for a night of rapture. As we were gazing upward the music on the hotel radio stopped for a special announcement from the Salisbury newsroom. Everyone stood dumbfounded, as though the world was coming to an end, and I remembered feeling a similar sensation at the time Mahatma Gandhi was murdered.

As we discussed the tragedy and its possible implications there came a familiar voice from behind me, 'What's the matter with everyone? You all look right glum.' It was Langley Brown. 'Aren't you supposed to be up there?' we chorused, pointing to his hotel room window. 'Yes,' he replied, 'but I need a drink!' That's what I was doing when Kennedy was murdered, while Langley Brown, who was supposed to be upstairs putting his act together, was certainly not doing what he was supposed to be doing. He stayed boozing with his guests for quite a long time. I don't know what happened to him or whether the marriage lasted: mine would not have survived the first night if I had pulled that stunt on Margery.

My early days of broadcasting were a shambles. I proved to be desperately mic-shy and while my stories were rated the tops, my reporting of them was downright embarrassing. Where Jim Biddulph had a confident, well-modulated voice I was stilted. A sympathetic producer, Ken Marshall, took me into a studio to try to improve matters. The type of microphone used was identical to those that can be seen in films of the thirties: large, black and intimidating. 'Don't think of it as a microphone,' said Ken, 'look upon it as a big ear and you are talking into it.' The exercise made not the slightest difference and it wasn't until I first appeared live on television – after I had left the FBC – that the mic-shyness fell away immediately and I reacted towards the camera as though it wasn't there. The same then happened with the microphone and some young women who found my voice too sexy to be contained to the air waves, persuaded me to do a taped voice over on the immortal recording of 'Je t'aime' by Serge Gainsbourg and Jane Birkin. The two words to be inserted at prescribed intervals which would send them into raptures of fantasy were: 'Donnez moi'.

Big international companies were now coming my way but it had been a long haul. I did some work for CBS but wasn't happy when they asked me to put on a phoney American accent – after I'd just found my own voice! Then Charlie Arnot of ABC News strolled into the office and began dropping $100 bills on to my desk. 'I want you to work for us,' he said. Until that moment, I'd intended to have some harsh words with him as Charlie, I knew, had been the recipient of mine and other journalists' tapes from the Congo War intercepted by Alistair McKenzie but his silver tongue was most persuasive and even though it would be difficult for some friends to believe, I actually asked him to stop dropping the notes after a very short time. There is a lot to be said for the adage, 'Easy come, easy go' as I have only had my pockets picked once and that was on the same day.

Before my first live TV appearance, I was asked to do a canned interview with Sir Roy Welensky for ITN. There were two very good reasons for being apprehensive: this was to be my first-ever TV interview. It was also my first interview with a prime minister who had such a commanding presence that when he died in December 1991, he was described as 'The last of the great imperial statesmen.' As the camera was set up and we took our seats the great man looked across at me and I must have appeared nervous for he leaned forward and gently patted me on the knee, 'Don't worry, Reg,' he said. 'You'll be all right.' It has to be the only time that a prime minister has said that to a television interviewer! We became quite friendly later and I would sometimes talk to him over his garden hedge and as we lived close to each other he would invite me to stroll round to tea and he'd even come into my office. Life was so informal and safe that he had no security guards.

At the annual meeting of the United Federal Party chaired by Welensky, the territorial government chief whip attacked the policy of the party. In a monotonous voice, this dull man read from newspaper cuttings and then went on to attack the very press that had supplied him with the paper cuttings for his witless speech. He resigned from the party on the spot and every journalist present assumed that was the end of him. In some ways I probably owe the man a favour for without him a part of my life might have been as tedious as his speeches. Few could have known then that the chief whip would become prime minister of Rhodesia and seize independence from Britain; that I would be constantly challenging his government in defence of press freedom, and even human justice. It had never occurred to me that such an eventuality would arise. But Fate was looking over my shoulder as much then as the day it led me to Fleet Street, and Rhodesia.

Enter Ian Smith

> No government ought to be without censors; and where the press is free none ever will.
>
> Thomas Jefferson

Margery concluded that I had to be out of my mind to resign a second time over censorship; I argued that this time, at least, it was with two senior colleagues who felt the same as I did. The resignation of the top three news writers caused such a hullabaloo that it was the front page lead in the national Sunday newspaper, the *Sunday Mail*, and it was also reported elsewhere in the world, including the UK. After the bold political and economic experiment of the Federation of Rhodesia and Nyasaland had been torpedoed and sunk by its very creator, Britain, and sliced up like leftover wedding cake as the matrimonial divorce settlement only ten years after the nuptials, new countries were formed to become Southern Rhodesia, Zambia and Malawi. The broadcasting corporation was similarly split and our departure came only five months after the break-up.

The writing was on the wall when Sir Edgar Whitehead's moderate UFP, the territorial wing of Welensky's party, was ousted by the Rhodesian Front during an election a year earlier when Winston Field became the new Southern Rhodesian prime minister. Countrywide, the party had been rated as a group of heavyweight right-wing extremists surprisingly led by a respected politician whom the hard-liners needed as a front to get into power. In this they succeeded by panicking the whites over near-imminent majority rule and having served his purpose, Field was toppled in a trumped-up sex scandal to ensure he would never return. I'd learned privately of the proposed coup by the cabal (though not the method) long before it happened and was told that the finance minister was the man to watch. He was christened Ian Douglas Smith but he might have been named Brutus for after totally supporting Prime Minister Field until they were safely in power, he and others then plunged the dagger in. Ah, what fiendish games politicians play! Welensky, who knew the political assassin well as his former chief whip, turned to me grimly over a cup of tea on the stoep of his home and declared, 'Now the malcontents are in power!'

The Federal disintegration had played into the hands of Smith and his co-plotters as they always knew it would and now they could carry on with the master plan they had drawn up – to declare independence from Britain. There'd been a deep resentment in the south that while Northern Rhodesia and Nyasaland (Zambia and Malawi) had been given their independence, Southern Rhodesia, a self-governing colony since 1924, had not. The whites of pioneer and early settler stock were particularly incensed because they'd had the option back in 1922 to link up with South Africa but preferred to stay loyal to Britain. Now, and with good reason, in their minds they felt double-crossed by the UK that having persuaded Southern Rhodesia to go into the Federation as the most sophisticated of three territories (but not the mineral richest), they were now being denied independence. The government supporters were also quick to argue that Britain had never given Southern Rhodesia a penny in financial aid so they had always been economically dependent through their own, mainly agricultural, industry. They knew they had the ability to make the country the breadbasket of Africa whereas independence under black majority rule would lead to economic disaster (how many millions has Britain poured into Zimbabwe only to be insulted by Robert Mugabe as he led the country towards economic ruin?). I'd much sympathy towards the farmers and industrialists because they really had turned a wilderness into a wonderful country where no one starved and I felt that genuine attempts were being made under the Federation to improve the lot of the African. All they needed was time but with cries of 'Freedom!' echoing worldwide, time was a commodity that wasn't on their side.

Ian Smith would play heavily on the emotional issue of British government betrayal when making his Unilateral Declaration of Independence (UDI), forever emphasising that there would be no black majority rule in his children's lifetime whereas under the Edgar Whitehead government, this had been anticipated with a transition over a period of time. Smith's vacuous prediction would later extend to 1,000 years! 'We can depend on our good friends in the south,' became his hackneyed phrase, possibly at the suggestion of his wife who was the sister of the South African finance minister. While this was meant to condition the whites to believe that the country would have to rely heavily on South Africa in the event of sanctions and insurrection, many of British origin who had emigrated to Southern Rhodesia after WW2 had grave misgivings that in return for help, they may have to adopt South Africa's apartheid policy. While there had been forms of racial discrimination within the country, the master-and-servant relationship between the blacks and whites was, in the main, good natured. But Smith knew he could count on the many Afrikaners in the country to support him together with the white artisans whose future would be clouded under black rule. He also played on justifiable fears that African states quickly deteriorated after independence and the inevitable begging bowl would be handed to the West for financial aid. In order to take UDI, Smith had to persuade the more British-than-British whites to his way of thinking, and also businessmen who had given dire warnings of the consequences of such an action. The Rhodesian Front government felt it was vital, therefore, to browbeat the media and most important of all, to control the newly titled SRBC.

Working behind the scenes was a man with a shady reputation, Ivor Benson, who was brought up from South Africa at great expense as an adviser to the government on the art of brainwashing the public. Benson had been in the Congo during that war where he reputedly always carried a gun and there were strong rumours amongst journalists that he had locked some Africans into a wardrobe and then shot it up. So far as I was concerned, it was only an unconfirmed rumour but what was known for sure were his pro-Hitler sympathies which led him once to give sanctuary to Britain's leading fascist, Sir Oswald Mosley. Benson learned his craft of persuasion by studying the techniques used by Josef Goebbels and in retrospect it was apparent that his advice was being taken even before he was officially appointed as a government advisor.

A news item had come over the agency wires which the newsroom decided would be included in the next bulletins, but for the first time, a directive from the chairman of SRBC told us it must be withheld. As it was a political item it was obvious an attempt was being made at censorship and the three senior news writers, Robin Drew, Geoff Preedy and myself, immediately announced that we'd resign unless the item was included. We won the day and shortly afterwards the chairman, Mr T B Rouse, resigned for 'health reasons' and a new chairman, Arthur Helliwell, was brought in. No one had ever heard of him but we guessed that he was hand-picked by the government and that the days of uncensored news were numbered. Helliwell's experience in broadcasting was nil and even worse, it was reported that he was a former police intelligence officer in Nyasaland. The showdown was a mere two months away.

The government declared that a referendum might be held on the possible seizing of independence and it was seeking advice on this from various organisations. The newsroom received an agency report that anthropologists and sociologists at the University of Rhodesia considered that all Africans not on the electoral roll should be allowed to vote on the issue. The news item was written but before the broadcast a telephone call from the new chairman directed that it should be struck out of the bulletin. Messrs Drew, Preedy and Shay again said, in unequivocal terms, that we would resign if the item was not used. Helliwell replied with an urgent memo declaring that the university group had released the statement intending to exert pressure of a political nature both on the government and the public. The memo said, 'I consider that in broadcasting this statement, particularly to an unsophisticated African audience at this juncture, the SRBC would have been lending its services to an undesirable exercise in political tactics.' He omitted to mention that the group had actually been asked by Government to express its opinion.

The three dissenters went to the Director General, John Parry, and handed in our provisional letters of resignation, declaring we'd be happy to withdraw them if an assurance could be given that the news service would be allowed to remain impartial. As no such assurances were forthcoming, we resigned and it was a crisis moment for all of us. We were offered jobs by the *Rhodesia Herald* but I declined as I doubted the situation there had changed but Drew joined and later became its editor. Preedy, whose uncle had been the first Federal prime minister, Lord Malvern, joined the BBC World Service newsroom in London. The loss of the three top news writers had come as a blow to the SRBC as there were only six newsmen left and some of these were relatively inexperienced. As for the dissenters, we were replaced by members of the police Special Branch!

The biggest disappointment to me was John Appleby, who stayed on as head of news but a few months later, after returning from holiday, he found he'd been replaced by another passionate Smith supporter, Harvey Ward. I was concerned that Appleby had severely compromised himself even though he'd felt it his duty to stay and I was truly sorry for him when he realised he'd been the real target of Helliwell. He later said to me, his moon-like face crestfallen, 'At least, Reg, you resigned with honour!' Those words deeply affected me and are etched in my memory.

When Appleby was fired he went first to England from where he was sent to Francestown in Botswana to set up an abortive anti-Rhodesian propaganda station. He then returned to Rhodesia for his remaining years as that is where his money was, and he died as an alcoholic sitting on a chamber pot in a nursing home at the early age of sixty years. His estranged wife, who clearly had no time for John either in life or death, coldly asked me to dispose of the ashes and to send her the bill. Partly out of cussedness but also with fond memories of John, I decided to send him off in style and hired a helicopter to scatter him where he was happiest, at Borrowdale racecourse in Salisbury. I'd been feeling fairly light-hearted when boarding the chopper and I recalled an incident John had once told me against himself. He'd been invited to an official dinner at Government House by the Governor, Sir Humphrey Gibbs, and as it was the first time such an invitation had been extended he was unsure of the events taking place after the meal. The black-tied men had retired to the lawns and the women to the cloakrooms and enlightenment dawned upon him just as the men were returning through the large French windows. In a state of desperation, John dashed outside and having found a suitable bush near the house he began to urinate. To use his own words, 'I was standing there all alone and in full flow when the floodlights came on!'

As the helicopter flew on, depression took over and an age seemed to pass before it reached the racecourse. There was more than one reason for my unhappiness as the helicopter had no door which did nothing to placate my fear of heights, and I could only sit and stare at John's ashes. Here was my friend and former boss, a superb broadcaster and author of thirteen novels who had come to my aid when I was out of work, and who was now reduced to a few cinders and ashes which I was holding on my lap. John wasn't even in a casket; just a worthless flimsy transparent plastic bag of the type that can now be found in any supermarket. This was the final 'scorpion' twist to the story of the man whose mystery tales I'd admired so much in the London *Evening Standard*, who was now about to be thrown by me from a helicopter into a void above a racecourse thousands of miles from England, where he would disappear without trace in a faraway corner of Africa.

My near-obsessive journalistic principles were seemingly becoming decidedly expensive, as Margery was quick to point out. It isn't usual for anyone to resign their job even once over censorship; now I'd done it twice, but I did wonder if anyone really cared? My only consolation was that I could live with myself while Margery on the other hand said that I should have stayed to fight the censorship from within the corporation if I had felt so strongly about it. She correctly reminded me once again that there was a problem of mouths still to feed and with the exception of the *Daily News*, a Thompson newspaper which was white-edited for African consumption, there was no one I could turn to for a job. I doubted the *Daily News* would survive long and only three months after I'd left the SRBC it was closed by police on orders of the odious Minister of Justice, Law and Order, Desmond Lardner-Burke, whose oppressive laws would one day, I predicted, be used against the whites under majority rule. At that stage, I was probably still the only white journalist to have spoken to Robert Mugabe and my comments were considered by many as treasonable.

I called on my friend, Eric Robins, and with him in the office was a good-looking young man, Peter Forbath, who was the American bureau chief for *Time*, based in Nairobi. I knew Peter already as a swinging party goer who didn't have much movement while dancing but his *suggestion* of movement had girls on their knees. As a journalist, Eric called him 'The Hoover' who sucked up every scrap of information available. He was a good operator.

'Say, Reg, I liked your stand and I wonder if you would like to become Eric's deputy on *Time*? He added that I would probably need some more strings and suggested I wrote to several American magazines and mention his name. I thus started as an international freelance journalist with Time-Life, McGraw-Hill Publications and *Playboy*. There's a lot to be said for sticking to your principles after all!

Eric had an Enterprise sailboat on Lake McIlwaine and Sundays were sometimes spent there with him and an Irishman, Tim Maginnis, but it was on land that the three of us would become involved in an escapist adventure of the type other people can only dream about. *Time* magazine was planning a cover story on Jomo Kenyatta and Eric chose to drive to Nairobi, a couple of thousand miles away and it was inconceivable that he should travel that distance alone on the mainly rutted dirt roads. I went along as his deputy and Tim came for the ride. I was also acutely aware that at some stage the Rhodesian borders to the north were likely to be closed and wanted to take advantage of them for road travel while they were still open. We both knew that the political situation in Rhodesia was closing in and either or both of us could be deported at any time.

Driving with Eric was ever an experience of some magnitude: with vivacious Marion Kaplan, we'd travelled through Mozambique in a clapped-out Volkswagen (I never knew him to have a car which suggested it might complete the journey) and the needle was staggering at around 40 mph when our whining engine disturbed an unseen herd of waterbuck. These are a large antelope which weigh up to 400 lbs and being nervous and shy, they are easily frightened and they will even take their chances against crocodiles in a river to escape humans, preferring to jump away from gunfights and into steel jaws. Their most unusual feature is white rings circling the backside, thus turning posterior into a target and the anus into a bull's-eye. This particular herd confounded the learned observations of naturalists by racing in our direction and a large bull sped across the road ahead of us. Then, before Eric could brake, a female leapt clear over the Volkswagen. Her timing and judgment were impeccable and it was truly poetry in motion to see four legs and a body glide over our heads with the grace of a ballerina. One false move on her part and she would have been through the windscreen, killing us all.

On another trip we nearly came to grief when our headlights picked up a reflection similar to the catseyes on British roads. Being pitch dark, we couldn't tell that they were slightly raised off the ground until Eric braked hard and began to swerve, careering from side to side as the car went through a herd of buck without hitting one. What the headlights had picked up were the twinkling eyes of the herd as they stood in the road, resting for the night. Because of these incidents I knew that our trip to Nairobi couldn't possibly be uneventful and few people looking at our disintegrating Opel would have given us fifty miles. We estimated that the journey there and back, not travelling as the crow flies, would be approaching 4,000!

On the morning of the great trek Eric switched on the ignition, accompanied by the indifferent sound of an engine yawning on being awakened, then nothing. He tried again… and again… and again. I questioned Eric only to learn that there'd been no such mundane thoughts of having the car checked over or serviced before we left; Eric was a man with supreme confidence in his vehicles. 'Tis me'self that will get it going,' said Tim, waspishly relying on the luck of the Irish to set us in motion. We knew he was very good at sailing boats, but with cars? Then came my turn – and this was a big mistake – for as I switched on the ignition it started like a dream. By a vote of two to one I was nominated as the man upon whose dexterity the whole tour rested: I became the official car starter. Eric took the wheel and we made good progress up through Zambia, arriving at Tunduma at about two o'clock in the morning, having covered around 900 miles. Each time we had stopped for refreshments, I was called upon to restart the car. Never before have I known a vehicle to fall in love with me, but the signs were unmistakable; I was the only one who could turn her on. What a pity, I thought, that she was such an old banger!

Tunduma is on the Zambia/Tanzania border and we arrived on a brilliant night when the moon was a suspended silver medallion and ice transformed the surrounding countryside into a Christmas card. It was also bitterly cold and we gazed longingly at a comfortable-looking inn. 'We can't wake up the hotel at this time of night,' said Eric despondently, while every word he uttered was punctuated with enough steam emanating from his mouth to equal Didcot power station. The air, meantime, was alive with the inviting smell of wood smoke which curled tantalizingly from the chimney of the hostelry. 'Sure we can,' declared Tim. 'I don't know,' was my negative Charlie Brown-type contribution. 'It's a bit unfair.' Thus it was that three hard-bitten journalists stood like idiots in the cold wondering whether we should disturb the slumbers of the hoteliers until we reluctantly reached a negative conclusion. 'We should have enough newspapers in the car,' I volunteered. 'That's what tramps use in London during the winter, they sleep under newspapers on park benches and underneath the arches to keep warm.' We stayed in the car all night and froze, each with a single sheet of the *Rhodesia Herald* covering him. Long after daylight we knocked on the door to the surprise of the couple who answered it; they were English members of a band of people who once made wonderful hoteliers in the middle of nowhere in many countries. 'Why didn't you wake us up?' they asked. 'That's what we are here for.' Eric and I avoided Tim's malevolent gaze. A hot bath and a shave with a good breakfast on the bougainvillaea-bedecked stoop soon had us on our way again but I did look regretfully at the beautifully clean and blanketed beds we'd had forsaken and all because we were too soft-hearted to knock.

Fifty miles inside Tanzania is Mbeya, a small town perched comfortably on top of an escarpment and after filling the car with petrol at a German-owned garage we made our way down the high escarpment with Eric driving. The Opel had found a new lease of life and travelled downhill with gusto while Eric handled her with masterly precision, seemingly ignoring the nasty mountain-sized drop on my side. As we approached the bottom we stared transfixed at an African lady walking in the road with a basket of bananas on her head and her back to us. It wasn't the woman that was so fascinating but we'd noticed a wheel that was speeding determinedly in her direction. The moment of truth dawned upon us just as the car gave off a crunching sound and Eric gyrated at the controls until we swerved round and came to a grinding halt with sparks flying as steel contracted with tarmac. In spite of our own problems, Tim and I still managed to watch mesmerised as our front offside wheel continued to career towards the pedestrian. 'Look behind you!' I shouted and I thought I saw her stiffen slightly but she carried on her dignified way without turning her head. The wheel then slowed dramatically and spun round a couple of times and collapsed a few feet from her bare heels. She still did not turn and never knew the drama that had taken place.

Such was Eric's faith in the invulnerability of his car that we discovered he carried neither spanners nor jack and it was after a twenty-minute wait involving consultation and recrimination that a passing motorist came towards us and promised to get help. Another hour slowly ticked by before a tow truck appeared and craned our proud supercar up the hill by the rear, its crestfallen headlamps lowered to face the tarmac as if in disgrace. We, in turn, had adopted the attitude that at least it had taken us to the bottom of the escarpment before shedding its wheel and should be cherished for that. The wheel was put back on at the petrol station and the German garage owner told us, 'Ja, your car, it is ready!' Eric replied that he'd like the brakes checked and when the garage owner said this had been done my friend's attitude changed and he said, icily, 'You drive it first.' 'I said it is ready,' said the German with a touch of arrogance. Having attended the Nuremburg trials with British military intelligence, Eric was not over-fond of Germans of the garage owner's age group who now lived in remote areas abroad, especially in places like the former Tanganyika which they had once colonised. He snapped an order, 'I said *you* try it!' The German garage owner almost clicked his heels before getting into the car and driving off. Marching ahead on the dusty dried grass verge of the road was a line of African schoolgirls in blue gymslips and we gazed with silent interest as the Opel went out of control and swerved from side to side as it headed towards the children. The situation seemed to be touch-and-go before the car veered off the road and stopped on waste ground. The German walked back towards us and any sign of arrogance disappeared. 'The brakes failed!' he explained. None of us replied; now we were all feeling decidedly cool towards him. Perhaps Eric had some premonition that all was not well; perhaps it was just his attitude towards Germans with steel-grey hair. Whatever, his insistence that the car be tried before we went back down the escarpment had saved us from certain death. Already under our belts now were two very narrow escapes.

Brakes fixed and tested, we were mobile and carefree again. In the middle of Tanzania and many miles from any form of civilisation, we came in the darkness of night to a road barrier. It was a rabies control post and a small, slim, elderly African dressed in an old, worn, thick brown jersey and blue shorts, detached himself from a large bonfire beside his kraal hut and looked us over. He didn't come across to me as a man of medical knowledge but he must have known a thing or two about rabies for by quickly ascertaining that none of us were foaming at the mouth, he diagnosed that we were not infected and with a smart salute he lifted the barrier to let us pass. Nothing happened – Eric had stalled the engine. As it was incumbent upon me to start the car again, I climbed from the back seat to do my duty. It was as I was walking back to reopen the rear door that the vehicle revved and shot off into the night while I stood in the road and waved, first forcibly and then limply until the tail lights disappeared in the distance. I was helpless in the middle of Africa with not the slightest hope of getting a lift to anywhere. As I was wondering about the possible attitude of the custodian of the rabies control post, he took me by the hand and led me to the fire where he introduced me to his wife and all the family, which included his mother, father and several children. He began talking but my knowledge of the dialect was nil and he then surprised me by speaking in Afrikaans and I decided he must have worked on the gold mines in Johannesburg at some stage. I had little knowledge of that language either, being confined to 'Ja', 'Hoo links' (keep left) and Nederberg Cabernet. Once, while on holiday in Cape Town my family had cringed in the back of the car when I called across to a burly, gun-toting, policeman and, airing my Afrikaans, asked, 'Oom Plod, can you direct me to…?' Fortunately for us, Enid Blyton was not on his book club mailing list.

I now sat in a crouched position between the compassionate rabies control man and his wife and pondered my fate. Those idiots, I mused, they could travel hundreds of miles before they realised I was missing and then they would wonder what had happened to me. I wasn't used to crouching and soon the bones of my knees were making their objections known by painfully forcing their way upward until they overstretched the thin taut layers of skin. Thank goodness the natives are friendly, I thought to myself and I wasn't joking. I'd heard from other travellers that Tanzania was a stroppy country where militant nationalists could be obstreperous and turn positively nasty towards white people. This, I comforted myself, was a nice homely family and with the help of the blazing fire I warmed to them quickly. Meanwhile, back in the car were two men racing towards Kenya, determined to do the journey as fast as possible. I later received an account of their conversation. 'Are you all right, Reg?' asked Eric solicitously, grateful that I had got the car going. No reply. 'It doesn't take him long to go to sleep,' Eric continued, as he drove onward. 'No,' said Tim, looking over his shoulder. There was a brief pause in this enlightened conversation before Tim made the startled pronouncement, 'He's not here!'

'Bullshit!'

'Be Jesus, Eric, I swear before God on the Holy Cross that he's not here!' Eric looked over his shoulder and when he could see neither my head nor my feet, decided to pull up and make a closer inspection, cunningly remembering to keep the engine running for there was no point in being stuck in the middle of an area known to be teeming with man-eating lions. After further inspection of the rear seat and car floor it was conceded that even my diminutive form couldn't be hiding and oaths were uttered. Hours might be wasted while going back to search for me and there was a *Time* schedule to meet. During a brief discussion they deduced that I may not have fallen from the car and been hungrily consumed by a nocturnal predator but may still be at the control post. It was worth checking.

After two hours of crouching, I looked up and saw headlights as a car approached and recognised the unmistakable griping sound of the engine. I was pleasantly surprised at the look of concern and relief on Eric and Tim's faces; they seemed happy that I'd neither been eaten by animals nor cooked for supper in a large pot. A warm handshake with my host and his family and, on recalling one more Afrikaans word, 'Totseins' (goodbye), the three good companions were off again, stopping at a one-ox town named Dodoma for the night.

Next morning we passed through Arusha, the home of Ernest Hemingway's son, but as he was away we decided instead to turn off to Moshi on the foothills of Kilimanjaro. There would be a half a day's deviation and we hoped that it would be worthwhile even though I had no doubt that it would be a total waste of valuable time. 'How exciting,' I sniffed with unconcealed sarcasm as we stood at the foot of the great snow-capped mountain and looked up. 'Piss off,' muttered Eric. 'Be Jesus,' exclaimed Tim. The mighty Kilimanjaro was only 100 ft high! Heavy cloud had come so low that visibility was a mere raindrop from our upturned faces. I'd seen more of the mountain from scheduled aircraft when its summit had pierced through an almost ever-present shroud. Dejectedly we returned to the car, which by now had collected really heavy cakes of mud, and headed for Nairobi. Eric assured us that the caked dirt would look impressive when we arrived back in Salisbury, and we all agreed. There was no question but that it must remain, even if it did put up the petrol costs through extra weight.

Eric had a military bearing: tall, with thinning grey hair and a tight military moustache. His eyes would peer straight through his thin spectacles and also the person standing in front of him. That he was shrewd and could be tough there was no question but one of his endearing charms was a gentle, yet dry sense of humour. Whenever we drove through African villages, children with their mothers would come out to wave and with a broad smile and an imperial wave back, Eric, who was anti-colonialist, would nevertheless call, 'Piss off!', deliberately mimicking what monarchs and heads of state might actually be saying to fawning flag wavers. Derisively, he insisted that it looked good to show that despite all the political eruptions, the big white bwana still cared. That was his theory which inevitably would have repercussions.

We reached Nairobi at sunset, parked the car, and headed for the New Stanley Hotel where Marion Kaplan was staying. After a quick drink with her we went to collect our baggage – which had disappeared! Thieves, expert at watching unsuspecting travellers, had speedily forced open the car door and taken several suitcases. Eric and I got off lightly but Tim lost the lot. We hadn't been used to thefts in Salisbury and expected Nairobi to be the same.

The following day, with the excuse of soaking up atmosphere for the major *Time* magazine article to be written, we went to the famous game park near the city and came across a herd of buck lined up in a row about half a mile long. Whether they had communicated through telepathy or ultrasonic language, I've no idea but stalking them were two cheetahs that were lean and hungry. The animal world knows instinctively when a predator will just stroll about and not attack – and when it will. We sat in the car and watched them with fascination for over half an hour before a man drove up and, in a very English colonial accent, called, 'I say you chaps, there are two cheetahs over there!' We looked at each other while Eric muttered a couple of familiar words and even though he couldn't possibly have heard them, the man obeyed.

Before the journey I'd contacted *Playboy* magazine to ask if they would like an in-depth interview with Jomo Kenyatta. They responded enthusiastically and suggested I send them seventy proposed questions to put to him. Writing seventy questions off the cuff isn't easy and I always prefer mine to be in response to what the interviewee has to say, but they were duly sent and were met with the full approval of *Playboy*. They were so enthusiastic that they chose to add two more, the first being: 'Do you have any qualms about being head of the Mau Mau?' Until the day he died, Kenyatta had denied being head of that bestial organisation and this was also denied to me by one of his ministers named Karioki who was proud that he personally had been a Mau Mau officer. Karioki wasn't to know that he too would be murdered, possibly by some of his former Mau Mau colleagues. The second question was even more challenging. Kenyatta had been a graduate of the London School of Economics and was, therefore, not as primitive as British Government propaganda had led people to believe. Surprisingly, he'd even been an extra in a film that projected the hazards facing white colonialists in Africa, *Sanders of the River*, starring Paul Robeson. So what was *Playboy*'s question? 'Tell me, Mr President, when did you last eat human flesh?' The interview was not granted.

One person Eric and I did interview was Kenyatta's communist vice-president, Oginga Odinga, a clownish-looking and humorous man who wore a colourful traditional African cotton dress. As we sat in his office he pointed to a small hole which had been drilled into the floor and asked, 'Do you see that?' We nodded: 'I came back early from lunch the other day and saw a man drilling the hole and as I sat at my desk he pushed some wires through it, which he then attached to my telephone.' said Odinga. What happened afterwards was Africa at its most endearing. 'Next day,' he went on, 'I went down to the floor below and opened the door of the room immediately beneath my office. Sitting at a desk was the same man with headphones on his head and a tape recorder beside him!'

In the build-up to a big festival when President Kenyatta would appear to the masses draped in a leopard skin, music blared out over the tannoys and one tune was repeated time and again. 'Do you hear that?' I asked Eric and he nodded as he grinned back knowingly. If there was one country hated more by black Africa than any other, it was South Africa. And if there is one tune that could be considered the soul music of the Afrikaner, it is 'Sari Marais'.

That night was spent at the home of our friend, George Clay. He and Ernie Christie had continued to shoot memorable film in the Congo for NBC. There was one of flamingos standing placidly at the edge of the Congo River and without the viewers' knowledge, George had thrown a stone and the flamingos flew gracefully into the air. Ernie then panned his camera to a nearby bridge where soldiers were throwing bodies into the crocodile waters below. They were a helluva team and incomparable.

The hours of darkness at George's house became the most bizarre I've ever experienced or ever wish to again as I shared my bedroom with a ghost that exuded indescribable malevolence. I've always accepted the presence of the paranormal and feel that while sceptics argue that ghosts defy logic and are a figment of the imagination, I reciprocate on whether logic really has the answer to all things or is really a comfortable protective shield behind which unbelievers hide while tossing their verbal bricks? Even Jung, who firmly rejected the existence of ghosts, sharply changed his mind while on a visit to Buckinghamshire when he turned in his bed to see the half face of a woman in his bed with her one eye open and staring at him. But then, he was an odd-ball anyway. A reason for my belief in the supernatural was that my mother, a practical person, had also seen a ghost. Sometimes she spoke of her childhood in her Cambridgeshire village and would tell me of a large Bible which was kept in her bedroom where, each night, she and her sisters would hear the pages being turned. She arrived home one day and walked upstairs to find a man standing on the top landing wearing a grey suit and a skullcap and as she was about to ask what he was doing there, he disappeared in front of her and inquiries suggested that he'd been the previous occupant of the large house. She also told of the family's St Bernard's dog which was terrified to go near the cellar door and how my grandfather awoke one night to say there was something wrong with the animal (why should he do that?) and went downstairs to find it lying dead outside the cellar door. The house eventually burned down as did much of the village, and some of the original walls of those homes still exist today even though the fire was in the late nineteenth century.

Anyway, on the night I stayed at George Clay's, there was no suspicion that anything untoward would happen. It was around midnight that we all went upstairs knowing there was a heavy schedule ahead next day but as we were about to enter our bedrooms the lights went out. No one thought much of it and by moonlight George showed me my bedroom which was at the top of the stairs and I was soon in bed and asleep. I don't know how long I slumbered; it could have been ten minutes, an hour, or two hours, before I was awakened by the persistent sound of running water and I realised that the water tank in the attic was immediately above my head. Presuming someone had flushed the toilet, I waited for the tank to refill but the running noise continued and I realised that it wasn't going to stop. Exasperated, I got out of bed and tried the light switch but nothing happened. As I stood at the switch by the bedroom door I heard rushing water downstairs and while this seemed odd, I didn't think too much about it. Following the sound, I went naked down the long grandiose marble staircase and turned right into a narrow hall which led to the kitchen. This was new territory for me but the silver moon lit the kitchen and I could see everything clearly: raised cupboards on my right while to the left was a draining board with pots, plates, cups and saucers. What particularly caught my attention were two old-fashioned brass taps which were gushing water into an old-fashioned stone sink. Assuming that either George or Ernie had left them on by mistake – the absurdity of this assumption had escaped me at the time – I turned them off and made my way back upstairs. That they had not been turned on by human fingers never entered my mind.

Soon after my return when I was back in bed, I was relieved to hear the sound from the water tank ease as it filled up and then stopped. Now for some peace! As I lay there, a sound of scraping came from the fireplace. Damned mice, I muttered and turned over with irritation. The noise was persistent and being still wideawake I swept back the bed sheet once again, this time with the murderous intention of finding a poker to dispatch the mouse. My feet never touched the floor. I'd only time to lift my head from the pillow and was beginning to sit upright when the room turned as icy as permafrost and I was entrapped in an aura of hostility and evil which I recognised with terror. On a visit to Rochester Castle in Kent with Margery and the children, the same oppressively cold and evil had insinuated itself upon us all but especially me, and we left the castle hurriedly. Now it was present again but the coldness and the evil were only part of the ordeal as the fluorescent outline of a man had manifested itself at the side of the bed and was leaning forward towards me. There was no face, just a hollow outline, yet I knew instinctively it was a man and even without a face and body he was staring at me and the sheer evil that emanated from him was terrifying. I was trapped as I couldn't sit up in bed without physically touching the outline whereas all I wanted was to get away from it. My hand stretched out and I grabbed the sheet and without even a hint of courage I threw it over my head and stayed there until there was an easing of tension. Gingerly poking my head out I was relieved that the apostle of evil had disappeared and the room had become warm again but the scraping in the fireplace continued until I went back to sleep. I've subsequently wondered why Hell has to be portrayed as being hot when my experience of evil has paradoxically been quite the opposite.

Next morning I told George of the incident and he appeared surprised and dubious. 'It's not haunted so far as I know,' he said. 'Several people have slept in that room and no one has reported anything unusual.' Feeling defensive, I pointed out that the lights had failed as we were about to walk into our rooms and to this everyone agreed. Naturally, it could have been a power cut and when we tried the switches the lights came on, but that didn't mean anything either way. Was it a hypnagogic hallucination? I was able to tell George exactly where his kitchen was and correctly stated where the cupboards were placed; where the sink was and described the type of old-fashioned brass taps that were there. This tended to validate my story and after some thought George was able to throw a little light on the matter. 'The house had previously belonged to an eccentric diamond millionaire,' he told us. 'He reputedly left a fortune in diamonds but no one has ever found them.' I inquired about his eccentricity and the reply was both chilling and amusing. Explained George, 'He became ill and knew he was for the chop so he ordered a coffin to be made and kept it beside his bed for two weeks until he died.'

'The bed I was sleeping in?' It was a rhetorical question but George answered. 'Yes, you were in the master bedroom and used the bed he died in.'

'And he was just taken out of his bed and dropped into the coffin?' George nodded affirmatively; I'd cracked it in one! Much later I asked myself why George didn't sleep in the master bedroom, which would be the natural thing for the house owner to do. That I was lying in the bed where someone had died with his coffin beside him certainly would not have put me off sleeping there. And what of those diamonds? They say you can't take them with you but it could be that the spook felt it was worth a try and perhaps he'd hidden them in the fireplace. I've also pondered if the ghost could have physically harmed me? It is easy to say no, that it was just an apparition. Yet with that being the case, how did it find the strength to turn on the big heavy taps? There was also another very disturbing thought which was very personal: why should I be singled out twice to be visited by such evil? The other side of the coin is that if such evil really exists, then forces of goodness must exist also. It also helped to confirm my strongly held belief that there really is life after life.

George invited us to spend another night but it was Eric who declined, saying that we had a busy day ahead and that George's home, at Karen, was too far to drive back to at night. He was absolutely right and I nodded vigorously in assent, feeling that the New Stanley Hotel would afford me a better night's sleep. It was the first and last time I would see the house and, sadly, George Clay. He went back to the Congo for NBC and was in a truck moving forward with Colonel Mike Hoare's mercenary force at Stanleyville when a bullet pierced the back of his skull and he died instantly. Because he was sitting upright, the cameraman with him, Klaus Krieger, did not realise that George was dead. I've never ascertained exactly what happened next but George's body was left out in the sun for three days as the battle raged and I cannot understand why it was dumped off the truck in the first place. It would not have happened if Ernie Christie had been around.

There were reports that Krieger had kept his head down so well during that three days that he would not go near the body. What was known was that Krieger and George's ex-wife, who were living together, began stripping George's home of all its possessions which effectively belonged to George's mother. But for another of Africa's larger-than-life characters, journalist-cum-lawyer, Denis Kiley, who dashed to the house and stopped the looting, everything would have disappeared. I ran into Kiley while in Nairobi and he suggested that he and I go for a Turkish bath. I can still hear his laughter after a steam bath when I was innocently led off by dusky maidens for a massage. The laughter was coming from the next cubicle and it had an ecstatic quality. The bastard!

Ernie Christie could never get over George's death and he told me how much he regretted not being in Stanleyville; the tension in his voice confirmed that he meant it. Ernie was as highly strung as a Steinway grand piano but I'm sure he wasn't frightened of anything. I once saw a beefy South African policeman try to grab his legs while he was standing on top of a police van at Cape Town Airport, filming the arrival of Robert Kennedy. Ernie smashed his camera into the interfering policeman's face and just carried on filming; he wasn't paid to argue with the law and miss the action. Fortunately for the policeman, he fell to the ground on his head and wasn't hurt and Ernie wasn't arrested, but later, when he was living in Johannesburg with a Rhodesian girl and former local TV personality, Donna Wurzel, he decided to put an end to it all. He reckoned that in addition to killing himself, he would also take Donna with him. Being the man he was, Ernie had to go out in style and on the morning of his death he rose early and drove to the airport to take off in his light aircraft, the same one in which he'd buzzed me. He flew at full throttle above the streets of Johannesburg, expertly avoiding the high-rise buildings. Ernie, the man of precision whether he used a dentist's drill or a camera, knew exactly where he was heading. He'd carefully plotted it all out beforehand, the direction, the floor and even the window of their flat and he nearly got it right as he raced forward determined to fly himself into the next world: he was just one window out and hit the flat next door, killing the occupants.

Having completed our *Time* cover story in Nairobi, Eric, Tim and I set off on our return to Salisbury. We'd heard that the local administrator at Arusha had just closed the Safari Lodge Hotel because he was affronted that during the proudest moment of his life, when he took President Sekou Toure of Guinea there to lunch, none of the diners stood up. The Safari Lodge is one of the most famous establishments of its type in the world, known to all international hunters and it was quite obvious that few of the diners recognised Sekou Toure or had even heard of him, and would see no reason why they should stand up anyway. To the administrator it was a humiliating insult to Sekou Toure, to Guinea, to Tanzania and most importantly, to himself.

A reporter in Arusha, Betty Roberts, advised me that the administrator was to hold a public meeting on the same afternoon of our arrival, in a local cinema where he would explain his actions. From the very outset we didn't take to him: 'A black Mussolini,' I whispered to Eric. After making a speech, he asked for questions from the audience. Clearly, he hadn't expected to find a small group of non-Tanzanian, white journalists there. Eric, always a quiet but penetrating interviewer, put forward the first questions, and then it was my turn. My tendency is to go for the jugular and it became clear that my questions were not well received. Eric whispered, 'We'd better get out of here, fast!' On stage the administrator was glaring hard and pointing at me; all around were the mumblings of his sycophantic supporters. We casually rose, saying, 'Thank you' and 'Goodbye' and walked out of the cinema. We could hear shuffles as others rose to follow and as we reached the street we knew that a mob was just behind. Fifty yards away was Betty standing beside her car – she had been at the back of the hall and knew what to expect. 'Jump in!' she cried as we raced to the car, followed by the angry mob which clearly had lynching on their minds. I have a great respect for many women drivers and for Betty Roberts in particular when, with her engine already running, she raced us away from the howling mob. It was a close shave in which she had risked her own life to save us! After we bade farewell and gave thanks to our courageous and forward-thinking benefactor, we half expected a telephone call would be made to Tana (the governing party) officials to arrest us en route. This wasn't to happen but as we passed through one village, Eric waved his hand and smiled magnanimously and he was about to exchange his usual greeting when the words froze on his lips. Waving their fists, the villagers shouted, 'Piss off!'

Back across the border and into Zambia, we stopped off for lunch at the Elephant's Head in Broken Hill and by now the car was thoroughly caked with dirt and we were very proud of it and even commented on how impressive it would be when we drove through the antiseptic streets of Salisbury. As we sat down in the restaurant, Eric looked across at a young lady sitting at a nearby table as if she had come from another planet. This was hardly surprising as she had pink hair and in the early 1960s in Africa, this was considered most unusual. She had more surprises to follow which I discovered when Eric nudged me, 'Do you see that?' From her cleavage emerged a nose and two beady eyes which began to survey the diners, one by one. This was too much for me and I gulped down my food and went across to interview her. 'Come to my room, dearie,' she said, invitingly. Eric overheard the conversation and dubbed her the Cockney Cleopatra! As I entered her bedroom in my ophiological pursuit, she put her hand down the top of her dress and produced a fully grown Egyptian cobra. 'Ain't it lovely,' she demurred. I backed away as for all I knew it could be a spitting cobra and I'd already had an eyeful. 'He's my pet and I take him everywhere,' she continued. I'd heard of girls with fetishes for snakes but never expected to be closeted in a bedroom with one. 'Do you have any more down there?' I asked with an appreciative glance at her cleavage. She smiled sweetly, 'No Ducks, one's quite enough for me.' As we sat on the bed she caressed the snake and I ventured, uncertainly, 'Do you sleep with it?' My mind was aroused at what she might get up to but, as if in answer, she bent over and stroked the cobra hypnotically as she put it to rest in a basket under the bed. During my interview I learned that the Cockney Cleopatra, whose talon-like fingernails would have torn an elephant's hide from its back, was a professional snake dancer. 'So what are you doing here?' I asked in wonder, for Broken Hill in Zambia is not a thriving metropolis; it's not even a metropolis. 'I'm travelling up to Nairobi,' she explained and I replied, chattily, 'I've just come from there.' The official version, as put out by Eric and Tim, is that I was in bed making love when she came out with the ultimate question while my totally accurate version is that we were doing nothing of the sort. But on learning that I'd just come down from Nairobi, she asked me in a voice choking with emotion, 'Do you know George Clay?'

As we left the hotel an African came up to us, beaming from ear to ear and he held out his hand, 'Money, please Baas.' We looked at each other suspiciously, and feared the worst. The glint in Eric's eyes was lethal as I stifled a choking sensation. 'Why?' we asked. 'For cleaning your car, it was very dirty!' The Opel had never looked cleaner, its green paint shining under the brilliant sun as the mud and dust collected over 3,000 miles of travel on dirt roads, over passes, down escarpments, through pouring rain, blistering heat and freezing cold, disappeared during lunch.

Our money was running low with still around 1,000 miles to go, and as we crossed into Southern Rhodesia we hadn't enough left for petrol. We called at an Indian-owned garage and I showed the proprietor my card from Broadcasting House and asked him if he would take a cheque. He studied the card for a long time, reading every word carefully with an occasional long stare at my features to confirm beyond doubt that I had the same face as that on the photograph. He then looked at the highly polished Opel and wrung his hands in torment and I felt his anguish as he declared with the passion of a mourner who has just lost his mother, father, brother and sister swept away in a great flood of the Ganges, 'Oh, goodness me,' in a voice that would later be aped by Peter Sellers, 'these are very unsettling times in our country when we don't know what is going to happen. It is a time that causes me much worry.' His hands and his body contorted as he stressed the seriousness of the political situation, before continuing, 'But in these terrible troubled times we must trust one another; we must help lame dogs over stiles.' 'Yes, indeed,' I replied, solemnly. 'Does that mean you will accept my cheque?'

'Ah, yes,' he said. 'I will give you petrol.' Then he added, staring hard first at me and then the cheque which he held aloft as if seeking holy guidance, 'But you must tell me – will it bounce?'

The Federal break-up caused turmoil in the minds of many, from the Asian garage owner to one of the most powerful men in one part of Zambia, the Litunga of Barotseland. An uneasy question mark hung over the future of the Paramount Chief as he had actively supported the Federation but now his territory came under the jurisdiction of the new Zambian government of President Kenneth Kaunda. The Litunga, the title meaning 'Keeper of the Earth', was Sir Mwanawina Lewanika III, a well-educated seventy-five-year-old, who had actually banned Kaunda's nationalist agitators from his domain and when Eric Robins and I learned that Kaunda was to take eleven of his cabinet ministers to a Kuamboka, we knew that this was something not to be missed. Like Kaunda, we'd never been to a Kuamboka; unlike Kaunda, we had never even heard of it and I even had to look on a map to check out exactly where Barotseland was. The Kuamboka, I learned, was a colourful African ceremony where the Litunga is taken from his summer to his winter palace and there is a practical reason for the move: during the wet summer season, the rains cause the vast Barotse plains to flood into a grassy lake 120 miles long and 35 miles wide causing thousands of Barotse tribespeople to get into their canoes to quant and paddle with the Litunga for six hours in ninety-degree Fahrenheit temperatures until they reached high land at a place called Mongu. It is this same water from the Barotse Plains that feeds the restless Zambezi River as it annually races downstream to cascade over the Victoria Falls with spectacular, ear-splitting force while making its way eastward to the Indian Ocean.

With Eric and Marion Kaplan, I arrived in Barotseland for the historic extravaganza, knowing that this could be the last of the Kuambokas. If Kaunda was unimpressed by the glorification of his former enemy and felt that it perpetuated unnecessarily an anachronism in the modern state of Zambia, he could simply ban it. On the other hand, by the act of being there he had tentatively expressed a spirit of reconciliation, accepting the olive branch handed out by the Litunga. I learned that by tradition, the Litunga had to travel in a large enclosed royal barge called the Nalikwanda. According to custom, the Nalikwanda has no windows and if the Litunga should get fed up with sitting in the dark and showed his face before reaching Mongu, he would be murdered by the tribesmen. There was one dyspeptic Litunga who wasn't remotely popular with his people and they, with regicidal cunning, plotted his demise during a Kuamboka. He entered his 102-ft long barge and was taken to the centre of the plains where the oarsmen sank the boat and were taken off by other canoeists. The Litunga sat in his enclosure, initially unaware that anything was amiss until the water began to rise about him. He found himself in a catch-22 situation for if he showed his face he would be physically killed but if he stayed aboard he would drown. Legend has it that he preferred the water to the spear.

Kuamboka with Marion Kaplan and Eric Robins

By tradition, the barge eventually becomes a tomb when it is sunk with the Litunga aboard after his death. In the past, many of the royal paddlers volunteered to go down with him in order to guide him through the clouds surrounding that great Kuamboka in the sky. Because of the length of the Nalikwanda, it has been subsequently likened to Noah's Ark, which is a misnomer as no female is ever allowed on board the royal barge. Such is the discipline, that any paddler who quants out of time with the rhythm of the others is thrown overboard. As we watched, the Barotse king left his summer palace on the dwindling island of Lealui, dressed elegantly in a cream silk frock-coat, matching trousers, and a grey top hat. It was an outfit that would have gone down well at Ascot. All the royal paddlers wore red hairpieces and the headgear was made from the hair of lions. Together with the hundreds of other canoeists, they also wore lion or leopard skins around their waists.

We were approached by a canoeist who offered to take us across the plains for a small remuneration. One look at him and I recalled a phrase used by every London bobby giving evidence at magistrates' courts: 'His eyes were glazed, his pupils dilated, and I formed the impression that he was under the influence of alcohol.' We boarded and began moving forward before the rest of the drum-beating armada so that we would be well out in front for Marion to photograph the whole scene. But our canoeist was in trouble from the start as we manoeuvred around in figures of eight. Laughed Marion, 'He's as drunk as a fiddler's bitch.' Another canoe was passing and we hailed it across and climbed aboard without our captain even noticing. Safely dug in on the dugout, we waved to him and he waved back, never realising that we were his passengers. I watched fascinated as some of Kaunda's cabinet ministers from the same Lozi tribe, paddled their hearts out as they took their leader across the plain, a sight of which Margaret Thatcher would have thoroughly approved. Drums beat furiously and the expert way they rowed to the rhythm of the drums suggested that some slave ships of another age might have netted expert crews from Barotseland.

Whether the Litunga was alone in his cabin aboard the Nalikwanda there is no way of telling, but I suspect he had both a valet and a candle, for when we at last arrived at Mongu, he had cast off his dandy apparel to emerge resplendent in the gold-braid uniform of a British Admiral of the Fleet, complete with dress sword and plumed tricorn hat! He moved towards the head of a procession to his winter palace with such dignity that the Royal Navy would have been proud of him. Only Africa can produce such an event; only innovative British diplomacy could have provided the uniform. I made some inquiries and the following account is less embroidered that it would seem to be…

There'd been an insurmountable problem of crocodiles dramatically decimating the Barotse population and the Litunga's father, fearful of a repetition of his ancestor's demise, reluctantly agreed with the tribesmen that his royal personage must do something about the carnage. Sitting on his reed-woven throne, he was perusing a four-year-old back-number of *The Times* dated 1896 which referred to the growing British submarine fleet, with particular reference to the recently launched all-electric number called *Nautilus*. This, reasoned the Litunga, was the weapon he needed and thinking of the money to be made from crocodile skins, he dashed off a cleft-stick messenger offering his friend, Queen Victoria, some lion and leopard skins, plus a rhino horn in exchange for the *Nautilus*. Here was a something not greeted with amusement by Her Imperial Majesty. Now that her consort, Albert, was dead, there would be no need by him for the aphrodisiac rhino horn for starters. The message had taken a year to arrive and it was now 1901. With the Litunga's request weighing heavily upon her ample bosoms, she retired to her summer retreat at Osborne House on the Isle of Wight and expired without the matter being resolved. Victoria's playboy son, Edward VII, who, being far too preoccupied with his social life, passed the matter over to the Colonial Office with a flippant and jocular, 'Why not make the old boy an admiral?' The merry monarch could not be taken too lightly and triplicate memoranda were trudged for several years between the Colonial Office and the Admiralty by lowly messengers to whom even a cleft stick had been denied. The deliberations seemed endless until it was finally agreed that the *Nautilus* could not be spared.

With the tact inborn in British diplomats, it was agreed the Litunga should be regretfully informed that the cost of firing just one torpedo at a crocodile would be economically prohibitive to Barotseland. The expenditure would far outweigh the revenue from the skins, a good one selling at around two shillings and fourpence. In respectful but unequivocal terms, the Litunga would be told that the world of *haute couture* was unpredictable, especially as it was dominated by the French, and that a sack of shrapnel-impregnated crocodile skins might even be rejected. 'What the Litunga really needs is to retain his authority and prove, that with British support, he is the most important paramount chief in Africa,' said the Colonial Secretary over lunch with the First Sea Lord. Then Edward VII's comment came to mind. 'I suppose you could make him an admiral; after all, no one would notice.' And so it was, in 1908, that the Admiralty officially denied the submarine request and presented the Litunga with the uniform of the Admiral of the Fleet.

It's difficult to understand why the Litunga should spend winter at such a desolate place as Mongu when, with such a splendid uniform, he could easily have cruised with the British Mediterranean Fleet. Mongu is as colourless as a parched maize patch in the Kalahari Desert, boasting only a straw palace, some administrative buildings, native huts and little else. At least, on the occasion when I arrived, something was truly happening. Here was the Litunga, the President, and the police band especially flown in from Lusaka. Officials' wives, too, had been flown in to be presented at the ball. Many people make boastful, exaggerated claims about their accomplishments, but they crumble in defeat on learning that I have actually been to a Saturday night hop in Mongu!

Eric, Marion and myself were twelve months ahead of other journalists in discovering the Kuamboka. Having read our reports, several turned up the following year and demanded a press launch, which was provided. They had already missed the boat so far as I was concerned but the one they travelled in did provide a modicum of excitement: it followed the watery course of the former Litunga and sank.

On another trip to Zambia, Eric and I visited the Valley of the Blind where we were to meet a remarkable man who was one of the world's leading eye specialists, Malcolm Phillips. As we crossed the Luapula River by ferry to meet Phillips, we were quickly reminded of the dangers of the area when a large water snake accompanied us swimming beside the boat.

Phillips had become an ophthalmologist with Dr Kenneth Kaunda's government but he began his work in the Luapula Province in 1949 and after nine years he produced the first detailed report of blindness amongst the 250,000 Africans in the province. He reported a staggering 3,235 blind per 100,000 people in the Kawambwa district of the valley alone. Of these, 83.2 per cent were blind by the age of ten years, and ninety per cent by the age of twenty. It was the highest blindness rate in the world. Compare this with England at that time which is the same size as the province, and average blindness rates amongst those under twenty measured fifteen per 100,000. Phillips had obtained the figures by simply getting on his bike and cycling much of the 200 miles along the river close to the Congo border. Where he found places inaccessible to motor vehicles, he cycled through the bush along almost unnoticeable footpaths without a thought for the predators which were around. During one tour alone, he performed 500 eye operations within a fortnight at just one village and many of the people he gave sight to there were blinded with cataracts before he was born. Responsible for much of the loss of sight were witchdoctors: 'There's no doubt in my mind that the main cause of blindness in the valley has been the use of native remedies for eye complaints,' he told me. 'It's an area which has suffered from frequent measles epidemics.'

As soon as the children's eyes began to ache, they were treated with primitive medicines, all prepared under filthy conditions which caused the destruction of corneas and eyes. Among the popular 'remedies' which the unsuspecting villagers paid the witchdoctors to help them and their children go blind, was chifufya, a preparation consisting of pounding a stone of copper carbonate to make a powder which is wetted. Soot from the roof of a mud hut is added and the concoction is then mixed together as a paste which is delicately applied to the eyes with a feather. Another is kameme, and to make this a portion of tuberous root is bored and the child then urinates into it. This is administered as eye drops. One 'remedy' that claimed many victims was made with leaves with a distinctly acid flavour plus watered snuff and the juice of crushed chillies administered as drops through a funnel made from a tree leaf. 'Most people are familiar with the effects of chillies, or red peppers in the mouth,' Phillips told me. 'Imagine what it must be like to have it as drops in the eyes!' It was truly a matter of 'blind faith' in the charlatan witchdoctors, but

Phillips managed to persuade the government into bringing in new laws with harsh penalties to those who use potions on other people's eyes which might endanger sight and an anti-witchcraft campaign was carried out telling people the truth about their remedies. While people who live primitively may not know any better than to use stinging substances, Malcolm Phillips made an analogy by pointing out that many men prefer the most powerful after-shave lotion they can find, just because they believe it is doing them good. They live in Britain, Europe and the United States... On a visit to Zambia and Zimbabwe in 1997 I was disappointed to see how much witchcraft had not only returned in strength to these countries, but was even welcomed with pride.

It's incumbent upon an intrepid journalist in Africa to possess a Land Rover; that was the excuse Eric and I used to convince ourselves into buying one. After all, we argued, the Land Rover was as much responsible for opening up the hinterland of Africa as the horse was to the American wild west. We bought a second-hand job but it was better than any of Eric's cars. Everything worked, even the starter and in order to keep it in such pristine condition we never left a tarred road to go into the bush – that was reserved for motorcars. But we did manage grand tours and on one trip we drove down to Lourenco Marques (Maputo) in Mozambique to meet Marion Kaplan who had just returned from an overseas trip. Marion, who was making a name for herself as a photographer – she later did work for *National Geographic* and became a journalist and author – had already hitch-hiked the length of Africa by herself and had the audacity as a Jewish girl to travel up the east coast of Africa on an Arab dhow. Later she spent five months on a dhow for the geographical magazine. Her courage is indisputable and she once forged a document in French, purporting to be from the president, to get into a forbidden area in the Congo where she went on a very dangerous mission with a group of mercenaries: a true war correspondent.

After picking Marion up we decided to drive back via Johannesburg which meant first travelling through mountainous Swaziland. We had no problems until we reached the South African border when the truck had a puncture. The South African police and border officials were surprisingly charming and they even changed the wheel for us. Marion had decided to make her home in Rhodesia with Eric and wanted to collect some boxes of books from Johannesburg which was duly done. Amongst the goods and unknown to me was a stack of papers belonging to the *New York Times* correspondent, Larry Fellowes, who had run foul of the authorities in Pretoria and had to leave the country in a hurry. En route, we stopped over at a small dorp for lunch and there were only two others in the restaurant, an elderly Afrikaner couple. During the meal we watched fascinated when the lady snapped her fingers and a black waiter came across. She pointed to a fly swatter resting on their table and then to a fly. With that, the waiter picked up the swatter and with a quick flip, deftly brought it down on the unsuspecting fly with a splat. Then he put the swatter back on the table and walked away. We were still laughing at the incident when we drove off and straight into another. 'Look a that!' yelled Marion before she creased into a raucous laugh. A white man was standing beside the road looking at our truck expectantly. Beside him was an African hitch-hiking for him with his thumb! We drove on.

On reaching the border post on the Limpopo River at Beit Bridge which separates South Africa and Rhodesia, we stayed the night at Peter's Motel and next morning we went to the border post as it opened. I glanced at a notice board inside the Immigration counter and saw a hand-written note which carried the number of our Land Rover and the names, Reginald Robert Shay, Eric Robins and Marion Kaplan. 'They're going to search us,' I reported to the others. 'I wonder what the hell this is all about.' As I handed over my passport, the Immigration man called over to another official who wore pince-nez spectacles and I noticed his pallid tight face bore a remarkable resemblance to Heinrich Himmler. He peered at me through sinister narrowed eyes, 'We vish to examine your vehicle,' he hissed between gritted teeth. 'Go ahead,' I replied.

He started the inspection with Larry Fellowes papers which referred to a famous communist-inspired bus strike in South Africa and these, with many other papers belonging to Larry, were studied in such a manner as if they were subversive to touch and he disdainfully held them, knowing he was soiling both his hands and his mind. After examining each paper he looked up at me menacingly without uttering a word. Then came Marion's books and on top of the piles was a biography of Jomo Kenyatta. The official stared in horror and disbelief as the black face of Kenyatta on the cover scowled back at him. Marion's eyes twinkled with amusement when, in disgust, he slammed the book on to the table in front of him. That we, three Europeans, should have a book with a kaffir's face on it in a purist country that had banned *Black Beauty*, was inconceivable. What was written on his face were the words, 'These are three blurry kaffir boeties.'

The books were placed in three piles. The largest – and all of these were slammed down – were those he had considered subversive. The next that might be subversive but he wasn't sure, were also slammed but with less severity. The third pile was very small but treated with great reverence when he discovered that one book was about his own beloved prime minister, Dr Hendrik Verwoerd. 'Man, I shall call a senior police officer from Louis Trichardt,' he said with a heavy Afrikaans accent. Louis Trichardt was about eighty miles away and I complained that we would be hanging around for some time. 'You can go for coffee across the street but you cannot go in your truck,' he replied, darkly. Over coffee, Eric and Marion voted two-to-one that as the Land Rover was in my name, I should take the brunt of the questioning. That sort of gesture from friends I can happily do without, but they were adamant. Perhaps they were relying on my simple, open, innocent and honest face to see us through. When he arrived, the senior officer from the secret police turned out to be pleasant; it was the classic pattern of the bad guy followed by the good guy. His questions were simple and I protested our innocence: 'I've never seen any of these things before and in the light of what is happening, I don't want to see them again,' I protested, and I heard Marion suck in her breath. 'You can take the lot if you wish but remember, we are taking them out of the country.'

This took him back a little and I explained that we had only picked up the books and papers for friends. After what seemed an age, he telephoned his superiors and said that we could go and take all our goods with us. We had been kept for twelve hours! So what was it about? The senior officer from Louis Trichardt had told me that when we went through the Swaziland-South Africa border post, the Immigration official had noticed that Ghana was stamped in Marion's passport. As Ghana was a black state hostile to South Africa it was believed she could not be up to any good and a message was sent to Beit Bridge to check us out. We crossed the border just as the post was closing and on the Rhodesian side it was clear they had received a message, and began to give us a hard time. This was too much for now that I was on my home ground I blew up, pointing out my citizenship. 'Miss Kaplan will not be allowed in as she hasn't the necessary funds to stay here,' I was told. I pulled out a cheque book and snapped. 'I shall guarantee her.' They backed down and we were through but Marion was very lucky.

My gallivanting around Africa had made Margery decide that she wanted to learn to drive and off she went to a driving school. After a few lessons I went out with her to see how she was progressing. We approached some traffic lights on the red and she serenely drove over them as cars on each side started to hoot and brake. It must have been an oversight, I thought; perhaps too much concentration on the gears. We came to more lights and this time there were cars waiting in front. She was about to crash when I pulled the handbrake and shouted, 'Stop!' It was a Bob Newhart situation. 'Didn't you see those cars?' I asked.

'Not until we stopped,' she replied.

'What about those earlier lights, didn't you see them?'

'Yes,' she said, 'as we were going over.' I knew there was nothing wrong with her vision.

'Why didn't you see them earlier?'

'Because I was concentrating on keeping the car in line with the kerb.'

'I don't understand. Why couldn't you keep the car in line and look ahead at the same time?'

'How can I do that?' I was becoming quite perplexed.

'What are they teaching you at the driving school?'

'That I should keep the centre of the car lined up with the kerb.'

'Yes, but what about looking ahead?' To my astonishment this well-adjusted, intelligent woman replied,

'They told me to keep my eyes on the road and line up with the kerb.'

I took her in hand after that and once she had got the hang of looking ahead, she passed her driving exam the first time. Margery became a very good driver. On one occasion we were travelling at night towards Zambia and she was at the wheel of the Chevy when a pantechnicon came towards us on the wrong side of the road with headlights blazing. We would have been flattened but for her quick reaction. She swerved to the right (the wrong side of the road), down a sharp water drainage ditch and sped along at an angle and speed which keeps 'Wall of Death' drivers from falling. Then we were out of the ditch and on the road. It was a breathtakingly superb effort.

UDI

The build-up to Ian Smith's Unilateral Declaration of Independence was reminiscent to me of 1939, providing as it did the same nervous anticipation of events when everyone knew that once the declaration was made, lives would be lost and life itself would never be quite the same for those involved. And as with WW2, each and every one of us would be involved in one way or another and Armistice Day, 11 November, was the date coldly and calculatingly chosen to appeal to war veterans worldwide. In Britain emotions ran deep amongst many people in favour of Rhodesians who had all volunteered to fight with them in the war, while most of the British immigrants were war veterans who had simply come to the country to look for a better life than their rain-soaked motherland could offer. Smith was aware that the bulk of the white population was pro-royal and insisted his move was honourable; that it was against the British government of the day and not the Crown to which he professed loyalty. Eric Robins, ever succinct in his assessments, declared to me with cynical and acerbic clarity: 'This is high treason in the name of the Queen!' Smith made much of 'kith and kin' ties with Britain and said the British would never send troops to fight against her own people. The Royal Rhodesian Air Force was equally convinced that the RAF would never attack their aircraft and in another of Africa's farcical situations, when Harold Wilson sent war planes to neighbouring Zambia immediately after UDI, they were actually talked down to the runway at Lusaka from the Salisbury airport tower!

Having announced that he had taken the illegal action to perpetuate white rule, Smith blandly produced a 'Declaration of Independence' which was purported to be based on that of the United States. And if that message wasn't appealing enough to the US government to support the rebellion, a 'Liberty Bell' was struck. My personal assessment was that Smith's variations on the American Bill of Rights were milked from George Orwell's *Animal Farm*. To the black Africans the bell did not ring true and the death toll fifteen years later from taking up arms would be an estimated 27,000 men, women and children of all races, but mainly black. White African youngsters propelled into the forces were later to become morosely bitter when it was realised that the deaths of their friends and sometimes their own maiming had been for nothing. Britain had been responsible for Rhodesia's defence and foreign affairs but in one stroke of the pen Smith had cast aside this protection and now there was no one to verbally defend the country at the United Nations and elsewhere, while physically there was no one from outside the country to defend it at all with the exception of a handful of South African security force police and helicopter pilots; mercenaries who were made to join up and be properly trained and, years later, a detachment of French Foreign Legionnaires who were not very good in counter-insurgency bush warfare.

The emergency meant that people of all races would be uprooted from their homes with many blacks going into detention without trial while some whites who objected were put on the next plane out at their own expense, making a nonsense of citizenship status. Smith was to split long-term loyal friendships and even marriages, which included my own. With the resignations of my colleagues and myself from the SRBC having been applauded by the public at large, it had been a matter of government priority now to denigrate the press and present journalists as being anything but people of integrity. Ivor Benson came into his own: Hitler had burned the Reichstag and blamed others to start his campaign of tyranny; Benson's Reichstag was a dustbin and a well-manicured lawn. Rumours soon circulated from the Information Department and then perpetuated by government ministers, that an overseas television team had been seen to throw coins or sweets into a dustbin and then filmed black children scrambling in after them. The object of the filming was to present the false picture that the blacks were underfed and scavenging.

The impact on the public took me by surprise. Despite television teams having the name of their companies labelled on the cameras and camera cases – BBC, ITN, ABC News, NBC, CBS, CBC, etc. – identity of the culprits differed. I found it remarkable how many people happened to be passing the dustbin when the incident occurred (reminiscent of the number of people who owned the Granada cinema crocodile!), and how many more people actually 'saw' the film in Britain and the United States.

This piece of fiction was followed by another Benson inspiration which claimed that a London national newspaper had published a photograph of Africans sleeping on the lawn of the city's Cecil Square with the caption, 'In Rhodesia, they don't even bury their dead!' These two cleverly orchestrated pieces of propaganda thus destroyed the credibility of the overseas media. Many claimed to have seen the newspaper which varied from the *Daily Mirror* to *The Times* but no one ever produced a copy. By using the carefully crafted fabrications, Benson had overnight changed the attitude of usually thinking whites into a people who were prepared to recklessly throw away their precious civilised standards, the very standards they were claiming to cherish. As the first victim of the Rhodesian Front government was the freedom of speech it became difficult to admit to being a journalist because this implied in brainwashed minds that I was a spy. I read one secret defence document some years later which actually stated that all journalists should be treated as enemy agents. There was even a 'Don't talk' poster (a nostalgic reminder of Britain during the war) with the listening spy in silhouette outline bearing a remarkable resemblance to myself! It beggared belief to me that men who had fought tyranny were now prepared to condone and even support it. By changing the public's attitude towards the press, the pro-Nazi Benson was also able to change its attitude towards life. While communist countries would prove to be a genuine threat with potential guerrillas being trained in communist countries, it was also the ideal bogeyman for propaganda.

I was particularly interested at the time of UDI when Ian Smith declared, 'We are the bastion of western civilisation against communism.' The phrase had a familiar ring to it and I recalled a *Daily Express* article many years before by Sefton Delmer in which he said that Goebbels and Hitler had used the theme at the inauguration of the Third Reich which sought to make the suspension of civil rights, the concentration camps, and the menacing military preparation palatable to the 'bourgeois' western world. It went, 'We are the West's only bulwark against the Bolshevisation of Europe. Without us to stand against it, Bolshevism will break through and you will all be lost.' As the years rolled on and the propaganda and the tolls of war increased, men who had fought in the world war were openly saying that perhaps Hitler's racial policies were right after all. Their attitude towards Jews was sympathetic (the Israeli government and security forces were secretly in constant touch with their Rhodesian counterparts) but if gas chambers had been created for blacks, I have little doubt that many heads would have turned the other way.

This would be borne out later when black villages were shot up or burned with home-made napalm in order to kill a possible terrorist in hiding. 'We should wipe out all the black bastards' was a common expression. Fascinated, I was watching a repeat of history from the pre-war German side, right down to the eventual building of a concentration camp where many children and elderly were to die on a daily basis.

Three British MPs came to Rhodesia on a so-called fact-finding mission shortly after UDI and following a talk with Ian Smith they held a public meeting in an hotel banqueting hall. Four hundred people turned up and in the light of the packed hall clouds of blue cigarette smoke flirted with each other until they interwove into a thick cloud which licked the air in anticipation of the storm ahead. A question was asked by a seemingly nice little old lady who was mystified and hurt that the British government was not supporting its own kith and kin. As one British MP began to reply, thugs moved in and during the resulting melee in which the three men were beaten up the audience applauded and hurled insults, 'Liars, yellow bastards, communists!' I knew at once it had all been pre-planned for as the MP began to speak the same lady held up a hand as a signal for the thugs to attack. The part she played was confirmed to me later at the Herbert Gibbons gymnasium that I used, as one of the bully boys was a member. Even the lady's part was too reminiscent of Nazi Germany to the point where Hitler had raised a hand to start the riot which landed him in the jail where he wrote *Mein Kampf*. Deep down I was very ill at ease at the hatred that had been engendered and once again wondered if I had made a terrible mistake in coming to Rhodesia to live permanently.

'There's a man threatening to beat me up,' cried a distressed Marion Kaplan who ran across the hall to where a small group of journalists were watching the fracas. 'He keeps trying to grab my camera and has accused me of taking "lying photographs".' Following her was a medium-sized, middle-aged man in a grey suit who tried to grab Marion before one of us told him to clear off. Unwisely he then went up aggressively to the apparent smallest in our group (usually it's me), delightfully selecting Peter Younghusband who was kneeling on the floor writing some notes. 'Come and fight,' snarled the aggressor. 'What's that?' growled Big Pete as he looked up, and like a giant bear being awakened from its slumbers he slowly rose and as he did so his huge frame unfurled until he towered over the belligerent. Peter rested his paw on the startled man's shoulder as he said quietly in his deep voice, 'I think you had better leave.'

Portraying Ian Smith as a great RAF war hero and fighter ace was another Benson projection. That Smith was a fighter pilot is without question; but the inference was that he was a Battle of Britain pilot defending Britain's shores was manifestly untrue. His patched-up face was portrayed as a visible proof of combat whereas he came down over Italy, apparently after he'd run out of fuel. I called on Government House to interview Smith and asked him in passing what medals he had collected. He was most charming, as he could be. 'None actually, but I was due for one.'

'Did you shoot down any German aircraft?'

'Well, no, I never saw one when I was in the air!' Smith had specialised in strafing, which was an essential and dangerous job in itself and he had also volunteered to fight which was very much to his credit. He had also fought with the Italian partisans which was highly commendable and took a lot of guts. But the portrayal of him by imputation as being a glamorous and illustrious dog-fight survivor was sheer propaganda which I'm sure he found embarrassing.

The advent of UDI meant that everyone wanted to interview Ian Smith and he fled to the quiet of his farm in Selukwe. *Life* magazine sent a staff writer, Jim Hicks, and photographer Terry Spencer for an interview. Terry told me he'd been a British fighter pilot in the war but that seemed to be all he had in common with Smith. We decided to drive to the farm about 150 miles from Salisbury and secrecy was of the utmost importance as we knew we would be stopped should the police get wind of our plan. Unfortunately, some other journalists had the same bright idea and talked it over in a bar where the ever-present Special Branch was eavesdropping and as we approached Selukwe we ran into a police road block where we appeared to be expected. 'Are you journalists?' asked the inspector in charge. It was when he asked for our names which they checked against a list that we realised why we were stopped, 'Oh, we've caught you in the net we set for others,' said the jubilant inspector.

We were ordered to follow a Land Rover to the police station at Gwelo, the main town in the area and Terry took a photograph through the rear window of the road block. 'I think they saw me,' he said and anticipating that any film would be confiscated he handed me the roll and quickly put another into his camera. As we followed the police vehicle I looked out of the window and noticed a public loo. 'Hold it, I need a pee,' I said and got out of the car to hide the film behind a cistern. Sure enough, at Gwelo police station a pompous superintendent demanded that Terry hand over his film of the roadblock. 'We're not fools, you know,' he said loudly for all the policemen in the general office to hear while Terry emptied his camera under protest and handed over the unused roll.

Despite giving the film away we were still being kept at the station and demanded to know why. Glaring at us in an unfriendly fashion, the superintendent walked away and began dictating a statement to a constable clerk, whose keyboard speed left much to be desired. I offered to type it for him but this was declined and after more than half an hour the superintendent presented each of us with a ten-line typewritten order which he had personally signed. I still have a framed copy for as we were reading it through, Jim Hicks howled with laughter and waved the document about shouting, '*Life* magazine isn't pornographic!' All the policemen stared curiously while the superintendent, his face colouring slightly with uncertainty, demanded, 'What do you mean?'

'Hear this, fellows,' called out Jim to the policemen, totally ignoring their superior officer. He had a captive audience of law upholders as he yelled, 'It says here that we mustn't photograph police erections!'

American television newsmen arriving at an airport in Africa tend to resemble Dr David Livingstone, with sweating black bearers carrying their multitudinous gear of all shapes and sizes. Their excess baggage costs are horrific by general standards but they work on the basis that they should never be short of anything to make a film successful. Conversely, most British teams carry the absolute minimum.

An ABC News team wanted to interview Smith at his farm and the car I hired was an automatic which was something new to me, and after they put their equipment aboard I took the wheel. As we approached Selukwe we reached the top of an escarpment and I began to drive down. I touched the brake on approaching a sharp bend but there was no response! On an ordinary gear change I would not have been unduly concerned as we weren't travelling fast but because it was the first time I had driven an automatic, and because of the weight of four men and all their equipment, I knew that I was in real trouble. Fortunately I managed to bring the car to a halt with the handbrake but it wasn't without sweat and then I broke the news to the others. Slowly I reversed the heavy shooting brake up the escarpment with luggage blocking vision in the reverse mirror, leaving me with just the offside wing mirror for navigation. By the time the brakes were repaired it was too late to see Smith and the trip was abandoned.

I was with the same group in the middle of nowhere when we were stopped at a tsetse control post. A uniformed African approached, saluted us and then slammed his fly whisk at an imaginary tsetse fly before smiling broadly to inform us with great confidence that we could now drive off in safety. We all agreed that it was truly comforting to know that this unassuming man had single-handedly protected us all from the dreaded tripanosomiasis disease. Further along the road we came to a very smart khaki-clad African policeman, his highly polished leather gaiters and boots reflecting incongruously against the sun-parched dirt and scrub surroundings. Raising an arm for us to stop, as though in the centre of a city main street, he ordered with solemn dignity, 'Excuse me, sir, but would you kindly activate your hooter?' I left the car to stretch my legs and the American who was driving was totally bewildered: 'Say, what's that you're telling me?' he asked the policeman nervously. Here he was in a foreign country being stopped by a black cop saying something in a strange unintelligible tongue. 'Would you kindly activate your hooter, sir?' My driver companion's face took on an unhealthy pasty complexion and the others looked decidedly uncomfortable. The driver asked in near panic, 'What have I done wrong, Reg?'

'He wants you to sound your horn!' As the policeman saluted, having been satisfied by the blaring sound which sent a herd of impala scattering for cover, I was now the one to look perplexed that the car didn't move off immediately. Having regained their self-assurance, my barbaric American companions showed no sign of respect either for the law or for the officer's perfectly correct use of the English language; they were quite literally doubled up on the floor in hysterics.

One ABC News man always took along a little wooden box wherever he went and that box must have been around the world a few times. I never saw him take it into an hotel; it was left in the car waiting for the moment when the owner would demand its services. There was nothing spectacular about it, nor sinister. The wood was solid enough, like that used as footrests by shoe-shine boys from as far afield as New York and Madrid. But I knew that if the owner ever lost it there would be panic; the box was his image maker.

So what was the secret? Height, for this man was vertically challenged and only slightly taller than me. Actors like the late Alan Ladd had it easy as it's common knowledge that his tall leading lady would merely walk along a newly dug trench from which she talked to him on the level. But what of an American TV news reporter who didn't have an army of diggers to hand? Usually if there is a height difference, reporters prefer to interview sitting down either in an armchair in a garden or the house. But there are times when there is no chair or there has to be a particular backdrop which necessitates standing: that's where the box came in. To the unconcealed amusement of interviewees, he brought the box from the car and stood on it with microphone in hand to conduct a serious interview.

Another ABC News man began to act so strangely that he locked himself in his hotel room for days on end. Sometimes I received a phone call from New York asking where the hell he was. Always being protective of the staff man on the spot, I'd say that he was out of town looking for some unspecified story. When he did eventually emerge he was either furtive or totally authoritative, demanding interviews with leading personalities. I'd know the people person-ally but to the consternation of the interviewees and embarrassment to everyone concerned he demanded that I leave the scene. At an important press conference with a leading political figure, he asked the same question nine times until he was told to shut up. There was little I could do or say as a staff man was my superior so far as his company was concerned and the whole matter was distressing as he must have been a fine reporter before he flipped his lid. Should I tell New York the truth? It was a difficult decision and I decided to ride it out, guessing that the film which was eventually sent back would give them an indication of what was going on. The crunch came for him when he said a few words to camera to open his story and he repeated them seventeen times. He was recalled.

When we first met, I asked him the truth of a story told of his adventures in Vietnam which was a joke amongst journalists who had been there, and he confirmed that it was true. There was a battle raging and he got his cameraman to climb up on to a ridge and then film him coming up over the top. Poor bloody cameramen; they have to take more risks than any of us in order to get their film. With sweat pouring down his shirt, our intrepid reporter was just at the top of the ridge and scrambling over to talk to the waiting camera when his leg was grazed by a bullet. 'I've been hit!' he exclaimed, and looked down to see blood oozing from the wound. Perhaps it was the professionalism or a little bit of the actor that came out in him – he always sleeked his hair back and reminded me of an old-time B-movie detective, Boston Blackie – for he suddenly ordered the surprised cameraman, 'Let's do that again!' Three times he climbed up to the exposed ridge with the vulnerable cameraman filming all the time while he put more grimace and surprise into his voice as he shouted, 'I've been hit!'

The problem with UDI from a news angle was that despite it being a huge international political story, after a time there was little to write about and even less to film. Scores of international journalists, photographers and cameramen found themselves running out of ideas and after a month they were getting restless. After all, there were other matters of interest taking place in the world such as the launching on 4 December, of Gemini 7 from Cape Canaveral with Frank Borman and James Lovell aboard. This was followed on my wedding anniversary, 15 December, by Walter Schirra and Thomas Stafford taking off in Gemini 6. A crowd of us were sitting in the midsummer ice-box foyer of Salisbury's Ambassador Hotel, the management having no idea how to work its air-conditioning system.

A radio was switched on and we heard the voices from Cape Canaveral and the atmospherical sounds from the spacecraft. 'It's looking good, yes, its good...' came the voice from central control. Aloft, through the crackling, a voice said that everything was fine until, 'We seem to be experiencing some difficulty here!' We all sat up and took notice. The lads up there were in trouble and as the drama unfolded everyone strained to listen to the fate of the astronauts. Were they were going to be forced down, to crash or burn up in the earth's atmosphere? The same thoughts passed through everyone's mind as we feared the worst. Then came the less confident voice, 'We're out of control up here, can you do something?' A voice from ground control cut in, 'We have your trajectory. Can you see the coastline of Africa?'

'Yes, we can see it clearly,' crackled the reply. After a pause the voice from the ground said, 'It looks as if you will be coming in across Angola and then down through Southern Rhodesia. With the course you are on you are heading for the capital city, Salisbury.'

'Oh my God, isn't there any way you can control this thing?' The radio was turned full volume and while everyone in the foyer knew it had to be a spoof there was still an element of uncertainty and the street outside became crowded with seasoned journalists and passers-by looking skyward at nothing. After twenty minutes came the fateful words, 'We're going to crash!' Then nothing. The jokers were from Canadian Broadcasting and they did a truly professional job from their hotel room.

Days passed and with Christmas fast approaching, everyone was becoming increasingly bored. Then a group of black children came along through the foyer carol singing. Under any normal circumstances, this was a 'must'; innocent black faces singing Christmas carols in the land of white supremacy… it was all there for the filming. But the journalists had all been told at the same time by their companies that they could go home for Christmas! As the choristers stood in the foyer they were almost trampled on by the cameramen in their haste to get out and get home.

Once the public became conditioned against the press, the purge of journalists was long and ruthless, and the toll was heavy. Amongst the early victims was Jim Biddulph, the public hero who had so nearly lost his life while reporting from the Congo. He was declared a prohibited immigrant, which meant he had to pay his own fare out and that of Marie and their six children who were Rhodesian born. By declaring them PIs the journalists and their families were treated worse than deported criminals as deportation meant the government had to pay their fares. Eric Robins was another casualty: he had lived in the country for thirteen years but as he packed his bags he said to me, 'I consider it an honour.'

After the forced departures, with those remaining wondering who would be next, censorship was brought in officially with Ivor Benson becoming the government's first chief censor. The *Rhodesia Herald*, being part of Anglo-American's South African Argus group of newspapers, objected strongly to government censorship and the deputy editor, now sitting in the top job through dead man's shoes, was told by the management to take up cudgels. As a result, the *Rhodesia Herald* produced blank spaces where censored stories should have appeared. It seemed to be a bold stand by the very man who had tried to censor me and cause my resignation. He was applauded overseas and condemned at home. Eric sent through a terse comment on the telex from Nairobi, 'He's very brave now!'

I called on my old chum Welensky for his political analysis of the situation and to my surprise he suddenly leaned forward with his huge bulk dominating my vision and I could see concern etched on his strong featured face. Welensky was a fighter and had once been the Rhodesian heavyweight boxing champion but his look was of one who was confused by the tactics of his opponent. 'Do you know there is a strong chance that I will be arrested?' he said. I was surprised but knew that he had totally lost popular public support with the break-up of the Federation and his incarceration would have upset few whites. His fears would not be realised but the comment was yet another indication of the paranoia taking place throughout the country.

The pro-African nationalist former Southern Rhodesia prime minister, Garfield Todd, fared less well and was incarcerated at his ranch. I once managed to break through the net to see Todd at his home and interviewed him to the sound of hippos snorting in the river below. After that interview he wasn't even allowed to talk to outsiders on the telephone and once he answered the phone to me, only to say guardedly that the government would not allow him to speak. New Zealand-born Todd (later knighted) was a former church minister and his daughter, Judy, became an unlikely firebrand. She shook like a frail autumn leaf when speaking publicly but she had the guts to put her message across against the incarceration of her father and the nationalist leader, Joshua Nkomo. Without question, she became the most hated woman amongst the whites and I privately feared for her safety but loved her spirit. Judy became the excuse for another journalist to be ordered out, *Time*'s Peter Forbath.

Hiding behind a veil of secrecy, it was easy to deport anyone the government either did not like, or just the organisation he or she worked for. The rapid removal of the mystified journalists was always accompanied by the comment from the public, 'He must have done something!' which could be likened to a policeman pounding an innocent bystander on the head with a truncheon and declaring, 'I am only doing my job!' I became tired of the phrase as it salved any vestige of public conscience there might have been and emphasised the ostrich-like attitude adopted by the whites as to what was happening to themselves. While no reasons were usually given for PI notices, I was actually told by the Information Department chief that Peter had met Judy Todd at London Airport and passed her secret messages, and that this had been seen by the Special Branch. Some years later I met Peter in New York where he became an author after covering the Czechoslovakian uprising from within that country, and I mentioned the purported London meeting. He wondered what I was talking about.

Before he left Rhodesia, Peter had the brilliant idea of writing a *Time* cover story on 'Swinging Salisbury'. Soon after he arrived in London, *Time* came out with a cover story on 'Swinging London' which was to harvest Britain millions of dollars in American tourism. He didn't write the cover but the coincidence was too much to believe that it had been thought of independently. UDI had caused a cataclysmic drop in Rhodesian tourism and I was able to retaliate the smugness of the Information Department towards Peter by enlightening them that the *Time* cover story could have been theirs had he not been chucked out with their connivance.

Time magazine, like the BBC, was a prime target despised by the government. Such was its fanaticism that it believed that *Time* was a communist magazine and that anyone working for it was a communist. Now that I was very much on my own as its sole representative living in the country, I was determined to stay without compromising myself. It was like being a trapeze artiste on a frayed rope from which two *Time* colleagues had already been pushed, but it was a challenge. Despite becoming chief correspondent for southern Africa I never once asked for my income to be raised above the minimum which I could well have done and been bountifully remunerated but there was a principle involved, press freedom, and I didn't want to be paid for defending it. It was also important to me (far more than to *Time* itself, I suspected) that the magazine should not be banned. All the facts reported had to be a hundred per cent correct, and it was to this end that I suggested to Eric Robins when he was still in the country, that all rewrites must be sent back to us for checking. There had been some embarrassing gaffes in the past by both *Time* and *Newsweek*. As a result of our open telex complaining of errors and our recommendation, which apparently caused considerable embarrassment within the magazine itself, we initiated a policy used by *Time* worldwide that all rewritten copy is sent back by telex for checking and approval of the original writer. It costs them a fortune but the money is well spent.

Another great American publishing house, McGraw-Hill, was also considered to be communist. When cabling articles to them before I had a telex, I would prefix the text, 'World News', meaning it was to go to the world news desk in New York. Five weeks after sending one such cable, a sneering post-office counterhand gave me it back. 'We didn't send it,' he said, accusingly. 'We don't give information to the communists.' Bewildered and angry, I demanded an explanation. Apparently, the London cable address of the communist *Daily Worker* was World News. That my cable was addressed to McGraw-Hill in New York was apparently inconsequential. No doubt a report went into my Special Branch file (I was told it was very large) that I was sending information to the communists.

It would have been very easy for me to get thrown out of Rhodesia. Some journalists came in with their particularly anti-Rhodesian stories already written in order to get deported and make a name for themselves. They helped Smith's propaganda machine enormously but did little to help my future self-inflicted role of defending the press. There were some stories which, if my name had appeared above them, would have meant instant deportation and glory but while journalists like to see his or her byline, I feel they should accept that the story is more important than the writer.

To put pen to paper favourably about any black leader would have been deemed tantamount to treason and so I secretly sent an article on the restriction of Joshua Nkomo, who was being held at a remote camp at Gonakudzingwa, close to the Mozambique border. The story was used for the cover of the American magazine, *Ebony Africa*. Questions were asked about its authorship. One journalist with whom I was friendly was Dick Walker, who later became a correspondent at the United Nations in New York. Dick was employed by the South African black magazine, *Drum*, which meant that he was earmarked for government-inspired departure. Dick was always a little vague and when he was asked if he wrote the Nkomo article, he would smile and, as the song goes, 'He didn't say yes, and he didn't say, no.' From this it was assumed he was responsible, and when it came to the government deciding whether he should remain in Rhodesia, without hesitation they didn't say, yes; they surely said, No!

Another story which tore at my journalistic heart strings not to acknowledge was a plot to assassinate Ian Smith by another nationalist leader, the Reverend Ndabaningi Sithole. At the time, Sithole was being detained in Salisbury jail and it was obvious that the source of the story was either the police or a prison officer. In order to protect my police source, I was asked by him not to publish the story for seven days. Because my contact was a member of Special Branch, I was not sure if I was being set up. As it was known that I wrote for the *Evening Standard*, I sent the story there with a Lusaka, Zambia, dateline and posted it in the ordinary mail, with an explanation. Naturally, I was kicking my heels and biting my nails wondering if my mail would be intercepted or if any other journalists would pick up the story. I was particularly worried about the *Daily Telegraph* which was considered a friend of Rhodesia and had exceptionally cordial relations with the government and Special Branch. Six days later all hell broke lose as the *Standard* led the scoop on its front page. Telephone lines were hot to surprised journalists in Lusaka who denied, reluctantly, that they knew anything about it. It was amusing that I had managed to play it even cooler than the *Standard* whose fingers were getting hotter as they held on to it. And it also appeared that I, like everyone else, had egg on my face for not getting the scoop.

As the years passed and the stranglehold on journalists was almost complete, the government set a trap by allowing a debate on television (the first such debate in years), entitled, 'Freedom of the Press'. The title was a mockery considering that such freedom didn't exist, and two of the men responsible were on the panel, Ivor Benson and his running mate, Harvey Ward. Facing them was the young freelance journalist, Peter Niesewand and myself. Peter's subsequent deportation some time later caused an uproar worldwide. In his book, *Secret Justice in Rhodesia* (banned in Rhodesia), Niesewand declared, '...Reg Shay and myself were left to defend the press, and by Rhodesian definition, the political left-wing. It was a heated discussion on predictable lines – Benson and Ward accusing the press of deliberate distortion, Shay and myself denying this…'

Peter said he believed the start of his downfall was that TV appearance and I am sure he was right. I am quite sure, too, that the trap was set for me, correspondent of the 'communist' *Time*, but he became the fly caught in the web. Some of the Information Department staff were already stringing for overseas periodicals and they actually believed that if I was thrown out, the chief correspondent for southern Africa, they could take my place with their propaganda sheets. The naivety was almost unbelievable for it never occurred to them that I might have a few words to say on the matter; that to be discredited inside Rhodesia was a badge of honour outside. If the TV appearance had been the start of Peter Niesewand's downfall, he still maintained good government contacts and the Minister of Justice, Law and Order, Desmond Lardner-Burke, actually attended his wedding. It was another TV appearance, to which I was not invited, which really led to Peter's departure when he innocently upset Ian Smith with a question about public money being spent on refurbishing Smith's bedroom.

Ian Smith's reign was akin to McCarthyism as you were either a loyal Rhodesian or you were a communist; there were no grey areas and the national press was almost totally subjugated, together with radio and television. Only a local financial newspaper, the *Financial Gazette*, showed any spunk and got away with it and continued to do so after Africans came to power under Robert Mugabe, who also felt it his right to control the media.

The anti-press propaganda not only affected the public generally, it was also causing serious problems with my marriage. As the children were all at school, and Margery was bored with being alone at home, she took a secretarial job with a large firm of plumbers. And it was the artisans, fearful of their jobs should the blacks ever take over, who helped Ian Smith to power. Everyone in the firm was pro-Smith and after a time this rubbed off on to my wife. Instead of backing my stand, she quite clearly became ashamed of me and my profession and with the chasm deepening with bitterness, there seemed little point in going home to a quarrel in the evening. With so many of my friends deported, I would go to the bar of a local nightclub and drink quietly alone. There was one thing I quickly learned; women cannot bear to see a man drinking by himself. It's rather like taking a crossword into a bar; sit quietly by yourself working it out and soon everyone wants to join in. Women were not the problem, however, and were not encouraged.

I discovered, too, that Ian Smith had his own set of informers and each night a different stranger would come up and start chatting to me, sometimes posing as an old friend. There would be casual questions and I knew exactly what was coming. The third question was, 'So what do you think about old Smithy, then?' I knew that the Special Branch were furious with Smith's own private police as they felt they were being usurped, or at the minimum undermined, and I mentioned the harassment to my SB contact as we sat in the gymnasium sauna. 'Let me know when it happens again,' he said, and gave me his phone number. I was drinking with a non-journalist friend, Peter Wild, and tipped him off that there would soon be a strange man coming up to join us and that he should keep him in conversation while I called the police. Sure enough, a man I'd never seen before walked in and started to chat. Soon the questions began with the third being, 'What do you think of old Smithy then?' and I asked if he was Special Branch. He smiled and said, 'Yes, as a matter of fact, I am. How did you know?' We talked and I excused myself and went to the telephone and called my contact. Peter, a little tipsy, told the man what I was doing. He almost ran out of the door and I must say the SB acted quickly, being there within five minutes. I was never again questioned by Smith's personal Gestapo.

There were other occasions when strangers would come up and engage me in conversation before asking, 'How would you like to work for us?' I never bothered to find out who 'us' was because I just wasn't interested in spying for anyone and the stock answer was always, 'Forget it.'

A 'piece to the camera' on UDI for ABC News. Picture: Paul Lazard.

Ian Smith takes UDI and signs independence document. Picture: Rhodesian Information Department.

Eric Robins: 'This is high treason in the name of the Queen!' Picture: Marion Kaplan.

Former federal prime minister, Sir Roy Welensky, expected arrest.
Picture: Life *magazine.*

Gold, Murder and Robert Kennedy

It was a slow news period, the time dreaded by every freelance journalist; the moment of racking brains for an off-beat story which will keep the family in food, clothes and entertainment. It's not a problem for the staff man whose salary and pension are assured, nor even for freelancers who compromise themselves by asking for financial retainers. I understand their reasons but believe such people tend to lose their edge and are no longer hungry for stories.

There came a glint on the horizon which would make a news feature, or even a fortune as a sideline; it was the same glint that drove men to the Yukon, South Africa, Australia and other parts of the globe: Gold! The price of gold was rising fast and Rhodesia was a gold-bearing country. A notice appeared in the *Rhodesia Herald* saying that the government was encouraging the opening of ancient disused gold mines which had been worked hundreds of years before. A six-night course would be held in Salisbury, one night a week. I enrolled for the course and soaked up the information. The class was told that the 'Ancients' worked one gold seam while, in all probability, there was another running parallel. Most informative was the revelation that outcrops of multi-coloured stones often spelled out the presence of the precious metal. We were told of the type of hills to look for which would be gold-bearing.

After this expert tuition, I was supremely confident and invested in a prospector's licence and a genuine prospector's axe. At that time I was living in a house perched on the top of a steep gradient with the Dickensian name of Hogerty Hill from which I had a view of possible gold-bearing hills for nearly eighty miles. Closer, however, only a few miles up the main road were even more hills in the African reserve of Dombashawa and I reckoned that if gold was to be found, it would be there. I dressed impressively in a newly laundered safari suit and bush hat with leopard-skin headband and set forth with axe in hand, poised ready to break asunder any rock which looked promising. I wasn't exactly sure what a promising rock looked like as that hadn't been explained, but intuition would tell me. As I approached the hills on foot there was a faint sound of the single beat of a drum in the background. Was I being watched? While Dombashawa was a reserve, surely it wasn't sacred territory like Mount Muozi. Confidently I moved forward until, with unsuppressed excitement, I came to the type of outcrop described in the classes. This was really extraordinary; success on my very first outing! It surprised me that other prospectors hadn't managed to find this obvious gold site on the doorstep of their capital city and I wondered if there was possibly something superior in a journalist's make-up; the trained observer who can uncover the unusual with unerring perspicacity. There was no doubt that here was I, a complete novice, hot on the trail of gold and not too far from the main road. This meant there'd be no need to build a railway extension to take the precious metal away; heavy trucks could do the job adequately. The outcrop was extensive and as I moved forward the metallic drumming became louder and now resembled the monosyllabic throbbing of a metronome. The painful realisation that I wasn't listening to a drum pounded into my brain as I gazed dejectedly at mounds of slag a few feet away. Before me was the creator of the noise; a stamp machine. I'd found myself at the face of a gold mine which was being actively worked! In disgust, I threw the axe down the shaft and went home.

At the bottom of the hill lived my milkman, Lt General Bob Long, former head of the Federal army, who now ran a herd of Jersey cows. I called on him and was surprised to hear military music: the band of the Grenadier Guards playing their regimental march at the Aldershot Tattoo. Over the music came the cries of the regimental sergeant major: 'Quick march, left wheel, 'alt,' and other familiar commands that took me back a few years to my halcyon days in the Royal Army Service Corps. Our less impressive regimental march was 'Roll out the Wagon'.

I followed the sound and came to a cowshed with all the Jerseys in their stalls being mechanically milked with the record player beside them. The milking of cows to music was not an uncommon practice: what surprised me was the milk was always fresh despite the curdling commands of the sergeant major...

Rhodesia contained a large hedonistic society and soon after our arrival Margery and I had received invitations to parties. Many were turned down because of the children, but occasionally we would find a baby sitter and go out. And when we did, the parties were always eventful.

One young lady who was so fat around the thighs that I unkindly dubbed her 'Miss Baobab', held a 'Parson and the Call Girl' party at her flat, with the men dressed as clergy and the women as tarts. Margery wore a tight-fitting leopard-skin dress with a slit up the side which did credit to her long shapely legs, while I went as a bishop. Inevitably, people in neighbouring flats complained to the police about the noise so late at night. The police liked to be called to the parties in flats as it was customary to be invited in for a nightcap. At around midnight a bespectacled reporter, John Miskelly, the epitome of a country parson, opened the door to find two policemen outside. 'We have had some complaints about the noise, sir,' said one. 'Oh dear,' replied Miskelly. 'I'll call the bishop!' The message was passed back that John's spoofing had been believed and I went to the door with a genial smile, ambivalent feelings and a glass which tinkled with ice and carried the contents of a well-poured Scotch whisky. 'Good evening, officers,' I beamed. 'I see you have discovered our little secret!'

'Pardon, sir?' Both policemen were staring hard through the open door with wide eyes. There was no comprehension in them, just downright incredulity. 'You shouldn't take too much notice of the goings on as this only happens once a year,' I said. 'These are missionaries who work hard and spend most of their time in the bush and I hold this little annual get-together so that they can let their hair down.'

'I see, Bishop,' said one, and the look in his eye suggested he was prepared to sacrifice the uniform of law and order for a cassock. Then came a divine intervention when Margery put her arms around me, murmuring, 'What's the matter, darling?' That gorgeous face, long, wavy golden hair and legs that went all the way, were too much for the policemen whose faces registered utter confusion. 'Would you care for a drink?' I asked, standing aside for them to enter. The pair looked at each other and nodded. 'No thank you, Bishop.'

'Your Grace,' I interjected.

'No thank you, Your Grace, it looks like a good party but please keep the noise down.' With that, they went off to discuss with their colleagues the secular pleasures of the clergy. Perhaps they had been enriched; they had said 'Grace' without receiving even a tiny tot!

Attending the party was a man who worked for the Federal Information Department, with his pretty English-born Chinese wife and after the call-girl beano, we attended another party sometime later which was two floors up in a block of flats. They had both drunk too much and quarrelled and in a fit of pique, the girl threw herself off the balcony. As no one had seen the incident, he stood there and wondered what to do. His feelings at the time, he told me afterwards, were that he would be accused of throwing her over the balcony and subsequently be charged with murder. In a balcony scene worthy of Shakespeare, the man from the Information Department plucked up courage and threw himself over the top with the intention of meeting the identical fate of his wife down below, which he did. They both stood up, brushed themselves down and agreed that such a terrifying experience called for a drink. We were all surprised to see them walk in through the front door.

Merle Fadness, whom I'd helped with her car at the near cost of son Peter's life, was the daughter of a gold miner and the next time I would see her was at the Arcturas gold mine, outside Salisbury, where her father was manager. I'd gone along for McGraw-Hill to look at a new drilling technique which involved my travelling several stages underground into the bowels of the earth in a bucket! For someone who has many of the phobias, disliking heights both looking up and down, plus being a bit claustrophobic, I had to be crazy to make the descent. But the apprehension was unjustified and it was a smooth trip even though the stage above the floor I arrived at was flooded and water gushed down the man-made chasm in a waterfall. Up above was a festive scene with African miners putting on little plays, each with a theme on mine safety, for Arcturas Mine under the guidance of Merle's father had won many safety awards. Amongst those watching the plays was a white member of the staff to whom I was introduced, a good-looking young man who was to bring great tragedy to the Fadness family.

Once a week Merle's father and the chief accountant drove to Salisbury to collect wages for the mine workers and when they turned off the main road to Arcturas with the money in strong box, they were fired on and both men were killed. At first it looked like a terrorist attack as the murder weapon was a Russian-made AK-47 rifle but things were not as they seemed and soon the good-looking young man was accused of murder and subsequently convicted. With sinister avarice he had deliberately staged the attack to look as though marauding terrorists were responsible. This very cold-blooded individual, (he had actually waved to Merle's mother from the dock), was later found dead in his cell; his throat cut with the top of a tin of Heinz baked beans. A verdict of suicide was brought in by the coroner but I've sometimes wondered if he really did kill himself: it isn't usual for a despised convicted murderer to be given the materials in jail with which he can cheat the hangman's noose.

With the onset of sanctions against Rhodesia, I broke a story reported around the world of the arrival of the oil tanker, *Ioanna V*, off Beira, Mozambique. It was a sanctions-breaking coup by the Rhodesians who had secretly purchased the ship bringing the oil and I flew to Beira for ITN but my cameraman used borrowed gear. I guessed the equipment would probably be faulty as I'd seen it before and, like its owner, was not up to top professional standard. It was Easter when thousands of Rhodesians always drove through Mozambique to the coast and to interview them on camera on the beach seemed a good idea. The first group were teenagers who decided to give me a hard time. Having been fed the anti-press propaganda, there was antipathy: 'You are not a Rhodesian,' they argued, 'go away.'

When I argued my case I was handed a litre bottle of strong lager. 'If you are a Rhodesian, you can drink this!' I promptly sank it fast. 'Now this bottle of wine!' Almost without a pause, I sank that too and handed over the empty bottle. 'Thanks,' I said. 'Now I'd like the interviews.' Inwardly, I thanked God for a strong constitution. All this time my cameraman was filming the booze-sodden youths – and this was only 10 a.m. They had a long day ahead of them out in the sun! I took one couple aside while they were still sober, to avoid interruptions from the others. On the third question my cameraman interrupted, 'Hold it, the sound's gone!' I told him to see what he could do with the equipment and make it urgent as I was worried that the drinks might begin to take effect on me. There was little chance of my getting drunk but the voice can slur after only one drink, not obvious in conversation but ruthlessly picked up by a microphone. A repair was affected and we restarted, 'Hold it!'

'What now?'

'The sound's gone again.'

'Why the hell did you have to get Hamlin's gear?' I asked bitterly. John Hamlin was a freelance cameraman who not only never looked after his gear but was so greedy that he made a contraption carried on his shoulders whereby he could carry a cine and two still cameras at the same time, filming all the while. As the sole freelance with his own gear, he was in great demand but the end result was always appalling. Twelve times the sound broke down and the youths wanted to get back to their friends. What the hell: 'Cheers,' I said, and let them go. Nothing else could go wrong, of that I was sure. There had to be enough of the interviews between the breaks to make fifty seconds. With some wild shots of the palm trees and the bathers with my voiceover, there would be a neat three to four minute package. Now came the most important part, the reason for my journey. 'You are quite sure the sound is okay?' The sound man assured me that it was, and the cameraman confirmed it. 'Right,' I said, 'let's do the intro to camera.' I stood on the sandy beach talking to the camera as the *Ioanna V* moved slowly past in the palm-fringed background in a remarkably cheeky sanctions-busting gambit. As I spoke, I expected the sound to break down at any time which would have created problems as the tanker was now moving out of sight. With relief, I heard the cameraman say, 'It's okay,' and the sound man put his thumb up.

I'd telephoned my office to put the piece over to the *Evening Standard* and *Evening News* which my secretary duly did. It would be good publicity for the film to be shown the following night on *News at Ten*. The thought that either newspaper might use my byline had never occurred to me as they had never done so before and nor had anyone else. Murphy's Law prevailed and the very last editions of both rival newspapers splashed their front pages with the arrival of the much publicised *Ioanna V*. Chance had it that this was the time when both decided to give me a baptism in bylines, something journalists could only dream about and is unlikely to have happened to anyone before or since! It was too late for either of them to change their minds but I had to do some fast talking to stay in the good books of the *Standard*. From then on, I used the pseudonym of 'Robert Webber' in the News. Sometimes, however, that newspaper would forget but by now Ronnie Hyde had accepted that I was a freelance without wanting the ties of a financial retainer which would have kept my work exclusive to the *Standard*. With my byline continually heading front page leads and frequent appearances on *News at Ten*, I'd unwittingly become something of a celebrity.

Armed with my precious film, I headed for Beira airport and on arrival I gazed at a blank patch of tarmac where my aircraft should have been waiting and was told that the pilot had flown off without me. He had been warned of a colossal tropical storm approaching and had decided that if he hung on any longer, there would be no chance of spending the night with his wife 400 miles away in Salisbury. I was livid. He had arbitrarily flown off in my chartered plane, leaving me holding the greatest piece of film since *Gone with the Wind*. Without giving the storm a thought, I called the airport tower and ordered him back. It's difficult to say which was the most supercharged; the atmosphere on the ground after he touched down and we snarled at each other, or the heavy clouds that had built up over the Inyanga mountains which would be directly in our flight path. My only thoughts were that the film must catch the night flight to London. We took off, just the two of us, as I had left the camera crew behind to watch developments on the ship's movements. As we flew towards Inyanga I could see the ominous build-up of the clouds ahead, like massive black wind-filled sails which lit up every few seconds as a huge generator released energy of such eruptive and foreboding force that only a madman would fly anywhere near it. The clouds reached to the ground, shrouding its mountains, and I knew that somewhere down there was the sacred Muozi, no longer sun-drenched, but forbidding and frightening, lusting for revenge against the climber who had so superciliously humbled it.

The pilot looked across waiting for me to order him to turn back. Under normal circumstances I might have done but this was not an option and I just stared grimly ahead. Having already flown out with the pilot, I knew that if anyone could get us through it would be him. Then we flew into Hell. I've flown in many storms and know what it is like to be buffeted; I've been in an aircraft when it hit an air pocket and plummeted as if a trap door had been released and I've watched an aircraft shoot in front of my charter plan just as we were about to touch down on a narrow escarpment. Other air incidents would take place in the future but indelibly etched upon my mind is the night I flew with the film of an oil tanker breaking sanctions for Rhodesia, of the pilot who didn't want to make the trip yet flew brilliantly; of the wings of that twin-engine Beach Baron aircraft which held on despite all the odds. Always in the back of my mind was the memory of the yellow-painted Airspeed Oxford I'd seen as a paperboy when its tail blew off.

For nearly 200 miles we were buffeted by the storm without the slightest sign of a let-up. The plane was pitched up and down, sometimes in darkness but usually in blinding light as lightning appeared to spotlight us in the way I had seen German bombers during the war before our Ack-Ack guns brought them down. Now I knew exactly how they must have felt; trapped in their metal coffins with nothing but hostility all around. I glanced at my pilot as he grimly held on to the controls and spoke by radio to the Salisbury control tower whose operator tried to guide us home. I looked at the windscreen wipers and wondered at their sheer futility as rain lashed against them with the force of firemen's hoses. There seemed little point in keeping them going when there was only torrential rain and cloud for as far as the eye could see, which was less than a foot. I could hear the tower as the operator, many miles ahead, spoke coolly but with a trace of anxiousness in his voice. It was obvious that he, like my pilot, wondered what madman had ordered us up there and refused to go back.

Being a sensitive fellow, I could tell by the pilot's demeanour that he felt I'd be directly responsible for making his loving wife a widow; he should be home by now, sitting down with his feet up and enjoying a large Scotch. I had always believed that lightning could not incinerate a plane but now I began to wonder: Zeus was outside unleashing flaming spears at our wing tips until they too appeared to be aflame as one flash after another tried to tear us apart. There had been a reported case some years earlier of an airliner being brought down off Beira through turbulence when there was no storm; the turbulence we were experiencing was powerful enough to bring down ten airliners and yet we managed to stay in the air right until the moment we went into a dive.

Through the noise of the storm outside the plane I could hear the tower as we plummeted earthwards. The controller in the tower seemed excited as he called out something like, 'Left twenty-seven, right thirty-six, left twenty-eight, right thirty-seven,' and so on, all in rapid succession as we were being talked down. At 400 feet, after seemingly an age of flying with the tension of imminent death, we broke through the clouds and spread out before us was rain-swept Salisbury Airport. On the ground, after we had run to cover, I turned to the pilot and shook hands. 'Well done,' I said coolly, and walked off. He just grunted. He'd done an incredible job but I felt that if he hadn't so arrogantly flown off we might have missed the storm anyway. I didn't want to show any warmth towards him just because he'd been so marvellous; he wanted to hate my guts and I wouldn't deny him that pleasure.

The pilot didn't have the same set of values as me over a piece of film and he would never understand mine; he wouldn't see that it was worth risking a life or two for a piece of film. Was I wrong? Perhaps. But journalists are a different breed. How many reporters and cameramen have been killed in war for just a few yards of news film? I got the package on the night plane to London and felt good. I telexed ITN in London to meet the flight next day which was done and the film rushed to the laboratory for processing. Eurovision was alerted and everyone stood by the great TV exclusive which already had such an incredible advanced publicity in the two London evening papers. Then John Mahoney, the ITN Foreign Editor came over the telex with the crushing sentence, 'Sorry, Reg, the whole film was out of focus. It can't be used!'

The international repercussions to the story had been enormous, so much so that the Portuguese had hesitated in allowing the *Ioanna V* to unload its precious cargo. I then found a cameraman who worked for an advertising agency who had a real, clean, working camera and we flew straight back to Beira to relieve the hapless pair with Hamlin's equipment. The *Ioanna V* had anchored just outside the harbour and now the sea was cutting up rough and the only way to recoup my losses was to interview the captain but there were problems. We'd have liked to have gone out to sea from the docks but the Portuguese officials took one look at our camera and decided we couldn't enter what was, they said, a prohibited area. To get to the *Ioanna V* would mean crossing treacherous sandbanks in a choppy sea and we looked for motor launches but none were available. After further searching we managed to get hold of a flat-bottomed rubber ski-boat with an outboard engine. Sometimes the rudder scraped the sand as we made our uncomfortable ride; at other times the water was deep. As waves lapped overboard we felt that far more important than our personal safety was to keep the camera dry. After half an hour we were close to the tanker and asked for permission to come aboard but a Greek seaman waved us away. 'The captain will not see you,' he kept repeating in broken English. And he was right; the captain did not see us. Dejectedly we made our way into the harbour as there was no point in risking the sands again. At least we had a close-up of the ship and the sailor aboard and filmed some of the port's installations. A customs official was waiting for us when we landed: 'Your film, please!' We'd objected strongly but the official had been adamant. Ron, the cameraman, handed him the film and we went off. Now that we were away from the harbour, I turned to Ron, 'You'd better let me have the film now,' I said, holding out my hand. 'Okay,' he replied, and handed it over. This time it was used.

The second time I was to recall an aircraft from the tower I chose a national airline. Philip Short (subsequent author of biographies on Hastings Banda and Mao Tse-Tung) had his own freelance agency in Malawi and wanted to pull out to join the BBC. I bought his agency as an extension to my existing operation in Salisbury and also as an insurance should I be deported from Rhodesia. But the move was a disaster from the outset. The country's leader, Dr Hastings Banda, was a megalomaniac who'd made himself Malawi's life president. He'd been directly responsible for the break-up of the Federation and at the Independence Day celebrations, which I'd attended, the African women supporters chanted with unbridled enthusiasm, 'We will open our legs for Dr Banda!' I'd put in a young journalist to run my operation and was surprised when he came through on the telex to say he couldn't cope (Malawi was not a thriving centre of news) but that a South African journalist wanted to join him. Faced with the collapse of the Malawi office, I engaged the South African as well, without seeing him. Stories he produced showed that he could write, and he was a worker. But when I did fly to Blantyre to see him, I was very unhappy. A heavy drinker and a thug, he introduced me to his girlfriend who had a shiner of a black eye which he had given her days before. She was terrified of him and so too was the young journalist who had asked me to take him on.

When I'd arrived at Salisbury Airport to fly to Malawi, a story was waiting for me in the airport lounge as Sir Roy Welensky was flying to meet Banda, his old adversary. We had a chat and as it was not a world-shattering story I filed it from Malawi as a piece with casual interest. Ten minutes later I received a phone call from the Malawi Government ordering me not to send the story even though they knew it had already gone. It was a method of covering themselves should the story hit the headlines and Banda would hit the roof. My telex was shut down for the rest of the visit, and so were my telephones. As for the South African, some time later he was deported for all the trouble he was causing around town and I happened to be in Malawi when he was due to depart. I went to the airport to ensure that he got on the plane, sensitive to all the trouble he had caused the agency during a very delicate time. The flight was called but he ignored it and was found drunk in the airport bar as the Air Malawi plane flew off. This was just too much for I considered the government was unwittingly doing me a favour in deporting him I got through to the tower and ordered the return of the plane.

It was a fascinating sight to watch it take off, circle, and come back again. I'd told the tower that the reporter was leaving on the president's express instructions and he must be on the aircraft. Later, when Air Malawi had done some checking, I received a bill for the fuel that had been used for landing and the second take-off. It was exorbitant and we came to terms whereby I promised to give Air Malawi a good write-up if they tore up the bill. They seemed more than happy with the bargain and I wrote the article on Air Malawi for just one newspaper – the *Malawi News*. The government then banned me from working there; it had planned to close the agency anyway as I'd been asking too many questions about corruption and police detentions without trial.

During my brief spell with the *Rhodesia Herald* when I was building up contacts, I met someone who would become a flying legend. He was sitting behind a large, utility-looking desk, in a Spartan office; the room of a man who might have risen from the rank of mechanic and felt uncomfortable there, or perhaps the office of a pilot who hated being grounded on promotion. Tears were in his eyes for outside his window was the mangled wreckage of a Dakota DC-3 aircraft, its twisted skeletal remains scattered among an air force bomb dump. I was surprised at seeing the bombs lying casually in the open, assuming they would be stacked neatly one on top of the other. The way they were spread about, however, made good sense once I had given it some thought.

The DC-3, a veteran of countless miles plus service in WW2, had belonged to Jack Malloch, the man at the desk. He would hire out the plane whenever and wherever he could as his business was flying people and cargo. Two hours ago, he'd watched it crash into the air force base only fifty yards from where he was sitting. There had been only three aboard; the pilot, his trainee co-pilot and an air hostess. What had caused the accident is conjecture and was never fully explained but Malloch believed his close friend, the pilot, had handed the controls to his junior companion on take-off and inexperience had robbed them of their lives. Only the hostess survived, having strapped herself into a rear seat.

When I met Jack Malloch again he had become probably the greatest air sanctions buster of all time but he was as modest as when we first met and declined to talk about his exploits except to say, 'I won't fly for individuals, only governments.' Even when we came to know each other well, he still gave me a polite but firm 'No' after I asked to write his biography. 'It would let too many people down,' he explained. 'To disclose names and places would be too compromising for the governments concerned.' As an example of this, I learned from one of his pilots who took part in the operation, that he once flew arms to an Arab country for the US and British governments in a covert operation. This was a very long time before Irangate. While some condemned Jack as a swashbuckling mercenary, others believed him a hero. Whatever the pros and cons, Malloch had his own set of principles and he stuck by them.

After that first, tragic meeting when he was so depressed, Malloch became personal pilot for President Moise Tshombe in the Congo and Tshombe later gave him a present of his own Dove aircraft, plus a Constellation. Later still, Malloch flew for both sides in the devastating Biafra war in Nigeria. He didn't take sides in that bloodletting but when his planes arrived with supplies at the dangerous narrow Biafran runway where lights would flash on briefly at night for a plane to land, Malloch was always in the lead aircraft. His younger cavalier pilots adored him.

Malloch was a personal friend of Ian Smith as both had been with the RAF during WW2 and both had gone down over Italy where Jack baled out and parachuted into a stone church wall breaking both his legs. He'd been flying a Spitfire at the time and it was in a Spitfire that he died, his beloved plane in his beloved country. On a plinth outside the air force base at New Sarum, Salisbury, was a wartime Spitfire. I had always felt a warm glow whenever I passed it; what Briton of my generation wouldn't? While the thought that it would fly again had never crossed my mind, Jack had other ideas. Twenty-six years after it was grounded as a relic, he restored the Mark XXII Spitfire and got it into the air. His company even won the British Rolls Royce Trophy for technical achievement in aeronautics in rebuilding the plane. On Thursday, 25 March 1982, he flew it for the last time. At the age of sixty-one years, he was piloting the Spitfire over the Goromonzi area east of Harare when it disappeared in a cloud bank. Following in a Vampire jet was a film crew who were making a feature on the plane's history and restoration. Jack and the Spitfire died as they had lived: dangerously. The bonus was that they died together.

Long before his death Jack unwittingly became responsible for my meeting someone who was far better known than him who would also die dramatically. Jack offered me a free trip to England aboard a DC-7C, a plane which made me feel I was riding a doodlebug bomb, especially at night when the red flames could be seen belching from the engines. Rita, our air hostess, was a very beautiful girl who would fantasise and enchant men with tales that she was a princess from India. She was, in fact, a mixed race girl from the back streets of Nairobi who abandoned her child to fly down to Rhodesia as the fiancée of a *Time* magazine bureau chief.

Jack Malloch landed our plane at Ile de Sol, in the Cape Verde Islands, a former Portuguese penal colony. As I sat talking to Rita, about thirty sex-hungry Portuguese men came along with chairs and formed an arc in front of us. They sat down and stared lustfully at the stunning girl without saying a word and I felt they would have willingly cut my throat to be with her. I was told they were prison warders who hadn't seen too many women recently and as Ile de Sol is the armpit of the world – hot, humid and ugly with a time zone out of keeping with anywhere else – I was relieved when Jack Malloch said it was time to board for Gatwick. We arrived in 'Swinging London' where money was a top priority but because of sanctions my bank account had been frozen. My Westminster Bank manager in Fleet Street was most accommodating and was of a breed of whom any customer would approve. 'As your money was earned in England, I cannot see why you should not spend it while you are here,' he said. This was a man of complete understanding. Entertainment ranged from cocktails with Hank Luce at his London pad (three miles and many light years from Khartoum Road, Tooting) to the occasional evening with other *Time* magazine folk at the Saddlers disco. Twice my bank account was opened up until the manager reluctantly felt he had been generous enough with my money, and closed it tight until I finally left for Rhodesia. When it was my time to fly back I telephoned Gatwick and the message awaiting me was sobering. 'Mr Malloch tried to contact you as he had to leave early,' I was told. Rita had searched London for me but without success. Now I had a problem; I had flown to London on a freebie but I hadn't enough money left to fly back, having blown the lot.

Before calling in to the *Time* office for an advance payment, I decided to visit the ABC News offices to suggest taping a couple of nine-and-a-half minute 'think pieces' which I had done several times before. The fee would help pay my return fare. As I breezed into their offices I was greeted with more than the customary open arms. An old chum, Peter Jennings, asked if I would leave immediately! He explained that Robert Kennedy was flying to South Africa for a three-day tour and only South African journalists were allowed on his plane and all foreign reporters were banned from entering the country. 'Can you smuggle yourself into South Africa and get on board Kennedy's plane?' asked Peter.

'No problem,' I said, seizing the opportunity to get home. 'Get me a ticket through to Salisbury (nice touch!) and I'll drop off at Johannesburg in transit and get on to Kennedy's aircraft.' This was the kind of coincidence I liked and I reckoned my chances were pretty good as I'd previously taken the precaution of having 'journalist' removed from my passport and replaced by 'Public Relations Consultant'. This was quite legitimate as I owned a PR company and the subterfuge had got me through many airports where journalists were turned away. Now, by the greatest stroke of luck, I was having my return flight back being paid for! Going through Jan Smuts Airport in Johannesburg was no problem and I bluffed my way aboard Kennedy's Viscount aircraft. The year was 1966. Kennedy had arrived on Saturday, 4 June, and was back at the airport on Monday, 6 June, to fly to Cape Town to start the official tour. That was when I boarded the plane. Who could have guessed the tragic events that would occur exactly two years later?

I'd always admired Jack Kennedy and liked what he had to say and I was looking forward to meeting his brother but my initial reaction was one of disappointment. On the tarmac, Bobby beamed with a fixed smile as he walked up rapidly to an African airport worker whom he warmly shook by the hands, fully conscious of all the media's eyes and cameras upon him. The African was taken completely by surprise and looked bewildered that the European baas should have picked on him; he hadn't the first idea who Robert Kennedy was, or what he was about. It was the good old American whistle-stop barnstorming tour which was aimed at showing the blacks just how much America, and Robert Kennedy in particular, cared for them. While being well aware of his background towards the blacks in the United States and his record on human rights, that first gut reaction was of a man who was totally ruthless and God help anyone who got in his way. I wondered at the time if he raced up to the manual workers at his home, the gardeners, cook, and other servants, with the same, 'Hail fellow, well met,' greeting but I was prepared to give him the benefit of the doubt. Even so, I was surprised that he had allowed rules to be laid down that only South African journalists would be permitted to cover the tour.

Despite being the only foreign journalist aboard the plane, there was another man who looked darkly around at everyone and acted most suspiciously. Perhaps it was his soft felt hat with a Tyrolean feather that first drew my attention to him; perhaps it was the way he took photographs as I counted sixty-nine shots on the same roll! Or perhaps it was his spanking new tape recorder bearing the words of the communist 'Yugoslav News Agency' on it. In a familiar Afrikaans accent he came to me, 'This is a new tape recorder and I don't know how to use it. Can you help me?' Naturally, I gave him every assistance and my companions ruefully thought I was pushing my luck a bit. He continually asked me about other journalists on the plane and eventually pointed to someone I knew well, whose home I had visited in the Cape. 'Hey, Tertius, our friend here wants to know about you now!' Tertius Myburgh's face reddened as he rose from his seat and turned on the obvious South African secret policeman who wilted under a torrent of abuse. Tertius was in a strong position. He was not only editor of the *Pretoria News* but, like Kennedy, had been to Yale University and was vetting Kennedy's speeches. What had amused us all was that I, the one person who should not have been on the plane or even in the country, was the man he had chosen as his confidante to ask about my companions. At no time did he ask anyone about me!

Whenever Robert Kennedy made a speech, he would mention 'My brother' so often that it became repetitive. In passing, I mentioned to him that the world knew who his late brother was and that a brief mention of him would seem appropriate and the comment went down like the proverbial lead balloon. We arranged that during the flight I would interview him so that I could tape record the sound of the aircraft engines in the background. This he agreed to do but it was quite apparent that our vibes were not in accord. Grudgingly, he said he would be interviewed for ABC News at 4 p.m. and at the appointed time I found him sound asleep, lying across two seats and wearing black eye covers. I was reluctant to awaken him but the interview was important as ABC News would want value for their money. The problem arose: how should I rouse him? There was only one thing for it. I looked across mischievously at Ethel, his wife, with whom I had a good rapport and her eyes twinkled. Then I shook the former American Attorney General by the leg and called, cheerfully, 'Wakey, Wakey!'

I doubt if anyone had ever awakened him like that before, perhaps Marilyn Monroe but not a man, and instinctively I knew it was not appreciated. As the black patches were removed, I met a pair of ice-cold blue ruthless eyes which glared at me and a pair of cold but usually warm blue eyes stared back with the words, 'It's time for the ABC interview.' The interview was good, perhaps because we didn't like each other, and ABC News thought it was money well spent. But the hostility went right on to the end of the tour which included flying over Robbin Island with dipped wings and a wave from Kennedy to an unseen Nelson Mandela. When the tour ended, Kennedy walked the length of the plane with Ethel to say 'Goodbye' to all the journalists aboard even though Tertius and myself appeared to have been the only two he had talked to and he gave everyone a memento – everyone except me. As he walked past, I asked, 'Don't I get one?' Grudgingly he came back and almost slammed a gold tiepin into my hand. It had a PT-boat motif. 'Ah,' I said, 'it's your brother again!' It was clear that, unlike myself, he didn't share his brother's part-Irish irreverent sense of humour.

Robert Kennedy's assassination two years to the day of his South African trip is well known. But there were other tragic sequels: a journalist dubbed 'Whispering Wallace' wrote about me in the *Johannesburg Sunday Express*, stating how I had smuggled myself into the country and aboard the plane. He even mentioned that I had Public Relations Consultant in my passport. Wallace had broken an unwritten law that we don't tell authorities what another journalist is up to, otherwise the chances of him repeating the performance are seriously compromised. Shortly after the incident Whispering Wallace went to London and under mysterious circumstances fell from an upstairs flat window and was killed. As for the plane we were on, I'm fairly sure it was the same one which crashed into the sea off East London, South Africa, drowning all aboard. I couldn't confirm this as South African Airways, whose charter plane it was, said in reply to an inquiring letter that they had no record of Robert Kennedy visiting South Africa. Their extraordinary missive read: 'On receipt of your letter, enquiring about the aircraft's name in which Robert Kennedy was flown around South Africa in 1966, I went through all our old records and archives and staff magazines, but I am afraid there is absolutely no mention of this incident.'

Broadcasting on the Kennedy trip was something of a problem. Because I should not have been there, I could not walk into the South African Broadcasting Corporation's studios and ask to do a voicepiece to New York. I therefore had to surreptitiously broadcast over the telephone from my hotel bedroom. Being a highly efficient organisation, ABC News likes to be technically perfect and hotel bedrooms, in addition to sometimes having disturbingly noisy spring beds, can also have a hollow resonance which is not conducive to broadcasting. I wrote three forty-second spots, got on the phone to New York and did a test piece for quality.

'Reg, where the hell are you phoning from?'

'My hotel bedroom.'

'Can't you get to a radio studio?'

'Not a hope. I'm not supposed to be in the country.'

'Okay, Reg,' came the soft west coast drawl. 'Don't worry. Why don't you try fixing up your tape recorder to the telephone and broadcast through the recorder's mike?' I knew the practice well and duly wired the tape recorder to the telephone, and tried again. 'We're still getting that hollow, Reg. I tell you what, get under the blankets of your bed and try again.' Fully dressed, I got under the blankets with my head shrouded. This presented certain difficulties – I couldn't see the script that I was supposed to read. 'Don't you have a torch, Reg?' No, I didn't, as I don't usually carry one but I would see what I could do.

With the blanket up to my nose, I found that by resting the copy on the pillow, I could read it. 'That's a lot better, Reg, but we could still do with a little extra quality. Why don't you run the tape recorder while we take the spots? Then, if that doesn't work, you can run the tape.' Hidden under the blanket with only eyes protruding, a tape recorder in bed beside me, I did my voicepiece and then I reran the tape. 'That's fine, Reg. Good quality,' I was told. 'Let's do a bit of Q and A. Keep the tape recorder running.' Now completely submerged under the blankets with sweat pouring off me, I had to reply intelligently and to broadcast quality, politically sensitive questions concerning one of the most famous and powerful men in the world.

That is how it was throughout the trip. First, submerged yashmak-style under a blanket and then total submersion. The great American public never even suspected what the Limey had gone through to tell them what their late president's brother was up to.

An Historical Expedition into the Okavango Swamps

The *Rhodesia Herald* carried a report that a nine-man team of doctors, dentists and students from South Africa's Witswatersrand University's medical school was to mount an expedition into the 20,000-square-mile Okavango Swamps in neighbouring Botswana. The object of their twentieth-century Rider Haggard-type adventure was to try to find and prove the existence of a race of man unknown to the modern world, the legendary River Bushman.

Feeling the need for a break from the strictures of Rhodesia while at the same time fulfilling my innate needs for adventure, I telexed *Life* magazine and pointed out that this was not a lost tribe but an actual race of man. I got the go-ahead to join the team. My Johannesburg-based photographer, Mike Irwin, met me at Francestown and we boarded an ageing DC-3 of Botswana National Airways. The plane and its pilot looked familiar and a couple of inquiries showed that the proud young national airline of the now independent African state had been leased all its planes by the irrepressible Jack Malloch. The wings of the Dakota were long and supple and suggested we were riding a latter-day Pegasus as the aircraft moved forward at a seemingly perilous speed and slowly lifted into the air with a full complement of passengers plus five standing. Instead of flying a direct 300-mile route to Maun on the edge of the swamps, (now better known as the Okavango Delta) the pilot chose a cook's tour of the arid Kalahari Desert, putting down at remote airstrips beside unmarked villages until there were only two passengers left – Mike and myself.

Nearing the end of our flight as we sat gazing out at the sand and scrub, our eyes filled with tears and we began to choke as acrid fumes from a faulty battery wafted towards us from the cockpit. It was possible that the crew had been overcome by the fumes already and I vividly pictured the first DC-3 I had ever seen, when Jack Malloch was also in tears. The fore cabin door was open and I shouted to the pilot over the noise of the engines, 'Will we make it?' There was silence before the co-pilot came back with the semi-encouraging words, 'I think we should; we are less than ten minutes from Maun!' As I wiped my eyes I knew that landing safely was only one of the problems that lay ahead for I was apprehensive about our reception on arrival. The leader of the expedition, Professor Richard van Hoogstraten, had made it clear that we would not be welcome. He argued that there was already one reporter with the team, a journalist from the *Windhoek Observer*, so why should he bother with *Life* magazine as well? During our negative correspondence, I pointed out that not everyone in the world had heard of the *Windhoek Observer* and in desperation I asked *Life* to pull strings (something I hate doing) with the university's renowned anthropologist, Professor Raymond Dart, who then contacted van Hoogstraten. It was not the ideal way of starting a month-long expedition with a hostile leader and possibly an equally hostile team.

We were met at the dusty Maun airstrip by a man known as the king of crocodile hunters. Far from being a keen-eyed, bearded, safari-suited giant with doe-eyed women dripping from his bulging muscles, Bob 'Nyangase' Wilmot was bespectacled, diminutive, restive and fast talking with the deceptive appearance of a city bank clerk and certainly not that of a man who knew the swamps better than the back of his hand. Nyangase, the local Tswana name for him, meant, 'Hurry here, hurry there'. I learned that he had spent weeks at a time alone in the swamps, travelling huge distances while living off game and fish. He knew more than anyone else about crocodiles and their habits, for he and his assistant had shot 32,000 of them in eleven years. His personal bag for one night was twenty-four! 'The expedition went ahead a couple of days ago,' was the news he greeted me with. 'Are they trying to avoid us?'

'They went in a hurry, just after receiving instructions that they must wait for you.'

'Can anyone take us to them?' I wondered if Wilmot had been asked to help keep us at bay by not providing a boat. Apparently not. 'I'll take you myself,' he said. 'I have a good idea where they are.' I took to him instantly and he led us to the tiny tin-roofed Riley's Hotel. It was there that the last illusion was shattered: when I offered him a beer, he refused. Bob Wilmot, arguably the greatest crocodile hunter the world has ever known, was tee-total. Instead of having a drink, he hurried off to work on a boat engine before taking us into the forbidding waters and this gave me a chance to look around the heat-blistered, dusty outpost called Maun. There were few houses but two banks which I learned opened two mornings a month. The airstrip came to life twice a week when the DC-3 arrived with hunters, mail and food supplies. The African women were dressed like nothing I had ever seen in Africa, wearing long, colourful Victorian-style dresses that could have come from the American deep south. I was told that the Herero women of Namibia wear similar dresses while in contrast, their children played in the white sand outside the mud huts clothed only with skin cache-sexe. The land was bleak yet nearby, reflecting the dazzling sun, were the clear fast-moving waters of the Okavango.

Kicking my heels after the ten-minute tour, I returned to the bar of Riley's where a group of hunters and a game warden had gathered. Among them were two Americans with telescopic lens rifles who bragged noisily about the defenceless animals they had slain. Surprisingly, I later found Bob Wilmot shared my sentiments over killing for sport explaining that he only shot crocodiles to keep his wife in luxury in South Africa. She had three homes and in contrast to her, he had a total lack of interest in both cities and in money. Also in the bar was a white hunter who had inherited a safari business from his father and word around Maun was that he was so terrified of wild animals that he had once dropped his gun and ran when he was charged. A charming man, I took to him but knew I'd never go into the bush with him without me personally carrying a weapon. Another hunter there was Lionel Palmer who would, during his career, find himself about to be killed and eaten by a pride of lions which were surrounding him. He had only six bullets and the situation looked very bleak indeed but Palmer was a cool man in times of trouble and he did what he was good at: with the six shots left to him he killed six lions and survived.

A game warden propping up the bar when I walked in proved to be exceedingly courageous and stupid. He had an awesome reputation for walking up to elephants and kicking sand in their faces, just to prove a personal theory that if you take the initiative against an elephant, it won't attack you. A year or so later I read in a Johannesburg newspaper of one jumbo who hadn't heard of this presumption and took exception when sand was kicked into its eyes. Trumpeting loudly, the jumbo raised its mighty bulk on to hind legs and then trampled the game warden into the Kalahari sand.

Mike and I spent the night at Wilmot's base camp which gave me time to brush up on the River Bushman theory so far. Few scientists believed that a pure-bred race had ever existed, arguing that the River Bushman was merely a Bantu-Hottentot hybrid who had moved into the swamps from Namibia. But in 1963, three years before the current expedition, van Hoogstraten visited the north-east side of the swamps and found hybrids who claimed to be descendants of a whole lost race, whose ancestral home was in the very heart of the swamps. Scientifically van Hoogstraten, himself the product of a country preoccupied with racial purity, had always been interested; now he was obsessed with the notion that somewhere in the swamps there really was a pure-bred River Bushman. His early findings had been treated with reserve by those who would not believe that an unknown race could possibly exist in the twentieth century. They argued that as Bushmen can live for a week in the desert without touching water, why should they bother to move into the swamps? Even the renowned American Desert Bushman expert, George B Silberbauer, had excluded the van Hoogstraten findings from his list of Bushmen, probably because the only swamp people found were hybrid. By chance, I met Silberbauer on a remote airstrip on the way back from Maun and was able to inform him first hand of the results of the latest expedition. Among those who had taken a keen interest in van Hoogstraten's findings, however, was the Australian-born Professor Dart who had achieved world fame with his Taungs Skull, which became known as the 'Missing Link' in Man's search for his own origins.

As it had taken Dart many years to convince the world that his Taungs Skull theory was correct, he encouraged van Hoogstraten to lead an expedition into the heart of the swamps to confirm what the young scientist already believed. I'm glad he did, for with the expedition I was to enter the world like that seen in *The African Queen*, a world that for most people exists only in books or on the Technicolor screen. The article I had read of the proposed expedition spoke of wide-eyed adventurous visitors to the edges of the swamps seeing web-footed lions and prehistoric pterodactyls that could carry off a buffalo like a stork with a baby. It was fanciful nonsense but it was in this remote and unreal atmosphere that the legend of the River Bushmen had fostered. They were first mentioned in print in a book by a German, Dr F Steiner, who had studied the Desert Bushmen of Namibia but he spoke of groups of Bushmen living on the banks of the Okavango River with predominantly Negroid features and a Bantu culture. Next reports were from two other anthropologists who studied the desert men, Doctors I Shaper and Hilliard Hurwitz. Both had led expeditions into the northern part of Botswana and reported seeing groups of river Bushmen living along the Okavango River but again, they were hybrids.

I awoke at sunrise in the quiet unhurried surroundings of a perfect dawn and walked down to the river's edge where Bob Wilmot was waiting to take us into the forbidding swamps. The clearness and speed of the fast-moving waters was astonishing; I had always believed swamps to be sluggish with dirty warm water, leaches and crocodiles which slowly broke through the surface covered in green slime, Crocodiles there were but the water was so clear that I could see the bottom and was assured by Bob that it was 100 feet down. As he started the outboard engine of his steel boat, smoke and noise brought the twentieth century into the Eden paradise and I knew that the noise of the outboard engine would be constant throughout the journey. Within hours we found the medical team near an island and the initial reception was so chilly that we were made to feel like gatecrashers until I spoke to van Hoogstraten and told him that once *Life* had finished with our photographs he could have them. Mike, who always reminded me of a secretary bird, nodded approvingly, even though I had just given away all the pictures he might have sold elsewhere at a later stage. The professor paused, smiled, and held out his hand, 'Welcome aboard!' He was looking rather pleased with himself and I took it to be the thought of all the free photographs. There was only one woman with the expedition and the only person not connected with the medical school, other than the Windhoek reporter. 'I'm a hybrid myself,' she was later to joke with me explaining that her mother was American and her father Scottish. Fiona Barbour was an ethnologist in charge of the Bantu Museum in Kimberley, South Africa, and her boyfriend was one of the team.

After a few days aboard van Hoogstraten dropped the bombshell and I wondered how an expedition leader could be so petty. 'We have found a pure-bred River Bushman already,' he confided and I noted the smugness on his face. 'It was on our second day out.' He wasn't given the satisfaction of my showing emotion; I can be like that. 'Are you planning to go back that way?' I asked. 'We have done our work there and we are now going further into the swamps to see if there are any more such men,' he said. One thing was certain; I wouldn't report back to *Life* that the expedition had found a lost race of man but that we had missed him. I decided to deal with the matter later for we were going to be confined to the swamps for another three weeks and there was no way I could hitch a lift on a boat going the other way.

The university team had struck lucky near the Caprivi Strip on the Angolan border while searching for a local ruler, a young hybrid named Phelo, who had once worked for Wilmot. They found him on a tiny island suffering from pneumonia and I doubt he could believe his luck that a whole university medical team should suddenly descend upon him. While Phelo was being treated, van Hoogstraten looked round at the gathered tribespeople and saw an elderly man named Tsatsa and knew at once that he had found his pure-bred legendary River Bushman!

With Tsatsa was his wife, Seditse, and their adult daughter who did the interpreting plus two women cousins who, like Seditse and the daughter, were virtually pure River Bush, but the team suspected about one-sixteenth hybridisation. A child of one of the women in the group appeared to have been fathered by a Bushman, but all the other children had obvious Negroid features. This small section of five claimed pure ancestry and it was later clear to the scientists that they were the remnants of a pure-bred people with Tsatsa apparently the only example alive of a doomed race. Subsequently others have been found but not by our expedition.

Tsatsa had an unknown click language which resembled that of the Hottentot. It was completely new to van Hoogstraten and was spoken only in that small section of the swamps, which itself was sixty miles by water from the nearest village. The three-click language later proved to be unique because the southern desert Bushmen have five clicks, while the central northern Bushmen have four.

Tsatsa was slightly taller than most Hottentots (or Khoisanoid) who, in turn, are taller than the Desert Bushmen and his skin colour was light brownish-yellow, which was similar to Cape Bushmen. Tsatsa spoke of his father and grandfather and therefore talked of life in the swamps for approximately 100 years. 'Up to fifty years ago, when the first Africans arrived, River Bushmen completely dominated the swamps,' he said. It was the news van Hoogstraten had longed to hear. The downfall of the lost race had been partly caused by the tsetse fly from which tripanosomiasis (sleeping sickness) had swept through their ranks like a plague, forty years previously; and also the over-amorous attitude of their women to the new African arrivals. By falling for the charms of the Yei tribe 'strangers in the night', who rested on the islands during fishing trips in their canoes, they had produced the hybrids who now occupy the swamps. Like all Bushmen, Tsatsa's group knew nothing about musical instruments but were quite happy to make music by clapping their hands and chanting. Unlike their desert counterparts, they carried no bows and arrows and didn't hunt for food on land. Instead, they were expert spear fishers and if they did go after an animal, it would be chased into the water and killed.

Tsatsa, the pure-bred River Bushman. Life Pix, Mike Irwin.

One of Tsatsa's most significant statements was totally overlooked by the expedition leader, which gave me reason to feel there was some slight retribution for van Hoogstraten's early attitude towards *Life* magazine. At the end of the trip I had to dash back to Rhodesia as I couldn't afford to stay away from the political situation any longer, and sent Mike back into the swamps to photograph Tsatsa and his family. Mike found Tsatsa and during the ensuing conversation he mentioned that before the Africans arrived in dug-out canoes, the River Bushmen had travelled on rafts made from papyrus reeds. When Mike returned to Johannesburg, I asked him to interview Raymond Dart and during the conversation, Mike casually mentioned the rafts. The response was electric as the elderly Dart jumped up and thumped his desk shouting, 'Then why didn't you get him to make you one?'

Dart knew at once that van Hoogstraten had bungled even while enjoying his personal triumph. Showing the same encapsulated vision that decided him no one outside of Windhoek need be told of his incredible find, he had totally overlooked the significance of Tsatsa's statement; that while he might have found a noncongeneric preadamite race, without realising it he had missed the significance of the reed craft implications. The reed craft culture has always been associated with Biblical Egypt, recorded back to Moses in the bulrushes, and at no time in Africa's history had there been a record of such a culture further south than Lake Chad in North Africa. The art of binding bulrushes together had also seemingly crossed the Atlantic to Lake Titicaca between Bolivia and Peru, hence the Thor Heyerdal expedition. How it travelled the thousands of miles down through the heart of Africa to the Okavango Swamps was a mystery to Dart; it couldn't have been by the colonising Negroes as they had no reed culture. The Bushmen, on the other hand, being the true indigenous people of sub-Saharan Africa, were known to have existed north of the equator and this may be an important clue.

The late and great anthropologist would have been interested in the discovery in 1993 – twenty-seven years after our expedition – of the Blombos cave high in a limestone cliff on South Africa's Cape coast which suggested a sophisticated style of living 80,000 to 100,000 years ago. As fish bones were found, these ancient dwellers' activities may have included fishing with both bone and stone-carved spears. The question that arises is: having entered the Okavango Swamps and learned to build papyrus reed craft, could it be that some nomadic Bushmen then took their boat-building and fishing knowledge further north to Lake Chad where, many thousands of years later, their skills were studied by another culture from north east of the Sahara Desert, the Egyptians? Egypt is only a long camel trek away from Lake Chad and Ptolemies and Macedonian kings who ruled in Egypt from 323 to 30 BC are believed to have been aware of the lake's existence. According to the *Encyclopaedia Britannica*, the lake was reputed to have been occupied by the vanished legendary Negroid Sao people but, I wonder, could they actually have been the San, as the Bushmen are known? The two words are so close that even today the Portuguese word for saint (an Israelite term) is 'Sao' whereas in Spanish it is 'San'. This is all conjecture on my part, but barbed-bone harpoons have been found in the Sudan and also the skull of a proto-Bushman. The possibility of Egypt's famous ancient craft actually being of Bushman origin which travelled north instead of south is tantalizing and possibly worthy of investigation by experts.

While we were in the swamps, a few members of the medical team went crocodile-hunting at night and learned first hand that it is not just a simple matter of shooting a croc and then skinning it. Wilmot's manager, Bill Cornuel, who acted as our expedition guide, led the hunt and shot a fifteen-foot monster which had at least four-foot of tail missing. Believing the croc to be dead, its hind legs were hauled into the precariously balanced boat. And then, to the horror of the terrified doctors the creature lashed out, pulled the boat into the reeds and then sank its teeth into the craft's steel sides. Cornuel put another five bullets into the head and still the crocodile struggled with the boat close to capsizing. He had only an axe left and it took several blows with that before the crocodile succumbed. Inside the stomach were found two partially digested whole young lechwe (type of buck); the head of a lechwe cow complete with horns; two vervet monkeys and two zebra hooves giving an indication of just how fast a crocodile can move. It is not unusual also to find the remains of African women who have been snatched away while doing the family washing.

The following night I went croc hunting with Cornuel anticipating the excitement of the night before, but it was not to be. The operation, however, came as a surprise as I had thought that the creature was picked up in the torchlight, a shot fired, and that was it. Nothing of the sort. I learned that when the torch is shone across the water, only the holder of the lamp can see the red eyes staring back. The hunter then moves the boat forward, keeping the eyes transfixed in the light beam until the boat is beside the reptile, and then a bullet is put into the head at point blank range. The croc then has to be caught with a hook before it turns over and sinks, the hook holder being careful not to damage the skin. The only croc we sighted declined to be mesmerised by the light beam and having quickly got the message, submerged into the water and disappeared as we approached. I wasn't sorry.

I've only deliberately killed animals twice. One was a huge male baboon which had been causing havoc with crops in a national park and I was with the warden at the time. The baboon was sitting in a tree when I shot it and after firing, the baboon continued to sit. 'You missed,' said the warden contemptuously, who then took another five shots before going up to the tree to find the creature was quite dead, high on a branch with blood dripping down like light rain. He took several more shots to dislodge it but the animal was still there when I left. Shooting an animal from a distance, I discovered, is quite impersonal but it is another matter being physically and psychologically involved. This happened when I went on a visit to the Zimbabwe ruins. It was evening and as I approached the dry stone-walled structure, a spring hare hopped in front of the car from about six yards away and I couldn't avoid hitting it. Spring hares are odd creatures which resemble kangaroos but are not marsupial. I left the car and found it sitting upright and shaking with fear but quite unable to move. A cursory examination showed its leg had been badly broken. I knew that it would be almost impossible to get it into the car without causing great suffering and if I had done so, there was not a vet for many miles around. On the other hand, if I just left it sitting there the chances were that it would be torn to pieces by a marauding leopard or hyena, or be left to die in agony in the sun the next day. There was only one thing to do. With reluctance and sadness I backed the car, put the headlights full on to mesmerise it, and drove straight ahead. The thud and the slight lifting of the wheels told me I had been an efficient killer...

When I joined the Okavango expedition there was still a very long way to go, hundreds of miles of feathery, pompom-topped papyrus reeds, bamboo and water-lily clogged swamps. Death was close at hand when we reached blockages caused by a pile up of trees and thick papyrus reeds which made navigation impossible. Cornuel had brought dynamite along which set one blockage free but even extra sticks of explosive were useless on two others and reluctantly we evacuated our heavily laden boats and hauled them across the blockages.

Being the only one who could not swim well, I was a little more apprehensive than most about falling through the reeds. I knew I would be unable to fight against the swift current. Fiona saw me hesitate and I detected a malicious smile. On some occasions I might be intrepid but the thought of travelling seventy-five yards under water – that was the length of one blockage – did not appeal in the slightest. Possibly because she was the only woman present who may have felt she had something to prove, it was Fiona who was first into the water, fully clothed, as she helped to lift the boat on to the reeds. To our horror and yells of warning, a crocodile moved in close to her and we watched helpless and tense as it approached but our shouts and the realisation that it was outnumbered must have distracted the reptile and it turned away. 'I didn't see it,' she said afterwards but the incident did not stop her from re-entering the water time and again. It took two hours to get the heavily laden boat over that blockage for while the reeds were thick, a pull on the craft meant the surface giving way and several of us narrowly escaped being swept beneath the reeds by clinging desperately to our precarious hold on the boat itself.

Despite moments of excitement, expeditions are generally ninety per cent boredom and some days seem endless. Often we spent twelve hours on the sun-crystallised water as the boats ploughed up to 100 miles from one night stop to the nearest palm-fringed island with nothing to see but papyrus. Because the team was so well equipped, there were times we wished something dramatic would happen in order that the large black box of medical equipment could be used for other than humdrum treatment of the locals we met. For this we knew we had to be the best medically-equipped expedition ever, anywhere in the world, made up mainly of both doctors and dentists! Carried aboard was a complete range of drugs and antibiotics which were for anything from asthma to epilepsy. A comatose patient could be handled for days; gynaecological conditions could be dealt with. Antidotes for all poisonous snakes in the area, including the rare mamba serum, were on hand. Deadly scorpions and spiders were not overlooked. Despite the careful and thoughtful packing of the chest, one item was curiously absent. When Dick van Hoogstraten got indigestion he was 'treated' by layman, Mike Irwin, with a proprietary brand of indigestion tablets.

On the small floating islands which housed single families, there was always a sick person needing help. And on the large, sprawling, Chief's Island, the biggest in the swamps, over 100 turned up in their makoros (shallow dug-outs) for treatment by the medical officer of the expedition, Dr Herbert Wong, a South African Chinese who, like van Hoogstraten, was a surgeon. His Chinese skills came to the fore when a medical student, George Beaton, trod on a burning twig with his bare feet and yelled out with pain. 'Pour petrol on the burn,' cried an African boat driver. The student hopped painfully towards the boats' petrol supplies before Dr Wong called him back. 'That's no good,' admonished the surgeon and the student blushed at allowing himself to be advised by the medically uneducated African boatman. Solemnly, the Chinese surgeon produced his own remedy: a bottle of soy sauce. It was rubbed into the burn, and it worked!

Wong was something special. He was the only one amongst us who could catch fish, and he was a remarkable cook. Realising South Africa's strict apartheid laws at that time, it surprised me that Wong should be on the expedition at all, let alone be its deputy leader. The Chinese were considered an inferior race with only the Japanese being classified 'white' because of their trade links and the South African attitude towards dark-skinned people was displayed by van Hoogstraten in his arrogance towards them when we landed on the islands. After looking around for possible River Bushmen, it never occurred to him to ask a likely candidate if he would mind being subjected to undignified treatment and I wondered what a white man would have done in the circumstances. Once a likely subject was found, van Hoogstraten ordered him to sit down before sticking two straws up his nostrils and smothering his face with plaster of Paris. The unfortunate guinea pig would never have the first idea what it was about.

On a freezing night – it was mid-winter – we sat around the camp fire and discussed the legends of the swamps; the lions with webbed feet and the pterodactyls, and decided the fables possibly had some foundation. There were plenty of lions about which, like all the other animals of the swamps, would swim through the fast-flowing, ever-silent waters from island to island. In the water they were no longer 'king', the crocodiles would see to that. But what of the pterodactyls? We actually saw the reason for the legend. At the time we were in an open area when a bird lifted from the water, its huge wing span appearing to cover the entire width of our channel. It was a memorable sight as the Goliath Heron swept low over the water. We never saw it again.

Nights in the swamps were beautiful, breathtaking, with more than a touch of magic. The stars were either distinctly separate, or massed together in clusters which illuminated the water. There was the ever-present sound of cicadas, the grunt of a lion, or a hyena laughing through to daybreak. I wrote descriptively one morning in my notebook: 'At dawn the swamps explode into a canvas of colour, and life. Wildlife is abundant: a black cormorant swoops down into the water in search of prey, only to rise without a fish. It flies dejectedly to a nearby tree stump and spreads its wings giving an appearance of crucifixion rather than hunger. A lily-trotter's matchstick legs make their way timidly across the swamps, carefully selecting each lily pad and gingerly standing on it with the other leg poised, preparing for the next delicate step. There are blue-faced Jacana and the white-and-tan dwarf geese. A saddlenose stork glides by and looks curiously at the camp. Back into the boat again and we pass islands with wild figs, sausage-trees and lalala palms which the swamp people 'bleed' to produce a potent mind-blowing wine. There are the rare shaggy sitatunga buck which prance through the shallow water with ease on their splayed feet. There is a beautiful lechwe which looks curiously at us with large brown eyes until a shot rings out. "We'll need that for the pot," says Cornuel, his rifle in his hand. We disembark on to a floating island where we find the creature still alive, but life fades from those uncomprehending eyes as we watch. Fiona is upset as the unfeeling Cornuel slits open the stomach to remove the bowels before we haul the carcass to the boat. Dr Wong says the meat will be far too hard today for steaks but he later makes a stew of the poor animal which, like us, had awakened this morning to enjoy the sunshine, but had only lived long enough to provide for our bellies.'

Two years after the Okavango experience and shortly after I received a letter from him, Bob Wilmot was dead. The legendary soft-hearted man who had shot all those crocodiles was himself killed in the swamps by a reptile, a black mamba, which struck him twice. It was then discovered that his trusted African assistant had forgotten to take along the medical kit containing ampoules of anti-venom which the medical team had given him just before we left for home. Bob, who is now a legend in his own right, is buried opposite his camp, I am told, on an island surrounded by the glistening ever silent and fast flowing waters of the Okavango he loved to death.

The Laughing Hangman

The news reverberated around the world with seismic impact: Dr Hendrik Verwoerd, the Dutch born pro-Nazi prime minister of South Africa, had been stabbed to death in parliament by a messenger. Ironically, although it was not appreciated at the time, the architect of apartheid who had so cruelly created laws which divided people of different races died at the hands of a mixed-race man in the very parliament where the evil law was passed.

Life magazine came through on telex as the news broke and asked me to fly to Cape Town urgently and write a feature on the assassination which was wanted in New York first thing next morning. This created problems as it meant flying to Johannesburg where I would have to change planes and arrive in the Cape at night, giving me no time for interviews on arrival. I picked up the latest information on the stabbing by telephoning colleagues and then sat down in the Mount Nelson Hotel to an all-night session of writing. I recollected the first time I'd been to Cape Town when I arrived with the family en route to Rhodesia, and how we sat in the gardens beside the parliament buildings. My article opened: 'As the whites sat on their "whites only" benches in Cape Town's parliament gardens and blacks sat on their "blacks only" seats; while brown squirrels ran up nearby trees, the architect of apartheid, Hendrik Verwoerd, was being knifed to death only a short distance away.' In an editorial turnabout through lack of pictures, *Life* decided to do a history of Verwoerd and passed my article over to *Time* which used it verbatim.

A week later I was back in South Africa for the funeral ceremony. With the government's paranoid dislike and distrust of the local and foreign press to rival that of Rhodesia, only a few selected South African journalists were invited to attend and a special press badge was produced to be pinned to their lapels. Come the event, the special area for the press was swarming with journalists, TV cameramen and photographers, all bustling about and doing their bit. 'How did they get in?' I heard one puzzled official ask, and quickly moved out of his way. He had been with the South African diplomatic mission in Salisbury and would have known I had no right, in the government's eyes, to be present. We were all indebted to Mike Irwin's wife who was an artist and she had sat up all night forging the official badge which was then distributed to those of us who needed them!

ABC News sent me to Cape Town to cover the trial of the messenger, Dimetrios Tsafendas, who everyone in court thought was white until he declared, 'I am a member of the Coloured race.' This time I didn't have to worry about going to the SABC studios as I'd entered the country openly and had no problems in getting a seat at the trial itself. At the radio station I asked for a studio, having already organised with America the time for my voicepiece, and was told that a Mr du Plessis would like to see me. Hello, I thought suspiciously, here comes trouble. Bespectacled Mr du Plessis came downstairs, shook hands solemnly and took me to his office. 'Mr Shay,' he said, in a broad Afrikaans accent, 'despite what you may have been told about us in the SABC, I want to assure you that we do not listen to other people's broadcasts and we don't tape record them either.' I didn't believe a word of it and didn't care; I could always return to my hotel room and broadcast beneath the blankets. 'Mr du Plessis,' I replied with equal solemnity, 'I'm very pleased to hear that.' 'Mr Shay,' he went on, 'we are a free country despite what you may have heard or read.' I had entered the heart of South African paranoia; its propaganda machine. Where else, I wondered, would a journalist asking to use a radio studio be subjected to this type of conversation. 'I take it, then, that I can use the studio?' I asked. He ignored the question and instead picked up a back copy of *Time* which was under some papers on his desk. By the way he looked at me I guessed he knew exactly who he was talking to; the post office would have sent a copy of any story I filed directly to the security police for perusal. It followed that when I asked for a studio, du Plessis would have checked me out. 'Have you seen this scurrilous article in *Time* magazine on the tragic death of our beloved prime minister?' he asked as he handed me the copy. I glanced through the offending article and told him I'd already read it. 'It looks straightforward to me,' I added, as I handed the magazine back.

We sat staring at each other in a cat-and-mouse situation; he realising that I was not about to lay claim to having written it while for my part, I knew that to have done so would have jeopardised my chances of using the studio. I wondered what his problem was and was about to ask when he broke the silence. 'It's the opening paragraph, Mr Shay,' he said. 'It is totally untrue!' With that he read aloud the familiar lines. 'That seems fair to me,' I commented and remembered vividly my first brush with apartheid at Cape Town station. 'I've seen for myself there are separate benches for blacks and whites in South Africa's parks.' I was close to adding that I knew there were brown squirrels in the park but thought better of it as this would only confirm that I was the author. 'Yes, Mr Shay, we do have separate seating arrangements in South Africa's parks but not the one beside parliament. Those seats are open to people of all races – they are not segregated!' Setting aside the total hypocrisy of the situation, I had chosen the one park in the whole of South Africa where there were not separate seating arrangements. Looking at du Plessis, it didn't seem tactful to laugh in his face but that small park did symbolise the whole irrationality of apartheid legislators and supporters; that here was one place where a black human being was considered equal to his white counterpart. Having made his point, du Plessis then gave me a conducted tour of the studios. We came to the showpiece, a large studio with stage and auditorium and it was impressive. 'We do have a problem here with the stage, Mr Shay,' he said. 'It has beetles.' The temptation was too much: 'I understood they are banned,' I replied blandly and he looked at me puzzled. 'Yes,' he said, 'we try to get rid of them but they keep coming back.' I knew that all Beatles records had been banned following John Lennon's remark comparing their popularity to Jesus Christ's and guessed that the very serious Mr du Plessis would not twig that I was mocking him. I had often wondered whether the Afrikaners, with their Calvinistic worship of Jesus, would have accepted Him as white should he materialise in the twentieth century. After doing my voicepiece, a taxi driver took me back to the hotel and I arranged for him to drive for me through the duration of the trial. The driver was a Cape Coloured and next day after I mentioned the inconvenience of driving the long distance from the court to the Mount Nelson to write my voicepiece, he took me to his home where I typed my script before going to the radio studio. It was a pleasing modern house and Charles introduced me to Alice, his pretty wife and their two children, a boy and a girl who were both under eight years of age, whose smiles of welcome made me feel that I was an honoured guest. 'Let me show you my garden,' said the taxi driver and he led me into a garden of trellised bougainvillaea, lawn and flowering shrubs of which he was clearly proud. 'I spend a lot of my spare time working out here,' he said. As we re-entered the house I was taken into the lounge to type my voicepiece and when they were done I asked if it was illegal under South African law for me to be there. 'You are all right here,' said Charles. 'This is District Six and so far as I know it's the only multiracial area in the whole of South Africa.' I replied, simply, 'Well, you have kept a lovely home and you have a beautiful family.' Sometime later came the news that all the Coloured people were forcibly moved out of District Six and their homes given to unsettled whites. I felt desperately sorry for the nice little family who daily gave me lunch and were so kind to me. The day following my first broadcast I returned to the SABC studios and was told that Mr du Plessis would like to see me again. As I entered his office he rose from his desk and beamed and shook my hand warmly, 'I want you to know, Mr Shay, that I have listened to a tape recording of your broadcast,' he said.

'Really?' By his demeanour I knew that he was a happy man; but there was little that could be controversial in a straightforward court report, anyway. 'Yes, Mr Shay,' he went on, 'and I want you to know that what you said was perfectly correct reporting and so everything is all right. You can go ahead and broadcast from here at any time!'

Back home, the government's vitriolic campaign against the foreign news media continued to take its toll. Most whites countrywide sincerely believed that journalists were traitors and should be treated like lepers and hostility was not confined to words as more than one visiting journalist was beaten up. Margery continued to be swayed more and more to the government's way of thinking by her artisan colleagues and the deep love that existed between us was turning to hatred and bitter quarrels increased and in bed I was sent to Coventry for two years which did so little for my ego that I felt I was becoming

Margery, just days before her paralysing stroke

impotent. While I'd put it down to Margery being ashamed of her husband being a journalist, there was more behind her aggressive behaviour than I appreciated. The verbal encounters were exacerbated by severe pains she was getting at the base of her head. 'For heaven's sake go to the doctor,' I remonstrated but when she did so our GP was away on leave and his young locum could find nothing wrong. She was sent to a bone specialist but as no fault could be found, I thought she must be suffering from migraine attacks. To me it was almost academic as by now we were not on speaking terms and I only saw it as a situation whereby the worse the headache, the worse her sour disposition. At last I came to a decision. Very reluctantly because, whatever our feelings towards each other, there had been a wonderful relationship between us and a lot of fun and we were both devoted to the children that had sprung from our love.

I took Margery out to dinner and told her that unless her attitude towards me changed, I would divorce her on the legal grounds of withholding conjugal rights. To my surprise she showed emotion, the first sign of this for a very long time. 'I'd like some time to think about it,' she said, and I gave her a month. I'd mixed feelings and realised that love and hate between the sexes are not parallel emotions but often intertwined. Neither of us could know that the time limit I'd dictated would be irrelevant; that the axe would fall, very cruelly and not in a way either of us could have anticipated. I was in my office two weeks after the dinner when a plumber rushed in and I was surprised to see him as I'd always viewed him with distaste as someone I suspected of chasing after my wife. He was distraught and the news he gave was a bombshell. 'Margery's collapsed and is in hospital,' he said. 'You must come quickly as she's not expected to live!'

Margery dying? This was impossible. He said she was getting ready to leave the office when she collapsed to the floor. 'She was lying there like a little old woman,' said the plumber and I thought this was a strange thing to say. Margery was thirty-seven years old but she still looked to be in her mid-twenties and I couldn't think of her any other way. During the late afternoon, it seems, she had surprised customers by commenting on the beautiful music being played on her miniature radio and they assumed she was joking as the radio was not switched on. As she was preparing to leave for the day, the telephone rang and she leaned over to answer it but the call was never received for at that same moment she crumbled to the floor.

The headaches had been caused by high blood pressure as both the locum and the specialist had totally neglected to give her a test, which I found incredible. For the next ten days she was completely unconscious and then semi-comatose for some time after that, having suffered a severe base-of-the-skull stroke – a killer had she been older. A ward sister, who handed over Margery's clothing, told me disparagingly, 'I think it's disgusting that a woman of her age should wear skirts above the knee!' It happened to be the fashion of the day and Margery could carry it off and the ugly sister then added, as if it gave her some inner pleasure, 'She won't wear them any more, your wife will never be the same again!' I looked at her in amazement, an absurd outsize dumpling with a small head topped with a butcher's 'Guard of Honour' hat normally seen on a stuffed roast crown of lamb. Her face, I decided, should have been put back into the pack and reshuffled. You frustrated old bitch, I thought but muttered through gritted teeth, 'You don't know my wife...'

Weeks turned into months and beyond as I daily visited Margery, first in hospital and then at nursing homes. My early visits were often perfunctory as her hostility was still there and the plumber would always be sitting beside her bed holding her hand. It was then that I realised that they were lovers and I felt deeply self-conscious and frustrated walking into the ward with all the other women patients staring as though I was an outsider butting in on the visits of the poor woman and her devoted husband. Margery, too, made it clear that I was intruding until her friend's visits ended abruptly when he learned that she would be paralysed for life. Divorce was now out of the question. Margery was resolutely determined to recover and I could not but admire her courage and steely determination. We began to talk more and she would say with the child-like determination and faith of a little girl, 'I'm going to get better, you'll see.' It was difficult to hold back the tears and I'd sometimes shed a few without her knowing.

Other than the ability to walk again, more important to her than anything else was to be able to drive her car. It was a goal she was determined to achieve and despite complete paralysis down her left side which was extended to the vision of her left eye – she could see straight ahead but not to the left – she fought at the St Giles' Rehabilitation Centre to walk, which she managed after a long struggle. First it was the parallel bars... one step, then two... four... Once proud of her gorgeous legs, she now had one that was thin and almost worthless. In tears she pleaded with me to tell the centre not to make a calliper for the leg but my request was to no avail. She hated it but one day I went to collect her and her eyes sparkled with anticipation as she said, 'Stay there, Reggie, look at this.' I was about fifteen feet away and with her unfeeling left arm flailing in the air with abandon, and the right one held out for balance, she slowly made her way towards me, berating anyone who came near in case she stumbled. She made the perilous journey and triumphantly fell into my outstretched arms! What I found quite incredible was that she could stay upright and keep her balance while walking on a foot which had no feeling to tell her whether it was on the ground or not. With the continuous squeezing of squash balls, (not now recommended) she was also able to get some slight movement in her left hand and fingers.

'Let's go for a drive and see how you get on at the wheel,' I said one bright sunny day. I watched the excitement in her eyes; the realisation of a dream about to come true. It would be proof positive that willpower could overcome any obstacle provided there was a determination to succeed. Now was her moment of truth. With the help of her calliper, walking stick and my right arm, we made our way to her car and triumphantly she sat in the driving seat and switched on the ignition. It was an exhilarating moment which was met with an immediate anti-climax as her foot slipped off the clutch pedal. 'This damned leg,' she cried with the same frustration I had seen so many times before. And then came the mumble, her lips set tight and a determined glint in her eyes, 'I'm not going to let it beat me!' I had a special bracket made for the pedal so that her foot wouldn't slip, and it worked. Soon she was driving slowly along quiet roads but I suspected she would never be able to go out alone, or on the main highways unless some miracle occurred. The miracle didn't come; much worse was to happen which would tax that courage all over again...

In March 1968, less than a year after Margery's stroke, the Rhodesian Government hanged three Africans in defiance of a plea from the rest of the world for clemency. The act was also in defiance of a reprieve by the Queen and the Privy Council and Her Majesty was subsequently labelled a tool of the British prime minister, Harold Wilson. Now, it seems, UDI had been taken in the name of a royal sycophantic lackey of the British government!

Richard Lindley was in Rhodesia to do an in-depth BBC *Panorama* feature on sanctions-busting oil being brought up by road from South Africa and he was in my office. 'I hear the public hangman, "Lofty" Milton, is boozing in the Norfolk Hotel,' I said. 'Would you care to come along to see him?' It wasn't the story Richard was assigned to work on but he came anyway. Never having met a public hangman, it seemed a good idea to have someone else around in case he and his boozing friends became difficult. Verification of what was said, too, could be important in the emotion-charged atmosphere of the country. Cardiff-born Milton turned out to be a most amiable hangman after a couple of drinks. He had enjoyed doing a good professional job on the three Africans, he said, and because his work was appreciated he was expecting to string up another 115 held in Rhodesian jails who were waiting for him to call! Lofty was not only a master of his odious trade, he was also a macabre comedian who told me he was known as 'The Laughing Hangman' who had put 332 human beings to death in southern Africa. Between beers he confided, 'I can hang three an hour, on the hour, every hour and after they drop I have a cup of coffee while a doctor examines the bodies.' When I asked how he could possibly drink coffee under the circumstances, he shrugged his shoulders and replied, 'I don't feel any emotion towards the people I hang.' He confirmed this by saying that he had actually arrived late at the jail for the three disputed hangings and when he walked in he joked, 'Well, where's the rope then?'

After dispatching the hapless trio, Milton sent a card to a friend at his home town, Karoi, in the north of Rhodesia. It read, 'Three in one', and was signed, 'Dropper'. He looked across at the two stony-faced journalists and licked his lips, declaring, 'That's a good one, eh? One Christmas, I sent out cards which carried a miniature noose tied with a hangman's knot.' I was curious about his psychological make-up. What makes a man want to become a hangman? He didn't come across as a pathological sadist; quite the contrary. To him it was just a straightforward job with no strings attached (he would have liked that one); but receipt of a wage packet at the end of the job just as any artisan would pick up. His laugh-a-minute approach to death, he explained, probably came during the Normandy invasion when he saw a lot of men die. This I could understand; humour can be a great safety valve in stressful circumstances but he had gone beyond the norm of mental self-preservation. Following WW2, Milton began his macabre career in the former British protectorates where each hanging earned him forty pounds which he shared with a colleague. Life in Africa is indeed cheap and Lofty declared to me with a knowing wink, 'That's what I call money for old rope.' As I plied him with beer, he was slowly tightening the noose around his own neck and he told me that the Salisbury gallows could only take six victims and he found them a bit cramped. 'I prefer the gallows at Maseru, Basutoland, where I can hang twelve people simultane-ously,' he laughed. 'Once I nearly wiped out a whole tribe which had been convicted of witchcraft killings!'

Throughout Britain there was a public outcry over the three Africans and here was I talking to the man who had hanged them and then joked about it. The story was political dynamite and now I was again in the invidious position of having a hot scoop yet knowing that I might be deported if I sent it. There was also the ever-present problem of what would happen to Margery's condition if she was uprooted at this critical stage in her life, especially as she was back in hospital. It was imperative that I should not be bylined and I decided to send the story exclusively to the *Sunday Mirror*, which was amongst the most hostile of the British press. Instead of using an open telex, I dis-patched the interview by air-freight together with a photograph of Milton in a local restaurant which I had commissioned Mike Irwin to take. The *Sunday Mirror* sent a telegram: 'We are going to use this like you would never believe.' They did, the front page was taken up with the picture of Milton while the whole middle-pages and the back page printed the story. In any other circum-stances the story and the difficult conditions under which it was obtained and written would have been an award winner. After the *Mirror* publication Milton was sacked on the spot for talking to the press and the witch-hunt was on for the treasonable journalist. By a stroke of good fortune he denounced Reuters and said he was looking for their staff correspondent, no doubt with one last hanging in mind. Lofty, it seems, had spoken to Reuters' bureau chief before I had interviewed him. I subsequently asked the Reuters man why he had not filed and he replied that he didn't feel the story would be of interest.

Having lost his job, Lofty Milton was not the type to personally stay hang-ing around for long, doing nothing. He started up a new enterprise into which his penchant for necrophilia was amply satisfied – making coffins.

I was visiting Margery in hospital shortly after this incident and she intro-duced me to a lady in the next bed, whose name was Catchpole. She came from Zambia and we chatted briefly until the lady's husband came in to visit, and then I turned to Margery with my back to them. As I spoke, a pair of probing hands moved gently around my neck. It was an uncomfortable and eerie sensation and there was something about the hands that told me that while soft, they were business-like. I stood up and spun around, facing him. 'You're Catchpole, the hangman!'

'Yes,' he said with a wistful smile. The Zambian hangman had been measuring my neck!

Whether being hanged is worse than suffering the fate of the early Christians in Rome is a moot point but I can advise from personal experience that anyone planning to walk into a lions' den should first ensure they are carrying a piece of tin, preferably about three-foot square. The West End actress and former film star, Jean Kent, and her husband Yusuf, were in Rhodesia when Jean said she would like to see some wildlife. As she was the lead role in a play she couldn't spend much time out of Salisbury and I suggested the lion park at nearby Lake McIlwaine. The owner of the park was Ossie Bristow, a fearless man devoted to his lions. 'We'll go for a walk through the park,' he said as casually as someone suggesting an afternoon stroll over the Sussex downs. 'In there?' I asked as I gazed with horror through the wire fence. Inside were several young lions and lionesses in prime condition sunning themselves on the ground and on rocks over which their bodies and limbs were sprawled. The high rocks, I observed, gave them an exciting vantage point to view an oncoming menu.

Yusuf was particularly keen to go as he liked danger. He told me how he had been in the French Maquis during the war and was surrounded by a German patrol. Carefully removing the pins from two hand grenades, he held down the spring levers as the Germans walked up with pointed rifles. 'If you shoot I'll take you with me,' he explained, and the Germans accepted the situation deciding that retreat was a preferable expedient to valour. Jean didn't share Yusuf's enthusiasm to enter the arena but she agreed to go and once she had assented Ossie called an assistant to bring him a sheet of tin. 'I see you don't carry a gun,' I mentioned casually. Bristow looked me up and down before replying, 'No.'

'Don't you think they might eat us?' I wasn't really thinking so much of myself as the rather outsized once-famous actress who would have made more than a desirable morsel to a whole pack of lions. I had visions of a disconcerted stage manager telling the evening audience, 'We are terribly sorry to cancel this performance but a lion has just gobbled up our leading lady.' My instinctive news sense told me this could make a good diary piece in the newspapers but my common sense explained that I might not be around to write it. 'Why don't you need a gun?' I added.

'If they attack I don't want to shoot them,' Bristow explained. 'They are such beautiful creatures.' This seemed reasonable; he was very fond of his lions. He had already been distressed recently when one had escaped and terrorised the surrounding area after a boy had capriciously cut a hole in the high wire fence. We entered the arena and as I looked at the lions gazing at us, Bristow advised that we should keep together. 'They're more likely to attack you if you go off by yourself,' he explained. As we walked, Bristow held up his piece of tin which the lions appeared to recognise as none came near us. I asked, 'What's it for?' We were now some 100 yards inside the caged area and there was no chance of escaping should the lions become playful or hungry. 'If they attack, I bang the tin,' Bristow replied. 'They don't like the noise and will stay away.' This was some sort of reassurance, I suppose, and it is true that the lions didn't attack us. But the thought did cross my mind as we wandered along that one of them might have been deaf.

Having survived the lions, I believe I might have been murdered if a certain army captain had known who was responsible for an incident which caused his demise. Even today, I don't regret what I did for he was truly objectionable and I'd heard of his unpleasant reputation before we met. He was head of the army band and played a beautiful trumpet once in Westminster Abbey, but that was all I had ever heard in his favour. We met at a local society wedding where the captain had his own small tax-free dance group made up of African members of the military band.

Drinks were dispensed on the lawn where the reception was held in true colonial style and the captain's group began playing a Hawaiian tune as genteel background music. There was polite laughter when, like wind exuding slowly on the dying note of a bagpipe, the music came to a halt as power drained from the electric guitars. Livid, the captain stormed into the lounge to find the overloaded electric plugs lying on the floor. Anyone with half intelligence could see they had fallen from the socket of their own accord but I was unfortunate enough to be standing nearby and he turned on me, a complete stranger, and accused me in no uncertain terms of deliberately pulling them out. He wanted to fight and I told him to behave himself and when he still wanted to fight I walked off. It was an embarrassing moment for me and the guests when the groom went up to him and sympathetically said he was sure it was an accident, and would he please start playing again? The thought crossed my mind that if the captain behaved like this to a wedding guest, what was he like with the troops? There were rumours that the army would have liked to get rid of him but he was not to know that one day I would do the army this favour by *really* pulling the plug.

The opportunity arose at a much-publicised big military procession when the Rhodesian Air Force was about to receive the Freedom of the City of Salisbury. The pageant was minutely planned and was to march past the back of my office, which was close to the Town Hall, and then swing round to the left 200 yards further on, left again, and parade in front of the dignitaries. People turned out in their thousands to watch and cheer. As one band went past the rear of my office block, followed by marching airmen, they were followed by an army band, led by none other than the captain. Fellow journalist Bill McLean and my assistant, Frances Louw, were standing at the office window with me and witnessed the moment I could not resist. With my inherited sergeant-major voice I yelled, 'Leeft wheeel...'

Without hesitation the captain did as he was ordered and police outriders also turned, manoeuvring in and out of road bollards and almost falling off their motorcycles. The captain, having made the fatal move, now realised he had to turn right to meet up with the others in front of the Town Hall. There came the biggest cock-up I have ever seen in a procession as army and air force bands marched head on and into each other, resulting in an entangled mess of drums, flutes, piccolos, trumpets, horns and tubas in front of all the other top brass including the president, their commanding officers, the mayor and civic dignitaries.

'What caused it?' was the question screamed across the front page of the *Sunday Mail*, which showed pictures of the cock-up. Only three people knew the truth, but we felt it would be tactless to reveal as this would almost certainly bring down more wrath against the press. Everyone pointed to the stupidity of the captain who had not followed the airmen in front, as he had done in rehearsal. In effect, he was being wrongly accused! The captain was hauled before the powers-that-be to explain himself, and I would have liked to be a fly on the wall watching him explain how he had been ordered to turn left. He was later dismissed from the army and is presumably playing with another dance group to a strict tempo, giving him time to reflect that it takes two to tango.

I was contemplating the steaming hot nostrils of an elephant in the gardens of Salisbury's Jameson Hotel when Bill McLean came along. The hotel had purchased elephant trunks from the Game Department after a culling exercise at the Wankie Game Reserve in the belief that they would be a tourist attraction. Future connoisseurs of this peculiar dish will declare that the tip of the trunk is more tender than the broader area near the face. Bill interrupted my meditation, 'I've remembered where I put my car,' he said.

Bill was a popular and fine journalist from Dundee (he became sports editor of SAPA in South Africa) who was the founder chairman of the Quill Club and to me, a very close friend. As he spoke I prodded my fork into the elephant trunk, slightly bemused. I couldn't get over those nauseating nostrils which glared back at me like a pair of closely set eyes. With revulsion, I wondered if elephants ever caught colds!

'Where was it?' I asked, forcing my fascinated eyes away from the food.

'Just down the road from here where I left it last week,' he grinned. At last the saga of the missing car was at an end, or so I thought. The week before Bill had got merry and then left to discover that his car was stolen and he reported the loss to the police.

'You're a piss artist,' I remonstrated. Bill left me in buoyant mood to fetch his car while I delicately cut into the meat around the nostrils. My elephant-trunk-steak meal was interrupted again, briefly, by the unmistakable sound of a police siren. Then I finished the dish, leaving the two holes.

Later that evening I saw Bill at the Quill Club and he was looking sheepish; clearly something was wrong. 'When I left you at the hotel I got into my car and drove off,' he explained. 'As I was travelling along the road the police chased and stopped me and I was arrested for stealing my own car!'

Elephants and their slaughter for ivory are emotive issues and yet I was to be in Africa for nine years before I even saw a live elephant outside of a circus and I was seriously beginning to believe they didn't exist; that steaming droppings I passed had been placed there by practical jokers. Before our Zambezi River saga, I went with Tony Down in search of them at 'A' camp in the Zambezi Valley, which was a leading hunting area in Rhodesia. It was a dark night under the canopy of trees with a blacked-out moon and stars but camp fires, that erupted like golden rain fireworks when fresh logs were tossed onto their midst, warned night predators of the whereabouts of their equally deadly human counterparts. Our vehicle stopped as a hunter materialised, his leopard-skin bush hat pushed above his forehead and his cream safari suit covered in sweat. He was nervous and his rifle was held in readiness for use. 'My God,' he called out, his voice shaking with tension, 'the jumbos are restless tonight.' 'Bullshit,' I replied casually, and drove on as he began to wonder if he'd really heard me correctly. Our visit to 'A' camp proved to be a complete waste of time for all we heard as we bedded down for the night was the roar of lions nearby, and as Tony reckoned they were a mile away and we didn't bother to light a fire.

The first time I actually came across an elephant in the wild was in the Zambezi Valley and it behaved in a remarkably civilised manner. I was with the family when we saw it close by on the far side of the tarred road. As I stopped the car and got out it flapped its ears, tucked up its trunk and charged forward. Then it stopped. Elephants have a reputation for making a dummy run to warn people away and I'd been advised that it is best to evacuate the scene before the second charge. This elephant was probably protecting its family, unseen but nearby, and by the same basic instinct I drove off to protect mine.

In another elephant incident I spent three days with the famous (some say infamous) Selous Scouts in the Zambezi Valley, watching them training. It was an exercise to show the press that the Scouts were merely trackers and not amongst the most efficient soldiers and killers that have ever been produced by any army. Men even transferred from the SAS to join this elite corps and not all of them passed the stringent training programme. Four journalists and a Selous Scout went off into the bush where we were to be tracked by another Scout. We surprised an elephant which ran towards us and then dashed straight past, about five yards away. Perhaps I was becoming blasé as I didn't consider the incident worth writing about but one local reporter, who had formerly been a staff man on the *Daily Mirror*, gave a graphic account in the *Rhodesia Herald* of how he survived an elephant charge. It was the second lead in the newspaper but anyone with the slightest knowledge of elephants would know that when a normal sized eleven-foot high, six ton jumbo charges with intent, there is little left to write a second lead story. This was realised by Togo Keynes, a wild game cameraman who was typical of his breed. Tanned of face, smallish, dumpy, sporting a beard and always wearing a bush hat, Togo was a well-known local character. He told me how he was in the middle of nowhere in the Kalahari Desert when he saw a herd of elephant. Leaving his truck, he set up his tripod, carefully mounted a cine camera and started to film. It was good material, even exciting, especially when the herd began charging. Togo carried on shooting like a true professional until he suddenly remembered that he was behind the lens of a camera and not watching a film. He looked up as the herd was almost upon him, leapt into his truck and drove off, leaving the camera on the tripod to continue filming its own destruction.

At Last, a Setback for Censorship!

Remaining in Rhodesia and not being declared a prohibited immigrant or jailed or hanged for treason, spying, or whatever incapacitating charge might be trumped up, posed real problems. It would have been too easy to be thrown out and received in Britain or America in a blaze of glory, and assured of work for years to come. But I had not emigrated for self-glorification or martyrdom – I just happened to be in Rhodesia when the big story broke – and the reason for leaving England remained. These problems were eased for a while after a local publishing house, College Press, approached me to ask if I would be co-author of a book on the build-up of the guerrilla war in southern Africa. At first, I didn't like the idea and was suspicious about the motive, and asked, 'Who will be the other writer?'

'Peter Hawthorne in South Africa,' was the reply and my suspicions were allayed. Hawthorne was a fine freelancer who had worked on the *Rhodesia Herald* with me and was now stringing for *Time* magazine (he later became a bureau chief). Knowing that he would brook no political nonsense, I agreed to write but shortly after I signed a contractual agreement, I was told that Peter had pulled out through 'Pressure of work'. This came as a blow as I too was under tremendous pressure – more than Peter – but I'd stipulated that I would only write about Rhodesia and none of the other African countries. I could understand Peter's withdrawing as the bulk of the writing would be thrown on to him. I knew, too, that he hadn't covered stories outside of South Africa which would have made his task very difficult. Other stipulations I made were that I'd write the final chapter summing up the situation without interference; that no politician would be asked to contribute; and that distribution would also be in Britain and elsewhere. 'Who's taking Hawthorne's place? I asked. 'A South African Afrikaner, Chris Vermaak.' That didn't sound good and I could imagine the bias. 'Never heard of him,' I said. 'He's news editor of the *Sunday Times* in Johannesburg.'

That was a fair recommendation and I didn't quibble as the *Sunday Times* had a good reputation for standing up against the apartheid regime. In the event I didn't meet my co-author until after publication of our book, *The Silent War* had gone to press. Using my police and other contacts, I set to work and never once went through official channels although, to my chagrin, the publisher picked up some Information Department photographs which led critics, especially in Australia, to claim that it was government sponsored. A reason for my decision to write was to publish a totally straightforward account of what was happening in the war, while blatantly defying government censorship.

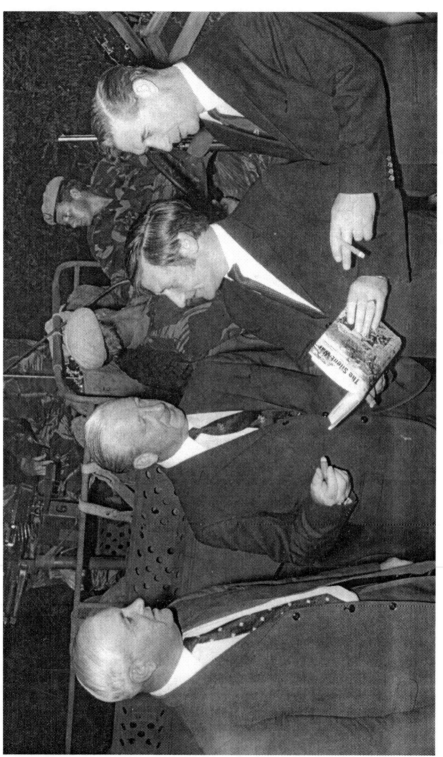

The Silent War is launched with police, military and Air Force chiefs attending. Picture: Rhodesia Herald.

Galaxie Press (Pvt) Ltd.

are proud to announce

the release on 6th May 1971 of

"The Silent War"

The Silent War is the most important book ever published on the conflict in Southern Africa.

Two top journalists combine to give a lively account of the war, often written with deep emotion.

Each episode is fully authentic.

Says the publisher, "This book should become prescribed reading for all thinking people....

"It serves to remind both Black and White of the many dangers which still lie ahead."

AVAILABLE FROM ALL LEADING BOOKSELLERS

The Silent War

DEPORTATIONS CAUSE LOSS OF SYMPATHY FOR RHODESIA: SHAY

Herald Reporter

DEPORTATIONS have a considerable bearing on overseas attitudes to Rhodesia and cause a serious loss of sympathy for the country, Mr. Reg Shay, co-author of the book The Silent War, said in Salisbury yesterday.

"This is, in turn, relevant to the support the African nationalists receive, b o t h morally and physically," he told a lunchtime meeting of the Chartered Institute of Secretaries.

"Whether the Government likes it or not, journalists writing for the overseas media carry considerable weight because of their vast readership."

Mr. Shay said that in the five-year period up to the end of 1968, 13 journalists had been deported or refused entry into Rhodesia, and that others had been similarly treated since.

"These were not little guys on the Alabama or Louisana newspapers — the converted whom we usually court — but men who carried tremendous weight."

Mr. Shay cited the case of Mr. Eric Robins of Time-Life, who had lived in Rhodesia for 13 years until he was deported.

"Eric had been senior British intelligence officer at the Nuremburg trials, and this had a great influence on him.

Naturally, he was concerned when we opened restriction camps and put people into gaol without trial.

"He was downright worried when we kept calling ourselves the bastion of Western civilization a g a i n s t Communism, as that was the phrase coined by Josef Goebbels back in 1937," he said.

"Eric and others may not have agreed with Rhodesia's politics but they liked us as people, otherwise they would not have lived here. After the treatment meted out to them I am sure their tone hardened towards us, and we lost any sympathy we may h a v e gained."

Citizenship

Mr. Shay said two colleagues from his own office had been deported and he was "convinced that in that emotion-charged atmosphere the only thing that kept me in Rhodesia was my citizenship."

On the subject of citizenship he said the deportation of Mr. Guy Clutton-Brock "could well be the biggest blunder the Rhodesian Government has made to date".

If a man took out citizenship it meant the country had accepted him.

"This does not mean, and never should mean, that he necessarily accepts the government of the day. He should have the right to protest and to disagree.

"Rhodesia has brought in a law by which citizenship can be taken away. Now no one can feel safe to protest, because he may not be a Rhodesian any more if he does.

"In effect the citizenship rights have been nullified."

LORD AVON HAS BONE SURGERY

London, Wednesday. — Lord Avon (74), the former Sir Anthony Eden and British Prime Minister from 1955 to 1957, underwent surgery yesterday to correct a bone defect.

A spokesman for King Edward Hospital for Officers said later: "He is quite comfortable and is expected to remain in hospital for a few days."—Iana-AP.

Hokonui Ranch,
P. O. Dadaya.
2nd June, 1971.

Dear Reg,

It was very heartening to see the Herald's report of your
speech to the Chartered Institute - at least, it may have
disheartened a number of people but it cheered me up enormously.
I hadn't realised that Goebels coined the famous phrase, but
I did note the fact that at a recent memorial mass for Hitler,
in Spain, he was remembered as the defender of Western civilisation.

I find everything very depressing in Rhodesia, not surprisingly,
and it doesn't help matters to find that most of my old friends
have left. But on the other hand the country, physically, is
hard to beat. One of the good things about going away is that
first morning back in Africa.

You are probably deluged with congratulations on your
book, so please don't bother to answer this note. I simply
thought that what I saw of your speech was courageous and
very lucidly expressed and I wanted to let you know how much
I appreciated it. I'm sure that many others did too.

Justin told me some time ago that he sees you now and again,
so I'm hoping that he will forward this for me as I can't
find an address for you in the Directory.

I hope that your family and yourself are well and happy.

With all good wishes,

Yours sincerely,

Judy Todd.

Letter from Judy Todd

By a recently introduced law, names of African nationalist leaders in detention and restriction could not be mentioned, nor proscribed organizations and people who had been declared prohibited immigrants. With grim humour I set to work breaking the ban and used banned African leaders' names in the context of purely straight reporting. Mentioned too, were unreported incidents that had taken place in the war which the security chiefs were quite unaware that anyone knew about. This was to indicate that one 'spying journalist' often knew far more than I wrote, merely using the information as background material. And it was with particular relish that, for the hell of it, I quoted from *The Thoughts of Mao*, Che Guevara's book on guerrilla warfare, and for good measure, Rhodesia's militant black leader, the Reverend Ndabaningi Sithole's *African Nationalism*. Sithole was, at that time, in Salisbury jail for plotting to murder Ian Smith. The book opened with a courtroom scene in which thirty-two African guerrillas were sentenced to death and showed incredible courage, singing 'This is our country. This is our Africa.' It showed that they were educated and were not afraid, as one put it, 'I think the hangman's noose has been made especially for me.' These were not words in the book welcomed by the government or Information Department.

Time bureau chief, Lee Griggs, meets Ian Smith.
Picture: Rhodesian Information Department.

I'd bought the banned communist and nationalist books overseas and while the thoughts of Mao and Che did not coincide with my own thinking, the publication of *The Silent War* signalled loud and clear that they were in my possession and what was the government going to do about it? I knew what they could do. A dismayed and astonished Portuguese press attaché friend, the fun-loving Mario Sampaio, had been ordered to leave the country some years before just because he had books by Mao on his shelf at home. The Portuguese were close allies of the Smith regime and to order out their press attaché purely because of his literature, highlighted their paranoia. In retrospect, the communists *did* take over Portugal for a time having infiltrated the armed forces but to Mario, having the books was just a joke about which he could boast and show off. It was important for me, therefore, that no one knew that Mao, Guevara and Sithole books were in my possession until after publication. In effect, that once-child who put a toy bird in the kitchen to see how his superstitious mother would react, was again playing the same game with much higher stakes. I later learned that there had been a rift between the government, which demanded that *The Silent War* be banned, and the security forces who insisted it be published. The latter saw it as a possible recruiting incentive! What I really enjoyed was that my flagrant breaking of several censorship laws would appear to be with apparent government acquiescence because they had not banned its publication. This meant it was now nigh impossible to prosecute anyone for breaking the laws I'd offended and no such prosecutions were ever made. It was also delightfully amusing that the country's security forces were directly responsible for aiding press freedom.

The army and air force co-operated fully with College Press, to organise the cover picture which showed a black and a white soldier together – the white soldier had already been wounded and his brother killed – and a helicopter hovering in the background. Photographer Mike Grant-Parke filmed from the ground while I went up in a helicopter for the first time. There were no doors, no seats and nothing to hold on to. One second we were on the ground; the next higher than the Empire State Building and as I stood there, the pilot turned the chopper in a circle a couple of times and I expected to fall out at any second, centrifugal force or not. I was absolutely petrified but somehow managed to appear cool when we landed.

Because College Press' main clients were African schools, which bought their educational books, they slyly changed the name of the publishers to Galaxie Press. I was given an advance copy and was surprised and irritated that an important promise had been broken: the publishers had approached Sir Roy Welensky who added a further chapter. Welensky hadn't known of my objections to political intrusion and I never mentioned the matter to him, suspecting he had written it partly as a favour to me. His other reason, I suspected, would have been to keep himself in a public eye from which he had fallen from favour. So much for it being a pro-government book; Smith and Welensky loathed each other. Had a government minister been brought in to write, I would have publicly renounced the whole book on the spot.

'We must have a launching party at my home,' said Frances Louw, who was my PA. A truly brilliant cook she also did any entertaining for me that was needed. It was quite a party with top service chiefs, including the new deputy police commissioner whom I had last seen objecting to police erections being photographed! As an added touch, the army sent along an armoured car which was placed in Fanny's garden with SAS troops standing guard. Members of the government were not invited. Later, I ran into an army colonel I'd never met before who stopped me in the street. He congratulated me on the book, adding, 'I read it in advance as I was the military censor who blue-pencilled some of the sensitive bits. You had things in there that even I didn't know about.' So it was censored; I should have known. Yet I hadn't noticed the removal of the sensitive pieces. It was then that I learned from the colonel of the government's intention to ban publication and the military's demand that it go to press, banned names and all!

The book was the country's biggest-ever bestseller having sold 10,000 hardbacks in six weeks, including three reprints, with demands for more. I suggested that we stop at the published figure and let them be collectors' items within Rhodesia, which they became. But College Press had failed to keep yet another promise; that they would distribute outside the country. This was despite rave reviews in the South African English-speaking liberal press (it wasn't even distributed there), and a mention at a Labour Party conference in England. It was heavily quoted in the Adelphi Papers of the International Institute of Strategic Studies in London and even Judy Todd wrote to say she enjoyed it.

More important from my point of view, it had strengthened my hand and even though I'd never made a speech before, I suddenly found myself addressing several important luncheons and also the country's major forum, National Affairs. The speech was totally unpublicised in advance and ignored by the *Rhodesia Herald* – the first time they had ever not pre-publicised a speaker at National Affairs or reported afterwards on the speech – and so I approached the *Sunday Mail* which gave it a page lead. To me, the new editor of the *Herald* who was praised abroad for the blank spaces in his paper in defiance of censorship, was still putting personal animosities above his very profession which I was defending. While the government had proscribed the mentioning of names of deported people, the public learned for the first time how many had been thrown out, and also those not allowed into the country. The gauntlet had been thrown down with the mentioning of names like Eric Robins, Peter Forbath and Jim Biddulph, but I was never prosecuted. I then publicly challenged the government to produce the English newspaper with Africans lying in Cecil Square and to name the TV company that had filmed the African children in dustbins but the response was a deathly hush. The constant suggestion that *Time* was a communist magazine was derisively put into perspective when I mentioned that its annual budget was greater than

Rhodesia's! My most dangerous provocation was to refer to Smith quoting Goebbels. At least, for the first time in years a journalist was able to stand up and hit back but I knew that this glory could not last for ever and that the authorities would bide their time.

Soon after publication of the book and possibly because of it, I became chairman of the Quill Club. I accepted with nagging misgivings but my qualms could not have foreseen the tragedy that would take place. It had already become disturbingly noticeable that more and more members of the Special Branch were coming into the Quill willy-nilly for they only had to show their identification cards which gave them entry to wherever they wanted. Originally, some entered as invited guests of a member such as the local crime reporter; now they were walking in uninvited. This was causing me concern but there was nothing that could be done about it and as a bloody-minded reaction I decided they should pay for the privilege. In other words, the ubiquitous secret police became official members of the press club. It was a mockery and something I looked at with cynicism but I had been interested in the enthusiasm of some journalists to make them members, even to propose them.

In the Herbert Gibbons gymnasium one morning, I met my regular police contact who was closely associated with the SB, without actually being in it. That's what he claimed, although I suspected he had been assigned to my gym to keep an eye on me as the police were known to have an excellent one of their own. As we talked in the sauna, a smile crossed his sweating face. 'I can't tell you who they are, but six of your journalist members of the club are police informers so the SB doesn't really need to be there,' he said. 'Any on the committee?'

'Yes, of course. We paid one of them a thousand dollars!' I had a strong suspicion who the person was; someone who hadn't been flush before yet now had some money to wave around. The same person later made vigorous attempts by lobbying to get me out as chairman, which was a good reason for staying. In the event, I resigned after three years to cover the war in Angola.

The SB introduced themselves to overseas journalists as being 'in the insurance business' and all who worked out of my office, and many who didn't, were warned in advance of their presence. I'd point to those who held the pen and the others who held the truncheon. During my tenure a law was introduce that forbade Africans to drink in the cities and towns after 7 p.m. Officially I should have ordered out black members after that time but as I considered the decree to be a disgrace to both justice and humanity, I ignored it and waited for prosecution. No action was ever taken against either the club or myself despite, or even because of the secret police infiltration. They took advantage of the situation in the most hideous way, however, against one black member, Dr Edson Sithole. Eddie was the most qualified lawyer in the country, black or white, and as he had some articles published, he genuinely qualified for membership. We had known each other since the trial of Michael Mawema for which he had helped prepare the defence brief. I knew him to be a nationalist and occasionally I'd get a phone call, 'The police are outside my house and I think I'm about to be taken away for detention.' Once I sat with Eddie and Robert Mugabe as they polished up their notes just before a press conference and when we walked into the conference room I saw faces amongst the journalists I didn't recognise and wondered what reports about me went back to police headquarters. In the event, of the three of us who had sat and briefly chatted, Mugabe would become prime minister and then despicable president, while I had more than a few perilous adventures to come. But Eddie… whatever happened to Eddie?

He was relaxed and enjoying himself at the Quill Club well after 7 p.m. before leaving to go to his car where his secretary was waiting to drive him home. A passer-by said they were approached by some white men outside the hotel who showed them their identification cards. Both Eddie and his secretary were taken away by them and this time he didn't have a chance to call me. I was in Angola, anyway. His car was later reported to have been found on the Mozambique border and Special Branch suggested that he had abandoned it to cross over and join the guerrillas. That is not what happened according to one of my reliable sources. My information, which I've never disclosed before, says they were taken to Goromonzi police station east of Salisbury and tortured to death. Their mutilated bodies are buried on a nearby farm.

It was Christmas and I was invited to do a charitable turn for the Mayor's Christmas Cheer Fund and tour the capital city on a veteran bright red Merryweather fire engine, dressed as Santa Claus. How could I refuse? I toured the city ringing a brass handbell of the type beloved by primary school headmistresses and shouting, 'Ho, ho, ho!' with crowds of passers-by in the street stopping to cheer. Being Santa is one of my weaknesses and strengths as I love being with children and treasure their innocence as they rush forward to collect their presents and cling to me pleading that I should not leave. The fire engine was followed by a truck of Coca Colas which had been officially handed over to me by a fully regaled mayor to take to a Coloured children's crèche. From that time on I seemed to become Santa Claus each year, handing out presents in hospitals. After one hospital visit, I decided to call on my Zambezi River friend, Tony Down, who was sick in bed in a room above the Quill Club at the Ambassador Hotel. I thought I would cheer him by turning up in my Santa outfit and did a few 'Ho, Ho's!' to the various guests in the foyer before going to his room. So far, all was well.

I came down in the elevator and was walking out of the hotel towards my car when there was a loud cry, 'Santa!' With horror I watched a large Sunday school class coming out of the cathedral and racing towards me. Whoever heard of Santa Claus without presents? A quick wave, three merry Ho's, and I dashed back inside the hotel. Santa vanished straight up a chimney which resembled an elevator and could be found sipping a quick gin in the Quill…

Guess who's Santa Claus? My cunning disguise for a charity trip.
Picture: Rhodesia Herald.

While the Quill Club was in the Ambassador which became the unofficial press hotel, most visiting journalists stayed at the plush Meikles Hotel, which I was to learn practised a form of apartheid. The annual conference of Ian Smith's Rhodesian Front was to be held, and *Life* sent down from Nairobi an Indian photographer, Priya Ramrakha. I knew Priya well, and was always fascinated how women were attracted to him despite his eyes not being quite aligned. That probably gave him some extra charm.

Having booked Priya into Meikles I thought nothing more about it but there was apparently consternation when he turned up. Having used his personal magic he had won over the receptionist who put him into the plush new wing as requested by me. Later that day, I received a telephone call from the manager, 'You didn't tell us that Mr Ramrakha was an Asian! Will you please tell him that he is being transferred to a room in Old Meikles.' Inside I was hot and livid but to the man on the other end of the line I became perma-frost. 'And can you tell me why a representative of *Life* magazine should be victimised?'

'It's not *Life*, sir, it's just that we don't wish to upset our Afrikaner clientele by having Asians in the new wing,' said the manager.

'If you don't keep Mr Ramrakha in the new wing,' I replied, 'I shall advise all the international correspondents coming to Rhodesia that Meikles is practising apartheid and I shall also write an article to this effect in *Time*. It won't be the loss of Afrikaners you'll need to worry about.' I knew that the hotel relied heavily on the media to fill its rooms during times of crisis and deliberately slammed the phone down. Fifteen minutes later it rang again: Meikles had decided that Mr Ramrakha could stay in the new wing after all! It was a small victory for the press against a self-imposed apartheid by management and I knew the practice would continue against other Coloured people not connected with the media but that was a battle they would have to fight for themselves. When he checked out of the hotel, Priya gave all the receptionists boxes of chocolates and flowers. They all loved him and pleaded with him to return soon but he never did. Instead, Priya later went to Nigeria to cover the Biafran war and as he was walking along a road with an army commander and other journalists he pointed to some soldiers on a hill. 'Don't worry about them,' said the commander. 'They are my men.' The soldiers then opened fire and the lovable Priya was hit in the stomach. He died in agony an hour later and his body was flown back to Nairobi to be cremated on a funeral pyre.

Back home, the government Information Department produced a press release concerning farmers and the need for them to fill in a form to apply for artificial insemination of their cattle. The notice said that farmers who already inseminate their own cattle need not apply! One man who inseminated his own was the chairman of the ruling Rhodesian Front, Des Frost, whom I went to interview one Sunday for ITN. At that stage cameraman, John Hamlin, was the ITN stringer, which gave me no authority over him. Frost returned from church in his Sunday-best clothes and asked to be excused for a moment. He took off his jacket, rolled up his sleeves and went into the cowshed. Anticipating that something colourful would happen, thus giving interest to a possible dull interview, I called the cameraman over but he refused to budge. Frost held up a giant hypodermic-looking instrument, lifted up a cow's tail and plunged his whole arm inside the female orifice. 'I'm giving her artificial insemination,' he explained. He then walked across to a tap, washed his hands, put on his Sunday-best jacket again and sat down for the interview. Bloody cameraman!

The same cameraman asked me if I would show him the scene of the murder of a white farmer, killed by guerrillas, who was a member of the police reserve. I'd broken the story in the London *Evening Standard* and knew the location. 'ITN wants a six-minute intro to camera,' he said. 'Six minutes?' I protested. 'They must have said six seconds.' The cameraman was adamant and so I went into the house where the murder had taken place. Chalk marks showed where the body had been and on a stand was the man's Rhodesian bush-type hat complete with leopard skin which was an obvious symbolic opener to pan from the hat to the floor but the Hamlin refused to film it. We then went outside and faced a line-up of reserve policemen, all friends of the dead man and the suspicions towards us was tense as I ad-libbed my intro. The sun was shining when I started but then a cloud came over. 'I'll have to change the exposure,' interrupted the cameraman. Then it got darker, 'Hold it!' This was the same man whose equipment later broke down in Beira. Four times I started and finally, in pouring rain with the policemen still watching closely, I talked for six minutes. ITN came back testily and wondered why I'd gone on for so long, confirming they wanted a six-second intro. As we left the murder scene, Hamlin drove ahead and disappeared just as my car broke down. Alone and in an isolated area where terrorists had just murdered, I was a sitting target as I repaired the fault alone by torchlight. It was an uncomfortable half hour but the trip was worth it as ITN sacked Hamlin and made me their official correspondent.

I held some sort of record with ITN for filming an incident which took up half of a ten-minute Sunday bulletin. It must have been a very slow news day indeed but the atmospheric story contained pathos and humour summed up the attitude of many Afrikaner farmers towards their black labourers. Everyone at ITN fell apart when they saw it: A gang of terrorists had attacked a remote farm and I drove to the scene next morning with a new camera team. The attack had lasted about five hours but the elderly couple emerged physically unscathed. First, I interviewed the wife on the doorstep of their homestead during which she told me how her husband had fired at the gang while she kept his guns loaded. This had been the method used during the Anglo-Boer war and during the interview the lady broke down in tears which spelled out the distress she was under. I'd spoken to the husband beforehand and knew there was a real ace up my sleeve and asked on camera completely deadpan, 'You must have been concerned that the guerrillas planted mines on your driveway, how did you eventually manage to leave the farm to get help?'

'That was scary, man,' replied the farmer, who turned and shouted across to an African labourer to re-enact his escape. The labourer ran to collect a pitchfork and then moved slowly along the dirt road of the farm, forcibly prodding it into the ground for hidden mines while twenty feet behind was the Afrikaner driving his car. Without the slightest thought for his farm-hand's safety, he just followed while looking to see if the employee would disappear with a loud bang and a puff of dust!

It was a guerrilla attack that was to unite me with a former colleague in the most unusual way. While I was working on the *Evening Standard* news desk, a well-scrubbed young reporter named Peter Fairley joined the staff, working on the awfully boring snob column, 'In London Last Night' whose job was to report on society parties. Years later, when he was reporting as a staff man for ITN, Peter came on a visit to Salisbury and David Holden, who was subsequently murdered near Cairo Airport, was in my office at the time and whispered, 'He looks like a fresh-faced young subaltern who might just make it!'

Reg Shay, News at Ten. *Photo courtesy of ITN.*

I had a tip-off that there was heavy rioting and burning of buildings at Gwelo in the country's Midlands which prompted Peter and me to drive there. To my surprise, there was nothing of the wimp gossip-columnist as he took the steering wheel and raced to the action about 150 miles away. There to meet us was Jake Sudworth, editor of the weekly *Gwelo Times*, who had tipped me off in the first place. 'I can't show you around the trouble spots because the paper comes out tomorrow and I have to rewrite it,' he said. Peter and I had an urgent consultation and solved the problem. 'You show us around, Jake,' I offered, 'and we will rewrite the paper.' And so it happened that two men who had worked on the *Evening Standard* in London many years ago now suddenly found ourselves writing the front page of a newspaper in a backwater town in Africa. The people of Gwelo never knew the high-powered teamwork that went into producing their weekly rag but Jake received many congratulations from the public.

Another guerrilla attack had also taken place in the south of Rhodesia and when I drove down to investigate, I came across two people who epitomised some of the extraordinary characters it's possible to meet in Africa. They were the Townleys, whom I interviewed after a chance chat in a bar at Birchenough Bridge. Spanning 1,080 feet, Birchenough at that time boasted one of the longest single-span steel-arch bridges in the world and is similar to the more famous Sydney Harbour construction. They were both designed by the same man, Sir Ralph Freeman and within one of the pillars of the bridge lie the ashes of the man it was named after, Sir Henry Birchenough. It crosses the hot, steaming, Sabi River and to burn your fingers, you merely have to touch its steel framework on a summer's day. The Sabi has an ancient history about which little is known. People who like to romanticise and claim that the country is the ancient biblical land of Ophir, believe that the Queen of Sheba once sailed up its waters from Sofala, Mozambique. The river had to be running a little faster then, as no sizeable craft could now travel along its sandbanked course except when a passing cyclone may cause it to flood.

I was having a refreshing Castle lager at an hotel beside the bridge and noticed a photo of a crocodile, which was prominently displayed. 'That's Wadoka,' said Doc Watson, the hotel owner. 'A mean-looking bastard,' I replied with distaste. Ever since the Zambezi attack, I've never taken kindly towards crocs. 'He's not too bad,' said Doc. 'He's fed by a woman who lives with her husband out in the reserve.'

'An African?' I asked in surprise. I have never met an African who felt any affection towards crocodiles. 'No, she's English!' My curiosity was aroused. Under the country's laws, it was illegal for white people to live in African reserves yet here was a couple who not only lived in a reserve, but one that was known to be heavily infiltrated by guerrilla bands. And she fed a pet crocodile! I asked for the direction to her home. 'It's about twelve miles away,' said Doc. 'Go half a mile down the main road where you will see a baobab tree beside a track leading into the bush. After two miles along the track, turn right at a second baobab, right at a msasa and then three miles until you come to some more msasa trees. You bear to the left for another few miles and you'll come to their house. You can't miss it!'

I wasn't too thrilled at the thought of the drive as terrorists had a disturbing habit of putting down mines on dirt tracks and also ambushing cars. The trip was not for the story but rather just to meet these extraordinary people. To write about them, I knew, could have sealed their fates for, as with Tony

Down and myself on the Zambezi saga, they would likely become terrorist targets just for the publicity such an attack would gain. The directions had been good and I didn't get lost. I came to a brick house, neat and tidy, which surprised me as by living in such a remote area, I'd expected the Townleys' retreat to be made of mud. I knocked at the door and when nothing happened, I knocked again. The door opened slowly and before me stood a grey-haired woman and I could tell at a glance that 'Billy' Townley was unlike any woman I had ever met. 'I'm sorry to have kept you but I couldn't find my blasted teeth,' she declared to the stranger. 'You're lucky I did, otherwise I wouldn't have come to the door.' Her dentures were clearly lodged as uppermost in her mind as they were in her facial orifice for she referred to them again when we entered the well-furnished lounge. Speaking through clouds of smoke, she cursed the loss of her own teeth. 'I used to smoke with this in my mouth, now I have to hold it,' she said, handing me her generously bowled billowing pipe to examine. When I admired a magnificent leopard skin which draped a settee, she declared, 'I shot that!' Defensively, she added, 'I know that by law I shouldn't have done, but what do you do when it's standing in your path?' From the intonation of her voice it was clear that she was well-educated and I was to learn that not only was her mother titled, but she was also a relative of the round-the-world yachtsman, Sir Francis Chichester. 'I can understand why Francis did it, getting away from everyone and facing a challenge,' she said, reflectively. 'Some people think I am mad living out here in the bush because it isn't every woman's way of life, but to me it's heaven.'

When I asked if she was worried about guerrillas, it soon became clear that the shoe was on the other foot. 'A couple of them were keeping watch on us from up there for a couple of days until I started taking shots at them,' she said, pointing to a nearby kopje. 'I haven't seen them since.' Billy was sixty-five years old and now she is dead from cancer, I'm told. She was an ornithologist and, like her entomologist husband, Dennis, was well known in museums throughout Britain and the United States. As we talked, Dennis drove up in a jeep, the front of it painted like a Walt Disney character's face, with the painted glass headlamps looking inwards with crossed eyes. Here was a couple I could empathize with instinctively and I explained the reason for my visit. 'Then you must be introduced to Wadoka,' said Billy and she led me from the house to a nearby small tributary of the Sabi River. 'There are seventeen crocs in that stretch,' she said as we neared the edge.

With the domesticity of an average country housewife about to feed the chickens, Billy stood near to the water's edge while, perched on the branch of an overhanging tree, was a fish eagle; its piercing eyes fixed on a bucket filled with meat Billy had brought with her. As she threw the small gift, the eagle took to the air and gracefully accepted the offering. Turning to the placid water at her feet, Billy then called, 'Wadoka, Wadoka. Come on you old baggage.' That was when any illusion of domesticity disappeared. A movement in the murky water and the sighting of a dreaded 'V' shape edging towards us warned me of instant danger and we both moved back a little. Green eyes emerged followed by a long snout as one of the world's deadliest reptiles, an eleven-foot crocodile rose from the depths and stood on the bank, glaring at us. Calmly, Billy threw a large piece of meat to her evil-looking pet about five yards away and watched it tuck in. I wondered how the rapport had come about but before I could ask the question, Billy spoke and disturbed my train of thought. 'The old baggage couldn't be expected to tell my hand from the rest of the meat, could she?' said Billy, explaining why she threw the meat instead of handing it over.

I've been told that Dennis went on to live there alone and that he had actually been known to go into the water to fix a small dam and not been attacked. Perhaps the crocodiles would not want to hurt someone who had befriended them; then again, possibly he didn't care too much about the dangers. For life in that lonely remote part of Africa could never be quite the same without Billy.

Another fascinating woman I met in Rhodesia before the war built up was an American named Alice Sanderson, who ran the Adult Literary Centre in Salisbury which concentrated on phonetic reading. Tall, bespectacled and thin, Alice could not speak a word of the African languages or dialects and yet she did more than anyone I know to teach Africans in the bush the three 'Rs'. Many of her pupils were taken raw, yet could read, write and keep written stock in ledgers of cow and goat herds, chickens, eggs and prices all listed and prices totted up, some within only eighteen days of starting their lessons!

There was a dramatic contrast between that good woman and Constable Coen, a South African policeman who came to Rhodesia during the Emergency. I never wrote about him as my tenuous position in the country would have been further jeopardised without anything being achieved, but for no apparent reason Constable Coen snatched a baby from its mother's back and in front of her, cut its throat. He was never charged with murder but quietly shipped back to South Africa. The South African police, who had come up to help the Rhodesians fight the guerrillas, were sometimes more an embarrassment than a help. Being quite contemptuous of the 'kaffirs' whom they believed would never dare attack them, one group piled up their weapons above the Victoria Falls where the current was not strong, and began swimming until a gang of guerrillas came along and shot them dead. One body was never recovered and was presumed to have gone over the mighty cascade. A strict security blanket covered the shooting but I went along to the South African barracks near the Falls, hoping to see the commander and with a photographer, I drove up to the barracks and straight past the guard, who saluted! The South Africans had been making claims on how well their barracks were protected and so the army commander, whom I had asked to see, was somewhat surprised at our presence. To put it mildly, he went ballistic and ordered us out with demoniacal gestures and untranslatable oaths in Afrikaans and I never knew what happened to the nice respectful guard.

In another incident at the Victoria Falls, a group of young Canadians ventured across the high gorges and down to the water's edge facing the Zambian bank. They then came under continuous and unprovoked fire from Zambian troops and two of the girls were shot and fell into the water. The Zambians subsequently claimed that the girls had been trying to swim across and were drowned without a shot being fired, an absurd statement considering the force of the current at that time. As a test, a railway line was later lowered into the water and it came up twisted!

With my regular local photographer, Mike Wesson, we followed the trail of the Canadians and as we climbed and scrambled down the basalt crevasses I was expecting us to be shot any time by the trigger-happy Zambians who would have had us in their sights. Then we went to the hospital and I interviewed a survivor who'd been shot and wrote a feature which was a good exclusive. Meanwhile a friend of mine, a leading journalist in South Africa, flew to Zambia and wrote a feature based on what he was told, which really was a load of nonsense. He hadn't faced any danger and basically took all the Zambian government propaganda which was fed to him. But journalism being what it is, he got South Africa's top journalist award for the story. As for myself, I've never even been considered for one.

During a quiet period with no massacres to attend and little money coming in, I let out one of my offices to an advertising man, Eric Edwoods, who was also well-known locally as a television personality. While he had a good sense of humour, Eric could be quite peppery at times and because the office was on the sixth floor, Eric had an aversion towards people who would get into the elevator on the first floor and ride down one storey to the ground. The day he blew up was when a fit-looking man entered the elevator on the first and went down. Eric glared at him. 'So, mate, wot's the matter with you then?' he asked nastily in his Cockney accent. 'You got a wooden leg?' The man was very polite and raised a trouser leg. 'Yes, Mr Edwoods,' he said quietly. 'As a matter of fact, I have!'

A Matter of Life…

Life magazine embarked on an ambitious and expensive project: The Rise of the British Empire. One look at an old map of the empire gives an indication of just how expensive a project it was and like the ambitious proposal of Cecil Rhodes to build a railroad from the Cape to Cairo, it was never completed. Flying some of the world's highest paid photographers to the four corners of the earth, paying correspondents, chartering aircraft and hiring cars, shipping film and using telephones and telexes internationally cost a fortune. The least expensive item *Life* had to pay for was the purchase of film.

After coming up with suggestions for pictures I was duly sent one of the world's top photographers, Dmitri Kessel, who was particularly interested in photographing a statue of Dr David Livingstone at the Victoria Falls. The crunch came when we stood at the foot of the statue and realised that Livingstone wasn't standing where he should be: 'He's too far back,' cried Dmitri dejectedly. 'He's not overlooking the Falls!' It was true: the famous statue of Dr Livingstone doesn't give him much of a view of the great cascade. 'I'll try to reconstruct,' said the photographer but I shall need to be able to stand above him so that I can include the Falls in the picture.' This was a challenge and at the Falls village I hired a single-decker bus, but just as I was about to drive it into the national park a game warden came towards me. I had no doubt he had been tipped off that the despised foreign press was around and decided to be difficult, 'No buses are allowed in that area,' he stated.

'Why ever not?' I inquired, explaining that a photograph in *Life* would help tourism. 'I don't care about that,' said the warden. 'The bus might damage a branch on a tree which we can't allow. If you so much as break a twig you are in trouble.' This was a setback but all was not lost. 'What if we put up scaffolding? Would that be acceptable? I had no idea if there even was scaffolding at the Victoria Falls as it was a largely undeveloped area. The game warden thought it was improbable too, for he agreed. 'Can you tell me where I can hire some?' I asked. 'No,' he replied with a smirk, 'probably Bulawayo. You won't find any around here.' His knowledge of the area proved to be less than that of the game laws as I found a small firm of building contractors who drove a heavy lorry much larger than a minibus into the park and erected scaffolding behind the statue. For two days Dmitri's life was in the ascendancy and descendancy as he studied and photographed Livingstone from behind before flying back to New York. Because of the enormous cost worldwide, the project was eventually shelved and *Life* as I knew it was soon to come to an end. The accountants moved in and precipitated its closure and it was only revived in a lesser form much later.

Another great *Life* photographer who came to Rhodesia was a Londoner, Larry Burrows, who had worked in the magazine's UK laboratories before being accepted as a photographer in his own right and now his home was in Hong Kong. He had covered the Vietnam war from the outset and one reason for sending him to Rhodesia was to get him away from the action.

I wasn't writing the particular article he was covering but Jon Hall, the *Life* staffer who was, asked me if I could talk him out of going back to Vietnam. The request had apparently come from New York as the magazine was gravely concerned about the risks he'd been taking and it was as if they had a premonition that he had already pushed his luck too far. Larry had certainly taken terrible risks and Tom Hopkinson, the former *Picture Post* editor, described him as 'The greatest war photographer there has ever been.' Jorge Lewinski, in his book *The Camera at War*, said there was no other (war) photographer to match Burrows' professionalism, his complete mastery of the craft, or his sense of composition and visual beauty. Larry stayed for a month and I treasure a photo he took of me being presented with a two-bell alarm clock on my birthday by *Time*'s Promotion Director, Bob Sweeney. *Time* seemed to like giving me clocks as I have one on the wall of my study at home which was presented to me in Nairobi, the clock being taken from the office wall! In the Bamboo Inn restaurant over lunch, I talked to Burrows like a Dutch uncle, pointing out that there comes a time when luck runs out. Larry knew exactly what I was talking about and we discussed the matter at length during which he admitted to having the gut feeling – not uncommon with genuine war correspondents who venture beyond their hotels and facility trips – that his luck was on the wane. 'Vietnam has been the real making of me, Reg,' he said 'and I've got to go back. I was there at the beginning and I shall be there at the end.' The slimly built Larry Burrows, who wore trousers that resembled those of an ice cream salesman, went back to Vietnam shortly after our talk and two years later the helicopter in which he was flying was shot down and he was killed.

A photo by Marion Kaplan of Douglas Collard 'Boss' Lilford, a millionaire cattle rancher, who was the money behind Ian Smith's Rhodesian Front party also appeared in *Life*. I didn't see the article before publication as it was written in New York but particular exception was taken by the Lilfords to a picture caption quoting Mrs Lilford as saying, 'Our dogs will eat an African a day.' They objected to the quote only because they'd mistakenly believed it said, 'Our dogs will eat a kaffir a day!' While Lilford could be the perfect gentleman – he had given Jack Malloch's air hostess, Rita, a record player for services rendered – he was also the leanest, meanest bastard I'd ever met and he was once taken to court for whipping an African farmhand; not surprisingly, he got off the charge. His lawyer had come to me before the case and with pointed finger threatened me with dire consequences should there be an error in my reporting. He was very pompous now that there was no one of the calibre of Aaron Maisels to challenge him in court; the last time we met he'd been prosecutor at the Michael Mawema trial.

After publication of the *Life* article, I went to my office to find my secretary,

Barbara Vandewaal, distressed. She said the Special Branch had questioned her and searched the office for copies of *Life* with the Lilford article saying that no copies were allowed inside Rhodesia. I was furious at both the search and the ruthless way Barbara had been interrogated and by coincidence it was South Africa's national day and I'd an invitation to attend a garden party at the High Commissioner's residence. Lilford, I knew, would be there. Still pumping adrenalin, I approached him and his wife on the immaculate lawn and harangued them for over fifteen minutes. It was an exhibition of gross bad manners on my part and the immaculately dressed guests stood around in a circle to watch with astonishment and embarrassment at the conflict in which the all-powerful and much feared six-foot-four lithe rancher was being verbally taken apart by someone nearly twelve inches shorter. Inwardly, I thoroughly enjoyed the scene and finally stormed off feeling that honour was satisfied. I wasn't invited back to another South African garden party for four years which was no loss; as for Lilford, his past caught up with him six years after the Zimbabwe celebrated Independence when he was murdered by African burglars on his ranch.

Tom Griffith, the editor of *Life*, came to Rhodesia with his wife, Caroline, for a holiday and we flew to the Victoria Falls where Dmitri Kessel had spent so many hours photographing Livingstone's posterior with his Haselblad and other expensive cameras. 'Here, Reg, let me take a photo of you with Caroline,' said Tom as he produced his camera. I gave a double take: this was no Canon, Pentax or Leica; it was the modern equivalent of a Kodak box Brownie. *Life* photographers were given several thousand dollars every two years to renew their cameras to ensure that nothing ever went wrong while on location: but this was not extended to the editor. He saw my surprise: 'I'm a writer, not a photographer,' he explained. 'I hardly know one end of a camera from another.' Not bad for the editor of the world's top picture magazine.

At the end of their holiday we went to their room in Meikles Hotel where I found the door unlocked. Inside was a man wearing white overalls and I demanded to know what he was doing there. 'I've come to repair the radio,' he replied and rushed out of the door, knocking me aside. 'What was that all about?' asked Tom. 'Special Branch,' I replied. The *Life* editor thought it was very amusing but I was incensed; the Griffiths were on holiday and hardly likely to get themselves involved in Rhodesian affairs, yet all the SB could do was to snoop. There was only half an hour left for them to pack their bags and leave for the airport. 'That's strange,' said Caroline. 'The cases I locked are unlocked and those that were unlocked are now locked.' The bungling intruder had been really caught in the act and Caroline had another shock: 'He's taken the keys of the cases that he locked!' she exclaimed. Downstairs, a blushing blonde receptionist denied that a radio mechanic had been sent to the Griffith's room. 'And the Special Branch?' I asked. 'I'm not allowed to talk about things like that,' she answered. I called for the manager but he was no

Ian Smith's backer, hardman Boss Lilford, murdered after Zimbabwe's independence.
Picture: Marion Kaplan.

45(31) New Horizons (C)

)0 (2) ● CAROL BURNETT PRESENTS THE JIMMIE RODGERS SHOW: Sharl Lewis, Stu Gilliam, comedian, guests (C)

(5) News: Bill Jorgensen (C)

(7) ● DICK CAVETT SHOW: Natalie Wood, actress; Pat McCormick, comedian; Drew Pearson, syndicated columnist; Beverly Sills, opera singer, guests (C)

(9) Burke's Law: Crime (R)

(13) Newsfront: Mitchell Krauss. "Perspective on Rhodesia," Reg Shay, Time-Life correspondent, guest; " 'Front Page' on Broadway," Robert Ryan, actor

(31) Brooklyn College Presents (R)

(41) Lagrimas Amargas

(47) News in Spanish (C)

:15(47) El Hit Del Momento (C)

:30(31) Cultures and Continents: "Indonesia: Between Two Worlds"

(41) Un Canto De Mexico

·00 (2, 4, 7, 11) News Reports (C)

I hit New York! New York Times.

more forthcoming. 'Then you had better ring the police and report a burglary and also contact the SB and ask for our keys back!' I demanded. A hastily called locksmith undid the cases and a race to the airport, which broke a few speed limits, saw them on to their plane.

New York: *Give My Regards to Broadway… Breakfast at Tiffany's…* Grand Central Station… Statue of Liberty. The films, the music, the photographs had all indelibly imprinted themselves subconsciously onto my brain and, like the Far East, Middle East and India, it was a place I knew I must visit before I die. In June 1969, I decided upon a ten-day holiday in the Big Apple, giving five days to myself just looking around, with the other five on semi-business. It's truly amazing that I can't even take a normal flight without incident.

The Portuguese TAP flight from Salisbury to Johannesburg, Lisbon and the Azores was long and arduous and I was looking forward to landing. Circling Kennedy Airport in a heat haze, it was possible to briefly see other aircraft stacked in a spiral and after what seemed an age of suspension, the aircraft came in to land. As we were about to touch down, I was gazing at the planes on the ground each side of the runway when, like a bolt from a crossbow, we shot back into the air thus breaking into the stack. I quickly realized we'd been only seconds from a nasty accident for on the way up I heard a sound familiar to all flight passengers – the pilot chose this time to put the undercarriage down! Until that enlightening moment, I had always thought warning bells rang in the cockpit while we were still high in the air. With perverse humour and pleased that the boredom had been relieved, I was quite happy with the situation and found it mildly amusing. This was not reflected on the sweating faces of the Portuguese Canadians we had picked up in the Azores who had a distinctly alternative and more realistic approach to the incident. But then, of course, they had never travelled with Tony Down!

My introduction to New York was a realisation that the scripts in some old movies were actually based on real life; the city really had its Mickey Spillanes. The porter put the baggage in my room and showed me the four locks on the door before retreating and five minutes later I passed him and a chambermaid talking in the hallway. As I waited for the elevator, I was transported into the world of James Cagney, Humphrey Bogart and Edward G Robinson: 'Now, Mary, you didn' hear nuddin' and you didn' see nuddin', okay?' said the porter almost *sotto voce*, believing I couldn't hear. In the same unmistakable Brooklyn accent, Mary replied in a distressed voice, 'Yeah, yeah. I didn' hear nuddin', and I didn' see nuddin'.' With that the elevator arrived and I heard no more but to this day I have wondered what exactly didn't she hear? Ah, well!

Having met up with a young Scottish surgeon who was also taking a holiday, we took a guided tour of Chinatown with a coach driver who exhorted the evils of drink throughout most of the trip. He didn't take too kindly to the raucous laughter of the two Brits who appeared to ridicule his protestations and he clearly felt we were beyond redemption and he was really upset when we were taken into a café basement where there was a golden statue of Buddha. With hushed reverence he declared, 'That statue is nearly two hundred years old!' As one, the surgeon and I looked at each other raised our eyebrows, and called, 'Two hundred years old?' That we should call out so loudly in a place of such reverence, and that our mocking cry showed we'd no respect for great age, seemed incomprehensible to the other tourists and our guide, who hastily led us from the shop. I wondered what he would have thought if we had mentioned that Edinburgh University, where the surgeon had studied, was by then nearly four hundred years old!

On the fourth day in New York the telephone rang in my room and it was the American magazine, *Business Week*, which had tracked me down and wanted to see me urgently: the holiday was over. Because of sanctions, the United States had put an embargo on the importation of Rhodesian chrome which, shared with Russia, was of the highest grade in the world. Having introduced the embargo, America felt compelled to buy from the Soviet Union at something like three times the Rhodesian price. It had shocked *Business Week* to learn that the wily Russians were buying the chrome cheap from Rhodesia and reshipping it to their real enemy, the US! 'Did you know?' I was asked. 'Yes,' I replied. 'I knew.' It wasn't easy to explain to people living in a free society that just by putting that information over the telex would have landed me in court for espionage.

Conversely, I was cynical that Ian Smith, who'd committed treason to hold back the twin evils of Red Menace and Yellow Peril, was using Russia and China quite heavily to defeat sanctions. *Business Week* was given a general run down on sanctions busting without going into specifics. The specifics could have been the tobacco being shipped from Beira, Mozambique, in bales marked 'Produce of Zambia' – (a friend who went to London saw a bale of tobacco with his own initials on it); the 2 a.m. flights of Jack Malloch's planes heavily laden with prime beef heading for Europe, usually Greece, where it was in great demand; the dresses selling in Marks and Spencer in Oxford Street which were made by David Whitehead in Rhodesia (the head of Whiteheads genuinely did not know how they got there); the forged cigarette packets with famous brand names for sale on overseas markets, including China (I considered that exercise quite dishonest); the importing of a hydrofoil from Italy which broke the Beira blockade (I watched it unloaded at Beira and travelled with it to Rhodesia); and many others, long forgotten. The Japanese were the first to move cars in with their Toyotas and Nissans, long before they were seen in Britain, while Italy sent Alfa Romeo kits and British-made reconnaissance aircraft. One aircraft regularly seen on the tarmac belonged to the Sultan of Brunei whom Jack Malloch told me was a personal friend of his. It made me wonder just how many true friends Britain had?

My next five days in New York were predictably busy with *Time* giving me an office complete with a beautiful and intelligent secretary. Within that short period I was on the radio three times for ABC; interviewed for twenty minutes on TV by Richard Krauss in *Newsfront* (Robert Ryan, star of a Broadway show took a back seat at ten minutes), given lunch by *Time* editors where the mind is grilled more than the steak; dinner with the Griffiths; twice visited the theatre as the guest of *Time*; had dinner at the home of the ABC News (radio) foreign editor, Mark Richards, who asked if I'd like to meet the mayor of New York and seemed surprised when I declined. When Hank Luce asked me to write a feature, I replied in the same tone as I'd used with Mark: 'Come on, Hank, I'm on holiday!' I suppose it was like Moses refusing to take the Israelites out of Egypt, but being the truly good fellow that he is, he understood. Immediately after my TV interview, a *Time* representative took me to a Manhattan apartment where a solemn cocktail party was taking place and, after introducing me to the hostess, he left hurriedly. As I entered the apartment everyone turned and I had the impression that they had watched me on the box with some distaste because I'd defended the British attitude towards Rhodesia rather than Ian Smith. No one talked to me and I wondered what I was doing there. At the end of the party and all the guests were leaving, I stayed behind for a chat with the hostess, a plumpish and rather ugly lady in her late sixties. 'I'd just like to thank you for inviting me and I thought we'd have a quiet chat,' I said amiably. She looked at me and there was a trace of fear in her eyes which I couldn't understand. With that, she said, 'You're not going to rape me, are you?'

Shortly before leaving New York, a stroll through Central Park at night was a must on my personal schedule, just to see if it really was as dangerous as people claimed. I could state categorically that it was a most pleasant walk in the moonlight and a wonderful place for lovers; I didn't see a soul.

While in the *Time-Life* building I ran into photographer, John Dominis, whom I'd last seen in the Kalahari Desert. While I like to believe that I am a red hot operator, this isn't always true and there have been occasions when I've missed the action completely: John was a reminder. He had arrived in Salisbury and was a very worried man. *Life* had sent him to photograph a leopard kill in the wild for a picture-feature entitled 'Cats of Africa'. It had seemed an impossible task: he had photographed a black panther in Pretoria Zoo but how was he to photograph an actual kill? From personal experience during my own nineteen years living in Africa, I never once saw a leopard in the wild and only as a tourist did I come across one in Zambia at night and it was only a few yards away. On that occasion the leopard knew exactly where I was as a firefly had flown into my trousers pocket making me a nocturnal flasher, but it was too busy dragging away an eland at the time to take a personal interest in me and my fly.

It was the redoubtable Eric Robins who rose to the occasion to help out John Dominis as he had learned of a man named Stanley Lester in Lobatsi, Botswana, who kept tame leopards. Their 'tameness' was questionable as Lester's daughter had received over sixty stitches to her face after a mauling by one of them. Eric contacted Lester who agreed to go on safari with his leopards for an extortionate fee. I drove Eric and Dominis to Lobatsi, which was over 1,000 miles away, and met Lester. John turned to me during the meeting, 'I've left a lens behind in the hotel room and I'm going to need it.'

This came as a nasty shock and was met with scant enthusiasm as I was tired from driving but there was only one thing to be done, 'Okay, I'll go back,' I volunteered reluctantly and climbed into my faithful Chevy As I accelerated over the sandy road, my lips revealing a slight case of the mutters over John's forgetfulness. Travelling at 100 mph on Kalahari scrub and sand, I came to a narrow bridge with a hump which sent the car into the air, slightly splaying the front wheels as it landed. Onward I raced, once scattering a herd of eland as my foot stayed hard on the accelerator.

Late at night I briefly slept in the car as there was no time to waste in an hotel and was in Salisbury before lunchtime to collect the lens and race back to Botswana before nightfall. At Lobatsi I received John's news with less than normal enthusiasm: 'I've just got some great shots,' he said excitedly. It seems that Lester's pet baboon had innocently come along to the photo-call just for the ride and without any desire to become the major participant in one of the greatest wildlife kills ever photographed with a still camera. Sadly, for him, it turned out to be a one-way trip and he never received a share of the plaudits given to John.

Lester's leopards, it transpired, had been taken out into the bush but not one of the five of them showed the slightest interest in catching game. They proved to be less than interested in anything until moments before I returned with the lens; that was when the baboon suddenly took off with the inner knowledge animals have that predators are studying them as a likely main course on their menu. In hot pursuit was one of the leopards and John's camera was instantly at the ready and he shot the whole sequence of the chase up a tree and down again, and then photographed the petrified the baboon as it turned to face the killer. The poor creature's face was contorted with fear and its hair stood on end as the leopard made one last pounce.

There were later accusations in the South African press that the photos were contrived but this was not true. The incredible alertness of the photographer who was able to take perfect shots on the spur of the moment marked the difference between a top professional who has his camera at the ready at all times, and a novice photographer like myself who had actually missed out on a flying hippopotamus!

I Take on Secret Police Torturers

'Reggie, what's happening to me? I'm frightened!' It was the voice of a little girl and the words were to presage a devastating change in Margery which would take all her courage and determination to overcome, over many years. We were sitting in her car which was stationary in a quiet avenue lined with flamboyant trees that had just come into their full majesty of crimson bloom, contrasting with the green-leafed jacarandas on the next road whose mauve crown of glory would wait another month to blossom. I'd driven to a little-used road where Margery would drive her car and opened the passenger door to take her round to the driving seat when she began to fall backwards and her left arm rose skywards while simultaneously her left bony leg began to rise into the air. 'I'm going away,' she cried out. 'Please hold me, don't let me go.' As I moved forward to catch her, the finger nails of her right hand clawed into the bare skin of my arm as a frightened cat clings to a tree; she blacked out and turned into a floppy doll. The seizure wasn't for long and when she returned to consciousness she was confused: 'I went back to my grandmother's kitchen,' she stammered and her face was filled with fear and bewilderment. 'Please don't let me go back again!' I drove her home and telephoned Dr Bernberg and after X-rays and consultations with specialists our doctor finally gave me the verdict: 'I'm afraid Marge is having a regression. The scar tissue on her brain is drying up.' Drying up? Scar tissue? What was he talking about? The answer left me with a feeling of foreboding in the pit of my stomach when he added, 'I'm afraid she is going to get worse!'

'Worse? How much worse?' 'We really don't know,' said Bernberg. 'The tissue could stop drying tomorrow, or next week, perhaps in a year, who can tell?' He shrugged his shoulders and smoke filled the room as he found space in his ashtray to stub out half a cigarette before lighting up another. 'The problem is, the longer it takes to dry up the worse she'll be affected.' He paused uncomfortably, a diminutive man in a white laundered safari suit, with black sleeked-back hair, thin moustache and narrow facial features which were clearly not at ease, and I knew he wasn't finding it easy to break the news to someone he had known for years. 'What exactly are you telling me?' I asked.

'I'm saying that Marge may very likely become a cabbage!'

My God! Visions of Margery as a human vegetable were too unreal to be-lieve, especially after all she had accomplished. To struggle against unacceptable odds of surviving this type of stroke only to be cruelly robbed of even the semi-normal life she had achieved was unthinkable. Blood pressure was still a problem, high one minute and low the next, but this was stabilised with pills. Her visits to grandmother's kitchen, spotlessly clean and polished with its old wood-fire cooker and the 'copper' for boiling linen; the giant family kettle and stewing pot; the line of saucepans; all of these had been totally destroyed by the German rocket but her visits back in time now increased to two to three times a day within seconds of her left arm and leg taking to the air. Sometimes I'd carry her from restaurants and once she vomited all over the floor in front of diners, for Margery was now suffering epileptic seizures. She was always worst just before and during menstruation periods which were long, irregular and heavy. Some time after the diagnosis Bernberg called me to his surgery for a private chat. 'Marge's periods are a serious problem,' he said. 'They are having a destabilizing effect and are associated with her epileptic fits. I've had a talk with the consultant who suggests a hysterectomy in order to telescope the approaching menopause but the decision is entirely yours. I must warn you that there is a chance this could kill her.'

I was astonished that the responsibility should be left to me, her husband who had been told that his wife was likely to become a physical, mental and even greater financial problem than she'd already been. Surely I was the last person who should have been asked to make the choice? 'I don't believe we should interfere but let nature take its course,' I replied. It wasn't a noble decision; I just believed that Margery should have been given the option, not me. In the event, the scar tissue took its toll on her which I felt at the time was worse even than her being a cabbage. She had become schizoid and developed a complete personality change. Whatever her personal relationship with me, or sometimes the lack of it, Margery had always been a popular person with a zest for life. Now she was turning into someone else. It is an experience almost impossible to explain to those who have not lived with it; and devastating to those who have. Since the stroke we had begun to build bridges again and were getting on well but all that was to change. At times she became furtive and withdrawn, eyeing people suspiciously as though they were conspiring against her. And she had also become an uncharacteristic needling tartar.

St Giles' Rehabilitation Centre contacted me to say that as she had cheered up wounded soldiers so much and encouraged them to get better, they would like her back again to cheer up the casualties. I warned, 'She is not the person you knew.' Perhaps, I hoped, being with people at the centre might help her to recover, too. Margery thought the whole idea was wonderful but on her third visit I received a telephone call at the office, asking me to call early before picking her up. I knew what was coming. 'Please don't bring her back,' I was told by a senior physiotherapist. 'We've held a meeting and decided she must go straight away. She's upsetting everyone here, including the soldiers.' Because the rehabilitation centre hadn't the courage to tell her themselves, Margery was convinced that I'd deliberately taken her away and I couldn't explain outright the true reason for her leaving. To have done so would have set her back even further and when I did try to explain that she was not quite the same as she had been and suggested a personality change, that was met with ferocious outrage. There really seemed to be no answer to the problem and life became very difficult again with quarrels being the norm through constant needling fuelled by the belief that I'd deliberately denied her treatment at the centre. Once more I loathed to go home except to be with my wonderful children but the atmosphere when I was present was so electric that it was better I kept away and only came home when Margery was in bed. The children were thus robbed of their father's presence and even their mother's love. I missed being with my children when they were growing up.

Robert was adult enough to look after himself and would either shut himself in his room to study and play tapes, or spend hours hitting a tennis ball against our courtyard wall or go off to play golf – he had a three handicap while still at school. This would later lead to him becoming a world-class sportsman. Annette, who was growing into a lovely-looking young lady, had a spirit as strong as her mother's and adamantly refused to become her servant, which was expected of her. She became extremely rebellious which, under the circumstances, was understandable but unhelpful and she mixed with some unsavoury-looking characters. Peter was the only acceptable member of the household to Margery and he was smothered with her affection. He did a fantastic job at home, never raising his voice and always giving a helping hand. While this was wonderful for all of us, I was worried that he might become something of a mother's boy but I needn't have been concerned. Relief came from a frustrated headmaster who would call me to the school to complain that Peter, who was assessed as having an excellent academic brain, was also the biggest rebel in class! It was refreshing news.

Lucy, our domestic, was the gem that sparkled and remained cheerful despite a tetchy Margery depending heavily upon her. But even Lucy's tolerance broke when she was expected to enter the room on her knees in an act of servitude and approach Margery in this undignified fashion. This new development had come about after I had breakfasted at the home of Bishop Abel Muzorewa, whom I knew well, and who became the country's first black prime minister. I mentioned to Margery that those who served him at the table came in on their knees, which was an African custom of respect. It was a trying situation with me strongly believing as I did on the one hand in human dignity but suffering a gross violation of it at home. Yet to mildly remonstrate would rocket Margery's blood pressure and put her into another epileptic coma. After a time, the dedicated and humorous Lucy left in despair.

I thanked God for the church! Boredom was a major concern for Margery who read novels avidly in the garden but because she had no visitors the greatest excitement of her life was to attend the Congregational Church on Sunday where she was welcomed. They were good people and genuine and Margery became interested in raising money for church charities by growing African violets which she did well and gave her an object in life. This was naturally encouraged but it did little to add to the tone of our beautiful home in Salisbury's elegant Alexandra Park suburb. The ballroom-sized lounge lost some of its decor with over 100 milk bottles at one end, each containing bloody African violet shoots in varying degrees of growth making it impossible to entertain at home. Even the Congregationalists' enthusiastic smiles began to wane when, week after week, month after month, Margery would arrive enthusiastically at the church with African violets for them to buy. The revenue went to charity; where half the flowers went to I can only guess.

There were African violets on the table of a dinner organised by the local press for the Minister of Information, an extraordinarily foppish character named P K van der Byl. The only information of any interest that emerged from the department during his tenure of office was that he had the biggest penis in the country, apparently and uncomfortably reaching his knees; it had entitled him to the sobriquet 'Tripod'. My retort on being given this news was that I couldn't imagine a better job for the biggest prick in the country. During the dinner, I felt a pain in the chest and on visiting the washroom the mirror reflected an extremely flushed face. Having excused myself from the meal I called at the local hospital casualty department where an Austrian woman doctor diagnosed indigestion. I didn't believe her as my suspicions of Austrian women doctors in casualty departments began years before in England, when I'd gone to hospital on a Saturday morning doubled over with suspected appendicitis. The Austrian lady there told me there was nothing to worry about and to come back on Monday. Within twenty minutes of my return on the Monday morning, I was being operated upon and my twisted appendix was considered so unique by the surgeon that he showed me a photograph he'd taken for the medical magazine, *The Lancet*.

This time, I was given two indigestion tablets and told to lie down for an hour. Still feeling uncomfortable but being assured it really was indigestion, I returned to finish my dinner. Next day my doctor, a specialist, a cardiograph and X-rays, showed I was having a minor coronary attack, with my heart being twice its normal size. It was a busy period and I carried on working for a week but half doubled-over before the doctor ordered me to bed where I fretted about the stories I was missing. Within a month I was back at work feeling much better, and within six months I was in the gymnasium lifting weights. While I don't recommend weight-lifting after a heart attack there is a slightly reckless streak in my nature which dictates there is a lot of living to be done. Subsequently, morning exercise at the gym followed by a sauna would keep me going all day and often, all night too. There would be many times I'd work for several days and nights, filing stories through the time zones of Europe, the United States and Australia. It was not the time nor the type of work which could afford the luxury of being ill when there was a family to feed.

The next time I met van der Byl was under bizarre, even surrealistic circumstances. It was dusk and I was driving towards Salisbury with my family in heavy traffic when I was passed by a black Mercedes in a clear case of speeding and very dangerous driving. It wasn't long before I saw the car again and it was stationary; nearby on the tarmac were the mangled remains of a bicycle. I stopped to see if I could be of help and recognised the driver as the head of a big fertiliser company which my press relations organisation represented. As I stopped he looked relieved, 'Reg, the police might impound my car as I brought in a few more rolls of film from Beira than I should have done. Can I put them in the back of your car?' Innocently I gave him the keys to the boot while wondering why the police should impound his vehicle because of a road accident and I couldn't understand why he thought his contraband was more important than a human life. As I was about to search in a nearby field for the cyclist who might be badly injured, another black Mercedes drew up and a voice I recognised called out, 'I say, can I do anything to help?' 'If you would like to direct the traffic I'd be obliged,' I said firmly to the owner of the voice, P K van der Byl. The former Service Corps sergeant knew how to give an order and as a former officer in the Hussars, P K knew what was expected of him. I reckoned he would have graduated with high marks as a traffic cop but at the time of the accident P K was otherwise engaged as the new Minister of Defence.

With Robert's assistance I searched a nearby field by torchlight for the body and grinned ruefully on glancing back at the bizarre sight of the Defence Minister waving on passing cars while a top businessman was busily transferring boxes of contraband film into my car right under his nose. So much for just a few rolls, I thought. For twenty minutes Rob and I searched not knowing if we would find an injured man or a corpse. The grass was long and the unfortunate cyclist could be anywhere and if he was alive his voice would not be heard above the noise of the passing vehicles. Eventually we gave up and I went back to the businessman and looked inside his now empty boot before turning to find him standing beside me. 'I can't find the body,' I said. 'It's in the car,' he replied. He lowered the lid of the boot and I saw the smashed head of the cyclist protruding through the rear window. I also felt damp and looked down at my favourite blue shirt and was upset to see pieces of brain on it which had dropped down while I looked inside the trunk. Perched over the front seat were a pair of feet and for me there was an unnatural eeriness about the pair of lifeless feet and legs wearing shoes and socks. I have seen it many times, mostly at massacres, and thought of the unsuspecting way we all put on our shoes and socks in the morning, sometimes carefully selecting them, without the slightest thought of whether we will be alive to take them off in the evening. Looking at the body I realised that on impact, the hapless cyclist had gone through the car windscreen like a bullet and I now half wished he'd hit the driver who had shown no remorse at killing a man; just fear that he would be caught smuggling. I walked across to the Minister and told him the body had been found and as he left to call for an ambulance, I drove off very conscious of the dampness on the shirt I was wearing. Back home I took it off and flung it into the wash basket for Lucy to put in the machine.

A couple of days later while she was hanging out the clothes on the line she turned to me and I saw she was quietly weeping. 'My uncle was killed riding his bicycle on the Bulawayo road on Sunday night,' she sobbed. 'He was a really nice man who had always been good to me. I often used to visit him and his family on my days off.' I didn't tell her about the accident nor the mess on the shirt she had washed and when I tried to wear the garment a few days later I felt ill at ease, as though the tiny parts of brain were still there. Lucy looked surprised when I gave my new shirt to the gardener. The businessman telephoned and he sounded officious and demanded that I drive to his office with the film. 'Come and get it,' I replied, 'and in the meanwhile I'm terminating our contract.' He sent his chauffeur-driven office car to pick up his smuggled film, the only offence with which he was likely to be charged. Accidentally killing an African on an unlit cycle at night was not an uncommon occurrence and considered of little importance as there were many thousands of Africans around the country using the same form of transportation without lights. As the Europeans (whites) used to say in frustration when they were held up by an African cyclist ambling in front of their cars, 'There's always one on a bicycle!'

Another of my press relations' clients with a problem was the Rhodesian rugby captain, Reg Neald, who had a large carpet business. He telephoned me and he was in a panic: would I call on him urgently? Neald was a Mormon and he had invited the BYU Sounds from Utah to Rhodesia to help raise money for the security forces in a series of concerts to be called 'Forces '74'. I already knew that he was very good at starting the ball rolling but quite hopeless at following it through and felt that perhaps it had something to do with initiating a move in rugby before passing the ball to someone else to make touchdown. The BYU Sounds, he said, were due in the country in ten days' time but only one hall in Salisbury had been booked for the series of country-wide concerts. Because I hadn't seen any publicity, I asked, 'What are the BYU Sounds?'

'They're the entertainments section of the Brigham Young University,' he replied. My reaction wasn't one of encouragement, 'You want me to organize concerts for a bunch of Mormons? Forget it!' The country was in the middle of a war and there was little sympathy for fresh-faced, well-scrubbed Bible punchers. It was usual for Mormons to have doors politely closed in their faces and unthinkable that the public should be asked to pay to see them. 'You realise that The Carpenters and The Osmonds started their careers with the BYU Sounds?' said Neald. 'I have a demonstration tape of some of the singers who are coming here.' I took the tape back to the office and played it in the studio. My spirits rose; they were beautiful and so was the quality of the tape. These were voices I recognised... The Carpenters, Barbra Streisand... it was unbelievable. I was on the phone to Neald, 'Are you sure these aren't the originals?' He assured me they were not, and that the BYU Sounds had three separate concert groups operating at the same time and all as good as each other. I had visions of clones of famous singers which reproduced in triplicate so that no one could tell the original when they gave a concert. 'Okay, I'll take it on provided we can agree on a fee,' I said. He had to be desperate as he immediately agreed to my high figure. 'Plus all expenses!'

The BYU Sounds were an immediate success and their performance was antiseptic enough to pass the censor with flying colours. The Rhodesian forces were about $50,000 better off and I was quietly amused when Ian Smith attended the last performance and came across to shake hands. I knew the Information Department would be furious but neither they nor the government knew how to handle me. I could stand up and castigate the government on censorship and other matters, write a book which ignored their censorship laws and yet, at the same time give support to the security forces. But then, for their own reasons, hadn't the security forces looked after me? and if my own home were under attack, who else could I turn to?

On the other side of the coin, many times there were facility trips where the Information Department ensured I didn't go when planes took off with a party of journalists. Fortunately, I had my contacts and sometimes as the press party plane raced along the runway to take off for them to spend a tedious six hours or so, they would return to have their copy mutilated by the censor while mine, which I'd not bothered to have checked, was already in the London *Evening Standard*. Part of the policy of leaving me behind was the hope that I would lose out on so many stories that my media clients would change their correspondent and to this end I had the honour to be the first journalist in Rhodesia to have his press credentials taken away. So far as I was concerned, it was a meaningless gesture and gave me licence to do as I pleased. The government did not see it quite that way and the credentials were quickly returned.

A new concept was arrived at with the formation of an official corps of Defence Correspondents and I was specifically invited to fill in an application form to join. The rules of the game had not been spelled out but I knew they would be inhibiting. I filled in the form, strongly suspecting what the outcome would be, and was told by a gleeful deputy Director of Information. 'We have now drawn up the list of official defence correspondents, and you are not on it!'

'Surprise, surprise,' came my tart retort. It amused me that apart from my opposite number, the young former army captain who, I believe, was never called up, I was the only Rhodesian citizen who applied. Had I thoroughly read the rules, I wouldn't have done so anyway. One paragraph read, 'Since every accreditation will only be granted to journalists considered by the authorities to serve the best interests of the country, every assistance and co-operation should be afforded to defence correspondents without prejudice.' How could any correspondent, local or foreign, carry a Defence Correspondent card and claim he was serving only the media? The first accreditation, I was told, went to the *Daily Telegraph*.

A new Minister of Information, Ely Broomberg, was appointed and all journalists were invited separately to speak privately with him on what was wrong with his department, and why the country had such a bad image abroad. I was prepared for a quiet chat but when I was ushered into his office, sitting down were two smug-looking members of the Information Department with whom I'd had many quarrels: the Director of Information and his deputy. The gasket blew! 'Congratulations, Minister, on taking over the worst Information Department in the world,' I snapped. 'These two characters here are what is wrong with the country's image as they haven't the slightest clue on how to handle the foreign press. As you are aware, Rhodesia has an appalling reputation abroad which gives an indication of their worth. Such is their integrity that when I was invited here today, it was to be a private meeting just between the two of us.' The berating continued as I singled out issues where they had been deliberately antagonistic by snubbing some of the most important news organisations in the world while toadying to the *Daily Telegraph* and obscure publications in America that no one had even heard of. It was a sheer merciless delight watching them squirm in front of their boss while I had relieved several pent-up feelings. It was an even greater pleasure when I added, 'Such is the limitation of their combined thought and knowledge that they actually believe they can hold intimate press conferences for the select few without anyone knowing what will be said.' The pair looked at each other and smiled knowingly, like intimate lovers who had a special little secret that only they could share. 'They have just held such a private press conference to which I was not invited, despite my representing a very large proportion of the world's media. At this conference, it was stated…' I went on. There was a stunned silence and two faces were white with shock.

'How did you know about that?' faltered the horrified Director of Information as the conference had ended only minutes before. Broomberg was affable and was clearly amused by the confrontation. Some days later he was sitting in the foyer of Meikles Hotel when I walked in and he came across to shake hands. 'I did enjoy that,' he said. 'I enjoyed it too,' I grinned back. But it didn't make any difference as Broomberg died a few weeks later and I remained virtually *persona non grata*. The situation was, simply, that I was always invited aboard the cramped, tin-seated operational DC-3 with its parachute lines still intact, to fly to the scene of a massacre so that I could write a 'correct' report; to be invited out on patrol, however, was out of the question. I was a security risk, pure and simple. Yet, as a dedicated non-spy, I was a safer bet than many of the visiting 'safe' staff men who were given privileged treatment and then had detailed debriefings when they got back home.

Working on the basis that one should always give back a little of that received, my door was always open to aspiring journalists, no matter what their colour or creed. There are African journalists now working in Zimbabwe (or jailed by Mugabe) and elsewhere who came to my office for advice, and they were always welcome. While I hadn't thought of this in terms of gain, it paid off handsomely with my being given pieces of information denied to my peers. Many probably would not have used the information anyway as much of it was highly contentious and dangerous to investigate. For me, that's what journalism is all about and it also helps the adrenalin to flow.

As his cries go unheard, he is beaten mercilessly until collapse

Torture victim, Anton Dzvinamurungu. Picture: author.

A Coloured reporter I encouraged had excellent potential and a name that automatically spelt success in the media: Shakespeare Johnson! How could anyone ever shut a door in his face with a name like that? 'There's someone in Highfield you should meet,' he said. 'He's been badly tortured by the Special Branch.' The man was Anton Dzvinamurungu and he was sitting on an old wooden upright chair in the garden of a friend in the Salisbury African suburb. Beside him was a gnarled wooden walking stick and I could see his bare feet were badly swollen. 'Look at this,' said Shakespeare as he pointed to Anton's matted hair which was separated by large bald patches. Anton was a supporter of Joshua Nkomo and he'd been in his kraal when guerrillas arrived and burned down the hut belonging to the local headman who was paid by the government. Everyone was suspect and because of his political affiliations, the

Special Branch hauled Anton off to jail in Salisbury. As we sat in the garden where water-starved maize leaves bore silent witness to their own struggle to survive, Anton told me he was then taken sixty miles away to Mtoko and thrown into a cell and made to lie face down on its concrete floor. He was then forced to raise himself on his hands in a press-up position while being severely beaten by two African police thugs using long clubs. 'They kept hitting me here and here,' he said, pointing to his buttocks and feet. 'Whenever my arms gave way they forced me to rise up and then they beat me until I collapsed again,' he said. 'They then turned me on to my back and held me down while a third man, a big heavy sergeant, sat on my stomach and put a green piece of towelling over my nose and mouth, and poured water on to it from a tin.'

Anton was put through this terrifying torture several times before the sergeant declared without compassion, 'I think this one is dead.' When the sergeant finally got up and Anton gasped for breath, he was dragged into a cell next door and was dropped on to a blanket where he slept on the floor. Next morning he was forced to walk to the nearby police station where a white detective inspector, named Anderson, and the black sergeant pulled out his hair in tufts. Anton screamed with pain but if that wasn't enough, the inspector then hacked away at his testicles with a pair of scissors, trying to force him to confess that he knew the guerrillas. After finally accepting his innocence, he was released.

'Could you take me to the cell where you were beaten?' I asked Anton and despite fear written over his face he agreed to show me. Because I felt I needed another witness, I asked Mike Holman if he would care to come along. Mike was an academically-orientated small-time stringer with a strong will and an incisive brain which didn't appear to limit his activities to journalism. He was closely associated with the Roman Catholic Justice and Peace Commission which investigated atrocities wherever possible and shortly after our investigation at Mtoko he fled the country dressed as a woman and then trod a successful path to Fleet Street.

I drove to Mtoko with Shakespeare, Mike and Anton who pointed across to some bush scrubland in the direction of where he believed the cell to be, saying it was inside a white building. Leaving Shakespeare in the car to watch over a very nervous and trembling Anton (there was no point in involving Shakespeare too much as retribution on him may have been far greater than upon ourselves). Holman and I came to a small whitewashed farm building which seemed pleasant enough but as we approached, gun shots rang out. Mike and I looked at each other and prepared to dive for cover. Were we being shot at? We could hear voices as though at a garden party and wondered if we were targets for a turkey shoot when we realised we were within yards of a police firing range on the other side of a tall hedge, only yards from the white outhouse. I looked at the thick doors on the building and noticed the small iron-barred glass-less windows. With some trepidation I pushed at one of the doors and to my surprise it swung open. As I walked inside I was momentarily stupefied as I hadn't really

Interview with a guerrilla leader near Beira, Mozambique. Picture: Moto.

believed that any evidence would be left lying around. But there it was: clubs had been carefully placed upright in orderly fashion against the walls where the torturers had placed them, instead of dropping them carelessly on to the stone floor. This indicated that a methodical and disciplined people had been at work; the most coldly sadistic of all torturers. On the floor was the green towel Anton had mentioned together with the tin which had contained the water to be poured on to his covered face. Stains discoloured the floor; Anton had said he urinated under torture and that he had seen stains there even before he was worked over. There was also some powder in a tin which I could not identify and thought nothing more about it. I took photos and hoped no one was around to see the flash and as I looked down at the implements of torture, I wondered how many men and women had been cruelly murdered in this squalid place. We didn't stay long; we had pushed our luck as far as we dared but the question now arose: what should I do with the information? Despite *The Silent War*, Margery's illness, and 'Forces '74', I knew that nothing would stop me being deported or far worse if I published the story in the overseas press. Mike Wesson developed the pictures as the only man I could trust with the negatives and I sent the story to the American black magazine, *Sepia*. They played it big with headlines of Nazi-type torture and the pictures prominently displayed. I had gambled that Ian Smith supporters in the United States did not read black magazines and this was probably right. While my byline was boldly featured, I had no comebacks.

Mike Holman wrote an article for a Justice and Peace magazine without a byline and one of my photos was used. A priest came to my office and asked to borrow the negatives which I loaned him and when I asked for them back he claimed they had been stolen from his briefcase. I had the distinct impression that he was lying but could think of no reason for it. Then the Roman Catholics asked me if I would give evidence against the Special Branch should they bring a case to court on Anton's behalf. Holman had already declined but I couldn't blame him; he too was treading a tightrope possibly greasier than mine. I called on Hardwicke Holderness, a respected liberal lawyer whom I knew well and asked for his advice. 'If you want to stick your neck out it's up to you,' he said, 'but don't be surprised if you get it chopped!'

This wasn't encouraging and with deep inner trepidation I decided to make a stand for Anton and thereby all the others who had suffered at the hands of the SB, and agreed to give evidence on his behalf. The case was held in the High Court in camera and this book is the first indication that it ever took place; even my closest friends were not aware of it. My appearance in court was short with questions about my interview with Anton; a verbatim type-written report from my shorthand notes taken at the time was presented to the court and identified by me. I told of the condition Anton was in when we met and of finding the cells and photographing inside them. The court already had copies of the photos, handed in by the J & P Commission lawyers.

'Can you tell the court exactly what you did when you found the building?'

asked counsel for the police. 'I went up to the door and looked in through a peephole!' Court shorthand writer: 'A what?'

'A peephole.' The South African-accented shorthand writer still looked perplexed and I leaned over and saw he was using Pitman's: 'Write a long thin line from left to right, going down through the line so that it's a double "P",' I advised. There was laughter amongst the few people in court, all Special Branch, and I looked around and grinned like a showman. The writer flushed crimson as he said, quietly, 'Oh, a peephole!'

After being asked about the contents of the cell and identification of my photographs, there were no more questions. It is possible that counsel, as with the one in Zambia after the car crash when I came out of the Congo War, realised that browbeating wouldn't work too well when I held the stage. In any event, I'd given all the evidence that mattered which would have been damning in any other court of law. Instead, by giving evidence against the forces of law and order who were protecting the country against terrorism, I would now be considered a traitor. A couple of days later I saw Judge Benny Goldin at a cocktail party. 'I've never seen anyone enjoy themselves so much in the witness box,' he said. 'Witnesses are usually overawed.' It hadn't been an act of bravado: if I was going to take on a bunch of police killer bullies and give evidence against them, it was better to say it with a smile. Only words, not smiles, go on the record.

Anton gave his evidence but claimed he didn't recognise Anderson as the man who had tortured him with scissors and pulled out his hair. He didn't recognise the black police sergeant who had covered his face with a wet towel and pulled his hair; nor even the constables who had beaten him with clubs. As a result, the case was thrown out. It had all been a waste of time and effort and when I saw Anton later, I was furious. 'Do you know how many people have stuck their necks out to help you?' I demanded. He seemed surprised at my vehemence. In his heart of hearts he probably thought that all whites stuck together and from what I learned in the gymnasium sauna he had been too terrified to expose the men who were glaring fixedly at him. The security police were exonerated and thus free to carry on as before with an extended licence to murder. In the incestuous atmosphere of Salisbury, who should walk into the Quill Club one evening but Anderson, now promoted to Detective Superintendent. He was later to rise much higher. With him was Kate McLean, who was divorced from Bill. They came in quite a lot after that and she asked me what Anderson had done that I should feel so hostile. 'Let him tell you,' I said. It's doubtful that he ever did and I'm glad that Kate didn't marry Anderson as Bill and Kate's daughter, Laura, is my godchild.

At a Joshua Nkomo open-air press conference shortly after the court hearing, one of his officials called me aside and took me round a corner. There, he dropped his trousers and presented me with his penis and testicles. 'Look there,' he said and showed me two smooth pieces of skin. 'What caused it?' I asked. 'I was tortured by the police. That's where they clipped a wire on my balls and gave me electric shocks,' he replied. Without my knowing it, word had got around on the African bush telegraph that I had helped Anton. It hadn't been my intention to become a crusader for human rights and I intended to remain an impartial observer as much as possible. I accepted that the Special Branch of any country has a duty to fulfil and I am realistic enough to believe that a shoot-to-kill policy may be necessary if innocent lives are to be protected against known terrorists. So far as I am concerned those who live by the sword can die by the sword; they voluntarily take their chances the same as I do when I volunteer to cover a war. But physical torture to satisfy sadism in the name of the law is indefensible when there are many other methods of extracting information. Knowing what was going on behind the scenes, I would sometimes look at Ian Smith with curiosity when he declared, with regular monotony, 'We will continue to uphold Christian civilised standards.'

If he did not know about the torture chambers and I subsequently learned there were plenty of them around the country, he *must* have been aware of The Cage…

My office messenger, Fanus, came to me and he was distressed. Even though I was the boss, Fanus and I were friends and we talked a lot. Over six foot tall and broad with it, Fanus had a capacity for getting into trouble in the most innocent way and seemed to rely on me to get him out of it. Once, at a large garden party, he had been co-opted with others to serve drinks but unfortunately he sipped too many dregs and fell down blind-drunk in the middle of the lawn to the disgust of the guests. I drove him back to the office, carried him up in the elevator and into the reception (thank goodness for weightlifting) and dumped him on to a settee where he slept all night.

When I gave Fanus time off for Christmas, he drove to his home in the forbidding Zambezi Valley to visit his family. Before he went I'd written a letter saying that he worked for me which was to be shown at police road-blocks. On his return he was almost on his knees with gratitude: 'You are wonderful, baas,' he said. 'You've saved my life.' This came as a real surprise as I knew that I hadn't done anything rash recently. Fanus explained that he and some friends were drunk and singing lustily on the back of a lorry above the Zambezi Escarpment when they were stopped by a white farmer and his sons. 'They all had guns and said they were going to shoot us as terrorists. I shouted, 'Don't shoot, I have a letter!' My note was produced and the farmer said, 'Oh, you work for Reg Shay. That's all right then!' and let them go. To this day I have no idea who the farmer was but to Fanus I was nothing less than The Great Protector!

I was seemingly in this role when he came into the office and tears were streaming down his big mahogany face, 'My father and mother are going to be put into The Cage,' he said. 'My father is a very sick man and he will die – he mustn't go in there.' I hadn't the first idea what he was talking about but his distress was clear. 'Why don't you make us both a cup of tea and then sit down and tell me about it?' I suggested. What he had to say caused me grave concern and I knew instinctively that there was more trouble ahead for me…

Because of the terrorist activity in the Zambezi Valley, where his parents lived, the authorities had pressed the panic button and built a concentration camp which the local Africans had called 'The Cage'. Fanus revealed that tribesmen were being herded behind the tall wire on two acres of land at Gutsa, his home village. 'Their homes have been burned by the soldiers who have also shot their cattle and goats,' he said. (That law of coincidence again; the last journalist the government would wish to know about The Cage just happened to have an office messenger who came from the area!) I wondered what the security forces were up to as even the dimmest white person knew that a rural African's wealth and status were measured by his animals. There'd been a spate of government propaganda about winning the hearts and minds of the tribesmen, and what Fanus was saying hardly corroborated the official line. 'Has your parents' house been burned down?' I asked as I glanced around at the safe luxuriousness of my office and mentally compared it with the fearful conditions of his home village. 'I don't know but it will be when they go into The Cage.'

'You say this Cage covers only two acres of land, have you any idea how many people are inside it?' I asked, and the answer came as a bombshell: 'Between three and five thousand!' Africans, like anyone else, are prone to exaggeration and they frequently say things they feel the listener would like to hear and if it hadn't been for his clear distress I would have been very dubious. 'Fanus,' I said, 'I don't know if you can get even one thousand people on two acres of land, isn't this an exaggeration?'

'No, sir. That is why they are now burying people outside the wire!' It sounded like an unfolding nightmare that was getting worse by the minute, but I like to absorb one point at a time. 'If you have five thousand people there, where do they sleep?'

'On the ground. Everyone sleeps out in the open on the ground but it's very difficult with men and women all sleeping together.' Yes, I thought, it must be. Africans are a rampant race of people but they have their own code of conduct which precludes communal sex. 'When you say, Fanus, that people are dying there, do you mean that these people who have died were being buried inside the enclosure where their families are sleeping?'

'Yes,' he said, 'but there is not enough room to bury them there now because of all the children dying!' The more questions I asked, the worse the answers. He went on, 'Children are dying on average five a day while adults die at about one a day.'

'Why are they dying?'

'I don't know but that is the average. I think the adults just die of old age but the children get sick and die.' I asked about medical treatment and was told there was a hospital in the camp which comprised four poles and a thatched roof where patients slept on the ground. A flying doctor called in once a week. There was no way that I could write a story of this magnitude on Fanus' say-so alone, and I knew I would never be able to get near the place and asked if it could be corroborated. 'Do you know any people I can talk to who have been inside this Cage? I would like to interview them for overseas television.' For Fanus' own safety, I didn't want him to appear as the SB would be able to identify him without difficulty and this could put his life in danger. While Fanus probably hadn't even given a thought to himself being watched, I felt it unlikely that my messenger would not be recorded on a police file.

Within a couple of days I drove out of town and into the bush to meet two Africans who confirmed everything Fanus had to say. They agreed to an on-camera interview and I said I would meet them the following week but first, I wanted them to take a risk: 'Will you go back to the Cage and photograph it from the inside? I want the pictures to include the hospital, the graves and the people.' Without hesitation they agreed to return and I gave them a still camera. They were taking an enormous risk for if they were caught they would be questioned and tortured and possibly murdered. They would first be kept in a truck with a tin roof for a few days where they would sweat under the Zambezi sun. They told me the truck was kept just outside the enclosure and always held two or three people who had protested against the building of The Cage; because no toilet facilities were available the air inside was foul. A week later they returned with photos of the wire, the mounds of graves, and the 'hospital', which showed a sick woman lying on the ground. There were few other people about which puzzled me but I was told they were now allowed outside the wire during the day but forced back inside before nightfall by curfew when anyone caught outside the wire would be shot.

I had used a cameraman I knew could be trusted for the interviews and back at the office I put a map on to a board and pinpointed exactly where The Cage was for a short on-camera piece, and quietly shipped off the film. A telex came back, 'Sorry, Reg, we can't use it unless we get the government's reaction.' I'm not heavily into four-letter words, which makes them more emphatic when they are used, but I'd hoped for a little more trust from ITN. Their request had been reasonable but I had hoped to break the story first and then get reaction. Now I was exposing my hand in advance. I put in a formal request to speak to the minister responsible in a television interview and, as was normal, I had to give the reason for the request and provide the gist of the questions that would be asked. When this was done a reply came back saying the Director of Information, Bill Ferris, would like to see me in his office the following afternoon. Ferris introduced me to the District Commissioner for the Gutsa area who had been flown down especially for the discussion. They both confirmed everything I had to say and I couldn't believe they would be so frank. They confirmed the children's deaths of five a day and said it had been caused by a measles epidemic, made worse by the cramped conditions. They also confirmed that the number of adults who died averaged one a day and they even agreed that the 'hospital' was totally inadequate with a flying doctor coming in once a week, and that there were only two acres of land for 5,000 people who were now held just at night. Even the burning of homes and shooting of cattle was confirmed. I could not believe what I was hearing. The explanation for all this was that the locals were being intimidated by terrorists and known to be hiding and feeding them. 'We are trying to help stop these people from being intimidated,' said Ferris blandly. 'Yes, I can understand your problem,' I said, adding, 'it's clearly important that you put that message across. I would like to interview one of you for ITN's *News at Ten*!' I'm sensitive to atmosphere and immediately knew that this wasn't what they had in mind at all but they were still being cordial. Ferris was the person who had blocked me in every way he could, right down to removing my credentials. Now they wanted something from me. 'Reg,' said Ferris, 'we've been talking totally off the record (this had not been mentioned in advance) and I'm afraid I must ask you not to publish it. You would be doing a grave disservice to Rhodesia by using this story.'

That sudden rush of blood pulsated: 'This has not been off the record and you are doing a grave disservice to Rhodesia by building this appalling place,' I countered. 'I've already filmed interviews with people who were incarcerated there and have photographs taken from inside!' Retorted Ferris, 'Then those films will be confiscated.'

'That will be difficult,' I snorted angrily, 'they're in London!' I telexed through to ITN that the story had been confirmed but that the government would not comment officially. Then I waited for the explosion to take place once it was shown and with my being charged with a nasty offence. Instead, a message came back, 'Sorry we can't use the story, Reg, as you put the map of the area on to a red background which is showing slightly in one corner.' That wasn't like ITN and I wondered what strings had been pulled behind the scenes on the old boy network. What really hurt was that ITN had asked me to stretch my neck out even further than I had already done by telling the government what had happened and then not backed me up. I thought also of the two men who had risked their lives so that the truth would be told and thus save others. But there was an up and downside: The Cage was pulled down immediately afterwards, disappearing without trace and I had the consolation of knowing that in a small way, I'd been directly responsible for saving an unknown number of children's lives and even some elderly, including Fanus's father. Now that AIDS is rife throughout Zimbabwe, I fear that many children may have been saved for an even worse fate. I also fervently hope that none of them became Robert Mugabe's young 'war veterans' who forced defenceless white farmers to leave the homesteads, sometimes murdering them.

The first officially recorded Protected Village was built the following year, in another area of Rhodesia. Not surprisingly, I was invited to take a look at it on a facility trip, probably top of the list. It wasn't a bit like The Cage, but a very smart place indeed! ITN's Mike Nicholson had missed the facility trip and asked me if I would find the new PV for him, which I did. He filmed inside before we were stopped, and then he deliberately lied that we had permission to be there. It was a stupid lie that could easily be disproved but all right for Nicholson as he was a staff man who could come and go at will. The finger was pointed straight at me for taking him there and Nicholson never lifted his own finger to say it was his fault. This time all my press hand-outs were stopped in yet another attempt to make me journalistically impotent. It was becoming a weary battle; until then I had always felt I could rely on people I considered my friends for support, no matter how ruthlessly ambitious they may be. Warning bells rang like a cheap two-bell alarm clock in my brain.

Amongst my memorabilia is a clip of spent bullets from a Russian-made AK-47 rifle and I've sometimes pondered why I keep it. Perhaps it's a war souvenir but as it is the only one I possess I doubt if that's the reason for there is nothing glamorous in the type of wars that I've covered. If someone points out a heroic revolutionary to me I will wonder how many innocent people he or she has either slaughtered or how many deaths they might be responsible for. The unpolished and darkening bullet cases come from the scene of a terrorist massacre in the bush in Mozambique and even now as I gaze at them the vivid memory floods back to the lonely Portuguese soldier who handed them to me. It's an enduring memory of only a couple of hours when we met in dangerous circumstances and then parted to carry on with our lives. As few people reading this book will be journalists, I'd like to invite you to spend just one afternoon in my life to get the feel of what it's like to cover Africa as a war correspondent; to share the ambience of danger, to meet brave and dedicated people; to face the stark reality of tragedy and ask the question: why?

I'm at Tete, just a few hundred yards from where I started the Zambezi River trip, and the helicopter I'm to use for the fifteen-minute flight looks as fragile as the Klepper rubber boat. 'Don't worry about the bullet holes,' laughs Luis Faria, the young Portuguese helicopter pilot and as soon as I'm aboard he takes off, racing forward only a few feet from the ground. I counted nine bullet holes in the chopper and Luis tells me there is another in his shoulder where ground machine-gun fire had given him an unwelcome birthday present six weeks ago. One dumdum had torn through the back seat just above the petrol tank and smashed a small fire extinguisher behind his head while another had sliced the earphone cord beside his neck. Most of the holes are in the wind-screen and are crudely patched with criss-crossed dark brown sealing paper.

The overhanging branches of a tree on a hill loom to the right, just a few yards from us, while five yards to the left are the new high-tension cables from Caborra Bassa's hydro-electric dam. It's exhilarating stuff and far better to fly at tree-top level when you have a phobia for heights, and as we breast a rise I see fleetingly below us the tarred road I'd driven along many times en route to Beira. Tar on the highway is supposed to cut the risk of mines but it's not really effective as Frelimo guerrillas have learned to open the sun-softened tar and place hidden mines, making it as deadly as a dirt road. Another tree looms up and this time we take off some leaves. The dial on the panel shows 130 mph and Faria grins. 'This is a safe height,' he shouts above the noise of the rotating blades. 'By the time the terrorists hear us we are overhead and it's too late for them to use their machine guns. The alternative is to go up to 9,000 feet to avoid their anti-aircraft guns and SAM-7 missiles and even then it isn't safe as they can attack us coming down!' Little wonder, I surmise, that Luis and a colleague are the only pilots left to fly seven helicopters and I wonder what madness keeps them going on their suicide runs. I decide it must be for the money for they will be relatively wealthy once they return to Portugal provided they are paid in US dollars.

We rise slightly and briefly to swing to port above the multi-voltage power lines, then swerve to the right to hop the same wires again! One false move and we'll be overcooked beef burgers, but young Luis tells me he survives by doing the unexpected and always changes his route. He has already flown to the death village six times today and knows the terrorists hope he will come the same way twice. It's a deadly cat and mouse game and when he says I'm the only journalist to visit the site I wonder who else is mad enough to join him. Nhacambo village, or what's left of it, is just ahead and we touch down. It's 4.37 p.m. and less than two hours to nightfall.

Even though the mutilated bodies are gone I am lucky that the diminutive, bespectacled representative of the International Red Cross, Antonio de Carvalho, has taken Instamatic photographs and has some to spare. They are not very nice pictures: the bodies, the children lying dead in the mud. Some people think of the Red Cross as nurses with white starched uniforms and disinfectant; it's not like that here in the bush. There's only de Carvalho and he risks his life to take pictures of bodies and write reports. That seems familiar… perhaps he should become a photo-journalist.

We walk around the village and look at the burned homes. 'There were 186 houses before the attack,' says de Carvalho, 'now only twenty-six are left.' The little school is gutted too but the neat rows of desks are still in place. Some of the children who laughed and played there won't be going back and stains of their blood discolour the ground. There's is just one other man in the village and de Carvalho says he is a Portuguese soldier. He doesn't look much like a soldier, not the type you would find in the British army. Whoever heard of a soldier walking around with bandages on his feet and no boots? No wonder the war has gone against the Portuguese in Mozambique if that is all they can produce. 'He was the only white man here when the attack took place,' says de Carvalho, 'just him and a handful of black militiamen.' The scruffy man comes towards us and holds out his hand with a shy smile. He is Corporal Tome Pereira Goncalves who is very happy to meet me. Yes, he will talk about the attack and I'm surprised at his command of the English language.

Sunday evening and Corporal Goncalves had just pulled off his boots and put his weary feet up on his bed. It had been a tiring day, keeping a watchful eye on the 600 villagers he was there to protect, never sure if terrorists had slipped in amongst them. Then came the onslaught. Sixty Frelimo guerrillas led by

Fernando Napulula hit the tiny hamlet with everything they had – mortars, bazookas, recoilless cannons, machine guns, grenades and automatic rifles. It was the seventeenth assault and Corporal Goncalves instinctively grabbed his machine gun and raced outside, firing as he ran.

He could hear the panicking civilians, women and children, shouting and screaming in terror. He could hear them dying, too. 'I called to two African militiamen to help me beat off the attack and then my machine gun jammed. Then I grabbed a mortar but as the terrorists closed in I switched to a G-3,' (automatic rifle), he says. 'I knew I could not save the village but only cover the civilians as they fled into the bush.' The three men fought for an hour until their ammunition ran out. Other militiamen – there were twenty-nine of them – also fought back but most were too busy helping the villagers into the bush, including their own families. With no ammunition left, Goncalves gave the order to his men to pull out. He expected the emerging killers to come after them but instead of chasing the militiamen, they decided upon a terrible course of plunder and death within the village itself.

They caught one little boy and chopped wildly at his arm with a panga but despite unbearable pain, the child did not faint. Blood streaming from the gruesome stump, his arm hanging from the elbow by the skin, he tried to run for it. He was shot in the back on the playground of his school and his small body was found next day, severed arm beneath it. And if that wasn't enough to satisfy the 'freedom fighter' leader's bloodlust, he was then disembowelled. A mother and her four small children were huddled into a corner of an underground shelter built as protection against mortar bombs and the crazed terrorists gunned them down before they were able to get out, leaving their bodies in a pool of blood in the shelter. 'That's them,' says the Red Cross de Carvalho as he produces his photographs again. 'You can have a copy and, come on, I'll show you where it happened.' We look down at the shelter with water inside, bloody muddy water. 'You see that hole in the ground,' says de Carvalho, 'that's where a woman was caught as she ran to join her children in the bush. That's where they bayoneted her, time and again until the bayonet made that hole beneath her body.' One terrified toddler had made a run for it; he ran as fast as a nineteen-month-old child can. There are the marks in the dirt to show he had fallen several times but the very fact that he was a toddler did not save him. He couldn't even plead with his killers for he had not yet learned to talk. By the time Frelimo left, seventeen people lay dead – two baby girls, three boy toddlers, three teenage boys, seven women and two old men.

Why did they have to die? It is a question I often ask myself when attending massacres of the innocents. In this case it was simply a personal vendetta by Fernando Napulula against Corporal Goncalves. 'We came face to face during an ambush I set, about three months ago,' explains the corporal. 'Rather than sit back to be attacked again, I had gone out with the militia to find him. Napulula ran away and I shouted "coward", and this damaged his reputation with the other terrorists.'

Without ammunition, Corporal Goncalves had run all night barefoot to the nearest army post at Marara for help. 'When I returned, I found a note left by Napulula which accused me of deserting my post and asking where my bravery had gone.' It is a challenge to Corporal Goncalves to stay and fight again and now, with feet bandaged and a loaded gun in his hand, and he smiles grimly at the challenge. 'But I don't want to see any more people hurt just because Napulula is out to get me,' he says.

Dusk is approaching and the Red Cross man asks if he can hitch a lift. As we casually walk towards the helicopter I stoop to pick up some spent AK-47 cartridges for no particular reason except, perhaps, as an aide-memoire to the article I will write. Seeing this, Goncalves' huge hand picks up some more and he carefully fits them into a magazine before presenting them to me. We shake hands and then wave as the helicopter rises a few feet off the ground. That's when I leave a very brave Portuguese soldier, one man standing by his post waiting for the return of a sadistic killer who he is determined to murder. Taunts in some overseas newspapers said that the massacre was a put-up job by the Portuguese troops but it's difficult to believe that type of accusation when you are there; when you meet such a kindly hero as Corporal Goncalves. Perhaps those who reported so eloquently on the attack should have been there too.

I don't know what happened to the corporal or to Fernando Napulula who possibly ended up with an important position in the Frelimo government. But peace can sometimes heal old wounds as I learned from one of my many strings, *Deutsche Presse*, or *DPA*. We had a good relationship. One of their staff photographers in Johannesburg flew his own plane and once I accepted a lift, sitting in the aircraft with two other Germans, both *DPA* journalists. As we flew, they began talking about wartime aircraft, Junkers 88, Heinkels, etc. and slowly there was an awakening. I asked, 'Were you in the Luftwaffe?'

'Ja,' they said, all three of them.

'And I suppose you're the bastards who used to drop bombs on me in England?' They looked at me and grinned broadly, 'Ja,' they chorused. Ah well; at least they weren't Gestapo, otherwise I'd have stepped off the plane.

The handover of Mozambique to Frelimo guerrillas by the new Portuguese government following the Lisbon coup created an air of unreality. The whites were certain they had been betrayed by the communist government in Lisbon and resented being called 'settlers' after being there for over 400 years. They felt strongly that they should have been consulted before such a major upheaval to their lives was decided.

In the port of Beira, I sat in the cocktail lounge of an hotel sipping iced coffee when a moustachioed Portuguese walked furtively across to me. He looked over his shoulder before producing a card from his trouser pocket which showed him to be a member of the National Coalition Party. 'I will call for you here at eight o'clock tonight,' he whispered darkly with enough garlic on his breath to keep any foe at bay. Surreptitiously he looked around the lounge to ensure he was not overheard. 'You will have the honour to meet our leaders,' he added before disappearing. Ten minutes later another man arrived the same way and he too produced a card, showing membership of 'The Movement for Free Mozambique'. 'Be here tonight at ten o'clock and we will talk to you,' he said, darkly and he too vanished into the night. As I was leaving the hotel I was tapped on the shoulder by another man, tall with a military bearing who claimed to be a member of the 'Dragons of Death', a sinister clandestine organisation believed to comprise disgruntled Portuguese army officers. He gave me a card to prove his credentials. 'We are ready!' he muttered and walked towards the carpeted stairs, 'I will contact you later.'

I thought of Peter Sellers, as I'd done with the Indian on the Congo border who'd accepted my cheque, and deduced that with each member of the clandestine organisations carrying a different card, a small printer somewhere in Beira must be doing a roaring trade in intrigue on his Arab business-card printing machine. I coined the phrase 'The Portuguese promise' when it became apparent that the Portuguese were masters of plotting but pitiful when it came to implementation; there was little wonder that Lisbon was the capital of foreign agents during WW2. When Frelimo eventually entered Beira, the secret organisations melted away like ice cream in the sun and it was their imminent arrival that had become the cause of the greatest concern. Farcically, when they did turn up they were accompanied and protected by their arch enemies, the Portuguese troops.

As the Frelimo guerrillas assembled at Dondo, twenty miles away, I drove out for an exclusive interview with their leader, Cara Alegre 'Happy Face' Tembe. He was pleasant enough; only twenty-eight years old and curiously he wore a large American Stetson, hardly the headgear of a militant Marxist revolutionary. When I say pleasant, I mean he was pleasant to me. At one stage during our talk he warned darkly that his spies in Beira had noted the whites who had come out to attend protest meetings and they would be 'dealt with'. It is not always the essence of these meetings that occupies the memory but the surrealistic intrusion of music which blares out over the camp radios. This time it was the Beatles singing, 'Hey Jude'. In a similar situation at Binga, on the shores of Lake Kariba, where Rhodesian black troops had set up camp against a possible lake-crossing by guerrillas from Zambia, machine guns were in place and the soldiers' torsos bristled with bandoliers of bullets. Elephant dung was in the middle of the camp to show that a jumbo had recently left a deposit and here the tiny radio was playing, 'Elizabethan Serenade'.

As tension reached breaking point in Beira, thousands of whites surrounded the local radio station and were held back by troops. At first they sang songs and hurled abuse until a demonstrator produced a pistol and as an army officer grabbed him the gun went off twice with one bullet piercing a wall and the other a demonstrator. Then came two explosions as hand grenades were thrown and this time an African riot-squad policeman was killed.

Into the middle of all this mayhem entered a Rhodesian diplomat. Sporting a Graham Greene-esque white suit, Bill Anlan, who seemed bemused at what was happening around him, told me he was on his way to Lourenco Marques (now Maputo) to become the new Rhodesian consul there. I'm not often stupefied, but this was breathtaking folly and I asked a question later to be used by tennis star John McEnroe, 'You cannot be serious?' Dressed immaculately and carrying a stick to help along an old war wound in the leg, he looked at me uncertainly, 'Yes, I am, very serious indeed.' I had always known that the Rhodesian government was out of touch with reality but to send a diplomat into the middle of this turmoil to present his credentials to the Marxist government was nothing short of criminal naivety. 'You'd better take the next plane back tomorrow,' I advised. 'There's all hell breaking loose in Lourenco Marques, even worse than here!'

Evening was approaching and the turmoil in Beira would subside until tomorrow once it was learned that the great entrance into the port town had been delayed for a day. This was agreed at the request of 'Happy Face' who was becoming very unhappy and worried at the reception he might receive. 'Let's go to the cinema,' suggested Anlan. 'You can be the guest of my government.'

'What a good idea,' I replied, and I was taken to an open-air cinema in Mozambique during a Marxist takeover by a representative of the Rhodesian government. I'll bet my name wasn't on the expense account, nor that of the unexpurgated film itself: *La Narankja Mechanical – A Clockwork Orange*! 'I didn't know it would be like that,' said Anlan afterwards, the very same words used by Ernie Christie on seeing his award-winning film in the Congo. 'No,' I replied seriously, but was inwardly amused. It wasn't the type of film the Rhodesian censors would have passed.

Next day, a Portuguese frigate quietly anchored offshore as the whites continued to crowd the main square and the radio station where they voiced contempt that Frelimo had insisted on a Portuguese military bodyguard to bring them into town. 'How can they head a provisional government and not have the courage to come into our second largest city?' one irate Portuguese man asked me. He answered his own question when he mentioned casually that he had three guns tucked away, 'Just in case of trouble.' A white teenage girl told me her hair had been pulled by some drunken Africans and she ran off into the crowd. 'If I'd cried for help, people would have come to my aid and that would have sparked off the trouble we are all trying to avoid,' she said. That was sensible thinking for a child of about fifteen years of age. I strolled away from the crowd and into a second-hand shop. There was an ashtray I'd admired in the window, which looked antique. It had a marble base on which was mounted a brass tray, and there was also a snuff box, a section for a matchbox, and above all this was a coat-of-arms. I asked the price. 'Seven thousand escudos,' said the ageing Indian proprietor. Intending to convey that I thought it was an antique bargain, I remarked, 'It's very old, isn't it?' The Indian studied me for a moment, then shrugged. 'All right then, for you it is seven hundred escudos!'

I'd been tipped off when Frelimo was expected to arrive and went out of town to meet them and travel behind their leaders who were being driven in a blue Land Rover behind a Portuguese troop bodyguard. It was another ridiculous African scene and I gave a couple of Eric Robins' derisive royal waves to what was clearly an anti-climax. Not a single grenade was thrown at us; not a bullet shaved our heads. Few people even realised who we were; it was hardly the entry of the gladiators. The Frelimo leaders went off into a shanty town while the Portuguese troops guarding them returned to barracks to pack their kit, and that was it. I never heard any more from the Dragons of Death.

Further down the coast in Lourenco Marques it was quite different. Violence erupted into a bloodbath following a call for peace by the local Frelimo leader. The capital's radio station had been seized by white extremists, then grabbed back by Portuguese troops who called in the Frelimo leader to broadcast his peace message. In true Evelyn Waugh tradition, he was to call 'Calo, Calo' (Cockerel), a prearranged signal to stop fighting. Not surprisingly, someone cocked it up as this was the moment the Africans went on the rampage!

Reports came through of more than 200 people being stabbed or beaten to death by gangs of Africans roaming the suburbs. But the journalists, with red-hot stories on their hands and their own breathtaking experiences to relate, found there was no communication out of Lourenco Marques. Of this I was blithely ignorant as I twiddled my thumbs in Beira with only a few killings to report. It wasn't until I went to the hotel telex and got through to a colleague in his Lourenco Marques hotel to inquire about the situation there that things began to jump. Suddenly, my colleagues realised an outside line existed after all and that Shay could get their copy away. From then on there was no rest. Having worked all night to move their copy, not one came back to say 'thank you'. Even worse, some left me with telex bills which were never repaid. Freelancers really should not be called upon to subsidize freeloading newspapers.

In Rhodesia, I had soon learned that the worst payers were the Swedes who found it obnoxious to enter the country of white supremacy and then, if they did venture forth, wondered why no one would hire out telex and radio studio facilities to them. They came to me as a last resort and I sent their messages even though it would compromise me further with the Special Branch. I was really cross when Swedish TV then found it morally inconceivable that they should send money into a white supremacist country and thus refused to pay for any journalistic help and left me footing their expensive telex and radio studio bills.

Watching the takeover by Frelimo would be my last trip to Beira, which didn't upset me particularly except that I would not see my old friend again. Carlos Brito was one of the kindest men I ever knew and a workaholic too, never utilising less than sixteen hours a day. He had started his commercial life as an insurance agent and gave water to the handful of Rhodesians who went to Beira on holiday. Then he was asked for food, which he provided; and then for accommodation. He turned his small home into a boarding house. Then more people arrived and he built a large flat complex, then hotels. In the end, Carlos Brito, now a millionaire, built a bank to help Africans. In his grand Dom Carlos Hotel, he entertained important people. I met an almost-deaf American senator there once who came most years; he was reputedly the founder and owner of Greyhound Buses. He liked going to Beira although I could never see why, but then, he too liked Carlos Brito.

Frelimo, by merely using the gun for persuasion instead of brains and industry as Brito had done, took over the hotels and the bank. I heard that Carlos had gone to Portugal, a penniless and disillusioned man. I've looked for him in Lisbon and the Estoril but he simply melted away.

An Introduction to Seductive and Deadly Angola

Following the April 1974 coup in Lisbon, the bureau chief of Associated Press in Johannesburg, Larry Heinzerling, telephoned to discuss Angola which was heading towards turmoil. Larry hadn't a clear picture of what was happening there as he relied primarily on reports from Mike Chapman, a public relations consultant who, to his great surprise and financial pleasure, had suddenly found himself in demand as a journalist. Mike was a huge, obese but kindly soul with a spitfire of a Portuguese wife who, after consuming the contents, would occasionally plant a wine bottle on his head, the results of which I had witnessed with compassion. Heinzerling was worried that because of Chapman's lack of journalistic experience and his own absence from the scene, New York would send out a staff man from the London bureau to Angola, thus diminishing his African parish. I liked Larry: he was young, ambitious and the son of a retired AP journalist I had long respected, and it astonished me that he had found himself too busy in Johannesburg to fly to Angola himself. 'Would you like me to take a look?' I asked, taking the hint. I hadn't been to Angola and felt that a visit there was overdue. 'I'll just confirm with New York and ring you back,' he replied a little too hastily. I hadn't realised at the time just how anxious London was to cover the Angolan scene.

The go-ahead came that afternoon and I touched down at Luanda Airport next day and thought what a dismal and depressing place the airport was. Slogans were daubed over the concourse walls, many in red, declaring in Portuguese, 'People's Power'. Other legends in black read, 'Hang Cortina', 'Shoot Cortina', 'Death to Cortina'. It didn't take an analytical brain to conclude that in some quarters, Cortina was not the flavour of the month.

My spirits hadn't risen when I went to the Tivoli Hotel where bored journalists sat around in the reception area. I didn't recognise any of them; nor did I recognise the drink they were cautiously sipping. Having introduced myself they, in turn, introduced me to Sbell, explaining that no other whisky was available. A local brand, Sbell had been invented by two alcoholic Scots some years earlier and its bouquet took me back to schoolboy cricket bats and linseed oil. The smell of its malodorous fragrance warned me of its potency and one sip was a hasty reminder that preserving my liver and the enamel on my teeth were of paramount importance. 'How did it get its name?' I spluttered through a moist white handkerchief with the foul taste assaulting and insulting my palate. 'They (the Scots) were always drunk and because they couldn't think of an original name for this piss, they transposed the "s" in Bells,' came a reporter's explanation.

Outside the heat and humidity were sauna temperature but the temperature in the foyer was as arctic as the ice in the Sbell and I was visibly shivering. 'It's bloody freezing in here,' I remonstrated. 'You'd think the management would turn the air conditioning down.' 'Not yet,' replied one of my new-found colleagues, conspiratorially adding, 'they can do what they like with it in a little while.' That was a peculiar remark and I noticed that despite the ice-box conditions the journalists all sat facing the entrance like Eskimos around a fishing hole, waiting with eager anticipation as they peered out through the smoked glass window. One glanced nervously at his watch as tension built up and muttered, 'Any minute now!' There was silence and then a conspiratorial whisper, 'Here she is!' The door opened to reveal a stunningly beautiful Portuguese woman in her early twenties, wearing a silver-blue, skin-tight outfit which clung like a sheath to her supple body. All their eyes were centred firmly above the navel to perfectly moulded breasts and an audible gasp was heard when the coldness of the foyer embraced them and they responded tantalisingly, the nipples popping forward with electrifying effect. Having come from the sunlight the young woman could not have seen the lecherous foreign press corps sitting like sneak viewers of a porn video anticipating the ecstasy.

After paying a courtesy call on Chapman and establishing that I could use his telex, I strolled from his office to the sea front. I'm not sure what I expected but I was forced to ask myself in wonder: where's the war? Unfurled like a mural was one of the most serene and magnificent bays in the world and commandingly situated on a nearby promontory overlooking the harbour was a Beau Gest fortress with white, sun-and-lime bleached walls reflecting a magnificent imperious mirage above an ultramarine Atlantic. A tropical beach invitingly stretched out its sands towards me and I quickened my pace, readily volunteering to be caught in its captivating embrace. After wandering across to the island (umbilically united with the mainland by a small man-made roadway) I gazed with spellbound admiration. I have never ever seen so many beautiful girls in one area, all clad in bikinis and sunhats as they lazed beneath thatched single-poled sun shelters, sipping gins and Pimms while wisps of scented smoke seduced my nostrils as the greatest exponents in the world of seafood cuisine wove their magic from the cornucopia of the ocean. I understood at once why the Portuguese called Angola their 'Pearl of Africa' and I forced myself to put aside my natural instincts of remaining for ever in paradise where I could overindulge in all things delectably palatable, and reluctantly left the island to write a scene-setter.

The glamour of life in Luanda did not reflect the ambience of the whole country. Resentment ran deep among the whites as they felt, like those in Mozambique, that they had been betrayed. Every white I spoke to said they would not remain under a government of the communist MPLA but would be content to stay under Jonas Savimbi's Unita movement. Could it be possible that half a million people would pull out, I wondered, or was it yet another

Portuguese promise? Would they give up a country they had settled before the Americas and Australia were even known by Europeans to have existed, let alone colonised? To them it was comparable to all the whites and blacks in the United States being ordered to hand back the country to the indigenous American Indians. What really got up the collective Portuguese noses was that they had won the war against most of the insurrectionists with only Savimbi's Unita surviving.

'We beat Roberto,' a Portuguese army officer confided to me. 'He had no troops left in the country at the time of the Lisbon coup, nor had the MPLA.' It is probable he was correct. Holden Roberto's UPA forces had withdrawn to Zaire (formerly Belgian Congo and now the Congo Republic) where his brother-in-law, General Joseph Mobutu, was president and the MPLA's troops had been pushed back into the Congo Brazzaville.

I wasn't shedding any tears for Roberto. During the civil war at Luvo, a village north of Luanda, 300 of his freedom fighters attacked forty-two white men, women and children at a sawmill. The marauders laughed as they stripped off their victims' clothes, tied them to planks and then sent them alive and feet first on a nightmare journey to the rotating saw blade. Roberto actually boasted about his troops' atrocities, including the sawmill incident, to a French journalist, Pierre de Vos of *Le Monde*. What had caused particular resentment towards Roberto and Savimbi, was that the MPLA was virtually controlled by Coloured people, and was an ideological rather than grass-roots nationalist movement.

Behind the MPLA was Rear Admiral Rosa Cortina, a hydrographer, known as the 'Red Admiral'. After the Lisbon coup he had become the unpopular governor of Angola, whose neck all the whites were craving to put into a noose. He nearly died at the hands of Roberto who had captured him and handed him over to Mobutu for imprisonment in Zaire. It was a move that Roberto was to regret. While a serving admiral in the Portuguese navy, Cortina disappeared from service for several months, reputedly spending the time in Moscow. A senior Portuguese officer disclosed to me that Cortina had attended an Iron Curtain conference where it was decided to infiltrate the Portuguese universities to find potential officer recruits for the communist cause. Under the guidance of Cortina, indoctrinated officers were brought out from Portugal just after the Lisbon coup. As a result, many Portuguese civilians found little or no help from their own soldiers when they were subsequently attacked and butchered by the MPLA. Cortina was responsible, too, for Eastern-bloc ships slipping into ports and inlets all the way down the Angolan coast, bringing in Cuban troops, arms and equipment which included Russian armoured cars and tanks.

I saw the Machiavellian Red Admiral only once. He was holding a private press conference for selected Portuguese reporters and when Stan Maher, a South African journalist, got to hear about it we gatecrashed the conference to see a smallish but extremely lithe and animated man, who reminded me of Yul

Brynner. Cortina was not pleased to see two western foreign correspondents present and we could see little reason to stay where we were clearly not welcome. Our decision to leave in a hurry was reached when Cortina was in the middle of a speech and pointed in our direction. At that time, the Portuguese civilians didn't even know he was in the country but if they had, there was one Portuguese promise that would have been kept...

While the city was peaceful with the exception of a few demonstrations, I could hear shooting at night in the museques, the black shanty towns where there had been trouble just before I arrived. 'If you go in there, you won't come out alive,' a Portuguese army officer told me. 'Can I go in with troops?'

'No,' came the reply.

I had the feeling that the Portuguese themselves did not care to go in and so I stayed away on this trip but wondered just what was going on as I sat on my hotel room's balcony at night and watched the tracer bullets in the museques. One thing was certain: intimidation and murder were rife.

For my next report I looked at Angola's economy and realised that its potential was probably greater than South Africa's. Rich in minerals and wealthy in agriculture – all its large coffee crop was sent to the United States – it also had oil in the Cabinda enclave to the north. I even broke a story during that short visit of Texaco discovering more oil offshore in Angola itself, a story strenuously denied by the company at the time. AP carried my story and then a retraction without consulting me which was humiliating, especially as I knew I was right. It meant that all the media worldwide who had read the original report under my name would now consider me suspect and it is of little comfort to know that oil is now being extracted from that very area.

There had been fighting at Cabinda just over the Congo River and I decided to fly there but by the time I arrived the FNLA and a local secessionist group had taken a pasting from the MPLA who were now in control. There were no Portuguese troops to be seen and as I walked into one shot-up building which had been the FNLA headquarters, I picked up a membership card as a souvenir. Then I realised that just carrying that card could mean death and put it in my sock knowing that my legs could handle dangerous cards, they had done quite well in the Congo War. I stayed the night at the American oil base where life for the occupants was politically uncomfortable but it was possibly the safest place in the enclave. The offshore wells were a sight breathtaking enough to spawn legends. Gazing at the moonlight reflecting ripples of diamonds on the Atlantic ocean, I was distracted by individual flames bursting from the water and twisting skywards into the night, their tongues licking the air and probing into the darkness.

I flew back to Luanda next day wondering at the privilege of being a foreign correspondent who sees so much more than most people, and shortly afterwards left Angola to await events. I did not have to wait long...

Reports were soon coming in that the Angolan situation was deteriorating fast and Associated Press asked me if I could go back urgently. As another favour to Heinzerling I agreed, but I really did feel that he should take a look for himself as my main responsibility was keeping an eye on the Rhodesian scene. My unexpected five-month stay became the longest of any foreign correspondent in the run-up to Angola's independence and beyond. It would be my most dangerous assignment ever and I will always wonder how I survived.

The return flight was eerie; an uncomfortable curtain-raiser to frightening events ahead. A few days before attempts had been made to shoot down a passenger plane coming in to land and as the TAP airline pilots were taking as few risks as possible, all the lights on the aircraft were switched off, both inside and out, as we approached Luanda. It was an ebony night where not even the passengers sitting close to me on the Boeing 707 were visible but I could feel their tension as they held their breath. There were not many on board – just five of us. Only stupid journalists and opportunist businessmen fly into war zones when everyone else is scrambling to get out. I felt as helpless as an English grouse on the 'glorious' twelfth of August; a moving target suspended in the sky, waiting for the missile that would send us crashing to the ground or the ocean. The only company was the low hum of the engines which, in normal times, would be comforting but the very heat they exuded could guide the SAM-7s to our destruction. I should have travelled in daylight as I have a false feeling of reassurance about light but I'd stopped over in Johannesburg to see Bill McLean who was lying seriously ill in hospital where a section of his pancreas had been removed. Perhaps my surprise hospital visit had helped to save his life as I stopped a foolish journalist friend of his trying to sneak Bill a beer. What was it the doctor said when I called him over? 'If Mr McLean has just one beer it will kill him!' The journalist was thrown out of the hospital and now, four hours later, I was sitting in an aircraft wondering if I would die instead.

How far off the ground are we? I wondered. *That's the real trouble; not knowing anything. If a missile hit us, could the other engines glide us in or would we drop like a stone?* My thoughts raced: *I suppose it depended on the damage to the wing. Would we crash into woods and perhaps be burned alive, or into the sea and scramble to put our lifebelts on? How does anyone put on a lifebelt in pitch darkness, or even find it? Air stewardesses always demonstrate how to inflate them and tell passengers the lifebelts are under the seats, which I've confirmed, but never explain how to deal with them in pitch dark. And the door: how would we find it?* I liked to think ahead in case of an emergency as in my profession it helps one to stay alive, but how could anyone plan in this situation? I hadn't expected all the lights to go out. *Wait and see,* I told myself, *that's the only answer.*

It was a long, long wait; an eternity. Finally a gentle bump told us eternity could wait, we were down... and now the engines raced in reverse. He was a good pilot, landing in blackout conditions with a touchdown that wouldn't displace a feather inside a duvet. Perhaps Luanda Airport would not be so bad after all, I wondered, but it was. What I saw filled me with shock, sadness and depression. Wherever I looked there were people lying on the stone floor hoping there would be room on a plane to take them away. There were old couples, young married couples with their families, a youth carrying a guitar with his girlfriend beside him. They were everywhere, tired, cold and hungry people who stared at me half vacantly, half disbelieving, that anyone should fly into the country while they were all struggling to leave.

I made inquiries and learned that they had come from outlying areas where there had been fierce fighting; they all talked of massacres. They had lost everything, their homes, possessions and even loved ones and all wanted to get to the safety of Portugal. There was a marked difference between these refugees and most others I have seen in Africa outside of the Congo; nearly all of them were white! This was going to be quite a different scene from my last visit…

A battered Mercedes taxi took me to the Tivoli Hotel, last bastion of the bored nipple-watchers and after booking into my room, I strolled outside and ran into my friend, Dave Ottaway, of the *Washington Post*. 'There's no point in staying there, they have no food,' was his greeting. 'You had better come to the Tropico and have a meal with me. Then I'll see what can be sorted out.' All the press corps had moved into the luxurious Hotel Tropico where there was now no room at the inn. David gave me a run-down on the bleak situation explaining that the three guerrilla groups were still at each others' throats while the Portuguese troops kept out of the way as much as possible. None of the conscripts wished to be the last soldier to die in Angola and they, like the refugees, just wanted to go home to Portugal. Shooting was still taking place every night in the museques and it was no longer safe to walk the streets in downtown Luanda after dark. With money, there was food to be had at some good restaurants which managed to stay open.

Two days after my arrival, David secured me a room at the Tropico but eating the food there could, at times, become suddenly indigestible as heavily armed MPLA soldiers would appear, pointing their guns. It happened three times while I ate there and on each occasion conversation stopped abruptly and an uneasy silence of frightened diners pervaded the room as the soldiers looked around menacingly with all of us nervously asking ourselves, 'Is it me?' The relief was audible after they spotted the person they were after and unceremoniously marched him out to a waiting truck. The poor wretch would not be seen again. This was a different Luanda to the one I had left: the MPLA reign of terror had now touched the city centre in an insidious form.

Shortly after I arrived back in Angola, the three political leaders, Holden Roberto, Augustino Neto and Jonas Savimbi, met at Nakuru, in Kenya, for what was dubbed a 'Peace Summit' and it started a day late because of Neto's delayed arrival, which suggested a certain contempt for his two rivals. Less than five months earlier, there had been a meeting on the Portuguese Algarve which resulted in what were called the Penina Independence Accords. An indication of the turmoil in Angola could be gauged in that at Nakuru a new ceasefire was called for – the fifth since the Penina Accords of January. The Nakuru meeting also repeated a call for the integration of the military forces into a national army, and the disarming of civilians. The National Defence Council stated that only Savimbi's Unita had given unfaltering co-operation with Portuguese forces in times of crisis, while the other two 'almost systematically' withdrew their elements from the mixed or integrated forces.

'There is to be a spontaneous demonstration at the Palace,' said Stan Maher with dry humour. 'We may as well take a look.' It was good to see Stan again. 'Spontaneous demonstrations' to the Palace had become commonplace and usually organised the day before by frightened people, both black and white. We drove to the Governor's palace and went inside to talk to the Information Department which, unsurprisingly, was dominated by the MPLA. Stan had not been inside before and he went along the corridors to the palace toilets and I waited for his reaction. Imbued with the sanitized conditions of South Africa, he had never come across some of the toilets on the European continent where used paper is thrown into baskets. His cheeks were as flushed as the toilet on his return and he was temporarily speechless. Then he blurted out the immortal words, 'If they can't manage a shit-house, how can they expect to run a country?'

Law and order was fast disappearing and I arrived at Mike Chapman's office one morning to see the plate-glass window of the Gestetner office below had been smashed. The manager shrugged his shoulders resignedly. 'It is happening all the time,' he said. 'They didn't steal any equipment; they are hungry. They just roam the streets at night in gangs looking for money.' Later that morning Stan and I made what was to become a regular pilgrimage to the palace and this time hundreds of whites had gathered. The massive front doors were slammed in their faces and they clamoured to get in, shouting and screaming and banging their fists against the unyielding hard wood. Many of the women carried babies in their arms, complaining they were losing everything because the world treated them as colonialists and had ganged up against them for their own political reasons. A middle-aged lady was dressed in black with a large plaster covering her head and she appeared dazed. She was just an ordinary Portuguese peasant-type housewife but she was the centre of attraction.

Maria Teixeira was her name and unbearable was her torment. 'Last night she and her twelve-year-old daughter watched as her husband was chopped to pieces by members of the MPLA,' explained a demonstrator, 'and then she and her daughter were raped by the whole gang!' The bewilderment, agony, hatred and humiliation that stirred in her breasts could not be imagined. How, I wondered, could anyone remain sane after such barbarism and what effect would it have on the daughter? The emotion of the crowd was volcanic and the passions were inflamed with the knowledge that one of the posters held up and calling for immediate repatriation was written in blood – that of Mrs Teixeira's mutilated husband. The Portuguese are a warm and passionate people who usually have a deep familial and social bond: how deep must be the feeling of Mrs Teixeira, I wondered, to allow men to take the blood of her husband to paint on a poster. Perhaps she did not give permission.

The doors of the palace remained firmly shut like an impregnable fortress and the frenzy of the crowd continued to build up until someone tried to grab the gun of a Portuguese municipal policeman. That was when all hell broke loose!

Stan and I were on the fringe of the crowd beside the palace wall when an MPLA soldier, a member of the misnamed United Force, lost his nerve and threw a hand grenade which exploded exactly twelve paces from where we were standing. Then he opened up with his AK-47 automatic rifle and bullets spattered the brickwork immediately behind us. Without a word, Stan and I looked for cover but there was none. Two Portuguese soldiers propelled themselves forward and grabbed the MPLA man and tried to pull his gun away but his finger stayed on the trigger and bullets continued to spew out and ricochet off the wall. Three people were wounded, two by the grenade and one by the bullets. It could have been much worse; it could have been Stan and me.

Only the day before, 1,500 blacks supporting Savimbi's Unita, which formed half the workforce in Luanda, had also paraded outside the palace demanding repatriation to their homes in the south. They told me they were tired of being beaten up, stabbed, or shot in their homes at night by armed civilians of the Popular Movement, the MPLA. Get away before the MPLA takes over was the uppermost thought in everyone's mind and panic was only thinly disguised. It was clear, even at this stage, that if any United Nations-sponsored general election ever took place in which the MPLA would inevitably win through murder, intimidation and deception, a civil war with Unita would seem inevitable.

I called on one Portuguese truck owner, stockily-built Guilherme dos Santos, who was planning to become a latter-day Moses and lead 3,500 Portuguese in a 2,500-car cavalcade to Portugal. They planned to drive 3,000 miles up through the Sahara and Morocco and across the Mediterranean into Spain. At the same time there was another cavalcade of 3,000 white refugees who were determined to drive south to Namibia, come what may, and were prepared to shoot it out with the MPLA if need be, dos Santos said as he helped his wife to pack the contents of their home. Unbeknown to them, Cuban troops were being landed secretly along their path. The refugees had hundreds of cars and 250 trucks, ripe pickings for the killers lying in wait. No news ever came back of what happened to the convoy. As I continued to watch the flashes of tracer bullets and listen to gunfire in the museques, another sound began to insinuate the darkness in the white suburbs until night after night came the timpani of hammering by unseen hands as the Portuguese made huge containers in which to put their goods. Should a ship ever arrive to take them away for ever, they were going to be ready. The tapping was not confined to Luanda, it was countrywide too as all the Portuguese prepared to leave their homes and take with them everything they could.

To many, this all night boxing-up of their precious belongings would come to no avail; when they reached the docks the wooden containers would be broken open and pillaged. It was the MPLA who now controlled the docks while panic-stricken crowds both black and white besieged all the western consulates. They called for ships and they called for planes to take them away from their homeland. Some consuls did not open their doors; others clucked sympathetically but all said they could do nothing. The American consul-general, Tom Kilhoran, and his staff were the most sympathetic and I called on Tom and saw a revolver lying on his desk facing the door. He had no illusions over the popularity of America amongst the MPLA. 'What can we do?' he asked me thoughtfully. 'This is a Portuguese problem. We can't repatriate these people unless asked to by the Portuguese government – and they are not asking!' The Marxist government in Lisbon certainly wasn't anxious to receive 500,000 people to swell the ranks of the destitute and unemployed (it was then standing at ten per cent in Portugal). And because of their ill-treatment, the refugees were now firmly right-wing, which would make them a formidable political opposition. It was true, therefore, that the Portuguese government of the day would have been happier if its own people had remained in Angola to be slaughtered; shamelessly, they did not want to know them. This was despite the fact that Portugal had claimed Angola and Mozambique were an integral part of the country and merely 'overseas provinces', with Portuguese citizen-ship being given to all, the indigenas and nao-indigenas distinction being abolished in 1961. But when the refugees did arrive in Lisbon, they found that even the Angolan escudo was seldom accepted. As a result, they were not only unwanted, but moneyless. Of those left behind, one African told me in a most matter-of-fact way, 'We are tired of being murdered.'

On a sultry evening I went to a downtown open-air cinema which was still operating. An MPLA camp was on the left-hand side of the cinema as we in the audience faced the screen. Elite, professionally led Portuguese troops were on the other side. During the middle of the film, shooting broke out and grenades exploded. Occasionally tracer bullets whizzed past but the audience took little notice; no one ducked as they had become immune to that sort of thing. The film was a western but all the action was off screen. That was how life had become in Angola; one minute a person could be watching a film, the next lying mortally wounded.

While eating with friends in a Chinese restaurant, an explosion took place across the road about thirty yards away. It came from what appeared to be an empty building. 'I'll just go over and have a look,' I said. We had become so dangerously blasé that there was little point in everyone's meal getting cold and I seemed to be the only one interested, anyway. On reaching the building I climbed three flights of stairs alone in the dark, with just my cigarette lighter for illumination. I tightened up a little at each floor in case the bomber was still there and hiding; on the third there were signs of an explosion. The bomb had been carried into the building in a newspaper as there were shreds of confetti newsprint littering the floor. With that I strolled back and we carried on eating; it was just another explosion. No one turned up to investigate because there was no law and order. Why had the time bomb been planted? We never knew as there was no apparent reason. If such a bomb had gone off in the capital city before the Lisbon coup, there would have been pandemonium; here, it was shrugged off. There was only a brief mention in next day's newspaper of another bomb which was thrown into the Portuguese airlines office, possibly a bid to frighten away the only airline left. MPLA rockets had hit the third floor of the university annexe of São Paulo hospital, killing three people while an ambulance taking wounded to the hospital had also been shot up. The Unita headquarters and other establishments of that movement were hit by MPLA rockets. Ten people in the HQ were killed and their bodies then mutilated. Eye witnesses told me that not only the dead but the wounded, too, had been chopped up. A communiqué from a Portuguese army colonel, Hector Almendra, described this as an 'Act of barbarism.'

And this was while the three political movements had a truce in Luanda for a peaceful run up to Independence. The corrupt MPLA became the government and Unita became their rebel terrorists. Before he was killed in action in February 2002, Savimbi had become a typical African despot but there were reasons for him becoming an embittered man.

A new threat loomed which was potentially worse than the bullets: the streets of Luanda began to pile high with garbage and there were genuine fears of a cholera outbreak. Then the water supply broke down! During severe fighting, the pumping station was damaged and it was difficult to find anyone qualified to repair it. Even worse, there were so many bodies decaying just outside Luanda with some of them in the reservoir, that an epidemic seemed more probable than possible. Portuguese troops were consigned to the distasteful task of gathering them up even though they had not taken part in the fighting and massacres. Heartbreak was contained daily in the newspaper with photographs of missing people, placed by mothers, fathers, sons, daughters, husbands and wives. There were captions: 'Have you seen my son? He disappeared in the centre of Luanda on Tuesday.' Many people disappeared trying to find safety; some vanished while breaking the dusk-to-dawn curfew, which we all broke, anyway. Most were believed to have been spirited away by the MPLA. In addition to the newspapers, large billboards were used to paste or pin on photographs of missing persons. After the September 11, 2001 outrage, there would be similar scenes in New York, catapulting the United States complacency at home into the real world of terrorism. The food shortage worsened to alarming proportions as MPLA troops blocked, then pillaged lorries carrying farm produce to Luanda. A Swedish ship stood idle in the harbour for weeks on end, anxiously waiting to unload food. Many ships, even in June when I'd arrived back, had been at anchor for over two months unable to drop their cargoes. Their captains were concerned at the amount of algae building up on the hulls which would slow their future passage and speed the depletion of vital fuel aboard. One East German ship, the *Alba*, was allowed straight in, however. Loaded with guns and ammunition, and some very large boxes on deck which could have contained tanks or armoured cars, it slipped into port at night. Next morning it was gone. Reports said that MPLA helpers had appeared as if from nowhere and totally unloaded it under the cover of darkness. And this was while the Portuguese were supposed to be in charge and keeping the peace, uniting the three factions, and helping to run the country during the transition! The Red Admiral Cortina had laid his plans well to turn Angola from a western to an eastern-bloc country. We know what eventually happened to the Soviet Union but I wonder whatever happened to him? On the grapevine, we journalists learned that three Portuguese reporters were tipped off that the unloading would take place, and had gone down to watch. Their potential scoop over the rest of us could not be confirmed as they were never seen again. What could be confirmed was that the MPLA were soon using 180 mm recoilless anti-tank guns and Soviet armoured vehicles. And within days of the Alba's departure, MPLA civilians were being handed guns *ad nauseum*, even though they had not been trained in the use of firearms. The volume of shooting in the townships at night increased after that and the MPLA's philosophy appeared to be if you are a revolutionary, we will give you a gun and ammunition; if you are a reactionary, you will receive only the bullet.

I finally managed to get a first-hand look at life and death in the museques, albeit briefly. Being members of the western press meant that some of us were not given facilities offered to those who supported the MPLA. And so, I thought, what else is new? The only British journalist to get full facilities from the Marxists was Jane Bergerol of the *Financial Times*, a good-looking woman who, I was told, hated my guts. This had come as a surprise as I'd never spoken to her other than to say a polite, 'Good morning.' Dave Ottaway learned of an MPLA press party going into the museques and gatecrashed the group. He was taken to a house which was used as a torture chamber by the FNLA, where five bodies had been found. He tipped me off, 'There's another press party going in.' I applied for the trip, was refused and gatecrashed it. After all, I had experience of torture chambers in Rhodesia and could now examine this one with professional interest. Unlike the Rhodesian police cell which had only bare walls and clubs, a towel and a tin for water, this was a house and there was finesse. Two ropes with nooses hung from the ceiling; a chair was completely burned out but there was an electric wire still attached to it, which was connected to a lamp. There were two beds – just springs, no mattresses – to which wires had also been attached. Also present were some familiar objects, cans and pieces of cloth – I knew how they had been used. And once again I was puzzled, for there on the floor was powder which was similar to that I had found in the Rhodesian police cell. I gathered some and put it into a used film canister for later identification by Rhodesian forensic scientists: it was the last I heard or saw of it.

The house of torture had a grave beneath the lounge floor and two outside. As we stood about, an excited African came up and took us twenty yards away into some scrub to look at another body he had just found. The MPLA and FNLA seemed hell-bent on decimating the population of the museques in the most unpleasant manner. Only Unita came out with honour; at that time I never once heard that they caused such suffering and it was some years later that I read a report that Savimbi had personally thrown people on to a fire.

I've never felt a great compassion towards the Japanese, possibly influenced by the death of my half-brother, Willie, who, as mentioned earlier, had been killed by them Burma during WW2. In the light of their behaviour towards prisoners of war, I had always thought of them as being sadistic but because of some of their wartime exploits, such as kamikaze pilots, I had also thought of them as tough and brave. I was surprised, therefore, on looking out of the office window in war-stricken Luanda, to watch with occidental curiosity, a Japanese television team come out of their hotel opposite. They looked to the left, and then to the right, before setting up a camera tripod. 'Hey, Mike, take a look at this,' I called to Chapman. He came across and we watched, fascinated. There was no fighting here, in fact, things were relatively quiet in the city at the moment and in a bid to normalise Luanda (a vain gesture), the council had sent out its painter who was carefully touching up the white centre line in the street. The Japanese crew swung into action, perhaps the most they had seen, and filmed the painter for over fifty yards as he slowly went past their hotel towards the sea. Having captured this momentous piece of Angola at war, they went back into the hotel, packed their bags and flew home to Japan.

A second incident concerned a Japanese newspaper photographer. A little chap, he carried a large label on his lapel. In English, Portuguese and Japanese, was the unforgettable legend: 'I am a Japanese photographer. Please don't kill me!'

I don't know if anyone did kill him but I never saw him again. It would have seemed patronising to point out to him that ninety per cent of the people of Angola were illiterate.

The Only Angolan War Correspondent Henry Kissinger Trusts

As the countdown to Independence continued apace and four months before the great event, all the western consulates in Luanda with the exception of the Americans, upped stakes and flew off. At first, I found it hard to believe. The situation was tough, it's true, but not desperate and I wondered about the reports they sent back to their anxious governments which had precipitated the action. From the British came the announcement that all UK passport holders wishing to depart must report to the Consulate-General and fly out with its staff. The plane was a VC-10 and having urgently advised everyone to exit, they were then told they would have to pay their own air fares for the privilege of flying on a government RAF plane which was travelling home anyway. It was the first time I did not feel proud of my country of birth for the twin reasons of pulling out so soon and then, having precipitated the departure of others, and charging them to leave. I learned afterwards that the French had complied with the British insistence that all governments should charge their nationals but with delightful Gallic dactylology to the rest, refunded the fares on their arrival in Paris!

The fleeing of the consulates boosted the Americans in my esteem and I don't believe it was just because I was representing Associated Press that we got on well. I had the greatest respect for Tom Kilhoran whose residence was some distance from the US consulate and between the two were barracks now occupied by the MPLA. Each night and each morning, the Consul-General's car made its way through the Marxist-controlled barracks, flying Old Glory pennants proudly. There was no one to defend him if he was attacked, and he knew he was a prime target for the MPLA's Fapla troops. The Americans really had every reason to be proud of their government's representatives in Angola.

Throughout my stay I watched the country change beyond recognition. Most of the once-smart Portuguese troops had become a rag-tail remnant of an estimated force in Africa of 150,000. Totally demoralised and subverted from within, they now moved about unshaven and with torn uniforms and made it clear that as national servicemen, all they wanted to do was go home. Only troops of the crack regiments stood tall. Most Portuguese civilians retained their sense of dignity but others cracked and noise became paramount as youngsters drove their motorcycles at speed with exhaust pipes deliberately removed or punctured. Their driving looked and sounded like a dirt track and then the car drivers caught the fever. I hired a green Volkswagen and soon found myself being edged off the road but after a couple of days of this, I adopted the London circa 1666 mentality and decided to fight fire with fire. Sometimes I drove as badly as they did, sometimes worse, but it was a way of staying alive. Word got around about the Volkswagen and I soon found cars swerving respectfully away from it as I traversed Luanda. A frequent passenger was Stan Maher, a two-Dan Karate expert, who was good to have around for reasons other than being a friend. Stan had a dry sense of humour and between us we named various statues; one was of the Portuguese poet, Camoes, who appeared to be winking. His face could also be seen on the country's bank notes and I dubbed him 'Mr Googoo'. Photographer Don Stephan, who was covering the scene for *Time* magazine, had explained that Googoo, was the name given to Mickey Mouse money. There was no shortage of that, it was openly sold in the market square. Another description was outside the Mercedes showroom which had the statue of a lorry driver holding a steering wheel in his hand. Noting all the crashes, Stan dubbed him 'Luanda's first driver'.

The suicide driving had begun in earnest in June, and if it was bad then, by August it was appalling, with people racing as if there was no tomorrow. For some this was tragically true as cars mounted pavements and crashed into walls. One wrapped itself around a tree in an embrace with the front and rear nearly touching. In another incident, a lorry careered down a main thorough-fare, crossed over a road island and knocked down a row of tall street lamps which took on the image of vandalized daffodils. The lorry then disappeared down the fifty-foot excavation site of a proposed new Sheraton hotel but if the driver had planned to become the fateful first on that death plunge, his last thoughts must have been those of disillusion: another car driver had beaten him to it and had plummeted into this new grave just two days before! The madness of the hellfire race of death continued apace. One wingless car found flight from the top of a high viaduct only to become a mangled wreck on the highway below, miraculously just missing flowing traffic. In another spectacu-lar incident, witnessed by American Consul officials driving past, a car mounted a pavement, leapt twenty feet into the air and disappeared through an advertisement hoarding.

Because of the tensions built up in the black township areas, few people driving near them stopped their vehicles to help anyone in trouble. I saw this happen only once, when a toddler was run over. The Portuguese driver jumped out of his car, grabbed the probably-dead black youngster by the arm and threw him into the back seat before he quickly drove off. If the child was still alive, I doubt if he is now. The driver knew that to leave him lying there would probably start a riot and even if he was compassionately whisked away to hospital, there was no room available for treatment as too many people slashed or shot during attacks in the museques had kept its bloodstained floors overflowing with the maimed and mangled.

A couple of days after the child incident, I drove towards the airport on the main road beside a township. Silhouetted fifty feet in the air ahead of me was the outline of a man, his arms outstretched and his head hanging Christ-like but without the wooden cross after a fast-moving car had catapulted him upwards. For a few moments he was just suspended: I don't know where he came down but it wasn't on the road and even if he had done so, no one would dare stop to help.

Murder was even rife at sea with bloated bodies washed up almost daily and it was difficult to tell if they were black or white. One leg that I could see from the road fascinated me; it was attached to a body that I never saw as the torso was hidden behind a group of boulders on the beach. As I drove past I could see the leg pointing skyward and I was told that it had belonged to a black man who had been bleached white by sun and water. Some Portuguese actually queued to view the body with macabre fascination; many would soon see enough bodies to have a gut-full.

Wilf Nussey, who had replaced my Congo-War chum, John Spicer, as editor of South Africa's Argus News Service, was with me in the Volkswagen when I found a skull lying beside the road. I picked it up and as it was still smelling I put it on to a boulder beside the country lane where it could be seen. Perhaps, I thought vainly, someone with a shovel might come along and give it a proper burial but wistfully decided it would possibly become a football. Wilf took a photo of me holding the skull but he wouldn't touch it. The Smithfield Market rocket was a long time ago and I'd changed mentally beyond recognition.

It was while I was writing up some notes in the hotel lounge that I was approached by a well-dressed and well-spoken Englishman who gave his name as Tony Bevan Lean. 'I had a large business here and now it is all gone,' he said morosely. It seems that amongst his many enterprises he had been the first man to export bananas from Angola and wore a pair of cuff-links, shaped like bananas, to prove it, a present from the Angolan Minister of Commerce. 'I am totally fluent in Portuguese and wondered if you would like an interpreter?' he asked. 'I'd particularly like to go up to the front with you.' I drove up to the front regularly and always by myself and sometimes I'd feel very lonely and vulnerable as I entered the approach road to Caxito where there was heavy fighting between the MPLA and FNLA. Using my usual 'beads-and-salt for the natives' approach, I would bribe the MPLA roadblocks with cigarettes and they would happily let me pass. My Portuguese was not good and so I welcomed the stranger and wondered what he would be like in the battle area. Tony and I became friends and only over the years have I unearthed that he is a former Lieutenant in the Royal Marines and a member of the SBS (Special Boat Squadron), the group that was later to do so well in the Falklands War. He mentioned once that during his RM training, he was on Britain's last battleship, HMS *Vanguard*, when the captain told him as an initiative test, 'This may seem unbelievable, Lean, but the engines are about to break down. I want you to get the ship going again.' He got the battleship moving at two and a half knots by using the quarter deck awning!

A subsequent check with the Royal Marines told me he was also the recipient, in 1957, of the Ralph Garrett Memorial Award, which had only been established the year before, and was to be awarded for the bravest act by a subaltern in peacetime in a year; in wartime it would have been recognised as a gallantry medal. A naval Sea Hawk was forced to land in La Spezia Harbour and Tony, who happened to be there, first checked that the pilot was safe and then persuaded the Italian authorities to locate and recover the plane. In a race against time to prevent sea damage, Tony spent long hours in the water using an oxygen set which had a maximum depth of twenty-five feet; he was working at forty-five feet! After only thirty-four and a half hours from the sinking, the plane was back on board HMS *Eagle*. The award spoke of his initiative, endeavour and daring.

Something else he mentioned in passing, helps to unravel further the secret of a sea mystery which involved 007-type espionage and murder – the finding of the headless and handless body of a British diving hero, Commander Lionel 'Buster' Crabb, in Chichester Harbour on 10 June 1957, over a year after he had disappeared. There had been much speculation over his death, and it was said that he was spying on the Russian cruiser, *Ordzhonikidze* at the time, and that he was not alone. Tony admitted to me that he too had been diving beneath the *Ordzhonikidze* which had brought Kruschev and Brezhnev on a goodwill visit to Britain. As he put it, 'I was "buddy" diving,' which suggests he was giving Crabb a friendly hand. They were diving together the day Crabb disappeared. Tony has always been reticent to discuss the matter and even today government papers on the case are locked away for 100 years and all requests by various people for a glimpse at them have been rejected. My friend has denied that he was working officially for the British government but despite this, he was a serving Royal Marines officer. 'I am quite sure Buster was detected and murdered by Russian frogmen although I don't know if they were using a detection device,' said Tony. 'The Russians chopped him up, possibly as a warning to others, and dumped his body off the Isle of Wight.' If this was a warning, it doesn't explain why they should remove the recognisable parts of his body, the head and hands. According to Tony, the hands were easily identifiable, being web, or club fingers. I haven't personally ever read any reference to Crabb's hands being chopped off. Syd Knowles, Crabb's often diving partner, has subsequently claimed Crabb was a Russian spy; I wouldn't know about that but the claim makes no sense unless Crabb was a double agent.

Explaining the scene on the night of Crabb's dramatic disappearance, Tony said the Vanguard was for'ard of the *Ordzhonikidze* in Portsmouth. 'Buster, myself and a Mike Cook had drinks in the Queen's Head and then repaired to the Vanguard, where we had a few more glasses in the wardroom,' he said. 'Buster had drinks with us in the wardroom the night before but this time decided to have another dive. He went into the water after midnight and that was the last we saw of him.' Tony Lean explained that both he and Crabb were working on recognition of the hulls, whereby one can tell by the way the water is distributed what type of ship it is; and also, by checking the hull, it is possible to note the speed a ship is capable of. 'Between the two of us, we had done several recces beneath the *Ordzhonikidze*,' he added. There was a cynical twist to the events of that night. 'We didn't know if Buster was dead or alive but next day all the officers of the *Ordzhonikidze* came aboard the Vanguard for drinks,' said Tony. 'They knew!'

Such was the man who asked to be my interpreter; but I didn't know his background then and it took some years to wheedle it out of him. And to think I wondered if he scared easily! He told me he did scare once; when he broke into a sunken U-boat and the upright skeletal remains of dead men came towards him. He got out fast!

Also sitting in the lounge of the hotel that memorable afternoon was Don Karl Steffan, the tall, lean, American photographer who knew about 'Googoo' money. 'Gin-con-gin' was his favourite tipple – gin with gin. These double gins, which he consumed neat and frequently, came up to three quarters of a large tumbler but I never saw him drunk. Whenever I subsequently sat down with Don in the hotel lounge or in the restaurant, it was fascinating to watch girls looking across at him. I knew that he was good-looking, but the attention he was getting would have equalled that of any Hollywood star. Then I caught on: photographers are amongst the randiest people I have ever met and I guess he was equal to the best. I noticed that he always placed his camera on the table or bar in front of him, with the zoom lens pointing upward. Very slowly his right hand would ease the long lens slowly up and down. The girls quickly got the message.

'Do you mind if I come along too?' he asked.

'Why not?' He was not competition and I was also a correspondent for *Time*, after all.

Next morning we drove up the Caxito Road, heavily armed with cigarettes. There was a group of sentries but I was recognised and automatically my hands went for the smokes as we stopped. Thirty miles up the road we passed a battlefield on the left; not an historical one – the fighting was still taking place! As I stopped we were surrounded by a large group of MPLA soldiers. This was the first time it had happened and I was surprised. Just as well Tony had come along to interpret, I thought. A young MPLA commander asked what we were about and I explained that we were covering a war. 'But there is a battle going on, you can't come here today,' he said, not appreciating what war correspondents were supposed to do. 'Can we come tomorrow?' I asked as a shell struck a tree branch thirty yards away leaving behind a smouldering stump which had been instantly cauterized. He paused and then, responding to a broad smile, agreed.

I went back next day toward the area where we had been stopped. Again we found ourselves surrounded and it was a tense moment until the young commander came forward. 'Drive off the tar road and on to this dirt track,' he ordered, grimly. I was apprehensive and wondered if we were about to be shot and asked, 'Have you checked that the dirt isn't mined?'

'No,' he replied. 'But the tar is!' He pointed to some soft tarmac just five yards from my front wheels, 'Come with me!' With that command we left the soldiers behind and walked across the open veld, just the four of us. Ahead were soldiers and I noticed Don and Tony look at each other and while I had assumed that the commander knew what he was doing, I wasn't too sure. Nor were they and uncertainty mounted with every step until Don could contain himself no longer: 'Christ, he's taking us across no-man's land,' he muttered uneasily. Turning to the commander and pointing to the soldiers, now less than a hundred yards away, I asked, 'Whose troops are they over there?'

'Ours,' came the confident reply. Memories of Priya Ramrakha flashed through my mind and I slowed our pace. 'Tell me, commander, how long have you been in the army?' I continued, casually. 'A year.' We all stopped and looked at each other. 'Hell's teeth!' whistled Tony and he was absolutely right; that is exactly what we were walking into. Those soldiers in front were not wearing MPLA gear, they were the *opposition* FNLA! Not only were we within shooting distance, more than likely we were in the middle of a minefield! 'That's far enough,' I ordered as Don took the commander firmly by the shoulders, turned him round and led him back to safety.

I took Tony and an Afrikaner journalist up the road, a giant of a man named Dionne du Plessis, and when we saw some MPLA soldiers in the bush we strolled over to them. As we approached, we all sensed that we were heading into trouble but it was too late to turn back even if we had wanted to. Men were secretly setting up the latest Russian-made weaponry and they looked at us curiously – we had stumbled into a forward command post! The commander came out of his tent and glared angrily and demanded to know who we were and what we were doing in this sensitive area. He was a middle-aged man with a voice like a rasp on the same steel that had moulded the ball-bearings he used for eyes. He gave the uncomfortable impression of being a gnarled and experienced warlord who would shoot first and then ask who he'd killed. It was a very dangerous situation and I explained, through Tony, that we were journalists and added, with beaming innocence, 'We have just come along to see you winning the war!' The commander was slightly taken aback at my outstretched hand which he took before demanding to see our passes. We produced our MPLA credentials supplied by the Information Department, knowing they were not exactly what he was asking for, and he growled, 'Your Fapla passes!' There was nothing for it but to feign surprise. 'Fapla passes?' I asked, knowing they were like gold dust. 'No one at the Information Department told us about them.' I asked him more about the passes, and when he hoped to capture the town of Caxito. He wasn't obliging but that was not important. It was vital to keep him in eye-to-eye contact so that he would not have time to consider getting through on the field telephone to Luanda for information about us. Dionne being a South African would have been enough to get us shot (I had already suspected he was associated with that country's military intelligence), and with me living in Rhodesia would not have helped, either.

Suddenly I held out my hand again and grinned, 'See you tomorrow – with the passes!' The commander had lost the initiative in this brief encounter and as Tony and Dionne also shook hands enthusiastically and with equally broad grins, we turned and walked towards the Volkswagen which was about fifty yards away. It was the longest walk we would ever make and we did not know if we would cover the distance. The commander and his men, we knew, were studying us and every seemingly casual step was a psychological countdown with tension tearing, screaming and wrenching at our nerves. We were walking with death and waited for bullets to tear open our backs. Each step was measured and I began to gesture with my hands and talk conversationally about the passes: to have quickened our pace would have given away our panic and the consequences would have been fatal. Framed ahead through low branches of trees was the Volkswagen, the green chariot that would carry us to safety. As we reached the car I turned and waved to the commander who was still staring, his men all carrying guns at the ready. He didn't wave back. I started the car and turned it slowly in the road before driving off gently and then accelerating, but it wasn't until we had gone several miles, and through the roadblock, that we began to relax. I'd been worried while still in the official no-go area that the commander might use the field telephone to have us shot or arrested. All three of us later admitted that we had felt the hair on the nape of our necks standing on end.

Beautiful Luanda has three ancient fortresses and a group of FNLA troops was holed up in one of them. They were led by a Portuguese mercenary. It was a popular sight to watch from the island as the MPLA fired mortars at the fort and missed time and again. Later, I inspected the damage and found that in one month they had hit it only five times! And modern-day mortar shells proved no match for the stone forts of yesteryear, making only pockmarks in the masonry.

As I was standing beside the beach on a brilliantly sunny afternoon, mortar bombs came across from the fort, landing in the sand about fifty yards away. One even hit a jetty and damaged it, the only accurate shot I had seen in the war, so accurate that I suspected they were aiming at the capital city itself. After about fifteen minutes, in which I was giving an account of the mortaring into my tape recorder, I decided to go back to the hotel and tell other journalists who might be interested. There were only two about; one American from the *New York Times* and the other British from the *Daily Telegraph*. I offered them a lift in my car and was asked to hold on a minute while they got organised. This seemed a little odd as the most that was needed was a notebook, pen and memory, the standard equipment of any journalist. I began to get irritated by their slowness and it took around twenty minutes to get them into my car. As I drove along the beach road in the direction of the fort and the Caxito Road, they became progressively jittery. 'Be careful going along here, Reg,' I was warned. 'This is ripe for an ambush.'

'What are you talking about?' I asked in astonishment. My routine had been to travel twenty-five miles beyond this point or even further. 'Look, Reg, I've had 'Nam experience,' said the American. 'We both know what it's like. You go slowly along here and keep an eye out for ambush.' This was at least six miles before we actually got near the Caxito road and several more miles from the cigarette-smoking guards. I pulled up near the shot-up jetty and commented that the shooting had stopped. As I was about to get out of the car, I was told, 'Hold it, Reg, turn the car round so that we are facing Luanda for a quick getaway.'

I couldn't believe it; we were still in Luanda! A couple of years later I was to read an article in the *New Statesman* by Chris Mullin. He gave an account of some war correspondents in Vietnam who summed up this pair: 'Correspondents who have spent any time in Saigon will recall that for many of their colleagues, reporting of the war consisted of a twice-daily trek down the 300 yards between the terrace of the Continental Palace Hotel and the military briefing centre. Here, one was in receipt of a perfectly typed English-language press handout, often describing the military situation in terms that were surreal. The intrepid correspondent then retraced his steps back past the Continental Palace Hotel to the Reuters Office where the handout would be transmitted whole, or in part, back to London or New York as the latest from Saigon. And that, together perhaps with some snippets of gossip from the diplomatic cocktail circuit disguised as "informed sources" was a day's war reporting.' I had not realised that the pair I was with were now only bar-and-facility correspondents, whatever they may or may not have done in the past, who were both good talkers with some influence but who would not go near the front line unless they were insulated by government troops.

Having acquired Fapla passes by mentioning the commander's name and his desire that we should be accredited (the man in charge was so impressed that he even presented me with an autographed book on the history of the MPLA he had written), there was another occasion on the same road a few days later when we were again in the lap of the gods. I was with Tony and Don Steffan and as I drove along the road we saw dejected Fapla troops coming in our direction and they appeared to be in a mean mood. 'I've never yet photographed an army in retreat,' Don commented agitatedly, explaining that troops do not like to be photographed when they are losing. I remembered the small, frightened boy on a train with a French-Canadian soldier who had returned from Dieppe and I knew what he meant. It was clear these soldiers had just lost a battle and we left the car to ask questions. While I was conversing with them through Tony, my interpreter, he said, quietly, 'Some others beside you said they want to kill us!' I turned to Don, 'No questions, just get into the car!' As we piled in, I gave my usual big smile, shook hands which seemed to take them by surprise and then gave a wave. Within seconds I spun the car round at speed as my foot hit the accelerator and we were off, still waving. Again we were waiting for bullets to rip into us. The soldiers, it seemed, liked the look of the Volkswagen so much that they had whispered amongst themselves, 'Let's shoot them and take the car.' In the car, Don turned to me, 'My God, you've got balls!' That meant a lot to me even though I'd never heard the term before.

There were two sequels: After one of my visits up the Caxito road I mentioned in passing to Tom Kilhoran where the fighting was taking place. He replied, 'That can't be right,' adding that the *New York Times* journalist had said it was elsewhere and pointed to a spot on a map on the far side of Caxito whereas my position showed it closer to the Angolan capital. I just shrugged my shoulders and left the subject. So far as I am concerned I've always tried to be 100 per cent accurate and if people don't accept what I say, it is up to them. But Don Steffan blew up, 'For Christ's sake, don't listen to that bullshitter,' he stormed, 'I've just come back from the front with Reg and he's telling you exactly where the war is!'

A few days later I called on Kilhoran and he had a meaningful look in his eye. 'I feel you would like to know that Henry Kissinger (then US Secretary of State) has sent a message to say he is relying solely on your AP reports!' I don't know what Kilhoran said to the other man but it would not have endeared him to me and he left with the *Daily Telegraph* staffer. Before the pair arrived in Luanda, AP had begun to send congratulatory messages when my stories started to appear on the front page of the American's newspaper and this was probably the reason for them coming. So far as I know, AP was never told of the behind-the-scenes drama or the Kissinger message and perhaps with hindsight, I should have mentioned it. While I hadn't been responsible for shaming the pair to the US government and have never mentioned the incident to anyone until this book, it certainly didn't endear me to them, either. Presumably, in order to protect themselves, I became the recipient of a very vicious character assassination. But even though I hadn't been responsible for exposing them, I have little time for such journalists: they cheat their own newspapers that put trust in them, they cheat the public, they cheat world leaders who rely on their reports and ultimately they morally corrupt themselves.

As the crunch time of independence approached, Mike Chapman flew out and I was sorry to see him go. I bought his news agency (being risky, payments were on a monthly basis) which contained all of the newspaper strings I had in Salisbury. This meant they would continue to have a correspondent in Angola and not be too miffed that I wasn't in Rhodesia. I retained my AP connection, but on a stringer basis which they were happy with as it saved them paying me a daily rate and expenses, including my penthouse suite at the Hotel Tropico (if you fear you are going to be killed, enjoy life beforehand and go out in style). One of the extra strings I had picked up was the *Daily Telegraph* to whom I filed daily. While researching for this book, I looked through library files of this newspaper and saw my stories – with his byline! It is quite remarkable how one can report on a war situation in Angola from Salisbury (Harare), Johannesburg and Cape Town, a couple or more thousand miles away.

A paradox to my way of life was that I'd be living dangerously in the afternoon and totally relax in the evening. With Tony and Don around there was usually something to do and some nightclubs had remained open while the Portuguese were still in the country and so by night we would dance with women; by day we would dance with death. The Angolans are a musical people and they insist that the Samba originated in Angola and not Brazil. It makes sense that the slaves took their rhythms with them. They are so musical that each political group had its own national anthem, each hoping they would come to power. The MPLA's tune was a haunting refrain which bore a strong resemblance to 'Delilah' and it was a challenge to come up with some lyrics. I started with: 'Bye, bye, bye, Angola. Why, why, why, Angola? You could see that Goo Goo was so good to me, forgive me, Angola, I just couldn't drink any more!' (That last line was by Tony.)

It was not a masterpiece but without my realising it, the lyrics had got around amongst the Portuguese. I'm seldom really surprised by anything but on entering a restaurant one evening I was astonished. As I walked in, all the Portuguese diners stood up, raised their glasses and sang, 'Bye, bye, bye, Angola!' It was a moment of great pathos and I looked around with dampened eyes; some of the people I knew, some I didn't. We were all aware that shortly none of them would be left in that lovely country, where most of them had been born. They would lose their homes, everything. But even they did not know just how bad their treatment would be when they arrived in Lisbon.

The snatch of another tune, sung briefly, was perhaps a little more amusing. Before Stan Maher had sensibly left the country, he and I visited the splendid white fortress overlooking the harbour (not the one containing the FNLA) and were taken to see the Portuguese colonel Officer Commanding. He personally took us round and then insisted we return to his office for a glass of sherry where we discussed the latest situation. He was very depressed and recharged our glasses and said, with a slight slur, 'Do you know this fortress is 500 years old?' Stan and I looked at each other and the temptation was too much. We raised our glasses, 'Happy birthday,' we chorused. The colonel's face lit up. 'Ah, you English. Yes, happy birthday to the fort.' We then sang happy birthday to his fortress in which he joined with enthusiasm and we left him a much happier man.

In similar light vein Tony Lean and I saw for sale an original 1931 Morris Minor. Open-topped, and complete with outside horn, the price was £100 which was exactly the cost when William Morris (Lord Nuffield) first produced it all those years before. We couldn't believe our luck and jointly became the proud owners with the original 1931 registration card. Miraculously, Tony produced for himself a Sherlock Holmes-type hat and we drove deliriously happy through the streets of Luanda in our new toy, which we named Pinocchio. We probably only went out in it three times as by now the political and war situation was bubbling to cauldron heat, and time for fun was fast running out. I was becoming uncomfortably aware that I could be the last western foreign journalist left and in the event I was the last British journalist to go. No one can be more stupid than that.

An interesting feature to the independence build up was that on previous Independence Days I'd attended, journalists would flood into the country about to be handed over the reins from colonial power. In Angola, they were flying out! Because I'd fallen in love with the country, I wanted to see it through independence, and beyond. It would be hazardous, I knew that, but it was my job and one I was good at. But by taking over the Chapman agency I had become particularly vulnerable in giving up AP as they would no longer be responsible for my welfare or my high-risk insurance. My main concern was that Luanda could become enmeshed in a pitched battle between the MPLA and the FNLA with no quarter given and nowhere to hide. Ideas flowed about methods of escape and I began to make plans for watching the possible battle from offshore. For some time, Tony and I had been admiring an old ketch in the harbour. The most I had handled earlier was the Enterprise sailboat on Lake McIlwaine and knew that I probably wouldn't be able to sail the ketch by myself. But Tony's background was different as he was an expert with sail. The ketch was smaller than HMS *Vanguard*, of course, but he liked the look of her and after a long search, we found the owners. 'We have only just bought it and we sail tomorrow,' we were told. The search for a funk hole continued. There was no point in considering driving south to Namibia, or north to Zaire. Luanda was surrounded by troops of the MPLA and they wouldn't let us get very far.

'I know someone who is selling a Bell's helicopter,' said Tony. That initially went down like a lead balloon.

'I don't like helicopters,' I said, 'and I can't fly one.'

'But I can,' he replied. Of course he could, there seemed to me little that he couldn't do. His training had included scuba diving, two-man submarines, driving a railway engine, parachuting, jumping from a plane into thick snow without a 'chute, swimming across a quicksand (on the Isle of Wight, no less) and heaven knows what else. I knew that his exploits had cost him one lung and two knees, both his knees having plastic plates beneath the skin. He also had back problems which had compelled him to leave the service.

'Will it get us down to Namibia?' I asked. I had visions of flying offshore to avoid being shot down. 'I doubt it, this is only a small job,' came the reply. 'But it should take us across the Congo River into Zaire.' We met the owner and he flew us around before handing over the controls to Tony, who proved adept. 'Would you like a go?' asked the owner. 'Not bloody likely,' I replied. My answer did not put the owner off: 'Let me show you how it works and I can also get you an official pilot's licence immediately, if that concerns you,' he said. I thought of the rigid examinations that pilots usually have to take but despite the offer there was no way I was going to handle the controls. 'No thanks,' I said. 'They terrify me.'

The asking price for the Bell's helicopter was just US$ 500. We were given time to decide whether we really wanted it but when we eventually agreed that Tony could be pilot and went back to the airport with the money, the owner was no longer contactable. His name had come up on a refugee flight and he was off to Portugal.

A few years later, I was having a drink with some *Observer* journalists in a Ludgate Circus tavern in London when one of them began to tell me of my remarkable purchases. To my surprise, I had become something of a legend amongst my colleagues, not so much for my reporting in Angola but because of the supposed transactions. According to Fleet Street gossip, I had bought an expensive motor launch with a high-powered radio transmitter (something that had gone through my mind for reporting on the possible Luanda battle, but I couldn't find one); a Mercedes car, a yacht, a private plane and a helicopter. All these things I had crated and sent out of the country. The worst fable had yet to come: I had supplied thousands of army boots to the FNLA! I wondered who put the stories around because they were basically as malicious as they were untrue. I could guess, of course. I had mentioned my escape plans to the two characters on the beach and even told them of a beautiful new Mercedes that had been left behind by its Portuguese owner in a public garage. To cover their betrayal of journalism it seems they felt the only way to cover their tracks was to demean me with their masterly piece of spin. To this day I wonder if they were responsible for the deadly trouble I found myself in; if so, it's unlikely that my death would have been on their combined conscience.

While helicopters came cheap, other items were at inflationary prices. Tony took me to a nightclub he knew well and we ordered a bottle of Scotch. It was a commodity which was running into short supply but he assured me we would be all right; he knew the proprietress. She came to us bearing an excellent Scotch in an earthenware bottle. I felt it was a little small for its age but it would have been gauche to make a comment. She had clearly dug into the depths of the cellar and I realised, knowing Tony, that she must have been a very good friend. There wasn't a floor show as performers were becoming difficult to obtain and so we just sat and chatted. We sank the bottle and asked for the bill. That bottle of Scotch came to US$ 112 and I reckoned that five of those could have bought me a helicopter and still left me with change.

One of Luanda's top night scenes during my first visit to the city was the Adeo. Now it was a disco with nothing to commend it. An article I wrote gave an insight into the decline of Luanda:

> Entering the Adeo is no problem. Walk past the fly-riddled garbage lying along the once proud Avenida Luis D Camoes; ignore the graffiti on the walls and windows all the way down the tree-less avenue, and you are there. Behind the bar is little José. Aged about thirteen years, the fair-haired Portuguese boy with the cheeky grin of a Cockney, is anxious to please and is always ready with a handshake. But this comes as a surprise: hands together, thumbs joined, and

then hands together again – pure African. But it's natural to José who was born in Angola.

The disco customers are jittery but the turned-up volume and toned down lighting don't make it apparent. A barman comes across, 'I'm flying to America on Saturday, do you have dollars? I'll give you a good rate.' It is the fourth request that day for everyone is leaving. One hundred thousand whites have already gone. Four hundred thousand want out before independence on 11 November, denuding Angola of technical skills necessary to keep even essential services going.

The airport tells the story. Families sleeping for nine days on marble floors. There are kids, including babes in arms, who feed from the bottle. Their mothers who usually breastfeed them are too embarrassed to do so in public and they don't want to take their children into the stinking toilets. The mothers will express their milk quietly behind the 'engaged' signs later. Who can spend nine long days and nights at an airport – two hours is enough – and hope to keep sane? It is even worse when you are never sure that a plane will arrive to take you out. A young couple lie back and he strums a guitar as she holds his arm. They pretend not to notice the queues of people with confirmed bookings in their hands fighting to get into the concourse to join them. But all the arm-twisting, the bribery and the string-pulling that has taken place in the past will have no effect upon the heavily armed Portuguese soldiers guarding the barriers.

They don't know at this stage that even Lisbon can no longer ignore them; that plans are taking shape to fly out the 500,000 in the three months remaining before the country is left to its own devices – devices that point to civil war. 'Cars are abandoned on pavements and in the middle of the streets. No one seems to care and there is no law to bring back order. The Liberation Movements have liberated many policemen of their guns under the threat of death; and no one wants to be the last man to die in Luanda.'

I mentioned that just up the road from the Adeo is a nearly completed apartment block filled with black refugees hoping to return to the Cape Verde islands.

No one seems to want them, and no transport has been laid on to take them away. 'If we reach our homes we can apply to live in the United States,' explained one. 'Now that Cape Verde is independent, there is an allowance of 20,000 people a year to live in America.' The piece went on to say that the Adeo was a good place to get away from it all, 'Because downstairs you cannot hear the shooting which takes place every night. Sometimes it is the troops firing at curfew breakers and sometimes it is the MPLA and FNLA having a shoot-out. And there is always firing coming from the sixteenth-century fortress of Sao Pedro dos Barra where a FNLA garrison has been besieged for several weeks. A popular Sunday afternoon attraction is to watch mortar and rocket fire being exchanged near the fortress between the FNLA defenders and the MPLA. None are particularly good shots and many shells land in the sea as a bonus for observers watching across the water from a safe distance.

The people in the Adeo are jittery because they don't know their future. Nearly all want to leave Angola – especially the whites – but know they will not be welcome in Portugal. Little José will probably be whisked off to another country where he will not be allowed to work behind a bar and where he will have to get used to the ordinary, old-fashioned handshake.

The finale of the besieged fortress episode came when the defenders agreed to leave, provided they were escorted back to the FNLA lines by Portuguese troops. We journalists and photographers turned up to see the event. I had always felt some sympathy for the defenders and at times had contemplated how I could cross the bay and interview their leader. It would have been impossible to enter by road as the MPLA would not allow a journalist to interview the 'general' they were attacking. And to go by sea would have meant attempting to climb a sheer cliff face – no good for my acrophobia. As we moved along the road towards the fortress, we could see black soldiers manning the ramparts. Their leader was a white mercenary who was out on the forecourt talking from a distance to the Portuguese troops who were lined up facing him. Photographers, using telephoto lenses, had captured the scene before we arrived. It was a pity that my camera didn't have a zoom lens.

I was more than disappointed with the mercenary. He was a nasty bastard, unshaven, unruly and unapproachable. As soon as he saw the photographers, he yelled, 'No photographs. We will shoot anyone taking photographs.' With all the Portuguese troops present, I thought that unlikely and decided to take a chance. Leaving the safety of the truck, I strolled nonchalantly into the forecourt with my camera held down by my side. Occasionally, without sighting, I filmed the mercenary and the troops lining the ramparts. It must have been one of the soldiers above that signalled to him. He spun round and pointed to me: 'You've been taking photographs!' I looked back, shrugged my shoulders and nonchalantly strolled towards my colleagues. As the mercenary hadn't actually seen me photographing, he was uncertain what to do. I too was uncertain. The Portuguese troops looked as though they could not give a damn if I was shot or not. The photographs were sent back to AP but I never told them of the drama, or inquired if they were used.

'Are you Reg Shay?' Dave Ottaway and I were lunching at the Tropico when my heart filled with dread as I looked up to see a man of mixed-race smartly dressed, with an Afro hairstyle. Everyone in the restaurant stared across and things didn't look good. I nodded, expecting the worst. The man had an American accent, which was not unusual as some of the MPLA had been educated in the United States. To my relief the man's face creased into a smile and that was most unusual. 'Well, hi there, Reggie, I'm Jim Giggams of ABC News. I've just come in!' His smile was infectious and he was anxious that I did some ABC broadcasts with him. He sat down and we filled him in on the current situation he declared, 'I want to get out of town and see some of the action. I want to go south and see Unita.'

Jim was something of a character. He had once objected to being hassled by the authorities at Rome Airport and as a protest, he stripped off all his clothes and ran through the airport stark naked. Now he was here in Luanda with that same air of bravado which brings sanity into a mad world. But I had to break the bad news to him gently. 'Jim, if you set foot outside of Luanda and into the hands of Unita, you're a dead man.' He was surprised but the smile was still there; I really liked him. 'Why is that buddy?' he asked. 'Because you are wearing the uniform of the MPLA,' I explained. Dave nodded in agreement. Jim did a good, competent job in Luanda, where there was plenty of news, anyway. So far as I know, he didn't venture beyond the capital city but it was an object lesson to the masters who send out their correspondents that they try to check in advance that their man will be all right. ABC News could be excused for this *faux pas* as it is the only time I've come across a situation where a man could find himself in a life-and-death situation for having the wrong hairstyle – possibly the first time since Samson.

Disturbing reports were coming in from Angola's second largest city, Nova Lisboa (now Huambo). The talk amongst the Portuguese was of thousands of refugees being shot as they tried to make their way to safety; of murder, rape and general mayhem. Nova Lisboa was to be the second springboard in the international plan to fly out the refugees. The problem facing those living in the outlying areas was how to leave their towns or farm areas in the first place. The second was how to get to Nova Lisboa alive. I boarded a Fokker Aero Commander with Dave Ottaway (I hope the *Washington Post* fully appreciated him), and American, freelance cameraman, Bill Mutchmann. As soon as we were on the plane I felt an inner trepidation which had nothing to do with Nova Lisboa and possible dangers there; the problem was far more immediate than that. Fokker put their wings above the fuselage which I find uncomfortable, always fearing that the wings will keep flying after the fuselage has come unstuck and dropped off. Looking straight down without the comfort of seeing a wing beside me has the same disquieting effect as a helicopter. What a wimp I am!

The scene at Nova Lisboa Airport was similar to that in Luanda, with hundreds of people milling around hoping to get out. Before leaving Luanda I had received a telex from Robin Drew in Salisbury, who was now news editor of the *Rhodesia Herald*. It was Robin who had resigned from the Southern Rhodesia Broadcasting Corporation at the same time as me and the message was personal: Would you please keep an eye open for a blue nun? The way the message came over was a little cryptic and I wasn't to know immediately if I was to look for a nun wearing a blue habit, or seek out a German hock! Then the rest of the message arrived: 'She has vanished in the Nova Lisboa area and everyone at the convent is terribly worried about her safety.' Look for a nun in the midst of thousands of people in a panic? There would be only one place she would eventually head for, I reasoned – the airport. During my stay in Nova Lisboa, which was another beautiful city and this time perched on a plateau with magnificent views, I made a couple of trips to the airport to look out for the nun. At the second attempt there, amongst hundreds of desperate people, including several nuns in black, was one dressed in blue. I went across, pushing my way through the throng and asked if she was Sister Theresa. 'Yes, I am.' She seemed quite taken aback, probably because I spoke English. This was very good news indeed as I wonder how many Sister Theresas there were in the world. 'From Salisbury?'

'Yes, I'm flying out today.'

A quick telex through to Robin with a story of her safety – there always has to be a story – and I'd almost forgotten about her. Later, Robin came through with a message of thanks, with a postscript, 'The nuns at the convent are now praying for your safety!' My safety? It was a thoughtful gesture and I was very touched. I would never have believed the time would come when anyone would pray for me, let alone a whole convent of nuns. They weren't to know that I'd given up Roman Catholicism at the age of one and a half years when my father died; or perhaps that didn't matter.

Despite the horrendous situation, there had been a large international trade fair taking place in Nova Lisboa which closed the day before I arrived. As it didn't appear that too many foreign companies from abroad were showing enthusiasm to come to the fair, it was decided to convert the grounds into a refugee centre. The three of us went along to the showground that evening, knowing that a column of 6,000 people was expected sometime during the night. It was bitterly cold. Someone once told me that Africa is a cold continent with a warm sun; someone was dead right. A trickle of refugees had already arrived when Dave, Bill and I turned up, and were seen by a young doctor, aged about twenty-four years, whose dark hair touched his shoulders. Unlike the hard-bitten trio of journalists confronting him, he wasn't used to war until a few weeks ago. His eyes were wild, for he had escaped from one of the outlying towns. 'I came here to get away from blood, blood, blood, always blood,' he said. 'I came here last week for a rest because I was dealing with twenty cases in twenty minutes and I couldn't take any more.' He paused and looked around. 'I'm only going to do first-aid work now. I've already sent three people to hospital with machine-gun wounds.' David asked if the hospital was adequate. 'No, it's too small to take many, and most of the doctors have left anyway.' As there were already 12,000 refugees in Nova Lisboa, I didn't think much of the chances of the 6,000 due to arrive to get medical treatment. And if the young doctor thought he would get away with just first-aid work, he was the only one who believed it.

David and Bill decided to kip down for a while until the main refugee contingent arrived. I tried to sleep but the plastic United Nations 'space blankets' provided were quite useless. They were ridiculously small; mine came from the shoulder to just below the knees so they would not even cover a seriously dwarfed Pygmy and I wondered what backhander had been used to persuade the United Nations to accept them without checking the size. Restless and cold, I decided to interview the local Florence Nightingale who was head of the local Red Cross. Usually I am cautious of overbearing women who head committees but I admired this lady tremendously. Exhausted from looking after the 12,000 refugees already in the city, Mrs Manuala Abranches carried on throughout the night without sleep, with only coffee, cigarettes, a strong will and a kind heart to keep her going. 'I have only 600 woollen blankets for 6,000 people,' she said. 'There was a warehouse fire last week which destroyed much of the food and blankets. We haven't food now for all these people and no way of making meals for them. And there is a health problem, too; we have only eleven latrines.' As we spoke, an old man came in on a stretcher and he was unconscious. Having reached safety, he would be cheated by the severe heart attack from which he was suffering.

'You look frozen. Would you like some whisky?' A man had come in from outside and seen me look longingly at the soup bowl from which Portuguese soldiers poured boiling broth for refugees. I had refused to ask for some on principle but now I was being offered whisky, which was quite another matter. This would not be depriving refugees. When I nodded affirmatively I expected the man to produce a silver hip flask from his pocket but instead he said, 'Follow me.'

We went outside and walked about forty yards within the showground, our breath vaporising into crystals in the night air until to my utter disbelief, we came to a disco nightclub still operating. Multi-coloured lights swirled around reflected from a silver ball which hung from the ceiling while pop music played but there were no dancers; it was reminiscent of a haunted ballroom. Nothing that has ever happened to me could have been more bizarre and I felt I was in a scene from a ghostly play. Suitably fortified with my favourite tipple from the free bar, I went back and found David and Bill were awake. 'You're not going to believe this,' I said, 'but there is a swinging disco next door and they're serving free whisky.'

'Horseshit,' said Mutchmann.

'Would I lie?'

They followed me out and the crusty Bill Mutchmann reluctantly gave out one of his rare compliments, 'Trust Shay to find it!'

As the refugees came in, the Red Cross workers struggled to look after them. The three of us broke our traditional journalistic neutrality and helped. Mutchmann, who always gave the impression that he had never helped anyone in his whole life, looked slightly embarrassed and muttered under his breath as he carried a bale of blankets probably feeling that he had to do something in repayment for the whisky.

Only a few of the many tales of horror and the bitterness that I learned first hand will be recorded here. There was the priest who told me he had seen sixteen whites thrown alive to the crocodiles; of the butchering of white families by the MPLA while the Portuguese soldiers looked on. Of the blacks who asked the MPLA for permission to cross a bridge, and were then mown down halfway across. Of Malanje, which once had 25,000 whites and was now an empty ghost town where, according to another priest, the water was poisoned by rotting bodies. Only 672 of the 6,000 refugees had managed to battle their way through that night; the others were still trying. A total of 150,000 were expected by the following month.

The next night David and I spent at a monastery and while there I wandered into an office and resting on a desk, glinting under the light of an electric bulb was a large metal crucifix. I picked it up, fascinated; it was the first time I had held such an object and in the silence of the room I just gazed at it as the owner must have done many times. First I noted the weight and realised how heavy it was to carry around the neck. I looked at the body on the cross but without feeling. It was an image in brass, not the real thing; the symbol of an atrocity many years ago not unlike what was happening outside these walls. What held my curiosity was the skull and crossbones at the base and I shivered. This was the symbol of pirates, the reputed cutthroat scum of the earth (I hadn't known at the time that they also happened to be quite democratic) and wondered what it was doing there before remembering that it was also an emblem of mortality. I then thought of Robin Drew and the nuns who were praying for my safety, and shyly kissed the area between the dead feet and mortality. It may have been a psychological reaction with a mental grasp at an indefinable safety net, rather like the lucky mascot that some people carry to survive in war. The knowledge that outside the monastery true Christians, including priests, were being horribly butchered, confirmed to me that life is a lottery. And yet, inwardly, despite being circumspect of religious organisations and a disapproval of icons, I felt that it was an important act – that someone really was watching over me. I didn't know what lay ahead; that within the next few weeks I would survive near-certain death too many times to be a normal coincidence. After interviewing Jonas Savimbi's army commander, I flew back to Luanda.

At three o'clock one morning at the Hotel Tropico I was awakened by a gentle tapping on the door and its very insistence warned me of danger. The tapping came again, quietly insidious and urgent. I reached for the telephone to call a colleague in another room. That was the first rule of the game – always let someone know when you are in trouble. If you disappear and no one asks about you, there is less chance of survival. An African answered the switchboard and I whispered a room number but the line went dead and I put down the phone. That tapping again. Someone outside would not take no for an answer. Yet, I reasoned with a professional instinct for self-preservation, it is better to stay in my room with the door locked, than open it. I tried the telephone again and the same thing happened; a voice, a click and nothing. The knocking persisted for five minutes before it stopped. There was no sound of anyone moving away.

After a short while, I slipped from my bed, carefully opened the door and looked outside, expecting to see someone standing guard. No one. Along the corridor was a light from an open bedroom door which I knew to be that of a journalist and I raced forward and into his room before pulling up short. With him were armed troops of the MPLA. This came as a relief for it meant that I was not being singled out to be taken away. I went back to my room and sat on the bed, with the door left open. Hurried footsteps came long the corridor and seven men burst in with AK-47s ready to shoot. The leader, a Coloured man with an Afro hairstyle, held a pistol pointed at my forehead and I smiled at him: 'I'm so pleased it's you, I thought it might be bandits.' He didn't return the smile and I showed all my passes, including the one from Fapla, which I had managed to acquire for going to the front. That did the trick, and they went away. Other journalists were not so fortunate and they were held for questioning, such was the knife's edge on which we lived. While the Nazi Gestapo would hammer on the door in their Teutonic fascist way, I believe the communist 'tap' was possibly more sinister because you didn't know what was outside.

An example of what could happen occurred to Luis Rodrigues. A part-time officer in the Portuguese army and BBC stringer, Luis was married to a very attractive and well-educated African lady. I was invited to their home several times for dinner and one day Luis came to ask if I would see him off at the airport. 'I've got to get out fast,' he said. 'and I'd like you to make sure that we get away.' It seemed odd that he did not call on some of his army friends to see him flee the country and I can only assume that the military was so infiltrated that he didn't trust anyone amongst them. What happened to him the day before was disconcerting.

Luis had been grabbed by some Fapla soldiers who beat him unconscious before throwing him into a car where he was driven to some woods outside Luanda to be executed. But when he came to, he protested vehemently and named names within the MPLA movement whom he knew as a journalist. One of his captors said, 'I think we have a big fish here,' and he was bundled back into the car and driven to Luanda and taken into a building. He was ordered to go through a door into an adjacent room where he was attacked by a huge African in Fapla uniform. Luis retaliated by kicking the man in the testicles and he fell to the ground in agony. 'I'm not sure what happened after that but I think another must have come in behind me as I was hit on the head and knocked unconscious again,' Luis told me. When he awoke, he demanded to be allowed to use the telephone to speak to an MPLA minister in the so-called transitional government. Luis' life hung on that call. Fortunately for him, the minister was available and immediately ordered his release. But the sympathies of both Luis and his wife were with Savimbi's Unita movement and he knew this was only a stay of execution. As I took him to the airport he gave me the keys to his apartment. 'I have a lot of books there in English which you can take,' he said.

This was the second time Luis had been in danger; the first time was with me when we were nearly killed in what would have been considered an 'own goal'. A couple of weeks before, we had been driving at night through Luanda after Luis had tipped me off about a shooting incident involving the Portuguese army. We drove along a main road, ignoring the curfew, and came to a Portuguese road block. Luis was recognised immediately and even picked up a couple of salutes. We were told by an officer that a car had been shot up after it tried to go through the road block without stopping. The wounded were just being taken away. 'I'd like to take a look?' said Luis. 'Of course,' replied the officer. 'The car is just fifty metres along the road.'

I drove to the shot-up vehicle and as we got out of the car, pandemonium broke loose. Materialising from storm drains on each side of the road were scores of agitated Portuguese soldiers and they were in a state of high tension. Everyone was shouting and pointing towards us and one was particularly animated, waving his rifle and then pointing it at me. Then he pointed with his trigger finger to a small object on the automatic rifle itself. As he was gabbling too fast for me to understand I asked a grim-looking Luis to interpret. 'He says, "I tried to shoot you, I tried to kill you but my safety catch was on,"' replied Luis icily. I would have taken the first shots as my seat in the car was closest to the soldier but as we were both still alive and unharmed, I couldn't think why Luis should be so serious. Personally, I felt more or less as amused as at the time when Tony Down and I had been attacked by the crocodile. 'Come on,' I said, 'that's worth a Scotch.' As we drove off the conscript Portuguese troops were still chattering animatedly. What a shower of an army, I decided.

It is probable that Luis' broadcasts on the BBC World Service were closely monitored by the MPLA and it's likely they contained some political bias. What became frighteningly clear to me after he had left was how closely watched he had been. Armed with keys to the flat, I called to collect his English language books for Margery. They were mainly detective novels which she would enjoy. At the apartment block, I went up in the lift, opened the door and saw that everything was neat and tidy just as though Luis was still living there and would come home in the evening. The Venetian blinds were shut and as I opened them slightly to let in some light, they made a clicking sound. Peering cautiously through the window, I noticed a heavily-built African woman walking across the courtyard with her back to me. She stopped and slowly turned and looked up at the window. I stood back so as not to be seen but she just stood and stared looking for some motion before hurrying off.

Luis was clearly a prolific reader in English for there were scores of books and I collected one armful and took them to the car. Then I went back for more. The second time down, a boy of about twelve years was standing by the car. He didn't say anything but just stood, as though on guard. My suspicions were roused and I was determined not to become paranoid and went back for some more. On my return a girl of about fifteen years was standing with the boy; neither of them saying anything. I decided that the next trip to Luis' flat would be the last. And so it was: standing by the vehicle now was a man who glared as I put books into the car. When I tried to get in he grabbed me and began shouting. I pushed him aside, got in and locked the door as he tried to reopen it; he then began hitting at the car with a bicycle rubber inner tube. As the tube slapped viciously against the side, I drove off at speed. I had no illusions that the MPLA Security had been telephoned and that I must get away before they arrived. I knew, too, that a full description of the car had been taken and that time was running out – fast!

It had been a very worried Mike Chapman and his wife whom I had also accompanied to the airport to see off as he, too, was concerned that he would be picked up. Only when they were inside the airport building did they consider themselves safe thanks to the large number of Portuguese troops controlling the refugee crowds. Taking over Mike's strings presented a particular problem as one of them was United Press International, embarrassingly, a rival to AP. I had always got on well with UPI who had been good to me in the past, and decided to send them routine stories. Their own staff man, a bureau chief from Johannesburg, had flown into Luanda before things really hotted up and told me that the atmosphere made him decidedly nervous: he was gone within three days. I believe that it was very wise of him to go if he was frightened and that was excusable even though he hadn't seen any of the action. But what he did subsequently was unforgivable. The MPLA, who had totally taken over Luanda by the time Mike and Luis left (the airport being the exception), were agitated at two reports put out by UPI. The first was that Luanda Airport had been bombed; the second was that Russian troops had arrived. Both stories were false and, unsurprisingly, the Director of Information, Luis d'Almeida, was anxious to know who the UPI correspondent was. As I had not written the offending pieces, nor even seen them, I felt it advisable to keep my mouth shut and let things cool down.

Shortly after my Nova Lisboa trip I arrived at Luanda Airport before dawn to meet Dave Ottaway who had stayed over. The evacuation to Portugal had just been completed and as I drove towards the airport entrance, my headlights picked up the body of a dead dog. This wasn't unusual for the insane driving that had taken place had killed many animals. Inside the concourse, the slogans remained daubed on the walls in red or black but otherwise there was nothing to show that only two days before there had been a mass of people queuing for their place on an aircraft to which they had been allotted. The Americans, Russians, British, French and others had all flown in to help rid Angola of the Portuguese colonialists they considered to be an unpalatable nuisance. The Russians would allow only one piece of hand luggage aboard their 'mercy' flights. Everyone tried to avoid the Russians.

I strolled on to the runway. There was no one about; no person in charge, no Customs and Immigration officials, no one in the tower. Before the half-light of dawn arrived, I'd become conscious, however, that I was not alone. I couldn't see anyone, but there was movement all around me. A strange, eerie sensation, being alone and yet not alone. What was it? No one touched me and yet I knew I was surrounded. With the first light the mystery was solved and before me was another tragedy. My companions could now be seen, dimly at first but enough to be identified: dogs! They were in all shapes and sizes, large, small, thin, and fat; German shepherd, poodle, Afghan, Corgi, Pekinese, thoroughbreds and Heinz 47. All were different and yet they shared three things in common: bewilderment, despair and hunger. The great humanity of the world which had plucked their owners away on a wing but with few prayers, found no room on the planes for their pets. The Portuguese owners had taken them to the airport, many clutched in their arms, in the desperate belief that some mercy would be shown. A forlorn hope. The world could see some mercy, and propaganda advantage, behind what was the greatest civilian air evacuation ever to take place. But for the 'settlers' to carry out their coddled pets would be too much; they must stay and fend for themselves. The dogs banded together desperately in packs after the world they knew had disappeared into the clouds above. They roamed the airport looking for scraps of food and in a few days they would be really desperate through hunger, and dangerous. Looking at them – there must have been forty to fifty in this pack and I saw another in the distance – I felt depressed at being alone with them and nothing to offer. Wherever I walked, they stayed with me.

The Fokker Aero Commander came in and I collected David. It was daylight now and as I drove away from the airport I counted another three dogs run over, possibly by the refugees themselves as they raced to the airport to catch their free flights to safety. It was then I knew that all the dogs would die. They would either be run over by the new car owners or, more likely be at the receiving end of a few AK-47s. After all, the gun-toting Africans were hungry too.

Two weeks before the last of the Portuguese had flown out, I was driving beside the bay one afternoon and saw some people staring out to sea. Curiosity got the better of me and I pulled over to see what was happening. One of the onlookers pointed to a shark close to the shore. Slightly further out to sea was a Portuguese man in a boat shouting instructions to his African assistant. The African was doing as he was told; he was swimming in the water trying to shoo the shark towards the boat where the man had a net. I drove off, wondering at the madness prevailing in Angola.

A Fight with Three Armed Bandits

I baulked at the idea of sitting in the office on such a bright Saturday morning but there was an important feature to be written with Independence only three days away. The office was ugly and depressing with three grubby rooms in open-plan style whose faded green walls needed a good scrub before being revitalised with a lick of paint. In my depressed mood, the office environment emphasised the physical and mental impoverishment that had overtaken Angola's capital city and the twin themes of my article were decay and lawlessness. I didn't have to look far to describe the former as the street outside my window was littered with rubbish. What I did not know was that lawlessness was about to confront me personally in the most dramatic way: armed bandits were stealthily creeping up the stairs.

My writing was interrupted by a gentle tapping on the door, which should have been a warning in itself as the hotel incident was still vivid in my mind. I walked across to the first office and opened the door to an African, 'I want to speak to Phineas,' he said. I'd seen this man two days before and on that occasion too, the messenger had been absent. 'Sorry, he doesn't work on Saturdays,' I replied and closed the door. As I walked towards the telex machine I felt, rather than heard, a movement behind me. The tingling on the nape of the neck crept up to the back of my head and I turned slowly to find myself yet again looking at the muzzle of a pistol. It was pointed directly between my eyes and behind the gunman stood two more Africans and I was relieved to see these two were unarmed. While I didn't like the odds as all of them were about twenty years of age, they were better than if all three had weapons. Realising this, I relaxed slightly and even though the adrenalin was running high I laughed to myself at the absurdity of the situation I was in. Looking down that little hole in a gun, it was difficult to comprehend that it was lethal; that it could eject a tiny missile which would have sent me straight out of this world. The man with the weapon motioned me to walk further into the office and as he did so he put his finger to his lips: it was his first mistake! The gesture made it clear that he was worried about making a noise, wrongly suspecting there were other people in the building. This gave me confidence and I guessed that I had a fifty-fifty chance of coming out alive. Uppermost in my thoughts was the imperative that the gangsters must not be permitted to tie my hands behind my back for I'd seen too many bodies of victims who had died helplessly with their hands bound. The thought of being knifed to avoid noise was less appealing than being shot.

From the action that followed it seemed they had worked out their strategy in advance and it was clear that the leader had been in the office before. I walked slowly, with my brain racing on the best method of attack and when I reached the telex machine, which was against the far wall of the third office. On arrival I turned to face them. The most heavily built man stood by the entrance door to stop any escape bid; the leader with the gun stood to my right and never once took his eyes or the gun off me, while the third gang member came straight towards me. I decided that he would be my first victim. As he got within arm's length, I grabbed him and threw him straight at the leader in the sure knowledge that if the heavy black pistol in his hands went off, I'd be left with only two men to fight and in the confused melee I might possibly grab the pistol as a bonus. The look of incredulity on the gunman's face as I attacked them was too much and I laughed outright with a sudden surge of confidence. For someone who will avoid a fight if at all possible because I loathe brawls, I was delighted to be thoroughly enjoying myself and their amazement turned to panic as they rushed towards the door, crashing into the third man who was standing open-mouthed. They scrambled out in confusion leaving the door open and as a precaution I picked up a heavy zebra-skin pouffe before moving forward to close it. Perhaps it had been a premonition for as I did so the leader came back and pointed the gun. This time he wasn't worried about the noise; he had been made a fool of and he needed to kill me to re-establish his authority.

Charging like a buffalo, I shouted and threw the pouffe in one movement but while it was a terrible shot and missed him totally, he'd had enough. With the pouffe and the mad Englishman coming towards him like a pair of heavies, he lost his nerve and ran. I slammed the door shut, moved quickly away in case he decided to put some bullets through it, and then laughed with exhilaration as I went to the telex machine. There was no point in calling the police; they didn't exist and I decided against going out on to the office balcony to see if they had run off down the street: I'd chanced my arm enough and there was no point in being hit by a lucky shot. I finished the feature and sent it off to the *Sunday Telegraph* and then ventured out of the office, down the dingy stairs and out into the sunlight. I wasn't sure if my would-be assassins were waiting to have another go but having established that no one was in sight, I quickly walked up the hill to my hotel. Every time I visited my office after that there was always apprehension as I ascended and descended the eerie stairs, especially in the dark.

My one regret over the incident was that John Monks of the *Daily Express* was not around to see the action. When I had first gone into the Congo War I'd been having a meal with John and Eric Robins when I noticed two mercenaries at another table were not wearing socks. I quietly commented on this and they overheard the conversation and immediately challenged me to a fight, which I refused. John, his pink face twitching with indignity, took up the challenge and had a lacklustre fight but I still refused to join in. I had no doubt that he thought I had a yellow streak but embarrassing though it was for me, there was no way I was going to be injured in a brawl when John Appleby was fretting over my safety, having allowed me to replace the seriously wounded Jim Biddulph. Now, in Angola, there had been no option but to fight and it was far more dangerous than satisfying the bloodlust of a couple of mindless mercenaries.

As the MPLA ruthlessly, illegally and with the help of foreign troops forced their rivals out of the capital city, I had my first glimpse of life under a new African Marxist state, even before the Portuguese army left. The relaxed drive to the 'island' was turning into a journey of extreme caution. A house near the entrance had been taken over and guards stood outside watching everyone pass. With the evening came the lowering of the MPLA flag and any misguided or uninformed person driving past at this time was shot. Everyone was warned that if Agostino Neto was chauffeured past, all cars must stop immediately. Factories were taken over by the 'Puevo' ('People') and workers' committees were set up to run them. The committee members were mostly illiterate and knew nothing of factory management and Tony Lean ventured to become an adviser to one committee in the hope that he would be able to stay on. The tractor company was Robert Hudson where he had been general manager before venturing into the export business on his own. Tony reasoned that he didn't have to agree with their ideology to try to stop the destruction of industry and the collapse of an economy which had taken so many years to create.

The most worrying aspect was the children who carried home-made guns. Youngsters of five years and upwards marched the streets in parades and to begin with onlookers smiled benevolently at their comical steps, even though there was concern at this early indoctrination. The guns comprised a piece of lead piping for a barrel, with equally makeshift stocks. A Portuguese army officer warned me they were not as innocent as they looked. 'One was killed yesterday when he fired it,' he said. 'There had been a live bullet up the spout and it exploded. According to the officer, the children were taught to aim their guns and fire in the event of an enemy attack, being put in the front line. 'If they kill themselves by accident it's too bad, if they kill an opponent it's a bonus. They are expendable,' he shrugged. The children were also taught to become informers on everyone, including their parents. Before Independence, every street had one house with an MPLA flag flying from it and in true Orwellian fashion, residents were told it was their duty to inform on their neighbours.

I was introduced by Tony Lean to Angola's top precious-jewel smuggler. It was well known in Luanda that he was a smuggler and he was respected because he was rich and seemingly generous. 'I'm leaving for Brazil and won't be back so you can take over my house and cars,' he said, waving his hand generously. Tony took advantage of the offer and it was good to get away from hotel life for a while. The house was large and well furnished but there was a problem with the cars as he inadvertently took the keys of the Mercedes to

Brazil and we had to settle for the lowly Fiat. Living opposite the smuggler was his closest friend who was leaving on the same plane. I'd hardly been introduced to the man opposite when he went indoors and came out into the street with a large plate full of cut emeralds and he insisted that I hold the plate. 'These are worth one million pounds,' he told me, glowingly, and I'm sure they were. Unlike the poor refugees who had suffered so much and were penniless, the pair flew out on a special Portuguese air force flight as guests of the army commander. The reason they received the VIP treatment was because the man with the emeralds happened to be the brother of the commander, who was also leaving Angola for the last time.

The number of western journalists left behind could be counted on one hand and I had the same sense of loneliness I always feel when the international media swarm in like bees, suck in the nectar of best stories and fly off leaving the scraps (and in this case the dangers) to whoever is left. Shortly before Independence, however, two reporters unexpectedly arrived out of the blue. I received an extraordinary telex message to say Roger Sargent and Chris van der Merwe of the Johannesburg *Sunday Times*, had arrived but were missing and could I find them? I was irritated that I hadn't been told that they were coming, knowing that their lives were being put at terrible risk. Inquiries revealed that they had flown in at night and booked in at the Tivoli Hotel, which was now almost empty. They had contacted their office to report their arrival and that was the last anyone heard of them. My suspicions, later confirmed, was that they heard a tapping on the door at night and were whisked away to the MPLA barracks and incarcerated. I made representations to Luis d'Almeida, the Director of Information, for their release and after some weeks they were allowed to go. I doubt if their departure had anything to do with my efforts but I was relieved they were safe.

A great loss to me personally was the withdrawal of the American consul-general, Tom Kilhoran, and his staff just eight days before Independence. The Americans had already advised everyone under their consular umbrella to leave Angola since their safety could not be assured. Kilhoran had asked Henry Kissinger for permission to stay but the answer was negative. A State Department spokesman in Washington said the move was a temporary withdrawal due to the 'uncertainty of the situation in Luanda.' Being British, I appreciated that understatement!

When the Portuguese officially pulled out of Luanda, I went to the Palace for the formal announcement of departure, made in a gilded ballroom, where the lowering of the flag also took place. It is customary in these circumstances to officially hand over the reins of power to the new leader but this was not to be. Instead, there was a brief announcement of their departure followed by the most realistic 'Beat the Retreat' I had ever seen as the High Commissioner, Admiral Leonel Cardosa, made it as fast as he could towards the docks without handing over to anyone the vast, rich country. They had expected to be fired upon at any moment but the MPLA let them go quietly and from the quayside

I watched Cardosa together with his aides and protective troops board the frigate. The warship moved off immediately the admiral was on board, leaving the MPLA to do exactly as they pleased in Luanda. As I was the major purveyor of news to the western world, it was inevitable that my days would be numbered too. The MPLA now controlled the airport, only TAP and eastern bloc planes were flying in and the Portuguese national airline cancelled all flights from Angola to southern Africa, which made me feel even more isolated and vulnerable and a very long way from home.

The 'Red Admiral' Cortina had assumed that with the aid of Cubans, the MPLA would easily take over the rest of the country. So far as he was concerned, it was a question of mopping up operations against the other two movements. The MPLA had control of the coastline and all the help they needed from the eastern bloc but Cortina was only partially correct, for he had reckoned without the tenacity of Jonas Savimbi. There has been much criticism of Savimbi that he accepted aid from South Africa without anyone explaining what else he could have done with all the odds, including the Cubans, against him. Should it be the case, even this cannot compare with the many atrocities committed by the MPLA. There was only mute criticism of the MPLA following a report in March 1993 that it had hired around 100 former South African troops as mercenaries to murder Savimbi. So much for ethics of both the MPLA and the continuous critics of the Unita leader who, at that time, unquestionably was hero to half the country's population in the south and who refused to accept the results of the elections.

I'd become chummy with a handful of communist journalists, including an Indian lady who worked for West German TV. As her name was almost unpronounceable, to most she was nicknamed Ndira and she was taken on a guided tour of the south of the country occupied by the MPLA and came back visibly shaken. An MPLA commander, anxious to please, had shot a prisoner in the head especially for her cameraman to film. A similar incident had happened some years earlier to Pulitzer Prize winning AP photographer, Eddie Adams, and cameraman, Vo Suu, when the South Vietnamese head of the national police, General Nguyen Ngoc Loan, deliberately shot dead a prisoner for the cameras. 'Come up to my room for a bite to eat and some vodka,' said Igor, a Russian journalist working for Tass. With him was a Pole whose name I didn't catch but now suspect it was Ryszard Kapuscinski, the well-known Polish journalist and author. Two things we had in common were our profession and sense of humour but another Russian, who stayed in the background of the hotel foyer when the invitation was made was very obviously KGB and I could see he didn't like the look of me at all. The feeling was mutual and he glowered at Igor when he overheard the invitation. I wondered what Ian Smith's Special Branch would have made of that, too!

One glance at Russian fare made me aware that eastern bloc journalists were not as highly paid as those in the west for the food was dried bread and bacon rind but at least there was vodka to drown it down. 'I've discovered a new drink,' declared Igor, triumphantly as he produced a bottle of Drambuie. He half-filled three very large tumblers with vodka and topped the other half with Drambuie. With that, he and the Pole downed the lot in one and carried on talking as though it was something they did every day. Their approach to alcohol was similar to that of a Russian journalist with an artificial leg I had met in Lusaka. Colleagues were quite convinced that the leg either contained a bottle of vodka or a radio transmitter and we asked him if he would like to look around the new cathedral, which was something of a Zambian showpiece. 'Does it have a bar?' he asked. We got the message...

A couple of days after lunching with Igor I saw him in the hotel foyer talking to a small group of MPLA and some people I had never seen before. They appeared to be Cubans but then Coloured MPLA members and Cubans are difficult to tell apart, which explains how they managed to assimilate so well. Igor was frowning and when he left the group I asked him what was wrong. 'There's a column of South African mercenaries coming up the road,' he said. 'The situation is very serious.' I had no way of knowing that the column was of South African troops and it was Mike Nicholson who broke the story for ITN when he got into the column without the South Africans realising it. Mike subsequently told me he regretted his action because Angola was lost to the West. I had been as concerned as Igor when he told me the column moving up from the south was a mercenary force as I was in a difficult position. What would be their reaction if they found me reporting from a communist-held city? And, alternatively, what would be the reaction of the MPLA towards a western journalist if they were losing the battle? I'd already experienced what it was like to be with their army when it was losing. At the same time as the South Africans were moving northwards, Holden Roberto's FNLA was moving south in an apparent twin attempt to take the city and I was beginning to feel like the contents of a sandwich just before the bite. The South Africans could have taken Luanda without many shots being fired had they realised the reservoir for Luanda was north of the capital, and the Cambambe Dam where the electricity was generated, was in the south. Cut off both and the city would be forced to capitulate. Neither happened.

11 November 1975 was a hot and sweaty day as Angola was now well into summer. In Rhodesia, it was a public holiday as Ian Smith looked forward to his annual Independence Ball where the 'Liberty Bell' would be struck ten times to denote the number of years of his rebellion.

Horst Faas and Ed Blanche, the London bureau chief of AP who had recently flown in, came into the office to say they would be going to the stadium to watch Angola's independence celebrations. I'd watched enough independence days, heard all the boastful promises for the future and seen the realities a few years later. I could imagine the drunkenness that would take place and there is nothing worse than drunken power-crazed men and women carrying guns, and I decided to leave the story to AP. As Tony Lean and I now lived in a quiet area, we decided to return home soon after dark and have a peaceful night but when I drove into our road there were guards who checked our passes, which was unusual. They hadn't been there earlier but they let us through without a problem. Happily, I'd had some large Rhodesian steaks in the refrigerator and we settled down to a meal which was sumptuous by any standards. Carrying a Courvoisier and smoking a large Cuban cigar, I went upstairs to the balcony to watch the celebrations at the stadium which we could see clearly in the distance. There was plenty of celebratory shooting and we saw the outline of an aircraft fly over the stadium as it came in to land. 'I hope they don't shoot it down,' said Tony. The sentiment had merit as the aircraft, which belonged to the International Red Cross, was found to have two bullet holes in the fuselage when it landed.

Then came shooting much nearer and we could clearly see flashes from guns. A battle had started right under our noses, directly below in the garden! Realising that we were silhouetted we gently eased ourselves indoors and switched off the lights before returning to the balcony to view the gunfight. Not that I actually saw anyone – a black skin is a perfect camouflage at night – just the flashes from the guns as they spat out their deadly missiles.

The question soon arose about our immediate future which was causing Tony a little concern. 'What should we do?' he asked. There seemed little point in shouting to the antagonists to be quiet as they might take offence and I knew that if they broke into the house, there was little we could do to stop them killing us. My thoughts flashed back to the Zambezi River, and another Tony, when we were surrounded by hippo on an island and faced instant death. 'We can't do anything about them,' Tony Down had said, 'so go back to sleep.' That was the answer! We went to our rooms, got into bed and slept while men down below remained hell bent on killing each other.

Next morning we went out on a recce. The wall of the house was shot up with lines of pock marks lacing it and the Mercedes in the lean-to garage was holed too, but there were no bodies. There had been a gunfight all right but who would have known except for the telltale bullet holes? Communists in Angola were taught to remove their dead so that their enemies could not take a body count.

A Dramatic Escape

It was Sunday, just one week after independence and I was sitting quietly in the dimly lit office writing on the telex an article on Angola's first week of 'freedom' with the enormous problems facing it. Throughout the day, though, I'd been pondering over the hurried wedding of my daughter, Annette, which had taken place the previous day. I should have been there to give her away but there were no direct flights to southern Africa and by the time I got to Salisbury via Lisbon or London and Johannesburg, it would have been too late. It's ironic, I thought, that I should be in the middle of a war while Annette's marriage had taken place to ensure that her husband, John, didn't get called up. He'd already served six months in jail as a Jehovah's Witness for refusing to accept his call-up papers; now he was due to go through the same humiliating process again. A few days ago I'd received an urgent telex from Annette and gave my consent to the wedding so that the loving couple could fly to the safety of South Africa to live. Importantly, I was now the only British journalist left to write the tragic story of Angola from a Luanda perspective but there were other good souls about: America was represented by Ed Blanche and Bill Mutchmann; German Horst Faas was with Ed, and Frenchman Jean Claude Pomonti of *Le Monde* was here too. The excellent, cool-headed Jean Claude had been keeping France well informed on the African scene for several years and was popular with all who knew him. New Zealander John Edlin had gone, leaving just five of us – three journalists, one photographer and a cameraman.

As I sat at the telex the telephone bell rang and reverberated throughout my uncarpeted offices like cymbals; I picked up the receiver. The voice at the other end was excited, 'This is d'Almeida. I want to see you immediately in your office.' My heart sank but I replied, 'Fine, Luis, come any time. What's it about?'

'I'll be there in a few minutes.' I was left holding the telephone, wondering what was so important that the powerful Director of Information (the BBC's perceptive John Simpson would later describe him as 'sinister') should call on me at eight o'clock on a Sunday evening. I knew it wasn't going to be a social call and my mind raced as I continued to punch out the feature on tape, ready for sending: it was a 'think piece' that would never be transmitted. I couldn't concentrate and kept asking myself: what does d'Almeida want? It had to be important... that's all I could think about. But why? My mind raced back to the stories I'd filed. I had been ultra careful not to upset the MPLA for silly reasons by not referring to them in my copy as Marxists because they objected to the term. In Rhodesia, I deliberately hadn't provoked Ian Smith's government by referring to the 'illegal regime'. Sensitive areas like that can be easily avoided and filled in at the other end if the policy of the newspaper dictates these terms should be used.

Luis and I had always got on reasonably well and only a month ago during lunch at the Club Nautico we had discussed Angola's MPLA party and its embodiment of Marxism. As the Portuguese wine waiter expertly warmed and poured generous dosages of Bisquit, Luis had smiled disarmingly and declared, 'We're not Marxist, how can I be a Marxist? I'm a Roman Catholic!' I had gazed out of the window at the passive warm Atlantic Ocean and thought of thousands of Cuban troops bristling with weapons who were disembarking along the coast; perhaps they too were mostly Roman Catholics. 'How would you describe yourselves?' I had asked. 'We are nationalists.' I'd mentally noted he did not say African nationalists for Luis, like so many of his colleagues, was of mixed race.

There was a soft tap tap on the door, and I braced myself. Outside stood d'Almeida with a tall young African, and I was relieved that they weren't accompanied by a bunch of gun-toting soldiers. Perhaps they are waiting downstairs in a truck, I thought, as his face confirmed to me that this wasn't a social call. I shook hands and the African was introduced as a member of Fapla military intelligence, which was ominous. 'Come and take a seat, Luis,' I invited, using my usual defence of a smile and affability but he ignored the gesture and came to the point, 'I've been told that you're working for United Press International. Is this true?'

So that was it: someone had viciously pointed the accusative finger at me. I could only think of three people who might do this: the pro-Marxist woman from the London *Financial Times* and the two miscreant 'hotel room' reporters. Whoever it was, this was an act of betrayal and totally unprofessional and, in my way of thinking, the person(s) responsible should have been drummed out of journalism. I'd thought the whole UPI episode had been dropped and forgotten; it certainly had been by me as I hadn't been concerned with it in any way: 'Well, yes and no, Luis.'

'What do you mean, yes and no?' Luis was certainly not the friendly man I'd known in the past, but I was determined to remain affable. 'I came to Angola for Associated Press and that is where my first allegiance is. When I took over Chapman's agency, UPI came with it, which was a bit embarrassing.'

'So you *are* UPI!'

I'd read about faces becoming contorted with rage but this was the first time I'd seen it first hand. I knew what was coming but knew I must stay cool; it was the only way I would stay out of trouble. 'It's quite simple, Luis. I file day-to-day stories to AP and only to UPI on request.' This wasn't strictly true now that Ed Blanche was in town but it might keep him away from the stories I knew he had in mind. Luis' finger jabbed at me accusingly and his brown eyes blazed with hatred as he screamed in uncontrollable rage, 'It was YOU who wrote those lies about Luanda Airport being bombed, and the lies about the Russians landing!' The intelligence man said nothing but twitched nastily and I began to wonder what to do if he came for me. Throwing him out of the window wouldn't help, even if I was able to, as there might well be others downstairs. It was a mad thought, but in hair-raising situations like this, one has to think of every alternative should the worse scenario come about. I replied, 'I did not write either of those stories and what is more, I don't know who did!' With feeling, I added, 'But I'd like to get my hands on him.'

'You're a liar! Both stories had Luanda datelines so it had to be you.'

I had never seen the reports; only heard of them. Presumably they had been published in Lisbon and elsewhere, that is how he knew of their existence. What he said about the datelines was damning but I resented being called a liar. 'And I tell you, I did not send those stories!' I was beginning to feel riled but knew that I must not lose my temper; I must play the innocent which, indeed, I was. 'Why don't you check back with the post office,' I said and our eyes met. He knew that I was referring to the monitoring that was taking place and turned to the intelligence man, 'Search the office!' Together they began to rummage through my waste bins – a futile gesture seeing that the story was at least six weeks old. They went through the filing cabinet and started reading every scrap of paper they could find. I'd never been through the files myself and kept my fingers crossed as I'd been tipped off that Chapman had actually done some intelligence work for Canada. Whether this was true or not I'd no idea; Angola had been full of rumours. We didn't speak for fifteen minutes as they poured over the files, not really knowing what they were looking for. Then the telex machine sprang to life, and on the other end was the *Star*, Johannesburg. This wasn't a good time for South Africa to come through and I cut it off.

D'Almeida began to question me again and once more the machine came to life and this time it was the Argus News Service from Johannesburg. I cut the machine off again and suspicion crept over d'Almeida's face, 'Why do you keep turning it off?'

'Because you are talking,' I replied.

'Leave it on next time!' he ordered. I shrugged; perhaps it wouldn't matter too much if South Africa came on. After all, he knew I lived in Rhodesia because I made a point of telling him so long ago. There had been no reason for letting someone else feed him that type of information. Now, I realised, I should have told him earlier that I was representing UPI.

My thoughts were that I might disappear that evening and be taken to the mosquito-infested barracks for a couple of weeks before being deported. It wouldn't be pleasant, I knew that, but writing a couple of false stories was not a hanging offence. That's the way I hoped they would look at it, anyhow. But I was reckoning without a twist of Fate; that in my office in Salisbury was a woman with a family history of alcoholism.

The telex came on again and I let it run before crossing over to see who it was. The call-back sign showed that it was my Rhodesian office but my blood ran cold. That stupid, stupid bitch! She had put the tape in the wrong way round and the whole message was coming across garbled. Luis d'Almeida strolled across and casually looked at the message; the effect on him was electric. He spluttered as he could hardly get the accusing words out. 'My God!' he yelled at last. 'That's code. You're a spy! You... you're a spy. You're a spy... I would never have believed it. You a spy!' I didn't know if the security man spoke English but he certainly knew the meaning of the word spy. He stood watching my every move excitedly while d'Almeida almost jumped up and down with frenzy, waving his arms about like the fanatic he had now become. Gone was any vestige of the mask of an urbane Director of Information; in its place was the face of a fanatical revolutionary who was after my blood. I tried to remain calm, to keep my voice controlled, 'Don't be crazy, Luis, that message is coming across garbled. I'll get a rerun.'

'No you won't – that's code and you're a spy!'

'That's *not* code and I am not a spy,' I answered in a very slow deliberate tone of voice. 'You've seen telex machines before and you know that they sometimes garble.'

'I know all about telex machines, everything.'

'Then you know that the message is garbled.'

'You are a spy.'

I wished he would change his course of thinking for the significance of the accusation was all too clear. I knew that unless I kept my cool, I would be taken away, tortured, 'tried' and convicted by a loaded People's Court, and then led to the nearby football field for execution. The thought flashed across my mind: did I miss Annette's wedding just to be shot as a spy? 'I'm going to get that message rerun,' I said.

'No you are not,' retorted d'Almeida, 'you'll do nothing of the sort.'

I ignored him, tapped the keys to stop the message coming through while d'Almeida tried physically to pull me back by pulling on my left shoulder. I sent, 'You're message is garbled; please rerun.' Frances at the other end clearly didn't like her work being interrupted and typed back, 'The message is not garbled!' Oh, you bloody fool. Sober up, woman! Then I tapped again: 'This is Reg Shay here and it is very very important that you resend that message correctly. Put the tape in the correct way round. Please do as you are told.'

There was a pause which seemed like an age. The reply came back, 'It's not garbled!' D'Almeida, convinced that he had caught a spy red-handed, ordered me to switch off the machine. I ignored him and retyped, 'This is very serious. Please send the message correctly.'

'Turn that machine off,' came the scream in my ears and d'Almeida tried to do it himself.

I turned on him and, knowing that I had nothing to lose, shouted back, 'What is the matter with you? Don't you want the truth?'

'I know the truth. You're a spy. You're a reactionary spy!'

He didn't say it with quiet menace; he was so angry that all reason had left him and he yelled the words like a demented maniac. 'Look Luis,' I said, 'why don't you just quieten down and let me prove my innocence?' I knew that I was arguing for my life. Instead of answering, he reached across and switched off the machine and I felt the hand of doom upon me, now I could see the firing squad comprised of a motley crew of Fapla soldiers who couldn't give a damn how many people they killed. Only a few weeks ago one of their own bloodthirsty army commanders, who had been rated a hero during the war, together with some of his comrades, had faced a firing squad on the football field for what was once a victor's bounty of rape and pillage. These were only minor charges to those levelled against me. To the MPLA, shooting an adopted Rhodesian would be a pleasure; shooting a reactionary, a duty; shooting a spy, mandatory. To d'Almeida I was all three! The vision moved in front of me with virtual reality; hands tied behind my back, eyes blindfolded, an order shouted in Portuguese and the 'Cheshire Cheese' would turn to Emmental as I crumbled into the dirt.

By comparison, facing the armed bandits in this same office only two weeks before had been something of a joke as I couldn't really take them seriously; when I was being mortared I hadn't been the slightest bit worried and didn't even bother to lie down in the sand alongside the Portuguese on the beach. I'd laughed when the soldier said he'd tried to shoot me, and regularly driving up to the front, usually alone, had been hairy all right but an accepted risk that goes with the job. A good drink of Scotch back at the hotel bar would soon remind me that perhaps it wasn't so bad after all. But this was quite different: espionage is a sinister business and being accused by fanatics that I was not only a hated reactionary but also a filthy spy put me into a category much lower than vermin. I wondered how I'd face the firing squad. I hoped I'd be brave but I was feeling far from that at the moment. I was more frightened than I have ever been in my life (except for the evil spectral appearance in Nairobi) and yet I have never feared death as such; there have been times when I have looked forward to it as an exciting new adventure. Now, I was hurt that people actually wanted to kill me. I knew that the kangaroo People's Court would be headed by a Portuguese mercenary with the sweet name of Commander Juju, who really hated reactionaries. I'd only spoken to him once and decided he was quite insane. The occasion of our meeting was a press conference at which he produced reams of meaningless 'statistics' to justify putting to death a large group of captured Portuguese and local African 'mercenaries' who were about to be shot.

I returned to my desk while d'Almeida and the security man pursued their search of my files with renewed vigour. I had time to think and decided to take a gamble. 'You won't find anything there, Luis, because there's nothing to find. I've told you I did not file those UPI reports and I am not a spy so why don't you just go away and think about it?' Seconds passed like hours and I felt Luis staring hard at me as I walked towards the door and opened it; this was the moment of truth and I had forced the issue. He spoke to the security man in Portuguese and then picked up some papers, including the garbled message and walked to the door where I was waiting for him, certain that he would say we should all go together. In anticipation of this, I held out my hand which they both shook, even if in a perfunctory manner. I knew there had been a temporary reprieve and that I must act fast.

Luis d'Almeida then did an astonishing thing by handing me back the garbled message! I held it in absolute disbelief. Having accused me of espionage, he now returned to me what he believed to be the incriminating evidence that could have me executed. So far as I was concerned this was a very Christian thing to do and feel that perhaps he wasn't a Marxist after all, but the Roman Catholic he claimed to be. Perhaps the nuns' prayers were being answered. However, there were more 'miracles' to come!

Was it possible that Luis wanted me to escape and didn't want my blood on his hands? I didn't know. What I did know was that because the security man was with him, he must put things into motion and I must get out of Angola fast. From now on, everyone would be after my blood. But how do I get out at short notice, I asked myself. I didn't have an air ticket, nor the first idea when the next plane left. Any possible escape vehicle went with the recent departure of Tony Lean. I wished he was still around, as there were scores of private aircraft left to rot at the airport and I knew that with him, we could have borrowed one. I closed the door and went to the telephone. 'Horst, can you come over to the office right away? I'm in real trouble.' 'What's the matter?'

'D'Almeida has just accused me of being a spy. It's really serious.'

'Is he there now?'

'No.'

'I'll be over.' One of the several unwritten laws amongst journalists is that if one is in trouble, others will do what they can to get him or her out of it. Minutes later, there was a Germanic knock on the door and I opened it to find Horst Faas and Ed Blanche. They had arrived in record time and I quickly explained what had happened. Horst's reaction was music to my ears: 'There's a plane out tonight for Lisbon and I have a ticket. You can get out on that.' This was a glimmer of hope; I expected the airport to be notified and watched but it was my only chance. We looked at our watches: 9 p.m. and we had to be at the airport by 10.30 p.m., an hour before take-off. 'Collect your things from home while we sort things out here,' said Horst. 'We'll meet you back at my hotel.' I dashed downstairs to my car and reached home in record time, grabbing my clothes and a few valued belongings although I knew I must leave most behind. Some of my clothes were missing but fortunately, as I was driving away, my domestic came into view and we drove back to the washroom where they had been ironed.

The domestic was a cheerful young African who Tony Lean had inherited from the house owner and he didn't seem in the slightest bit surprised that I should want my clothes at this time of night, and then drive off with them.

Many African employees seem to accept philosophically that all white 'baases' are crazy. I gave him some money and said I was leaving for a while. On the way from home I drove past the Hotel Tropico in my little Fiat and saw Luis d'Almeida standing outside talking to a group of notebook-carrying journalists whom I didn't know. The last thing I wanted was to be seen and I ducked down behind the steering wheel. It was fortunate that d'Almeida was too intent on what he was saying and the journalists, too intent on listening. Otherwise they might have looked with some surprise to see my car going past driverless.

I pulled in at Horst's hotel almost opposite the Tropico and went up to his room where we looked down on d'Almeida who was still talking. Horst went down and listened and when he returned his words were not encouraging. 'You're right, Reg, you really are in trouble. He says the MPLA are looking for you and that you are to be tried as a spy, and executed!'

I looked back grimly and knew that I was shaking inwardly; reaction was setting in. This wasn't like me but there was nothing I could do about it. The extreme tension of the previous hour's screaming was taking its toll and I knew that the odds of my getting away were 99-1 against. I vividly remembered an incident in my childhood in Leatherhead when I watched a pig escape from the local slaughterhouse, chased by a man with a bloodstained knife. I remembered the abject terror in the pig's eyes as it brushed past me and the way everyone stopped and laughed at its plight. The pig had known it was about to be murdered and it hadn't got a friend in sight. It was caught later that afternoon and killed to become bacon on the breakfast tables of people who had never undergone the terrible torment it had endured. Had I escaped temporarily only to be recaptured and suffer the fate of the pig – die to give only casual interest to people reading their newspapers at breakfasts of egg and bacon?

Only a few hours ago I was contentedly going about my work with little more concern than thinking of my next article. Now everyone would be on the look-out for me. Even Horst's hotel wasn't safe as the MPLA had plenty of spies of their own amongst the porters and switchboard operators. At 10 p.m. we left, with Horst, Ed and Jean Claude (I was glad he had come along) leading the way. I passed Mutchmann but he stayed behind without a word, even though I had given him plenty of work in the past. We drove to the airport without incident, past the spot where I had seen a body flung into the air by a car, and entered the concourse where there had been so many refugees lying on the bare marble floors.

On the way, we had stopped for Ed to throw out some papers he had found on my desk. I wondered at this for there was nothing incriminating in them even though they included the garbled telex; did Ed think I was a spy too? The man at the airport desk took my ticket and I was relieved he didn't ask to see my passport which would show my name was not Horst Faas. The first hurdle was over and next came Immigration Control. I was given a questionnaire card which I filled in and handed back. The African Immigration officer took my passport, studied it closely and applied his stamp before returning it. With my escort, I walked over to some seats where we sat and waited.

At eleven-fifteen a man hurried out from a nearby office, picked up my filled-in questionnaire and disappeared into a back room. I knew now that the MPLA authorities had rung the office to find out if I was making my getaway and I looked at my colleagues who returned my unanswered question with glum expressions. There was little conversation and each of us occasionally glanced with forced casualness towards the airport entrance, just to make sure. But we knew that when they arrived there would be no need for furtive glances and we would all be in trouble. I wanted to tell the others to go away as staying only endangered them too but at the moment, I needed their company badly and said nothing.

Eleven-thirty passed and the plane was still sitting on the tarmac. This was the time we should be taking off. Now I was positive I wouldn't be leaving and asked myself: what is keeping them? They have stopped the take-off so why don't they come and arrest me? When we arrived we saw some soldiers at the far end of the airport: perhaps they wanted to come in style, led by that insidious little bastard, Juju. That's it, I thought, of course, they are waiting for him! At last I turned to my companions, 'I think perhaps you had better go.' No one made a move, and I lit a small cigar to soothe the nerves but it didn't work. Midnight passed and there was still no sign of aircraft movement. I tried to take my mind off my plight by watching a cockroach, about two inches long, marching across the hard floor as though defying anyone to tread on it. It seemed to have the same choice that Luis d'Almeida had given me – fly away or be crushed. The seconds ticked by, each one taking its time and none of them doing me any favours: 12.30 a.m., and the tannoy pierced the silence. 'Will all passengers please report to the transit lounge?' All passengers! That was a joke; there were just thirteen of us.

I shook hands with the valiant trio and went through to the departure lounge. The other passengers had gone already and I was surprised to find my way blocked by a small man, shorter than me. Surely the authorities would not have just one man to stop an escaping spy? No. He merely wanted to check my baggage and search me. I smiled casually with my hands up as he did a quick, expert recce of my clothing: 'No guns,' I said. If I'd been carrying one it would have loused up the whole thing: Luis Rodrigues had left a palm-sized Gestapo gun behind for my protection but I neither wanted it nor ever carried it and later he would be cross that I didn't bring it with me as it was worth £2,000. The airport security man smiled back and let me go through.

Another hour passed, this time in the comfort of the departure lounge which had upholstered chairs and even a carpet. The bar was closed but that didn't worry me; at least I was one step closer to freedom. The tannoy came to life again, this time more muted, and called us all to the waiting TAP plane. Could it be that my accusers were not taking the elementary precaution of checking the airport? That was too much to believe. Luck had been so much against me earlier in the evening, why should it change now? As I walked up the steps to the plane, I saw my three journalist companions watching me go aboard. We waved to each other, none knowing what fate held in store for any of us. But at least they knew I was safe and unknown to me they drove off, sensibly picking up my incriminating car from the hotel and parking it outside my house. For a while, sitting on the plane was comforting but then I began to fidget. *Why doesn't the damned thing take off? What the hell is going on? Don't tell me that I have got this far, only to be robbed of my getaway at the last minute?* I looked at my watch: 1.30 a.m. The strain was unbearable. *Why don't they close those bloody doors and get into the air? That is the vital thing; get airborne and out of radio range. Only then will I be safe. Every minute I stay is another minute of danger.* My nerves were so taut that I began to imagine that perhaps the MPLA were playing a game of cat-and-mouse with me – just letting me sweat until they came to pluck me off the freedom wagon. They had played this game with Unita and the FNLA when they were sharing in the transitional government; when they mortared the homes of ministers belonging to these two movements as they slept and thought they were safe.

I kept looking at my watch until it was 2 a.m. There was no good in keeping on asking myself why we weren't moving. A steward was standing near the open door and I dragged myself out of the seat and walked forward. Casually I asked, 'Why are we still here?'

'We are recharging the batteries.'

'But you were doing that when I came here at ten o'clock tonight.'

'Yes, they are taking a long time but they should be ready soon.'

I didn't believe a word he was saying. It was ridiculous to wait all this time in war-stricken Angola to charge some batteries on a plane that had been flying until this evening. The steward was lying, that was crystal clear. Or perhaps that's what the pilot had told him to say. I returned to my seat in despair and sat down heavily. To have got this far, even on to the plane, and then be thwarted. Yet another half hour passed before and the steward came towards me and I stared hard before his face creased into a broad smile, 'We'll be taking off in a few minutes, will you please fasten your safety belt?' After going to the other passengers, he walked back and closed the outside door. Could it be true? There was still time for those bastards with guns to come rushing along. The engines sprang to life and we began to move towards the runway. I looked at my watch yet again: 2.30 a.m.! The lights of the plane were extinguished as we stood ready for take-off. The engines revved to screaming pitch and we surged forward, the pilot seemingly almost as anxious as myself to put Luanda as many miles behind him as he could. For half an hour I waited to see if there was an alteration of course, when the pilot would swing about and return to the Angolan capital. But he went straight on and then, when I was sure we were out of radio range, I called the steward, 'A bottle of champagne, please!'

It was good to arrive in Lisbon, but as I booked into the five-star Savoy Hotel I thought of the thousands of Portuguese refugees who had landed in the capital of Portugal only to find they were largely unwanted. I was worried, too, about Horst and Ed for after calling in at AP's Lisbon office, I was shown an all-round telex from AP, Johannesburg. It read,

> Ed Blanche and Horst Faas in Luanda have been interrogated for spying. They slipped out a message saying that under no circumstances should anyone write a story about Shay's expulsion that could harm them. They also said not to pick up any stories from South African or Rhodesian newspapers while they are in Luanda, and they are planning to get out today if at all possible. They also said that no one in southern Africa should call Reg's office in Luanda since the MPLA now think it was a spy base.

I did not know at the time but AP, UPI and BBC TV had all contacted d'Almeida protesting my innocence. The message from the BBC (*Panorama*) was particularly gratifying considering that I did not work for them. They did know, however, something of the stands I had taken in Rhodesia even though I had not personally told them. Richard Lindley, for instance, had been with me when I interviewed hangman Lofty Milton and would remember my protectively hiding Polly Toynbee in a rather unusual way. The following afternoon in the hotel foyer, I ran into the gargantuan frame of Mike Chapman and I thought of the time we first met, only a few months ago, and what had happened since then to both of us. While he had made a lot of money during the crisis, he had nevertheless lost his business and his home.

James McManus, then with the *Guardian*, came across and was over the moon because he had just bought a pair of almost knee-length boots of pure leather: 'You'd better read this, Reg.' He gave me the afternoon newspaper and there was a rather nasty-looking page lead spread across four columns relating to a press conference held in Luanda by the insidious Commander Juju. The opening paragraph spoke of me as the UPI correspondent who had escaped Luanda and, to my discomfort, stated that I was now at the Hotel Savoy in Lisbon. It associated me with other wanted men, Mike Chapman, Luis Rodrigues and Bruce Loudon of the *Daily Telegraph*. Bruce had not even covered the events from Luanda but had been with the FNLA filing good 'on the spot' stories and so he would have been far from popular with the so-called Popular Movement. His reports showed he was certainly not a 'hotel room' war correspondent.

Juju's deductions and conclusions were probably the most absurd I had ever read and merely confirmed my impressions that he was a political fanatic in dire need of psychiatric treatment. Under normal circumstances I wouldn't have bothered about my hotel being named and considered the finding of my staying there a piece of good journalism which should have been followed up with an interview. What the newspaper, *A Capital*, had actually done was to hand an invitation to the MPLA supporters in Lisbon to 'go and get him'. I had already seen plenty of the Afro hairstyles walking around the Portuguese capital, identical to those in Luanda, and was not keen for a repetition of the quiet tap on the door in the early hours of the morning. I went upstairs, packed my bag and checked out of the hotel and called in to the AP offices to say I was flying to England provided there was a plane. There, in the offices, were Horst Faas and Ed Blanche. 'My God, you're lucky to be alive,' said Horst. 'Did they want you!'

Ed was surprisingly hostile, blaming me for Associated Press being thrown out of Luanda. It was a preposterous assertion considering all the risks I had taken on behalf of AP plus the additional prestige I'd brought to their coverage by Kissinger's reliance upon my reporting, but I was told that I would never work for the company again. 'Why not?' I asked in astonishment. 'Because you got AP thrown out of Angola!' he replied, his face wreathed in hostility. Losing the agency string didn't bother me but I had gone to Angola as a favour and I thought that was some thank you! It was then that I realised how much I had unwittingly put Ed's nose out of joint by going to Angola for Heinzerling and not letting London deal with it. Until we met in Luanda I had never even heard of Ed Blanche.

In reality, Ed had got himself into trouble by crazily calling at my office, a major misjudgement considering the circumstances of the night before. Those offices were the last place to go near, as they learned to their cost. They had entered at 9 a.m. to use my telex machine but as they walked through the door they were in trouble. Horst told me that each had a revolver put to his head, and someone said, 'Where's Shay?' My office was full of armed Cuban soldiers and being ransacked. Horst said he did not know where I was, and when the question was repeated Horst said he believed I had taken the night plane to Lisbon. 'That's a lie!' snapped the officer in charge. 'He couldn't have.' Just how narrow my escape had been was then revealed and is the reason why I sometimes wonder how much we really control our destinies, for what the officer was about to disclose goes beyond normal chance. He declared, 'There was no flight to Lisbon last night!' adding that the schedules had been checked on the night of my departure and they showed there was no flight. And in order to confirm this, he had telephoned the airport but the lines were down!

It transpired that the TAP flight schedules had altered from summer to winter on 1 November; I had escaped on the seventeenth but the MPLA had checked the wrong flight schedules. Why the telephone lines should have been down I couldn't say, for they had worked all right at one stage as I distinctly heard one ring. When taking into account, also, that Horst just happened to have a ticket which he gave me; that there was no check that I was not he when I went through the ticket barrier; there were simply an awful lot of coincidences which contributed to my getaway. It is amusing now to reflect, just briefly, that I was the Angolan government's Most Wanted Man: Dead or Alive!

The hapless Horst and Ed were then ordered to give directions to my house. They denied all knowledge of it despite having been there a few nights before for dinner, and had also parked my car there after I departed. Guns pointed menacingly at them until Horst said carefully, 'I know that at the entrance to his road was a church with a big wooden cross (one of Luanda's landmarks), and that he had a big house with a big dog.' With that they were driven to the church, followed by a lorry loaded with armed soldiers. As they went down my road, a dog I'd inherited from the previous occupant, a Rhodesian Ridgeback, jumped over the wall. 'There, that's the house,' cried Horst, 'and that's the big dog!' Inside the drive was the Mercedes with the bullet holes in it; and outside was the Fiat that Horst had parked. The military vehicles screeched to a halt, and then backed away from the house, which was immediately surrounded. Slowly, the trigger-happy troops moved forward before rushing inside and grabbing my astonished and frightened house servant. They pulled him into the garden and began beating him and demanding to know where I was. Horst and Ed overheard the conversation and watched the beating which went on until the servant produced his MPLA card. Shaking visibly, he told them that I had visitors who came at night but he did not know who they were. This was true: two of them were sitting on the pavement outside! After searching the house for me, they returned to the Fiat which they seemed to know was mine. Horst still had its keys in his pocket with 'Fiat' on them, and as they were close to a drain he hastily deposited them through the grill. Suspicious that the 'master spy' had put a bomb in the car, they produced a long rope and tied it round the door handle before a group of soldiers tugged from some distance away, forcing open the door. When it didn't blow up, they opened the bonnet and pulled out all the wiring. The car was then towed away for further inspection.

Satisfied that the bird had indeed flown, the officer-in-charge then drove back to the Palace to report the bad news to Luis d'Almeida. Horst and Ed were ordered to wait outside in the reception area and what happened next gave them some indication of what I'd been through. 'For something like half an hour we heard shouting from inside the office,' said Horst, 'and most of the shouting was done by the intelligence officer. In the end, d'Almeida came out and he was shaking like a leaf. I'd never seen him like that before, and it was clear he was being held directly responsible for your escape.' In a way, I felt sympathetic towards d'Almeida on hearing this as he had, wittingly or not, given me the slimmest of opportunities to get away. Horst and Ed were then driven to the army barracks for interrogation; the place I knew I would never leave alive should I ever be taken there. That is where the Robespierre-type trials were held after torture, where people disappeared for ever.

The couple were taken into a bare, long, whitewashed room with two desks which faced each other from opposite ends. 'We were ordered to empty our pockets and place the contents in the centre of the room,' said Horst. 'It was the same method the Russians use. Then I had to go to one table and Ed to the other.' Behind each table sat a chief interrogator, and behind him stood five others. Said the unflappable Horst, 'It was unnerving.' Even more unnerving were the finger marks on the wall beside each desk, and other marks too, made by the thongs of whips which had cracked on to the backs of prisoners before striking the walls. The interrogation lasted for two hours before they were driven back to their hotel and told to pack their bags. And the MPLA this time looked up the correct flight schedules as they were bundled on to the next plane for Lisbon.

Because of the Lisbon newspaper story, I was not yet out of the woods and the AP office told me there were no planes to London that day and so I booked the 10 a.m. flight for the following day. Meanwhile, the problem came as to where I should stay. Hotels were out: the MPLA and their supporters who were still strong in the Portuguese capital would have little difficulty in checking out where I was. A young Portuguese AP employee offered me the room where he was staying, and I gratefully accepted. He drove me to his quarters: it was a doss house! Five men were sleeping in one room but I was given a separate one for myself, with just a glass door between us. A five star hotel one night; a doss house the next. There was a Congo War ring about it. I didn't sleep and it had nothing to do with the snoring of the down-and-outs. Perhaps I had been through too much recently for I kept a sharp letter-opener beside me, just in case…

Next morning I flew to London and went to Waterloo Station to make my way to Leatherhead to see my brother, Warren. I was transported into an unreal world of the past. People in London were the same as they had always been; it was the same station I'd come to every day when I started work as a child. There was no sense of fear, or was there? I put my suitcase down and went for a cup of coffee at a nearby trolley. As I stood drinking, I noticed some policemen looking at the case. Slowly, five of them moved towards it. I finished my coffee and strolled across.

'Is that your case, sir?' asked one.

'Yes.'

'Don't you know that you shouldn't leave suitcases lying about, sir?'

'No,' I said. 'Why is that?'

The policeman looked angry. 'You really don't know about the IRA bombs, sir?'

'No,' I teased. 'What's all that about?'

'Don't you read the newspapers or listen to the news?'

'Well, yes, I happen to be a journalist but I live in Africa and have just come from Angola. They have bombs there too, you know.'

They knew of Angola all right so they must have read my reports and a couple of them even recognised me from ITN appearances. We chatted amiably for a while and then four of them moved off. The one who remained had something on his mind. 'Excuse me, sir,' he said, 'can you advise me how I can join the South African police?' Having advised him against such a rash move I got on to the Southern Region train and travelled down to my brother's home, to Fetcham where I grew up and even though there had been bombs during the war, it was the one place I had always felt safe.

Later, on my return to Africa, I stopped off in Johannesburg to see the UPI bureau chief. It was the same man who had admitted quite frankly to me that he didn't like the atmosphere in Luanda and flew off in a funk. I asked him about the two stories which had caused all the trouble and he casually told me he had monitored propaganda broadcasts from Unita and the FNLA and filed them from Johannesburg as gospel truth – with a Luanda dateline! His only concern on seeing me alive and well was to ask how much I would charge him for the expenses incurred while representing his company.

NOVEMBER 23, 1975　　　　　　　　　　　　　　　　**Page 9**

RUSSIA'S GAMBLE IN ANGOLA

In Angola last night moderate African nationalist movements were reported to have surrounded Henrique de Carvalho(main base for Russian military intervention in the territory.

RUSSIA has already played an important rôle in fanning the flames of war in Angola, and because of her intervention a r m s a n d ideologies the once-prosperous territory is wracked by a civil war which has been taken out of the hands of the Africans fighting it.

Even on the fields of battle the commanders in charge are foreigners to Angola, except for former Portuguese and white Angolan soldiers who aligned themselves with the three liberation movements.

The United States Secretary of State, Dr. Henry Kissinger, had kept a personal watch on reports sent in by his consul-general in Luanda, Mr. Tom Kilhoran, until he was recalled just before independence on November 11.

With Gulf Oil producing 650 million dollars' worth of crude annually from the Cabinda enclave the continued A: t presence seemed justified. Offshore oil resources found by Texaco at St. Antonio Bay at the mouth of the River Zaire are known to be larger than those at Cabinda. But Angola's output at present ranks only seventh in the world.

A major purpose of the American presence was to keep an eye on Soviet activities and influence. The consulate offices overlooked the harbour where Eastern bloc ships could be easily spotted if they used Luanda to land arms supplies.

For the real reason for concern about Angola is its vital strategic importance.

Unlike the treacherous coast of South West Africa, the Angolan coastal belt is a haven for

By REG SHAY

Reg Shay left Luanda last week after four months' reporting of the Angola nationalist forces' battles.

ships. Recently in the news have been the comparatively small ports of Mocamedes, Benguela and Novo Redondo which have been retaken from the M.P.L.A. by the mercenary-led armoured column moving north. The country's largest port, Lobito, was also re-captured. In addition to its giant harbour, Lobito also has modern docking facilities which were used to export copper transported from Zaire and Zambia over the British-built Benguela Railway.

Last July the M.P.L.A.'s army took control of all these ports south of Luanda. The action was so swift and well-calculated that few believed the military moves were masterminded by the M.P.L.A. The seizures were made at a critical time when

U.N.I.T.A. had weapons for only just over a third of its 30,000 troops. The F.N.L.A. while well armed by Zaire, lacked leadership and direction.

Yet almost overnight the positions changed, and a united U.N.I.T.A. and F.N.L.A. formed a blended fighting force which sent the M.P.L.A. reeling. Clearly the West had reacted, probably through Kilhoran's reports, and it now seems probable that American collusion with South Africa was responsible for the arrival of the armoured column from the south. Arms were also poured into Nova Lisboa airport for U.N.I.T.A. They came from American-backed Zaire.

This has resulted in the position becoming critical for Russia, which has backed the M.P.L.A. to the hilt. While two large airfields, Luanda and Henrique de Carvalho, are still available for landing Soviet supplies from Congo Brazzaville, Luanda's port is the only one left for sea shipments.

Because Luanda has the second largest docking facilities, the largest airfield and the recognised seat of Government. for Russia's gamble to pay off it is vital that the capital does not fall into U.N.I.T.A.-F.N.L.A. hands. Otherwise hopes of a free run of the Atlantic by Soviet

warships from Angola are doomed.

The Americans estimate that 4,000 Cuban troops and an unknown number of Algerians, have been poured into the fray to bolster the fading M.P.L.A. forces. But the Cubans and Algerians, like the rest of the liberation forces, are trained as guerrillas, whereas the war has now taken on conventional overtones.

The next few weeks must therefore show whether Russia is prepared to commit herself by providing tanks, fighters and troops. So far she has been bluffing. Only armoured cars have been thrown in to support the Cubans, and the 20 Russians allegedly captured are likely to be military advisers.

Now the bluff is being called, and Russia has to decide whether the strategic importance of Angola is worth the gamble and its international consequences.

'Russia's gamble in Angola', Sunday Telegraph, *23 November 1975*

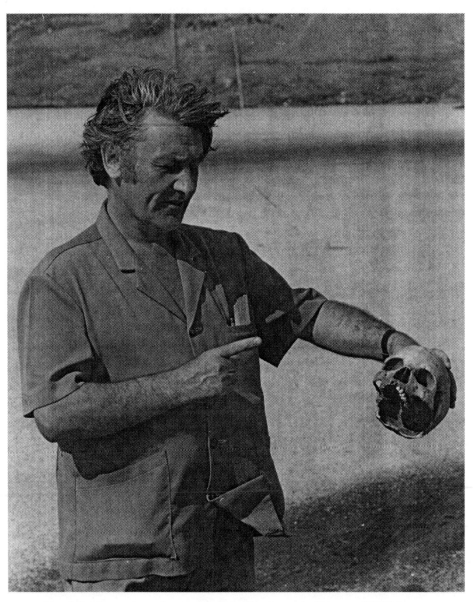

Death by the road – a decomposing skull in Luanda. Picture: Wilf Nussey.

Now Reg Shay knows

HAVE YOU ever wondered what you would do if you were suddenly looking down the business end of a revolver in the hand of someone who appeared ready to use it?

I have not given the matter much thought because as a firm believer in discretion being the better part of valour, I am reasonably certain that I would simply do what the man said — perhaps throwing in "Yes, sir" as often as possible without actually grovelling — at least until the situation looked brighter.

Salisbury journalist Reg Shay says that he used to wonder what he would do, now he knows.

I should first point out that he is of Anglo-Irish stock and stands little more than five feet nothing in his stockinged feet.

In Angola

But he is stocky, and although normally genial it is known that this former Fleet Street reporter can get stroppy if pushed too far.

Being a journalist who chases headlines he sometimes finds himself in trouble spots — such as the Congo during the Katanga nonsense

Now he is in Luanda, Angola, where he has taken over a news agency.

Despite attempts to wipe our banditry, Luanda is a little unhealthy, he says. For example: the other morning a man entered his office and asked to see the messenger, who was out, so he left.

But he was back again within minutes with two of his mates. All three were Africans in their early 20s.

Closing in

Writes the Salisbury journalist: "Seconds later I was staring down the barrel of a revolver brandished by the first man, while the other two were closing in on me."

Perhaps it was the Irish in him, but as one made a grab for his pocket Reg Shay threw him off and charged at the gunman

Taken aback, the three bandits retired, but not before the gunman turned in the doorway and pointed his revolver at the journalist again. So Reg Shay let fly at him with a heavy zebra-skin stool.

Which was the last straw for the bandits, who having decided it wasn't their day, made off empty-handed.

Angola bandits, Rhodesia Herald.

CORRESPONDENTE DA U.P.I. FOGE DE LUANDA PARA LISBOA

LUANDA, 18 — Fugiu para Lisboa o correspondente em Luanda da agência noticiosa UPI, o qual fora referenciado como tendo ligações suspeitas com a Rodésia. O correspondente da UPI, Reginald Shay, encontra-se desde ontem em Lisboa, no hotel Tivoli, após ter embarcado apressadamente no último avião de anteontem, aquele em que seguiram delegações de partidos políticos portugueses convidados para as festas da independência.

Shay fora acusado ontem de ter emitido para o estrangeiro uma notícia falsa, segundo a qual o aeroporto de Luanda fora inutilizado por bombardeamentos.

O nome de Shay fora referido há cerca de dois meses em Lisboa, após haver conhecimento de que procurara adquirir os direitos de correspondência de agências noticiosas e jornais, nomeadamente da Reuter e do «Finantial Times», ao então representante das mesmas, Michael Chapman, entretanto interdito de trabalhar em Angola.

Michael Chapman era agente comercial e desempenhava como missão «jornalística», desde há bastante tempo, a de correspondente da Reuter. Chapman fora acusado de elaborar um boletim «noticioso» com informações colhidas na rua e não confirmadas, a maioria das quais boatos, que distribuía, ou vendia, a empresas e representações diplomáticas.

Durante as averiguações sumárias efectuadas, verificou-se que Reginald Shay enviava para Salisbúria mensagens em código, assim como textos em africaans, inglês e alemão, cujo conteúdo permitiu definir as actividades suspeitas de Shay.

MANUEL BATORÉO escreve de ANGOLA

actividades estejam relacionadas, também, com as de um antigo correspondente do «Daily Telegraph» em Lisboa, Bruce Loudon, que actualmente se encontra em Salisbúria. Bruce Loudon foi o jornalista inglês convidado pelas autoridades fascistas portuguesas para «testemunhar» que não houvera massacres em Wiryamu.

Fontes dignas de crédito admitem que seja verdadeira a indicação, entretanto posta a correr nalguns círculos. ginald Shay é cidadão rodesiano utilizando documentação britânica.

Informações ainda não confirmadas dizem que Shay dispunha de um barco com equipamento de rádio, o qual se encontraria ancorado ao largo de Luanda, ou mesmo nas proximidades da baía. Fonte autorizada relacionada com círculos diplomáticos britânicos citou há cerca de um mês Reginald Shay como tendo justificado a existência desse barco e respectivo equipamento de rádio como forma de garantir a emissão de noticiário caso Luanda ficasse isolada de comunicações.

Contactos com Kinshasa

Observadores locais admitem ainda que Reginald Shay tivesse contactos com um jornalista angolano agora em Lisboa, Luís Rodrigues, o qual foi identificado como tendo simpatias pela F. N. L. A. e mesmo contactos com Kinshasa: shasa foram detectados no respectivo local de trabalho, o «Diário de Luanda», embora Luís Rodrigues tenha dado explicações acerca dos mesmos, segundo as quais esses contactos nada teriam a ver com actividade política.

Fonte oficial angolana indicou que será brevemente dada uma conferência de Imprensa, durante a qual ficarão esclarecidas as actividades de Reginald Shay.

Por outro lado, ainda, refere-se em meios ligados à Imprensa angolana que tanto Shay como Luís Rodrigues tinham ou têm contactos com indivíduos anteriormente ligados a órgãos de Informação de Angola, os quais se encontram actualmente em Lisboa e fazem parte dos quadros responsáveis pelo jornal «O Retornado». Em nota publicada há dois dias, o «Jornal de Angola» referia com críticas particularmente duras e citando aspectos desagradáveis do respectivo «curriculum», os nomes de Mimoso de Freitas, Jorge Ligne, Adulcinir

A spy in Lisbon, A Capital *newspaper, Lisbon, 18 November 1975*

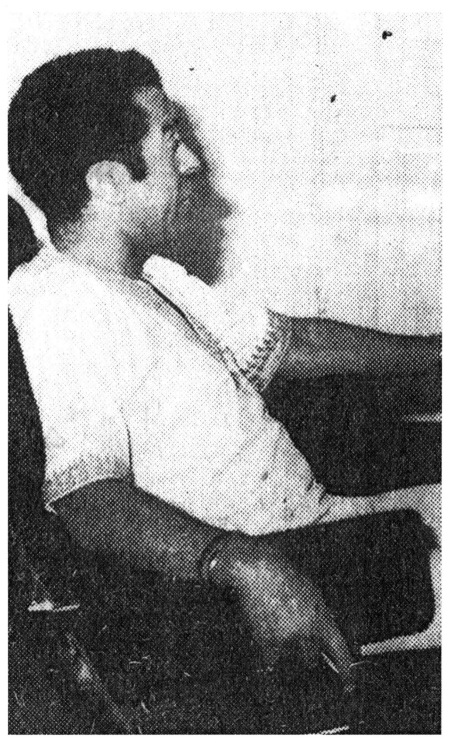

Luis d'Almeida, who accused me of being a CIA spy.
Picture: Luanda newspaper, O Comércio

THE FEAR THAT NOW GRIPS LUANDA

Reg Shay, who has been covering the Angola war for four months, fled from Luanda this week after the Marxist M.P.L.A. accused him of being a C.I.A. spy. This is his despatch:—

HUNDREDS of whites in Luanda are living in fear.

They know that if the forces of the rival nationalist movements—U.N.I.T.A. and F.N.L.A.—succeed in their pincer advance on the capital, they could be shot as collaborators.

Even before Luanda falls, the informers of the Soviet-backed M.P.L.A. forces can accuse them of spying — a charge which brings death by firing squad.

I had to fly out of Luanda hurriedly because officials mistook a garbled telex message for an espionage code.

Meanwhile U.N.I.T.A. has reported the capture of 20 Russian soldiers in a battle

The front page of the Daily Express

A Vampire Witchdoctor

Shock of a different kind greeted me on my return from Angola. 'We've no money left,' said Frances. 'What do you mean, no money?' I'd had a standing float of £5,000.

'You heard what I said,' she answered belligerently, and added to emphasise the point, 'The telex has just been cut off because I couldn't pay the bill.'

Having just spent several hair-raising months nearly having my head shot off in order to keep the business in good shape, I was not amused. I don't worry about money when it is there; only when it is not. What bothered me far more was that my umbilical cord, the telex, had been severed. The phones were still working and I telephoned ITN and *Time* to send me money urgently in advance of future expenses and they responded magnificently.

I also called Nick Kruger, the head of Lonrho in Rhodesia, who said I could use their telex. I'd once interviewed Lonrho's chief, Tiny Rowlands, and he had said that if I ever had telex problems my news agency could always use Lonrho's. The chance that such a situation might arise had seemed remote at the time and I certainly didn't want to be beholden to the international company. Rowlands was a great adversary of Ian Smith yet Lonrho was one of the biggest sanctions' busters, there being no sentiment in business. Nick would actually show me his confidential Rhodesian balance sheet which showed that after UDI its income had leapt by ten million pounds a year. The company itself, which derived its name from London-Rhodesia, was a dirty word within the country and Nick Kruger had a difficult job. He not only had to contend with Rowlands to whom he was devoted, but also the Rhodesian government, sanctions busting, and worst of all, deaths of his staff. Beneath his cold and forbidding exterior, he was a soft-hearted man who would become deeply depressed with the murder by guerrillas on Lonrho's estates of people whom he had personally employed. I was the only journalist he would ever talk to and we lunched on average once a month at his request at the Salisbury Club. On one occasion when he came back from London, he was looking brighter than usual after a session with Tiny. 'Krisman,' ('Christ man') he said in his heavy Afrikaans accent, 'I was sitting in Tiny's office in London when two police officers arrived to interview him about sanctions busting by Lonrho. As they entered the office, they said they would particularly like to interview Mr Kruger from Rhodesia. Tiny turned to me and said, "Thanks for the talk, Nick, I'll see you later," and I walked out.' The Scotland Yard detectives never knew that the very man they were seeking was actually in the room with them!

I didn't use the Lonrho telex for long, just one day in fact. The post office telephoned Nick next day to say that press messages could not go out on his machines, otherwise Lonrho would be cut off! Such is the arrogance of little men with authority and such was the censorship that we were both closely monitored. I called at the post office and made my position clear – that if the machines were not restored immediately they would never be paid the £7,000 that was owed. 'Restore the lines and you will have the money by the end of the week,' I demanded. It had an immediate effect and the money was paid on time.

I had no option but to fire Fanny when the bailiffs arrived and started moving out the furniture. It was the end of a long relationship reminiscent of Clint Eastwood's film *Play Misty for Me* which started as a one-night stand followed by phone calls from her. Later into the relationship, she would feign suicide attempts – her ten-year-old son once found her unconscious in bed and contacted me after she'd taken a measured overdose of pills knowing it was not lethal – or drive up to my home at 4 a.m. with her hand on the hooter, awakening Margery and the neighbours. A search of her desk produced piles of unopened letters and bills addressed to me which I'd never received, going back before the months I was in Angola. Her desk drawer produced a glass with brandy still inside; there was mould around the rim so she could not have been drinking from that glass when she put through the taped message backwards on that fateful evening. What a pity that someone who was so good at public relations and promotions and who was also a trained chef – as well as being the highest paid woman in the country – should have been so useless at running an office. She didn't use the money for personal gain, but was just totally incapable of handling it and, in my absence, she somehow became chair of the Quill Club through my resignation and got that into debt too! I've no doubt she was in love with me which made things worse and I recommended her for a job with some misgivings. Sadly, she died after I left the country.

Another surprise on my return to Rhodesia was an invitation to address the government's Defence Committee in the parliament building! I'd been asked earlier to make an hour-long off-the-cuff speech at a meeting of a school's Old Boys, to be followed by another hour of questions. At the same time, I agreed to address International Affairs at the university, partly from the quiet satisfaction that I'd neither been an Old Boy nor a university student. It had been indicted that the OBs' meeting was a far more influential forum than even National Affairs, and I was intrigued. The intimation was correct as they were subsequently addressed by Ian Smith, the former Southern Rhodesian prime minister he had incarcerated, Sir Garfield Todd, and the British negotiator at the United nations, Ivor Richards (later Lord Richards) making us a very diverse bunch of honorary members. My subject was Angola and someone in high places was listening that night for the next morning a former high-ranking Air Force officer, and Member of Parliament telephoned. 'We would very much like you to address the Defence Committee tomorrow afternoon.

Perhaps you would have lunch with me first?' Was this a joke? The voice at the other end suggested that it was not. There was good reason to be incredulous. On the one hand the government was being as obstructive to me as ever and yet had the effrontery to ask for my help and advice. I was caught at the right time, being unhappy towards my treatment in Angola. The size of the committee was larger than I would have expected and it proved to be particularly interested in the amount and type of new weapons being used by the MPLA. 'Stalin Organs' were also of prime concern and they wanted to know what it was like being at the receiving end.

The invitation to address the Old Boys had been extended by an old friend, Colin Black. The robust and genial Colin had been the Federal Government's Director of Information and he'd had a lot going for him so far as I was concerned because he was the only government press officer I've known who understood the demands of the press. When the Queen Mother came to Southern Rhodesia in the early sixties, Colin accompanied her and did first-class work. He had been constantly plagued by journalists, day and night, but enjoyed that as part of his work and would personally take responsibility for answering awkward questions. At night around a barbecue for journalists, he would bring out a banjo and sing suggestive but not crude songs. A journalist's dream, everybody wanted to know him – he was 'Good old Colin'.

After the Federation broke up, Colin was pensioned off and he tried his hand at writing articles but without much success and eventually his health began to fade. There was a general election and by coincidence, Ian Smith and I used the same polling booth during which he would unknowingly cancel my vote. Cameramen and journalists crowded around waiting for Smith to arrive and cast his vote after which the hoards of journalists then dashed off to write their deathless prose while photographers sent away their pix on the wires. I too was moving away and then stopped abruptly: standing on the pavement looking on wistfully was the skeleton of a man. I left the pack and walked across to him, 'Hello, Colin, what are you doing here?'

'Just watching.' There was sadness in his eyes and as I didn't feel that Smith casting his vote for himself was such a hot-shot story, I stayed for a while before following the pack. Later that evening, in the Quill Club, a journalist said, 'That chap you were talking to, I think I know him.'

'Yes,' I replied. 'We all used to.'

The war in Rhodesia began to heat up when Robert Mugabe's forces found access into the country through Mozambique following the Lisbon coup. The two first and worst hit areas from this onslaught were Centenary and Mount Darwin, in the east of the country where guerrillas had sent a rocket into a house and wounded two little girls. Living nearby was an incensed farmer, Chris Kleynhans. Imbued with Smith's propaganda about white superiority, he declared in the national newspaper to the guerrillas, 'Come and get me, if you dare!' It was a foolish gesture to throw down the gauntlet because they did come and Kleynhans' bold words cost the life of his wife, Ida. I went to see him in hospital where he told me that a hand grenade had come through the bedroom window and landed on Ida's stomach. He threw himself on to the floor but she wasn't quick enough. Several more grenades were lobbed but despite being wounded, he survived. Kleynhans then had to live out his life with the awful knowledge that he was directly responsible for his wife's death. At first he stayed on at the farm and I would call on him if I was visiting the scene of a nearby terrorist attack. The last time I saw him he was very dejected and said he was leaving his home, adding, 'There are too many memories.' The naive Chris Kleynhans abandoned his farm a broken man who would always ponder how a silly gesture could have such devastating consequences.

Robert was at university and during his vacation I asked if he would like to see a little of what his dad did as part of a day's work. We drove towards Mount Darwin to see a farmer friend, Jim Rankin, and to observe the prison-like conditions under which the farmers were now living. As we passed the fortified farmhouses, many encircled by brick and wire fencing, I was able to point out the various places where attacks had taken place and these included the now empty farm of Chris Kleynhans. Jim, a respected cattle judge, showed us a prize Brahman bull he was particularly proud of and feared it might be inhumanely butchered by guerrillas. We talked of the most recent attacks which were being stepped up as more and more gangs infiltrated from Mozambique. Jim proudly showed us an additional protective wall complete with gun slits he had recently built and I wondered how it would stand up to hand grenades, rockets and mortars. 'Shall we have tea on the lawn?' asked Pauline, Jim's wife. It was bliss, sitting there in the shade, several yards in front of the wall without a care in the world, just sipping tea and chatting as birds of varying colours flew down from nearby bougainvillaea to peck at cake crumbs on the grass. Peace and tranquillity in a pastoral atmosphere were the order of the day. Thirty yards away was the farm labourers' compound which seemed to be unusually quiet even for a Saturday afternoon when the men go off for a beer drink. Usually some of the wives and children stay behind to disturb the peace but none of us had given their absence even a casual thought and too soon time came to leave as I did not wish to drive home after nightfall, especially with my son as a passenger.

At 10.30 a.m. next day the telephone rang; it was Jim Rankin. This was the first time he had ever called me and I knew something was wrong. 'I feel you should know that while we were drinking tea, we were being watched by terrorists hiding in the compound buildings. There were thirty-five of them!' he said. Thirty-five? That was a small army and their combined fire power would have blown that protective wall to pieces within minutes – and we were relaxing and sipping afternoon tea in front of it! I was curious to know if Jim had any idea why they had not attacked the obvious sitting ducks. 'My boss boy (foreman) told them that I treated my labourers well and so they decided to leave me alone,' he said. Phew! I was relieved that Jim had not thrown down a Kleynhans-type gauntlet – being a section leader in the police reserve he knew better.

I've interviewed a vampire only three times in my life and it was always the same man. He didn't look anywhere near as impressive and frightening as Bela Lugosi, Vincent Price or Peter Cushing, and he did not come from Transylvania either. The only thing going for him was that he was the real thing. A suburban African, he was a modest and charming little fellow despite his totally obscene practices.

Ian Smith had claimed that terrorists were using spirit mediums to persuade unsophisticated tribesmen to follow them and this was the peg I needed to get my vampire witchdoctor on television for ITN. In order to place an obvious feature story onto a news bulletin, there has to be a news story to which the feature material can be 'pegged'. The vampire's name was July Mwanda, and I found him in an African township near Salisbury. July professed to be a faith healer and also claimed to be a practising Roman Catholic. His tiny grey house, set near the corner of two dusty dirt roads, gave no hint of the kind of alternative medicine he meted out to his patients except that the 'Faith Healer' sign above his door, like the Angolan monk's crucifix, bore a skull-and-crossbones. The first time I interviewed July he was about to treat a three-year-old child with a malady that was never explained. We walked into his back garden where he picked up a white chicken which was pecking contentedly at a discarded maize husk. How kind, I thought, as he tenderly stroked the hen, he likes animals. It was then that his schizophrenia manifested itself as his mouth opened wide to reveal a strong pair of brown-stained incisors. His head went back and forward in a single movement as his fangs enveloped the neck of the unsuspecting chicken and they remained embedded until the head fell off into the sun-bleached dirt beside the husk. 'That was most interesting,' I murmured with feigned indifference. 'Why did you do it?'

'This is a sacrificial chicken,' July explained, while using the arm of his shirt to wipe away blood which had splattered his face and dark sunglasses. Delicately, he then removed feathers from his teeth before digging the incisors into the chicken again in order to grip the bird in his mouth. He then stooped to pick up the severed head which appeared to be a significant appendage to the cure and he rubbed the neck all over the bewildered child's chest until it was covered in blood. Taking the chicken from his mouth, he turned to me with a look of triumph one would expect from a surgeon who had performed a triple bypass. 'He's cured now,' said the witchdoctor and he dismissed his young patient with a pat on the head while the mother curtsied and clapped her hands in respect and proffered a few coins.

The next time I called on July, I was invited into his house like an old friend. On the wall of his filthy front room was a photograph of himself beside an idealized picture of Jesus Christ. Another picture was on a calendar from a township butcher which showed a haloed Jesus, the Good Shepherd, tending a flock of sheep. Mangwa wasn't interested in either sheep or even chickens on this visit: this time the vampire was in the market for a goat. 'A lady is coming here who is dying of cancer and I must have a goat,' he confided, 'and as I don't happen to have enough ready cash to buy one, I wondered if you would kindly oblige?' Always happy to donate to a good cause, and this one might even interest cancer research scientists, I assured him there was no cash flow problem and we went off to find a goat. Fortunately, he knew exactly where some were grazing and after agreeing the price with a herder, he put the nervous, smelly goat on his lap and we drove back to his home in my sparkling clean Mercedes.

The lady was waiting in the garden on our return and he took her into the house where he ordered her to remove her shoes, stockings and knickers, and to lie on the floor and lift her dress. Then he ordered her to open her legs. Is this going to be a vampire's orgy? I wondered uncomfortably. She wasn't exactly a young maiden, probably in her late thirties, and the thought entered my mind that perhaps his vampiring had depleted the township of pubertal virgins. Completely fascinated, I awaited the next move. With a flourish, July produced a ram's horn and showed it to me with a knowing look and a professional nod. Seeing the lady lying there and looking very vulnerable, I was by now truly apprehensive about his intentions. He knelt between the woman's legs clutching his horn and began poking her. I asked, 'What are you doing?' as he probed her stomach with the pointed end of the horn before listening through the hollow end. He replied, simply, 'I'm locating her cancer.' How foolish of me, I thought, to ask such a stupid question, but he wasn't put out. A few seconds later he looked up and grinned while pushing his horn hard into the woman's stomach and declared, 'Here it is!' With that, his mouth opened and the fearsome fangs dug into the woman's belly. She didn't even murmur or show any sign of emotion as he stayed there and sucked for several minutes before spitting out the contents of his mouth into an unsterilised chipped blue bowl. There was a strange slimy foreign body in the bowl which I could not identify. 'That is the cancerous growth!' he said triumphantly.

We walked into the garden and he produced a long knife. 'I have to complete the cure now by releasing the evil spirits into the goat,' he said, and slit the creature's throat. It wasn't a sight for the squeamish; the poor animal stood uncomprehending until life slowly ebbed from its eyes as its blood poured into a tin saucepan. July drank some of the warm blood before going inside to pour the rest of it on to the woman's wound. I looked again at the calendar from the friendly butcher who loved Jesus and would, no doubt, receive the carcass for a price. That I should have paid for it didn't seem quite kosher, even if the goat was.

I saw my friend the witchdoctor only once more, when I took my son, Peter, along as an extra curricula fillip to his education and he repeated his chicken feat. Having cut open a child's head with his teeth, he appeared to suck out a bone which he said had been bothering the youngster. He then

My friend, the vampire witchdoctor. Picture: author.

walked with the dead chicken's body in his hands and the severed head in his mouth, to the nearby hungry crocodile waters of the Hunanyi River, where he completely submerged his patient before handing him back to his mother. Unfortunately for July, he then lost his footing and began to be carried away by the current, the bird's head still in his mouth and his brown fur hat firmly wedged on his head. 'Are you all right?' I called, realising that he couldn't swim. This was another stupid question and as I watched his arm stretched out and grasped an overhanging branch and quickly he pulled himself ashore. I should have realised that vampires do not drown; they are put down with wooden stakes.

Some months later, I was chatting with an African counter hand at Salisbury's main post office who had read an article I'd written on July. To my surprise, he said that he knew the vampire witchdoctor. 'My daughter was unconscious in hospital for three months and I was told that nothing could be done for her and she would die,' he told me. 'I discharged her and took her to July Mwanda. He cured her within minutes.'

While I have known several Jesuit priests – they would probably be disturbed to learn that one of their flock was a vampire – I have sometimes wondered at the attitudes of the Roman Catholic Church. A case in point was when I was attending the visit of Pope Paul VI to the Ugandan capital, Kampala, where he was to consecrate ground for a new cathedral to commemorate a handful of martyrs. There had been nine Roman Catholic martyrs in Uganda compared to over 100 Protestants. Ironically, the subsequent advent of that blighted country's genocidal political leaders may have tragically helped to redress the martyr imbalance.

Thousands upon thousands of bedraggled Africans, most with their clothes in tatters, waited to cheer the arrival of God's locum. As they lined the road, I watched the diminutive white-robed pontiff bless them all along his route where some had even placed banana fronds on the road where he rode, not on an ass but in a smart large black Mercedes limousine. So inspiring was the occasion that the Pope's driver was overawed enough to drive past the entrance to the proposed cathedral and the blessed hands of the Pope began to wave Italian style.

At the time, I was commenting on the arrival into my tape recorder for an 'On the spot' relay to ABC News and as I spoke, I stepped backwards and trod on a toe. There was a sharp dig in my ribs and I turned to look into the very angry eyes of Julius Nyerere, President of Tanzania. Until now, my treading on political leaders' toes had been in literary form; now it was literal and I wondered what his gang of thugs in Arusha would have done if they had seen it! Another President who was with him, Kenneth Kaunda of Zambia, recognised both me and my predicament and threw back his head with laughter to the further chagrin of Nyerere.

After His Holiness entered by the exit he alighted from the car to be solemnly led by a cluster of cardinals to a newly constructed altar built specially for the occasion. Amid total silence, he knelt before the altar and symbolically kissed the ground before moving off to a man-made island on Lake Victoria where he conducted mass for the masses. Degrading the whole stage-managed scene were Catholic priests who went amongst the devout followers carrying sticks with bags on the end demanding money. This was no feeding of the multitude with bread and fish from the lake but a hard-nosed game of collecting cash from the poorest of the poor for the privilege of seeing a stage-managed show aimed at a world audience. While the Pope was away I strolled back to the altar and watched queues of African women, their babies tied on to their backs with frayed towelling or other pieces of cloth, move forward to emulate His Eminence by kneeling before the altar and kissing the ground. As they rose, shoved right under their noses was a bag held by a priest. I felt truly incensed and pointedly commented loud enough to be heard by the Father that I doubted that when Christ washed the feet of his disciples, that he held out a bag demanding they chip in for the Last Supper.

I commented on the begging bags to Eric Robins, who had flown in from Nairobi only to have his own unlikely experience. Eric had called at the presidential palace and when he entered the elevator a drunken African held out his hand: 'Good afternoon,' he said with a slur. 'My name is Obote!' Milton Obote was the President of Uganda at the time and there was already talk of murders committed by his regime. He was later overthrown by Idi Amin whose mass slaughter shocked the world, only to be overthrown himself by Obote who continued the practice. If ever a country suffered retribution for whatever reason it has to be the hapless Uganda and now it is plagued with AIDS. As for Pope Paul VI, there's been talk of making him a saint.

Africa has been a fertile ground for religion and other mystical beliefs but I watched an incredible ceremony by a sect that was taking southern and central Africa by storm. I was one of only half a dozen whites who had witnessed the annual gathering and doubt that even today many more have seen it. For some years I had been fascinated, when driving in the eastern districts of the country, to occasionally see Christ-like white robed figures standing alone halfway up a mountain side. They would be statuesque and I once stopped my car to watch a man for twenty minutes without there being a sign of movement. They are known as the 'Apostolics' but inquiries showed that little was known about them amongst the whites. One journalist who does know of them is Peter Godwin who, in his fascinating book, *Mukiwa*, disclosed that as a child he attended a small village Apostolic ceremony with an African servant and became 'possessed'. He has not, so far as I know, been to the annual shindig that I attended and may not know of it.

About the time the young Godwin entered his trance, I paid a social call to the home of Professor Marshall Murphree, a lecturer at the University of Rhodesia, who held the Chair of Race Relations and we discussed the Apostolics, or VaPastori we Johanne, to give them their true title. Rhodesian-born of American parents, Marshall was also a Minister of the American

Baptist Church. He told me the Apostolic sect was a breakaway from the US Baptists and that their annual Penta ceremony (short for Pentecost) was to be held shortly and would I like to travel with him to the eastern districts to see it? The journey was around eighty miles on tar and then a further forty miles on a chassis-breaking track which wended like a drunken elephants' trail into the heart of the bush until we came across thousands of men garbed in white robes and carrying crooked staffs – everyone a black religious disciple. Murphree said that during the ten-day Penta, there were never less than 15,000 worshippers present, their occupations ranging from gardeners, cooks and barmen to bakers and shoemakers. All the men had billiard-ball heads but wore beards while the women wore shawls over their heads; all were barefoot. As the curtain of darkness was drawn, the scene before me revived memories of James Hilton's *Lost Horizon,* and the old Ronald Colman movie I'd seen with my long-armed friend, Sid Creek. Dusk soon gave way to a night of pure magic as I watched many thousands of white-robed, happy-faced men holding staffs in one hand and flickering burning torches in the other, chant continuously throughout the Penta. Seeing their equally happy, smiling womenfolk and children I knew that I had found the inhabitants of the real Shangri-la; not in the snowbound mountains of Tibet but in the heart of Africa.

Their chant was as haunting as it was sublime and deep in my consciousness I knew the theme but it took quite some hours before I identified it as an adagio of 'Nkosi Sikelele Africa' which I'd first heard at the African nationalist meetings. Even hearing it sung at a different level, it still retained a majesty that came deep from the soul of the continent. At an unseen and unheard command, all 15,000 people sat down in a single movement but the chant continued even though the huge expectant congregation was separated with men sitting apart from their womenfolk throughout the Penta; there would be no cohabitation even between married couples. I thought of how different this was from the 'civilised' western world of pop festivals, of drugs, drink and sex.

Above the chanting a voice rang out and a small, cadaverous-looking man holding a huge Victorian bible, ran between the dividing lines of the congregation. He warned of the evils of drink (even Coca Cola and leavened bread were forbidden at the Penta!) but he was suddenly drowned by the good-humoured but increasingly strident chanting of the listeners who had clearly become bored, and was forced to sit down. Another man stood up, even older. Grey-haired, bearded and bent-backed, he ran between the aisles as nimbly as Ron Moody's Fagan and was even more vehement than his predecessor. I turned to Marshall, 'What's his pitch?' My professor-preacher companion grinned broadly, 'He's extolling the virtue of young maidens marrying elderly men who can provide a good home for them!' Loud groans emanated from a group of teenage girls and once again the chanting reached a crescendo as the ambitious, lecherous old codger was sung out of business and forced to sit dejected and humiliated on the ground. The night was bitterly cold – it was mid-winter – and women huddled with their children on the hard earth away from the congregation, trying to sleep. I tried too, but the continuous chanting and near hypothermia decreed somnambulism could wait.

Next morning all the adolescent girls were rounded up and led into nearby woods by women elders. Marshall delicately explained they were being taken for 'a physical examination'. Half an hour of tension amongst parents passed until joyful singing could be heard from the woods and a group of laughing girls holding hands came dancing out to the waiting crowd. The woman leading the singers held up a green leaf: it was a sign of purity. Mothers' faces lit up with relief and they rushed forward to congratulate their daughters. These nubile maidens were followed by a second group who were quickly surrounded by crowds of men and this time the woman leader held up a leaf punctured with a hole – the unwise virgins. Some of the girls looked sheepishly at their stone-faced parents; others grinned back smugly at the male admirers.

During our journey to the site, Marshall Murphree told me that the VaPastori, like some other religious sects, disdained modern medicine and relied completely on God to protect them. This posed many problems, particularly when it came to inoculations on a continent which is so tragically rife with disease. The VaPastori we Johanne, which means 'Apostle of Johanne', was founded by former American Baptist Church member, Muchabaya Ngomberume, who took the name Johanne after his resurrection. Ngomberume had once been a member of Murphree's own father's congregation but he suddenly claimed to have died and to have risen again on the third day, after seeing God. I recalled an occasion while I was with the FBC when one of our reporters covered the massacre by Kenneth Kaunda's Zambian soldiers of 700 followers of the Alice Lenshina sect because they would not carry his political party's cards. They raced towards the guns with spears shouting 'Jericho' as bullets tore into them, many women with babies on their backs. It made Sharpeville look like a picnic but because it was black killing black and there was no black-white apartheid involvement, the carnage never received Sharpeville's publicity. Alice Lenshina also started her sect by claiming to have risen from the dead after three days.

The VaPastori has around 100,000 members in Zimbabwe alone with their tentacles stretching far into the two Congos, South Africa, Mozambique, Zambia and Malawi. They interpret the Bible literally; holding their meetings each Saturday (not Sunday) where it's forbidden to carry cash. They also gather in fields in preference to churches, quoting Acts 7:48–49: 'Howbeit the most High dwelleth not in temples made with hands; as saith the prophet, Heaven *is* my throne, and earth *is* my footstool: what house will ye build me?' saith the Lord: or what *is* the place of my rest?' Amongst the 'sins' are witchcraft, adultery, theft, anger, pride and covetousness – all of which helped to make them the gentlest and happiest sect in the world. Johanne had claimed several visions as a teenager, but the movement started when he was twenty years old when he claimed a great light shone on him, and the voice of God said, 'You are Johanne, the Baptist the Apostle...' That was in 1932. Johanne had fourteen wives, which made adultery seem irrelevant, and when he died they were passed on to his brother who already had five. This proved too great a burden for the sibling who survived only another two years.

We had timed our arrival for the Saturday towards the end of the Penta, knowing that Sunday would be the eve of the climax. Throughout Sunday men gathered wood to build a gigantic and twenty-foot high fire while all the time the chanting continued as preachers extolled their interpretation of the Bible. Soon the heavens too would be ablaze with light from the southern stars and as dusk approached a silence befell the gathering as everyone waited in anticipation. I watched, curious at first and then entranced with near-disbelief as a boy of no more than five years of age walked to the head of the massed sitting crowd. He raised his hands with the air of a maestro and pointed to a group of men in front of him who began to sing; then to another group. In VaPastori tradition, he ran up and down the aisles bringing in various separate groups of men, women, boys and girls of all ages, in varied descants. The timing was impeccable as he conducted, chided and exhorted all the while with his tiny mesmeric hands. The little boy was controlling the voices of many thousands of ordinary people with spectacular precision; a task that would daunt even the finest professional choirmaster. Then a blazing torch was put to the wooden pile.

As men detached themselves from the chanting throng, they too fired the tinder-dry wood and flames leapt and sparks frolicked into the freezing air. This was a confessional blaze where all those present would purge themselves of their sins. As the chanting continued, white-robed men ran beside the blaze, ignoring eighty-foot high flames which licked at their garments with fiendish tongues, ever eager to snatch and draw their victims into the inferno. Men and women shouted as they raced tauntingly beside Hell itself: 'I have stolen!' cried one man. A woman screamed, 'I have committed adultery!' Sweat poured from ebony bodies that moments before had been near-frozen. Young and old alike ran the gauntlet, heedless of the fallen embers that burned beneath their unclad feet. For over an hour they ran, never slackening the pace, while others fed the hungry inferno with fallen trees and bushes. 'I've seen them deliberately walk barefoot over a long carpet of smouldering embers and it doesn't seem to hurt them in the slightest,' said Marshall Murphree as we watched. He explained that when the runners were completely exhausted they believed they had been purged of all evil, and he pointed to six double entrance gates to a large arena. 'Those are the twelve gates mentioned in the Bible and going through them is trial by ordeal.'

'Prophets', their eyes closed, lined each side of the arena's isles, blocking the paths of those who wished to enter. The queues seemed endless as the exhausted runners waited patiently for their turn of admission. Suddenly the eyes of one prophet would open and gaze piercingly at a passing figure and point accusingly. I watched as an attractive young woman was accused of pride;

a man was accused of being a thief and he did not argue. There was another adulteress and one man was accused of practising witchcraft. The miscreants then crossed to a smaller blaze where some old men were sitting and this was the 'judgment fire' where the elders were the judges. It was a revealing insight into their psychie to see the offenders kneeling to confess aloud of their misdemeanours. One adulteress threw herself to the ground and spread-eagled herself. A judge, who showed no emotion, nodded his head imperceptibly and the woman rose. 'Tatenda,' she whispered and made her way gingerly to a gate reserved for those who had been forgiven. I watched tensely and it reminded me of the Customs Hall at Heathrow Airport when, as the first person to gather his luggage and having genuinely nothing to declare, I walked a gauntlet of over a dozen Customs officers each staring piercingly at me as I made my way through the green route feeling as guilty as hell. Now, as I held my breath, I watched the woman pass the test: the prophet's eyes remained closed. I too passed through the gates without difficulty but Marshall told me that one white man he had taken there was turned back as he had unwittingly broken the rules by forgetting to take cash out of his trouser pocket. As he approached the gates the prophet immediately became agitated and opened his eyes before pointing to the pocket in question. After the offending money was removed, he was forgiven.

Freezing weather and an icy wind continued into the next morning and as we walked towards the nearby Muroti River where Johanne had carried out the baptism of 160 converts within a month of seeing the light, I was glad I had brought an overcoat. Because it was the dry season his 'River Jordan' was little more than a mountain stream, but it was deep and cold yet neither this nor the wind blowing through the Msasa trees stopped the baptism by total immersion of scores of naked children, including two three-month-old babies.

The mantle of Johanne had fallen on to one of his sons, Abel, whom I met briefly in a hut in which he had stayed throughout the whole Penta. There was nothing special about him; just an ordinary man of medium build who had little to say. But then, the VaPastoris are just ordinary folk whose simple lives are transformed for a few days each year. After the baptisms, Abel emerged from the hut with his twelve apostles and walked towards a long table set with twelve plates of unleavened bread. At his bidding, the apostles and the congregation took the bread and sipped fruit juice… the finale had been reached. The last supper seemed to me as something of a disappointing anti-climax, possibly because no Judas had been allowed through the gate. A pity really; he would have made a good peg for a story.

Multiple human deaths in Africa are usually caused by tyrants, disease or starvation but I was present immediately after the instant deaths of 426 people of whom 390 were Africans and 36 white and they had died through nothing less than stupidity and neglect. It happened at a coal mine at Wankie, near the game reserve now called Hwange, and might never have occurred if elementary precautions such as putting down gravel had been carried out. Keeping explosives just fifty yards inside the tunnel entrance did not help when they blew up. There were three explosions, and I wrote at the time:

> At 10.29 a.m. green paw paws hung from the trees lining the pithead of Wankie's Number Two colliery. The sun was high on this balmy autumn day. An African policeman stood in his brick duty box a few feet from the entrance. At 10.30 a.m. the paw paws were dead, charred to a cinder. The policeman was dead too, blown fifty yards, his box nearly demolished. Also feared dead were hundreds of miners working 300 feet below.'

Some indication of the force of the explosion could be gauged by a heavy steel trolley used for carrying miners which shot out of the shaft like a ballistic missile and smashed into a wall lining the top. When I arrived, hundreds of widows of both races had gathered to stare desperately at the tunnel; the African women wailing in their traditional manner, totally bewildered by the enormity of the disaster. Deadly methane fumes and carbon monoxide flowed freely through the shaft vents to the surface, making it dangerous to get too close. The date was 6 June, when people throughout Europe were celebrating the anniversary of D-Day.

Next morning, sixteen South African rescue teams arrived to help. These teams are amongst the most experienced mine rescue operators in the world but they were far from optimistic that anyone would be found alive. There are times in life when people in charge have to make appalling decisions and on this occasion the Anglo-American Corporation, owners of the mine, had to decide whether to allow the deadly gases to flow out and prevent further rescue operations, or blow them back. They decided on the latter, which meant that the chances of anyone surviving in a pocket of air would be blown away once four huge ventilator fans, brought up from South Africa, drove the gasses inward. Before the decision was reached, sixteen rescue teams went in relays down the shaft, 3,000 feet along the tunnel, using the age-old method of detecting gas by carrying two canaries with them. If the canaries lived, the area was clear; if they died, it was not. A bell rang seven times: it was the tolling of death and it reminded me of the plague of London and the pit opposite the Fleetway House. After the bell tolled for the seventh time, a trolley slowly rose from the depths with two bodies on it, wrapped in red and black blankets. It was a moment of nail-biting intensity and black screens were placed around the shaft for fear that the African women would become violent in their grief when they witnessed the scene. In the mortuary area the wailing increased to such intensity that only African men who knew the miners were allowed there. When women were told they could not view the mutilated remains, one official told me nervously, his body shaking, 'This could be nasty.'

As he spoke a policeman came across and ordered pompously and ridiculously, 'Don't talk to the press about this!' Some people, I summed up, can reveal their mentality with as few as just seven words. As the policeman marched off the bell tolled again; only one body this time and gas had bloated it beyond recognition, so that it was even impossible to tell his race.

The police, who usually had an antipathy towards the church because of its identification with African political aspirations, now welcomed a Methodist minister, William Blakeway, who became a hero of the scene as he moved amongst the women, comforting them. He was accompanied by an African priest and between them they helped to defuse a very nasty situation.

As so often happens at a time of tragedy and tension, something ludicrous occurred. A school bus drove up to the mine with a handful of white children. 'What the hell are they doing here?' snapped one of the weary white wives. A little boy waved to his mother sitting on a bench, not knowing that he would never see his father again. In another bizarre move, convicts were let out of their cells to dig hundreds of graves in anticipation that they would be filled. Then the decision was made that everyone was dreading: Number Two shaft would be sealed as a giant tomb. A white woman who had stayed for days and nights beside the entrance from the moment she had heard of the disaster, screamed, 'You must try again!' On the Sunday immediately following the decision, a service was held on a football field with the Salvation Army band playing, 'Abide with Me'. Ian Smith was there, so too was the head of the Anglo-American Corporation, Harry Oppenheimer, who flew up from South Africa in his Lear jet but arrived late. After the service I went back to the tomb where all the widows of both races had gathered with their wreaths, waiting to be given words of comfort by Oppenheimer. Perhaps no one told him they would be there, or perhaps he felt he just could not face them. I shall never forget their expressions of disbelief when they looked up to see the Lear jet soaring into the air. The message that came across was that Mr Oppenheimer was a very busy man.

John Kelley, the news editor of the *Rhodesia Herald* came to the scene and later produced a charcoal tie with the date in red 'W/1972'. I was fascinated that my chum could have such bad taste.

Macbeth and Murder

In the name of white supremacy and independence from Britain, even the whites living in Rhodesia were suffering from increasingly oppressive legislation but accepted it as the price they had to pay for retaining their way of life without fully comprehending that this very life was being eroded. One law after another was rubber-stamped limiting individual freedom under the convenient guise of necessity; a word used by countless dictatorial regimes. Draconian powers used by the government were such legislation as the Law and Order (Maintenance) Act; Emergency Powers; Land Tenure Act; and Deeds Registration Act. Under the latter, white residents had to register conditions of residence in their areas which would prohibit Asian and Coloured people living in white-settled zones. Blacks had been banned already except for servants and their families. Now servants' children were not allowed to live with their mothers and fathers, which forced many white housewives to close voluntary private schools they had created to teach their servants' children. The law also meant that a husband and wife domestic could not live together in a white area unless they were both employed by the same household, which was rare, and frequently police would arrive to inspect their quarters. Despite the experience of South Africa's Sharpeville shooting, Smith even introduced pass laws for Africans. Not carrying a pass meant a fifty pound fine or a year in jail.

Censorship increased and life was becoming even more challenging. By law, journalists had to submit all copy relating to military activities to censors and it was tiresome that my exclusive stories would be deliberately held up and frequently shown to my opposition in order that they could file my information first. Any true journalist would have refused to accept such a gift on principle and there were times when my own copy was handed back, looking unrecognisable. I wrote a strong letter of complaint against the ethics of this duplicity but there was no reply. Here is a brief example with regard to censorship:

> The Rhodesian security forces, using ground troops, helicopters and jet fighters-bombers were mopping up today a guerrilla band which was taken by surprise by a small patrol at Rowa, ten miles south of Umtali which borders Mozambique. The band of insurgents was discovered near the main road leading from Umtali to Birchenough Bridge and South Africa. Over 100 guerrillas were found by the patrol at a two-acre camp and when the Rhodesians opened fire the insurgents fled, leaving behind dead, arms, ammunition and pamphlets which attacked the internal settlement. Unconfirmed reports say that during the attack and subsequent hot pursuit, over fifty have been killed so far.

Those two opening paragraphs were cut to: 'The Rhodesian security forces are continuing follow up operations south of Umtali.'

The stage was reached where journalists could be censored before they had even written a story. The *Daily Mirror*'s Nick Davies came to my office and he was in trouble. 'My photographer, Peter Stone, has been arrested and I am sure the authorities are after me. Would you mind coming with me to my hotel room as I'm sure there's an Immigration official waiting to take me away?' Bloody marvellous, I thought. Davies had not had the courtesy to tell me he was arriving or that he was actually here, and now he wants me to stick my neck out and show the authorities that I am the *Mirror*'s correspondent while they are still looking for the writer of the 'Lofty' Milton story. I went along and waiting inside the hotel room was a man from Immigration. He was courteous enough and Nick was led away to the remand prison and then sent back to the UK.

Some time later over the telephone from London, Nick (by now the *Mirror*'s Foreign Editor) mentioned that he had been strip-searched at the remand prison. This is a humiliating experience, which includes a rectum examination, and once again I blew my top and demanded to see the Information Minister, Ely Broomberg, to protest vehemently. Even he was shocked as the pair were PI'd only because they represented the *Mirror*. 'I wish you to tell Mr Davies and Mr Stone that they are welcome back into Rhodesia at any time, and that I would like to apologise to them personally,' said Broomberg magnanimously. 'From now on, the *Daily Mirror* is welcome in Rhodesia!' This was an incredibly significant victory but Peter Stone had been unnerved by his ordeal and would not return. Nick, however, appreciated that he was now in a situation where he could do no wrong and purred with delight. I soon learned how much he loved power politics and particularly enjoyed plotting and so it did not surprise me, years later, that he became front page news following the death of Robert Maxwell. Nick was sacked and branded a liar by the press when he denied being an arms deal manipulator for his late boss.

A month after Nick had returned to Rhodesia the government introduced new regulations in which foreign correspondents were compelled to have work permit accreditation renewable after thirty days. The government's overreaction against the world press was publicly revealed by P K van der Byl, whom I had once asked to direct traffic. He was now the co-Foreign Minister (his shared duties were not too onerous as no country had recognised Rhodesia's independence) and he disclosed that a survey of 4,717 editorial and other items on Rhodesia had shown only 298 items to be unfavourable. 'The vast majority were factual and unbiased,' he conceded.

There were blushes in the corridors of America's CBS who were singled out for praise because of co-operation by their producers. Having seen the end product of a TV commentary on Rhodesia, van der Byl declared, 'This is one of the finest pieces of pro-Rhodesian propaganda I have ever seen!'

Two months after this comment more 'D' notices were introduced and it became an offence for local papers to publish information relating to defence, public safety, public order, the economic interests of the state, or any information that could cause alarm and despondency 'and other allied matters'. This made even the pro-government journalists wonder what was left to write about. I smiled cynically at an editorial comment in the local *Sunday Mail* in which the editor declared that he had already imposed self-censorship in order to please (a synonym for appease) the government, adding, 'and often sacrificing journalists' principles because we put patriotism first!' And if that wasn't enough, the editorial went on to bleat that it was sometimes embarrassing that cabinet ministers now praised the Rhodesian press 'as some sections of the outside world are calling us lackeys of the government.' Despite his mental torture, I noted that the editor did not resign in protest even though his same newspaper had carried as its lead story the resignation of myself and two colleagues some years earlier in our direct protest against government intervention. Our action had been taken before censorship was even official!

The imposition of ruthless and usually absurd censorship was not confined to the media. A surprised West End actress, Sandra Duncan, who was expected to bare her breasts in the Simon Gray play, *Otherwise Engaged*, was ordered to wear a bra at all times. When it was pointed out that many black women walked around bare-breasted, we were told that this was different because it was 'traditional'. And when the visiting British comedian, Norman Wisdom, let slip the obscene word 'Bum' in a television interview, it evoked a whole column of comment in the *Sunday Mail* which then went on to advocate greater freedom of expression.

It was African freedom of expression in art form which many whites particularly resented. The director of the National Gallery, Frank McEwan, was one of two men who had recognised the potential of the indigenous people as artists, particularly as sculptors. The first was Canon Patterson who saw their art to some extent in terms of souvenirs from which they could earn a living. Patterson and McEwan were as philosophically unalike as any two men could be with the latter being an artistic heavyweight. Through him their sculptures, first in soapstone and then serpentine, became recognised worldwide and McEwan encouraged his charges to great heights. He had started with his own gallery attendants and eventually had up to seventy-five sculptors who were producing works in an exciting three-dimensional form. Frank told me he'd turned down the offer as director of the new museum in Fort Worth, Texas, to take up the post in Rhodesia because he saw the potential of Africans. But the civil war, which dispersed many of his artists, and public opinion which was against him for swamping the art gallery with what most whites considered to be rubbish, forced him to resign.

Their loss was reflected in May 1988, when Frank McEwan, at the age of eighty-one years, re-emerged at London's Barbican, at an open-air exhibition of 'Contemporary Stone Sculpture from Zimbabwe'. It was opened by Prince Charles, who has several pieces.

Because of the Luanda bandits' episode, I had become staircase-conscious and as I'd taken over a suite of offices in an oldish building, I tended to tense up when I entered it late at night when the unlit surrounding area took on a sinister air. Emerging from the elevator one night, I turned right towards my office and heard a sound behind me; a human voice, then 'Shh...' I turned quickly but there was no one in sight and I hesitated wondering what to do next. If they were bandits, were they armed? There was only one way to find out and only one place they could be, back past the lift and along the darkest end of the corridor and in a small alcove to the right. Here we go again, I thought, and with that I plucked up courage and marched loudly down the dark corridor and demanded, 'Who's there?' Out of the darkness came five Africans; four men and a woman. Perhaps they were terrorists; there had been a lot of activity in the town recently. 'What the hell are you doing here?' I snapped authoritatively, a tactic which can work wonders. To my relief they cringed and the men put their hands in their pockets and produced identity cards and shone a torch on them. 'We're policemen, Baas!' said the leader. I asked him what they were doing huddled in a corner on my floor.

'Protecting the building, Baas. There are a lot of totsis (crooks) about,' he answered and the others nodded in agreement. It was a highly unlikely excuse, especially as they were all together on the second floor of a building where my office just happened to be situated. Perhaps the visitors were about to break into my rooms when they heard the lift coming up, and had hidden. It didn't matter; they were too alarmed to be aggressive and it was a cold night. 'You had better come in for some coffee,' I said. At two o'clock in the morning I sat in the office drinking coffee with four policemen and a woman and never knew what they were really up to.

Many times I worked for several days and nights if there was a big running story, just crashing out for a twenty-minute siesta in the afternoons. After a day's writing and broadcasting (including TV) for Europe, I would frequently sit down for an in-depth article for *Time* magazine, starting at 10 p.m. on an open telex. I kept the line live as it was the only way of ensuring there would be no interruptions on the machine with incoming calls, which would then come through on my other telex on to which I would quickly tap out the required story. The bulk of a lengthy *Time* article would be written between three and four hours and as soon as I had finished, the *Washington Post* would inevitably come up and there would be another hour of writing. Sometimes the Australian Broadcasting Corporation would want a voicepiece from my studio followed by the *Sydney Morning Herald* asking for a story. The world is a twenty-four-hour business and I could be assured that every word I wrote or broadcast was read or listened to by many millions of people, by world leaders, and by... the Special Branch.

There were four telephone lines to my office, three of them linked to the internal switchboard while the fourth was my private line. It was lunchtime and I was sitting in the office when a fast-tinkling sound came on one of the

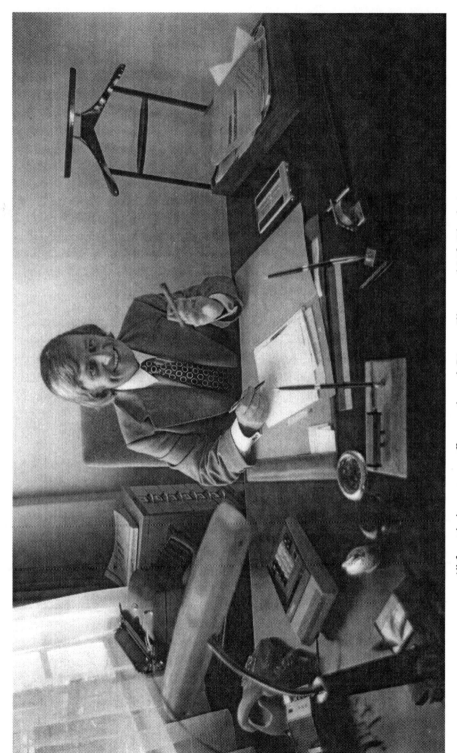

All four telephones to my office were bugged. Picture: Illustrated Life Rhodesia.

switchboard lines – my secretary having put them through before going to lunch. I picked up the phone. 'Oh,' came a surprised voice.

'Who are you?' I asked, knowing full well who it was. 'It's the Post Office. We are just testing your line,' came the reply and the man at the other end immediately pulled out the plug. I'd always suspected that the lines were tapped, together with my radio link and the telex, but it was nice to get confirmation. Then the direct line on my desk came to life with the same strange ringing. I picked up that telephone. 'Is that a new tapping device you're fixing?' I asked. This time the plug was pulled without even a reply. As I eased back in my chair, the office took on the sound of an old clockmaker's workshop with all four telephones being intermittently rung. For a while after that, whenever someone telephoned I would begin the conversation, 'Before you say anything, I should warn you that this line is being tapped.' It was amusing to irritate the post-office listeners and the secret police.

The telephone rang and I picked up the receiver, 'Hello, Reg, Jim here. Get to the airport straight way, New Sarum.' New Sarum was the air force base. 'Hi, Jim, what's up?'

'Facility trip.' I could talk to Jim Brady, we had known each other for years, he and his wife, Rosie, being good friends. He was the government chief press officer; it was his superiors with whom I always quarrelled. 'What's it about this time?' As a non-accredited defence correspondent, a pariah, I was only invited on facility trips when the government knew I would write 'objectively'. 'It's another massacre,' said Jim. An unpalatable truth that I had come to terms with, was that I'd become blasé over massacres. The distorted faces, bodies and gaping wounds, the crawling flies and the stench of death now meant very little. The first time I had been taken to see mutilated and putrefying bodies I wondered what my reaction would be. Would I be sick? Would I be seeing a sight that would haunt me for ever? It surprised me how detached I was and not affected at all; now I was seasoned, one of the most seasoned of all the forthcoming assembled company – the Congo, Mozambique, Angola and Rhodesia itself had seen to that. I reckoned I had become so immune that if I'd lived 2,000 years ago, I'd have reported deadpan on the crucifixion of Jesus and then produced a parchment think-piece on the political implications. Was I totally immune or was I kidding myself? This would be a fateful day. 'Sorry, Jim, I can't make it this time. I'm busy.'

'I think you should go, Reg, it's a bad one.'

'Where is it?' Jim Brady knew from me that my telephones were now tapped and would not say where the murders had taken place. He had already gone as far as he could to ensure that I did not miss the big story. 'Just get to the airport, quickly,' he said. I put down the phone, picked up my tape recorder and spoke to my secretary Carole Hodge, 'Cancel all appointments. It's the big white bird, again.' She looked down at the open diary on her desk: 14 June 1978. 'Going anywhere nice?'

'Do I ever?'

Carole was the young mother of two children, very attractive with long dark hair but what was most important to me was that she really loved her job. She would sing quietly to herself as she worked, the happiest and most efficient secretary I have ever known.

I drove to the New Sarum air force base where a collection of pressmen's cars were already assembled at the main gate. Among those present was Dave Ottaway, and he had brought his wife along for the ride. 'We were going on a picnic this morning,' he smiled and held up a small bag. 'We still have our sandwiches.' David is the only person I know to have taken his wife to a massacre as compensation for not going on a picnic. True journalists really are an extraordinary breed.

A familiar camouflage painted DC-3 was waiting which meant it was going to be an uncomfortable ride. We journalists knew the old Dakotas well and there was only one with decent seats; it had belonged to the wartime South African prime minister, Jan Smuts. I'd only flown on it once and that was in the days of the Federation. The one we'd now be riding in would have the spine-breaking steel seats and parachute wires we had all become familiar with. As we walked to the plane, a visiting British reporter spoke with astonishment. 'How the hell did they get these?' Dotted around the airfield were reconnaissance planes, British-built Islanders. No one answered. Just because Britain and the world had brought in sanctions against Rhodesia, it didn't mean that their latest aircraft could not be smuggled into the country. Some of Nato's member countries with exports in mind were privately very happy when Ian Smith took UDI. At breakneck speed the DC-3 once again raced down the runway, its wings flapping until they eventually forced us into the air, seemingly through sheer vibration. Never in the field of flying has one plane appeared to travel so fast and yet move so slowly. We touched down at the heavily guarded air strip at Umtali, in the eastern districts and jumped into waiting army lorries. It was cold and none of us had been prepared to travel in open trucks around the Vumba mountains. 'Where are we heading for?' I asked a man from the Ministry of Information. 'I don't know,' he said. He was probably speaking the truth as the Info Department was not noted for telling its own people half of what was going on. At first I did not recognise the terrain but then it became disturbingly familiar. 'Are you sure you don't know?' I asked. 'Nope, only that it is a mission station. The Elim Mission, that's all the advice I've been given.' I replied, 'Never heard of it,' but this was very familiar ground.

As we alighted from the truck the info man dropped his rifle and the bullet almost shaved my head. I didn't give it much thought as I was too preoccupied with the surroundings but other journalists were highly vocal and voiced their displeasure in no uncertain terms. We walked forward and as buildings came into sight I recognised them immediately. 'I've been here before,' I muttered. 'That's Eagle School.' Two years before a friend, John Hillis, who was chairman of the Board of Governors, had taken me there to see if my publicity company could do anything to promote the school. Several parents had taken their children away because of the war situation resulting in a general fall in the number of pupils attending.

A special play had been put on by the children for John Hillis and we sat through the performance as the youngsters struggled with their parts. Impudent sprogs with conical hats dressed as the Three Witches produced a pallid version of Shakespeare's haunting masterpiece, *Macbeth*, as they stirred the cauldron with gleeful mocking faces and chimed, 'Double, double, toil and trouble; fire burn and cauldron bubble.' What dark forces were these innocents reaching out to as doting parents sat and watched their small darlings play out roles they could not possibly comprehend? Evil was about, outside the school and on both sides of the border where men and women had taken up arms to kill in whatever fashion they chose. But how could I or anyone present suspect that a real horror would be enacted here only two years later, a horror which would have such an indelible imprint on my mind that it took years to overcome? The lush Vumba area had been free of attack until the collapse of the government in far away Portugal but now: 'I'm pulling my children out,' a mother told me after the play was over. 'It's not going to be safe here soon.' The school was eventually closed but unknown to me it was taken over by the Elim Mission whose members would pray to the living God they believed in; missionaries whose children would not be allowed to dress up playfully as witches to stir a cauldron steaming with hate.

Morning mist, cold and chilling to the flesh hovered above the football field. It hung like a shroud, shameful of revealing to curious eyes the terrifying testimony to collective depravity and madness at its most obscene; an unleashed malevolence even greater than that contained in Shakespeare's play. Children had been the witches and children would be amongst the victims of the ghoulish psychopaths who ventured out on that terrible night. Armed police and reservists now stood around the sports field, many of them in tears. They were battle-hardened men who had fought in the bush and killed yet they all stood with ashen faces. I recognised one of them and walked over to him: 'I just can't believe it,' he mumbled. 'How could any human being do this? It's a nightmare. If ever we catch up with those bastards, there won't be one left alive.'

Beneath the mist was an area where blankets and thick plastic sheets were spread out and I knew that bodies would be beneath them. Walking closer, I gazed down and through that strange misty haze was a face, the eyes looking up at me. It was a very pale face, that of a child; a little boy, and he was dead. The men who had covered the bodies had accidentally missed his face; perhaps they had hurriedly pulled over the covers, unable to look any more at the horror lying at their feet. Slowly I walked back to the waiting journalists, knowing for sure that I would really hate this assignment.

A man from Lancashire introduced himself to us as head of the mission station. He was not an endearing person but then he may have had a conscience – he knew full well the reasons why Eagle School had pulled out but totally ignored advice from the security forces and set up the mission there and then. Having put everyone at risk, he personally chose to live in the safety of nearby Umtali town. As he introduced himself to us he was instantly disliked by journalists who resent being talked down to: 'I want you to behave with respect and not go amongst the bodies,' he ordered. 'Remember, these people have relatives and so you must show mercy when you take photographs. Precious little mercy was shown here last night.' We took into consideration that he was probably overwrought and just murmured back a few words. Of course we would walk amongst the bodies; that was why we had been brought here. Did he think we were going to tread on them? As the covers were pulled back the first three we came across were the usual scene – men with their hands tied behind their backs and stabbed to death. I stared down grimly and remembered the bandits in my Luanda office and how I had been determined they wouldn't tie my hands. Being missionaries, they would have probably accepted the situation passively. I hoped they had been the first to go, to escape the horror which was to take place next to their wives and children, but I knew it was wishful thinking.

Slowly, more covers were removed one by one, and the full horror of what happened revealed a night of frenzied terror and orgy where evil reigned and man debased himself beyond belief. I gazed down through the low, hanging, curling mist at what I first took to be a life-sized doll, still clothed and wearing tiny booties. It wasn't a doll: Pamela Lynn was nearly three weeks old when the crazed terrorist plunged his bayonet into her head. Pamela had been something really special to her thirty-six-year-old midwife mother, Joyce, who for years had wanted a baby of her own, as she had put it, 'Before it's too late.' It was clear the baby had been forcibly snatched from her mother before she too was bayoneted several times. As I stared at Pamela, memories flashed back to the morning when Margery screamed and I raced into the nursery to pick up the lifeless body of Alan. How Joyce must have screamed.

Another young mother had a hatchet in the back of her head. I am not going into all the names and details. The women had been stripped of their lower underwear and were lying with their legs apart. In a necrophilic lust, they were raped before and after death. Only one wasn't raped as the killers showed sensitivity towards sex with a woman going through her menstrual cycle. Bayonet holes in her lower abdomen revealed their displeasure. As I walked through the bodies, talking quietly into the tape recorder, a photographer nudged me, 'Look at that bastard!' The head of the Elim Mission, who had warned us to be respectful, was walking amongst the victims taking photographs. 'He probably wants to send happy snaps to the relatives,' I snorted in reply.

I broadcast to both ITN and ABC News. Margery, who was living in England at the time in a village with the unlikely name of Pratts Bottom, said I sounded emotional and that it was a good broadcast. ABC gave me a rare accolade in their monthly newsletter and even the *Sunday Mirror* mentioned me on their front page, which was an extreme rarity. None of this meant much to me. I was concerned to realise my own fallibility; that I could feel emotion as a professional and was not as hard as I liked to believe. Perhaps if Alan had not died it might have been different, I don't know, but I felt that I never wanted to see another body again, that I was losing my zest for covering wars.

In London, the Labour MP Andrew Faulds claimed without the slightest foundation for saying so, that the massacre was carried out by the Rhodesian security forces. Countrywide, emotion against him ran high and those of us who knew kept very quiet that his gentlemanly soft-spoken brother had actually been standing amongst us at the scene, working as a cameraman for ITN. Some liked to claim that the outcry was because those killed were white, suggesting that if freedom fighters murdered blacks nobody cared. There could be an element of truth in it, of course and looking down at the bodies of white children, I could more naturally identify them as being my own, but I get choked at seeing any dead children, no matter what their colour.

Was it the work of Rhodesia's Selous Scouts? They were trained killers but they were taught to kill as quickly as possible, and silently if possible. Their commander, Lieutenant Colonel Ron Reid Daly, once mentioned to me that he was trying to find out where to purchase crossbows for his men for silent night-killing. The scene at Elim on the night of horror was far from quiet with shooting and screaming. A lecture on the virtues of Marxism was given to the black children of the mission who were forced to assemble outside. A surviving missionary who hid under his bed, (I was refused the opportunity to interview him) reportedly had no doubt the killers were Robert Mugabe's nationalist guerrillas. There is now a monument on the site claiming it was the Selous Scouts and even though I have subsequently stayed at a house only 200 yards away, I could not go back to view it. The monument is a lie if only because the Selous Scouts would never have given such a lecture; there would be no reason to. But to paraphrase Goebbels, 'If you tell the lie often enough, and it is big enough, people will believe it.'

I don't know if the Ottaways enjoyed their picnic sandwiches but something similar to their experience could have happened to Peter Snow and his new bride, Ann. Peter had been to Rhodesia on assignment for ITN and now, having just married, brought Ann out for their honeymoon. There had been another attack in the Umtali (now Mutari) region and I decided to drive to this beautiful area and have a look around. Peter immediately said he would like to come along too, and asked if he could bring Ann. We drove to where the guerrillas had been operating but saw nothing. It doesn't usually cross my mind that some of my friends are household names in Britain and America – as I suppose I was in Rhodesia – but the thought did strike me that a photograph of the happy couple spending their honeymoon in a terrorist area might be of interest. Peter agreed, but then spoke to Ann privately. 'No, you had better not, Reg,' he said. 'Ann shouldn't be here, she might lose her job!' Ann was working for the Canadian Broadcasting Corporation and was concerned they might find out she was playing hooky on her honeymoon in war-torn Rhodesia.

An American girl photographer came to the country and she carried a gun. She was very attractive but spoke with a squeaky voice which I found irritating. I confess to a certain bias because I'm always suspicious of some good-looking women correspondents who have a tremendous sexual advantage over their male counterparts by using their charms when it comes to eliciting information from over-sexed generals. I met her when Sandy Gall and I were having a quiet drink in Meikles Hotel. Sandy had beside him a case of wine and the girl came across to ask for a bottle. We were planning our next ITN story and we both quietly hoped she would go away and eventually she got the message and departed clutching the wine.

While I'd considered her to be rather insensitive, the assumption proved to be quite wrong. She had become involved with a Rhodesian army major and during her visit to our table she produced a service pistol he'd given to her for protection. The major had said that he would take her with him on operations which, I felt, was pushing their relationship just a little too far. What I hadn't appreciated was her feelings towards the gallant Rhodesian army officer with whom she had fallen deeply in love.

Sadly, it was an affair that would end in tragedy. Shortly after the wine bottle incident, the officer went out on an operation without her, and he was killed. The shock of losing her lover proved to be too much for the tall blonde American I had so completely misjudged as being insensitive. On hearing the shock news, she took the pistol from her handbag and used it for the first time.

War correspondents come from all walks of life, with Winston Churchill being one of the best-known to be drawn from the aristocracy. Another aristocrat who came to try his luck was Richard Cecil. I realised there had been some behind-the-scenes negotiations with the snob Defence Minister, P K van der Byl, for Richard, correctly titled Lord Cecil, was given the red carpet treatment. He was sent by ITN and I found it slightly irritating that he was allowed to go out on operations with the troops when I, who had supported the forces to some degree, was held back by the Information Department.

I liked Richard and on a trip to Umtali he pointed to the Cecil Hotel. 'Wherever I go I seemed to be surrounded by the ghosts of my ancestors,' he said with amusement. Even the capital had been named after one of the clan, the late British prime minister, Lord Salisbury. Richard particularly sought my advice about adverse trades union reaction towards him in England. He was acting as a war correspondent without either qualification or a union ticket and this was causing a stir back home. Personally, I couldn't see why a member of the British elite shouldn't have a ticket like anyone else if he was doing the job and I advised him that as the unions could not touch him in Rhodesia, he should just get on with the job he was sent out to do. Richard had done parachute training in Britain with the SAS and had experience in jumping at low altitudes. He found the Rhodesians were jumping even lower than he had attempted. 'I'm going to the sharp end tomorrow,' he told me. 'We are jumping at a very very low altitude, probably 400 feet!' I admired the young lord who would throw himself out of an aircraft at such minimal height, which hardly gave the old-style parachute time to open and in my reasoning that fully entitled him to be given the accolade of war correspondent. Next morning, Richard boarded the waiting DC-3 Dakota and when he was over the battle area he jumped alongside other parachute troops. He landed safely but before he could unbuckle his 'chute, a guerrilla who was hiding in the long grass shot him dead.

It's one thing to stand in front of a camera and pontificate briefly as an intro to a news story you are producing, but it is quite different to be in the studio reading the news. When ITN's *News at Ten* was presented with two newscasters, they would read from a teleprompter and at the end would smile 'goodnight' and talk briefly to each other as they picked up the news bulletins from their desk. It always seemed very chummy and many newspapers would ask what they talked about.

On one of my annual visits to ITN, Sandy Gall and another old pal, the late Reggie Bosanquet, suggested I went with them to a rehearsal of *News at Ten*. I watched the teleprompter doing her mangling as she turned a handle round at the correct speed for the reader and as I sat between Sandy and Reggie an almost invisible earphone was put into my ear so that I could hear the producer ordering what item to read, where to drop a paragraph, and so on. The rehearsal went okay and as the deadline for going on the air approached, a technician asked me to leave. As one man, both Sandy and Reggie turned round and demanded that I stay. It turned out that I was one of only five people at that time to sit in on the programme as it went out live. It soon became clear that Reggie and the lady producer did not always see eye to eye. I'd known him to be difficult at times but Reggie, when he was in full flow, was one of Britain's best-ever newscasters. If he could be difficult, so too could the lady producer. As he was reading one item, her voice came through the earpiece, 'You fucking stupid clown, what the hell are you doing? I told you to drop that fucking paragraph!' Sandy got better treatment but then, despite that wonderful beaten-up face, he has a very *sang-froid* temperament. The tirade went on until the end of the bulletin and as we went off the air, Reggie's smile vanished and he jumped from his chair. 'Let me get at that bitch,' he snarled as he went to the production room. They had a humdinger of a set-to as I'm sure they did most nights, and when they came to the Green Room for a drink they were still at it. I'm not decrying the producer, she was great and Reggie had some nice things to say about her in his autobiography. But it took a true professional to stand up to that battering of insults and carry on reading while it was going on.

During another visit to ITN, Reggie and I were having a drink when I asked him if he had got everything he wanted out of life. 'I've been very lucky,' he said. 'Everything has gone right for me.' We went on to chat about that lucky life. He was in the process of being divorced and he said it was all going very smoothly. The next time we met, everything had changed and he was distraught. 'My wife's got an American lawyer and she's taking me to the cleaners,' he said. He added that he would even have to give up the home he had bought from Rex Harrison. Reggie then appeared drunk on TV and his toupée slipped. He got into deep trouble for an article which appeared in a Sunday newspaper and the last straw came when a woman tried to sue him for paternity. He won that case but the lucky streak was brief as the one thing Britain's most popular newscaster did not tell viewers or friends was the worst bit of luck of all: that he was dying from cancer.

When Reggie first came out to Rhodesia he gave a dinner and invited Eric Robins and myself. It was then that we realised just how good he was as a wine connoisseur. Rhodesia was just beginning to produce its own wine, and Arlington Vineyards marketed a remarkable vintage which I'm sure could even rust stainless steel. As a 'thank you' for dinner, we presented Reggie with a bottle of the wine but suggested he should not open it until he was on the plane to London. Reggie later said he had tried to throw it through the window of the aircraft. Fortunately, we had also secured a bottle of Côte de Nuits Burgundy which was savoured with relish.

I went to see the man who produced the remarkable Arlington wines and casually mentioned what I had thought of them. He was most understanding and apologetic and as we spoke, I couldn't help noticing that he was sprinkling salt around the base of his vines, and asked, 'Why are you doing that?' He replied with the mesmerised air of someone who had carried out an in-depth study of great foreign vineyards. 'I reasoned it out this way,' he said. 'Some of the best wines come from the Mediterranean area where they have salty sea air. I am sure that salt is what my grapes need.' I never saw Arlington wine on the shelves again.

On a further visit to ITN, Sandy Gall suggested that we go to the announcers' room for a chat. A very lovely girl in her twenties was sitting down at a desk and we were introduced. 'Reg,' she said with a smile that would encourage knights to chase dragons, 'How nice to meet you at last.' I assumed she was the announcers' secretary and marvelled at how lucky they were. Then she said to Sandy, 'I have to open a fête tomorrow.' I didn't have to be too intelligent to know that secretaries do not usually open fêtes. Because I lived in Africa, I only saw British TV on visits to London and therefore could not know who was introducing my films and voice reports. And so, I had the unique distinction that while she knew me, I was probably the only person in the whole of Britain who talked to and yet had never heard of the gorgeous Anna Ford!

The best nightclub in Salisbury was La Bohème. It was owned by Currie L'Estrange, a man who walked with a heavy limp as a memento from WW2. Because of world sanctions, good artistes were difficult to come by but one evening Currie came across to my table and asked if I would do some local publicity for his next singer. He could hardly contain himself, 'I've got Guy Mitchell!'

'You're kidding!' I didn't think that Currie had the sort of money needed to fly out a big name like Mitchell and I couldn't think why he would entertain at a small nightclub in Rhodesia. There had to be a catch. With a broad grin Currie told me, 'He doesn't cost much, I've got him for a song!' The smile was to disappear later when he found out why the former world's number-one songster was going so cheap. For the star who became the darling of mothers and daughters with 'Trudy Fair', 'She Wore Red Feathers', 'Pawnshop on the Corner in Pittsburgh, Pennsylvania' and many others, turned out to be a drunk whose first-night openers were corks drawn from a bottle. His song, 'I Never Felt More Like Singing the Blues' was more than appropriate. Instead of seeing the once trim-figured cowboy of a dozen films who had cut twelve golden discs, the audience watched a bespectacled, roly-poly man of 225 lbs. It did nothing to calm Currie L'Estrange's qualms when, just before the opening of each show, the singer quaffed a bottle of Mateus Rosé. 'It soothes the throat,' he explained, swaying like a palm tree in a hurricane.

Days went by and Mitchell missed some performances altogether. To the man who had topped the London Palladium bill more than anyone before him, Currie was forced to say, 'I'm afraid I shall have to terminate your contract.' Pathetically, Guy Mitchell simply said, 'Please help me.' L'Estrange invited the singer to his luxurious home where he was encouraged to play tennis and golf. His tennis partner was my son, Rob. I also took him to my gymnasium where he trained daily. Currie also gave him a horse to ride while I got him along to Alcoholics Anonymous, which I was startled to find was housed in my office block! 'I've had three wives and I've lost three million dollars,' Guy told me as one of his excuses for hitting the bottle. 'Divorces can clean you out.'

Guy Mitchell had one really good friend in the world, Congressional Medal of Honour hero and film star, Audie Murphy. The pair had starred in a television series in the States and the bond of friendship ran deep. Without drink, Guy was now turning up on time for his performances and he began looking fitter than he had done for years. His weight dropped to 186 lbs and his waist went down to thirty-three inches. When he eventually left he was very fit and bronzed. It was shortly before his departure that I heard on the radio that Audie Murphy had died. We waited until the end of Guy's performance before breaking the news and it was as though he had been shot in the stomach. This was not the kind of news to break to a man trying desperately to fight alcoholism but it was better to break it while people who were trying to help him were around. Currie told me later that he thought Guy had begun taking a few drinks again, but he wasn't sure. I was glad, therefore, when he made his comeback at the London Palladium where he no doubt sang 'Heartaches by the Number'. Currie, too, had a heartache: his wife upped stakes and left him to fly to England and chase after Guy.

About a mile from La Bohème is one of the best repertory theatres I have been to, Salisbury Reps (now Harare Reps). The performances there were matched only by the after-show parties. Producer Adrian Stanley put on Shakespeare's *Julius Caesar* in a modern setting. Principal actor, John Keeling, for example, was Caesar dressed as Mussolini. Tons of sand had to be put on stage each night for the final act, which was a battleground in the western desert. The Rhodesian army helped out by producing some very loud bangs which came from a field gun on stage.

After the last show was a 'Beira Party', which meant a lot to Rhodesians as Mozambique's Beira was no longer available to them as their seaside holiday resort. I turned up in swimming trunks, flippers, straw boater, beach umbrella and a bicycle tyre round my waist. I'd begun changing in the car before the end of the show when a final blast of gunfire shattered windows of the theatre. It was a dismal evening and pouring with rain as I stepped from the car hopefully to hasten unnoticed into the stage door entrance. To my surprise, a police reservist in uniform cycled towards me and stopped. I adopted a casual stance: 'Excuse me, sir, but can you tell me where the terrorist bomb went off?' he inquired politely.

'That wasn't a bomb,' I explained. 'It was gunfire on stage.' Clearly, because of my unusual attire I wasn't to be taken seriously.

'That's quite incorrect, sir, it was definitely a bomb.'

'No, it was quite definitely on stage; I've seen the show and so I know. They're doing *Julius Caesar*.'

'An explosion in *Julius Caesar*, sir?' He was looking at me a little peculiarly. 'Yes, it happens during the desert war scene,' I answered, defensively. 'The desert wa... are you sure, sir?' The story was too long to explain and the rain was bucketing down. It wasn't too bad for me as I was more or less suitably dressed (or undressed), but the part-time bobby was suffering discomfiture. I couldn't decide whether this was because of the weather, or the thought that he was dealing with someone of lower intelligence than himself. 'Well,' he said, dubiously, 'I don't think any bang on stage could be heard from my house which is over 300 yards away. It had to be a bomb.'

'Suit yourself,' I replied, clinging to my tyre and umbrella with one hand, and raising my white boater in farewell with the other. I would sometimes wonder about the report he turned in at the police station, and whether he mentioned a chap standing in the rain in his swimming trunks who talked of *Julius Caesar*. Perhaps they put him away, knowing as I did that there was no bomb in Salisbury that night.

The Reps was always a source of human interest and one member with human attributes was Jim, a big bluff Yorkshireman and a former Arnhem paratrooper. He liked to quaff a pint or two and was never noted for going home early. In Reps Bar there was plenty of talent about which wasn't all on stage, and moral standards were not always as high as the censors would have people believe. Jim and a girl he knew there had a sudden lust for each other which they could not contain. Surreptitiously, they slipped outside and got into his car and such was their passion that he not only took off the girl's clothes but his own as well. It was a hot, sultry night with the stars of the Southern Cross creating a perfect ambience for sub-tropical romance. They opened the car window during the build-up of their heated ecstasy before they were lost to the world. Only too soon it was time to dress again and go home to their respective spouses. What they had not noticed was the sneak thief who put his hand into the car and ran off with Jim's clothes. 'Wot will I tell the Missus?' asked Jim. 'I can't go home in the Noddy!' Now it was the girl's turn to rise to the occasion. She not only had a key to the building, which was locked up, but also the stage wardrobe where she helped to fit out costumes. Soon she came out with a bundle of clothes. 'Here you are,' she said. 'It is all I could find in your size.' Jim went home dressed as Long John Silver. This is the first time that I have parroted on him.

Amongst the great pleasures of freelance journalism is the opportunity afforded to meet a variety of unusual people. Whereas a staff man either specialises or, as a general reporter will interview someone and then dash off for the next story, a freelance can stay around and get to know a person better. A man who interested me was mindreader Jon Tremaine. There are many who will say that ESP is trickery (I wonder if their closed minds and determination to cling desperately to logic to prove them wrong at all costs are not a sign of insecurity?), while others swear by it. I am not qualified to give an opinion but if Jon Tremaine based his act on trickery, he was exceedingly clever. He certainly got me to do something unusual.

During one part of his act, he would call a person on to the stage and say they had won £25,000 in a lottery. The answer to his questions varied but an example was: 'What will you do with the money?'

'Buy a caravan.'

'How many wheels?'

'Five.'

'Five wheels? That's unusual. How many windows?'

'Seven.'

And so it would go on. Jon would then get an assistant to hand the man or woman a sealed envelope which was then opened. On the sheet of paper, written in Jon's hand and read out by the lucky winner of £25,000, would be the answers, stating the caravan, five wheels and seven windows. Another of his inexplicable performances, to me, anyway, was to tell people exactly how much cash they were carrying. They, personally, had not a clue until they emptied their pockets.

I invited Jon to my office for an interview and told him, 'I reckon that unless you have a different stooge every night, the only way you could have done the act on the caravan was to write out the card with the answers in advance and then, instead of reading the man's mind, you actually planted the thoughts into it.' Jon smiled and with a stammer, replied, 'Yes, that's right.' He asked me if I had any playing cards and I quickly sent out for some. Then he asked me to spread them out on my desk, faced down, and run my finger above them until I chose the card I wanted. It was a normal ESP test but I have never claimed ESP. 'I'll take the Queen of Clubs,' I said, and then picked out that very card. I shuffled and repeated the performance, this time choosing the Two of Diamonds. Again I picked out the correct card. On the third occasion I got it wrong and Jon's face was a picture of perplexity until I mentioned that I had briefly lost my concentration. After he left the office, I tried several times to repeat the two successful performances but failed dismally. Jon, who has appeared on British TV and entertained the Royal Family at Windsor, read the mind of Prince Charles when he was a child.

So if Jon Tremaine really did have ESP and could read minds and also implant thoughts into others', how had it come about? He told me that during the evacuation of London after WW2 broke out, he was sent to the country and lived with a family which detested him. One day the elder son, a bully, tied him into a high chair at the top of the stairs and pushed him down. The traumatic experience left Jon speechless for many years but his mind remained alert and after a period of watching people he would know what they were about to say. His mind reading developed from that. Slowly his voice returned, but with the stammer.

The only other time I had come upon ESP was in London during the Ferrari years which impressed me with the mental relationship between humans and other animals. A man claimed that he and his German Shepherd could play noughts and crosses and demonstrated to me with the dog barking out the number of squares where it wanted to put a cross. When the dog won I asked for it to be put into another room with the door closed before they played another game. The dog barked at the correct squares and it won again.

Goodbye, Africa

Eartha Kitt came to Rhodesia and I took her to lunch with freelance journalist, Justin Nyoka. They got on well and Justin was embarrassed when the internationally famous star insisted on going to his humble township home to meet the family. I'd known Justin for many years as a BBC World Service stringer and as he'd never been to Bush House we decided that as I was about to make my annual pilgrimage to ITN, we would travel to London together. We kept quiet about our departure as news of it would have reached the ears of the Special Branch who would come to all sorts of imaginative conclusions. En route we stopped off at Nairobi as I wanted to call on Eric Robins. Nairobi Airport proved itself capable of yet another farce which only Africa seems capable of producing: Justin was held at the airport and not allowed to leave because he had 'Rhodesia' stamped in his passport while I, a white man from the same plane which had flown in from the south, had no problems.

Eric's reception was cool, explaining that he'd heard my book, *The Silent War*, supported Ian Smith. When I protested that this was nonsense, the warm-hearted Marion Kaplan in her ever-friendly way said, 'Don't bother to explain, you know what he's like.' I left after a drink with him at a nearby hotel and rejoined Justin at the airport, never to see Eric again. This piece of deliberate misreporting had been given him by the *Daily Telegraph* reporter who could personally do no wrong in the eyes of the Smith Government and was given the most favourable treatment by the Information Department. It was the same correspondent (whom I'd sometimes help and was even a guest of when I invited Joshua Nkomo to a dinner party), who had been one of the two reluctant journalists I'd later taken to see the mortaring on Luanda beach and who left Angola after their hotel room misreporting of the war was revealed by the CIA.

The secrecy surrounding the London trip lasted no further than Rome where another of my many extraordinary coincidences took place. As we climbed steps inside the Sistine Chapel, a voice was heard from above: 'Hello, Reg, Hello Justin.' Incredibly, waiting at the top were two non-journalist members of the Quill Club! Could we never get away?

'Let's find a beer garden,' I suggested on our arrival in Munich. As the Oompah band played, we sat down on wooden seats beside a German family which included two teenage daughters, and as we chatted a couple of youthful dropouts edged around trying to attract the girls away. I didn't know that Justin had noticed but after a while he called the youths over and then stood up and publicly harangued them for a good ten minutes on good behaviour

I take Eartha Kitt to lunch. Picture: Rhodesia Herald.

and manners. The band stopped playing and the beer garden became silent as the former schoolmaster held the stage. When he sat down there was a brief silence before the whole beer garden erupted into standing ovation as the youths slunk away. It was a remarkable performance by any standard but especially from a man who had never seen Europe before. I felt proud of my companion.

Travelling with Justin was an illuminating experience. A well-educated person who could quote Shakespeare at will, he nevertheless had preconceived ideas on the importance of Africa to the outside world. He also believed his skin colour united all blacks and overrode loyalties to their countries of birth or adoption. During our flight conversations Justin had declared, 'You Europeans will never understand the Africans,' and I threw back that we probably understood them a damned sight more than he realised. In London we rode on the Underground and on the escalator Justin raised his arm in salute to every black man he saw and sometimes called, 'Hello, Brother.' He carried on with this in the streets and couldn't understand why he was totally ignored. The look of puzzlement on his face was revealing and I commented dryly, 'Not every black man in Europe understands the Africans.' For a moment our eyes met and the subject was dropped although I would have liked to ask him why the Muslim religion is so popular with the blacks when it was the Arabs who were the original perpetrators of black slavery. Once on a trip to Tunisia, a coach driver pointed out a small village as a tourist curiosity, 'They are the only blacks in Tunisia,' he declared and laughed, 'We shipped off all their ancestors as slaves!' The word 'kaffir' which has been used as a derogatory word to describe Africans in South Africa is actually a Muslim word for infidel.

A pleasant summer's afternoon had greeted Justin's and my arrival in London and in the evening I booked into an hotel before going for a stroll. When I returned, there was a message for me to ring a certain telephone number. As there was no way anyone could know where I was staying. I threw the note away. At 7 a.m. the telephone rang, 'Hello, Reg, it's Charles here.' We had met briefly in Salisbury when he came out with a British mission and I, together with a journalist friend of his, had seen him off at the airport. I was impressed that Charles should not only know of my arrival but where I was staying as not even Justin, whose activities I suspected extended beyond journalism, knew of my hotel as it was chosen at random. 'I wonder if you would care to join me for lunch?' We dined at the Travellers' Club and while there I was asked a couple of probing questions but nothing of substance. During lunch I was surprised to be asked who would come to power, if not Robert Mugabe. There was no question that Mugabe would make it and I was sure Charles knew this too, so I gave the name of an obscure nationalist who sometimes came to my office. I was curious to see how much Whitehall knew about the nationalist hierarchy and it was enlightening to see Charles's reaction of disbelief as he knew all about the man I mentioned. I concluded that he had comprehensive tabs on every African nationalist in Rhodesia and strongly suspected Justin was the source of this information. I left London on a South African Airways jumbo jet without Justin and as I looked through a window at the queue of people on the tarmac waiting to board, there was one man whom I instinctively knew would sit beside me. The jumbo was full and I was travelling tourist yet the stewardess had said, 'Here's your seat, Mr Shay.' As I looked hard at her she turned away quickly: there are no names on tourist boarding cards. The last man aboard sat next to me, the same man I had mentally picked and he immediately introduced himself as an architect from Johannesburg. Many journalists can spot a policeman a mile away and this one was much closer than that. All this attention was flattering but I had no idea what it was about or why anyone should think I was worth watching. Sometime later I was advised that the intelligence organisations of five countries were keeping an eye on me.

There was a sequel to the trip. Throughout our visit to Europe, Justin would gently sing in a pleasant voice, 'We are going, we are going, heaven knows where we are going.' It was prophetic. In August 1978, he disappeared from a ranch he'd mischievously bought in Enkeldoorn, the heartland of Afrikanerdom in Rhodesia, and was taken away by an armed band of Africans who called at his home. There was a whip-round at the Quill for his wife, Esther, but no one knew if she was a widow. We didn't know if he had been taken by the Special Branch or by guerrillas and if it was guerrillas, which group? Justin had previously supported Joshua Nkomo but changed his allegiance to Robert Mugabe when he realised the way the wind was blowing. I'd feared for his life but fortunately for him he was taken away by Mugabe's men who told him he was about to be visited by the SB. After African independence he became Zimbabwe's Director of Information and people called him Comrade and if I had stayed in Zimbabwe we would probably have been on opposite sides of the fence because of my brushes with censorship. He died in a car crash, but the general impression amongst journalists was that he had been murdered, but by whom? I wouldn't know as I wasn't there, but I do know it's very dangerous to be mixed up in politics in Africa.

Justin had been with me when African nationalist leaders were holding a meeting to see if their two sides could unite in their struggle against Ian Smith. The meeting was held inside a shop in the Highfield township while the main road leading into the township was lined on either side with thousands of Mugabe and Nkomo supporters facing each other. A handful of journalists were present and as we stood in the centre it soon became clear that there was still no love lost between the two sides. They were kept from each other's throats by armed police with dogs who were totally outnumbered but we few pressmen were thankful for their presence as tension mounted all along the dusty road. Inside the shop the arguments became so heated that at one stage, an Nkomo man decided the room needed ventilation and as we watched, one of Mugabe's top men came hurtling through the plate-glass window. This

A tense moment as Rhodesian police shoot thirteen dead. Picture: author.

antagonism provoked war chants and fist waving by the two sides and one man waved his fist at me. I decided to keep an eye on him but believed it was all posturing until thirty yards away shots rang out. Pandemonium broke loose amongst the Mugabe supporters as police fired their pistols all along the line and ran into the crowd with their dogs. I watched men fall as bullets tore into their backs while they attempted to run away through a field behind them which led to a broken-glass-topped wall they had to scale to escape. Most of them made it regardless of torn hands but one man was shot in the chest before attempting to run. I guessed he had been earmarked by the police and wondered if he had deliberately stayed to attack someone he didn't like. As I gazed down at his lifeless eyes, I knew he would not angrily wave his fist at me any more.

The Information Department put out a report that the police took action to prevent trouble, that they only opened fire when attacked. This could be true and I should be grateful to the men who possibly saved the lives of the journalists standing there defenceless. I hadn't seen any sign of the scuffling which was supposed to have triggered the killing of thirteen people, I only saw them being shot. But two policemen with dogs did themselves little credit afterwards when a black nun walked past on a visit to a friend. She could have been courteously asked to leave the area rather than be shouted at and told to 'Fuck off'. The second dog handler walked past me and it was clear the shooting had made his day. He had a song in his heart and his voice echoed along the dusty road and over the field of death where the bodies of the slain were still lying. His song: 'Oh, what a beautiful morning...' I got through to ABC News (Radio) in New York and suggested a voicepiece backed by my on-the-spot reporting and tape recorded sounds of shooting screams of the dying. 'I'm sorry, Reg,' said the foreign news editor, 'but we're full up with domestic news today.'

Amongst the pictures on my walls at home is a large sketch of two big cats snarling passionately as a prelude to sex. A remarkable feature of the sketch is that it was executed with a felt-tipped pen which never left the paper until the work was completed. The signature at the bottom is simply, 'Jeni'. I had a lot of time for Jeni which I suppose was mutual, for she executed the work for me as an unsolicited gesture. Tall and angular, Jeni was not beautiful but she had both a great sense of humour and of fun.

After I had resigned as Quill Club chairman, the committee decided to waste club money on putting up a metal barrier between the bar and the drinking area even though doors were locked at closing time. The club was based on the first floor of the Ambassador Hotel and I pointed out that if anyone broke into the club rooms, they could get behind the bar despite the shutters. 'Not so,' I was told; that was something like throwing down the gauntlet. By chance, I ran into Jeni and she was looking very unwell and a little sad. She had told me earlier that she was dying of cancer with only about a year to go, and had been to the hospital for treatment earlier in the day. 'Do you feel like breaking the law for a beer?' I asked, and her eyes lit up mischievously. After club (and licensing) hours, we went to the Ambassador and climbed out through some first floor windows and on to a low roof which led to the Quill. I opened more windows which led to behind the grilled bar and took a couple of beers before leaving and entering through another window into the club lounge where we had a drink. After I had left two empty bottles and some money on the counter we went back through the window. I never told the new chairman about his ridiculous bar grill; it seemed nicer to keep it as a little secret between Jeni and myself.

Jeni had mentioned that she had met a very strange German who lived out in the bush and kept a rest camp for troops. 'His name is Willie Walderich and he really is odd,' she said. 'He told me he was an officer in the German army during the war.' My curiosity was aroused. A former Hitler officer running a rest camp for soldiers in the middle of the Rhodesian bush didn't make a lot of sense. Bill Zimmerman of ABC News was in town at the time and I suggested we charter a plane to Binga, on the shores of Lake Kariba, where Jeni would set up a meeting. Bill and I arrived at Binga and paid a courtesy call on the District Commissioner, with whom we had tea, before going to the local pub to meet Herr Walderich. He drove up in a Land Rover with an automatic pistol over his shoulder and a Luger in his waist-belt holster. Over a Castle lager, he began to explain himself. 'Ja,' he said. 'I vos an officer in ze German army. I fought in Crete, I fought in Monte Cassino, I fought on ze Russian front.' 'How very interesting,' I said, hoping to coax him into what he was doing now. 'On ze Russian front, it was bitterly cold and full of snow,' said Walderich. 'There was no food and I was very hungry and I thought I would starve.'

But Providence shone upon Willie Walderich to prove that God moves in mysterious ways. 'There vos a lot of shooting and then my colonel, Ja, my colonel, he vos shot dead. Do you know vot I did?' By this time Bill Zimmerman was looking uncomfortable and had already formed his own opinion of Walderich. 'What did you do?' he asked. 'I ate his leg… I ate my own colonel's leg!' said Walderich. Bill looked at me reproachfully. 'Christ,' he said. 'We've come all this way just to meet a fucking Nazi cannibal!'

We never did find out what Walderich was up to in Rhodesia as the District Commissioner rushed into the bar in a flaming temper. He had checked back with the Information Department to find that I was persona non grata. To him, we were clearly journalist spies. 'You will leave Binga immediately,' he ordered. And we did. He, and Rhodesia, were welcome to protect Willie Walderich against citizens such as myself.

The District Commissioner for Kariba had been presented with a new motor launch and a press party was invited along for a ride. Also aboard was an Under Secretary for Internal Affairs, Bob Woollacott, who was a personal friend for despite his high position and also being of Rhodesian pioneer stock, Bob was not a UDI supporter. Kariba, once the largest man-made lake in the world, being 175 miles long, was subject to highly dangerous storms and while we were out on the lake, the wind strengthened and the water became choppy. Soon we were in a real storm but the District Commissioner was so serene that I half expected him to raise his hands to calm the troubled waters. 'There is absolutely nothing to worry about,' he said. 'Remember, this is a brand-new boat with all the latest in safety equipment on board.'

I asked, as if tempting Fate, 'What happens if the engine packs up?' A tall man, he smiled down condescendingly to the little fellow who obviously knew far less about boats than he did. 'I don't think there is any chance of that, do you?' In answer to his question there was a coughing sound from the engine suggesting it was in its death throes. I noticed the smug grin disappear when the engine choked and stopped altogether but the smile soon returned. 'There is still nothing to worry about, it's a twin-engined job, you know.'

'And there's not much chance of that packing up as well?' I ventured. By this time the boat was rocking so much that I found it easier to hang on to an overhead cross beam than to have my feet permanently on the deck. 'The chances of both these new engines failing are one in a million,' he assured me. It is amazing how those million-to-one shots can come off. He'd hardly uttered the reassuring words when there was another splutter as the second engine failed. Never one to take these situations seriously, I asked if he had a back-up paddle but he was not amused and rushed to the radio in panic to call, 'May Day!' I didn't feel in any real danger even though we were heading for some rocks; more interesting to me was the certainty that that we were drifting helplessly towards the hostile Zambian bank. As Zambia harboured anti-Rhodesian guerrillas loyal to Nkomo and a few trigger-happy troops of their own, I felt there was far more possibility of being shot than drowned. The alarm was answered and another large boat appeared on the scene to throw us a line and pull us away from the shore when we were less than fifty yards from being wrecked. Bob Woollacott told me some years later that it was sheer coincidence (yet another?) that the other vessel was in the area and that it was the only one on the lake capable of rescuing us. I don't think that my guardian angel was particularly looking after the District Commissioner: it was he who was responsible for setting up The Cage.

Most airports can be likened to spiders' webs. After entering them it's often difficult to get out and the reasons for flight delays are seldom given. But I was privileged to be let into the secret of why a Boeing 747 was delayed from leaving the mausoleum-inspired Jan Smuts Airport in Johannesburg. The explanation came from a very attractive petite blonde wearing the uniform of South African Airways ground staff. As I sat and waited bored and agitated, she materialised like a vision of loveliness and sat beside me, immediately taking my hand which she held on her lap. My pulse throbbed with excitement at this unexpected and deliriously exciting turn of events – and I confess that my jaundiced view of Jan Smuts Airport changed immediately – when the young woman said, 'Your plane is late taking off and so I thought I would come and sit with you.' 'Yes,' I sighed.

'I heard the announcement.' Then I realised that this was the same girl who had given me my boarding pass at the counter. With clear and mischievous blue eyes, she declared, 'They are having a lot of trouble with that plane!' My mind flashed back to the nurse who had casually mentioned during my wardroom frolics that I might be suffering from a malignant growth. Should this delightful young enchantress be revealing all to a passenger waiting to go aboard? I plucked up courage and asked the inevitable question, 'What sort of trouble?'

'It's one of the toilets,' she said, hardly able to contain her bubbling laughter. 'They've already spent half an hour trying to get the seat down!' Flushing toilets has sometimes caused problems for me as I've searched in frustration for the necessary implement of waste disposal. Hotels and trains in Europe have been particularly troublesome, ranging from the old chain to buttons on walls, the floor, and even behind the seat flap. All too soon the tannoy burst into life calling passengers to the plane and I found myself empty-handed as the SAA girl took her leave. I was in half a mind to forget the plane and spend an ecstatic night in Johannesburg but wisdom prevailed and I boarded the SAA plane only to be frustrated for the second time that afternoon when I couldn't find how to flush the toilet. Finally I put the seat down in despair and then I realised what the girl had been talking about: that was when it flushed.

On another unlikely airport occasion, I was flying back to Rhodesia from Heathrow, having just visited Spain. I'd bought a large South American-type sombrero, complete with tassels, for one of the children but it was so awkward to carry that I put it on my head. Also at the airport was my good friend, Robert Marple. Robert was principal of some African private schools and many whites thought this high-living scholar was a 'kaffir boetie' because the schools had been privately set up to help youngsters who could not get a proper education under the government system. Such was the delicacy of the situation and the tightrope he walked that the children themselves (aged up to twenty years), and not knowing his background, once went on a terrible rampage of destruction and Robert locked himself in a lavatory to avoid serious injury or death, while they searched for him.

At the airport, I saw that Robert had brought a yard-of-ale glass in a long round box, strapped to his back. It resembled a quiver. The plane was crowded but the British Airways girl at the counter had seen that here were two passengers who could be trouble – a veritable Mexican Pete and Robin Hood. We boarded the plane and were greeted with cheers by several of the passengers already on board who knew either one or other of us. It is surprising just how many people we did know on that jumbo. To our delight, we were given a whole row of seats to ourselves. Both Robert and I believe in living first class even if we do sometimes travel tourist and we sipped sherry before the meal, washed down the food with palatable wine, finishing off with coffee and cognac. The film was watched in comfort and then we stretched out on the seats for the night while other passengers who had laughed at us, suffered the agonies of sitting upright throughout the flight.

Flying in Rhodesia, however, posed more problems than lavatory seats or uncomfortable seating accommodation. An old-timer who had started his own newspaper was 'Flash' Seaton. He was a hard-working journalist and his public relations son, Roger, had always told me that his father would die on the printers' stone. Because of censorship harassment, Flash eventually moved to South Africa and worked on a Johannesburg newspaper and he was on duty when the shock news came through that a Rhodesian passenger plane had been shot down in the north of the country, near Lake Kariba. It was a great tragedy. After the Russian-made SAM-7 missile struck the plane, the pilot skilfully managed to crash-land in thick, rocky bush before he was killed on impact. There were eighteen survivors, including young air hostesses. They lived until the guerrillas came along who, instead of giving them a helping hand, shot everyone dead. Two children were amongst those murdered but a couple who had gone for help escaped to tell the tale. The crash had not meant a great deal to Flash, other than it being a good story. Then, while at the stone, he read the names of the dead. I like to think that Roger died with a gin in his hand; he had always ordered one on take off...

During a holiday flight to Spain with Margery, (she'd returned to Salisbury to live some time ago) I bought a villa on the Costa Blanca at the very beautiful coastal resort of Javea. For some time I had felt my days were numbered in Rhodesia and it was as well to purchase a funk hole into which I could retire. Margery chose the villa which overlooked the sun-drenched glistening Mediterranean. The area even boasted hillside terracing built by the Moors which would be a nostalgic reminder of Inyanga.

I had always determined that I'd retire while I was still young enough to enjoy life but there was more to it than that. It was clear that Robert Mugabe would come to power at some stage and I'd no reason to believe that life as a journalist under his rule would be any different than with Ian Smith. The journalists who had bowed to Smith would do the same to Mugabe who, in turn, would use the same repressive laws brought in by Ian Smith's govern-ment. There would be no long-term place for me, a freedom-loving freelance journalist and so-called maverick. It was noticeable to me how few stories came out of Zimbabwe since independence until Mugabe sent out his millen-nium message which encouraged his followers to invade white farms and take them over by intimidation and murder. My own granddaughter and her husband were amongst the first to suffer from the seizures – their neighbour was murdered in March 2002.

Shortly after our flight home from Spain an assistant commissioner of police, Mike Edden, approached me in Reps Bar and his demeanour was reminiscent of the enraged Luis d'Almeida. He was spluttering at the mouth, and shouted for all to hear, 'Are you for us, or against us? Are you for us, or against us? Are you for us or against us?' He kept repeating the same words in uncontrollable rage as he prodded my chest with his forefinger. I wondered what he was on about and was concerned because, as a head of the Special

Branch, he wasn't the type to cross swords with too often. 'Mueller,' he snapped. 'You sent a message about Mueller!' It was true. That morning I had telexed my co-author, Chris Vermaak, in Johannesburg, asking if he knew of a South African army major named Mueller who was masquerading as a colonel in the Rhodesian army. The monitored telex must have really got people jumping as Chris told me later that he was hauled before the highest military authority in South Africa and seriously reprimanded for receiving my message! Rhodesia, I decided, was becoming very sick indeed and the paranoid reaction to my telex indicated just how quickly my every monitored message was being sent to men with power. As with Angola, there was no guarantee for my safety, not only from the guerrillas but from the very people I was working amongst. I was also becoming weary of the African political scene; the blatant lies of half-baked politicians, black and white, who had no scruples and who frequently brand journalists as liars whereas, in reality, most of us are basically honest and merely quote liars. The journalists most hated by extremist politicians, left or right of the political spectrum, are those who are prepared to risk their careers and even their lives in search of truth.

It was shortly after the Mike Edden row that I was driving along a very difficult guerrilla area and was expecting to be blasted into eternity by a mine or an ambush at any moment when I thought: what the hell am I doing here when I could be relaxing beside the Mediterranean? I put the proposition to Margery and she agreed that perhaps it was time to go. 'Would you like a last look at the country?' I asked.

'Yes, I'd love that,' she replied without hesitation. She knew the dangers of flying on the same schedule as the Viscount that had been shot down killing Roger Seaton, but shrugged it off. She too found it exhilarating flying at tree-top height for some distance after take-off. We made the trip and I was particularly impressed by the courage of the two young air hostesses, attractive girls in their teens who were very attentive to Margery. By flying this route they knew they were living at the cutting edge.

It was a couple of days after our return to Salisbury that I telephoned Derek Ebben, who was head of the United Touring Company in Rhodesia, and suggested our weekly lunch be held on Friday. One of Nature's gentlemen, Derek had suffered imprisonment by the Japanese during WW2, and subsequently was eased out of his job as Director of Tourism in Zambia through 'Africanization'. This was a form of apartheid, acceptable in Africa, where top jobs are reserved for blacks and the former white bosses, who understood the business, were kept on to run the show as advisers. In Britain it would be considered racial prejudice.

Derek was a very close friend of mine and once, during a trip to Geneva, I telephoned Zurich where I knew him to be and he flew over for dinner which we shared with a tall, blonde, beautiful German travel agent. After a trip to the Pussycat nightclub the three of us set off in high spirits down the sober streets of Geneva dancing the steps of 'We're off to see the Wizard'. A couple of months later I was invited to Derek's home for lunch where I inadvertently disgraced myself. His wife, Peggy, enjoyed the social graces and there was just a handful of guests for lunch and quail, which was the main course, was exquisitely served. I prodded my quail with a fork and was so surprised at what happened next that I exclaimed in a loud voice, 'Good heavens, it's laid an egg!' This was greeted with hushed silence of the kind to be expected when Hercule Poirot is about to disclose the name of the murderer. I should have realised the gaff; that cleaning the bird had been left to the domestic help who probably thought that leaving an egg inside was a bonus for the finder. But seeing the egg with the complete shell around it was so fascinating that I prodded again and out came another egg, this time with half a shell. 'This really is extraordinary,' I declared to the assembled company. 'It's rather like a production line.' The guests' attention was immediately captured by Peggy who began a conversation totally unconnected with the source of my wonderment. A third prod and a third egg came out, this time with no shell at all. 'I can't believe it,' I exclaimed. 'Look at that!' Derek smiled across bleakly, 'Yes, old chap. Aren't you lucky?' The rest of the meal was uneventful and I can only guess why I was never invited back.

During our phone chat, Derek suggested we postpone our usual Friday lunch to Monday as he had to fly to Kariba on business. I was in the office when Jim Brady telephoned to say that another Viscount had been shot down and I went to the telex to dash out the story, happy that so far as I was aware, I didn't know anyone on the plane. Suddenly I stopped typing the news item and dashed to the telephone; the girl receptionist at the United Touring Company was in tears. The plane my dear friend took was the same that Margery and I had been flying on the week before carrying the same pilots and air hostesses. There were no survivors.

One person within my own profession who was also partly responsible for my planned departure was a colleague, ITN's Mike Nicholson. Mike's bravery is as indisputable as the quality of his television reporting and he has picked up many awards but there is another side to him. He has sparks of mischief which could get him into trouble and that includes sneaking up to people and pushing them into swimming pools, a practice of which I, as a poor swimmer, thoroughly disapprove. He told me that he did it once in Cyprus and the recipient of his frivolity went looking for him with gun in hand and murder in his heart. I feel that anyone over the age of ten years who pushes people into pools has to be watched, and Mike has been watched by millions on TV. It was, therefore, with some apprehension that I felt for any unsuspecting sailor who might be gazing over the rails of HMS *Gloucester* in the Gulf War once I realized Nicholson was on board! I learned of this weakness when standing innocently beside a pool after he had driven off from Frances Louw's home following a luncheon, but what I had not realised was that he'd run back over the lawn and within seconds I was treading water.

The first friendly retaliation occurred as we drove towards Mount Darwin, past scores of empty kraals with roofless huts which had been burned by the security forces to stop guerrillas sheltering in them. Because it was a long journey I decided to take a picnic lunch and amongst the goodies were hard-boiled eggs which I casually threw to the camera team to catch. For some inexplicable reason I had kept one egg in my office refrigerator for about a year, knowing it would come in useful one day. This one I had not cooked and I tossed it to Mike. He was good, very good, as instinct told him there was something wrong and he let the egg crash to the ground.

We were out on another occasion following a particularly grisly guerrilla attack – a marauding gang had carried out brutal murders the day before – when we stopped beside a bridge for a leak. I had just begun to pee when I heard the car doors slam behind me and my three companions were away. There was a conspiracy, I knew, but what was it about? They could not really intend to leave me on the bridge to be murdered; that was unsporting. They had disappeared on to a path in a wooded area instead of carrying along the main road, which was puzzling in itself. Fifteen minutes later the car swung out from the trees and on to the road and stopped to pick me up. All three were looking smug but refused to disclosed what they had been up to. Next day was my birthday and a small party was held for me. The ITN team headed by Mike solemnly presented me with a cake box and wished me a happy birthday and I mumbled my thanks with a gruff voice choking with emotion and opened the box. The reason for their shooting off into the bush and leaving me to my fate in that lonely terrorist-saturated area suddenly crystal-lized as I gazed into the cake box. They had spent fifteen minutes collecting bullshit! Score two–nil for Nicholson.

I hadn't forgotten Mike's penchant for swimming pools and decided he really should be taught a lesson, preferably hoist by his own petard. Frances (this was before my Angolan experience) was holding a party once again at her home, this time for Mike's birthday, and she had put a balloon in a cake which she'd made. Naturally, he was invited to do the honours and cut the cake! Once again his uncanny sixth sense told him something was wrong and he refused to push in the knife. I, meanwhile, had written a note before leaving the office: 'Tell Mike when I've gone, that his car keys are in the pool.' It was winter and because Fanny's pool was untended during the cold season, it was murky and filled with algae. Mike's Mercedes was parked just inside the drive and, with Till Eulenspiegel mischievousness, I removed his car keys and threw them into the deep end of the pool before walking in to enjoy the lunch. I'd reversed my car anticipating a possible quick getaway and towards the end of the party, I apologised for having to leave early and handed the note to our hostess, asking her to hand it to the birthday boy after I'd gone. Mike saw the exchange and suspected skulduggery was afoot. He grabbed the note and read it as I was making for the door, then looked up in disbelief with the words, 'You wouldn't!'

'Take a bet?' I called back as I raced for my car with Mike in hot pursuit. I was in and away just before he reached me and he went back to his car and realised the keys were indeed missing.

Back at the office, I received a call from Frances which disclosed that my Machiavellian scheme was working beyond all expectations. Pandemonium now reigned and I was wise to have avoided such goings on. I knew that Mike had a short fuse which, it seems, was actually ignited by cold water. He and the soundman stripped off and dived into the murky depths while the cameraman and a girl companion stood beside the pool watching, entranced. Frustrated, Nicholson's slimy body emerged and he didn't resemble the suave TV journalist in the slightest degree. Enraged at seeing his still-clothed cameraman and the girl, who was wearing an expensive new dress, he hurled them both fully clothed into the water before diving back in. Indignant at the treatment, the cameraman then emerged to throw in both Nicholson's and the soundman's clothes. Tensions by now were running dangerously high and it was only after fifteen minutes of searching the icy bottom of the pool that the keys were recovered. The cameraman and the girl stayed at the house while their clothes dried; Mike and the soundman, meanwhile, drove back to the hotel with only towels to cover their nakedness. While driving towards the centre of Salisbury they saw an African hitch-hiker who couldn't believe his luck when the sparkling Mercedes stopped. He sat alone on the luxurious back seat and through the rear-view mirror the pair could see his face change when he realised he was in a car with two naked white men. They hadn't gone far when the passenger suddenly disclosed that Salisbury was not his destination after all, and he left hurriedly. On arrival at the plush Meikles Hotel the couple walked nonchalantly and with great panache across the foyer and asked for their keys as though nothing was untoward. In the true tradition of best hotels, there was not even a raised eyebrow as they went to the lift, still clad only in their loaned towels. Score two–one.

It was therefore with shock some time later that I learned that Mike and another of his many camera teams, Tom Phillips and Mick Doyle, were missing in Angola. I had given them a swinging party shortly before they left on the dangerous trip. I was in London when the new foreign editor told me they were stuck in Angola with the Unita movement and there seemed to be no way of getting them out. Desperate measures were called for and Mike Morris, then deputy FE, was put in charge of attempts to save them and he devised a scheme to snatch them away in a charter plane. I returned to Salisbury with an assurance that if this method failed, I would have a go. Their reluctance to agree probably had something to do with my own experience there and I knew what would happen to me if I was caught. But I reckoned that with my bush knowledge, and that by taking some part-time members of the Rhodesian security forces who were expert trackers, we should be able to make it. In the event, Mike and his team were eventually saved by the charter aircraft although the pilot wasn't told what he was letting himself in for. They returned to England in a blaze of glory.

After the fuss had died down, they came back to Rhodesia and I gave a celebratory party. Tom and Mick came along but Mike failed to turn up, which surprised me especially as we had corresponded over the telex while he was in London and I'd sent him ten new story suggestions which he described as 'impressive'. Impressive or not, next day he fired me with the lame excuse that, despite the suggestions and that he was taking all the stories, I was not being active enough. I never got to the bottom of it; perhaps he listened to the made-up stories about me in Angola, or perhaps he was concerned that I was exceedingly highly paid by ITN and disapproved of a freelance earning more than some staff men. I knew, too, that Nicholson had an insatiable appetite for the limelight and the thought of sharing it (unlike Jim Giggams of ABC News) was anathema to him. This meant that even though I'd started and built up a successful ITN operation, I was now just feeding Nicholson's appetite for stories thus losing my main source of income. I was interested, therefore, on reading his autobiography, that he claimed to have come up with sixty ideas of his own. He had used forty of mine and the only original idea he had for a story in Rhodesia was to travel briefly on the footplate of a steam engine! Whatever, it was a poor reward for all that I had done, especially as my Africa reporting had put the BBC into the shade. As a top figure in ITN, Nigel Ryan, said to me later, 'You watched ITN's back.' My mumbled reply was simply, 'But no one watched mine!' I don't think he heard.

Despite opposition at home, Nicholson had come to Africa to stay because he liked Rhodesia and South Africa and he had been well looked-after by me. He startled me once when he said how much he admired Mike Edden, the SB chief, and how well he got on with him. I guessed at the time that the 'loose cannon' (my words) would have come under some discussion during their talks which possibly had some bearing on my being fired. Now that I was vulnerable I was told that I would be called into the police reserve despite being fifty years of age with heart problems. This was in defiance of letters from my doctor and heart specialist declaring that I was unfit for police duty of any kind. Clearly people were out to get me and I was tipped off that I would be sent to a Protected Village and was warned darkly, 'Anything can happen to you.' I didn't fancy being shot in the back by one of my own people and with this background knowledge I decided to leave before the papers arrived. Ironically, three days before my departure the deputy head of Information, knowing there would be a change of government, approached me. 'I think we should get together and have a new understanding,' he said. I ignored him.

A couple of weeks before I left, a poignant incident occurred in which I actually felt sorry for Ian Smith. Guerrillas had set fire to the huge oil storage tanks in Salisbury which virtually spelled the end of the road for UDI; expensive oil that had come into the country despite sanctions through the ingenious conniving of government and private enterprise. A group of pressmen had been invited by the Information Department to the scene and I was advised that I would not be welcome. Smith's private secretary, Sandhurst-trained sanctions buster, Costa Pafitas, (the same Greek would soon be bearing gifts to Robert Mugabe by becoming his private secretary when power changed hands!) told me that I was not rated as a journalist of any significance and would be turned back if I went along. He knew through Nicholson that I no longer represented ITN but I went anyway and saw Pafitas standing beside Ian Smith. When he saw me his eyes blazed like the oil tanks.

After a reporter asked Smith what significance the guerrilla attack would have on the country's future, the rebel prime minister turned and put his hand on my shoulder in front of the assembled TV and press cameras and declared emotionally, 'We Rhodesians must stick together.' I looked across to Pafitas who stared back without comprehension and I thought of how different things might have been for me if I'd compromised my principles. Ian Smith hadn't compromised either and I'd admired him for that but now neither of us had any future in the country. We had been unknowns who had peaked in our own way but having peaked, it was now over. He would go down in history, admired and hated for the stand he had taken; I would return to virtual obscurity.

A small farewell party was held for me by two very close friends, Gil and Mary Buss, but just three months after my departure, they were divorced. Mary always said I'd kept them together.

Retirement, Spain and My National Daily Newspaper

Retirement to many people comprises pottering around the garden, pruning the roses, taking a morning and afternoon constitutional with Fido, and then returning to a centrally heated lounge to watch television. Some people with high pensions like to continue their working-life practice of getting in a couple of rounds of golf during the week.

My press relations company's clients had included Rhodesia's largest building society and we were asked by them to organise a golf tournament. I turned up with every intention of teeing off last but to my surprise and horror, I was invited to go first. 'But I can't play,' I protested lamely. Everyone looked at my smart Wilson clubs and informed me with knowing winks that they had heard these excuses before. I was trapped. 'You had better stand back,' I declared and they laughed politely.

Swinging the club in practice had been fine, no problem at all. Only when it came to hitting the ball did everything go awry. Down came the two-half wood which made contact with the ball; at least I hadn't missed the damned thing. Putting my hand to my eyes to shade them from the sun, I gazed with sudden confidence to where it might land. 'Can you see it?' I asked my opponent. There was no reply and as I turned for a possible polite handclap, those waiting to tee off appeared to be suffering from abdominal contractions. Convulsed with hysterical derision, they pointed fingers over their shoulders to an area fifty-feet astern. I had sliced the ball which had ricocheted off a boulder thirty yards to the right, before landing to the point directly behind me. It was a successful PR exercise as none of the competitors was made to feel inferior when they muffed a shot.

Then the press challenged a group of businessmen and I was brought in. No decision had been made as to who would partner whom but I happened to put my ball on the tee and swung the club in practice. To my astonishment, the wood made contact and the little white missile shot off like a rocket, straight down the fairway.

One of the press corps' top golfers, George Nicholas, who was agricultural correspondent of the *Rhodesia Herald*, looked on in admiration. 'I'm partnering you, Reg,' he said with a broad grin. 'I hit it by accident,' I faltered. He didn't believe a word when I said that he might be the agricultural correspondent but that I was the biggest divot digger of all time. 'Nonsense,' he declared. Golf, like sailing, can give an enlightening insight into human character and as with the sudden overpowering dominance of Tony Down, once we were on a boat travelling down the Zambezi River, so too came an unexpected personality change with George. From a mild nature-lover, he transformed into a snarling maniac but in all fairness to myself, the Country Club was a difficult golf course with plenty of rough and high grass which gobbled up golf balls – twelve of which I'd borrowed from George.

The third golfing incident took place in Javea when I played with Rob and his friend, John Clark. I was invited to tee off and gave a mighty swipe to which the ball did not do justice. It bounced into long grass ten feet away, never to be seen again. The second ball didn't even leave the ground and bulldozed its way through the same grass to be reunited with its golf-bag companion. The third ball rolled in front of a tree, this time it remained in view, and with disdain Rob and John then teed off with excellent shots. My next shot hit the tree with force and I looked into the air to try to find the trajectory of the ricochet. I was still gazing skyward when I heard Rob shouting, 'John, John, are you all right?' The prone figure of John Clark was lying flat on his face and forgetting about the ball I ran forward, believing he'd suffered a heart attack. John lay perfectly still and I wasn't even sure if he was conscious but I had a growing uneasy feeling that whatever fate had befallen him, I was somehow responsible.

'What happened?' I asked Rob, and he looked at me balefully,

'You hit him with the ball!'

'Oh, God, where?'

'In the centre of his back.'

At least, I consoled myself, it wasn't his head. Then came another thought: perhaps I had broken his spine! As we knelt beside him there came a moan, then another which confirmed that he wasn't dead. Then he rolled over on to his side which he couldn't have done if his back was broken. Slowly John recovered and being a fit sportsman, he eventually rose to his feet and even managed to carry on with the game. Even more of a sportsman, he assured me that it wasn't my fault; that he should not have been in the way. Nor was he after that as he watched me studiously for the next seventeen holes. That game was good for Rob as he became the possessor of a good set of Wilson clubs!

My retirement to Spain became a series of disasters but through no fault of the Spaniards for whom I have a great affection. Some miles south of Javea along the Mediterranean coast is Benidorm, reputedly the largest holiday resort in Europe and certainly the place people love to hate. In summer it is hot and crowded with thousands of down-market tourists, but it is always spotlessly clean and caters well for the holidaymakers. In winter, it has the most equitable climate of any place in Europe.

I'd met a couple of men working there during my first visit from Rhodesia: George Webber, an old Fleet Street hand, and local lawyer, James Seth-Smith. George had a fortnightly newspaper called the *Sun News*, which was quite a good tabloid but short of money. James and I advanced some finance on condition that it was not used to pay off old debts but to turn the newspaper into a weekly. With that, he paid off the printers and closed down the *Sun*

News and disappeared to Fleet Street where he later became deputy night news editor on the *Daily Mirror*, the position once occupied by Lino 'Dan' Ferrari.

I next invested in the formation of a glass-fibre company and that was another disaster. The two men who talked me into putting up the money were work-shy which was very silly of them as the project was good and they would be wealthy by now. They did manage to produce an excellent hard-top mould for the jeep-like French Mahare and this was sent to a Spanish factory for production. Alas, shortly afterwards, the factory suddenly went into liquidation and the mould disappeared!

Next to disappear was Margery. Until we arrived in Spain she had been taking twenty-one tablets a day which I always felt was over the top. Not long after our arrival she had a slight regression which at first seemed like another stroke, but a brain scan proved my fears wrong. An officially non-practising English doctor who lived in Javea on retirement, Chic Carter, took her off all her tablets except for two and the recovery was remarkable. I'd put in a swimming pool at home where she spent endless hours floating in a rubber ring but her remarkable mental recovery caused by the removal of the drugs gave her a new awareness combined with frustration at having little to do. So much had she come to her senses that one day she was able to say to me, 'We can't go on living like this!' With that she flew to England, wheelchair and all. Since then her progress was truly remarkable. Much of her pre-stroke confidence had returned and she got heavily involved in charity work, selling flags and visiting patients in hospitals. She was introduced to Prince Charles when he visited Milton Keynes and was subsequently interviewed on British TV's Sunday programme, *Songs of Praise*.

Miraculously, her operatic voice returned to some degree, even if she did sing slightly slower than before. She once wrote to me a letter with the poignant sentence, 'People applaud me but I don't know if they clap because they like my voice, or they feel sorry for me.' I am sure they applauded because they admired her.

When Margery left Javea, she also left behind a unique place with unique people. On my first arrival I had been assured that it was a peaceful place where British, Dutch, German and even some Americans had decided to spend their latter years before going to the wall. The wall? The hole-in-the-wall is the local cemetery where the deceased, incarcerated in varnished wooden boxes, are levered heavenwards on a primitive crank which sways too and fro while mourners, hands to their mouths, watch with bated breath as the chain-smoking cemetery hand attempts to kick the precariously-perched coffin into an empty hole. The allotted holes become vacant from time to time dependent on whether the incumbent, possibly engrossed on flying to a higher plane, forgets to pay the rent. Should this occur, the bones are removed and quietly disposed of. Even a new incumbent cannot be assured of eternal slumber, rent paid or not. During my retirement to Javea, one wall collapsed and eleven bodies fell out.

Occasionally some of those interred are given an Egyptian send-off. At the funeral in neighbouring Denia of a retired Indian army officer, his widow turned up and, to the horror of the mourners, ordered the coffin to be opened. Clearly intent on sending her husband to the Pearly Gates in the style to which he was accustomed, she then placed into the coffin a bottle of whisky and a box of Havana cigars. It was only after the lid had been closed again and his coffin pushed into the wall that a woman friend commented, 'Darling, you forgot to bring a glass and some matches!'

Brochures depict the Mediterranean as a calm sea with palm-fringed beaches and near-naked bathing belles. But there is another side to the Med and it can be as dangerous as any ocean. I was walking below the harbour wall when someone shouted urgently from a nearby yacht, 'Get back. The waves are coming over the top!' I retraced my steps just as a giant wave crashed over the high wall. Even though Javea was supposed to have the safest harbour along the Costa Blanca, many small boats moored there were sunk. Smashed shop fronts on the far side of the beach road bore testimony to the sea's force and expensive new furniture in one shop was washed out to sea. A catamaran in the harbour was plucked from safety to become matchwood as it was flung across a coast road; a large glass-fibre 'gin palace' launch in the harbour was sunk by a floating ladder that had broken away from another of the fifty boats that became reunited with it in Davey Jones' locker. Further along the coast were more sinkings with ships running aground or washed on to rocks. At Altea, near Benidorm, a large cabin cruiser was swept on to the coastal road and was crashed into by a car being driven at night killing a woman passenger. It is rare for car passengers to be killed by boats that have floated from the sea and on to the highway.

I drove down to investigate the tragedy and on my return along the motor-way, a strong gust of wind swept me off the road and into a storm gully. Sitting upside down in an overturned car five feet below the highway raised certain complications for I tried to open one door only to find it was wedged against a wall of earth. Concerned that fire might break out, I then tried the other door and forced it open. My attitude had been that there was no point in waiting for a crane in Spain to pluck me from the drain! As I scampered up the bank unscathed, a lorry I had previously overtaken stopped and the driver came out and surveyed the scene open-mouthed. He'd seen the accident and didn't expect to find me alive… and shook my hand enthusiastically. Then a toll-gate keeper, resplendent in a dark blue uniform, shook hands in wonder. He had also witnessed my departure and called the emergency services. Then two policemen of La Guardia drove up and after surveying the scene they too shook hands: 'A miracle,' they said, looking at me in awe. The ambulance arrived and the male nurses and driver all gazed at me and my hand was being pumped like that of a barnstorming American politician. It was becoming tiresome. 'You should be dead,' they all agreed. How little they knew!

The following year, and an event as unlikely as the big storm took place: Javea had an earth tremor. There had been an earthquake in Greece and the shock waves travelled the length of the Mediterranean. Altea had the worst shakes but some apartment blocks in Javea were affected at their foundations. 'That's also never happened before,' was the universal comment. The reaction of the Spaniards during the tremor was astonishing as they hurriedly left their beds and raced to the beaches for safety! I suspect they are unlikely to do that again following the Indian Ocean tsunami.

There was something else Javea had never before experienced – snow! 'We get it on the surrounding mountains but never in Javea itself,' I was told, but I was in Javea when it snowed heavily. The snowfall, like the storm, was probably unique as photographs of it are shown on café walls and even on tourist cards. As many of the locals had never driven in snow before, motor scooters were particularly vulnerable and their drivers looked in disbelief after braking to find they were still propelling forward. Villa owners on the side of the local mountain, Montgo, and other hilly areas were housebound for up to five days, unable to get their cars down the slopes.

It was on the side of Montgo that John and Aurea Davies lived and if anyone tells me a hard luck story I immediately think of them. On the night of the snowstorm, some close friends from Singapore arrived and despite being fitted out with the latest gadgets in their kitchen, which is a chef's dream, Aurea found herself unable to cook because the electricity failed. It meant they had no lights in their villa except for some candles, and no heating. As they sat and froze the water supply iced up too and stopped flowing. 'I'll make some sandwiches,' said the doughty Aurea, which she produced by candlelight. While he was munching a sandwich one of the guests chose this moment to die. John was a doctor but there was nothing he could do for his friend and they were now in the nightmare situation of being huddled around the candles with no electric light, no heating, no water, a corpse, and a new widow to console. The telephone was still connected but they had to sit with their deceased friend until 4 a.m. when an ambulance forced its way up the steep slope to the house. Surely, they thought, nothing more could happen. Next morning they went out to their cars, one of them a brand new top-of-the-range Mercedes John had imported from Germany, only to find their roofs crushed. The weight of the snow had caused their garage to collapse.

Another couple sharing the same name – Davies – were Dick and Mary who also suffered from the Javea winter cold that night. Dicky, was a submarine commander in WW2 and had once damaged his submarine in the 'placid' Mediterranean during a storm. He also had the rare distinction of having knocked out Prince Philip during a rugby match at the Royal Naval College, Dartmouth. How he did it I cannot say as Dicky was only a half-pint, like myself. The couple were well-known imbibers at local hostelries and their problem arose after they arrived home after midnight following a party. Mary had insisted on keeping the key to the house, knowing that her husband could not be relied upon to look after it. 'Oh, God, I've lost the key!' she exclaimed as they stood outside the front door. Dicky impatiently muttered some incomprehensible words as Mary searched her handbag and her pockets. They searched the car, too, but without success. There was nothing for it; the night would be spent in the car. Like moonstruck lovers they huddled together in the now-freezing vehicle, waiting for dawn. As the sun rose, they drove to a telephone box and called the local odd-job man. Armed with a hacksaw, he soon demolished the expensive wrought-iron burglar bars and broke a window before entering the house. Soon the front door was opened and the hapless couple went into their bedroom, eager to catch up on some sleep. The atmosphere between them was cool at the time but it froze like the weather outside when Mary removed her bra and the key fell to the bedroom floor.

My penchant for knowing people who have subsequently met violent deaths didn't end when I arrived in Javea. On the evening that the snow began to fall I was at the home of an American friend, Charles Fagan, and his wife, Patty. Charles was elderly and Patty a young waitress he had met in New York who was wild-eyed – I am sure she was on drugs – and so wild-natured that she once managed to drive her Mercedes sports car into the sea. Tragedy occurred when Patty brought home a stray Spaniard who, during the course of conversation, took a decorative sword off the wall and stabbed her in the stomach. As Charles rose from a chair to come to his wife's assistance, the Spaniard raised the sword and brought it down on Charles's head, slicing it in two. Patty survived and was able to give evidence against the killer who was jailed for over forty years. Now a millionairess through her inheritance from Charles, she went back to America and fell into the company of drug smugglers and was shot dead by police on the Mexican border.

The day the first sunbather removed her bra on Javea's sandy beach, she was observed by two municipal policemen. The usual Spanish bravado towards blonde foreign girls disappeared and they were overheard arguing and the senior said, 'I'm ordering you to tell her to put her top on.' The junior policeman was adamant, 'No. You're the boss... you go.' In the end, neither approached the blissfully unaware sunbather. To prevent further exhibitions of such public indecency, the municipal policemen produced a handwritten notice which was put up at the entrance to the beach. It was meant to advise all English-speaking sunbathers that such immodesty was forbidden because it was a family beach but that was where their problem arose. Dutifully the two guardians of public morality put up their notice which read, 'This is a familiar beach!' The floodgates were opened and Javea has never been quite the same.

Ann Mason, who owned the English Library in Javea told me of the day she went to the lost property office at the municipal police station. On the desk was a row of keys and she pointed to one in surprise after reading the name tag, 'Don't tell me they have been lost?'

'Yes,' came the reply. They were the keys to the slammer!

Twice a year, Javea has its running of the bulls. As with Pamplona, the bulls run through the streets, but unlike Pamplona, they thankfully only run one at a time. The roads are cordoned off, and in some areas, planks are nailed together like steps, so that crowds can dash to them and climb as the bull charges. It's all macho-bravado and I reckoned that I was too old to mess around with that kind of caper. Sometimes I would stand slightly bored on the sidelines and watch others do stupid things. Frequently a teenager, over-anxious to prove himself would be gored and rushed to hospital.

My complacency came to an end when Rob arrived in Javea for a holiday and promptly went over the barriers. 'Come on, Father,' he called. Came the terse reply, 'I'm too old and too fat.' It's fine when you are in your late twenties and a world-class squash player but for a decadent journalist in his mid fifties it's something else. But how could I show cowardice to my son? Reluctantly, I climbed into the arena and ran across to a raised platform. For twenty minutes I was safe as I watched, not without a little boredom, as a young bull occasionally trotted past. Then I left the platform with Rob and ran across the road towards the shelter of some temporary safety steps just as a bull suddenly charged towards us. Young Spaniards and Rob all scrambled upwards in front of me, forgetting the common courtesies of making room for the elderly, but I saw a small niche amongst a battalion of buttocks and started to climb. 'Senor!' yelled a chorus of Spaniards, who waved their hands to indicate that there had been a near miss. 'Up yours, too,' I muttered. 'That was close, Father,' said Rob. 'Its horn missed your backside by an eighth of an inch!'

It was in the port of Javea that one bull went off the end of the jetty and swam round to the beach where a group of girls were sunbathing. Two young English lasses looked up just in time to see it rise from the sea and head towards them. They collected their towels later…

Journalists pontificate with the pen, typewriter and computer on all matters: moral, political, religious, industrial, arts, finance and related business in general. Their fallibility comes to light when they leave their desks and attempt to practise their wisdom. While they may exist, I have yet to meet a really good journalist who is also a good businessman. I don't know if I am a particularly good journalist but I'm certainly in their mould when it comes to business…

Partly because of my retirement investments based on good ideas but poor judgment of character, my coffers were disappearing fast and something dramatic had to be done. With hardly a penny or peseta in my pocket, I made a far-reaching decision. If I was to live comfortably for the rest of my life, I'd have to become a millionaire even though I have no particular interest in money, per se. No matter how much I spent, surely I couldn't lose a million pounds or so? 'If you are going to start again, stick to what you know best,' said a Javea friend, Tony Ross who had been appalled at the glass-fibre debacle. But hadn't I also lost money on the *Sun News*? Even though I was short of cash, there was a pro to offset the cons: I'd become very fit. Having been forced to sell my car, I walked everywhere which was seldom less than fifteen miles a day and usually much more. Chopping down trees for firewood at home was also physically rewarding. The trees were iron hard as they had been burned in a flash fire which nearly took my home.

In the next villa to mine was a Dutch couple, Anton and Martha van Brink, who were something special. Anton, an electronics expert with Phillips for many years, had been interned in Dachau concentration camp by the Nazis, where he proceeded to surreptitiously make radios for the inmates. It was there he contracted diabetes which meant he had to inject himself with insulin for the rest of his life with never a word of complaint. Not long before his death on Lisbon Station and long overdue, he received a medal which he proudly showed me. The medal was in recognition of his work with the Dutch Resistance. As for Martha, she had courageously browbeaten the Gestapo into allowing her to visit Anton in Dachau, and had subsequently become a leading light in the Dutch women's rights movement, lecturing in India at her government's expense. We had something in common: Martha and her daughter, Antoinette, were journalists.

'I'm planning to start a national daily newspaper to compete with Fleet Street,' I told Anton and Martha. Lesser people would have laughed in my face; they weren't even surprised and were quite sure that I would do it. One of the problems of living abroad is that English newspapers usually arrived a day late, sometimes two or three. They were also costly, too expensive for many of the thousands of retired people who live only on their pensions. In order to raise money for the project, I virtually gave away my villa, and the person who bought it said subsequently, 'I stole it off you.' and it was sold by him for treble the price a year later. But now I had some capital for research and a full assessment of the pricing structure. This had included flying to Barcelona and Madrid to check out the prices of printers and the equipment available and making contacts both countrywide and in Britain. After a year or so, money was again running low and in Javea I bought an ageing and rusty Volvo for fifty pounds with a view to driving it by roundabout route from Javea to London to raise money for the project itself. A very nice little chap who liked to help people and he could do anything with his hands, Jack Little, (what parents could name their son Little John?) spent hours fibre glassing the rust together and repainting the car yellow, yet he refused all offers of payment. My intention was to drive the 'Yellow Peril' down to the south of Spain, up through Portugal to Lisbon, across to Madrid, up to Paris and then to England.

The great day came and I set off in the early morning, negotiating the precipitous snake-like pass between Javea and neighbouring Teulada quite successfully. Unfortunately, the winding road was a test too far for the car's aged steering mechanism and I delicately nursed it back to Javea and Jack Little who found the fault and fixed it before I was off again. By now it was getting late in the afternoon and I decided to spend the night at a Benidorm hotel. The following morning I strolled out on to the balcony only to watch with dismay as the Yellow Peril was towed away into the sunrise by the municipal police.

On paying a fine to retrieve it, I learned that there would be a parade later in the day and my car, which had been legally parked overnight, had become illegal for just that one day in the year! Several hours later and several pesetas lighter, I re-embarked on the trek to Marbella a few hundred miles away and the journey went without a further hitch. Andrew Linn's name had been given to me and I went to see him. Andrew, a shrewd entrepreneur in Marbella, was enthusiastic and I earmarked him as Managing Director of Shay Publications in Spain. The next leg was Lisbon, via Gibraltar, where I wanted to find out the size of the British population there, and also take a look at the Portuguese Algarve but unfortunately I took a wrong road and missed Gibraltar completely by two miles – it isn't everyone who can miss Gibraltar!

Lisbon was a disappointment as friends I had wanted to meet with newspaper connections were away on holiday. From Lisbon, the Yellow Peril took me back into Spain and across to Madrid and then up to Paris. There was one friend in Paris I particularly wanted to meet – Tony Lean. Tony had been divorced in England for the second time and then remarried, to a French girl. When we met up he looked terrible. While he was deeply in love with his new wife, she was disenchanted with their marriage and beamed hate at me as if I had been responsible for their ill-fated love match. Tony Lean, the man who had marched so confidently with me over no-man's land in Angola, was drinking himself into a Paris gutter because of marital problems. This was a terrible blow for many reasons, not least that I had plans for him to become Chief Executive of my British operation as he had the business acumen, and experience. After three days of trying to console him, I drove on to England to continue my quest.

Before I left Paris, I mentioned to Tony how shocked I had been at being approached by child prostitutes in Lisbon. 'Tragic, isn't it,' he said. 'The last time you saw them they were toddlers.' Because the refugees from Angola and Mozambique had not been made welcome in Portugal, many found themselves homeless and jobless. These proud people, who had lived comfortable lives, were left without any possessions and some of their daughters knew of only one way to bring money home. And I thought that I was having problems!

The Yellow Peril covered thousands of miles without a hitch. She was British registered but having taken up residence in Spain, the road tax on her was two years out of date. She also had no MOT (something I'd never heard of) and also, while I was crossing the Channel, the insurance ran out without me realising it. It was just my luck to be stopped for speeding on a motorway! She had paid me back well for giving her a new lease of life by travelling around 3,000 miles and because I had developed an affinity with the car, I'm sure that she saw me accept the speeding ticket with some pride. Sadly, as I arrived at a friend's home in Kent the Yellow Peril spluttered her last gasp as her stout-hearted engine gave up the ghost for ever.

For the next two months I concentrated on making a Business Plan and then approached my brother to ensure that I had added up my figures correctly. Warren had done well for himself, having retired as Director of Finance and deputy chief executive of London's Sutton Borough Council and he introduced me through a friend to the international accountants, Coopers & Lybrand, who were incredibly helpful. I'd now gone to the top and intended to stay there. Then, as if from the blue, a dejected and wiser Tony Lean turned up, having driven from Paris in an old French ambulance which still contained bullet holes from the Algerian campaign! Tony also had a brother who was the British naval attaché in Madrid and at their mother's home in Ascot – the lodge to Mrs Wallis Warfield Simpson's home where it once all happened with Edward VIII and I asked Tony if he knew any millionaires. 'Don Bilton,' he said, and his eyes lit up. 'He's a South African but I believe he has a yacht in Spain.' After several telephone calls to South Africa and Spain, we finally contacted him in the Cape Province. 'Why don't you stay aboard my boat at Duquessa?' he said. 'I'll be there soon.'

Duquessa is part of the Costa del Sol's millionaires' playground. And so, two near down-and-outs flew to Spain and took up residence for a month on the millionaire's large, comfortable catamaran. Tony was still very depressed and was still drinking quite a lot, but he had a new problem: whenever we walked up the gangplank he kept falling into the water and it was only then that I learned of the plastic plates in his knees. Clearly, his days of walking the plank should have been over and he confirmed this one morning by saying he had fallen off the plank at 1 a.m. while I was tucked away in my bunk and had been hauled out of the sea without a life jacket at 3.30 a.m. by a security guard. He had banged on the side of the boat for two and a half hours in a bid to awaken me without success.

Tony's courage came to the fore once again when a speedboat went up in flames at night, probably through arson for insurance purposes. It was the type of boat, said to be worth £100,000, used in the south of Spain for smuggling drugs from North Africa. We knew that if the inferno reached the speedboat's fuel tanks, Duquessa's harbour could go up, as several yachts and launches were moored nearby. He boarded the blazing craft (after falling into the water first) and I threw him a hosepipe before grabbing another pipe to spray both him and the flames. After fifteen minutes we were on top of the situation, and that is when the harbour's security guards arrived. Quite deliberately, and maliciously, they sprayed Tony with a gaseous substance which quells flames – their thanks to the man who had done their job for them unless, of course, they were responsible for the fire. Tony was ill for some time after for it had been during a gas exercise in the Royal Marines' SBS that he had lost a lung.

Don Bilton then arrived and read my business plan with enthusiasm. 'This is tremendous, it's the best plan I've read in twenty years,' he declared. He was very charming but did not tell me if he would put up any money but Tony had a chat with him before he flew back to South Africa. Tony then advised me, 'Don said he would guarantee £175,000 if you can find the other half.' I had been looking for £350,000, a trifling sum with which to start a national daily and Sunday newspaper, but I was sure I could do it. I had some reservations on the strength of the Bilton offer; but at least I now had a name and a guarantee, and decided to use them as bait.

In Duquessa was a former wartime submarine commander, David Teare, who told me of yet another former submariner with Throgmorton Trust in the City. We met up in London and went to see him. During the negotiations I learned an important lesson on raising money; City financiers do not like to fill the basket with only their own eggs. Throgmorton Investment Management Ltd said they would put up half the money if Bilton put up the rest. It was a firm offer and I had it in writing but all attempts to contact Don failed. Then another man purporting to be a millionaire, Barry Haynes, came on the scene and agreed to put up the rest. The day before the formal signing of the agreement, in which the monies would be paid over, Haynes disappeared to Brussels and I haven't seen him since. I was told, subsequently, that many people of perverse nature get a thrill out of going along with negotiations until the time they have to pay up.

It was a nail-biting time as Throgmorton threatened to pull out unless I came up with a backer within two weeks. As the deadline approached, Andrew Linn, who had helped me with the negotiations, came across to London with two entrepreneurs who agreed to put up the rest. One of them had attended a dinner of Marbella's top businessmen where I had been guest of honour. Also in my favour was Tony Trembeth of Coopers & Lybrand, who had given me considerable help and provided me with temporary offices within the Coopers building which stood on the site of the old *Evening Standard*. In my temporary office, I found myself standing exactly where the news desk used to be! And I also learned that they had offices in the Fleetway House where I had started out as a messenger! At one point, when the cheques were paid over, I sat back and laughed at the absurdities of life. Barclays Bank had telephoned and I gave instructions, 'Put £300,000 on weekly deposit at nine-and-three-quarter per cent and leave the rest in the current account' The reason for the laughter? I had been down to my last £25!

The uniqueness of my project was to have the newspaper made up in England, at Maidstone in Kent, and then send it by satellite overnight (faxing was in its infancy and I hadn't yet heard of it) to printers in Madrid and Marbella for simultaneous printing. It meant that the British would have their newspapers on the morning of the same day they were published and at less than half the cost of the Fleet Street newspapers which would arrive the following day. I would rely heavily on agencies to begin with and then build up until I had a full reporting staff before expanding throughout Europe. My personal knowledge of computers was nil but I knew the project could be done, even though I was the first in the field with this particular type of venture. I'd advertised for staff and was pleased with the response. One man particularly impressed me, Paul Rafferty. He appeared to have good credentials and told me he was a member of the Institute of Directors and took me to their London offices on a pretext of collecting some papers. As he had newspaper and computer experience I decided to appoint him as my totally trusted right-hand man, with a view to becoming a possible managing director. He claimed he had set up newspapers before, which was a boon and I was also particularly interested in his knowledge of computers. What I did not know was that Rafferty had bankrupted at least one newspaper and was an undischarged bankrupt himself. I did become a little suspicious when he introduced me to his girlfriend with pride as 'the youngest ever woman bankrupt in Britain'.

The launch of the Daily Standard *with the British ambassador, Lord Nicholas, Gordon Lennox and Andrew Linn. Picture:* Daily Standard.

One of my objectives had been to give employment to some of the older and experienced ex-Fleet Street journalists who had lost their jobs because of huge staff cuts that had recently taken place. As Tony Lean was still mentally convalescing, I also thought I would give a young man a chance, hence Rafferty. I shall not go into the gory details but it is true to say that the person I had brought in as my loyal and trusted right-hand man began to sabotage me from the beginning so that he was able to strut into the newsroom one day and declare, 'I got rid of Reg Shay in five weeks!'

I hadn't realised that he was screwing up my cash flow – always assuring me that everything was fine – and withholding my mail. Computer equipment he'd told me we could get cheaply was unsuitable and I didn't know at the time that he had been doing a private deal with the computer company which gave him a brief holiday in America as a reward. Too late I discovered what Rafferty was up to and realised more money would be needed before we even started publishing. The shareholders, led by a fussy little Maltese man who supported Rafferty because, as he put it 'he's hungry' (a euphemism for greedy) came down on me like a ton of bricks and demanded that my shareholding be reduced to fifteen per cent (it had been fifty-one per cent) and I become a non-executive board member, or they would not put any more money in. I agreed only in order to protect the jobs of the staff and was appalled later when told the board intended to sack half of them once the paper was up and running. My demand that Rafferty be removed was totally ignored and they were to reap the harvest. One black day was Friday 13, 1986. It was on Friday 13, 1967, that the engine on the rubber boat had packed up on the Zambezi expedition and I had stood armed with a paddle, ready to strike out at any hungry crocodile. I concluded that a mauling from a croc was preferable to one from some businessmen.

Having suffered a humiliating boardroom session (described in my diary as a day of infamy), I took a taxi and drove down the Mall towards Buckingham Palace. Deep in thought, I gazed through the cab window and realised I was staring at a young lady's bare bottom. It was travelling along the Mall at the same speed as my taxi and my driver was taking more than a casual interest. Three girls in their late teens were laughing merrily in another cab and one had decided to emulate the Maoris (the Queen had recently been to New Zealand and was given the bare-arsed treatment as a calculated insult) by saucily pulling down her knickers and placing her bottom out of the cab window for all to see. My immediate problems evaporated as my sense of humour returned.

The atmosphere created by Rafferty and his girlfriend at the Maidstone offices was far from humorous and after paying them a visit, I came to call the offices Stalag 9. Rafferty sat at one end and his girlfriend (known as 'Boots') at the other, and the staff even had to ask permission to get a paper clip from the locked cupboard. Journalists I had appointed were disposed of although my deputy editor, Geoff McCormack, had put up a gallant fight. I was totally ashamed of the layout of the early editions and the high Fleet Street standard of publication I needed was never achieved. Even the work I'd done to arrange pre-launch publicity had been ignored. I had wined and dined a former colleague who had become a senior editor in the BBC World Service news-room and knew that the launching of the newspaper would be a world service news item. McCormack, who had worked with Derek Jameson on the *Daily Mirror*, had organised a meeting so that I might appear on his early morning BBC Radio 2 show to talk about the project. The board said Jameson was not important as he was not on Radio 4, and the project was dropped. Serious as the situation was, once again there was humour as a safeguard to sanity.

I'd once mentioned to Rafferty that I would have liked to have been able to afford an airship to fly along the Spanish coast as a publicity boost and subse-quently the publicity campaign-which-never-was came in the form of a balloon. I was in Spain when it arrived sometime after the newspaper had been launched. 'What are you going to do with that?' I asked Bob Holt, a friend of Rafferty, who had been brought in as the chief publicity officer despite no previous experience. He was holding a large deflated balloon with the same neutral-grey colour that would have resembled a WW1 army-issue condom. 'I shall get it blown up and fix it to the top of my car and then drive through the streets of Benidorm,' he declared. 'You'll have to get permission,' said Jimmy Ruddock, whom I had previously appointed as the local publicist. 'We don't have to worry about that,' replied Holt and he disappeared, only to return a few hours later, crestfallen. 'I was blowing it up at a service station when the police came and made me deflate it,' he said. Jimmy and I exchanged glances before Holt came up with another wonder plan: 'I'll blow up the balloon and hire a speedboat so that I can take it along the Benidorm coast.' Said Jimmy, 'You'll have to be 350 yards offshore and no one will be able to read the advertisement from that distance.' We watched the performance from a nearby bar and next day Holt returned, 'I blew it up but it wouldn't go into the air,' he said. 'It just kept going round and round in the water.' I ventured, 'Perhaps you needed helium gas.' That was the last I saw or heard of the bloody stupid balloon, and it was the only publicity the *Daily Standard* received along the whole of the Costa Blanca with the exception of a couple of local broadcasts I made, plus pictures of the first edition coming off the press on Spanish national television organised by Andrew Linn. But Spanish TV, not surpris-ingly, is in Spanish for the Spanish. The distributors, who had been hostile from the beginning because they feared the *Daily Standard* would interfere with the revenue they received from the British newspapers, also managed to put a spoke in. They told the newsagents to withhold the newspaper for a day and I only found this out by chance when I was given the previous day's newspaper instead of the current issue, which was hidden in the back of the shop. Said the newsagent, 'We were told that the British like their newspapers a day late!' I had visited the distributors in Barcelona before setting up the newspaper and asked them to handle circulation but after I named the price I intended to charge, just fifty pesetas, a director told me that was the sum he would charge to distribute. 'That's extortion!' I snapped. 'Yes,' he replied with a smirk, 'but we are the sole distributors!'

NEWS

Deposed editor tells of Spain daily in-fighting

by Jon Slattery

REG SHAY, the man who planned the *Daily Standard* — the paper aimed at British expatriates and tourists in Spain — claims he lost out in a power struggle for control of the title.

While rescue attempts are still being made to save the *Daily Standard,* which has ceased publication, Shay says he lost any influence over the paper before it launched.

Although the paper was published by Shay Publications and Shay was announced as editor-in-chief and chairman, he claims his ideas for the paper were ignored.

Shay still believes that an English daily for Spain, beating the Fleet Street nationals on price and appearing on the same day of publication, is a winning formula.

Shay, a former freelance television reporter and war correspondent, spent 18 months planning the project and raising finance. He said he was against the *Daily Standard* setting up editorial offices in Maidstone, Kent, and spending in excess of £100,000 on the high-tech equipment needed for the paper to be transmitted by satellite to printing centres in Spain.

"I didn't want a very big set-up. I wanted to go in small and build up. Once the money was spent on equipment we had cash flow problems. Like all journalists I am no businessman. I am convinced the idea was a good one but greed and power

'Pushed out': Reg Shay.

combined to destroy it."

Shay at one time held 51% of Shay Publications but his holding is now down to 11%. He said he was persuaded to give up the major part of his shares after being told that was the only way extra capital could be put into the project.

Shay claims that he was so out in the cold that he was not invited to see the first edition of the paper being produced.

Another person out of the picture before the launch was former Fleet Street journalist Jeff McCormack, who was recruited by Shay. McCormack was given the title deputy editor, production but resigned just before the launch.

McCormack claims he was given just two months to handle the editorial side of the paper and bring it to launch but with six weeks to go was left with an unfurnished office in Maidstone. He also alleges that 600 replies to a job recruitment advertisement placed in *Press Gazette* were never passed on to him and there was a clash with the paper's general manager, Paul Rafferty, over editorial control.

McCormack said: "The project should have succeeded and we should have been able to sell 40,000 copies a day in Spain but I was hamstrung, not given enough backing or staff. There were things beyond my control that caused the final situation."

Shay also had a number of disagreements with Rafferty although he had recruited him to help set up the paper. Before joining the *Daily Standard,* Rafferty worked for the *Brighton Entertainer* and previously launched a free paper in Birmingham which collapsed with debts of more than £100,000.

Any rescue package for the *Daily Standard* will have to be approved before a creditors' meeting due at the end of this month. Thirty staff, including 14 journalists, have been made redundant by the paper.

My newspaper, the Daily Standard, *folds. Picture:* UK Press Gazette.

I still haven't the slightest doubt that had I been left alone with a little more money, the *Daily* and *Sunday Standard* would have been success stories. Because of their attitude towards me, I had long decided the board could stew in their own juice and when I was eventually asked how to save the newspaper, I shrugged my shoulders; there was no way I would bail them out and by now I *wanted* the project to fail. Considering all the problems outside the production of a newspaper, I reckon something could be learned by some that I could produce a daily and Sunday newspaper for such a small sum which survived for four months before being deliberately wrecked when it was close to breaking even. After the collapse, Rafferty went to other newspapers to sell the *Daily Standard* know-how, made up of all my ideas. Whether he went to Robert Maxwell I do not know, but shortly afterwards he came out with the very expensive publication, *The European*, and that was produced only one day a week. Then the *Sun* became the first national British newspaper to publish in Europe, followed by others.

Since the collapse of the newspaper I have moved to Birmingham in England. It became the only place where I have been mugged, being attacked from behind after aiding a girl who had also been assaulted. I was punched to the ground and kicked and limped for two years having had a bone broken in my foot. The mugger ran away when I kicked back.

Other than that, I tour Europe extensively and spend time in Melbourne and Sydney with my son, Peter, who now lives in Australia. I've now met more members of my family by my father's first marriage who have sought me out. But enough of the present. I'll close my life's story with an interview I did in Rhodesia, where I met and wrote a syndicated feature of a man who also had a remarkable story to tell. He was David 'Tommy' Lewis who, during WW1, had been posted to France to join the Third Flight of the Third Squadron of the Third Brigade of the Third Army. Three was his lucky number for although his Sopwith Camel was shot down by the Red Baron to make him von Richthofen's eightieth and last victim and despite the famous Snoopy song, he actually survived. To know that you were the last man to be shot down by the Red Baron could be a cross to bear; difficult to live with. Imagine Tommy Lewis's situation when someone asks at a cocktail party or over a bar: 'I say, have you ever done anything really interesting?' After a suitable pause, he could say, 'Well, yes. I was flying a Sopwith Camel over France one day when who should appear but the Red Baron. He shot me down, you know... I was his eightieth victim.' There would be no point in continuing as his new companion would be either looking for someone else to talk to or telephoning for men in white coats.

In similar circumstances, I could say, 'Well, I was once attacked by a crocodile, which was at the time when I scared a hippo which jumped out of the Zambezi River and into the air!' or, 'Three Africans held me up at gunpoint but I attacked them, of course, and they ran away,' or... 'The United States government was relying on me!' (Muffled yawns.): 'Oh really?' Before leaving, I will notice a mobile telephone being taken surreptitiously from a coat pocket and soon police and ambulance sirens will be heard...

Margery died suddenly on 30 October 2004 after being semi-paralyzed for thirty-eight years. Shortly before her death she was stopped by police and cautioned in Milton Keynes for speeding on the pavement in her electric wheelchair. She was seventy-five.

My family: Rob, Margery, Annette and Peter. Picture: author.

Printed in the United Kingdom
by Lightning Source UK Ltd.
123004UK00001B/63/A